PUBLICATIONS
OF THE
NORTH CAROLINA HISTORICAL COMMISSION

RECORDS OF THE
MORAVIANS IN NORTH CAROLINA

EDITED BY
ADELAIDE L. FRIES, M.A.
ARCHIVIST OF THE MORAVIAN CHURCH IN AMERICA
SOUTHERN PROVINCE

VOLUME IV
1780-1783

RALEIGH
EDWARDS & BROUGHTON COMPANY
STATE PRINTERS
1930

THE NORTH CAROLINA HISTORICAL COMMISSION

TABLE OF CONTENTS

PART I

PAGE

General Letter from Unity's Elders Conference.................................. 1494

Brotherly Agreement of Bethania.. 1498

PART II

1780. Fall of Charlestown. Defeat of Americans at Camden. American success at King's Mountain. Tories defeated on the Yadkin. Moravian towns over-run by American troops; supplies furnished by the Brethren in large quantities. Prisoners from King's Mountain quartered at Bethabara. Lawlessness of wandering parties of militia. Visitation of Bishop Reichel. Organization of congregations at Friedland and Hope............................. 1511

1781. Quartering of American troops in Moravian towns. Sick and wounded soldiers in Salem. Passing of English army under Lord Cornwallis. Small-pox epidemic. Lawless actions of Whigs and Tories. Defeat of Cornwallis at Yorktown. Meeting of the Assembly of North Carolina in Salem.. 1656

1782. Second meeting of the assembly of North Carolina in Salem. Title to Wachovia confirmed to Frederic William Marshall. Traugott Bagge elected to Assembly. Continued lawlessness of militia and highwaymen. Gradual improvement in business. Death of Bishop Graff............ 1784

1783. Jubilee of Moravian Mission to Greenland. Gradual reduction of American army. Peace celebration in Wachovia, July Fourth. Economic and social conditions returning to normal. Wild animals plentiful. National Day of Thanksgiving. Epidemic of measles.................... 1834

Memorabilia of the War as it touched Wachovia.................... 1875

PART III

Diary of Bethania, 1779.. 1889

Travel diary, Lititz, Pa., to Salem, N. C., and return, 1780............ 1893

Letters. Reports to Unity's Elders Conference. Orders for supplies for army.. 1896

Proclamation for celebration of Fourth of July, 1783................ 1919

Men resident in Wachovia, 1775-1783.............................. 1922

ILLUSTRATIONS

Rev. Frederic William Marshall, From Pencil Sketch in Salem Land Office..*Frontispiece*

Facing Page

Bishop August Gottlieb Spangenberg Writing the Idea Fidei Fratrum in the Summer-house at Barby. From Silhouette Belonging to Miss Adelaide L. Fries........................ 1698

Map of Salem, 1783.. 1806

The Psalm of Joy, July 4, 1783.. 1864

PART 1

INTRODUCTION

[The two papers which follow are placed at the beginning of this volume because they set forth, in a rather remarkable manner, the ideals of the Wachovia Moravians of the Revolutionary period, in religious and civic lines.

The letter from the Unity's Elders Conference is a challenge to complete devotion in the service of Christ, worked out along the practical lines of gratitude, brotherly love, obedience, contentment, responsibility, and readiness for Christian service wherever and whenever called.

The Brotherly Agreement of Bethania, under the numerous details appropriate to local circumstance, shows the basic principles of co-operation, interest in the local affairs of church and village, submission to properly constituted authority, good order, decorum, honest business, clean streets, definite property lines, prompt payment of taxes and other obligations, carefulness in money matters, justice among men, charity toward the helpless, good understanding between neighbors.

That many fell short of these ideals goes without saying, but an understanding of the aim of the Brethren is worth while, and throws light upon the story of the difficult days of 1780 to 1783, which tried their souls to the uttermost, but brought them out to a position approved of the men who lived about them. Cleared of all charges of lukewarm loyalty, confirmed in their temporal possessions by act of the Assembly, citizens of acknowledged value to the Province that had been, and to the new State that had come to be, the close of the Revolution brought to the Brethren good reason to review their trials and their blessings and sing their "Psalm of Joy":

> Peace is with us, Peace is with us,
> People of the Lord.　　　　　]

A General Letter from the Unity's Elders Conference at Barby, to the Moravian Congregations. Dated September 13, 1780.

[Translated in full.]

Dear Brothers and Sisters,

Through love to our Lord and Saviour and the work which He has entrusted to us, we, your servants in the Lord, the Brethren of the Elders Conference of the Unity, feel ourselves impelled to have a heart-to-heart conversation with you. We hope that as you read this you will have the same feeling that is in our hearts as we send it to you.

First we must say that to this day God our Saviour has done much for His people, the Brethren. If we did not honor and praise Him for this we would have cause for shame in our unthankfulness. But we beseech you to join with us in thanking Him for the Goodness, Faithfulness, Wisdom and wonderful Leading of the Lord, which He has hitherto made known among us in so remarkable a manner, and to adore Him in all humility.

Next we must not omit to mention our hope that He will continue to show us His favor in increasing measure. He has given us His word that He wishes now to bring us back to the first grace, love and simplicity. The beginning He has already made in respect to certain important matters among us. For example: He has given us in general more love for one another and more confidence in each other,—although some persons still show little enough of this. He has led us to more simplicity of doctrine and hymns, and this causes us to believe that He will bring us back in those things in which we are still lacking.

Now we will mention one thing, namely the great call which we have to serve Christians and heathen with the word of God. When, by grace, the Lord sought us, and by baptism brought us into one body, we promised Him solemnly that hereafter we would live not for ourselves but for Him. This pledge have we often renewed, especially when He so graciously revealed to us that He Himself would be our Elder.[1] Even had we made no such promise He is in truth our Lord, and we owe Him body and life and all. We should therefore truly say: None of us liveth unto himself, and none of us dieth unto himself, but if we live we live unto the Lord, and if we die we die unto the Lord.

It is therefore only just that each Brother and Sister should firmly decide: I am not my own master, I have a Master, Who bought me

---

[1] Sept. 16, 1741.

for His own with His own blood, and Who redeemed me from the slavery of Satan. All that I do or leave undone is to be ordered according to His will; my part is to be always ready, and to await His word. Shall the Lord my Saviour expect less from me than did the Roman Captain from his soldiers and his servants? Of them he said: "I have soldiers under me—I am a man under authority—but if I say to this man 'Go' he goeth, and if I say to another 'Come' he cometh, if I say to my servant 'Do this' he doeth it."

Who does not abide in this spirit, so that he will do with joy whatever the will of the Lord for him is, he belongs not within the covenant which the Saviour has made with us and we with Him.

It is of course true that the Saviour does not call every one to His great work among souls, but each member is bound to be content with the Lord's will, and to apply himself to that which is his duty for the time, carrying on his handicraft or other business that he may have bread to eat and may serve his neighbor. And if a man does this for the sake of Christ, faithfully and with his whole heart, so is the Lord pleased with him, and accepts as service for Himself what we do with the work of our hands for our neighbor.

It may easily happen that with the best of intentions a man drifts into worldly ways. For example: if he is not content with having food and clothing, and worries about the future; or if he takes the world for his pattern, and copies it in his clothing, his household, his furniture and other things; or, again, if he allows his children to follow the customs of the world in regard to marriage, and tries to secure for them a good living, without finding out whether the plan accords with the will of the Lord our Saviour in their regard. A man may become so busy in providing for his support, so intent upon gain, that he puts himself out of reach if the Lord would like to use him here or there in the service of the Gospel.

How good it would be if our Brethren and Sisters, married or single, would ever keep this thought in mind: What a great joy it would be to lead souls to the Saviour, or to serve them with the Gospel. Oh how happy we would be to be counted worthy of that!

But a man may say: Oh well, people can always be found to bother themselves about other people. I prefer to carry on my business, and to take my rest; I can serve God within the Congregation. Journeys are much too hard for me, especially on the ocean. I can not stand the cold, and heat does not agree with me. When I am at home I can rise when I will, and lay me down to rest when I desire; I can follow my usual course, and that suits me best. Who goes abroad must be pleased with sweet or sour. Among the heathen one must face many dangers. The man who has these thoughts forgets the precious promise, given by our Lord Jesus Christ: There is no man that hath left house, or brethren, or sisters, or father, or mother, or wife, or children, or lands, for my sake, and the gospel's, but he shall receive an hundred-fold now in this time, houses and brethren and sisters and mothers and children and lands, with persecutions; and in the world to come eternal life. Mark X, 29, &c. The man of the spirit which chooses easy days forgets the hard path which the Lord our Saviour trod for us, the weariness of His life upon the earth, and His bitter sufferings for us. For He endured the cross, when He might have chosen all joy.

Oh how we would thank and praise God if there were in each Congregation a group of Brethren and Sisters, known not only to God but also to the Congregation, not only single but married as well, who had dedicated themselves to be of service to the Lord in His kingdom. Then each would seek to have this spirit: I will try to be of real use to the Congregation, so long as I am a member of it; to grow in grace and in the knowledge of Jesus Christ shall be my daily aim; I will never forget His sufferings and His death upon the cross, and His blood shed for the forgiveness of my sins; whole-hearted and tender communion with Him shall be my dearest business; Him will I love till death, for He is my Lord and my God; I will learn the teachings of Jesus Christ and His disciples, and will treasure them in my heart; I will support with my prayers the work of the Brethren among Christians and heathen, of which I always hear on Unity Days, and of which I read the printed accounts; if I find opportunity to touch a soul and be of help to it, I will do it with diligence, so long as I am in the Congregation; I will be faithful in my present calling, and will do the work expected of me with industry and loyalty; in food and drink I will be content with what is necessary, and not accustom myself to luxury; I will not use my salary for clothing which does not suit my origin and education, but will keep myself in accordance with my condition in life; when I can help the sick or poor I will do it gladly, and I will take part in the appointed collections according to my means; I will give my body the needful care, but I will not pamper it, when I go somewhere I will go on foot, so that walking will not be too hard for me when it is necessary; I will not accustom myself to things which a pilgrim can not always have where he is being used by the Lord, and which one can well do without, as Paul has said: "A soldier abstains from all things which would hinder him in his calling," and in another place it is written: "All things are lawful for me but not all things are expedient, not all things edify."

See, dear Brethren and Sisters, so have our Brothers and Sisters thought, in whom the first love and grace and simplicity ruled; and this is what the Saviour desires that we have once more.

That in the Elders Conference of the Unity we resolved to send this letter to our dear Brethren and Sisters was brought about by the following circumstances. We have thought much about the work among Christians and heathen which our Lord Jesus Christ has committed to us, without our deserving or being worthy of it, and we have spoken much with each other and with the Saviour about it.

We are often astonished at the grace of the Saviour, Who has honored the Unity of Brethren by using its members as helpers in His work. At the same time we have seen that some Brethren and Sisters are needed, who could be very useful here and there, and among those who are in the service some need to be reminded of many things. Who shall and who can help? God alone!

Therefore, dear Brothers and Sisters, let us pray to the Lord with one spirit and one mind, first, that He will prepare more Brethren and Sisters and make them willing and able; then that He will point out those whom He, in His grace and wisdom, has chosen for His service, and that He will strengthen them in that purpose; and third, that He will give new grace to those who are called to labor in the vineyard of the Lord, that He will fill their hearts with His love, open their mouths to speak His praise, strengthen, keep and increase their power of body and soul; teach, lead and direct them through His word and His Spirit; give them patience in tribulation, forgive their sins and short-comings, and richly bless their work.

Remember particularly Cairo and the Copts, Jamaica and the Barbadoes, the Brothers' Garden and Nicobar, the free negroes of Surinam, the congregations from among the heathen on the Ohio, the Kalmucks and Sarepta, and any others of whom the Holy Spirit reminds you.

Pray also that He will keep, renew and increase the Witness-spirit, which hitherto has rested upon the Unity of Brethren.

Finally we commend ourselves to your love and thoughts, and to your faithful prayers, for many important matters are committed to us, and who is sufficient for these things? We wish and hope that each of you will set apart a time each day for communion with the Saviour, over his own needs and concerning His kingdom on earth.

Here, you are commended to the Lord and to His grace by your servants in the Lord,

THE ELDERS CONFERENCE OF THE UNITY.

[In the Salem Archives there are three copies of the Brotherly Agreement of Bethania, adopted in 1780. One is in German, with names of signers attached; probably the last eight names were added later. One translation was made in large part by Frederick William Marshall, the change in handwriting, capitalization and phrasing showing where it was finished by another hand; the other translation was begun by Traugott Bagge, but was largely the work of Abraham Steiner. The Marshall translation is given below, with the final paragraph supplied from the Steiner translation and the names from the German copy.

Each of the Moravian congregations in Wachovia had its Brotherly Agreement, with provisions adapted to the local conditions. Bethania was a village of farmers, whose plantations surrounded the town, hence the items regarding meadows and orchards, party lines and cattle; but the underlying principles were the same in all the Agreements adopted, which magnified religion as the foundation of successful community life, supplemented by rules of conduct to which all had agreed.]

Brotherly Agreement Concerning Congregation Rules, for the Town of Bethania. Adopted April 2, 1780.

Whereas we the Inhabitants of Bethany have been brought together in this place by a particular providence of our Lord, some of us having taken refuge to the United Brethren of Bethabara during the Indian War, where they heard the merits of the Gospel of Jesus Christ preached with Impression upon their hearts at a time when some Families of theirs were going to settle the place called Bethany, which occasioned these Refugees to stay there for some Time with the 7 Families of the Brethren by their Consent, at first only for a Time, untill a great part of them had joined the Brethren & this Congregation was formed. And being convinced by several Years Experience as well as by the Consideration of our common Frailty & the Deviations and Disturbances thence to be feared, whereby the chief aim of our living together might be lost, we find it both usefull and necessary, jointly to agree together about certain Orders & Regulations, to the faithfull and conscientious Observance whereof each of us has freely consented & thereto doth bind himself before our dear Lord and Saviour, & in his presence, in the most solemn Manner.

First of all we declare that it has never been the Intention of our settling here, either to grow rich or to acquire worldly Advantages, but properly to save our own & our Children's Souls, that leading a quiet & peaceful life in all godliness and honesty, we may also bring up our

Children to the Lord who has purchased us, and God's benevolent Intention with this Place & all its Inhabitants may be generally fulfilled. May He himself graciously preserve this mind unto us as long as Bethany shall stand.

It is therefore a main Concern of ours that so as our Saviour has in a particular Manner owned the Unity of Brethren, whereof we look upon ourselves as being a Part, he may take the Lead in our Congregation also, that our Congregation Regulations may be made accordingly, that we ourselves may live unto him, & also bring up our Children for him. And whereas thro' Grace we have been brought to a People, to whom He has given a particular Call to proclaim his Glory unto all Nations, we wish also in this respect not to fall short of our Election, but that he may fit out People even among us and our Children, so as he has blessed the small Beginnings of our first Brethren, for the spreading of the Gospel in all the World, whereby Numbers of Brethren's Congregation Places have been settled in so many different Countries, who enjoying the Merits of Christ, have received the same Faith & are joined together in true Communion of Faith. This Communion, the Effect of our Saviour's Intercession in his Highpriestly prayer, John the 17th, for his People, we will highly esteem as a great Favour, preserving it uninterruptedly by the Assistance of our Lord, and ever encourage the Service of the Gospel with all our Might.

The Doctrine of our Lord Jesus Christ & his Apostles, as contained in the holy Scriptures, both in the Old & New Testament, is to be the rule of our Walk, in our Families, in the Place[2] among one another, and towards those that are abroad. And so as we esteem it an essential Character of a Congregation of Christ, that the Word of God be preached among them pure and clear, so we will also make it our Endeavour to lead an holy Life accordingly.

Our Congregation Orders are not so much intended for a correction in Case of Transgressions, as rather to prevent & remove beforehand as much as in us layeth every Thing that could be hurtfull or an Occasion for Sinning. And whereas Congregation rules referr properly to the human Heart, our Wish and Intention with regard to all outward regulations is, that first of all a living knowledge of Jesus Christ may be planted in the Hearts of the Members of the Congregation, thereby to be convinced how useful and wholesome good Order & Discipline be, & what Harm would ensue if there were none, so that not only the Ministers and Servants be obliged to watch over it, in Consequence of their Function, and scrupulously to keep to it, without Distinction or

---

[2] Moravian communities in which civil affairs as well as those of the church were controlled by church boards were sometimes called Place Congregations,—a literal translation of Gemein Ort.

regard of Persons, but that all Members of the Congregation be equally bound to make it their Concern. For our Congregation is properly to be ruled by Principles and Orders, adopted & acknowledged by us all, whereby Harmony and a Conformity of thinking is promoted and kept up amongst us, so that the Business of the Ministers is only to see that these Principles may uninterruptedly govern in all Respect.

We therefore request the Elders Conference in Wachovia, at this Time residing at Salem, under the Guidance of our Lord, to take the Direction of our outward & inward Regulation into their Hands, the same as in the other Brethren's Congregations in this Country, looking upon them as appointed to watch that the Laborers[3] & Committee from Time to Time here employed, may not be disturbed in executing their Offices & maintaining the Congregation Orders.

According to the Rule given by the Apostle: *Is it so that there is not a wise Man among you?* next to these we have chosen sensible People to be the Executors of these Congregation rules, whose Object is the spiritual as well as temporal Prosperity both of the whole Congregation & of every Individual, in endeavouring to prevent Hurt or Harm & to judge & rectify between the Inhabitants. This is the real Intention for which the Committee has been chosen, viz[t] to make it their Business to bring all Congregation Regulations, Morality, Uprightness, & proper Decorum in the Behaviour of the Members of the Congregation into Execution, & to be Overseers in a proper Sense. Next to this they are to keep the Accounts of the Congregation, both receits and disbursements & to account for it to the Congregation Vestry or Meeting of the Heads of Families, and to see the Points hereunto annexed concerning the Families, the Place, Lands & Fields &c. put in practice. Of this Committee the Minister & Schoolmaster for the Time being and for the present four Members nominated by us thro' the plurality of Votes and confirmed by Decision of our Saviour by Lot,—according to the Custom of the Brethren's Congregations—are to be the Members, who are to be newly chosen in the same Manner every three Years.

And whereas the holy Scripture expressly ordereth us to be subject & obedient to the Higher Powers, for they are the Ministers of God to us for good, we will cheerfully submit ourselves to the Laws & Regulations made for the benefit of the Country, e.g. on Sundays not to do any but necessary Work, which can not be helped, not to dry linen, not to hunt, nor discharge Guns in the Streets, or do any other offensive & unbecoming Actions. In like manner we will regularly discharge the Taxes both of the whole Country and the County, and whoever shall withdraw from this Christian Duty can not be a Member of the Congregation.

---

[3] Ministers.

In general we look upon ourselves as obliged to seek the Peace of the Country where the Lord has established us, and to live in neighbour-like Love & friendship with all Men. We will not meddle in religious Disputes, nor persecute anybody on account of his Persuasion. We will as little meddle with Political Disputes or Party Affairs, but follow Peace with all Men.

Among ourselves we will submit to one another according to Scripture, receiving brotherly Admonitions in a brotherlike Manner, particularly giving Place to Advice of the Apostle: *We beseech You Brethren to know them which labour among You, & are over You in the Lord, and admonish You, & to esteem them very highly for their Work's sake, and be at Peace among Yourselves,* and accordingly we will conform to our Teachers, Labourers, and Members of the Committee and obey them, for they watch for our Souls, as they that must give Account that they may do it with Joy & not with Grief, for that would be unprofitable for us. We will earnestly pray for them.

If any body should desire leave to live in this Congregation, the Committee is first of all to examine all his Affairs, to be perfectly acquainted with the real Ground & Intention of his Desire, & send an Account thereof, together with their Opinion, to the Elders Conference, that it may appear as evident as well can be whether such Desire proceeds from an upright, well considered Intention to live with a People of God. According to Circumstances it may be well to be informed whether the Person be of Age; whether bound to any body; whether promised in Marriage; whether in Debt; and if the Person be married, who & what Sort of People belong to their Family; with what Business they intend to get their Livelihood; that neither the Congregation nor the Persons themselves may thereby suffer unexpected Losses. If there be no Objection found either in the Elders Conference or Committee, it is mentioned to the Congregation Vestry, & if even there no Objection be made the Committee giveth him Leave to be an Inhabitant, in the Manner hereafter mentioned. Riches, profitable Business & other worldly Views are not to be reasons for any body coming to live here, much less to possess an house.

We also own it as a fundamental Principle that no body, whoever it be, ought to be received as an Inhabitant or Member of the Congregation upon mere Hopes, unless there be convincing Proofs of the Work of the Holy Ghost on his Heart, and his being called to us.

For as there is no other Intention in our joining as a Congregation, & by the Grace of God never shall be, but to live together in a true Communion of Faith & brotherly Love, according to the Mind of Christ, it is a natural Consequence, that no body can prosper in it, except he be really blessed with this Mind by being born of God or that he heartily desire after it.

The Intention with our Choirs being such, that every Person may obtain Grace to learn to know our Saviour as well as oneself in an evangelical Manner, & according to Age & State to be clothed with Jesus in Heart Soul & Body to enjoy His Merits, we look upon it as one of the most important and usefull Regulations in our Congregations that the two Sexes be kept separate, in proper Order & Decency, without Exception, thereby to prevent any Hurt of the Souls as well as the loss of our Glory in Christ. We the Heads of Families will therefore make it our particular Business to order our Families accordingly.

As to that most important Point, the Education of our Children, to train them up in the Nurture and Admonition of the Lord, we bind ourselves by the Grace of God to one another, to the faithfull Observance of the following Theses:

1) That we are never to forget that our Children are the Property of Jesus, bought and acquired with holy precious Blood, whom therefore we are to bring up solely for our dear Lord, bestowing all possible Care to keep them from Offense & Harm, which requireth

2) That we Parents approve ourselves in all our Behaviour as Men of God; edifying our Children by our Priestly Walk and provoking them to Imitation, which is the most efficacious Way to have a good effect upon them, as well as to promote our own Blessedness.

3) We will also steadily observe that the Children be not permitted to run about from house to house without sufficient reason, & if it should happen we will ask them what they want, & when their Business is over, we will send them home again. In like Manner it will be well in general that a Parent seeing Children in the Street or in Places where they have no Business send them home, though they be not his own, nor will we take it amiss of one another. We will also not suffer them to ride like mad when they water horses or at other Opportunities.

4) Not thro' a Notion of particular Holiness, but convinced of our human Frailty and Sinfullness, we will strictly observe that all unnecessary private Conversation between Persons of different Sexes be wisely avoided and no ways connived at, thereby to prevent Hurt and Danger. For it is not sufficient that the Opportunities for Disorder and sinfull Actions be cut off, but that no secret Connections & Engagements may happen, and Promises of Marriage be not made except in proper Order.

5) Still less would it become us, & it is therefore not at all to be suffered amongst us, that our young People be suffered to rove about in Troops, perhaps of both Sexes or mixed with those from other Places,

thro' the Woods & Fields, or other Plantations, whereof nothing but hurt, Excesses & Transgressions are to be expected. In like manner our Boys & Girls are not to be indulged in libertine Connections with other People on Sundays, neither in the Houses nor in the Streets. From the same Principle it shall not be suffered amongst us, that young People of both Sexes be bespoke to meet in the Harvest for Husking & other Work, or for Weddings, or that lightminded Conversation be allowed. But if notwithstanding all the Care taken it should happen that single People by a clandestine Connection should contract Marriages, or that others had concurred therein, then such single People, as well as those that have been accessory to it, are to be excluded our Congregation.

We will no less keep those Strangers whom we can not well do without, in Time of Harvest, or at other Times for spinning & other Work, in good Order and Decorum, and those of ill Repute, against whom we are warned, we will remove as soon as can be, tho' they might have been employed before now, without running the risk of Mischief arising by it. Whoever doth not conform to these Regulations with his whole Heart, can not be looked upon by us as a Brother.

We all will hold fast the form of sound Words of the Scripture in our Diet, Dress, Lodgings & the like, minding to add to our faith Temperance, honesty, Modesty & good Oeconomy, truly avoiding by the Grace of God all Extravagancy, Vanity & misapplication of temporal Matters, not forgetting that even in the Times of the Old Testament God highly resented in his People the Extravagencies in Clothes & other Excesses. On the other hand the Christian Decorum in outward Matters, whereof Cleanliness is a main Part, is not to be neglected in a Congregation Place, such as, the Cleanliness of the Streets, that no Dung, Rubbish, dead Creatures or the like be suffered to lay about, that every house have its own decent Necessary house, & if Cattle should die in the Stables to have it removed & buried as soon as possible. To this also referreth the Carefulness in regard to fire, & walking about with Candles, which the Heads of Families are to be carefull about, thereby to prevent Harm to themselves and the whole Village, and if the Fire Inspectors should find necessary to remind any thing to conform to it willingly.

Being Members of the same Body, whereof Christ is the Head, we look upon ourselves as bound by the Communion of Faith, Love & Hope, to which we are called, each to be helpers of the other's Joy, bearing good and bad Events in common, and therefore every Member is the more bound, not to undertake nor to occasion any thing whereby an other or the whole Congregation could suffer harm or Damage, or be brought into bad reputation.

Whenever a Brother or Sister amongst us, whoever it be, should see any thing whereby sinfull Actions or harm could ensue, or our Glory in Christ be lost, such Person is bound neither to keep it secret, nor to speak of it unguardedly or in the wrong Place, but to inform thereof the Committee or the Labourers for the Time being without delay, that it may be examined into, and all Harm be prevented, whereas it shall not be suffered that personal Matters be reported & made public, to the Detriment of Individuals.

Every Inhabitant is to work, according to the Rule of the Apostle, & to eat his own bread, & whoever neglects this or thro' Negligence gets into Debt, must not expect any Assistance from the Congregation. But if thro' Age, Sickness, or otherwise without his own fault, a Member should become helpless, so as not to be able to maintain himself, & he should have no Relatives to provide for him, of such the Congregation will in Love take Care. More particularly we will make it our Business to provide for Widows & Orphans, and if no Guardian be appointed in the Testament, the Committee will do it, so that the Widow may know whom to advise with, & he again may have recourse to the Committee, which is to care for the Widows & Orphans as well as Time & Circumstances admit of it, that also these Children may become usefull People.

And whereas we gratefully acknowledge the good temporal Subsistance of every Member, as a peculiar Blessing & Benefit of the hand of God, we will also beg it of him as a particular Favour, that Greediness after lucre or willingness to be rich may never become our Aim. In all Trade & Business we will study what is fair & honest, abhorring all Deceit. Nor will we extend our Businesses, such as Distilling, so as thereby to encourage Immoralities or Things not becoming this Place, but rather conform to such just & brotherly limitations as may from Time to Time be agreed on amongst us.

If any body should want to borrow Money we look upon it as proper that he first mention it to the Committee, and have their Advice, & that no Money be lent or borrowed upon Interest, within or without the Place, without it, much less that he pawn any Thing for it.

All Inhabitants look upon themselves as obliged to take Share in all Regulations jointly made for the Benefit of the Congregation & the whole Place, whether it be in Expences or in personal Help. Of this kind is among the rest the Maintenance of our Minister, of the Congregation-house, and what is required for our Meetings, or such Collections wherein we as Brethren & Members of the Unity take a free-willing Share, in like Manner of the Burying Ground, and what shall be jointly approved of for the good Order of the Place.

In general both in our civil Connections with one another, and in the Behaviour towards Strangers and Travellers, the rule of Christ should be of wholesome Effect: As ye would that Men should do to you, do ye also to them likewise.

From this Principle derive several neighbourly Duties incumbent on us, particularly with regard to the reciprocal management of our Plantations, such as not to allow Cattle to range freely if they are known to leap Fences, to clip the wings of Fowls, not to fell Trees into the Creek, nor to leave Fallgates open of joint Fields in going in or out, nor to allow young People to take of the Neighbour's Fruit or Vegetables. And in Case by such Neglect Harm be done, it shall be estimated by Neighbours, & the Damages be made good by the Guilty.

In general we determine, that an express Agreement be made among ourselves concerning the Land which we do jointly possess, which every one is to observe, & regularly to pay the Rent of the Land as well as his Share of the Taxes when due.

As also, that no body may raise an House, Barn or other Building of Note, without previously acquainting the Committee, or upon Occassion the Meeting of all the Heads of Families.

And whereas much Damage or Dissatisfaction may be caused by bad Fences, it is resolved that all Fences, whether of single Pieces or in common, are to be kept in as good Order as possible, & if thro' any one's Neglect harm should ensue, he whose Fence is found deficient is to pay the Damage.

It is also just, that if any body should take up Land adjoining an other, that he be bound to make and keep up one half of the Fence between them, and in Case two who border upon one another should resolve to make a Middlefence, it is to be upon their Line, but if the other should not choose to make a Middlefence he can however not forbid the other, if he sets it entirely on his own Land.

As to the Orchards, it depends upon the Inhabitants whether they choose to have Middlefences, in which case each is to make & keep up his Share, but if they could not agree about it then the plurality may finally decide it & so it is to remain.

In the same Time we determine that no body be allowed to put any Cattle whatsoever into joint[4] Orchards, Meadows or Fields except they be guarded, & whoever transgresses this shall pay unto his Neighbour full Damages. And if after Harvest, Fields & Meadows might be depastured, it shall not be done by any body before all those that are adjoining are previously agreed about the Manner & how it shall be conducted. Therefore no Turnip seed shall be sowed, & no Flax spread on

---

[4] Here the handwriting changes in the translation.

such Fields whereby the enjoyment of the Pasture could be prevented at proper season.

In like manner we determine that all public Fences, wherever they are, shall be repaired and put in Order in the Month of November & December, & that in those Meadows where it is necessary, profitable and for the best of the Community to have Ditches, that they be made, and that each partaking Brother of the Land & Ditches be bound to keep them in proper order, and that they be cleaned and renewed yearly, in the above said two Months, that the Water may not be stopped in its course to the Damage of the Community.

And as thro' length of Time the original dividing Line posts & marks between the Fields have been lost, we will in their stead set up Stones, to which purpose some Brethren from the Congregation shall be appointed.

But in future no Wood Land shall be surveyed for any Person before he has cleared his old share of upland & meadow Land.

Concerning the woods & the using of Timber, every one who uses the same for his Trade & sells the same again, shall also pay for the same as it shall be valued. Wood for building & Fences may be taken Gratis, but for Hickory 6d and for other wood 3d per Cord shall be paid.

Should any new Errings & misunderstandings arise among the Inhabitants it is their Duty first according to the Rule of Christ to converse with one another on the Subject in Love, but if the matter is thereby not compromised, they shall take some other Brethren as they like to it, and it is to be hoped that their equitable decision in the Matter that may be judged by the Rules of the Congregation will appease the parties best.

And in case an inhabitant should be guilty of transgressing these Rules, he shall first be admonished privately, and if it does not avail, then he shall be reprimanded by the Committee or by a Compagnie of Brethren chosen for that particular purpose, and should he also not mind this, the case shall be laid before the Congregation, and if he dont mind then, he can not be lookd upon as a Member of the Congregation.

Should it also happen (which God forbid) that an inhabitant of Bethany, who has swerved with his heart from the Lord, should fall into gross Sins, as whoredom, Adultery, Theft, Boxing, Drunkenness, defrauding, &c., such an Offender can forthwith not be deemed as one of our members, nor suffered to be among us, except a thorough conversion and change of heart & mind renews his capacity to the communion of Faith & to the living in the Congregation.

Lastly we determine that every one who is appointed by the Congregation to any thing, be it as Minister & Schoolmaster, or a Member of the Committee, receiver of Rent, Surveyor, Inspector of Fire, Waiter in the meeting Hall, or what ever name it may have, shall be acknowledged in his Office, and in his official transactions and desires assisted and treated with Decency.

Permission shall not be given to any body to live in Bethany, or to be a possessor of a Lot there, before this our Brotherly Agreement has been laid before him, and he with mature deliberation & clear knowledge of the whole why & whereto the Congregation has made this Agreement hath determined to agree thereto, and before he to the inviolable Observation thereof has either solemnly given his hand, or if he intendeth to be a possesser of a Lot before he by his manual Signature has bound himself to these Rules in presence of the Committee.

Now therefore after all the above written regulations & Orders have been well considered by us, & being thoroughly convinced of the necessity and utility of the same, we engage & promise one to the other, jointly & separately for the Lord's sake and by his Grace to observe the same truly & conscientiously, and pray God our Saviour, who hath moved us to this Disposition, that he may preserve the same in us, take the execution thereof into his own hands & support the same against all difficulties which may arise against them, and we impower those Brethren who are from Time to time appointed in the Service of the Congregation, inviolably to guard having regard to persons, that every inhabitant live accordingly, and that they proceed against those who should have the misfortune to lose this point of view, according to the herein established Maxim.

And[5] in case we should at any future Day deem it necessary for the benefit of the Congregation, to add, diminish, or otherwise to alter any thing in these Congregation Statutes, then these Alterations, after having also been unanimously agreed upon, shall be as powerful and binding as if the same were added hereto at this present, word by word. And as many as walk according to this rule, peace be on them, and mercy, and upon the Congregation of God. Now, the God of peace, that brought again from the Dead our Lord Jesus Christ, that great Shepherd of the Sheep, through the Blood of the everlasting Covenant, make us perfect in every good work, to do his Will, working in us that which is well pleasing in his Sight, through Jesus Christ, to whom be glory, also, from the Congregation at Bethany for ever & ever.   Amen.

---

[5] This paragraph is wanting in the Marshall translation, but appears in the German, and also in the Steiner translation.

In Witness whereof & by Virtue of a brotherly Covenant this is subscribed by all the Housefathers of this Village with their own hands, at
Bethany on the 2nd day of April, 1780.

Joh. Jac. Ernst[6]

Got fried Grabs

Michel Rank

Heinrich Shore

Peter Hauser

Adam Cramer

Henry Sponhauer senr

Michel Hauser

Joh. Balthaser Hege

John Beroth

his

Peter X Sehnert

mark

George Hauser senr

Philip Transu

Casper Fisher

Johan Christoph Kürshner

George Hauser junr

Samuel Strub

Philip Christoph Vogler

Wilhelm Grabs

Abraham Transu

Gottlieb Kramer

Carl Gottlob Opiz

Michel Hauser junr

Johannes Conrad

Gottlob Rank

Michel Seits

Simon Peter

Petrus Hauser

Adam Buttner

Johannes Transu

Johann Nicholaus Bockel

---

[6] Ernst was pastor of Bethania in 1780. The names are taken from the German copy; the
translations omit them.

PART II

PART II

1780

[As the Revolutionary War approached its crisis England found herself entirely surrounded by enemies. France had openly espoused the cause of the American Colonies; Spain had defied her on her own account, and in 1780 Holland did the same; while the other nations of northern Europe were leagued in an armed neutrality which was hostile to British interests. The problems of King George were further complicated by troubles within the Empire, for there were riots in England; Ireland, asked to raise an army to repel a threatened French invasion, took advantage of the state of preparedness to demand and secure independence for the Irish Parliament and the Irish Courts, and more freedom for Irish Catholics; and in June a rebellion broke out in India, led by Hyder Ali, a native prince, but instigated by France.

In 1780 Joseph II, idealist and would-be reformer, succeeded his mother, Maria Theresa of Austria. Catherine of Russia continued her campaign against the Turks. Germany, unlike the rest of Europe, was enjoying Peace, Prosperity and Letters under Frederick the Great. The poet Lessing, in the ducal library of Wolfenbüttel, was within a few months of the end of his life and work. Goethe, a privy councilor of the Duke of Weimar, was already in what is known as the second period of his literary production. Kant, professor of logic at the university of Königsberg, had written a good deal, and was about to publish his "Critique of Pure Reason." Schiller, a regimental surgeon at Stuttgart, was on the eve of giving his first Tragedy to the world.

In America the fortunes of the United Colonies sank to their lowest level during 1780. The Continental Congress was fairly united in opposing England, but was split into numerous cliques, each pushing the interests of its favorite general. Washington, though handicapped by this lack of solid support, held the British forces in check in the north, but in the south they had everything their own way for the first half of the year. Georgia and much of South Carolina had been overrun in 1779, and in May, 1780, Charleston fell before Sir Henry Clinton, who had come south with heavy reinforcements. When Clinton returned to the north, Lord Cornwallis took command of the southern part of the British army. Against the wish of General Washington, Congress sent General Gates to take command of the American troops in the south, and in August his small army was disastrously defeated at Camden, S. C. Meanwhile a guerilla warfare had been carried on by Marion, Sumter, and others, who at least gave the English great annoyance, and forced them to be constantly on guard.

The first encouragement for the American people was the battle of Ramsour's Mill, June 20, 1780, near the south fork of the Catawba River, in North Carolina. The real turning of the tide of their fortunes came in October, 1780, at King's Mountain, N. C., where Ferguson and his men were defeated, largely through the efforts of frontier militia, who came to repel the invaders. In December, General Washington was permitted to send Gen. Nathanael Greene to supercede General Gates, with Col. Daniel Morgan, Col. William Washington and "Light-horse Harry" Lee holding commands under Green.

North Carolina troops suffered severely in the disasters of 1780. Washington had sent all North Carolinians of the Continental Line to the support of Charleston, and when that city was forced to surrender all of the men who had not been killed were captured. Many died from harsh treatment, and only a remnant ultimately returned to their homes. Some North Carolina Militia were lost at Charleston, and many more at Camden. But Tarleton's butcheries, probably intended to strike terror to the souls of the patriots, had an opposite effect, and contributed not a little to the zeal with which the frontiersmen from Carolina, Virginia and Tennessee gathered to defend the Old North State, meeting with a success which encouraged them as much as it surprised and dismayed Lord Cornwallis.

In civil and military affairs there were many changes of leadership during 1780. It is only necessary to mention that when Governor Caswell's term expired he was ineligible for re-election, and was succeeded by Governor Abner Nash.

In the Moravian Settlement of Wachovia, in 1780, Rev. Frederic William Marshall was both Proprietor and Administrator, that is, he held title as Trustee to the land in North Carolina which belonged to the Unitas Fratrum or Moravian Church, and represented the Unity in all that concerned its management, in addition to his services as minister of the Gospel. Bishop John Michael Graff was still pastor of Salem, and careful diarist. Rev. Lorenz Bagge was in charge of the congregation of Bethabara; Rev. John Jacob Ernst was at Bethania; Rev. Valentine Beck served the country congregation of Friedberg, and Rev. John Christian Fritz was stationed at Hope; Toego Nissen, an Akoluthe, was in charge of the society of Friedland, until succeeded by Rev. Johann Casper Heinzmann. Several of the Brethren in Salem assisted by holding services from time to time, as needed. Traugott Bagge was still the Merchant in Salem, and was virtually a purchasing agent for the American forces in the vicinity of Wachovia, though without definite commission. John Jacob Bonn was the community physician and surgeon, as he had been for a number of years. The Assembly had recognized the loyalty of the Moravians by altering the wording of the Affirmation to the form they desired, and by giving them permission to pay a three-fold State tax in lieu of all military service, since the bearing of arms was against the conscience of many of those who had long been members of the Unity of Brethren. Others who had more recently joined the Unity and did not have the same scruples, or young men who were not communicant members, served in the militia, no objection being made by the Church officials. What additional services the Moravians rendered, and how they bore the trials of the months which saw the tide of war steadily drawing nearer their peaceful abode, will appear in the following translations of the diaries and other papers of 1780, filed in the Salem Archives.]

Memorabilia of the Congregations in Wachovia. 1780.

[Translated in full.]

During the Night Watch we passed from the old year into the new with the reading of the beautiful Doctrinal Text: "Grace and Peace from God our Father and from the Lord Jesus Christ be with you and with all those who call upon the name of our Lord Jesus Christ in all their and our settlements," and "let all who this desire say from their hearts 'Amen'." So we began the year with the hope and faith that this Text would be fulfilled for us, in all our towns, and committed ourselves anew into His care and guidance with manifold joy. At once our faithful Lord answered our prayer in the most blessed manner with His Yea and Amen during our participation in the Holy Communion; and during the year we have had countless evidences of His presence, so that with joy we can praise His gracious control. He comforted us concerning our weakness and the insufficiency of our tenderest love toward Him and for each other, of which we were reminded as we read the Minutes of the General Synod last year and reread them this year, and He strengthened our hope that we might become His joy.

The continuance of the war unrest during this year has often encircled us with danger and difficulty, but we have clearly perceived the almighty care and protection of our heavenly Father, and have seen that He Who is with us is stronger than he who is with our enemies, according to the Text of Sept. 13th, as was particularly manifested during a night attack of Light-horse on Br. and Sr. Fritz in the English School-House. Bethabara also felt His care in many ways, especially during September, October and November, when as many as 2,000 men were quartered there at different times, and had to be supplied with most of their provisions. His fatherly forethought was also fully proven in the way our material necessities were supplied, for we had to meet many unusual expenditures and demands, and our trade and handicrafts brought us more loss than profit, and yet we must continue them for we could not refuse service to our neighbors. The continual depreciation of the currency was particularly disastrous, and we must thank Him that He has fed us and provided for us, that He gave us a rich harvest of all kinds of grain and fruit, and has graciously guarded us from all harm.

Among the blessings which our good Lord has given us, we mention the Visitation of our dear Br. Reichel, from June 15th to Oct. 5th, and especially his addresses to the Congregations and to the Choirs, his attendance in the meetings of the Conferences, and his personal talks with the Brethren, also the talks of himself and his wife with the Sisters and the Married People. During his visit the Classes and the Visiting among the Married People were reinstituted, this taking place in Bethabara and Bethania during August. Already in January the Minutes of Synod had been read in Bethania, and in March the Rules and Regulations had been signed by the House Fathers of that town, and the Committee, which had been out of existence for a while, was reorganized with four Brethren. The good result of this movement has been seen among the young people, some of whom have taken more part in that Congregation while others have moved to the Choir Houses in Salem. The Societies of Friedland and the English Settlement have been organized as Country Congregations, the latter receiving the name of Hope; there have been Receptions of members, and the Holy Communion has been held with the Brethren and Sisters designated by the Saviour. During Br. Reichel's visit to Friedberg a prayer-meeting was begun there, and also classes for the young people of both sexes; and in all our towns arrangements were made for the instruction of the children in the doctrines of Jesus, and also for the preparation of candidates for the Holy Communion, according to the suggestions made by Synod. A Conference of the ministers of all the Country Congregations will be held every four weeks.

Br. and Sr. Reichel brought with them some new assistants for the Congregation of Salem, some from Europe, others from Pennsylvania. Br. Jeppe Nilson had been appointed Vorsteher of the Congregation, and with his wife was to help in superintending the Choir of Married People; the Single Brother, Friedrich Peter, had been sent to be secretary of the Conferences, a Reader and musician. But fourteen days after his arrival Br. Nilson was called away by the Saviour from the duties of his office, without any period of illness, and to our great sorrow.

The Congregation Council, Aufseher Collegium and Grosse Helfer Conferenz, as organized last year, have continued their work with blessing, and various Brethren and Sisters have become new members thereof according to the instructions of Synod.

Among the Memorial Days which have been observed, those of Aug. 13th, Sept. 16th, and Nov. 13th, stand out as most important. On the first-named of these days, in addition to the celebration of the Holy Communion, there was the baptism of our only negress, Mary, formerly called Edy. On the 27th of August, in Bethabara, Br. Reichel baptised our negro Christian, formerly known as Frank. On Sept. 16th there was a reception of Akoluthie, the two Brethren Fritz and Samuel Stotz and the three Sisters Fritz, Elisabeth Colver and Maria Elisabeth Krause; and this was followed by the ordination of the three Brethren Heinzmann, Fritz and Friedrich Peter as Deacons of the Unity of Brethren. On Nov. 13th we were particularly conscious of the presence of our faithful Chief Elder among His poor, weak followers; and on the 18th of November there was a post-celebration of this Festival in our Country Congregations, where in each there were Receptions of members and readmission of Brethren and Sisters to the Holy Communion. The Festival of the Chief Elder was observed for the first time in Friedland and Hope. At Christmas also there were especially blessed days, among others that on which our negro Abraham, formerly Sambo, was baptised. Before Easter, Br. and Sr. Fritz moved to the School-House Hope, which was later consecrated during a visit of Br. and Sr. Marshall and others from Salem, and the membership there became a formal Society, and later, as already stated, a Country Congregation was organized. In August, Br. and Sr. Heinzmann moved to Friedland to take charge of the Society there, he having married the widowed Sister Reuter; and Br. and Sr. Toego Nissen and their two children returned to Salem, having served Friedland for five years. The office of Vorsteher of the Single Brethren, so made vacant, was undertaken jointly by the Brn. Petersen and Samuel Stotz, Br. Praezel becoming the Pfleger of that Choir. On the 25th of June the Jubilee of the Augsburg Confession,—published in 1730,—was solemnly celebrated with a Psalm of Thanksgiving.

Among the mercies we have all enjoyed belongs also that we have been permitted to exercise the privilege granted to us by the Act of Assembly, passed last year in our favor, in regard to military matters, and this in spite of the fact that several serious attempts were made to class us among the hated Tories. But our faithful Lord, by ways and means unknown to us, has caused the leading officials of this country to acknowledge us as peaceful and loyal citizens. According to the above-mentioned Act we have paid the Provincial tax three-fold, but the County Court decided that it was unjust to make us pay the County tax three times and has been content with the regular rate. The Court has also rendered no decision regarding certain pieces of property belonging to the Brethren which might be declared confiscated under a new law. Br. Reichel's coffer, which was stolen at the Potomac, and which contained the General Deed for the Wachovia Tract, has been found and has been delivered to Br. Marshall.

We had an unusually long, hard winter, such as was remembered by no one in this country, and we heard of various travelers who were frozen to death. This was followed by an equally hot summer, so that at times laborers were obliged to give up their work in the fields; but the harvest was abundant, which made up in some degree for the repeated calls for grain and cattle for the soldiers, and the Brethren and Sisters were able to meet the expenses of their congregations, and to contribute toward the Unity expenses, the collections for foreign missions and for the schools for the children.

Correspondence with Bethlehem has been somewhat difficult, on account of the conditions existing in the country, and a few letters have been lost, but a hearty, reciprocal connection has been maintained; and several times we have received fairly large packages of Gemein Nachrichten from Europe, by way of Bethlehem, and also the Wöchentlichen Nachrichten of the Unity's Elders Conference, and the Memorabilia for the past year of 1779. All of these have been read to the Brethren and Sisters, and have been heard with thankful interest.

In Salem, in January, a regular school for smaller boys was begun, taught by the two Brn. Heckewälder and Schober. Later the school was transferred to Br. Triebel's house, near the Brothers House; and after Br. Heckewälder went to Pennsylvania, Br. Schober took charge of the school, with Br. Martin Schneider to assist in the supervision of the smallest boys. We thankfully acknowledge the growth of the boys in the knowledge of holy truths and of other useful things, but various incidents have occurred which lead us to pray that they may have a true change of heart. Sr. Catherine Sehner has taken the school for girls succeeding Sr. Oesterlein, who has been married. A *Congregation Account* has been opened in Salem, as in other congregations, since the Diaconie could no longer meet all the expenses. The Masters who carry on businesses or trades for the benefit of the Congregation or Choir Diaconies have given written Bonds, in accordance with the recommendations of Synod.

The repeated passing of soldiers, the moving hither and thither of poor families in flight, have given many opportunities for deeds of kindness

to friends and strangers.   Our friends and acquaintances on Haw River
have again been visited by Br. Heinzmann; a woman from there brought
two of her sons to us for safety and in hope of their salvation.   Br.
Lorenz has also visited his acquaintances in the German Settlement on
the Yadkin, and has served them with the preaching of the Gospel and
the baptism of their children.

In thinking of the numberless times that God has protected us during
this year we must say first that through His angels He has often turned
away the misfortune which the Evil One had planned and intended;
then we will mention certain special proofs of His care which have been
seen in Salem.   On one occasion vicious men threw stones through the
windows of the Brothers House, and one stone passed directly over the
head of a Brother, struck the stove and broke a tile.   A Brother was
saved from drowning in the Petersbach.   That the new bell-tower was
erected without injury was proof of the care of the angels, and we acknowledge it with thankfulness; they also shielded several Single Brethren from imminent danger when during the night part of the plank ceiling and the flooring above it fell into the sleeping-hall between some of
the bedsteads.   In spite of the frequent acts of robbery and murder which
have taken place in our neighborhood, our Brethren have traveled in
safety.   The flood of the 4th and 5th of May tore away the sluice above
the dam at our mill and broke a large hole in the race, but the mill itself was not injured.   The Saviour has protected us from illness.

Many changes have taken place in our towns, especially Salem and
Bethabara.   The widowers Gottfried Aust and Jacob Blum went to
Bethlehem in the spring to be married, and returned with their wives.
Then Br. and Sr. Blum took the place of Br. and Sr. Johann Schaub,
Jr. in the Bethabara tavern; Br. Schaub went to Bethlehem to learn
the art of indigo dyeing, and returned.   Br. and Sr. Peter Rose moved
from the Salem farm to Bethabara, to do the same kind of work there;
and the Single Br. Philip Vogler moved from Bethabara to the Salem
farm, and married the widow Steinmann. The Single Br. Schreyer
married the widow Baumgarten and moved to her farm.   The three
Single Brethren, Carl Opitz, Peter Goetje and Johann Reuz came from
Pennsylvania; the first went to his feeble parents, the Kirschners, near
Bethania, the second became Master of the shoe-shop in the Brothers
House, and the third settled in Salem as a hat-maker on his own ac-
count.   The Single Br. Walther moved from the Tavern into his Choir
House, and Br. John Holland took his place.   Br. and Sr. Meyer sent
their two eldest children, Jacob and Maria Magdalena, into the Choir
Houses.   The four Single Sisters who have served the Oeconomie in

Bethabara for some years exchanged places with four other Sisters from Salem.

Besides those already mentioned the number of residents in Salem was increased by the coming of the Single Sister Maria Magdalena Reuz from Lititz, the Older Girl Anna Johanna Fockel from Bethabara, the Single Brother Balthaser Christman from Haw River, and seven single persons from Bethania, namely the youth Abraham Transou, the boy Kirschner, Juliana Hege, Maria Magdalena Transou, Maria Christina and Gertraut Hauser, and the two Single Sisters Barbara Christman and Dorothea Schumacher who had formerly lived in Salem; little Christian Nissen was the only child born here this year. Altogether eighteen persons were added to Salem, but the number was reduced by six through the death of little Abraham Steiner, the two little girls Anna Blum and Magdalena Kapp who returned to their parents in Bethabara, the negress Maria who also moved to Bethabara, the Single Brother Christian Heckewälder who went to Bethlehem, and the single Johann Nilson who was dismissed.

Besides the two little girls and the negress the congregation of Bethabara was increased by three, namely by Sister Elisabeth Blum who was married to Br. Blum in Bethlehem and came hither with him, and by the birth of twins, Johann Lorenz and Maria Christina Bagge. The congregation lost two, namely the girl Johanna Fockel, already mentioned, and Br. Richter who went home in peace.

Bethania had an increase of eight, namely George Hauser, Jr. and his family, the Single Br. Carl Opitz, Anna Barbara Pfaff from Friedberg who married Wilhelm Grabs, and the two children Catherine Fischer and Catherine Rank who were born in the town. There was a decrease of seven, the youth Johann Schor went home, Margaretha Hauser married and moved away, and five others moved to Salem as already noted.

There have been Received into the Congregations:

in Salem 13, among them one negro and one negress by Baptism;
in Bethabara 1 negro, also by Baptism;
in Bethania 11;
in Friedberg 7;
in Friedland 13;
in Hope 8;
a total of 53 persons.
In the same places there were 25 Confirmed for their first participation in the Holy Communion.
Nine couples were married.

At the close of this year the congregations stand as follows:

Salem,

24 Married Couples 48
Widows 2
Single Brethren, Youths and Boys 48
Single Sisters and Older Girls 27
Little Boys 13, Little Girls 9 22

Total .... 147 persons.

Bethabara,

16 Married Couples 32
1 Widower, 2 Single Brethren, 2 Boys 5
Single Sisters 5
Little Boys 12, Little Girls 15 27

Total 69

Bethania,

18 Married Couples 36
Single Brethren 2, Youths 15 17
Young Women and Older Girls 8
Little Boys 11, Little Girls 19 30

                                                             91

Living outside the town but belonging to the
    Congregation 32

Total 123

Friedberg,

Communicants 40
Received 13
Society members 55

Total, not counting the children 108

Friedland,

Communicants 10
Received 15
Society members 31

Total, not counting the children 56

Hope,

Communicants 6
Received 8
Society members 56

Total, not counting the children 70

Grand total, 573 persons, [exclusive of the children in the Country
Congregations].

The Diary of the Congregation in Salem for the Leap Year 1780.

[Extracts translated.]

Jan. 1. New Year. In the Night Watch the congregation passed blessedly into the New Year with the reading of the Text: "Zion hears and is glad; and the daughters of Judah rejoice because of thy judgments, O Lord";

> We commit ourselves unto Thy guidance,
> And in all Thy blessed ways,
> With thousand joys,
> Good Shepherd, Thou wilt lead us.

The Doctrinal Text was: "Grace and Peace from God our Father and the Lord Jesus Christ be with you and with all those who call upon the name of our Lord Jesus Christ in their and our Settlements."

> Who this desire,
> Say from the heart "Amen!"

At 10 o'clock in the morning the festal service was held, Br. Graff preaching as usual from Luke II. In the afternoon the Memorabilia of various German and English Congregations for the year 1777 were read. At 7 o'clock the communicants assembled for the first time in this year for the Lord's Supper.

Jan. 2. In the afternoon at 1 o'clock was the funeral of little Abraham Steiner, who died on Dec. 30th at the mill. This time only the Brethren went to God's Acre, for snow fell all last night and continued today, clearing up toward evening with a cold west wind.

Jan. 3. The wind was from the north-west, and it was very cold, so only the twilight service was held, with the reading of Nachrichten from St. Croix [West Indies] and Zeist [Holland].

Jan. 4. The Aufseher Collegium met in the morning. Among other things notice was given that the Single Sister Barbara Christman, who has been living with Br. and Sr. Stockburger, and Juliana Hege are now permitted to move into the Sisters House. Official instructions were given to four Brethren;—Heckewälder and Schober concerning the little boys who begin school with them today, Br. John Holland who moves to the Tavern, and Walther who leaves the Tavern and returns to the Brothers House. In the afternoon the good news was announced to Sr. Christman by several members of the Collegium, to her great joy, and she gave her hand in pledge of obedience to the Rules and Regulations of the congregation, which have been explained to her during the last few days. Toward noon Br. Marshall returned from Bethania; yesterday and the day before he read to the communicant members there the most important parts of the Minutes of General Synod.

Jan. 5. The Aeltesten Conferenz met during the morning. At 7 in the evening there was a meeting with the House-Fathers who will send their sons to the day-school; the new organization of the school was explained to them, and the necessity for their contributing to the support of the two Brethren who will teach the boys, and they declared their willingness so to do.

The wind was from the west today, and especially toward evening it blew heavily and brought a bitter cold.

Jan. 6. Epiphany. At twilight, instead of the liturgy, there was the reading of the sermon that Br. Reichel preached on the Mission Festival of 1778; reading of the Nachrichten concerning our heathen congregations and posts was postponed to next Sunday. On account of the intense cold, which must be the worst of the winter, the singstunde was omitted, but there was a meeting of the Grosse Helfer Conferenz, in which mention was made of the decision to have the Brn. Holland and Walther exchange work.

Jan. 7. Sister Bachhof brought Sr. Graff an affirmative answer to the proposal that she marry Br. George Schmidt. In the twilight, reports for the first half of 1777 at Fulneck [England] were read. The second service was omitted because it remained as cold as yesterday, with a strong wind from the west-north-west. Br. Johann Krause came from Steiner's mill and reported that not only had the water-wheel frozen fast, which has never happened before, but the ice had also sprung the wheel which will now have to be fastened with iron screws.

Jan. 8. The Single Sister Juliana Hege moved from Bethania into the Single Sisters House here. In the afternoon the betrothal of Br. George Schmidt and Sr. Bachhof took place in the presence of the Brn. and Srs. Graff and Marshall. The severe cold continues.

Jan. 9. The Widows had a Choir meeting, during which Sr. Baumgarten received the Widow's ribbon.

Jan. 10. The new arrangements for the Boys' School went into effect, with Brn. Heckewälder and Schober as teachers. In the afternoon a lovefeast was held for these two Brethren, with the former teachers, Fritz and Jens Schmid, and the Brethren of the Aeltesten Conferenz present as guests. May the Saviour lay His blessings upon this school. The children will be in the school from 8 to 11 in the morning, and from 1 to 4 or 5 in the afternoon, but will eat and sleep at home. For the present eleven will attend, including the two older boys, Aust and Bonn, who are still in school. Br. Marshall collected the contributions for foreign missions from the members living in town. In the twilight there was reading of Br. Joseph's[1] sermon, delivered on Dec. 25, 1777. The singstunde was omitted on account of the bad weather, for today it has alternately snowed and rained, with wind from the south-east.

Jan. 11. Poor Sr. Bachhof came to Sr. Graff and positively refused to marry Br. George Schmidt, saying she could not rest until she had made up her mind to do this. It is the first case of the kind that has ever occurred here. Perhaps it will be good for both of them. The weather cleared with wind from the north and west, and in the following night it froze.

Jan. 12. The wind changed to the north-west, and all day the sun was unable to thaw the ground. Many people declared that it was the coldest day we have had this winter. A neighbor, Rosenbaum, who passed through the town, coming from Holston River, said that an entire family had been frozen on their journey to Kentok [Kentucky]. Sr. Bachhof came to Sr. Graff and took back her refusal of yesterday in regard to her marriage, and said "Yes" instead, but we will wait to see whether she sticks to it.

Jan. 13. In the twilight there was a liturgy, with the Hymn

> Appear, O congregation,
> Before the Trinity.

Congregation Council should have met later, but was postponed on account of the bad weather, slippery paths, and the sickness of several members.

Jan. 14. The weather has moderated somewhat.

Jan. 16. The negro, Jacob, who formerly belonged to us, came from his master, Robert Lanier, and wanted to get his clothes, but he was sent away empty-handed, for in the first place they did not belong to him, and in the second place he had done much damage here.

In a congregation meeting in the evening the widower George Schmidt was married to the widow Rosina Bachhof. Each is 61 years old, and this is the latter's third marriage.

Jan. 17. The newly married pair, with their two children, had a pleasant breakfast with Br. and Sr. Graff. Br. Fritz began to teach the Single Sister Maria Elisabeth Krause to make gloves, so that branch of the leather goods business can hereafter be carried on in the Sisters House. The weather has been moderate for some days, but this afternoon a strong wind from the north-west brought with it a piercing cold.

---

[1] Bishop August Gottlieb Spangenberg, affectionately dubbed "Br. Joseph."

Jan. 18. Br. and Sr. Marshall returned from Bethania. They have spoken very frankly with the Brethren and Sisters there, and many have expressed their regret for their lack of conformity with the Rules and Regulations, and have said that they wish to follow the foundation principles laid down in the Minutes of Synod. Br. Marshall has told the Bethania members that the test of their intention to remain a congregation of the Unity of Brethren will be that in secular and spiritual things they, and their children as well, will do as other congregations do, and the children will not act merely according to the ideas of their fathers.

The angels again protected the teamster's wagon from damage. It was standing in front of the Gemein Haus, when the ringing of the bell frightened the horses and they ran away. The leading pair turned and fell on top of each other, which stopped the second pair until the teamster could get to them and straighten them out, and so no harm was done.

In the afternoon the four Brn. Herbst, Heinzmann, Bagge and Bonn went to Bethania to take the taxes to the sheriff for the residents of Salem and for the Administration.

Jan. 19. The four Brethren who went to Bethania yesterday have returned. They wished to pay the County taxes at the regular rate, and the sheriff said the County tax should be paid three-fold like the Provincial tax; so the sheriff postponed receipt of the taxes until the next session of the Court could rule on the matter. Sr. Rosina Schmidt moved today into the home of her husband.

Jan. 20. The Aufseher Collegium decided that Br. and Sr. Meyer should send their two older children into the Choir Houses, as they cannot be cared for properly in the Tavern, on account of the rough people who gather there.

Jan. 21. There were several gentlemen here, who came by or from Hillsborough, from Charlestown, etc. They looked over our town and expressed *satisfaction*. One hears from various directions a rumor that peace will be made between England and France, but the report lacks confirmation much as one would like to believe it.

Jan. 22. The bitter cold has moderated a little.

Jan. 24. This morning it snowed a little, and tonight the north-east wind has again made it very cold.

Jan. 25. Br. Fritz went to our English Settlement, and in the home of Mr. Markland held the funeral of a young man by the name of Crampton, a grandson[2] of his wife. As the young man was felling trees his skull was fractured by a piece of wood. The newly selected

---

[2] The Death Record in the Hope Church Book calls him a stepson of Matthew Markland.

3

place for a God's Acre was consecrated with a prayer, and a sermon was preached to a large audience.

Jan. 30. At close of day the *Hymn of Praise to the Father* was sung. For several days the weather has been milder, and today the ice and snow have melted rapidly.

Jan. 31. Br. Graff began the doctrinal instruction of the little boys, according to the printed outline of the teachings of Jesus and His apostles. The boys were very attentive, and looked up the indicated Bible references with interest; the smallest boys sat like little priests, and listened intently.

From a Virginia newspaper, which carried news to the end of December of last year, we saw that all the sea powers of Europe were pushing equipment, which proves that the rumored peace between England and France is not yet near.

Feb. 3. The Communicants gathered in the Saal and various announcements were made. Among the rest they were told of the recently published Unity writings,[3]—the new Hymn Book, the little book of Doctrinal Instruction for Children, the History of the Brethren's Mission in Three West Indian Islands, and so on,—and any who wished to order them were asked to notify their Choir leaders.

Feb. 4. Friedrich Lang, of Deep Creek, was here yesterday. He is one of Br. Fritz' awakened hearers, and he and his brother George have several times expressed a wish to move away from their present place and come nearer a School-House of the Brethren, so they could send their children to school. Br. Heinzmann told him of the plantation which Br. Rose has had in rent, and which he is giving up, and asked whether he would like to take it; he looked over it and liked it, but asked for fourteen days time before answering, partly in order to consult with his wife, and partly to see whether he could rent his present plantation.

Feb. 5. Since yesterday the wind has been from the north, so it is cold again, and does not thaw much during the day.

Feb. 6. Br. Fritz preached in the English Settlement. Br. Herbst accompanied Wilhelm Grabs to Friedberg to see about his marriage, and returned in the evening, hoping that there would be good results.

Feb. 7. Shortly before noon a hard storm of rain and sleet came up from the east, and continued all day and into the night, so that no evening services could be held.

[3] Gesangbuch, zum Gebrauch der evangelischen Brüdergemeinen. Barby, gedruckt durch Lorenz Friedrich Spellenberg. 1778. C. G. A. Oldendorp's Geschichte der Mission der evangelischen Brüder auf den caraibischen Inseln S. Thomas, S. Croix und S. Jan. Herausgegeben durch Johann Jacob Bossart. Barby. 1777. Der Hauptinhalt der Lehre Jesu Christi zum Gebrauch bey dem Unterricht der Jugend in den evangelischen Brüdergemeinen. Zweyte Ausgabe, Barby, 1778.

Feb. 8. The weather has cleared up cold from the north-west.

Feb. 10. This was the first warm and pleasant day of the winter, with wind from the south.

Feb. 11. It rained all day, with a south wind, and melted practically all the ice and snow, and began to thaw the earth which has been frozen a foot deep. Toward evening there was a thick fog, and during the night it did not freeze for the first time this winter.

Feb. 12. In the prayer meeting Br. Graff spoke on the Text: "One is your Master, even Christ, and all ye are Brethren," * * * and presented several matters for prayer, for instance he said that next week the County Court would decide whether the County taxes must be paid three-fold and that their decision would affect our future, and have an influence on other attempts that might be made against us.

Feb. 13. During the liturgy the Single Sister Mary Handson and the Older Girl Elisabeth Hartmann were Received into the congregation with the Kiss of Peace. Br. George Hartmann came from Friedberg for the Reception of his daughter; from him we heard that several of them had been to the Court in Salisbury about the twelve-fold tax which had been demanded of them, and the favorable decision had been given that they were only to pay the three-fold tax. General Rutherford had proved himself to be a just man.

Feb. 14. The three Brn. Heinzmann, Herbst and Bonn went to Richmond, to hear the decision of the Court concerning our taxes,—see under date of Jan. 19th,—and then to pay the taxes. The two lawyers, Mr. Dun and Alexander Martin, passed on their way to Richmond, and each of them was told about the matter under consideration, so that in case of need they might speak for us.

Feb. 15. It was rainy all day. In the meeting of Communicants Br. Marshall spoke impressively on the text: "The peace of God, which passeth all understanding, shall keep your hearts and minds in Christ Jesus." Br. Bonn returned this evening from Court, bringing the good news that without further consideration the Court had decided that we should pay the County tax only once instead of three-fold, and he brought a written order of Court to that effect. The sheriff will come here himself to collect the taxes. This was a confirmation of the text, for which we give our humble thanks to our good Lord.

Feb. 16. In the morning the Aeltesten Conferenz met, Br. Lorenz [Bagge] being present. Br. Meyer went to the burial in Friedberg of the Society Brother, John Müller, who died day before yesterday. The two Single Sisters, Marie Transou and Juliana Hege, who recently moved into their Choir House, gave their hands to several members of the Aufseher Collegium in token of their promise to abide by the

Rules and Regulations of the congregation. The wind today was from the north-west, and during the following night it froze.

Feb. 18. Br. and Sr. Marshall, Brn. Graff and Heinzmann and the Single Sisters Quest and Colver went to Friedland, to join the Society there in celebrating the anniversary of the organization of their Society and the consecration of their meeting-hall five years ago. In the first general meeting there was a sermon on the purpose of the association of this group, which was that with the Unity of Brethren they might be grounded on the sufferings and death of Jesus, and might live for Him. The second service was a lovefeast for all, young and old, who belong to this School-House, during which the story was told of the families who moved hither from Broadbay in 1769, 1770 and 1771. The third meeting was for members of the Society only, including seven who joined today, and Br. Marshall read to them an extract from the Minutes of General Synod.

Here, in the twilight, Br. Pretzel read Nachrichten from the Diaspora of Upper Lusatia. The day was closed with the hymn:

> As Jesus hung upon the cross.

The weather was pleasant; toward evening it clouded up, and did not freeze.

Feb. 19. Today we received warning from Bethania that search was to be made in our towns for provisions for the soldiers destined for South Carolina, and wagons and horses were also wanted. In the Brothers House a quantity of wheat was put out of sight. Friedrich Lang wrote that he would not be able to rent Rose's plantation.

Feb. 20. Br. Marshall went to Bethania, to read to the members there the Rules and Regulations as revised for them.

Feb. 21. Michael Hauser has said openly that a plan is being made against Wachovia, the intention being to declare it an English property and to confiscate it for the present Government. This afternoon there was a rather hard rain which continued into the night. In the twilight there was reading of reports from Wetteravia and the Palatinate.

Feb. 22. It rained all day. During the night a heavy storm came up from the north-west, and toward morning it froze.

Feb. 23. It was reported in Aeltesten Conferenz that the Bethania congregation is well satisfied with the parts of the Rules and Regulations that refer to conduct and religion, but find it necessary to give further consideration to the part concerning town affairs, especially regarding the purchase of their land, and arrangements to be made for their common ownership and use of the same. There was a sharp wind from the north-west all day, and it was bitterly cold.

Feb. 24. Br. Marshall had a conference with the three Brn. Graff, Bagge and Bonn regarding land affairs. The Deed to Wachovia, whereby Br. Marshall succeeds James Hutton as Proprietor, and the Power of Attorney to the three Brethren aforesaid to transfer the twenty pieces of Metcalf land to Br. Marshall, must both be registered at the next term of General Court. It is a little less cold today.

Feb. 25. Br. Heinzmann is 58 years old today. Through Mr. Frederic Miller we hear that the Assembly at New Bern has scattered, there being too few members present to form a House.

Feb. 26. Last night it did not freeze; toward evening there was a little warm rain which put out the bush-fire which yesterday crept in across our God's Acre.

This afternoon a group of bad young men gathered in our Tavern, sons of our good friends John Padget and Doughted, and hitherto friendly. In the evening as they were leaving they threw several stones at Br. Heinzmann, whom they saw as they passed the Brothers House; they also threw a stone through the window of the shoe-shop, which fortunately did not touch any of the Brethren who were in the room, though it struck the stove and broke a tile. There appears to be much unrest at present, for the English troops are probably not far from Charlestown; paper money has fallen to 2d on the dollar, and people are bringing quantities of it to our town in order to buy things with it.

Feb. 27. Br. Fritz preached in our English Settlement, and Br. Herbst went thither with him. Br. Fritz told Padget and Mr. Doughted of the misbehaviour of their sons yesterday; they were very sorry, and promised to speak to their sons about it.

Feb. 28. The Single Br. Biwighaus was sent to Salisbury to see about several things, especially the falling value of the currency. Br. Grabs and his son returned from the home of Br. Pfaff, and told us that the betrothal of Wilhelm and Pfaff's daughter had taken place. There were many strangers in the Tavern, who attended the two services in the Saal. The weather was spring-like.

Feb. 29. Again many people came to town to get rid of their paper money.

March 1. In the evening meeting mention was made of the first organization of the Brethren in Bohemia and Moravia 327 years ago, in spite of the severe persecution then existing. At 8 o'clock the Single Sisters had their Choir Liturgy, using No. 2.

The sheriff came for the taxes, of which £2000: had already been paid according to his order. Br. Biwighaus returned from Salisbury, and brought from Mr. Bude[4] a copy of the Will of Mr. Montgomery.

---

[4] Boote.

Mr. Bude wrote to Br. Bagge that the currency had fallen to fifty for one; also that the English had landed 7000 men at Blue Ford.

March 2. This evening we saw the Northern Lights.

March 3. The Northern Lights were followed by a strong wind, and tonight it froze, though not hard.

March 4. Today we first heard what purported to be a true report that the English had taken Charlestown. A few minutes later it was stated as a fact that a Spanish fleet had arrived there and that the English had left.

March 5. In the morning the Church Litany was prayed, and after this there was the reading of a sermon which Br. Fries[5] had written on the text: "Show Thy marvelous lovingkindness, Thou Saviour of those who put their trust in Thee." After the Children's Meeting the interesting diary of the Negro congregation of Antigua for May, 1776, was read, and was heard with close attention. Then the Married People had their Liturgy, using No. B. Sr. Marshall continued reading the history of the West India Islands to the Single Sisters. In the evening gemeinstunde Br. Praezel spoke tenderly on the text: "We are members of His body." The weather was quite pleasant. Toward evening a number of people arrived from Salisbury; among them was Mr. Bude, who was on his way to the Wilkes County Court. The visitors attended the service in the Saal.

March 6. The Brethren of the Aeltesten Conferenz and the Aufseher Collegium had a conference concerning the falling value of the paper money. We have heard from Salisbury and other places that everywhere the dollar is reckoned at 2d instead of 4d. It was resolved to inform the entire communicant congregation of this, which was done this evening at 8 o'clock, and as no one offered any objection the dollar, from tomorrow on, will be received and paid at the value of 2d. Care must be taken that outsiders can not say that we have reduced the ratio, but they must be told that this is the rate everywhere and no one will give us more for the dollar than that.

Br. Biwighaus was sent to the Wilkes Court-House, on the Mulberry Fields, to register the Mortgage on that land, given to us by the now deceased Hugh Montgomery.

A beginning was made with the digging of a trench between the potter-shop and George Schmidt's. It is to lead to the first standpipe, so that the water which runs free there may be taken in pipes to a cistern, partly for use in wetting clay, and partly for protection of that part of town in case of fire.

---

[5] Rev. Peter Conrad Fries, a member of the Unity's Elders Conference.

March 7. Mr. Buthe left for Salisbury, after having made certain inquiries here concerning the Montgomery purchase of the Mulberry Fields; he seems to have something to do with the settlement of this estate, and therefore gave us information about the matter.

It is said that General Rutherford has written to Col. Joseph Williams, urging the marching toward Charlestown of the soldiers enlisted in this County, for an English fleet is lying there.

After midnight it began to rain, and continued all morning; toward evening it cleared, but was not cold.

March 9. The Aufseher Collegium met to consider various matters, especially the election of a new Assembly, which will take place tomorrow and day after tomorrow. Certain Brethren were selected, who will cast their votes for those candidates who are opposed to the division of our County; certain men are working hard for the division in order to further their own interests.

While this conference was going on two men came to the Tavern, stopping for an hour or two on their way to Lancaster [Pa.]. A package of letters, the Diary for December and the Memorabilia for last year, and the Diary of January of the curent year, were wrapped and given to them.

It began to rain this morning and continued into the night; it also thundered and lightened for the first time this spring, wherefore only the twilight liturgy was held. The "Hymn of Praise to the Father" was sung, and six strangers stood outside and listened reverently and with folded hands.

March 10. Br. Graff held doctrinal instruction for the younger girls.

Eight Brethren went from here to Richmond, and cast their votes for Mr. Sheperd and Cummins and Freeman for Assembly-men, returning this evening. The Commissary, Mr. Henderson, has demanded six beef-oxen from us, that is two from each town, for the soldiers enlisted for service in the South, so a meeting of the Aufseher Collegium was held this evening, and it was decided that the Brothers House should furnish the two required from Salem, but that the entire town should share the loss.

March 11. The Brn. Marshall, Graff and Petersen, and the Srs. Marshall, Graff and Anna Maria Krause, went to Friedberg today to join in the Festival of the Congregation and Society there. It rained today, and there was heavy thunder.

March 13. The Commissary, Mr. Henderson, came to inspect the two beef-oxen promised from Salem. Through him we heard that Mr. Sheperd received the most votes for Senator, and Mr. Cummins and

Freeman the most for the Lower House; all three are against the division of our County, and therefore our Brethren voted for them as did others. The opposite party call it a *Moravian election*. We hear that the troops which are marching from Pennsylvania to Georgia are taking another way and will not pass through our towns.

Br. and Sr. Fritz moved today to the English School-House taking the little Blum girl with them. We wished them the blessing and support of the Saviour in their new work.

All day there was a cold wind from the north-west, and during the following night it froze.

March 14. A traveler from New England, who had passed through Bethlehem, reported that a colony from Europe had recently arrived there. The man is a merchant, and had with him all sorts of articles for sale; he had crossed the Roanoke on the ice, and could not say enough hard things about the winter in the north.

March 16. The Commissary, Mr. Henderson, brought two men to appraise the two beef-oxen and to take them away. Two men from New River offered to bring Br. Aust 2000 lbs. of lead; he will burn it for glazing as no other glazing can be procured now. Pipes have been laid to the new cistern; the water runs from two stand-pipes, one in front of Aust's house-door and one into the cistern.

March 17. Mr. Henderson paid £500: for the two beef-oxen, partly currency and partly notes on the Assembly. He took the oxen away, and promised to spare us further demands for provisions. Br. Steiner returned from Salisbury; he had been summoned as a Juryman, but had been released because he is not a free-holder. Yesterday and today there was a raw wind from the north-east, but it did not freeze.

March 18. Br. Marshall and the other Brethren who left with him on the 13th, returned from Salisbury with nothing accomplished. While they were there no Court was held, it being impossible to secure a Grand Jury; in general there was no desire to do anything.

March 19. Col. Martin Armstrong passed, coming from Charlestown. He gave us little information, but it looked as though he were seeking safety for himself and his belongings, which he had with him on a wagon.

March 20. Spring began with frost last night, for it had cleared with a cold wind from the north-east. Probably there was snow further north, when we had the cold rain. The Single Br. Christ went to Salisbury, to try to buy glasses at the sale of the departed Montgomery's property.

March 22. Br. Aust went to Bethania, and Justice [Michael]

Hauser signed his Pass for the trip to Pennsylvania. Br. Rudolph Christ returned from Salisbury, having accomplished his object.

March 23. Maundy Thursday. Br. and Sr. Toego Nissen came from Friedland, and Br. and Sr. Fritz from the English Settlement, to the Communion. At 2 o'clock the congregation gathered, and listened reverently to the reading of the High Priestly Prayer of Jesus, and the account of His institution of the Pedilavium and the Lord's Supper. The edifying sermon which Br. Joseph preached before the Pedilavium on Maundy Thursday, 1778, was then read to the communicants, and we knelt before our gracious and merciful High Priest, asking to be absolved from all our short-comings and faults. Then the Sisters, and after them the Brethren, had the Pedilavium, according to the command of our Lord. In the evening at 7 o'clock was a second reading from the story of this day,—of the deep anguish of His soul and His bloody sweat in Gethsemene, of His arrest, of Peter's denial, and so on, an account that pierced our hearts. At 8 o'clock the communicants gathered to share in the Testament which on the night in which He was betrayed He gave to His Disciples and to all those who should believe on Him through their word. At the beginning of this service two Single Sisters, Anna Maria Hege and Eva Hein, were confirmed for their first participation in the Sacrament by the laying on of hands. There were 80 communicants; three Single Brethren remained away of their own accord.

March 24. Good Friday. Early in the morning there was the Post Communion, with three Brethren and Sisters. The reading of the story of this day continued morning and afternoon, the reading being interspersed with suitable chorals. At the beginning of each service the choir sang an appropriate anthem or choral, with instrumental accompaniment. After the words: "He gave up the ghost," the congregation fell upon their knees, while the verse was sung:

> Most holy Lord and God,
>
>   * * *
>
> Grant that we may never
> Lose the comforts of Thy death,
>
>   * * *

and thanks were given to our faithful Lord Who loved us even unto death. With melted hearts and moistened eyes the liturgy was prayed which portrayed His agony and death, and that led to the account of the opening of His side. A short service was held at twilight; and a brief anthem sung at eight o'clock brought the blessed day to a close.

This morning the Brn. Toego Nissen and Fritz went to their posts to read the great story of the day to their little congregations. Old Jacob Christman came from Stinking Quarter to visit his four children here. This morning there was a fine rain for about two hours, which refreshed the gardens; this evening it cleared.

March 25. Great Sabbath. This morning the man Spek, who went to Pennsylvania last fall, returned from there, bringing two small packages of letters, and four copies of printed Daily Words, though without the Doctrinal Texts, which they did not yet have in Bethlehem. He also brought several copies of the Nachrichten. The letters from Bethlehem were dated Jan. 31st, those from Yorktown were written in February. Nothing was said about the arrival of Br. Hübner and company from Europe, so the verbal report brought on the 14th of this month was without foundation. The above-mentioned traveler had been obliged to sell his horse at the Potomac and come the rest of the way on foot, carrying the packages, for his Congress dollar would be accepted nowhere for more than 1d.

In the afternoon there was a blessed Sabbath lovefeast, during which the Brn. Nissen and Fritz returned, and after the service they and their wives went back to their homes. At the close of the day the several Choirs had their own Evening Blessings.

March 26. Easter. Soon after five o'clock the congregations assembled in the Saal, and having received the Easter Greeting we went to God's Acre and prayed the Easter Liturgy, with a blessed consciousness of the presence of our risen Lord, and besought Him to keep us in everlasting fellowship with the five Brethren and Sisters who went home during this year from this congregation, and also with the 25 Brethren and 13 Sisters, servants of the Lord, of whose calling home we have heard. It was a beautiful, clear, fresh morning, and there was some frost. Not in many years have there been so few visitors present at this service; we saw only several traders. At ten o'clock Br. Graff preached the Easter sermon on the words "Ye seek Jesus—which was crucified—He is risen." (Mark XVI.) In the afternoon the Diary of Bethlehem for July and August of last year was read; and at the close of the day the touching account was read of the appearance of our risen Lord to His apostles. Br. Heinzmann preached in Friedland.

March 27. Easter Monday. This was observed as the festival of the Incarnation of Jesus, and also as Gemein Tag. Br. Graff made the festal address to the four Older Girls, and Maria Magdalena Meyer was added to their number. * * * There was a meeting of the Brethren and friends who have supervision of the roads; they came from the various parts of Wachovia, except Bethania, and made plans for carrying on the work.

Br. Aust went today to Bethabara, and tomorrow he and Br. Blum will leave for Bethlehem to see about their marriages. They will take a package of letters for Lititz and Bethlehem, but much is left which will be sent in George Hauser's wagon next month.

March 28. The Brethren and Sisters Marshall and Graff set out early in the wagon, and Br. Prezel followed them to the School-House in our English Settlement. This is now to be known as *Hope,* and as Br. and Sr. Fritz are now stationed there the name was publicly announced during this visit and the House was dedicated. The Text for the day was most appropriate: "Except the Lord build the house they labor in vain that build it." During the lovefeast five single men and nine single women, one married negro and two married negresses, were received into the Society. The entire group was filled with joy and hope at this gracious visitation from the Saviour.

March 29. It has continued to be dry, with warm days, but the nights are cool and occasionally there has been a little frost. In spite of this the peach trees are beginning to bloom freely.

March 30. Two Brethren of the Aufseher Collegium went to Br. Peter Rose, took a pleasant leave of him, and arranged the matter of his two-year unpaid rent for the farm. In the afternoon Br. Rose, his wife and little son, and their baggage, drove to Bethabara, where they will take care of the farm for the present. The Salem farm is left without care until new arrangements can be made. Three companies of travelers passed through; they started to Kentucky, but lack of provisions forced them to turn back at New River.

March 31. Martin Schneider left in Friedrich Müller's wagon for Cross Creek to buy leather with paper and other money. About noon there was an unusually severe storm from the south, then the wind blew from the north-west and it was rather cold, though the wind prevented much freezing.

April 1. The Single Br. Johann Nilson came from Bethabara to work in the leather goods shop here.

April 2. Last night the frost was heavier than during the night preceding, but many of the fruit blossoms escaped, and today the wind shifted to the south making the weather milder.

April 3. A standpipe was set in the water-main opposite Br. Miksch's house, and a barrel placed there, for the accommodation of families on that side of the street and also for the use of strangers. Marriage was proposed to Br. Rudolph Christ, who has been put in charge of the

Pottery for the time being, and also to Br. John Holland at the Tavern, and both accepted it.

April 4. In the morning the Aufseher Collegium met, and among other things passed a resolution that among ourselves receipts and disbursements of every kind, including debts made prior to this time, shall be paid half in hard money and half in paper; also that necessary articles shall be sold to outsiders for paper money at 2d to the dollar. The reason for this action was that several Brethren in our town have refused to accept paper money, which created much complaint among our neighbors, and several men who are friendly to us have warned us that to refuse to accept the paper money would bring us into all sorts of difficulties and dangers. In the evening at 7 o'clock this resolution was announced to all adult residents in the town and no one made any objection to it; the Brethren and Sisters were also earnestly admonished not to discuss political matters with outsiders, and the Brethren were urged to demean themselves according to the Affirmation which they have taken.

It rained most of the day. The wind was from the north-east and rather cool, but the rain was very good for the crops, which have not been growing during the recent chilly, dry weather.

April 5. The Aufseher Collegium had a short meeting about the erection of a new bell tower, as there is danger that the old one may collapse. Br. Meinung and Br. Miksch went to Friedland to survey some land on Muddy Creek.

April 6. Mr. Commens, a Representative from Surry County, passed on his way to the Assembly in New Bern. [*Marginal note.* He did not go to the Assembly this time.] As he had given us warning about the paper money Br. Bonn told him of our recent action in the matter and he was entirely satisfied. This afternoon there was the betrothal of Br. Rudolph Christ to Sr. Elisabeth Oesterlein, and of Br. John Holland to Sr. Maria Strub,—it was a pleasing circumstance that this was the birthday of Sr. Strub's father.

April 7. Last night or this morning there was a light frost, but the day was warm.

April 8. It rained all day from the south-east. In the afternoon there was a thunder storm, but it remained warm, the first good, growing, spring weather we have had.

George Hauser of Bethania came with his wagon, and loaded the packages destined for Lititz and Bethlehem [Pa.]; he also took the letters Br. Marshall has written to Bethlehem. Yesterday and today many travelers have passed, coming from Kentoki; they could not say enough about the poverty and misery of the large number of people there. In Kentoki there is neither bread nor salt, nor forage for their cattle for the canes have been frozen, and large numbers of the cattle have died; moreover the Indians have been murdering frequently, and many men have left the frontier.

April 9. About twenty men passed in several parties, going, they say, from the Lower Counties to Kentok, but one suspects that there are other reasons why they are going aside. In the evening there was a hard storm from the north-west, but it was not followed by frost.

April 10. The Representatives, Commins and Freeman, passed on their way to the Assembly.

April 11. Just at the hour for the singstunde there was a hard thunder-storm, so the service was omitted.

April 12. Martin Schneider returned from Cross Creek. He spent all the paper money he took with him, getting leather, salt, etc. The rate was 2d to 3d for a dollar.

April 15. The weather was still cloudy and cool, with wind from the south. Br. Fritz came from Hope, largely for a supply of provisions, for food is already very scarce in that settlement. In the afternoon there was a little lovefeast in the girls' school as a farewell to Sr. Oesterlein, and a welcome to Sr. Catherine Sehner who takes her place. The Brn. Christ and Holland also had a lovefeast with a small company in the Brothers House as a farewell to their Choir.

April 16. Sunday. In the congregation meeting the choir sang: "Speak peace to Jerusalem," * * * and at the close of the service Br. Rudolph Christ and Sr. Oesterlein, Br. John Holland and Sr. Maria Margarethe Strub, were united in marriage by Br. Graff. There was a strong sensation of the presence of the Head of our Church.

April 17. The two newly married couples took breakfast in the Gemein Haus with the Brn. and Srs. Marshall and Graff, and also dined with them at noon. This morning there was a light frost in low places, but the day was warm and promised rain.

April 19. The afternoon was stormy, with thunder and rain, and there was probably hail to the north of us, as it became cold.

April 20. Yesterday several of the carpenters went with Br. Johann Krause to the pine woods near Hope to fell tall trees for the building of the new bell-tower. Br. Herbst went to the home of Br. Pfaff, where the marriage of Wilhelm Grabs to Pfaff's daughter is to take place today. Br. Meinung and Miksch returned from the Wach, where they have surveyed land for Peter Schneider and young John Hartmann. The weather was stormy and cool, though the wind was from the south, and at night there was a light frost. We did not expect such weather after such a hard winter.

April 21. George Bechler took leave with tears prior to starting on his return journey to Pennsylvania; he had been much touched by the love which was shown him by the Brethren here. The carpenters returned from the woods, and the wagon brought the heavy timbers cut for the new bell-tower. At close of day the hymn: "Oh Head so full of bruises" was sung, and during the service a party of about thirty Light-Horse, belonging to the militia in Guilford County, arrived to spend the night in the Tavern. They are moving to the Hollow because of a rising there, led by certain men with a large following, many of whom are believed to be horse-thieves. The pretext for the rising is that they wish to support the cause of King George. All circumstances indicate that people everywhere would like to have peace.

April 22. The troops who came yesterday left for Richmond; they maintained fairly good order. Br. Heinrich Stöhr came from Bethabara for the letters for Lititz and Bethlehem, and with them our Diaries for February and March. At 8 o'clock the communicants gathered, * * * and they had scarcely reached home after the Communion when a hard thunder-storm broke, with a frightful wind, and the roaring noise of an earthquake. The storm continued until nearly midnight, and was accompanied by rain which was very good for the crops. God be praised for all the grace and protection which He has vouchsafed to us this day.

April 23. Br. George Biwighaus, accompanied by John Hartmann, set out for Wilmington, on business for the Store.

April 25. The bell by the Gemein Haus was taken down; the support on which it hung, of which one post was rotted quite in two, was torn away, and part of it was again set in the ground so that the bell could be hung in it temporarily.

April 26. A suggestion that Peter Rose's former plantation should be rented to Philip Vogler was approved by the Saviour. There was a cold rain from the east all day.

April 27. The Single Br. Philip Vogler came from Bethabara, looked over the plantation near Salem, and said he would like to rent it.

April 28. Since the 26th it has been cool, and today there was a cold rain from the east. There was a light frost in the morning, but it did not hurt the buds.

April 29. The company of Light-Horse mentioned on the 21st returned today. We hear that they failed to find any Tories who were planning a rising.

April 30. About 9 o'clock the Light-Horse marched away, having behaved reasonably well. The Saal Diener and Dienerinnen had a lovefeast for encouragement in their office; their number has been increased by Br. and Sr. Rudolph Christ, and diminished by the withdrawal of Br. Jeremias Schaaf who has to care for the lamps in his Choir House. The month closed with a storm from the south, but the blossoms remain unhurt. The elder Vogler came back from Bethabara with his son Philip, and went from here to the plantation; he was much pleased with his son's new work, and will help him plant corn, etc.

May 1. Michael Seiz came with his wagon, bringing salt, leather, rice, etc. from Cross Creek for Brn. Heinzmann and Bagge. A number of persons came to the town to buy pottery. Some men met in the Tavern, apparently by appointment, in order to tell each other the news of the war conditions in the south; no notice was taken of it. A man from New Bern reported that 8000 militia-men are to be called out, and 3000 more volunteers are to be enlisted; he also said that Abner Nash has taken Caswell's place as Governor, and so on. Philip Vogler has moved to the plantation and has begun ploughing, with the help of his brother from Friedland.

May 3. The Aufseher Collegium presented the rental contract to Philip Vogler, who accepted it. He takes the plantation for two years, and will pay one-third of the crop as rent.

May 4. A cold, heavy rain began in the morning, and continued all night with a stiff breeze from the north-east.

May 5. It continued to pour all morning, and in the afternoon cleared up warm from the south. Everyone thinks that the water will be high. George Hartmann, of Friedberg, brought a small package from Pennsylvania, which had been brought to Salisbury by Leonard Kreiter, who left here on March 9th with a package of letters for Pennsylvania. The package had been lying in Salisbury for eight days, and contained the Bethlehem Diary of October, November and December, 1779; there were no letters from Bethlehem, but only from Br. Neisser and Jacob Blum, dated Yorktown, April 8th and 9th. The latter reported the pleasant journey and arrival there of himself and Br. Aust; Br. Neisser announced that the Brethren and Sisters from Europe, who had been so long and eagerly awaited, had finally reached Bethlehem on the 30th of March, namely the Hübners, David Zeisbergers, the widower Martin and two Single Brethren. They had had a long and dangerous voyage of eighteen weeks, but had been wonderfully sustained by the hand of God.

May 6. Br. Steiner notified us that the high water had washed away part of the race, but the mill had suffered no damage. We were concerned for the mill at Bethabara, but Br. Kapp came hither himself and told us that no harm had been done there, except that the bridge below the tavern had been washed out and the fence also. We thanked God that it has turned out this way, for the water has not been so high in nine years.

Mr. Doughted and his wife came this afternoon, asking for Certificates for their three unmarried sons who have recently been Received into the Society at Hope. They were given written authority to ask the Justice, Capt. Phelps, to permit them to take the Affirmation, and when that has been done they will receive the Certificates.

May 7. We hear from New River that several days ago three inches of snow fell there.

May 8. Several Brethren from here went to Steiner's mill, and the mill race was repaired with the help of men from the neighborhood. Br. Fritz came from Hope on a short visit, and through him we learned that the Atkin had not risen very high, and no damage had been done to houses or fields.

May 9. A large number of Brethren worked on the bridge over the Wach which was badly injured in the recent flood, but they did not finish it enough to make it possible to cross. The work done on the race yesterday has been washed out again.

The Single Br. George Bibighaus returned safely from Willmingtown and Cross Creek. He could not say enough about the high prices and the damage done by the recent high waters. He had to pay $100.00 for one night's lodging in the tavern. It was fortunate that he had taken corn for his horses. Otherwise the country was quiet.

In the singstunde reference was made to the calling-home of the Jünger,[6] twenty years ago today.

May 10. Some of the Brethren worked on the bridge again. Br. Krause and his men raised the new bell-tower this afternoon. It is pyramidal in form, and about the height of the Gemein Haus. The work was done quickly and safely, and the pulley did its desired part. The weather was very hot and humid, with much lightning in the east.

May 12. There was probably hail to the east yesterday, for today was raw, and in the following night we feared frost, but it was cloudy so did not freeze.

The Aufseher Collegium had decided that instead of a little roof over the bell there should be a cap with a weather-vane, as is usual on towers, and as this was ready it was raised and placed. It was hard to do, and looked dangerous, but the angels warded off all accident, for which we give praise and thanks to our dear Father in heaven.

---

[6] Count Zinzendorf.

May 13. The bell was hung in the tower, was rung, and the hours were struck. The sound could be heard further and more clearly than hitherto, and we were the more thankful since all had been accomplished without injury to any one.

Again today, as almost daily recently, people passed taking wagon loads of corn from Dan and Smith Rivers to the Lower Counties, where at present there is great need in many places. Sr. Steinmann was here, returning from a visit to her parents, Br. and Sr. Graeter; it was proposed to her that she should marry the Single Br. Philip Vogler, and she seemed not averse to the idea.

May 14. Whitsunday. Most of the day there was an unfriendly rain from the east, but in the evening after the liturgy we were able to close with the "Hymn of Praise to the Holy Ghost."

May 16. Sr. Bonn took little Magdalena Kapp to her parents at the mill near Bethabara. They will now take charge of her; Sr. Bonn has cared for her with unfailing patience and faithfulness for a year and a half. Br. Lorenz reported from Bethabara that this afternoon Br. Philip Vogler and Sr. Johanna Steinmann would be betrothed; this will be mentioned to the congregation here this evening for their remembrance before the Lord.

May 17. A report spread that a man had been taken prisoner to Salisbury, and that on him had been found a list of the members of a *Combination,* and among the names four Friedberg Brethren. Martin Walk, one of those named, happened to come here, and from him we learned that the man was a vagabond named Graef, who passed here on the 2nd, going to Muddy Creek. During a conversation with Abraham Dancey he had written several names in his note-book, and he had been arrested because of questionable remarks which he had made. The weather has cleared up nicely.

May 18. The Brethren of the Aufseher Collegium and Br. Johann Krause went to Steiner's mill and selected a place above the dam where a spillway is to be built in the race to guard against a recurrence of damage from high water. John Brown and three men began to make brick in our brick-yard. A gentleman passing through from New Bern allowed us to read a copy of the new Militia Act passed by the Assembly now in session, and we saw that the Act regarding us had not been repealed.

May 19. The Brn. Marshall and Bagge received a summons from the Commissioners appointed for this County to confiscate the land of those who are under English rule, and so on. The three Commissioners are Prox [Brooks], Major Phelps and [blank] and the Brethren must ap-

4

pear before them tomorrow in Bethania. The Old Testament Text for today is: "What He ordains is worthy of praise and glorious,"[7]

> To Him leave choice and action,
> He is a Prince all-wise.

May 20. The Brn. Marshall and Bagge left early for Bethania, in response to the summons received yesterday; we wished them the good counsel and support of the Lord. They have not returned, and it is the work of the Evil One to let this happen on our Communion day.

May 21. The Brn. Marshall and Bagge returned from Bethania, where they celebrated the Holy Communion yesterday with the congregation. They were gently and courteously treated by the two Commissioners, and discussed the land matters with them. No question was raised as to Wachovia, and Br. Marshall explained the Metcalf lands and other such tracts, and how they were managed. The Commissioners made no comment except that they would report to the County Court. In short the gentlemen were just and modest men. Yesterday a man named Jolibet, a member of Assembly from the Holston neighborhood, reported in passing that the Assembly had taken action which was favorable to us, both in regard to the ownership of our land and in respect to militia service. We recognize the influence of the Saviour in this, and thank Him heartily for it.

May 22. The wagon from Bethabara brought Sr. Steinmann and her belongings, as the bride who will be married tomorrow. She will lodge with Sr. Utley for several days. Her little son was left temporarily with Br. and Sr. Stach.

May 23. The marriage of Sr. Steinmann was performed by Br. Graff in the evening meeting of communicants.

May 26. Br. Heinzmann, accompanied by Daniel Christman, set out for Stinking Quarter to visit the old friends there.

May 27. The heat was very oppressive. Yesterday and today storms came up but went around us. From various quarters it is reported that Charlestown has surrendered to the English. Br. Krause has about finished covering the bell tower.

May 29. There has been a gentle rain yesterday and today. Travelers coming from Pennsylvania report having passed two wagons, and it seems probable that the expected Brethren and Sisters are on the way. There are conflicting rumors regarding Charlestown, so we will

---

[7] There are many minor differences between the Martin Luther translation of the Bible and the King James Version. This Text is from Ps. 3, iii, which in the German reads "Was er ordnet, das ist löblich und herrlich." The editor's task of identification of texts quoted from time to time in the diaries is made possible by a *Biblisches Spruchregister*, arranged by Ed. Bernoulli, and published at Basel in 1836; in this book the texts most used by the Brethren are arranged in alphabetical order.

have to wait for facts, but people are coming from that section who seem to be in flight.

May 30. The place for a small house for the night-watchman was laid out on the lot next to Miksch's,—it will be 16 by 13 feet. Report is confirmed that Charlestown has been taken by the English, and that the camp of the Burgoyne prisoners will be changed. The Militia from this neighborhood,—of whom one passed through,—were released on condition that they would appear before the English when called. The weather continues cloudy and damp, but it is not actually raining.

May 31. Bachman, who lives near Bethlehem, sent us the pleasant word that three Single Brethren had come in his wagon and would arrive today. This took place toward evening, to our great joy; they were the Brn. Johann Reuz, Peter Goetje and Carl Opiz. They brought letters and Gemein Nachrichten. Br. Reichel wrote from Lititz, whither he had come on the journey hither, that he and his party,—that is the Jeppe Nilsons, Blums and Austs, and the Single Br. Friedrich Peter,—expect to arrive about eight days after the three Brethren who came today.

During the night Br. Heinzmann and Dan Christman returned from Stinking Quarter. Last Sunday Br. Heinzmann preached in the little church of our friends to a fairly good audience, and afterwards he visited in their homes. He was heartily welcomed, but there is no real awakening among the souls there.

June 1. Br. and Sr. Phillip Vogler brought their little son from Bethabara, and moved to the plantation. Many people passed, who appeared to be much excited and concerned over the progress of the English. We hear today from various militiamen, who have been discharged at Charlestown and are returning, that the British troops have reached Mecklenburg County. Among the things received yesterday was a complete Text Book from Europe, and now the Texts can be made known to the congregation each day. We also received the chest, which was in London already in 1775 but could not be sent over; it contained, among other things, the remaining volumes of the Life of Zinzendorf, Reichel's Study of the Bible, and so on. In the evening the Congregation Council met; the Single Br. Proesing and the Single Sr. Catherine Sehner were present for the first time, in accordance with the rulings of the last Synod.

June 2. Br. Marshall and the three Brethren who arrived day before yesterday set out for Bethabara and other places. Mr. Horatio Hamilton came to Br. Graff and asked for a Certificate on account of the General Muster called for today at Richmond; he was given a written declaration that he belongs to a Society of the Brethren. At present there is much confusion among the people; some want to withstand the English, who are making incursions as far as Salisbury, and advise throwing up breastworks against them, while others rejoice in the good success of the English, and hope for better times. At midnight there was a heavy storm, with rain which was very good for the parched land.

June 3. Toward noon Br. Marshall returned from Bethabara with the Brn. Reuz and Götje, Br. Opiz remained in Bethania with his parents. The men of Friedland and Hope returned from the Muster held yesterday at Richmond; of those who belong to us only Philipp Kroen was drafted. Those who were taken in the draft must appear tomorrow ready to march, and we hear that horses are to be pressed, therefore our horses shall be put out of sight so far as possible. Several gentlemen came in flight from Georgia, bringing their negroes and cattle. Among them was Col. Joseph Haversham, who called on the Brn. Marshall and Bagge, and was provided with one and another necessary article, and he was both appreciative and satisfied, for he had heard that we were Tories, and had not expected such courtesy. On the contrary he had not been treated well by the so-called *Liberty men* in Salisbury, who had refused to let him drive his oxen through the town, whereby he had lost some of them and some negroes. A man passed with a wagon load of salt from Cross Creek. He reported that last Thursday the English troops, 4000 strong, crossed the Peedee River, divided into two parties, and marched toward Cross Creek and Salisbury. They were looking for depots of ammunition.

Br. Lorenz went to Deep Creek to baptise several children.

June 4. In the three morning services of our Gemein Tag we read the diary of the long and dangerous voyage from England to New York of Br. Huebner and his company, also the diary of the Indian congregation on the Muskingum river.[8]

Mr. Haversham went on toward Dan River with his negroes, most of whom had camped at Steiner's mill; Br. Oesterlein was sent with a letter from him to Col. Martin, who passed through here day before yesterday. Br. Oesterlein returned the following day, and had found no food for himself or his horse until he came back into the Bethabara neighborhood.

June 5. This morning early fifty soldiers came to our town looking for a deserter, who they said had passed through here within the last ten days, but we knew nothing of him. [*Marginal note.* This was a wandering party from South Carolina, who were either amusing themselves, or were out spying for Tories.] As they left, a Captain came with twelve men, asking for the same deserter. They took up quarters

[8] In Ohio.

in our Tavern, and Br. Bagge incidentally learned that they belonged to a Corps which had been defeated by the English below Charlotta Town.[9] The Captain sent his underwear to the Sisters House to be washed, and the blood stains showed that he must have been in the engagement. He ordered rations for his men, and it was decided to let them stay in the Tavern as long as they are here.   We also heard that people have spoken evil of us as Tories, and threatened to burn the town, so another Brother was appointed to assist the nightwatchman during the following night.   The above mentioned officer and his men attended the evening service, in which an impressive address by Br. Reichel was read, closing with a singstunde.

June 6.   Col. Armstrong and other officers of the local Militia, with a guard of about twelve horsemen, passed on their way to Salisbury. At present everything is confused, but we are in peace, thank God, and we look to Him, and wait for what He will do with us.   In the afternoon we had a little rain; the weather is good for the crops. [*Note.* The Militia had really come to find out where and why Br. Oesterlein was sent across the Atkin day before yesterday.   They thought we were corresponding with the Tories of that neighborhood, but Col. Armstrong did not believe that, and when we explained truthfully they rode away to the place from which they had come.]

June 7.   The Captain who came day before yesterday, a Hessian, born a Swede, left this morning for Virginia with three or four of his company.   His suite had been made up of three companies, who happened to meet in their flight, and some of them left yesterday.   A certain Colonel from Georgia arrived yesterday with his wife, a little child nine weeks old, and a number of negroes.   They were also fleeing, and today went on to join Mr. Haversham.   Peter Volz brought us word that in camp on Abbots Creek, near Masinger, there was a party of soldiers in flight, who were accompanied by many wounded who were moaning piteously.   They were seizing all the horses they could find, so the residents of that section were hiding their horses where they could.   From Bethabara came the news that the recently drafted soldiers, ready to march, had been ordered home until further notice, because the English had been defeated at Willmingtown.   We also hear that the Virginia troops have been called home, and all this must mean something.   In the afternoon a certain Captain, named Washington, and a Cornet, came to our Tavern. Each had three or more of his company with

[9] On May 29, 1780, Colonel Buford's troops, retreating from Charleston, were overtaken by Tarleton's troops, near the line between North and South Carolina. Tarleton's report of the engagement says that Colonel Buford's force consisted of 380 Virginians, a detachment of Washington's cavalry, and two six-pounders. According to the same report the Americans lost 113 killed, 150 paroled because they were too badly wounded to be moved, 53 taken prisoner, and about one hundred escaped, while the English lost only 12 killed and 5 wounded.

him, and they were following the other Captain mentioned, but they stayed here over night because of a hard storm with heavy rain. In the evening they came to the Saal, but were rather critical in their demeanor. The Captain had taken possession of Br. Graeter's mare, he got it back here, but had to pay $200 to redeem it. Philip Kroen came from Friedland on his way to Capt. Schmidt, and asked Br. Graff for a Certificate, but as he has been drafted none could be given to him. He was told that he would have to offer to pay three-fold taxes, and then another time a Certificate could be given to him. The men of Friedland did not pay the triple tax last year, as we advised them, but went to muster, so the privilege granted by the Act of Assembly cannot apply to them until they begin to pay the three-fold tax.

June 8. The officers who came yesterday rode away with their subalterns. We feared that the wounded men from Abbots Creek would be brought here, but heard that they were being taken to Virginia. Three of them came hither on foot, but had neither money nor food, so Br. Bonn bandaged them and gave them half a loaf of bread, and they left again. The Collect under the Doctrinal Text today was:

> Lord, teach us both faithful and useful to prove,
> That friend and that foe may believe in our love.

These soldiers gave us some details concerning the bloody action at Hanging Rock. Before they were aware of it they had been surrounded by the English, and laid down their arms, but as the English commander rode up one man seized a gun and shot at him, and then the massacre began.[10] Between three and four hundred were killed or taken prisoner, and those who could ran away. The militia were released until further orders, but the regulars were held.

It rained most of the day, but cleared toward evening. After the meeting for communicants the Grosse Helfer Conferenz was in session until nearly ten o'clock, for the difficult question of the constantly falling value of the paper dollar came up again, and some of the Brethren have not followed the ruling of the Conferenz that payments should be half silver and half paper.

---

[10] Bishop Graff, writing in the Salem Diary, speaks of the Buford and Tarleton engagement as taking place at Hanging Rock, but that name is usually applied to another engagement which took place in August at a place not very far away. Colonel Buford's note to Colonel Tarleton, refusing to surrender, is dated from the Waxhaws. Tarleton's "Campaigns of 1780 and 1781" presents the English side of the story, while the "Memoirs of the War in the Southern Department of the United States," by Lieutenant-Colonel Henry Lee, gives the American account. In his foot-notes to the latter book Gen. Robert E. Lee accepts Tarleton's figures as to losses on both sides. Later historians, from Bancroft down, have also accepted Tarleton's figures, but have denied the rest of his story, accusing him of ruthless massacre and sustaining the validity of the use of the term "Tarleton's Quarters" as synonymous with heartless brutality. Even General Lee, in his otherwise generous foot-notes, refuses to credit the English claim that the Americans threw down their arms and then fired, which gives unusual interest to this story of retreating soldiers, told as they passed through Salem immediately after the engagement.

June 9. Br. Heinrich Stöhr, who reached Bethabara yesterday after a trip to Pennsylvania, came this morning and brought word that he had found our beloved Br. and Sr. Reichel on the other side of James River, and that they and their party were well when he left. He also told us of the unpleasant experience they had had, which Br. Reichel also mentioned in a short letter,—which was that on the further side of the Potomac River, during the night when no watch was set, Br. Reichel had lost his coffer, in which were his clothes, his papers, and worst of all the Deed to Wachovia, which had been attested in Pennsylvania. A sack of clothing belonging to the teamsters was also stolen, but Mr. Coly found that his mulatto had it, and brought it back to the wagon, which gives us hope that the coffer will also be found. The teamsters were not willing to wait, so nothing could be done except notify a Justice in the neighborhood of the theft, and post an advertisement in which a reward of £50 was offered for the return of the coffer. This unfortunate occurrence was the subject of a conference with several Brethren, and it was decided that as soon as Br. Reichel arrived a Brother should be sent with legal authority to reclaim the coffer from the ferryman. More parties, with negroes, passed through fleeing from South Carolina. We heard that four days ago the English were still in Cross Creek.

June 10. The Aufseher Collegium considered sending a wagon to meet Br. Reichel and his party, to render their further journey more comfortable.

Several Society members from Friedland,—George and Jacob Lagenauer and Michel Vogler,—came for Certificates from Br. Graff, in order to be free from drill and draft. It was explained to them that they had waited so long that Certificates would probably not help them, for Col. Armstrong had received orders for a large number of Militia. Several more families came to our Tavern, fleeing from South Carolina with their families; there was also another soldier, wounded in the action at Hanging Rock, who came to Br. Bonn, had his wounds bound up, and then went on.

June 12. Haymaking began in several places today. Col. Joseph Williams and several other men came here with the Bethabara wagon, which they have taken for the public service; here they took for the same purpose 120 gallons of brandy, and a quantity of leather and iron. We had to submit, for they are needed for the war.

June 13. In the morning there was a thunderstorm with heavy rain; it cleared toward evening.

June 14. In the morning the Brn. Marshall and Herbst set out in the Brothers House wagon to meet Br. Reichel and his party, the Brn.

Stöhr and Proesing going along as teamsters. An alarming report reached us that a party of soldiers was coming to seize all food that they could find, so that the English might not get it, as it was believed that we had plenty stored up for our own use. We committed ourselves to the care of our Father, remained quiet, and nothing unusual happened. Yesterday a family came in flight from Georgia, bringing about twenty negroes; like those who preceded them they camped in the woods opposite the Tavern, and the place looked like a negro village. The weather was clear and breezy, and good progress was made with the hay harvest. Three Brethren supplemented the nightwatchman in his service.

June 15. Br. and Sr. Graff spoke with the married people in preparation for the Lord's Supper, and they were found in a proper frame of mind, though several had been affected by the recent alarming reports. We thank the faithful Saviour for turning aside the dangerous intentions against us, which were dropped, as we hear, when news came that the English were planning to land at New Bern, and the soldiers were ordered thither in haste. This may have been the reason that the gentlemen who have been at the Tavern for several days left with their negroes, seemingly friendly and satisfied though hitherto they have been complaining and dissatisfied.

At noon Br. Herbst returned bringing word that Br. Reichel and his company would arrive toward evening, and about six o'clock we had the pleasure of welcoming these dear Brethren and Sisters, who were well and in good spirits. In the party, besides Br. and Sr. Reichel, were Br. and Sr. Jeppe Nilson, Br. and Sr. Aust, Br. Friedrich Peter, and the Single Sister Reuz. Br. and Sr. Blum left them this side of Dan River and went to Bethabara.

June 16. The two wagons,—George Hauser's and Christian Conrad's,—arrived safely with the baggage of those who came yesterday. Br. Steiner reported that his three day-laborers wanted to leave, because of news that the English have advanced past Hanging Rock.

Our dear Br. Reichel spent the afternoon seeing the town, and made several families happy by his visits; and he made a fine address at the evening service. After that Br. Reichel had a short conference with the leaders of the Choirs who had spoken with the Brethren [preparatory to the Communion].

June 17. The Choir leaders who had spoken with the Sisters had a short conference, and then the other members of the Aeltesten Conferenz joined them in the meeting hall of the Single Sisters, aside of the Saal used by the congregation. Br. Reichel opened this first formal conference by praying that the Saviour would give His presence, wisdom and counsel in each conference that should follow, and that the Holy Spirit might lead the members into faithful and united efforts for the best interests of all.   Then he explained in some detail the object of his visit to our congregations; and he announced that Br. Jeppe Nilson was sent as the congregation Vorsteher, and with his wife should assist Br. and Sr. Graff with the married people, and also that the Single Br. Friedrich Peter would act as secretary for the Conferences, and would help in the Saal and in his Choir as a reader and musician.

A small log house for the nightwatchman was quickly and safely erected near Br. Miksch's house on the street.

At five o'clock in the afternoon the entire congregation, including the children, had a happy lovefeast welcoming Br. and Sr. Reichel and their company.   Announcement was made of the appointment of Br. and Sr. Nilson and Br. Peter to their offices, and affectionate appreciation was expressed for the service of Br. Herbst as Vorsteher ad interim. Finally the hymns of welcome were sung,[11] and love, joy, praise and thanksgiving filled all hearts.   But still more impressive was the Holy Sacrament which followed in the evening at eight o'clock, in which Br. Reichel presided and led the liturgy.   This service set the seal upon our covenant to remain true to the Cross of Jesus until we go to Him. The communicants numbered ninety-five, including Br. and Sr. Blum from Bethabara, thirteen more than ever before.

June 18.   Br. Reichel and others went to visit the little congregation of Bethabara.   Some of Col. Polk's friends came from Mecklenburg in flight; they returned the following day to try to save more of their property.

In the gemeinstunde Br. Reichel preached on the Text: The Lord hath done great things for us, whereof we are glad.   He said that when we think of Herrnhut, for example, founded fifty-eight years ago, and of the many other congregations and towns which have arisen since then, and remember how the Lord Himself has brought them through all kinds of dangers from within and without, and especially when we consider our congregations here in America during this time of war, we can in truth apply to ourselves this Text and say: The Lord hath done great things for us.

June 19.   Mr. Bachman, who brought the three Brethren and their baggage on the 31st of last month, is returning in his wagon to Pennsylvania, and Br. Reichel and others sent letters to Lititz and Bethlehem.

June 20.   The Aufseher Collegium met, and Br. Reichel introduced Br. Jeppe Nilson as congregation Vorsteher.   In conclusion Br. Reichel begged the Brethren and Sisters not to be carried away by self-made

---

[11] Filed with the Diary.

anxiety and concern over the dangers of the present time; and urged them not to mix in political affairs, but rather to be constant in prayer to the heavenly Father of this poor land, asking Him to forgive its sins and our own, and the Saviour would surely hear our prayers and send help at the right time. Br. Jeppe Nilson held the singstunde for the first time.

June 21. Col. Armstrong and his brother the Major were here. The latter went from here to his Company, which at present is in Mecklenburg with others under the command of Gen. Rutherford. An English Corps is about twenty miles south of them.

June 22. The Brn. Reichel, Marshall and Nilson went to Steiner's mill to see the work that is being done on the mill-race. Just now there is a shortage of laborers, for the men who have been working there were deserters,[12] and they have left. The heat was very oppressive, but most of the hay was brought in. Toward evening there was a heavy thunder storm, with much rain.

June 23. Br. Bonn left for Richmond to bandage a patient, but heard in Bethabara that there was a rising on the Atkin of the so-called Tories, and that Col. Armstrong would march against them with some of the Militia, which will probably result in an engagement. We had heard similar reports from the Catawba River,[13] so Br. Bonn turned back at Bethabara, and brought us letters from the Brn. Lorenz and Ernst, which contained the same information. Capt. Schmidt has ordered his Company to meet at Richmond today, and has refused to accept the Certificates of Michel Vogler and George Lagenauer, just as we told them he would because they were presenting them too late.

June 24. Johannes Tag, and the Festival of our little boys.

June 25. Today was the anniversary of the publication of the Augsburg Confession, in 1530, and solemn mention of it was made in the congregational meeting in the evening.

Mr. Frederick Miller and his wife came from Friedland. He was much perplexed over the present situation, for the so-called Tories have become active against the other party, and visa versa, and he wished for advice as to what he should do. It was apparent that he wanted to move to Salem, but as Br. Reichel was not present he hesitated to say so openly. Capt. Heinrich Schmidt and some twenty light-horse came to our Tavern. They had orders to take all arms and any doubtful persons, and wanted to make Br. Meyer go with them on

---

12 Evidently deserters from the English army, since it was the Tories they feared. See Salem Diary, June 27, 1780.

13 On June 20, 1780, Colonel Locke, with a force largely composed of militia from Rowan County, fell upon and defeated the Tories who had gathered at Ramsour's Mill, on the south branch of the Catawba River.

an untrue charge that he had recently given lodging to two English officers. They were really South Carolinians, but he will have to answer the charge before a court martial. It is evident that this is a critical time, which must turn one way or the other, and may the Saviour guide affairs for the best interests of His kingdom.

June 26. In the morning Capt. Schmidt left with his horsemen, going in two divisions and by two roads, one toward Hope and the other toward the South Fork. The latter party met old Br. Graeter, and tried to take his horse, threatening to shoot him; he risked that and they let him alone. About ten o'clock that night Major Goode arrived with about thirty light-horse, with the intention of seizing arms, just as the party planned yesterday, and like the others these had to be fed, in spite of the fact that at Belews Creek, whence they came, they were nearer to their homes than to us.

June 27. We hear that the Tories are out in force in the Abbots Creek settlement.[14] During the night our neighbor, Mr. Friedrich Müller, came from the Friedland settlement to our Tavern, and remained until morning, fearing that the Tories in camp on Abbots Creek would raid his house during the night.

Several Brethren were sent to Steiner's mill to help in placing the spillway, as the day-laborers there have left for fear of the Tories.

June 28. Br. Schaub, Jr. came from Bethabara and received from Br. Reichel written authority, to claim the coffer stolen at the Potomac, and the necessary affidavits, all properly attested before several Justices, and Tobias Hirte, who is returning with him, will serve as witness. He also took written authority from George Hauser, [Sr.] of Bethania, regarding the coffer. Again today there were numerous storm-clouds in the sky, but they brought no rain here.

For the past two or three days everything has been quiet, and there have been almost no visitors in the town, which is good for the bakery.

June 29. Major Winston sent written notice that he and a company of light-horse would spend tonight here. This came to pass, and a company of infantry also arrived and had to be cared for in our Tavern. They feared an attack from the Tories, and set guards on all sides, but during the night learned that the report was without foundation. In the evening Br. Reichel held a public service, to which a number of the soldiers came. He spoke on the Text "The gates of hell shall not prevail against my congregation," explaining that by "congregation" we were to understand all those who could say with Peter: "Thou art the

---

[14] Seven or eight hundred Tories had joined Col. Samuel Bryant by the time the men he raised west of the Yadkin had crossed that river and marched down the east bank to Abbotts Creek. (Ashe, History of N. C.)

Christ, the Son of the living God." * * * The hearers were very attentive and orderly while he so bore witness.

During the fourteen days that he had been here, our dear Br. Jeppe Nilson had been well and in good spirits, and today he was about the town taking up the collection for Foreign Missions. But for two days he had noticed a sense of drowsiness, which led him to retire this evening earlier than usual, and during the night he suddenly had a stroke. Br. Bonn at once opened a vein, aud the blood flowed freely, but without bringing him back to speech or consciousness, and about two o'clock in the morning the Lord took this His faithful servant home into His everlasting joy, while Br. Reichel and several Brethren who had gathered sang a liturgy and united in prayer. We were all deeply touched by this unexpected home-going, for we had looked for much benefit from the services of this Brother, but it is better humbly and with childlike trust to accept the oft strange way of our wise and faithful Lord than to speculate about His purpose.

June 30. Early in the morning the home-going of our dear Br. Nilson was announced to the congregation by the musicians in the accustomed tunes, and all of our towns were notified.

The troops who came yesterday left today, the horsemen going by way of the Shallow Ford and the infantry through Bethabara. They were drawn up before our store, and their commander, Major Winston, in their name gave friendly thanks to Br. Bagge for their kindly reception and the good attention given to them. They took two of the horses from the Brothers House for use for two days in carrying their baggage, but did not promise to return them. We have no complaint to make about them, if it leads to our being left in peace, though the expense of their entertainment will probably not be refunded to us.

In the congregation meeting this evening the home-going of Br. Nilson was remembered in the accustomed liturgy.

July 2. In the afternoon at two o'clock was the funeral of our Br. Jeppe Nilson. The number present at the burial was so unusually large that there was a double row all around God's Acre. The weather was threatening all day, but it did not rain until the gathered people were under roof, and then after raining a while it ceased so that they could go home, then there were several storms and rain for several hours.

July 3. The Single Brethren and others began to cut wheat, the weather having cleared.

At present all is quiet, for the Tories, who have recently made much disturbance, are said to have gone to join the English.[15]

After the evening meeting the Congregation Council met, having been postponed from eight days ago. Sr. Aust was present for the first time, and she will also be a member of the Grosse Helfer Conferenz. Br. Reichel rejoiced over the large number of members of Congregation Council, and laid upon the hearts of all that they should think of the best interests of the congregation. Among other things the Brethren were instructed not to permit the hated name "Tory" to be applied to them, for they have proved the contrary by taking the Affirmation and paying the three-fold tax.

July 5. Again there was a storm, and it rained fairly hard.

July 6. At twilight there was a meeting of all the Brethren and Sisters, and Br. Reichel spoke on John Hus, who 365 years ago sealed his evangelical testimony with his martyr death at Constance. He pointed out that we have cause to be interested in this, for thereby was laid the foundation for the Union of the Brethren of that day in Bohemia and Moravia, who had maintained his teachings not by force of arms but through prayer and sufferings, making of the Unity of Brethren a witness-congregation.

The Single Br. Johann Reuz was sent this morning to Richmond, to see about the two horses which Major Winston took from here on June 30th. He brought them back this evening, but had been obliged to go some miles beyond Dan River for them. In that neighborhood there was a cloudburst last Sunday, making the river very high, and washing away whole fields of corn.

June 7. In the afternoon a company of militia under Captain Meredith arrived; they had been in Bethabara for several days. They were followed by Col. Armstrong. To our joy Captain Sheppard and his troop of horsemen marched by outside the town; some of the horsemen were in Bethabara last night and behaved badly. The foot-soldiers marched away toward evening. In the evening service a sermon was read on the Text: "I will fear no evil, for thou art with me."

July 8. Through a sergeant, who came Express to Col. Armstrong from Salisbury, we learned that the English were about sixteen miles from Salisbury; the Express went from here to Richmond bearing orders that many troops should be sent down quickly. In the afternoon a party of light-horse came with a drove of cattle which they had taken from people on the Atkin; they were driven toward Richmond next morning. The heat is very oppressive these days.

---

[15] Discouraged by news of the defeat at Ramsour's Mill, Colonel Bryant and his Tories, by forced marches, hastened to join the British under Major McArthur. They took part in the engagement at Hanging Rock, Aug. 5, 1780.

July 9. In the morning Br. Marshall led the congregation in praying the Church litany, and mentioned the name of Br. Jeppe Nilson in connection with the petition for "everlasting fellowship with the church triumphant."

July 10. In the morning there was Bible instruction for the little boys. After that there was a conference with the Brn. Prezel and Petersen in regard to the filling of the position of Vorsteher of the Choir of Single Brethren, as Br. Heinzmann has asked to be relieved. Then Br. Reichel had a conference with the officers of the Choir of Married People, especially with reference to the care of the Choir, and particularly of members just entering it. Proposal was made to Sr. Reuter that she should marry Br. Heinzmann, and in the evening she gave an affirmative answer. Br. Friedrich Peter led the singstunde for the first time, following the thought of the Text: "Unless the Lord keep the city the watchman waketh but in vain."

July 11. Last night Br. Reichel was taken sick with another attack of flux, and had a high fever without perspiration. The flux gradually ceased, but the high fever continued, so he was obliged to remain patiently in bed, and let his duties go for the present. The Aeltesten Conferenz met in the afternoon. Among other things it was mentioned that Br. Heinzmann had been relieved of his duties as Vorsteher of the Single Brethren, and that Br. Peterson would take over that office, with the assistance of Br. Samuel Stotz, while Br. Prezel alone would serve as Pfleger. Also that Br. Heinzmann would take Br. Toego Nissen's place in Friedland, and would therefore marry Sr. Reuter.

July 12. Br. Reichel was bled, and from the condition of his blood it could be inferred that he had taken cold, probably on the journey hither, and through this change he will gradually improve.

Toward evening news came from Steiner's mill that the day-laborer Berger, who has worked there for some time, and has often come here on Sunday, had suddenly passed out of Time. He was here this morning, but had been complaining for several days, and he passed away suddenly while taking a fresh drink in the heat of the afternoon.

July 13. Br. Prezel held the funeral of the day-laborer who died yesterday at the mill; he was buried in our God's Acre for Strangers. Br. Reichel was somewhat better and stronger, and the perspiration began to come again.

July 14. In the afternoon there was the bethrothal of Br. Heinzmann and Sr. Reuter, in Br. Marshall's room. Br. Reichel was not able to be present, but was out of bed most of the day, and feeling stronger. For several days there has been a strong east wind, and several Brethren have complained of a return of flux.

July 15. The passing of various young people to and from the English has caused much confusion, for example cattle have been driven away, Joseph Booner was beaten half to death, and so on. During the afternoon a company passed through, on horseback and afoot, going to the corps of General Rutherford at Salisbury; they behaved in quite an orderly manner.

At six o'clock in the evening there was a Communion lovefeast, during which interest was expressed in the fact that this was the 77th birthday of our dear Br. Joseph, and we gave thanks that our good Lord had blessed this faithful servant of our Unity for so many years. At eight o'clock ninety-two partook of the Holy Communion. Br. Graff held the service, and Br. and Sr. Reichel received their portion at the same time as the congregation, a Brother taking it to their room from the Saal.

July 16. Br. and Sr. Graff, with the Meyers and Br. Petersen, went to Friedland. In a private service Christian, the little son of Br. and Sr. Toego Nissen, born on the 9th of this month, was baptized into the death of Jesus. In the meeting of Society members Br. Graff announced that Br. and Sr. Toego Nissen would be replaced by Br. Heinzmann and Sr. Reuter, who would be married for that purpose, and expressed the wish that this change might be accomplished in love and peace and with the blessing of the Lord.

With great pleasure Br. Reichel received a letter from Mr. Beard, Jr., of Salisbury, wherein he mentioned that Mr. Noly[16] (that is the ferryman on the Potomac whose negro stole Br. Reichel's coffer) had sent him a Deed and some letters "For the Rev. Mr. Reichel," by a traveler. He gave no further particulars. [*Marginal note.* Mr. Beard had himself received these things from the well-known Heyl who lives near the Potomac, and had brought them with him.]

It is said that an Express from Col. Armstrong passed with an order to Mr. Joseph Williams, saying that no more men should be sent to Salisbury because the English had retreated, but we dare not put much faith in such reports.

July 17. Br. Biwighaus was sent to Salisbury for the articles mentioned in the letter received yesterday.

Capt. Moseby and several men passed on their way home. They had brought some captured Tories from Salisbury to Guilford Court-house, several of whom had escaped on the way.

July 18. Early in the morning Br. Bagge received a note from the Capt. Paschke who was here last spring with the Pulaski cavalry, saying that he and about sixty men, partly Virginians and partly Irish,

---

[16] Spelled Coly in the entry of June 9, 1780.

were coming and wished quarters and provisions. They arrived during the morning. Some of the men were lodged in Triebel's house, and some in the Tavern. The Captain announced that the real purpose of his coming was to collect all available food-stuffs and create a depot of supplies for an army to be gathered at the Atkin. Similar contributions have been called from Rowan County, and soldiers are to make forcible collections in other sections. We may be thankful that the above-mentioned Captain has come here, for he is a friendly man. He sent an order to Bethania to the two Justices Hauser[17] to come here for a conference with him.

Br. George Biwighaus returned from Salisbury, and brought to Br. Reichel the things lost on the Potomac, in so far as they have been found and handed over to Mr. Heyl, who wrote about them to Br. Reichel. They consisted of the certified Deed to Br. Marshall for all Wachovia, which was of the greatest importance; also Br. Reichel's books and papers; and strange to say nothing had been hurt. They were found in the woods by a woman who was looking for her cow. We thank the Saviour for His special help in this matter.

July 19. In the afternoon our land received a fine rain, which was needed by the gardens and especially by the corn fields. Justice Michael Hauser was here, and received order from Capt. Paschke that his district must send five or six wagon-loads of wheat to Steiner's mill.

July 20. This morning half of the soldiers from here marched north and south from Salem to carry on the taking of grain. They were hardly out of the town when poor Sr. Baumgarten came to complain that all her butter was taken from her milk-house last night. The soldiers lodged in Triebel's house ate it on their bread this morning and the broken crock, in which the butter had been, was found behind the house. Br. Pfeil lost his silver shoe-buckles, taken from his shoes before his eyes; and several pieces of clothing belonging to Br. Schaaf were stolen out of the wash-tub. Soon after his arrival Capt. Paschke had warned us to look out for our property, for he could not answer for his soldiers. The Helfer Conferenz was not held, as many of the Brethren and Sisters dared not leave their houses for fear of thieves.

July 22. All the soldiers except the Captain and a few others marched to the Quaker settlement to get grain. Last night the soldiers at Triebel's found a keg of wild-grape wine belonging to Martin Schneider, and drank all of it, refilling the keg with water. One man became very drunk and received a good beating. Some of the drafted militia returned from Salisbury, as they had no food there.

---

[17] Michael Hauser and George Hauser, Jr.

Br. Heinzmann turned over the cash-box and the account books of the Single Brethren to the Brn. Petersen and Samuel Stotz. Br. Reichel had so far recovered that he was able to hold the meeting for members of the Hourly Intercession.

July 23. The Single Brothers' Choir had a happy lovefeast, during which the Single Brethren bade farewell to Br. Heinzmann, after his faithful service as Vorsteher of this Choir for six and a half years, and at the close he showed his love for each Brother by giving to each the kiss of peace. In the evening meeting Br. Reichel spoke on the Text for the day, * * * and with special reference to Br. Heinzmann and Sr. Reuter, and after the singing of the usual marriage liturgy by the Choir they were united in holy wedlock in the name of the Trinity and with the blessing of the Church. Br. Heinzmann moved into the Gemein Haus.

July 25. This evening two English deserters came to our Tavern. They were examined by Capt. Paschke, but he secured little trustworthy information. The weather was cool and rainy today.

July 26. In the afternoon several Brethren had a conference about listing the Wachovia land for taxation.

July 27. Some of the men from Capt. Henry Schmid's company brought to Steiner's mill the grain that they have collected.

Br. Heinzmann moved into his wife's house, where they will stay until they go to the place to which they have been called; little Anna Steiner and the maiden Elisabeth Hartmann were therefore transferred to the Sisters House.

July 28. Various men rode through today, who recently fled to Virginia from Georgia and South Carolina. They had heard a report that the English had been defeated on the Waxhaw and had retreated, and they were returning to see after their plantations. This report[18] was contradicted by a man who was in the camp of General Sumter last Sunday, [July 23,] and found all quiet on the Waxhaw.

July 29. This morning two men and a negro boy came to our Tavern, and soon after Mr. Hunt, Lanier and another man arrived. Mr. Hunt found in the possession of the first party a horse which had been stolen from him, so they arrested the two men and examined them. It was found that they were father and son, from Georgia; that they had stolen the negro boy from a Mr. Rainord on the Catawba River; and much paper money, counterfeit silver and gold, and other suspicious articles were found in their pockets, without counting what might be in

---

[18] On June 17th Gen. Griffith Rutherford was informed that Lord Rawdon had retired toward Camden. On July 20th Maj. W. R. Davie intercepted a convoy of provisions and clothing four and a half miles from the British post at Hanging Rock, and a few days later he intercepted three companies of mounted infantry returning to Hanging Rock.

5

their saddle-bags. The two scamps were bound and taken to Shallow Ford, where they will be properly examined.

The Brn. Bagge and Herbst went this afternoon to Sr. Baumgarten's farm and sent away an Irishman, who has worked for her with reasonable industry for several days, but who was trying to force her to marry him.

July 30. In the evening it began to rain, and continued all night. Through responsible men we heard today the distressing report that in Kentok two settlements had been attacked by seven hundred Indians and one hundred white men, and had been destroyed in a barbarous manner. The Bryants have been living in one of these settlements. The Indians had treated the people so cruelly that the English had left them.

July 31. It rained all day, with an east wind which blew down much corn, but the rain was not heavy enough to cause the streams to rise. However, the ground was thoroughly soaked.

Br. Beck reported from Friedberg that a band of thieves was lurking in the neighborhood, robbing milk-houses, and that twice shots had been fired at Weesner and his wife, though without injuring them. Roving soldiers had taken a mulatto, and shot him through the arm; he had been serving as a spy, but betrayed the ringleader. [*Marginal note.* We learned later that his statement was largely false, and that the thieving was done by several negroes, not by whites.]

Aug. 1. Br. Reichel and others returned from Bethabara. While there a man returning from Pennsylvania brought unpleasant news, speaking of unrest in that province and of attacks from Indians.

Mr. Frederick Miller came to list the property here for taxation, and that of some of our neighbors.

Aug. 3. Captain Paschke returned, presumably from a visit to the troops on the Peedee. In the Grosse Helfer Conferenz the citizens' watch was reorganized, and each night, according to circumstances, one or more men will assist the regular night-watchmen. For several days the weather has been very hot and humid, with thunderstorms.

Aug. 5. Br. Marcus Hoens came from Friedberg, and asked Captain Paschke to release his wagon and team, which has been hauling meal for the army, but he could not get it back. All the wagons from the neighborhood have been pressed for this purpose; so far our wagon has not been taken. The people on Abbots Creek have been much disturbed by a wandering party of light-horse.

At Steiner's mill Br. Bulitschek changed the shorts-mill so that it would grind flour, in order to hasten the work with the much wheat brought in by the troops.

Aug. 6. In Friedland, Br. Reichel preached to a large congregation, on Luke 18. Then the Society members and their children had a happy lovefeast, with an address on the beginning of this settlement; and at the close of the service Br. and Sr. Heinzmann were introduced to the congregation, with the announcement that they would take charge in place of Br. and Sr. Toego Nissen.

Aug. 7. The Single Br. Johann Reuz began his work as a hat-maker, in the lower story of the former skin-house. The boy, Ludwig Blum, went to him as apprentice on trial.

Aug. 8. All day and until late in the evening wagons passed from Bethabara, Bethania and the neighborhood, going to Steiner's mill for the flour which has been ground there, and which they will take to the army on the Peedee. During the past days the heat has steadily increased and has become almost unendurable. This evening there was a hard storm, and it rained until about ten o'clock, so that no evening service could be held.

Aug. 9. It was clear and somewhat cool. The negress Ide was told that she might be baptised next Sunday, of which she was very glad. It was proposed to Br. Schreyer that he should marry the widow Baumgarten, to which he assented.

Aug. 10. Toward noon Br. and Sr. Toego Nissen arrived from Friedland with their children and their baggage. They moved into the little house belonging to Br. and Sr. Heinzmann, and the latter moved to their place in Friedland, taking as many of their things as could be packed into the two carts which brought the Nissens. The tears shed in Friedland when the Nissens left showed the love felt for them by their people.

Aug. 11. As the wagons taken by Captain Paschke's soldiers had left for the army in South Carolina with the flour ground at Steiner's mill, the Captain left this morning with the rest of his men. He seemed fairly content, though he was not as friendly as he was when here last year, and he was also sick. He paid for his own entertainment, but for his soldiers he gave a due bill against the public account. He left a very sick soldier here to be nursed, but it was necessary to move the man from the Tavern into the adjoining smoke-house, as the stench was intolerable.

Aug. 13. On this memorable anniversary of the Unity of Brethren the congregation met for the first service at half past eight in the morning. Br. Reichel told the story of conditions in Herrnhut fifty-three years ago, of the meeting in the church at Berthelsdorf for the Holy Communion, of the heart-melting which came over the entire congregation during this Communion, and of the love, and harmony, and the covenanting together to live according to the mind of Jesus, which followed in the prayer meeting in the Saal in Herrnhut; in short they felt themselves born anew. * * * It was an indiscribably blessed day of remembrance for the congregation of Salem, and will not easily be forgotten. There were clouds around the entire horizon, but it scarcely rained enough to lay the dust and lessen the heat a little.

Aug. 14. Br. Samuel Stotz, accompanied by Br. Martin Schneider, left for Cross Creek to see whether he could exchange some of the paper money for goods; may the Saviour be their Protector on this journey. The Brn. Marshall and Bagge went to court at Richmond, on business connected with the Metcalf lands.[19] Br. Charles Holder also went thither, having been called for the third time. He did not go on two calls, and will probably be fined. Toward evening Col. Alexander Martin came to our Tavern, on his way to Richmond. He was friendly, as always, and attended the evening service. The weather was again very oppressively hot.

Aug. 15. Again various persons passed toward South Carolina, believing that the English have been driven back,[20] and that they can again take possession of their plantations, which remains to be seen. Sr. Baumgarten, who had declined the offer of marriage with Br. Schreyer, came to Sr. Graff and with tears and regret said that she had not done right, and that she would now accept the proposal if it was still open. Her refusal had already been made known to Br. Schreyer, and now the matter must rest until we hear what he has decided.

Aug. 16. The Brn. Marshall and Bagge returned from the court in Richmond, and the former reported to the Aeltesten Conferenz that the court had not taken up the land matter, and only one Commissioner had appeared. Charles Holder was dismissed without fine.

Aug. 17. Our little girls celebrated their Festal Day. In the afternoon there was the formal betrothal of Br. Peter Schreyer to Sister Baumgarten; Br. Reichel officiated, in the presence of the Brn. and Srs. Graff and Marshall.

Aug. 18. At noon Br. Heckewälder, as school-teacher of the boys, held the burial service, on our God's Acre for Strangers, of the soldier William Brown, who was left here sick on the 11th of this month. He

---

[19] The "Metcalf lands" consisted of between eleven and twelve thousand acres, in twenty tracts, scattered along the water-courses in what were then Rowan and Orange Counties. The land had been granted by Earl Granville to William Churton, his surveyor-general, in 1762; Churton sold to Charles Metcalf, an English Moravian; and Charles Metcalf sold three of the tracts to his sister, Mary Metcalf; Bishop Graff, Jacob Bonn, and Traugott Bagge, had received a Power of Attorney from the two Metcalfs to sell the land to Frederic William Marshall as trustee for the Unitas Fratrum. By 1780, therefore, the Metcalf land was the property of the Unity.

[20] Aug. 5, 1780, Colonel Sumter, of South Carolina, and Major Davie, of North Carolina, attacked the British at Hanging Rock. The English and Tories were driven from the camp, which was looted by the Americans, who then withdrew, taking the captured stores with them.

died last night. While still alive his body began to mortify, and was eaten by worms.

Aug. 19. A report spread,—told by various men and confirmed by Moser's son, who had fled from the Continental army,—that last Wednesday there was an important battle, near Pinetree,[21] between the English and American armies, in which the latter was totally defeated and scattered, lost all the arms and baggage, and many men were killed and taken prisoner. Among the rest the English were said to have taken four hundred wagons, and we are much concerned about our wagons from Bethabara and Bethania, which set out some ten days ago to take meal to the Continental army. The Daily Texts during these days have seemed to suggest trouble and difficult circumstances, such as they may be obliged to undergo.

Aug. 20. Br. Kremser took a large package of letters, and our diaries of May, June and July, to Bethabara, and they were entrusted to a man returning to Pennsylvania.

Mr. Friedrich Müller arrived, having come from the meal-wagons, which he left at a ferry on the Peedee, about forty miles from the place of battle. A Captain and one hundred militiamen were at the ferry, and would not allow our wagons to recross, although they were in danger of falling into the hands of the English.

The Brethren of the Aufseher Collegium had a short conference concerning sending our Tickets to the Assembly, and it was decided to hold them for a while. They were for provisions furnished the soldiers. It was also decided to refuse to accept articles which persons might wish to store here for fear of the English. Shortly afterwards Mr. Robert Walker, Sr. came to Br. Bonn with just this request, but he refused to keep anything for him.

Aug. 21. The dry, cool weather continued, with wind from the east. All day soldiers and wagoners were passing, who had been in the battle near Pinetree. Most of them were on foot, hungry and without money, and bread was given to some. Among other things they brought the news that Captain Sumter and his rather large Corps had been totally defeated.[22] One man brought word that a company of cavalry was on the way hither from beyond the Atkin, but they crossed the river higher up. Toward evening the Brn. Samuel Stotz and Martin Schneider returned from Cross Creek, whither they went eight days ago. They reached Cross Creek just in time, before news of the unfortunate battle

---

[21] Aug. 16, 1780, Lord Cornwallis defeated General Gates a few miles from Camden, S. C. The site of Camden was formerly known as Pinetree Hill.

[22] Aug. 17, 1780, Tarleton surprised Sumter eight miles from Rocky Mount, recaptured the British wagons and stores, took Sumter's artillery, etc. Out of eight hundred Americans engaged only three hundred and fifty escaped death or capture.

had been received, and so were able to exchange their large store of
Congress money for salt. When they were safely on the return trip
they were stopped by an officer, who was camped with his men beside
the road; but when they showed him their Pass he permitted them to
continue, with their wagon and horses.

Soon after their arrival, the Brn. and Srs. Graff and Marshall returned from a visit to Friedberg. Last Saturday,[23] General Gates and
other officers took breakfast with Mr. Kleinert, but were in haste.

In the congregation meeting Br. Reichel told the story of the beginning of our Mission among the negroes in St. Thomas forty-eight years
ago, by the Brn. Leonard Dober and David Nitschmann, and pointed
out the rich blessing and success that had attended the work among the
negroes on the islands St. Crux and St. Jan.

Aug. 22. Toward noon Colonel Armstrong and his brother the
Major arrived. They had been in the battle, and through them we heard
that Brigadier Rutherford was taken prisoner. An attempt will be
made to gather the scattered troops, and half the militia are to be called
out. The people are in the extreme of fright because of the English.
In the meeting for communicants Br. Reichel spoke on the Text: "In
the world ye shall have tribulation, but be of good cheer, I have over-
come the world."

Congregation Council met to consider the matter already discussed
by the Aufseher Collegium this morning, namely the North Carolina
paper currency. This is nowhere accepted any more, and if the Branches
in town take it in exchange for necessities they cannot stand. It was
decided that for eight days we would lay aside this paper currency
among ourselves, and use either hard money, or Congress money at the
rate of 125 for 1 (or 1d for a dollar), or buy on credit, and see whether
by that time a value would be established or utterly lost. We cannot
refuse to accept this money from strangers who have no other and
are in distress, but it must not be taken at a higher rate than it can be
used again.

Aug. 23. There was an interesting meeting of the Aeltesten Conferenz. Br. Heinzmann brought a report from the Friedland Society,
and yesterday Br. Fritz reported for Hope, and it was resolved that a
small congregation should be formed out of each Society.

Again several soldiers passed; they had escaped in the battle.

Aug. 24. Br. Meinung surveyed the cleared land beyond the Wach
which belongs to the Plantation, so that a proper Contract can be drawn
up for Philip Vogler. Again soldiers passed in flight after the battle

---

[23] August 19, 1780.

between the English and General Sumter's Corps. It is oppressively hot,—the rain is too long delayed. Second-crop hay was hauled in. A congregation meeting was held by Br. Reichel, during which the Single Br. Peter Schreyer was married to the widowed Sr. Maria Baumgarten.

Aug. 25. Toward evening several of the light-horse arrived, with captured Tories who are being taken to Hillsborough. A shower cooled the air a little.

Aug. 26. This morning Col. Armstrong and Mr. Sheppard and Mr. Commans [Cummings] arrived, on their way to Hillsborough. The first-named told Br. Bagge confidentially that men were speaking angrily against us as Tories, from whom an uprising might be expected, and a troop of light-horse was expected from Virginia, who were known to deal sharply with such people. He promised to give the necessary orders for our protection, for he did not consider us Tories.

Br. Schreyer moved to his wife on her plantation, and Br. and Sr. Graff went along to introduce him to the children, who rejoiced to have a father again.

In the evening Br. Reichel and the Marshalls returned from Hope, where they had spoken with the members of the Society, and had received John Padget and his wife and Benjamin Chitty and his wife into the congregation, so forming the nucleus of a Country Congregation, to the great joy of that group. Now they have a great desire that the Holy Communion shall be celebrated there.

Circumstances made it advisable to observe this evening, instead of tomorrow, the anniversary of the beginning of the Hourly Intercession, fifty-three years ago.

Aug. 27. Sunday. Br. Reichel and a number of Brethren returned from Bethabara, where the negro Franks had been baptised with the name of Christian.

With the usual liturgy, the Single Sr. Dorothea Schumacher was received into the congregation. She is the first of the Schumacher family to join a congregation here; the older and younger Schumacher men were present.

Aug. 28. The Aufseher Collegium had a conference with Johann Ferdinand Schreed. He was formerly a soldier, has worked here for over a year, and on last Brothers' Festival was awakened and asked permission to remain here. He expressed the same wish today.

We hear that a company of light-horse, under Captain Caldwell, are on a Tory hunt in the neighborhood. They have beaten several men, and threatened Br. Steiner, claiming that he had spoken against *Liberty*. May the Lord mercifully turn this aside from us. At present much pressure is being brought to bear on men, who must either take up arms against the English, or be rated as Tories.

Aug. 29.   The Single Brethren had their Festal Day.

Aug. 30.   Br. Heinzmann reported from Friedland that Peter Schneider and Lagenauer had reached there in safety, having left their wagons thirty miles away, all right except that two of their horses had been stolen.   Other horses will be sent to bring the wagons in.

Colonel Campbell, who had come to Bethabara with two hundred light-horse from Virginia, sent for Br. Bonn to attend a soldier who had fallen from a horse; the man had been left in Bethania, so Br. Bonn had to go thither.

Br. Reichel had a conference with the parents, and the Brethren and Sisters who have supervision over the boys and children.   He read the first four sections of the ten points brought out by the Synods of 1769 and 1775, and they were thoroughly discussed.

Aug. 31.   Br. Reichel visited the school for little boys.   At ten o'clock Br. Graff held the children's meeting, and made an address to them, in which he urged them to be true in heart, and daily renew their baptismal covenant with the Saviour.

Afternoon an Express came from Colonel Campbell, from Bethabara, informing us that he and his men were coming here, and toward evening he arrived, accompanied by Col. Martin Armstrong and eighty cavalry-men.   The latter immediately took possession of the Tavern meadow for camp-site and pasture, but for today and tomorrow made requisition only for bread.   They behaved in orderly manner, and many of them attended the evening meeting in the Saal, having asked and received permission to come.   The Colonel slept in his tent among his soldiers.

Sept. 1.   The month began with damp, cloudy weather, promising rain.   Christian Conrad came to visit Br. Reichel, and told him much of his trying trip with his wagon.   The load of meal, taken to the Peedee, had to be taken from there to Hillsborough.   During one night twelve horses belonging to the wagon train were stolen from a fenced pasture by soldiers fleeing from the battle.

This afternoon the cavalry rode away in small parties.   They will scour the surrounding country for grain and cattle for General Sumter [Sumner]; he and his men are in Mecklenburg County, and are in great need of food, for neither grain nor cattle can be found there any longer.   In Hillsborough, General Gates is trying to gather another army, that he may wage another battle with the English.

Sept. 2.   Early in the morning it began to rain, and continued until after night-fall, so that no services could be held.   We were very thankful to our dear Father for this rain, for it was very dry, the great heat had drawn all moisture out of vegetation, and nothing could be planted.

Toward evening a party arrived from Colonel Campbell's company, and after them an Express with several men from General Smallwood's Corps, which was said to be at Guilford Court-House. The latter behaved in so brutal a manner that the former said among themselves that we ought to give the fellow a ball in his head. Scarcely had they left next morning, when an Express from Colonel Campbell brought them back, with orders to go to Bethabara, where they had been posted previously.

Sept. 3. Colonel Campbell marched through with his company, on their way to Bethabara. He came through the Friedland settlement, where he ordered a supply of grain, but at a fair price. He and Colonel Armstrong, who was with him, have found that not as much can be secured in this district as Captain Paschke had led them to expect. Apparently Captain Paschke had intended to bring General Gate's army here, but Colonel Armstrong will try to prevent this.

Br. Reichel, Br. and Sr. Marshall, returned this evening from Friedland. Today they have spoken with the Society members there; and this afternoon, in a special service, Michael Rominger, Sr. and his wife, Jacob Ried and his wife, were Received as the first members of a congregation at that place, to the joy of all who had desired the beginning of a congregation there.

Sept. 4. The officers who were here yesterday, to whom horses had to be furnished, brought them back today. In the afternoon an officer from Hillsborough came to the Tavern, but we could not find out what he wanted.

Sept. 5. Sr. Graff has had fever for several days, and so has Br. Bonn. Probably the coming of fall weather has been at least partly the cause.

Eight Sisters came from Bethabara to their Choir Communion. There is much distress in Bethabara, for 300 soldiers from Virginia are there, who have camped in the orchard, where they do as they please. The Aufseher Collegium considered the written order, sent by General Gates to Major Hartmann, that 1000 pairs of shoes should be made here. The Major knew perfectly well that this was impossible, so he ordered a quanity of leather for uppers and for soles, which we should take to the army, and he gave us written Protection that neither leather nor wagons should be pressed here until this order had been filled.

In the afternoon the Single Sisters had a lovefeast in their little prayer hall, which was quite filled. Br. Reichel congratulated them on the increase of this Choir, which was begun in 1766 in Bethabara with

troops. Balzer Christman went as teamster, Br. Biwighaus as accountant, and Br. Gottlieb Strehle to select the hides. The little boys moved from their old school-room into Br. Triebel's house, where a lovefeast was held for them by Br. Reichel and the other Brethren of the Aeltesten Conferenz. The boys were told that Br. Schober would hereafter conduct their school, in place of Br. Heckewälder, who was to go to Pennsylvania with Br. Reichel, and Br. Martin Schneider would assist in looking after them.

During the following night there was a hard thunderstorm, with strong wind and heavy rain from the north-west. Otherwise all is quiet these days, and we have heard nothing about the war.

Sept. 27. Colonel Armstrong and Mr. Commans were here; they signed the Pass for Br. Reichel for his journey. The weather was rather cool, and here and there one saw signs of frost for the first time this fall.

Sept. 28. Ten of the light-horse appeared, sent by General Butler to guard the leather sent yesterday from here to Hillsborough. They missed the wagon, but will probably catch up with it today, on information brought by old Jacob Christman, from Stinking Quarter, who came to the doctor, and who had met the wagon.

In a meeting of the Communicants and Received, Br. Reichel read from the Nachrichten recently brought from Pennsylvania. They were partly from the end of last year, and partly from the first of this, but some numbers were missing, and probably some packages have been lost at sea. Count Henry 28th sent greetings to the congregations here; he is now the correspondent for North Carolina in the Unity's Elders Conference. Br. Reichel also reminded the congregation that this was Br. Graff's 61st birthday, and sang for him several hymns of blessing.

From Salisbury came a report that our troops, which have been in Mecklenburg County, have withdrawn to this side of the Atkin, and that the English are following them.

Sept. 29. Michaelmas. In the afternoon there was a happy lovefeast for the Brethren and Sisters who serve in the Saal, as musicians, and with the children. In the morning Br. Reichel had made a talk to the children on the care of the holy angels for them. Br. Pfeil was sent to Bethabara to wait on Br. Richter, who is sick. Soldiers who have been serving in Mecklenburg passed through today, singly and in groups, returning to their homes. Many fugitives also came from Salisbury, in wagons, on horseback and on foot, and more passed on the highway leading to Virginia.

Sept. 30. Br. Reichel and other Brethren of the Aeltesten Conferenz spoke with the Brn. Spisike, Oesterlein and Johann Stotz, who have the oversight of our Older Boys.

Oct. 1. Br. Reichel preached on the Gospel for the day, Matt. IX. The congregation was so large that both the small rooms by the Saal were filled, for Brethren and Sisters had come from all our towns to see Br. and Sr. Reichel once more and bid them goodbye. In the afternoon, following the children's service, Br. Reichel and the Brn. Marshall and Graff went to the Brothers House, where there was a farewell Lovefeast for the three Brethren who were leaving the House, namely Br. Heckewälder, who will go to Pennsylvania with Br. Reichel, and the Brn. Reuz and Yarrell who will be transferred into the Choir of Married People. Br. Reichel urged the Brethren to hold fast to the Principles of their Choir, and to be ever more firmly grounded in the fellowship of Jesus Christ, * * * and his tender kiss to each in turn was a sign of the covenant, and was accompanied by a feeling of love on both sides. Then there was a conference with the Masters who superintend the professions carried on for the benefit of the Choir House Diaconie.

Meanwhile a Company of Virginia Cavalry passed through our town, led by Colonel Armstrong; they did not stop but went on toward the Atkin. In the evening meeting the two couples already mentioned were married, Br. Reichel making an impressive address. Colonel Armstrong and Mr. Commans were present.

Oct. 2. Early in the morning Br. and Sr. Reichel and Sr. Graff went to Bethabara, where the Reichels took leave of the Brethren and Sisters in a lovefeast. Br. Reichel also blessed the Single Br. Richter for his home-going, which followed soon after.

Here in the forenoon Br. Graff held doctrinal instruction for the little boys, and at 10 o'clock the children had a liturgy, as they will have each Monday from now on. They will also have a meeting on Friday, making three services a week for them.

Many people continue to pass, bringing with them their small store of goods and chattels. They come from this side of and beyond Salisbury, and go to Virginia, where, it is said, some thousands have taken refuge.

Oct. 3. Some of the Single Brethren went to Bethabara to the burial of the departed Br. Richter. Our wagon returned from Hillsborough, bringing a load of raw hides, and a friendly letter from General Gates to Br. Bagge, in which he expressed his satisfaction with the leather which was sent. He offered to give a Ticket for the balance of the bill, or to pay in money as soon as some came; expressed his willingness to serve us in any way; and sent a Pass allowing Br. Bagge to get salt from Cross Creek. Br. Bibighaus had heard from a certain Major

Penn that they had not really needed the leather, but that they had wanted to test our sentiment toward this State, for we had been described to Congress as Tories, and it was well for us that we had proved the contrary.

Oct. 4. In the morning there was the last session of Aeltesten Conferenz which Br. Reichel and his wife will be able to attend here. In the evening meeting he preached his last sermon on the Texts of these days, especially that for tomorrow: "The peace of God rule in your hearts." In a service that followed he and the communicant members of the congregation bound themselves in the Cup of Covenent to submit themselves wholly to Jesus, Who died for them.

Last night the weather changed to rain, which continued all day. We heard with sorrow that a party of Tories had raided Capt. Shepperd's house and ruined it, and he had escaped with difficulty.

Oct. 5. This morning our dear Br. and Sr. Reichel set out for Pennsylvania,[25] after a Visitation here of nearly four months, upon which the Saviour has been graciously pleased to bestow a rich blessing. Our hearts and love will accompany them with prayer to the Saviour on their journey in these perilous times. Br. Heckewälder went with them to Bethlehem, for he seems to have played out here and hopes to find there an employment which will suit him better.[26] The teamsters are Peter Schneider and Michael Hauser, Jr. Br. and Sr. Marshall accompanied them to the noon halt, returning in the afternoon. The weather was cloudy, with a rather cool air from the north-east, but favorable for the trip.

Oct. 6. The weather continued as yesterday. Br. Johann Krause accompanied the party who left yesterday as far as Dan River, and saw them safely across it; he brought back their hearty greetings.

Colonel Armstrong, Major Henrich Schmidt, and Mr. Comans returned from the camp on the Atkin, whither they had escorted a wagon loaded with powder and lead. Last night three riding horses and one draught horse were stolen from them out of Christian Frey's stable. Young Schumacher brought back the empty wagon; he had driven it for them. The officers went on to Richmond to suppress the rising of the Tories.

Oct. 8. The weather was unusually pleasant and clear.

Oct. 9. The two young married couples, Yarrells and Johann Reuzes, moved into the houses which they are to occupy for the time, the former into Fritz' house and the latter into the old Skin-house.

---

[25] See Part III, this volume, for full notes on the journey of Bishop Reichel and his party.
[26] In 1781, in Bethlehem, Pa., he married Anna Maria Nitschmann. He died in Hope, N. J., in 1803.

Andreas Volk's son came for the doctor for his brother-in-law Johann Krause, who was shot in the leg yesterday while standing guard at Richmond, which was again visited by a strong party of Tories under Gideon Wright. The bullet had remained in his limb; Joseph Dixon was sent to bind up the wound. The Tories had expressed sympathy for the injured man, saying the ball had not been meant for him but for some one else, and so on. What consequences this may have remains to be seen.

Oct. 10. The members of the Aufseher Collegium went with Br. Walter, who is Road-master, to decide where repairs shall be made on the road to the bridge. Again many travelers and refugees passed.

Oct. 12. Last night it began to rain, continuing gently all day, and more heavily during the following night.

Oct. 13. Br. Peterson set out on horseback for Bethabara, but heard from the younger Schumacher, who was returning from there, that a large party of Tories were in that village. About 500 Tories had marched past the mill, but without molesting anything. It looks now as though the entire Tory party had risen, both in this neighborhood and on Abbots Creek. Br. Peterson therefore turned back.

The Aeltesten Conferenz met with the three Brethren who have charge of the boys, and those fathers whose sons still live at home, and it was agreed in which hours the boys should be in their parents' homes and when in the Boys Room.

Oct. 14. Br. and Sr. Marshall went to Hope to hold the first Communion there for the four communicants.

Almost no outsiders were here today, probably out of fear, for both parties are under arms, and have been stationed only a few miles from Bethabara, at the bridge near Andreas Volk, in preparation for a small engagement. Shortly after the prayer meeting there was a heavy rain, which continued through the night and into the next day.

Oct. 15. The 42nd week. The 21st Sunday after Trinity. In the morning the Church Litany was prayed, and then, instead of preaching, a sermon of Br. Gregor's was read. This closed the congregational services of the day, for yesterday already a certain Captain from General Smallwood's troops had informed us that a part of his Detachment had camped at Friedrich Müller's in Friedland, and would be here today, and they arrived during the forenoon. There were about 150 horsemen and 30 foot, with three wagons, and they were joined by a small company of militia from Guilford, and Capt. Lapp with 12 men came from Bethabara, where Col. Shepperd and Major Schmidt had arrived with about 200 men. All these men and their horses had to be fed. They kept good order, cooking in the open place by the Tavern

6

in the heavy rain. They were being held in expectation of the rising, but stayed here all night. It is reported that Gideon Wright's party was defeated at the Shallow Ford by Capt. Gambly, and completely routed. Br. Bonn was asked to come and bind up the wounded; he sent his apprentice, Joseph Dixon, next day.

Oct. 16. Br. Ernst came from Bethania to Conference, and Br. and Sr. Beck from Friedberg, in spite of the high water. General Smallwood and his officers, who are still here today, wished to attend a service, so at twilight Br. Graff held a bright singstunde, in which voices and instruments joined in harmony, and at the close the New Testament benediction was sung. The weather has cleared; it is somewhat cool but not cold.

Oct. 17. Early this morning General Smallwood and his troops left for the camp on the Atkin. During the forenoon another Corps of some hundreds of infantry arrived from Dan River. (They expected to be joined by the horsemen from Virginia under Col. Armstrong, but the latter did not come.) All these troops had been in Bethabara for two or three days, and had eaten all the food there; and here they did not find enough bread left in the Bakery that each might get a little, and so they marched on to the Atkin.

Oct. 18. Last evening a soldier came from the Atkin for Br. Bonn, who must ride thither with him this morning to attend an officer who is so sorely wounded that Joseph Dixon does not consider himself able to care for him. The soldier made harsh threats that he would bring 150 Virginians here in three days to burn the town, (but he will not be able to do this unless our Lord gives His consent). About ten horsemen from the Atkin passed on their way home to Virginia; they report that the English have been driven back.

The weather was cool today, and last night there was a sharp frost. For four days the wind has been from the north-east.

Oct. 19. Yesterday Br. Bagge went to Bethania, and returned today by way of Bethabara. The five wounded men had been taken to Bethania, and twenty men had been left to guard them; Capt. Campbell and the rest of the Virginians will march back to that State, and will not come to Salem. A Proclamation of General Smallwood had been published, in which he stated that any soldier caught robbing would be brought to the camp and hanged. This order will have a good effect, for barbarous and unjust treatment has driven many to the Tories who would gladly have remained peaceful.

The weather has become mild, with wind from the south. Br. Bonn came home this evening. He had bound up the five wounded who were taken to Bethania, and also the one Tory who lay in a house near the battle field, and whom he had attended by permission of the Virginia Major. The Major had treated Br. Bonn most politely, and by his advice had left only three men in Bethania to wait on the wounded instead of the proposed twenty. We see in this the gracious hand of God, Who turned aside the threats of these people,—to Him be the praise!

Oct. 21. The Brn. Peterson and Sam Stotz took to Mr. Lanier the Tickets for provisions furnished the soldiers and received $20,000.00 paper money, for which they gave receipts. Bethabara received the same amount in the same way.

Oct. 22. Br. Kühnast came from Bethabara in great concern because a large number of Tories, captured in an action on the Catawba River,[27] and the Whigs who are guarding them, are marching toward Bethabara.

Oct. 23. Four Brethren from here were sent to Bethabara, to assist in the work caused by the arrival of a large number of soldiers and prisoners; all of them and their horses must be taken care of, and no notice had been sent in advance. Everything was in confusion, there was no help in man, and our only comfort and stay was the Saviour, according to the Text of the day which was: "The Lord is near,"

> Lord Jesus mine, Thy being near
> Into my heart brings peace and cheer.

To Him we commended these difficult and distressing conditions, being diligent in prayer and supplication for the strengthening of our poor Brethren and Sisters.

Oct. 24. All day there were many visits from the soldiers stationed at Bethabara, not only militia officers but also English, who were permitted to move about freely and were not watched as closely as the Tory prisoners although they also had a guard. A load of meal was sent to Bethabara for the soldiers and others, as the supply there was exhausted. Br. Bibighaus set out yesterday, with a wagon hired by the store here, to bring a load of salt and other things which have been bought in Cross Creek; from there he will go to Hillsborough, taking the Tickets given for leather which he will exchange for money. Br. and Sr. Graff and their companions returned this afternoon from Bethania; they came by way of Bethabara, but were not hindered by the soldiers camped there.

Oct. 25. Br. Bonn was called to Bethania to attend the wounded, it being said that the elder Allen was in very bad case, though he was not in as serious a condition as was reported. Yesterday an officer or soldier hired his horse for a couple of hours, but he did not bring it back until

---

[27] The battle of King's Mountain was fought on Oct. 7, 1780, and was a signal victory for the Americans.

today, and then lame and worn out. Again all day there were officers riding to and fro; several horses had to be furnished to take them to the Atkin. In the evening Bible Reading we commenced the 1st Epistle to the Corinthians. Br. Marshall made a talk to the Single Sisters. The weather continued cloudy, but not cold.

Oct. 26. This morning Colonel Campbell, Shellwy [Shelby] and other officers arrived, took breakfast at the Tavern, then all except Captain Campbell went on to the camp on the Atkin. Again several horses had to take them to the other side of Atkin. In the afternoon Br. Herbst went to Bethabara to see whether Colonel Cleveland, or any one else, would pay for the provisions furnished from here, as they are going to leave tomorrow.

Oct. 27. Soon after ten o'clock there was an eclipse of the sun, which could only be seen now and then when the sun came from behind the clouds. Br. Herbst returned from Bethabara; he had received the hides of the cattle they have killed in place of money. When no other animals are available they kill one and another of the cattle which they drive in from the woods near Bethabara. They will stay until Tuesday or Wednesday.

Oct. 28. Br. Marshall accompanied Br. Bonn to Bethabara to see the distressing conditions there. Br. Bonn visited his patients in Bethania. Br. Graff sent a letter to Br. Reichel by a traveler named Bach, who was on his way to Pennsylvania; the man would only wait one hour. The weather was unusually pleasant and warm; it rained a while during the night.

Oct. 29. Several Brethren attended the thanksgiving sermon which Mr. Hill preached in Bethabara in view of the victory over the Tories.

Oct. 30. We were afraid that the troops at Bethabara would move their camp here today, but the arrival of Colonel Cleveland freed us of apprehension; he said it was quite enough that they had stayed so long at Bethabara. We heard that General Gates and 600 calvarymen had been taken on their way to camp, but this was a false report.

Oct. 31. The Aufseher Collegium completed the Agreements with the Masters and superintendents of the Gemein Diaconie Branches. Br. Oesterlein returned from Bethabara, where he has been helping for eight or ten days. No one knows when the troops will break camp. Br. Herbst brought from Bethabara a load of hides from slaughtered cattle. Some of the Tories, who had joined the English, are surrendering themselves and receiving Pardon, but they must serve three months. In the afternoon there was a hard storm from the north-east which made it cold, and during the following night it froze a little.

Nov. 1. Remembering that we shall go to a heavenly home, and thinking of the company of those whose life on earth has ended, the evening address was on Hebrews XII: "Ye are come unto Mt. Zion." A company of English and other officers attended the service. The officers, Cleveland, Winston, and others, who visited here yesterday were given a good meal, without charge, at the Tavern, with which they were *well pleased,* and this may have influenced them not to move the entire army hither from Bethabara. From that village we hear many reports of violence, for instance Giery Wright was shot in his own home; very likely he had intended to give himself up, as many are doing at present. The weather continues cold, and it froze tonight.

Nov. 2. Nothing particular happened. Refuges from Georgia passed through. We heard that in that state there had been a rising on the part of some who did not wish to take the oath of allegiance to the English, and planned to overthrow them,[28] but they were defeated and scattered.

Nov. 3. This afternoon the Single Br. Biwighaus returned from Cross Creek, and the four wagons loaded with salt and other things arrived during the night. They had not been hindered on their way, though their horses were tired out and some of them were sick. The salt was immediately unloaded, during the night, and the wagons went home. We were afraid that Colonel Armstrong, who had come toward evening, accompanied by the Commissary, Mr. Brooks, might press the goods *for Continental service.* Mr. Reed, of Hillsborough, had also come, probably to see about the captured Tories.

Nov. 4. Br. Rose brought a package of letters and Nachrichten, which Br. Johann Schaub had brought from Pennsylvania. Br. Schaub had met Br. Reichel, whose party had traveled without interference to Manakesy [Md.] making the trip in fourteen days. There were no letters from Europe, but extracts from letters written to Bethlehem mentioned the great *tumult*[29] in London last July.

Many people came to the store for salt; for some weeks they had not so much as a grain left.

Nov. 5. Br. Friedrich Peter preached here for the first time.

Nov. 6. Br. Schaub came on a visit. He reported that last night three officers escaped from Bethabara. Here there was a great sale of salt in the store.

William Barton Peddycoard and his family are moving back to Maryland, as he is disturbed over the question of military service. Letters

---

[28] In the middle of September, 1780, Col. Elijah Clark led an unsuccessful attempt to re-take Augusta, Ga. [29] Probably the Gordon "No Popery Riots" are meant.

were sent by him to Br. Reichel and others. The weather is dry and mild.

Nov. 7. The demand for salt continues, though the people can pay for it only with grain, as they have no hard money.

Ten men from Major Phelps' light-horse came to the Tavern, expecting the rest of their command to come tomorrow.

Nov. 8. The other light-horsemen did not appear, so the ten men returned to Bethabara. While they were here they had to be entertained *at county expense,* which probably means a loss for the congregation Diaconie.

We hear that most of the captured Tories who live in this section have been released, on condition that they serve six months in the American army. Before beginning service they were allowed to go home and wash their clothes.

Nov. 9. With the approval of the Aufseher Collegium, Br. Meyer quietly took down the Tavern sign, so that he could not be forced to sell strangers so much brandy.

Nov. 10. About one hundred of the Tories, who have been prisoners in Bethabara for nearly three weeks, and who have obtained their freedom by enlisting in the American army, came here and went on to the mill, where they secured provisions, and on the next day proceeded to the camp at Salisbury. With them came about twenty English officers, and it looks as though they would remain here for some time. They were lodged in the Tavern, to which came also a number of sick soldiers with their doctor. Those who could not be lodged in the Tavern were placed in the large kitchen under Fritz' house. The day was closed with the liturgy: "As Jesus hung upon the cross," and some of the above-mentioned guests attended the service. The weather has been cold and raw, but it cleared during the night. Mr. Brooks, Commissary for the soldiers, came to Br. Miksch and asked for a room, as he desires to have some quiet.

Nov. 11. The English officers asked that they might leave the Tavern and be given quarters where they could cook for themselves. The Aufseher Collegium met, and arranged to place them in various houses. The sick were taken away, and other men who have been in camp by the mill were brought here. In Bethabara there was the funeral of the man who was carelessly shot by a boy.

Nov. 12. We had expected that the cold weather would bring snow, but instead there was rain, gentle at first, and then heavy, which continued all night. Yesterday a chimney in the Gemein Haus caught fire, and today the same thing happened in the Tavern; fortunately there was no wind, and no damage was done.

Nov. 13. This important day of remembrance among us was again observed, and was marked by a real sense of the grace of our faithful Chief Elder. In the first service, at nine o'clock in the morning, Br. Marshall spoke of the great importance of this day in 1741. In the festal lovefeast the congregation thought particularly of the consecration of our Gemein Saal, nine years ago. It rained all day, and we were not disturbed by persons from outside the town.

Nov. 14. Several wagons passed, going to New Bern on business for our store. The weather was clear until toward evening. Some of the English prisoners attended the service in the Saal.

Nov. 15. Four more wagons left for Cross Creek, and Br. George Biwighaus rode with them to make purchases for our store.

Nov. 16. Mr. Commans passed, and from him we heard that the court in Richmond adjourned yesterday, and nothing was done, except a few absolutely necessary things. No jury was chosen, there were scarcely twenty men present, and not a single lawyer.

Nov. 17. From an adjutant in General Smallwood's army, who came from camp, we learned that the troops remained in their recent positions, that the rest of the Tories had been taken as prisoners to Salisbury, and that the English have landed in Virginia.

Nov. 19. While the younger Schumacher was attending the services here his house was robbed, probably by a vagabond who passed through this town and saw him here. A company of forty men arrived, and camped in the woods below Salem.

Nov. 20. The English prisoners, who have been here for a week, moved to Hillsborough, by order of General Gates. They went unwillingly.

The wagon, which left for Pennsylvania last month with Br. and Sr. Reichel, returned, bringing letters from them, dated at Yorktown [Pa.] on Oct. 26th. The wagon brought a load of iron and other things for the store. The wagoners had heard nothing of the war unrest, either going or returning.

Nov. 21. In the sleeping-hall of the Single Brethren the angels prevented a serious catastrophe last night. Some of the ceiling boards, and the flooring above them, came down with a great crash, but fell between the beds, so that the Brethren sleeping in them were not injured.

Nov. 22. Br. Jens Schmidt had to be brought back from Bethabara because of a suspicious sore on his tongue.

Nov. 23. Br. Walter, with some Brethren and a cart from Friedland, went out to work on the roads.

Nov. 26. The elder Christman's son Jacob and his wife came from Reedy Fork, and attended the [Sunday] services. He and his father ask that one of the Brethren may come to them as school-teacher for their children, and hope that among the neighbors some will join with them in the movement, but the people seem not to know what they really want, and we cannot act on such an uncertainty.

Nov. 27. The Brn. Meinung and Miksch surveyed a piece of land on the Wach, below the mill, for John Peddycoard.

This afternoon a scamp was taken to Major Schmidt. He was arrested near Peter Frey's, for stealing, and another party tried to steal near the elder Greter's, but was driven off with the help of the neighbors. At present there are many highwaymen about, who steal and even murder. In Abbott's Creek settlement, recently, a wagon-load of stolen articles was found in a hollow tree.

Br. George Biwighaus returned from Cross Creek, and during the night the wagons arrived safely, loaded with salt and other wares.

[*Minutes of the House Conference of the Single Brothers' Choir, Nov. 29.* Br. Stotz has bought a Clavecin for the House meeting-hall. It was resolved that at a Choir meeting proposal should be made that a collection be taken to help pay for it.]

Dec. 2. The weather changed into rain, with some glaze-ice.

Dec. 3. The First Sunday in Advent. Br. Graff preached on Matthew XXI: "Behold thy King cometh unto thee."

Dec. 4. The Brn. Biwighaus and Flex went to Salisbury, to see whether General Gates would pay the Tickets issued for the leather sent to Hillsborough, or what direction he would give about them. The air was cold, with a raw wind from the north-west. The negress, Mary, was given a proposal to marry the negro Brother, Johann Samuel, and she assented.

Dec. 5. The Aufseher Collegium met, but several members were called to the Tavern, where several evil men were trying to plague Br. Meyer.

Dec. 7. The negro Br. Johann Samuel came from Bethabara, and was formally betrothed to the negro Sr. Mary.

Dec. 9. Our town was unusually full all day. Six Virginia officers came from Salisbury to the Tavern for a rest. The Brn. Biwighaus and Flex returned from camp. They were given a cordial reception by General Gates, who gave a friendly recommendation of our Society to General Green; however, instead of getting payment for their Tickets they were given a draft on the Treasurer in Maryland or on the Governor.

Dec. 10. Some of the officers who came yesterday attended the morning and evening services in the Saal. Toward evening four wagons arrived, loaded with lead from New River. The men spent the night in the Tavern; they are taking the lead to camp. The weather has cleared, but not cold.

Dec. 11. Spach's and Hartmann's wagons came here for wood-hauling and other work. In this way they will avoid the men who are pressing mounts for the light-horse.

The Virginia officers returned to camp, and were followed by the wagons with lead.

Dec. 19. There was a heavy rain storm, which seemed to end the recent rainy spell, and after that it cleared.

Dec. 21. The two wagons returned from Willmingtown, bringing salt for Mr. Commans and our store. Four other wagons that belonged with them arrived yesterday. They had set out for New Bern, but on the way Mr. Commans heard that nothing could be done there, so he went with them to Willmingtown.

[*Memorabilia der Gemeiner in der Wachau ins Ganze und insonderheit.* Six wagons arrived, most of them loaded with salt which had been made on the Virginia coast and had been taken to Willmingtown by water. Some loads were for Salem, some for Richmond, so for the present this neighborhood is well supplied.]

Dec. 22. The Brn. Meinung and Miksch went to survey land for Mr. Moses Martin, on the Carteret.

Dec. 23. All day the town was full of people, buying and selling. The weather continues fine.

Dec. 24. The Fourth Sunday in Advent and Christmas Eve. Between the morning and afternoon services we received a package of letters and Nachrichten, together with the Daily Texts for the first four months of the coming year,—this was a beautiful *Christmas present.* In the evening was the Christmas Eve vigil, which was attended by a number of young people from Bethania and Friedberg. First there was the Christmas lovefeast for the children, about thirty in number. An Ode was sung with instrumental accompaniment, and at the close a written Christmas verse and a lighted candle was given to each child, and they carried the lighted candles to their homes. The weather was calm and pleasant. Later the adult members had a lovefeast.

Dec. 25. Christmas Day. Br. Graff preached the festal sermon. A storm from the west brought cold and frost.

Dec. 26. In the afternoon our only negro, Sambo, was baptised, receiving the name Abraham.

Dec. 29. A large package of letters, and our diary for August, September, October and November, was given to Mr. Beard, of Salisbury, who will take it with him to Pennsylvania.

We were somewhat disturbed by a report that a company of soldiers from Virgina were on their way hither; but we were quieted by further information that they were marching by the upper road to the Atkin.

Dec. 30. The Holy Communion was celebrated for the last time this year. Br. Marshall and Br. Friedrich Peter served the Brethren, the latter for the first time, and Br. Marshall and his wife served the Sisters. There were ninety-one communicants. Shortly before the service an officer and two men came from the Continental Army to get leather and shoes, but they made no disturbance, and went on next day, with the promise that the leather ordered should be delivered at Guilford Court-House.

Mr. Lanier brought slaughtered hogs to Br. Herbst, in payment for the negro Jacob, who has run away from him. He said he would have to send his cattle away, for men were shooting and killing them in the woods, both his and those belong to others.

Dec. 31. We heard that the Virginians, 140 men, reached Bethabara yesterday, but camped in the woods, and made no trouble except that meal and meat must be furnished them. They will be here tomorrow.

The New Year's Eve service began with a lovefeast at half past eight. The second service was at half past ten; and at half past eleven the congregation assembled for the last time, and heard the Memorabilia of our congregations with thankful hearts. Shortly before the reading was finished the musicians gave the signal of the changing year, and the congregation fell upon its knees singing:

Now thank we all our God,

This was followed by a prayer for the whole Church of God, for our rulers, and for this land. Rising, the choir sang:

Holy Lord God!
Holy Almighty God!

The service closed with the Benediction; and with a gracious sense of the presence of Jesus Christ, and the peace of God, the congregation went home for a few hours of rest.

Minutes of the Salem Boards. 1780.

[Extracts translated.]

Jan. 4. (Aufseher Collegium.) Br. Bagge's draft of a petition to the Assembly was read; it asks that the county of Surry may not be divided.

Jan. 6. (Helfer Conferenz.) Sister Micksch, as Saal-dienerin, becomes a member of this Conferenz. The fire-inspectors, having made their rounds during the past days, reported a new fire ladder and three hooks. There are seven fire-buckets in the Brothers House, three at Br. Herbst's, and one extra. Inquiry shows that most of the Brethren have money in hand for the payment of their taxes.

Jan. 8. (Aeltesten Conferenz.) The older and younger boys are to be kept separate in school, but when one Brother must leave the room the connecting door shall be opened so that the other Brother can supervise both classes. A hymn shall be sung at the opening and close of school, both rooms uniting; in this way the boys will learn to sing better. In winter the school shall be in session from eight to eleven o'clock in the morning, and from one to five in the afternoon. In summer it can probably begin at seven o'clock. The parents shall take their little children to school; the two Brethren shall see that they are taken home. On the days when the children go to meeting, Br. Heckewälder shall keep them at the school until the bell rings, and then take them to the Saal.

Jan. 11. (Auf. Col.) Br. Meinung reported on the price of sending letters, etc. It remains as fixed by the Collegium on Sept. 9, 1772, with the following exceptions:—For letters to and from Pennsylvania, 2d apiece; newspapers 4 sh. per year; small packages 6d apiece, and larger packages in proportion.

Jan. 20. (Auf. Col.) Taxes for this year are:—To the State 25 sh., to the county 3:6d, for Salisbury Court-House 4d, on the £100. The sheriff had orders to collect the entire tax from us three-fold; the Brethren proposed that they would pay the state tax three-fold and the others straight. After consultation with Brethren in Bethania it was decided to accept a suggestion of the sheriff, and postpone payment until February Court, the Brn. Bagge and Michael Hauser going surety that the Brethren would then pay the taxes according to the decision of the Court.

Jan. 20. (Helf. Conf.) Clipped silver shall be accepted at the following rates:—A piece weighing four pennyweight, 2 sh.; 3 pennyweight, 1:6d; 2 pennyweight, 1sh. There shall be no allowance for overweight between the amounts specified.

Jan. 26. (Aelt. Conf.) The Bethania Committee will hereafter consist of the Brn. Michael Ranke, Peter Hauser, Grabs and Schor, together with Br. Ernst.

The fence around the Bethabara God's Acre needs thorough repair, and as the Brothers' side is almost full it shall now be widened, as may be determined after looking over the place.

Feb. 1. (Auf. Col.) A summary of the cost of the waterworks was presented, with the receipts and disbursements in 1779. Receipts were about £42:18:—, including £13:4:—paper money; expenses were £69:17:6, including £23:6:6 in paper money. Counting the paper money at 1 sh. for a dollar the expenses were £49:9:3 in good money. It is evident that the receipts have not exceeded the expenses, and this shall be made known to Congregation Council, or to the entire congregation, for then no one can object to the payment of 9d each four weeks, in good money.

There was a discussion of the ordering of books from Barby and England, for instance the new Hymn Book of the Unity, the little book for doctrinal instruction, the Idea Fidei Fratrum, Spangenberg's Short Account, Layriz on the Instruction of Children, History of the Mission in St. Thomas, English History of the Church of the Brethren, and so on, not only for the use of the congregations in Wachovia, but for private parties. The matter will be brought up in the next Congregation Council, and any person wishing one or another book shall mention it to one of the officers of his or her Choir, and then the order shall be sent according to the number required.

Br. Melchior Rasp is very old and feeble, and shall be excused from congregation dues.

Feb. 8. (Auf. Col.) Br. Triebel is unwilling to rent or sell the logborer, is also unwilling to have the work done by anyone except himself or his apprentice. If he continues to do the work, it must be with the express understanding that if any log is not accurately bored he is to make another, without charge for the faulty one.

The property[1] of the departed Br. Johann George Baumgarten was listed on the 5th of this month, and appraised by the Brn. Herbst, Schnepf and Michael Hauser. According to the Contract the land reverts to the Administration, as it has not been paid for, but the Administration does not wish to enforce this, but will let the Baumgarten heirs take it under the terms of the original Contract, if they wish to

---

[1] Now occupied in part by the Methodist Children's Home, in the western part of Winston-Salem, N. C.

retain it. Should the widow decide to change her condition in life it will be only fair that the person who takes possession should pay her present children two-thirds of the difference between the original price and what it would bring in sale. Br. Bagge and Michael Hauser shall talk this over with the widow, for in view of his long service of the Oeconomie the departed Brother had been given an unusually low price on the land, and it is only just that his children should reap the benefit on the part that belongs to them.

Sheriff Hudspeth has offered to present our case to the Court, and to recommend that outside of the State tax we shall pay the taxes straight, as he has recognized the justice of this. We will therefore not need to employ a lawyer, but can secure one at the time, if necessary, from among those present at Court.

Feb. 9. (Aelt. Conf.) Br. Aust has been told that at the last Conferenz meeting the Saviour did not approve his proposal to marry Sr. Reuter. Neither he nor we can suggest another suitable Sister here, and he has asked whether he could not be helped out by a Sister from Pennsylvania, and has further suggested that he should go north to see about it. Conferenz therefore laid the matter before the Saviour in the three following lots:

1) The Saviour approves that we shall write to Pennsylvania concerning a Sister for Br. Aust.
2) The Saviour approves that Br. Aust himself shall go to Pennsylvania.
3) Blank.

The second was drawn: The Saviour approves that Br. Aust himself shall go to Pennsylvania. Now the matter of Br. Rudolph Christ's marriage must be taken up at once, as the Pottery cannot be managed except by a married couple.

Feb. 16. (Helf. Conf.) Br. Bonn reported that the sheriff had presented the matter of our taxes to the Court, and had been supported by two lawyers present, and the Court had granted our request.

Some of the Brethren do not approve of the decision of the Conferenz regarding the accepted value of silver money, and think there should be allowance for extra pence in value. No man receiving such a piece of silver is obliged to spend it, but he may take it to the goldsmith, where he can get full value, and any man can accept such silver pieces at such value as he pleases without binding others, so the resolution of the Conferenz remains unchanged.

Feb. 17. (Auf. Col.) Br. Meyer has recently bought wheat at 20 sh. good money for a bushel; the price is too high, and will have an ill effect.

Orders for the books to be brought from Europe now stand as follows: In German,—41 hymn-books, 9 copies of Reichel's work on the Bible, 11 Idea Fidei Fratrum, 4 History of the Mission in St. Thomas, 48 little books on Doctrine, 4 Layriz on the Instruction of Children, 3 Berthelsdorf song-books, 3 Life of Zinzendorf, parts six, seven and eight, 49 Halle octavo Bibles; Arnolds' German-English dictionary; in English,—6 History of the Mission in St. Thomas, 6 Cranz' History of the Brethren, 14 Spangenberg's Short Account of the Brethren's Unity, 1 History of the Greenland Mission, 12 hymn-books, 3 Bibles, large octavo. As we do not know the exact price Br. Wollin will be asked to send them from England and guarantee payment; this will not increase the cost greatly, as they will not be shipped until peace has come. A list shall be made and laid aside, so that when the books arrive there shall be no confusion as to the order.

Feb. 22. (Auf. Col.) It was suggested that as wheat is scarce and high a bread of mixed flour and corn-meal, or corn-meal alone, should be furnished to guests at the Tavern. Further, that it would be worth the trouble to try to raise spelt, as it is not so much in danger from weevils.

It was remarked that if we are asked to take part in the next election of Assembly-men we should send several Brethren to the election, for it is our duty to participate in anything that pertains to the welfare of the country.

Feb. 23. (Aelt. Conf.) Br. Ernst orders three hymn-books for Bethania. He inquiries what he shall do if Samuel Strub asks him to publish the Banns for his approaching marriage? As Strub has not been baptised it will be better for him to get a License.

March 10. (Auf. Col.) At the Election in Richmond, the Commissary, Michael Henderson, told Br. Bonn that he had instructions to press half of the beef-cattle, needed for the army, from the Brothers House, but that he would be satisfied with two head from each of our towns, if one from each place is fairly good. We will do as he desires, and as he seems inclined to favor us we will endeavor to satisfy him. The Single Brethren shall provide the cattle, but in cases like this, where there will probably be a loss, the loss shall not fall on the party that furnishes what is ordered but on the town as a whole, since the order was really to the community. This shall apply in the case of a recent loss, where a bill for provisions furnished some time ago has only been paid in these last days.

March 21. (Auf. Col.) George Hauser plans to go north with a wagon early in April, but it is uncertain whether he will be able to bring back more than the Brn. Aust and Blum will wish to load.

Packages which he is to take north shall be assembled at the store, and packed together in a box or barrel.

March 29. (Aelt. Conf.) On Easter Monday certain young people, of both sexes, from the upper part of Bethania, dined in our Tavern, and returned to Bethania riding two by two. Br. Ernst shall be informed of this.

March 30. (Auf. Col.) Last Monday the Collegium met with the Road-masters:—from Bethabara, Schaub, Jr. and Stöhr; from Friedland, Philip Green, Jr.; from the English settlement, Markland, Sr.; from Friedberg, Peter Pfaff in place of Johann Jacob Schott; from Salem, Charles Holder. No one came from Bethania. It was recommended that at steep places there should be cross ditches dug at the top to lead off the water, so that the track should not become impassable so quickly. The division of work on the roads shall now be as follows:—

Bethabara, Walker's road, as far as the Town Fork road to Salem	6 miles
the Town Fork road, 2 miles, the Mill road, 1 mile	3 miles
from Bethabara to the Spangenbach on the road to Salem	2 miles
Salem, Town Fork road to Wagner's	8 miles
from there to Walker's	4 miles
the Shallow Ford road from Salem	4 miles
the Belews Creek road	7 miles
toward Bethabara as far as the Spangenbach	3 miles
Friedland, from Beroth's to Salem	2 miles
their road	5¾ miles
The English Settlement, from the cross-roads to the Shallow Ford bridge	4 miles
from the Shallow Ford road to the lower bridge	5 miles
Friedberg, from Peter Frey to Isaac Beroth	5 miles
from the mill to the Shallow Ford road coming from Salem	2 miles

Br. Aust's accounts of the pottery were considered. Br. Meinung shall write them out fairly, and shall include the old Proclamation money, writing it before the line, so that the loss sustained through it shall show properly.

Br. Stockberger was reminded not to let his cattle stray about the town, and not to permit the animals to stand much in his neighborhood, as complaints are often made.

April 4. (Auf. Col.) As Br. and Sr. Graff cannot live on their present salary, because all necessary articles of food and clothing are very high, it was decided that it would be fair to raise their salary from £4: to £7: for each four weeks, beginning with the first of January of this year.

April 5. (Auf. Col.) The Collegium considered and approved the plan for the new clock-tower. The foundation shall be twelve feet square, and above, under the little roof, the tower shall be two feet square. At the bottom there shall be a door, and for the height of the door the wall shall be of frame-work faced with brick. Above that it shall be covered with *feather-edge* boards. Br. John Krause will build it, with the help of a carpenter. The long posts will probably be of pine. As the matter concerns the entire congregation, and the members will have to contribute to it, it shall be brought up at the next Congregation Council.

April 6. (Congregation Council.) The plan of the bell-tower was laid before the members, was considered, and the entire proposal was approved.

April 11. (Auf. Col.) An upright pipe, with a crane, like the one recently set opposite Miksch's house, shall be set at the lower corner of the Square, opposite Reuter's house. Then it will not be necessary to have the water run constantly on the Square, but only as needed. If the Tavern gets too much water, more can be turned to other places.

After his marriage, Br. Christ will occupy the former Meinung house, and asks that the gate between his garden and Holder's shall be fastened. Br. Herbst will attend to this at once.

April 12. (Aelt. Conf.) The Single Sisters propose that Sr. Sehnert shall take Sr. Oesterlein's place as school-teacher for the children, and Conferenz has no objections for she has frequently substituted for Sr. Oesterlein. It will be well to arrange that she shall teach arithmetic. Lenel Kapp will enter the school, and next Saturday the school will have a lovefeast.

Next Sunday, in the gemeinstunde, the marriage of the Brn. Christ and Holland will take place. This shall be mentioned to Br. Ernst, so that he can notify Maria Strub's parents.

April 14. (Aelt. Conf.) Br. Ernst reported that George Hauser, Jr. wishes to take the boy Joseph Binckele as his apprentice for two years, and without this help he cannot well carry on his work as a smith. He promises to be responsible for the good behaviour of the boy, and as the lad has a good reputation, and the Bethania Committee has no objections, Conferenz also will not object. In connection with this George

Hauser and his wife have stated that they wish to be permanent residents of Bethania.

April 25. (Auf. Col.)   Br. Christ's salary from the pottery shall hereafter be £60: good money per year, and the pottery shall pay his house rent.

Br. Holland shall have £30: good money per year from the Tavern, in addition to food, drink, lodging, etc.   Br. Meyer's salary from the Tavern shall be raised from £30: to £40: per year, and the Tavern shall pay the expenses at the Brothers House and Sisters House for his children.

By the moving of Br. and Sr. Holland to the Tavern there will be one less room available there for the better class of travelers and for families passing through.   It was therefore decided to build a one-story block house, with a chimney, in the Tavern yard, especially for the convenience of families.

The worm-fence around Stockburger's land, on the street, shall be replaced by a fence with posts, so that the line may be preserved better.

The vacant lots between Miksch and the Two-story house are now to be fenced in, and as Stockburger's house stands out across the line, it was decided to open the lane by the Two-story house, forty feet wide according to the plan of the town, and to extend the fence to Stockburger's garden.[2]

May 2.   Br. Meyer sends a letter, saying that he would like to take the land opposite the Tavern and clear and fence it for a pasture, and asks that he may have it free of rent for ten years.   There is no objection except that this shall not include the Strangers' Graveyard, which lies on that land, and also that right is retained by the Collegium to use young timber and gravel suitable for street repairs.

Br. Herbst reminded the Collegium that there should be a map of the Strangers' Graveyard, so that the graves could be placed regularly. Hereafter a charge of 5sh. to 8sh. good money, shall be made for place for each grave, which will maintain the fence.

Several thousand clapboard nails will be needed in covering the clock-tower, and at present they will be difficult to get.

May 3. (Aelt. Conf.)   Br. Philip Vogler has accepted the proposal to take charge of the Salem plantation, and has begun work there, so it is necessary to think of his early marriage.   The Single Sisters suggest Sr. Catherine Leinbach as a woman well fitted for plantation life, so instruction was asked in the matter and the lot was drawn: "The Saviour does not approve that we take up the matter of the marriage of

---

[2] The Two-story House stood on the north-west corner of Main and Bank streets, the latter being the "lane" here ordered opened.

7

Br. Philip Vogler and Sr. Catherine Leinbach." Then Eva Hein was suggested, and the lot was drawn: "The Saviour approves that we take up the matter of the marriage of Br. Philip Vogler to Sr. Eva Hein." After the Sisters' Festival the matter will be laid before Br. Vogler.

May 9. (Auf. Col.) Br. Heinzmann will lend the nails for the clock tower, but they must be returned in kind.

The man Brown now offers to make brick for 13sh. the thousand, he to do three-quarters of the work; we must furnish one man and feed them. He is to be paid according to the number made, but as some are generally lost in burning payment shall be only for those that can be used. Food and lodging are hard to plan, but if they can be fed from the Brothers House kitchen they can be lodged in the huts on the brick-yard, where Cornelius Sale formerly stayed while at work there. We will be very glad to have several thousand brick made in this way.

May 10. (Aelt. Conf.) The Single Sr. Eva Hein has declined the proposal that she should marry Br. Philip Vogler, saying that at least for the present she prefers to remain undisturbed in her Choir-house. Br. Vogler has suggested that he would like to have the widow Stein-mann, and as Conferenz has no objection the Saviour's direction was asked, and the lot was drawn: "The Saviour approves that we take up the matter of the marriage of Br. Philip Vogler to the widow Stein-mann." This will now be reported to him; and as she will pass through here today, on her way to visit her parents, she shall be asked to stop on her return, and then the proposal can be made to her.

May 16. (Auf. Col.) A contract has been made with Brown, who will burn brick here for 12sh. per thousand. He is to receive in addition the food for three men,—we must furnish a fourth man. They are to have two quarts of brandy a week, and the food will be furnished from the Single Brothers kitchen. If they can not make place in the huts in the brick yard they can spend the nights in the shed on the plantation.

May 23. (Auf. Col.) Br. Meinung sent a letter stating that the house[3] in which he lives is greatly in need of repairs, that it leaks badly even in an ordinary rain, and was literally flooded in the last storm, when the water came in through the roof and through the walls. It was resolved to cover the house with shingles as soon as possible, and save the tiles that are good for repairing other houses. It might help the walls to plaster them on the outside, if we had some one who could do it, for Br. Melchior Rasp is too old for such work.

May 23. (Aelt. Conf.) Before Whitsuntide two brothers, Mattheus and Christoph Reich, came from Haw River on trial, to work on the

---

[3] The Two-story House.

plantation of the Single Brethren. Both like it here, and the wish has been expressed that another visit might be made to their neighborhood. Br. Heinzmann is willing to go, and Br. Daniel Christman has said that he would gladly see his parents again, so it was decided that the two Brethren shall set out next Friday, and visit those whom we know [*Marginal note:* in Stinking Quarter,] and if there is an opportunity Br. Heinzmann shall preach for them.

Br. Mücke needs help in the brewery and distillery in Bethabara, since he has lost Br. Philip Vogler. As there is no one here at present whom we can propose for the place it was suggested that perhaps Abraham Transou, of Bethania, might do. He is a well-behaved, industrious man, and his parents would like to see him become a full member of the Unity. He has shown no desire to move to the Choir House in Salem, but this might be the first step.

May 25. (Helf. Conf.) Br. Marshall mentioned that the Single Brethren Walther and Heckewälder had received the most votes in their Choir for filling the vacancy in this Conference occasioned by Br. Christ's marriage; and of the two the Saviour appointed Br. Walther. He was therefore present for the first time, as was also Sr. Christ. Now the communicant Single Brethren must elect a Single Brother to take Br. Walther's place in the Congregation Council.

May 31. (Aelt. Conf.) Br. Ernst reported that young Abraham Transou does not wish to go to Br. Mücke in Bethabara, giving as his reason that he would have no companions of his own age, but only old Brethren.

June 1. (Congregation Council.) The Single Br. Johann Henrich Walther has become a member of the Helfer Conferenz, and in another election the Single Br. Andreas Bressing has taken his place in this Council. The Single Sr. Catherine Sehnert was also present for the first time as a member of the Council, she having taken Sr. Christ's place as teacher of the girls' school.

The three Brethren who arrived yesterday from Bethlehem brought Gemein Nachrichten, Text Books, and other books. Those who wish Text Books shall make it known; and those who wish the new volumes of Reichel's Work on the Bible and so on, can get them.

June 6. (Auf. Col.) In discussing the German books recently received it was remarked that those who have early volumes of certain series should come for the additional volumes. We can hardly sell the Text Books for 3 sh., for they cost 2 : 10d in Pennsylvania, not including transportation.

A detachment of Virginia cavalry arrived yesterday to spend several days. In a conference with Br. Meyer and the Captain last evening, it was decided to feed them at the Tavern while they are here, which will be better than to have them take supplies by force, and we are not in position to issue rations.

It was definitely stated that without delay corn-meal must be used in baking bread, in order to increase our supply, for we neither can nor will refuse to feed the hungry who pass in numbers every day.

The accounts of the Single Brothers House and of the notions store were considered. Both have made considerable losses, which have come in large part from the repeated fall in the value of the currency.

June 8. (Helf. Conf.) All this week soldiers have been coming and going, some of them asking sternly for deserters, with an idea that we were harboring some. We also hear that some persons have been misled into a premature declaration in favor of the English, and have given them horses, and have even exchanged letters with them. This makes another occasion to remind our people to take all needful care, all the precautions called for by such a time, so that no one slips into something which would be dangerous.

As the present confusion in the value of paper currency is producing ill feeling among us, and the recent agreement did not find favor with all, and the congregation Branches and the Choir Diaconies are suffering, the matter was thoroughly discussed. It was decided that it would be best hereafter to count the dollar as worth one penny, especially among ourselves, and we will continue to make payments half in paper and half in silver. Those who work for wages shall accept payment in full each four weeks, not leaving part to be paid in good money later, the intention being that no one should try to avoid taking his share in the hardships and losses of the time.

June 9. (Congregation Council.) The old rule was renewed that the back bench by the organ should be left vacant for visitors when there was to be no organ music; also that the young Brethren should sit on the front benches, and that the married people should occupy the corners.

Finally it was remarked that in connection with several recent occurrences, especially marriages, there had been much prior unnecessary and unseemly inquisitiveness and talk, which did harm and no good, and the Brethren and Sisters were asked to guard against this, as something which was of no benefit to themselves, the matter under discussion, or the parties involved, and which was not suitable in a congregation dedicated to Christ.

June 13. (Auf. Col.) Br. Herbst reported that during the past year his household expenses had been eleven or twelve pounds more than his salary. He was authorized to take this from the business.

Last year the congregation Diaconie lost £99 : 4 : 5, (valued in good money) through the depreciation of paper currency.

June 13. (Aelt. Conf.) Br. Ernst reported that at the last Muster there had been much complaint because certain men from Friedland, Hope, etc., had brought Certificates, claiming that as Brethren they were not obliged to drill, and it was said that in other respects their conduct was not that of Brethren but like other worldly persons.

As our dear Br. and Sr. Reichel and party are expected before the next Communion it was thought proper to plan that the Communion lovefeast should be for the entire congregation. Br. Graff promised to compose a hymn for the occasion.

June 17. (Aelt. Conf.) The letter from the Unity's Elders Conference to this Conference, concerning the mission of Br. and Sr. Reichel, was read once more. Br. Reichel remarked that most of the items mentioned had already been attended to by Br. Marshall, so it only remained for him to become personally acquainted with the Brethren and Sisters, to attend the meetings of the Boards, to confer with the Aeltesten Conferenz as to whether changes might be needed here and there for the best interests of the congregations, and to talk with the Brn. Marshall and Graff and consider whether the work of God in Wachovia would be strengthened by any changes in the personnel.

June 20. (Auf. Col.) Br. Reitz, who recently arrived from Pennsylvania, will begin hat-making on his own account. For the present he can work in the lower story of the former Skin-house. The Congregation Diaconie will have to furnish the outfit.

June 21. (Aelt. Conf.) The young men of Hope, Friedberg and Friedland who count themselves Brethren and have taken Certificates, and who appear to their neighbors not to behave as such, must be admonished. Br. Pretzel was asked to go to Friedland next Sunday to see them. In all only ten Certificates have been given, and Capt. Heinrich Schmidt encouraged it, but Colonel Armstrong shall be told about it.

June 27. (Auf. Col.) Br. Friedrich Peter, who is to write the Minutes for the congregation, copy the Diaries, and help in other ways, is granted a yearly salary of £40 : good money, and if this proves to be insufficient it shall be increased. The Diaconie shall pay his room rent, and he shall not be expected to contribute to the Congregation fund.

July 3. (Congregation Council.) It is not only wisdom but our duty [said Br. Reichel,] that as Children of Peace we keep quiet during these days of turmoil in the land, without partisanship, for which the Saviour will give us the needed grace. Our Brethren shall not permit themselves to be called *Tories,* which slanders them. We must put quite away from us the idea that we will be in danger from the English if we are not Tories. The Lord, who moves the hearts of the contesting Powers according to His pleasure, and directs all events according to His will, can give us favor with them, and can help us through all critical times if we commit all the circumstances of the country to Him in prayer and in faith, relying on His help.

If the warring factions threaten us with press and other demands, the best way, it seems to me, is to meet them in a friendly fashion, whereby we will save four or five times as much as we would otherwise lose.—In this connection Br. Meyer stated that the quartering of the soldiers in the Tavern last week had caused a great loss, which the Tavern was not in condition to meet. It should be noted that the Tavern has spared the Brethren and Sisters from having the soldiers quartered in their homes, so it would not be fair to expect the Tavern to bear all the loss, and Congregation Council must consider how this can be made good. It will be well for Br. Meyer to make out an account, and present it at the next Congregation Council.

We must bear our fair part in the calamities of the times, said Br. Reichel, and must not think that as Children of God we shall escape the general trials of the country. If the Saviour will only hold us together and let us keep our homes in these turbulent days we have great reason to give Him thanks and praise.

Notice was given that Br. Peter Goetje was to be master-shoemaker.

July 5. (Aelt. Conf.) The wish was expressed that two or three Sisters would take up tambour embroidery, and we will try to find some who have talent for it. Sr. Nilson is willing to teach them and to draw patterns for them. Br. Traugott Bagge will give all possible assistance, as soon as the times improve.

July 6. (Helf. Conf.) After singing:

> The chief command is: Love thou Him;
> The second: Serve His people here:

Br. Reichel spoke of the chief mission of the Helfer Conferenz as reorganized by the Synod of 1775. We shall be a congregation of Jesus, in which all is done honorably and in order, according to His heart. This cannot be achieved by the ministers alone, and therefore the dear Saviour has appointed Brethren and Sisters as helpers of the ministers, who will aid us in carrying out this desire of the Saviour. Members of this Board shall have ears and eyes to note evil that has crept in and good that can be furthered, and shall speak of it plainly in this meeting, whereby useful plans can be made for the promotion of the welfare of the congregation. Moreover, through this Board additional servants of the Lord will be secured, for when there is little business to come before it the more interesting parts of the Synod Minutes shall be reviewed, which will familiarize them with the foundation principles of the Unity, and prepare them to help in carrying out the foundation principles of the congregation and its choirs, and thus to grow in the service of the Lord.

July 11. (Aelt. Conf.) On Sunday evening the boys Blum and Jacob Bonn went to walk alone. Boys who do such strange and doubtful things should be kept in better order.

July 11. (Auf. Col.) The recent collection in Salem for foreign missions resulted in £5 : 3 : 6 good money and 39 paper dollars, together £5 : 6 : 9 good money.

Br. Meyer shall not build a worm-fence around the piece of land recently cleared opposite the Tavern, but shall use posts, which Br. Herbst will lend him. This will give a straight line. The road by the Tavern and on to the meadow shall remain sixty feet wide.

This is the time of year to cut down the bushes and weeds in our streets and lanes, and the streets especially shall be cleared.

July 25. (Auf. Col.) Congregation Council shall be notified that Justice Friedrich Müller will be here in eight days to list the taxes. Those men who are over fifty years of age shall state the fact to him, so that they can pay the tax straight instead of three-fold.

The preliminary report on the congregation Diaconie accounts was read, and Br. Reichel made the following remarks:—The schools of a congregation, according to the action of Synod, should not be maintained solely by those who have children in the schools, nor by the congregation Diaconie only, but should have the individual support of members of the congregation. Here in Salem the congregation Diaconie has been obliged to bear not only the general expenses of the congregation but also the support of the ministers, and no private individuals have contributed. The store has furnished most of the money from its annual profits, for what has come from other Branches has largely been used for other purposes. But times have changed, these Branches have lost money instead of making it, and the plan of Synod is that ministers' salaries should be borne by the members, so it is only fair that this should be done in this congregation. It was remarked that the residents in Salem are still poor, and have little which they can give; this was freely admitted, but it was pointed out that in most places the beginning of contributions to church causes had taken place in times of need, not in seasons of prosperity, and it was the general opinion that, without the help of all the members, the congregation, by which they all profit, can not continue to bear its load.

July 26. (Aelt. Conf.) It is only fair that the congregation should maintain its schools. School matters should be so arranged that teachers receive proper salaries, so that they may be in good heart for their tedious job. The teacher of the girls' school, who has been getting only three shillings a week, should have an additional shilling.

July 27. (Congregation Council.) The reading of the Minutes of the last meeting brought up the question of war expenses, which have recently fallen upon the Tavern, the Brothers House, Br. Triebel, etc. It was unanimously agreed that the congregation in general was responsible, and should reimburse those who had suffered. The war-load is the load of all, and the entire congregation should bear it.

Notice has been posted in the Tavern that Friedrich Müller will be here on Aug. 1st, to list the taxes of all who are in Captain Smith's District. A room in Br. Fritz' house shall be placed at his disposal for meeting with the Brethren, and apart from that he shall be given free room and board at the Tavern.

Aug. 1. (Auf. Col.) A letter from Bethabara was read concerning the negress Susy. It was agreed that it would be better for her and her husband to remain together in Bethabara, and a reply was sent to the Brethren there saying we had no doubt they would be willing to pay Salem £5: good money for her, and then they could take entire charge of her.

It was agreed to hold by the custom of charging off 2½% each year on the House account.[4]

Going through the mill inventory again, it was agreed that every effort should be made to secure for Salem the toll taken at the mill, and to haul it from the mill without delay. Br. Merkly will begin hauling tomorrow, and Br. Bagge will go with him to the mill, and in case the sergeant stationed there raises any objections Br. Bagge will explain the matter to him.

Br. Bagge reported that a Brother told him recently that L—B— was a really bad boy, and was leading the other boys in the Brothers House into sin and harm. Careful inquiry shall be made among the Brethren to see whether this is a matter of prejudice or a matter of fact.

Persons living in the upper part of the town are complaining that since Stockburger has begun driving his cattle to the upper pasture the cows drink from the trough from which cooking water must be brought, and it is very disgusting. We cannot forbid Stockburger to

---

[4] A "Fund for answering the Decrease in the value of Houses" was opened April 30, 1774.

take his cattle to the field, so the water must be fenced in or protected in some other way, which can be best decided on the spot. Since Aust has put up the stand-pipe at his house Stockburger has lost the use of the overflow from the trough, which he had formerly led to his barnyard. * * * Stockburger must have water for his cattle, which cannot drink from the run because of the leather-dressing business, but we wish he and his cattle were outside the town.

Aug. 7. (Aelt. Conf.) The Bethabara wagon and two-horse team have been pressed, and it is doubtful whether Johannes Samuel should be sent with them.[5] It will be better if a competent man will take charge of them as though they were his own,—perhaps Michael Ranke, of Bethania, who has been called as wagoner for the Continental troops, can be commissioned to do this, and then a younger man from Bethania can be sent as driver, and can be constantly in Rancke's company.

Aug. 9. (Auf. Col.) Br. Heinzmann has sent word, by the two Brethren who went to see him, that in consideration of the circumstances Toego Nissen may have his house for the annual rent of £8, on condition that the room in the upper story is reserved for the use of Br. and Sr. Heinzmann when they come to town. He also stipulates that this price shall not be given to any other renter, as the house cost over £200.

Aug. 16. (Auf. Col.) Br. Petersen mentioned that various persons from our town have been cutting poles in the Single Brothers' woods, though they could get them from other woods by notifying the forester. Br. Reichel remarked that we should be careful of the wild cherries and chestnuts, and the gathering of wild grapes should not be according to individual preference, but all should be done in good order.

Br. Triebel asks 20 sh. good money for expenses in quartering the soldiers; this is fair and shall be paid, and charged to Public Expenses.

In regard to the extra nightwatch of the citizens it has been said that as the Single Sisters do not take part in it they ought to take over all the cleaning of the Saal. This was not approved; we will thank God if each Single Sister can get through without making debts.

Until school dues are regulated, Sr. Sehnert, who holds the girls' school, shall be paid 4 sh. a month out of the school fund, as there are so few children that she can not live on their fees.

It has been suggested that Br. Toego Nissen could begin to support himself by making gutters for the store and Gemein Haus, but he will probably not succeed with making something for which he has not been

---

[5] He was a slave.

trained. It will be better for him to make chairs, spinning-wheels for cotton, wheel-barrows, and the like, to which he is accustomed.

Aug. 22. (Auf. Col.) Br. Triebel is willing to have the boys' school in his house, and proposes to let them have the entire middle floor for £8: a year. As the Diaconie bore the expense of improvements, something shall be deducted from the rent for two or three years until the cost is covered.

The abstract of the Congregation Diaconie accounts was read, and it was perceived with sorrow that there is a deficit of over £1000: and in the present hard times it will probably not be better this year.

Br. Stotz, who returned safely last evening from Cross Creek, stated that North Carolina currency no longer circulates there. He was forced to let ours go at a very small value, one hundred and twenty-five Continental or two hundred North Carolina for one hard dollar, and it is probable that things which have since become known concerning conditions in the land have caused the North Carolina currency to be discarded altogether. The Single Brethren, the store and the workshops can not continue to furnish the necessities of life at a great loss; and if North Carolina currency no longer has a value, to sell for half the payment in that and half in hard money would be actually to give half away. We think it will be best for the next week to pass no North Carolina paper money among ourselves, but to buy goods on account, and we can meet again in eight days and see what shall be done further. Meanwhile the Continental currency shall be rated at one penny for a dollar. Regarding outsiders, we will do the best we can to avoid taking North Carolina paper money, but will not refuse to accept it from soldiers, or from others in need, where it might lead to the taking of supplies by force or have other bad consequences. Prices must be set accordingly, but it is better to suffer loss than not to keep peace.

Aug. 23. (Aelt. Conf.) Yesterday a contract was closed with Br. Yarrell, whereby he takes over his lot and business on his own account.

Aug. 28. (Auf. Col.) Br. Reichel said concerning Bethabara and its relation to Salem, that according to the repeated instructions of our dear Saviour, Salem should remain the town in Wachovia where the chief work-shops should be located, and that no change should be made in this. That, according to the same instructions, Bethabara should not be given up, but should be developed, but only those industries should be carried on there that were needed for the residents and the neighbors, for instance a smithy, shoe-maker shop, tailor shop, etc., and these should not, as in Salem, have a master and several journeymen or apprentices. Bethabara therefore could not have an independent store, but only a branch of the store in Salem, and not so large in trade or in stock.

Br. Bagge presented a written statement that today Br. Yarrell had traded with certain strangers for nails, steel, coffee, and allspice in exchange for breeches leather. * * * The following remarks were recorded:—No one except the store should carry goods for retail. Anyone who acquires goods in these hard times in order to get rid of his bad money shall offer them to the store at the purchase price, but shall not sell them in small quantities. The old rule should be followed, and when store goods are offered in exchange at the work-shops the person offering should be sent to the store. If the store buys, a certificate or ticket can be given, which can be used at the work-shop and later redeemed by the store. If the store does not buy, no one shall. Each man may buy what he needs for his household or shop, and where he can do it best. The Brothers House Vorsteher may keep a supply of sugar, coffee, etc. for the Brethren working for the House, but shall sell nothing to other Brethren in the House unless he buys in quantity and sells without profit, or it is something which the store does not keep in stock. No one in town, except the store, shall accept store goods to sell on commission.

It was mentioned that the shoemaker was selling shoes made in Cross Creek, which were not very good, and Br. Reichel remarked that it would be better not to carry articles made elsewhere.

Br. Bagge stated that recently Kremser has not been able to climb his chimney, though other larger men have done so. Br. Kremser, through another Brother, explained that this chimney and one at the Tavern ought to be made larger. Collegium could say nothing except that it would be well to have a thinner and more energetic man for this job, but if none could be found Br. Bagge would have to enlarge his chimney when he had a chance.

The single man, Johann Ferdinand Schroed, who has worked here for about sixteen months, has repeatedly asked permission to become a citizen of the town. He was called in by the Collegium for a conference, before his desire is laid before the Conferenz. In answer to questions he gave the following account of himself:—He was born Sept. 29, 1750, in Tulpe, Trumberg, district of Würzberg; learned farming but no handicraft. In his seventeenth year he became a Würzberg soldier, then entered the Hessian service. He came to this country with the Hessians, was captured by the Americans in a skirmish near Germantown, and they held him prisoner for three months at Lancaster. There need forced him to take service for one year in Pulaski's Corps, though he received no written certificate of surrender. When he had served over a year he asked Colonel Kowatsch for his discharge, and when it was not given he, and others in the same fix, left the army. He had made no promise of marriage. The reason that he wished to remain here, and asked for fellowship with the Brethren, was that he wished to live only for the Saviour, and give himself into His hands, and he believed he would find opportunity to do this among us. Although he had been brought up a Catholic he had no scruples about denominations and would dispute with no one about them, for there is no other name whereby we can be saved but the name of Jesus. He promised to obey the rules of the town, which Br. Stotz would read to him, and to accept and follow advice; agreed also not to be displeased if the Saviour did not give him permission to become a resident of the town, but would remain as a guest as long as it was convenient. An answer to his request was promised.

Aug. 30. (Aelt. Conf.) The wearing of soft leather shoes is to be discouraged, and it would be best to instruct the shoe-maker, Br. Goetje, not to make them.

The Aufseher Collegium has spoken with the single Johann Ferdinand Schroed, and makes no objection to his Reception into the congregation. The lot was drawn: "The Saviour does *not* approve that Johann Ferdinand Schroed shall receive permission to become a resident of the congregation in Salem."

Sept. 1. (Aelt. Conf.) Br. and Sr. Reichel were in Hope eight days ago, and spoke with the Society members there. Many asserted with tears their desire for a closer connection with the Unity, saying that they had come from Maryland to this place with that in view. The two communicant couples, Elrods and Daniel Smiths, were particularly urgent in their desire for a fully organized congregation. Permission was given by the Saviour for the Reception of John and Mary Padget and of Benjamin and Mary Chiddy. A fully organized congregation will be established at Hope, with the Holy Communion every eight weeks.

In Friedland the organization of the congregation can take place next Sunday, since the men who have been away with the pressed wagons have returned.

George Hauser, Jr. has signed the Rules and Regulations of Bethania, and will remain there as a permanent resident.

Men of Bethania are distilling peach brandy, and offer it at five to six shillings a gallon. The common price is one gallon of brandy for one bushel of grain, which is now worth one hard dollar, so no one will buy for more.

Sept. 1. (Congregation Council.) The verse was sung:

> He, He shall do, shall govern,
> He is a Prince all-wise.

Br. Reichel pointed out that we should keep this verse in mind during the vicissitudes of the continuing war unrest. Distressing thoughts may easily afflict us, and then it will be well to remember this verse. Do not worry, He can do all things and He will direct all events. * * * We have had proof that the Saviour works wonders. He helped our Brethren and Society members from Bethabara, Bethania, Friedberg and Friedland, who took their wagons to the army, and brought them back without personal injury and having recovered most of what they had lost. It is also a cause for thanksgiving that we suffered no damage from the soldiers who were here yesterday. In spite of all the *insolence* which people give us during these times we must remember that in war nothing is done that is right and praiseworthy, and must thank the Saviour that we have been shielded from serious harm. * * * He can turn the hearts of kings and princes and of the wildest men, and will make known to all men that we are loyal to this country, even as we have taken the Affirmation in the sight of God.

The expense account of the clock tower was presented. It amounts to £58 :6 :—, and it was decided to apportion this sum among the Brethren and Sisters, and the Aufseher Collegium shall work out a plan.

Sept. 5. (Auf. Col.) A certain Major Hartmann arrived yesterday, coming from General Gates. Today he told Br. Bagge that he was sent to order a thousand pair of shoes for the Continental army, for quick delivery; and if these could not be furnished he was to take an equivalent quantity of shoe leather. There are no shoes here, so he was referred to Br. Herbst. It was estimated that fifty sides of sole leather, at $20 a pound, forty sides of upper leather, at $200 to $300 a side, and several calf skins, can be furnished in three weeks from date, which we must ship in a wagon to the army. If good hides can be found there we will accept them in payment, otherwise we will demand Continental currency. We will also ask for a *Protection* against press of leather or wagon for the next three weeks; and if the Major is authorized to give a *Pass,* so that we can send a wagon to Cross Creek for goods for the store and for the Single Brethren, we will ask him to give us one. We will also ask whether a *convoy* for the wagon and leather can be sent to us.

Congregation Council shall decide whether the Brethren alone shall pay for the clock tower, or whether all adult Brethren and Sisters shall pay in proportion to their contributions to the congregation fund. In the first case each Brother will pay twenty shillings; in the second case each Brother will pay fifteen shillings and each Sister seven shillings, six pence.

Matthew Markland, of Hope, who is road-master for that district, has let us know that the bridge over Muddy Creek, on the Shallow Ford road, has broken down, and it is so rotten that it cannot be repaired, or at least is not worth it.

Sept. 12. (Auf. Col.) Complaint was made that Br. Christman, the cooper, was not giving as good service as he should, but it is not altogether his fault for sometimes he cannot wait on people as promptly as they wish.

In the last Congregation Council it was said that the Collegium ought to regulate the relation of the store to the work-shops. The store should not keep for sale articles made elsewhere, if the same article is made in this town, of the same quality and in sufficient quantity; it is another thing if the store buys in quantity from a local master-workman, and sells in retail for the same price which the shop gets for retail trade, making a small profit thereby. There are exceptions, however, for if the store should be forbidden to carry certain articles which can be brought in more cheaply than they can be made here the only result would be to drive customers away, to the injury of the store without helping local shops; moreover this would tempt outsiders to open independent stores in the neighborhood as has already been tried. Among these articles have been mattocks, shovels, spades and other iron farm implements. The store has also taken iron or steel cow-bells in exchange from other smithies in the neighborhood, and has sold them at a slight profit, and this without injuring our smith who is always busy with other work, and has only a few on hand. In regard to the leather-dresser and the saddle-maker it should be remembered that the store established those trades and built them up until they were taken over by men trained in the craft, so it is not unjust if now and then the store has a dressed deer-skin or a pair of leather breeches for sale, though it will happen seldom. It will not hurt the hat-maker if the store continues to carry the coarse wool hats bought outside, for while they cost less than those made here they are also of poorer quality, and when the local hat-maker has on hand a supply of various good hats those who wish them will not buy the coarser, inferior kind. The store has taken finer hats from outside hat-makers, in exchange for dye-wood and other things which they needed in their business, and has sold them at the current price, with little or no profit;

but it will be well for the Brn. Bagge and Reutz to discuss how this shall be handled in future.

There are not many grapes in the woods this year, but it will be well to ask the Brethren not to go out alone to gather them, and to give notice if they do go, so that they may not fall into the hands of evil men hidden in the woods. It might be better not to go out this year.

Sept. 13. (Congregation Council.) Agreed that each Brother should pay seventeen shillings and each Sister five shillings toward the expenses of erecting the clock tower, assessments to be payable in two installments.

The abstract of the congregation and Saal expense shows a deficit of £102:4:10 for the year May 1, 1779 to April 30, 1780. Lovefeast expenses have been £11:16:7.

Council listened to an abstract of the expenses of the congregation Diaconie, which this year has a deficit of £1060:11:6, partly because of the falling value of currency and losses in the Branches, partly because of unusually heavy expenses. In Europe, when a new congregation was begun, each member was expected to pay a weekly sum toward the support of the ministers. Here the congregation Diaconie bore the expenses in former years, but last year fell far short. There have been the expenses of delegates to and from the Synod, the Visitations, the sending of new ministers for the local congregation, for which the members have not hitherto had to pay. It is very evident that the local congregation Diaconie can no longer pay all the salaries of the ministers, especially as few of the Branches are making any profits, and each member will need to support the work by free-will contributions. In all European congregations each member has felt himself pledged to aid in the support of the ministers; and the local congregation has the same pledge in its Rules and Regulations, but something should be done, actually, not only with respect to ministers' salaries but also for the school, which is also a concern of the entire congregation. It is the duty of each member to help, even if the membership can not yet bear the entire load, being still small and the times hard. First of all the congregation should pay for the Gemein Haus, which is booked at £1200.[6] The Council should arrange to have each member of the congregation make a weekly free-will payment toward the support of the ministers. These proposals were approved by Council, but nothing definite was done.

Sept. 13. (Aelt. Conf.) Matthes Nöting, who has been working for Volz, Sr., in Friedberg, has asked Br. Pretzel to give him work, and to plan how he might support himself here; his master, also, has spoken

---

[6] The cost of building had been borne by the "Diaconie of Administration," that is by the Unitas Fratrum through its local office in Salem.

a good word for him. He was a soldier in Hessian service, was captured by the Americans at Charlestown, and as a prisoner was forced to do service on an American ship for four weeks, after which he was released and made his way hither. Conferenz has no objection to his coming on trial.

Sept. 15. (Land-Arbeiter-Conferenz.) Br. Reichel said: We rejoice greatly that in spite of the unrest in the land we again have an opportunity for conference with those who labor in the country congregations. This Conference shall consider conditions in the country congregations, and whether anything can be improved.

At weddings, or when guests are invited to a meal, there shall be no gathering of unmarried persons of both sexes, and no frivolity, which is not seemly in connection with a wedding which has been performed according to the ordinance of God.

In Friedberg and Friedland schools are held four days in the week from October to Whitsuntide. In Hope there is school every day from eight in the morning to five in the afternoon, which leaves Br. Fritz too little time for his other duties. In Bethania school is held five days a week throughout the year except during harvest, the boys attending on one day and the girls on the next. It would be well in Bethania, for the sake of those who live outside the town, to hold school four days in the week for the boys and girls together; the same arrangement can be introduced in Hope.

The Land-Arbeiter-Conferenz shall meet every four weeks.

Sept. 20. (Aelt. Conf.) Wish was expressed that young married people, who are well and entirely able to work, should do their own house-work, and not keep servants purely as a matter of convenience.

Sept. 20. (Auf. Col.) It is wiser to let the congregation know how bad things are than to keep silent hoping for better times. Otherwise trouble might come which timely knowledge would have prevented, and the present officers could be accused of negligence by their successors and the congregation.

Sept. 21. (Congregation Council.) Unanimously agreed to begin at once the contributions to the support of the ministers and the schools. Each member should be guided by his circumstances in determining the size of his free-will offering to the ministerial salaries. If the congregation approves of this it shall be explained to each Choir, and then each house-father, each Single Brother and each Single Sister, shall have opportunity, privately, to pledge what he or she expects to be able to spare weekly; this shall be written down, and collected in each Choir monthly.

God's Acre is a place which the Brethren and Sisters like to visit, remembering their fellowship with those who have passed into the heavenly congregation. It should always be kept in such order that it is pleasant to see. Br. Schnepf has been mowing the grass there twice a year, and Br. Herbst will remind him to do it now. It was suggested that a few sheep might be turned in to eat the wild grass, and then fine grass could be sown. The wish was expressed that the grave-digger, now Br. Schnepf, should take the customary care of God's Acre and beautify it; Br. Herbst will speak with Br. Schnepf, and if he can not undertake this the oversight shall be given to Br. Aust, who can hire men to dig the graves and to do other work there under his supervision.

Sept. 25. (Auf. Col.) In spite of all effort no wagon and teamster have been found which can be hired for the journey north of Br. and Sr. Reichel, and we must see what can be done in our own towns. Colonel Armstrong and two Justices will be asked for a Pass for the party.

Final accounts of the departed Br. Wutrobe's estate were read. According to his Will, Br. Stotz will give £78:4:1 to Br. Reichel, to take to Wutrobe's youngest sister in Germany.

Br. Koffler was asked to have cord-wood cut, for the use of the town this winter.

Sept. 27. (Aelt. Conf.) Br. Kühnast has engaged the wagon and two horses from Bethabara, and two horses from Bethania, for Br. Reichel's journey.

When the children have had some practise in singing they shall have a short song service once a week, or a liturgy that is partly singing. Occasionally the memoir of a child shall be read to them, which will have more effect on their hearts than a sermon.

When Br. Reutz has married he shall teach singing to the Sisters.

Adam Schumacher, Jr., and his wife have been awakened by the Spirit of God, and hope to become members of this congregation. * * * We can not refuse to make arrangements for Brethren who should belong to a country congregation but who wish to be united with this congregation. They may be received into the congregation, and may come to Communion once in eight weeks, and may attend all services suitable for a country congregation, but will not be eligible for membership in the Congregation Council or in the Grosse Helfer Conferenz. Their children may and should attend the schools. They shall be visited like other members living outside of the town.

Sept. 28. (Auf. Col.) Boys shall not be left at home alone when the parents go out.

It shall be decided at what hours the older boys shall be in the Brothers House, and when they shall be with their parents, so that one does not depend on the other, and in the end no one know where a boy is.

A number of years ago it was discussed that there ought to be proper written contracts with the masters who carry on businesses for the congregation or for the Diaconie of the Single Brethren. This shall be done at once, and in the contracts shall be stated their year's salary, and their entire relation to the Diaconie. It is not wise to give a master part of the year's profit,—an annual *douceur* is preferable.

It is probable that the ware in the pottery is being sold too high, as it is not glazed because of lack of glazing, but instead is burned two hours longer. However, it is hard to judge.

Br. Reichel announced that the bad conduct of the single J— N— made it dangerous to allow him to live longer in the congregation. This afternoon he was called before the Collegium. He said he did not know why he should be dismissed, he had not been drunk recently, but he was advised to know himself better; he was told that he must leave, and was permitted to depart.

This is probably the last time that Br. Reichel will meet with the Collegium. * * * The Collegium must serve as congregation Vorsteher, as there is no other, and that will make more for it to do. Until another appointed Brother can come, Br. Marshall, in addition to his numerous other duties, will advise on all important matters; Br. Herbst will continue as vice Vorsteher, as arranged before Br. Nilson's death; and Br. Bagge will help where he can. Br. Reichel promised to bear in mind that this office should be filled as soon as possible, and hoped that the Saviour would supply a Brother before he (Br. Reichel) left America.

As the Communion wine is nearly out, the wine in the Tavern shall be bought from Br. Meyer for hard money.

The contract price for taking Br. Reichel to Pennsylvania is as follows:—For John Rank's wagon two shillings a day; for each horse two shillings a day, (two horses belong to Michael Hauser and two to Bethabara); to Michael Hauser, Jr. and Peter Schneider, teamsters, four shillings each per day. If the horses rest several days on the return trip less will be paid for those days. The teamsters will board themselves; we will furnish feed for the horses. Br. Heckewelder will pay eight pence a pound for his baggage from here to Lititz; if the wagon does not go so far proper reduction must be made. An attempt shall be made to get iron and nails for a return load, and Br. Heckewelder has been asked to see about it.

An Order shall be delivered to Charles Holder, authorizing him to fine, or if necessary to arrest, soldiers who misbehave here, and to call men to assist him; and another Order shall be delivered to Br. Meyer, forbidding him to sell liquor to a soldier without order from a ranking officer. Colonel Armstrong has sent the Orders to us by George Schmidt, in view of the disturbance on the 16th of this month.

Sept. 30. (Auf. Col.) The Brn. Stotz, Bagge, Koffler and Merkly met and talked with J— N—. They asked him whether he had any complaint to make against any one in the town, or whether any one owed him anything. He said no one had injured him, and no one was to blame for his being sent away except himself. No one owed him anything except Stockburger about eight shillings—this was promptly paid. He asked for a written recommendation, and was referred to Br. Schober, his last master.

Oct. 3. (Auf. Col.) We were happy to have Br. Reichel with us once more.

It was suggested that George Schmidt ought to make a Will; his wife has been drawing a pension from the Widows Society, which ceases since she has remarried.

Incidentally it was remarked that we ought to have a larger stock of grain on hand, and that it would be safer to store it in private houses than in the Brothers House.

Oct. 4. (Aelt. Conf.) Jacob Stolz, eighteen or nineteen years old, wishes to move into the Brothers House, that he may belong to the Saviour, and leave himself entirely in His hands. He was drafted but was released, and his parents are willing to have him come, so an attempt shall be made to find work for him here, and if he remains of the same mind the Saviour will be asked whether he shall become a permanent resident.

George Hauser, Jr., has asked for a Certificate, as he would like to be recognized as belonging to the Brethren, and would consider it an honor to be reckoned among such a people. Colonel Armstrong shall be consulted, and if he approves George Hauser must pay the three-fold tax, and must give up his offices, which, indeed, is his intention.

We must insist that the residents of Bethania pay a joint rental for their land, not individually. It would be well if the Bethania land could remain a possession of the Unity, and the residents pay a joint annual rent.

Johannes Samuel, of Bethabara, ought to be married soon. As we have only one baptised negress, Maria, who is working in the Salem Tavern, there is no question as to who should be his wife.

Oct. 10. (Auf. Col.) Br. Marshall mentioned that Sr. Nilson will remain here, in the service of the congregation.

Stockburger had a corn-husking last evening, to which some of the Single Brethren were invited. He shall be told that he must not do this again, for there is too much danger of frivolity.

Oct. 12. (Aelt. Conf.) Br. Aust has taken charge of God's Acre, and has begun to bring it into good order. Next spring he will make a form, three inches high, and two inches wider below than on top, so that all the graves may have the same shape. He will keep this form at his house.

It was decided hereafter to use the English type of coffin.

It was further agreed to clear and plow a strip a rod wide around God's Acre, to prevent the approach of forest fires.

Oct. 16. (L—A—C.) If because of sickness or other circumstance a man needs the help of his neighbors in gathering his corn, and does not turn it into a frolic, this does not conflict with the rule that we shall not have the merry-makings customary in this country on such occasions.

Concerning secret mariages it was remarked that some of our country members have believed that we wished to prevent them from marrying. Occasion shall be taken to tell them plainly that we think marriage necessary for them; that the fact that there have been few marriages in the town congregations has been owing to circumstances and has nothing to do with them; and that if a marriage seems advantageous they may with full confidence discuss it with the minister and his wife, who will help them with advice. House-fathers shall be plainly told that they should observe tendency toward marriage on the part of their children, should ask them about it, and should lead them to seek the help and counsel of their parents. A house-father is responsible for all that goes on in his house, and nothing should be done without his approval; children should not be permitted to marry as they please, but should consider the wishes of their father.

Oct. 17. (Auf. Col.) The house into which Br. and Sr. Reutz have moved is booked at £249. He may buy it for £210, or may rent it for 6% of the book value.

The land to which Stockburger plans to move will probably lie best if he takes fifty acres on this side of the Wach, and fifty acres on the other side, on the line of Vogler's farm. That will give him about one hundred acres. For this and the cleared bottom land he can pay one shilling per acre rent.

The mulatto Maria (formerly Iddy) is to have a change, and Br. Meyer shall be notified. She was bought for £285: currency, which was then about £71 :5 :—in good money. Since then she has grown, and is much more useful. It was discussed whether she should be sold for her purchase price, or for £75: good money; it would probably be best to buy an equally good negress in her place, and rate her at the same price.

Oct. 18. (Aelt. Conf.) An estimate shall be made of the taxes which must be paid the end of November, and how much we can pay in *Tickets.* If the Tickets amount to more than the taxes we must consider how we can get money for the balance; if the Tickets will not be sufficient to pay the taxes we must try to get more currency.

Oct. 19. (Congregation Council.) It is our duty, in speaking with outsiders about our position in these political circumstances, that we allow no one to doubt that we are faithful subjects of the State. Even without an Affirmation our conscience would have required that we be loyal to the State, according to Romans 13, i,[7] but in addition we have taken the Affirmation in the sight of God. Our character as an honorable people requires that we maintain this position, so that every one may acknowledge us as faithful subjects of the State, which will give us standing with this party, and will not bring us into danger from their opposers, for in all the world it is required that fidelity be pledged to the party of government that is in power, and that due submission shall be made to it. It is painful for us, it is unendurable, and in the end dangerous, if we permit ourselves to be accused of being Tories, and we are to consider this term of reproach as an injury, not as dishonor to be borne for the sake of Christ, and we shall not let it rest upon us.[8]

As we hope to pay the next tax in Tickets, steps must be taken to have them approved and ratified by the Auditors, who are now at Hillsborough.

Br. Bagge told us that according to an Act of Assembly there is a corn-tax as well as one to be paid in money. With each £100 paid in cash one peck of corn must be delivered, but for the corn a Ticket will be issued, which will be accepted as cash in the following tax payment.

Oct. 25. (Aelt. Conf.) Br. Graff has commenced instruction for the Single Sisters who are candidates for confirmation for the Holy Communion. Several Sisters who are already communicants wish to attend the instruction, which is approved.

---

[7] "Let every soul be subject unto the higher powers. For there is no power but of God: the powers that be are ordained of God."

[8] This is striking testimony to the loyalty of the Moravians in North Carolina to the American cause. In date it preceded by three days the receipt of news of the battle of King's Mountain, and falls therefore into the period when the American success seemed most uncertain, and when the inducement was greatest to join those of Tory sentiment.

The wish was expressed that the Single Brethren might have similar instruction, and Br. Graff is willing to undertake it.

Oct. 26. (Helf. Conf.) Br. Tycho Nissen has agreed to dig the graves. He can probably make the grave-stones also, and is to try one. Care must be taken that he cuts good letters, and the inscriptions should all be in one language, not German, English or Latin according to fancy.

The grass in the God's Acre for strangers should be cut from time to time, to keep it in proper order.

It is wiser for our Brethren not to take up stray horses, for at present it has far-reaching consequences, and often instead of receiving the thanks of the real owner the man who takes up a horse must pay the costs. If any one wishes to catch a horse which has been running about here for a long time and is really a menace, he shall first consult with several Brethren, Herbst, Bagge or Bonn for example. He shall not ride or drive a stray horse until it has been registered, otherwise it is theft in the eyes of the law.

Oct. 27. (Auf. Col.) Br. Reitz has decided to buy the house in which he is living, and will pay £210 for it. The Lease[9] shall date from last Michaelmas.

Br. Herbst reported that Br. Schober asked eight shillings per week, and Br. Schneider four shillings, for their service in the boys' school, and no objection was raised.

Oct. 31. (Auf. Col.) The contracts between the Congregation Diaconie and the masters were signed and executed,—Br. Bagge for the store, Herbst for the tannery, Meyer for the Tavern, and Aust for the pottery.

Br. Aust said that he had sold an unglazed crock for five pence and a glazed for six pence; and that he was now asking six pence for the unglazed crocks that had been burned for a longer time, and twice as much for glazed crocks when he could furnish them, for glazing is very expensive now.

Nov. 9. (Auf. Col.) It was decided that gold coins should be weighed, and should pass here according to value, not by piece.

Nov. 9. (Helf. Conf.) In order to know one grave from another in the God's Acre for strangers, it was decided to finish the row which has been commenced before beginning another, and to write the name on the place of each grave in a map which is to be made.

When Continental officers come asking for horses, and the person approached can say that he has none, he shall not suggest another man

---

[9] For explanation of the Lease System in Salem see Vol. II of this series, pages 710-713.

who has a horse which can be pressed, for that is not neighborly, still less brotherly, conduct.

Nov. 14. (L—A—C.) Members are beginning to feel the spirit of freedom in the land, and to think that as soon as the children attain their majority they are at liberty to do as they please, and no longer give their parents respect or obedience. The true idea, in conformity with the Bible and the foundation principles of the Unity, is not contary to the law of the land, as some have supposed, for law does not abrogate the Fourth Commandment. The law does not prevent a child from being obedient to a parent, but only prevents a father from refusing to let a child set up a separate household because he thinks it would be to his advantage to keep the child at home. According to English law a child is obligated to respect his parents, and to care for them in their old age.

Few households have family devotions, and parents in our country congregations should be urged to have morning and evening prayers in their homes.

Nov. 16. (Congregation Council.) Counterfeit currency shall not be received or paid out knowingly. If any man is doubtful about a bill he shall take it to Br. Bagge for inspection, for Br. Bagge has been appointed for this county to write the word *Counterfeit* across any false bill.

To bring the chimney-sweeping into better order Br. Kremser shall be told to divide the list, sweeping part each month, and sweeping certain chimneys every month. Each house-father shall see that his chimneys are swept regularly.

As three store-houses are to be prepared in each county,—four in Rowan County,—it was decided that if one is located in Salem the mill should be suggested as the place, which would keep out of the town the soldiers appointed to guard the stores.

Nov. 16. (Auf. Col.) Martin Lück has attained his majority, and so has become free from his master, the cabinet-maker, Johann Krauss. As is customary they shall exchange the indenture papers.

There was a conference with Balthaser Christman, who has asked permission to become a permanent resident of the town. He says that he was born Dec. 9, 1760; that he is here with the knowledge of his father, who is willing for him to remain; that he has given no promise of marriage, has not bought land, nor made any contract which would interfere with his staying here; and that he has never been drafted for militia service. He believed that he could, and promised that he would, obey the rules of the community.

Nov. 21. (Auf. Col.) Br. Jens Schmidt has a sore on his tongue which looks like a cancer. He shall come from Bethabara to the Brothers House here, where he will be cared for.

The fire-inspectors make the following report:—At Christ's there are no bricks in front of the fire-place. The chimney in which the potter burns his ware has holes in it, and boards in the curves; it is sometimes red-hot, so that the flames shoot out above, and sparks fall on the roof. We will speak with Br. Aust about it; the pottery ought to have a separate kiln. Christ and Holder have wooden poles in the chimneys, on which to hang meat for smoking.

Yesterday Mr. Lanier brought corn on the cob to apply on his debt. It shall be offered to Br. Meyer, and carefully measured.

Nov. 22. (Aelt. Conf.) It was agreed that if a Continental Store is placed in Bethabara we should try to have Br. Heinrich Stoehr appointed Commissary; and as one of our houses would be pressed for the purpose we should offer to clear out the old store building. Br. Blum should do all that is possible to avoid having the tavern cellar used.

The elder Christman has said that he would build a small schoolhouse for his children, and thought other children would join them, if a Brother would come to them as school-master. This would open a new door for the Brethren in that neighborhood, but the idea can not be carried out until the people there show a real longing for the Saviour and for a closer connection with the Brethren. Meanwhile a Brother shall visit them now and then.

Br. and Sr. Marshall visited Hope last Saturday and Sunday. William Douthit has expressed a desire to be Received into the Society, but it will be better to wait until he is cured of his affection for the Tory cause. Meanwhile he and Stephen Riddle may attend the Society meetings. The elder Elrod has stated that his son Christoph will marry the elder Douthit's daughter Sarah, and the Banns will probably be published next Sunday.

Nov. 28. (Auf. Col.) The house in which Br. Christ lives stands on the books at £163; the original cost was £140, and the rest for the room in the second story and for making doors and windows. It was decided to let the pottery have it for £150.

Robert Cochran, merchant and tanner in Cross Creek, has proposed that Br. Bagge sell tanned leather for him on commission. Br. Herbst has gotten many hides this year, and will be able to supply the town and the neighborhood with leather next year, so we cannot accommodate Mr. Cochran.

It was recommended that the huts on the brick-yard should not be repaired. It seems impossible to get roof-tiles made, and brick-making does not require such expensive buildings.

Dec. 2. (Aelt. Conf.) Maria shall be given the proposal to marry Johannes Samuel. It is not necessary to publish the Banns, but they shall be commended to the prayers of the congregation here and in Bethabara.

Dec. 13. (Aelt. Conf.) Br. Marshall will accept payment for the Bethania rent in corn, at four shillings a bushel.

George Hauser, Jr., asks to be Received into the congregation. He is sick, and says with tears that he wishes to belong to the Saviour; that he will keep out of political affairs, and will bear the abuse which this will bring him. His Reception was approved by the Saviour.

Dec. 15. (Auf. Col.) Two traders have been here recently who wished to put their goods on display for three or four days. They spoke to Br. Bagge, who did not forbid them to sell, but did not encourage them to display their wares for so long a time. They did not show anything of much value, nor did they offer to sell cheap; but some of the Brethren and Sisters thought they might have goods for sale which would be serviceable in this time of scarcity, and did not like what was done. It was decided that in future such traders may be permitted to show their wares for one day, but not for two or three; Br. Bagge is not forbidden to buy from them in quantity for the store. Brethren may buy for others in town, but may not buy to sell at a profit, or carry on a private trade with them.

Dec. 19. (Auf. Col.) The rule must be observed that no brandy is sold by the quart in the still-house except to people bringing grain or to persons passing through, who will not stop at the tavern, otherwise the tavern gets too many drunken men, and there are quarrels and fights. Br. Meyer shall sell it to strangers when he must, and it will be well to sell at a reduced price to those who buy as they are leaving the tavern.

Br. Aust stated that the glazing recently burnt from lead cost four shillings a pound, instead of the former eight pence.

Br. Bagge laid before the Collegium the Tickets recently received from General Gates for supplies furnished. The Tickets were drawn on Thomas Sim Lee, Governor of Virginia, or the Continental Treasurer of that state. They totaled $38111 34/90, of which $1829 belongs to the store, $190 to George Smith, $800 to Jacob Bonn, $5607 to the tavern, $10439 7/8 to the Single Brethren, $4831 to the mill, $480.49 to Bethabara, and $13907½ to members living in the country. The amount granted was $27 more than the total of the Tickets. There was

discussion of how to get the money for them; decision was left until later.

Dec. 20. (Aelt. Conf.) With the beginning of the year 1781 Br. Graff will resign the writing of the congregation diary to Br. Friedrich Peter. The Choirs shall make notes of matters belonging in the diary and shall hand them to Br. Peter each week.

Br. Beck wrote from Friedberg that Fishels thought to give their daughter in marriage to the younger Tanner, if Conferenz approved. No objections were raised, so the matter may proceed.

As Texts for the year 1781 we will use those of 1776 until the new ones arrive from Pennsylvania.

Memorabilia of Bethabara, 1780.

[Extracts translated].

The peace of God, with which we entered upon the new year, has been particularly felt as we partook of His Body and Blood in the Holy Communion, and this great grace was vouchsafed to the congregation thirteen times during the year.

The festal days of the Church and of the Unity have been observed with the grace of Jesus, and were days of real blessing. The Gemein Nachrichten, the sermons from the Wochen, the weekly reading of the Bible, were a comfort and blessing to us in all difficult situations. The Holy Ghost has declared Jesus to us, has kept us in one mind, and has shielded us. The Visitation of our dear Br. and Sr. Reichel, and their visits to the congregation, were accompanied with blessing.

After reading again the Minutes of Synod, the Committee here was reorganized. A girls' school was begun this year, with Sr. Engel as teacher.

In spite of the continuing unrest in the land we have experienced the merciful protection of our dear heavenly Father. At various times our town has been full of soldiers, some of them antagonistic to us. More than two thousand have been here, and the chief burden of their care fell upon the town. The last men, nearly a thousand in number, were here for eighteen days; we had much pity for these soldiers, of whom many were in the most needy circumstances. Many of them had opportunity to learn to know the Brethren, and to see what spirit animated us. We can believe that we have earned a good reputation among friends and foes. We thank our good Lord that He has protected us in body and soul, that we have been able peacefully and quietly to carry on our work and to hold our church services. Oh God, give to us and to all inhabitants of this land an honorable peace! We acknowl-

edge with many thanks that we have retained our health under the hard and oppressive conditions. In the face of all the loss experienced by the residents of this town and by our neighbors, we acknowledge with thankful hearts the blessing of God in the harvest from fields and orchard, the latter larger than for a number of years.

In our town we have seen the protection and service of the holy angels, especially when so many fires were built around our old houses.

In Pennsylvania, Br. Blum married the Single Sr. Elisabeth Koch; and on their return they took charge of the tavern, where Br. and Sr. Schaub, Jr. have served for seven years. Since Br. Schaub returned from Bethlehem he has begun indigo dyeing.

The congregation consists of 69 persons, and in addition there are two at the mill,—George Wagemann and Margaretha Schor,—a negro and negress at the tavern, and a negro boy on the plantation, a total of 74.

Bethabara Diary, 1780.

[Extracts translated.]

Jan. 10. This morning it began to snow. Threshing was continued in the sheds.

Jan. 16. All the communicants assembled for Congregation Council. The Saal expense amounts to £2:—:6 for the half year, to which eighteen Brethren and thirteen Sisters will contribute, the Brethren paying 1 sh. 6d, and the Sisters 1 sh. each.

The fence around God's Acre needs thorough repair, or perhaps a new one. Three Brethren from the Committee and three from the Council shall look at it and decide what shall be done, and then appoint a member of the Committee to attend to it.

Since the calling away of Br. Lung there has been no regular grave-digger. The younger Br. Schaub was willing to undertake it, and was elected by the Council. It was decided that twelve shillings should be paid for digging a grave, this to include filling the grave and hauling away the extra dirt. He shall also mow God's Acre twice a year, and straighten the stones before Easter.

It is unseemly that when some one has been called home persons come at once to buy this or that; they should give the bereaved at least four weeks time, even when there is no Will.

The Brethren were reminded that the taxes must be paid in Bethania, to the sheriff, next Wednesday. Whoever does not wish to go in person can give his taxes to Br. Blum or Schaub; Br. Kühnast will go also.

Jan. 17. At twilight there was a hard storm from the west.

Jan. 19. It was unusually cold.

Jan. 21. The mill has frozen in the cold weather, and can hardly be made to run. On the Atkin $20 is being paid for a bushel of corn.

Jan. 27. It was decided to move back the fence half a square on the Brothers' side of our God's Acre.

Jan. 29. In the evening at seven o'clock the local communicants had a happy lovefeast. About eight o'clock the communicants reassembled for the most Holy Communion, 36 persons partaking.

Jan. 31. There was a discussion about fire-inspectors, and the Congregation Council shall select two Brethren to serve with one from the Committee.

Feb. 6. Sunday. At nine o'clock the Church litany was prayed. At ten o'clock was preaching, and several of our neighbors were present. In the evening at eight, instead of gemeinstunde there was a singstunde.

Feb. 7. The contract between the elder Br. Schaub and Hoft Heintz has terminated, and he has rented his place to Mr. Brachten for 1/3 of the crop. It began to snow, so there was no evening service.

Feb. 8. The melting snow and glaze ice made it very wet.

Feb. 11. Johannes Krause was here asking for the baptism of his child, so Br. Lorenz went thither today, and held a service in his house. The child received the name Andreas; sponsors were George and Maria Schulz and the elder Andreas Volk. About fifty persons were present, half of them children, for the school-master of that neighborhood came, bringing the school.

Feb. 13. Sunday. Unity Day began with a service at nine o'clock.

Feb. 14. The Committee met. Br. Kühnast stated that the affairs of the departed Br. Nilson had been arranged according to his Will, and Br. Blum will take the money for his children to Pennsylvania, and get receipts from them.

Oats were threshed in the sheds. Six hogs, weighing 1000 lbs. were slaughtered for the benefit of the Oeconomie.

Feb. 15. Br. Mücke returned from Dan River, whither he went yesterday to see about promised grain. The Brn. Bonn and Blum returned from Court, with the news that the court had considered it fair that we pay the county tax straight. The sheriff did not have time at court to take the money, and offered to come to our towns for it.

Feb. 18. The shoe-maker, who has been working with Br. Stöhr for two weeks or so, ran away during the night, leaving debts in various places.

Feb. 21. Br. Marshall came on business. Boundaries were fixed for the lot on which the still-house stands, and for the hop-garden;

they are each twelve rods wide, and the former is two hundred feet deep.

Feb. 22. It was a rainy day. Threshing was finished.

Feb. 26. Saturday. In the evening at eight o'clock the congregation met for the Holy Communion. Immediately after this service Sr. Lenel Schmidt received the Communion for the Sick.

Feb. 29. Plowing was begun for summer grain.

March 2. A day-laborer by the name of Daub, who has worked here for nearly a year, took his departure. He said farewell with tears, and with regrets that his circumstances did not permit him to stay longer.

March 3. Plowing continued and fences were mended.

March 4. Br. Blum went to Bethania to see about a wagon and team for the trip to Pennsylvania; George Hauser, Sr., will go.

March 9. General Muster was held in Richmond today.

March 10. For a quarter of a year various people on this side of the Atkin have been asking for a service and for the baptism of their children, so Br. Lorenz went thither today and held a meeting in Nicholas Doll's house.

March 11. Yesterday and today there is voting in Richmond for new Assembly-men, so several Brethren went from here today.

March 13. The Committee met. It was said that Mr. Henderson would be here, to get meat and corn for the militia about to be enlisted. That we must give something is beyond question. The Brn. Kühnast, Schaub and Blum shall speak with Mr. Henderson when he returns from Salem. It was known that he wanted meat, corn and oats, so it was agreed to offer him six bushels of oats, ten bushels of corn, and two cows. He agreed to this, except that instead of two cows he wanted one cow and one ox.

March 14. Several acres were sowed in oats.

March 15. The Brethren of the Committee, the Brethren and Sisters who serve in the Saal, and the musicians, had a happy lovefeast. There were thirteen Brethren and eight Sisters present.

March 16. Br. Bonn went to Richmond to Colonel Sheppard, who has a sore eye. Mr. Henderson ordered the promised corn and oats taken to Richmond today.

March 19. Palm Sunday. The litany of the Life and Sufferings of Jesus was sung. * * * The cost of the fence around God's Acre was laid before the Congregation Council. It amounted to £4: 4: —. It was agreed that each Sister shall give two shillings, and each Brother two shillings, six pence. This amounts to £3 : 10 :—, but three Brethren

offered to give £2 : 16 :—so a new fence can be built the rest of the way around.

March 20. Colonel Armstrong came from his journey to the south, his wagon also arrived with a load of various wares, which he offered to sell here for a fair price.

Plowing continued, and a beginning was made with burning along the fences.

March 23. Maundy Thursday. Br. Ernst sent word that Johannes Schor departed at seven o'clock this morning, and the burial will be tomorrow afternoon.

At two o'clock the congregation assembled in the Saal to hear the story of the sufferings of our Lord. * * * At eight o'clock the reading of the story was continued; and at nine o'clock the communicants gathered to partake of the Lord's Supper, on that night in which He was betrayed.

Today, while burning about the fences, the wind was so strong that a standing tree caught, the wind drove the fire into the fence, and if help had not come quickly the entire fence would have been consumed. As it was, 150 rails were burnt.

March 24. Good Friday. The congregation met at nine o'clock and listened to the story of His sufferings, interspersed with the singing of hymns. In the second meeting the account of His crucifixion was heard with deep feeling. In the second hour of the afternoon the account of His death was read. * * * At three o'clock there was the reading of the opening of His side, followed by a liturgy. In the evening we heard the story of His burial; and the day closed with a hymn concerning His precious wounds and death.

March 25. Great Sabbath. At two o'clock the congregation, including the children, had a happy lovefeast, rejoicing over the holy incarnation of Jesus, and over His rest in the grave. The day closed with prayer and a liturgy.

March 26. Easter. Early in the morning the congregation met in the Saal, greeted one another with the words: "The Lord is risen," "He is risen indeed!" and after a hymn we went to God's Acre and prayed the Easter Liturgy. Several outsiders were here, among the rest Gideon Wright.

At ten o'clock was the preaching service; * * * and in the afternoon the quarter-hour for the children. This was followed by reading the story of His resurrection and appearance to His disciples. The day closed with a singstunde.

March 27. Easter Monday. It was Unity Day, with the reading of Nachrichten in three sessions.

March 28. The Brn. Blum and Aust set out for Pennsylvania, Mr. Thomas Cummings going with them. Colonel Armstrong was also here.

March 31. There was a strong wind today. For the close of the month we sang: "Oh Head so full of bruises."

April 2. The married people had a conference concerning the beginning of the school for girls. Five girls will attend for the present, and those that come all day will pay four shillings a month, and those who come only half the day will pay two shillings.

April 3. The five little school-girls and their mothers had a love-feast, and Sr. Maria Elisabeth Engel was introduced to them as their teacher.

April 5. The girls' school began today, and will be in session from eight to eleven in the morning and from one to five in the afternoon. The girls attending the school are:—Elisabeth Fogler, Anna Maria Kapp, Susanna Elisabeth Bagge, Elisabeth Fockel, and Johanna Elisabeth Stöhr.

April 9. It was announced that during the week the communicants will meet Tuesday and Thursday evenings at 7:30; services for all will be at 8:30 each evening, except on Saturday, when the members of the Hourly Intercession will meet at eight o'clock. The children's meeting will be on Thursday at ten in the morning.

This afternoon our Assembly-men, Cummings and Freeman, arrived, accompanied by a gentleman from South Carolina. Colonel Armstrong came also, and when they had eaten they went on to Salem. From the lower part of North Carolina a large party of gentlemen came with their servants, on their way to Kentucky;[1] they remained over night. This party, seventeen in number, attended the evening meeting.

Announcement was made of the approaching marriage of Br. Rudolph Christ to Sr. Elisabeth Oesterlein, and of Br. John Holland to Sr. Maria Strub.

April 10. George Hauser, Sr. came from Bethania, and loaded his wagon for Pennsylvania. The weight of the load was over a thousand pounds, and he borrowed a horse for the trip.

April 11. Tobias Hirte, who has been here with his brother-in-law for nearly half a year, left with George Hauser's wagon for Pennsylvania.

April 12. Br. Lorenz went to Salem to Conference.[2] Commissary Henderson came, asking for beef cattle and for corn.

---

[1] Lorenz Bagge, diarist of Bethabara, spells the name phonetically *Cenduck.*
[2] This entry is made nearly every month.

April 14. The gentleman from South Carolina, who has been here for several days, went to Richmond.

April 19. Br. and Sr. Marshall came from Salem to speak with the Brethren and Sisters before the approaching Communion. Colonel Armstrong was here on private business.

April 24. Br. Heinrich Stöhr left for Pennsylvania, accompanied by George Biehler. The former will visit his father, and will see whether he can get a Brother who is a shoe-maker to move here; the latter has been here and with his brother-in-law George Holder for several months, and has attended our services frequently.

Br. Schmidt has undertaken to blow the horn when it is time to stop work.

April 26. Corn planting began. In the afternoon it commenced to rain, continuing until in the night.

April 29. The company of Light-Horse, who passed last week going after Tories, came back saying that everything was peaceful, and they had found nothing to do. They stayed here several hours, taking their mid-day meal here, and were well content with what was served to them. They behaved so quietly that one hardly knew they were here. They left at seven o'clock, going toward Salem.

May 1. Elisabeth and Johanna Stauber began school today. They will attend half of each day. There was a hard storm, with rain from the west.

May 4. Ascension Day. At eight in the morning there was service, with a short address, and the reading of the story of the Ascension of our dear Lord. It began to rain again.

May 5. The rain continued all night, and until afternoon. The water was so high that the bottoms were flooded.

May 6. The water fell rapidly. All the fences and bridges needed attention.

Sixteen soldiers passed on their way to Hillsborough. Colonel and Major Armstrong were here.

May 11. Br. Meinung has been here making the inventories and monthly reports of the businesses; he returned to Salem today.

May 12. Our team hauled saw logs to the mill today. From the court we heard that Mr. Lanier has been made Treasurer of this county.

May 14. Whitsuntide. The congregation met in the Saal at half past eight in the morning. * * * In the afternoon there was a service for the children. * * * In a meeting for communicants there was an

address on the Text for the day; then the Cup of Covenant passed from hand to hand, while a blessed liturgy was sung. It rained most of the time after mid-day, and yet the members living outside the town attended the services.

May 15. *Monday after Whit-Sunday.* Our Unity Day began with the hymn: "Be present, God the Holy Ghost." Reports from Bethlehem for the months of October, November and December were read in two sessions. In a third session the 18th Woche from 1778 was read. * * * The evening gemeinstunde closed with the Old Testament benediction.

May 16. This afternoon there was the betrothal of Br. Philip Martin Vogler to Sr. Johanna Elisabeth Steinmann, maiden name Moll.

May 21. Br. Stauber was here for the service, and on his way home stopped to see old Br. Schulze. He had hardly started on his way again when something stung his horse, which began to kick, and he was thrown, hurting himself badly on head and one arm, though nothing seems to be broken.

May 25. Colonel Armstrong and Mr. Cummings were here, the latter returning from the Assembly.

May 29. Hoeing and ploughing corn began. Also a beginning was made with covering the stable.

June 3. Br. Heinzmann came from Salem to hold the services during the absence of Br. Lorenz, who left this morning for Deep Creek, accompanied by Br. Kapp.

June 4. Br. Lorenz reported concerning his trip to Deep Creek, that although it had not been announced he had visited in several houses, reaching Friedrich Lang's home about eight o'clock. Valentine Riess, who had shown him the way thither, went on that night to announce his coming in another neighborhood. A little daughter had been born to the Friedrich Langs on May 30th, so Sunday morning there was a meeting in his house * * * and the child was baptised, receiving the name Elisabeth. From Lang's they went to Valentine Riess' where a company had gathered, and eight fathers were waiting to ask baptism for their children. Some of the children were nearly a year old, but under the circumstances no one was refused. It was a great baptising, but there was no disturbance. There seemed no advantage in further visits, for all were full of the present unrest in the land, so Br. Lorenz decided to go straight home. On the way he and his companion met a large company of cavalry, who said they were going to Alexander Martin, and to a man who was in Salem with many negroes;—Br. Lorenz knew nothing of either. When asked where their journey would end, the men said in Guilford.

9

June 5. Br. Opiz came from Salem, on his way to Bethania to his parents. He brought two copies of the *Daily Texts,* and one copy was sent on to Br. Ernst.

From various persons stopping at the tavern we hear all sorts of news, and that our whole neighborhood is stirred up;—may our good God protect us from tumult and uprisings and the shedding of blood.

June 6. Colonel Armstrong was here, and said he had orders to press brandy in our town. Br. Mücke promised him some.

June 7. Br. Lorenz went to Salem to Conference; he returned about five o'clock, just as a heavy storm broke from the west, with hard rain. Corn ploughing was finished today.

June 8. Br. Stöhr returned from Pennsylvania.

June 10. The Brn. Triebel and Göpfert came from Salem on a visit.[3]

June 12. Two German day-laborers, who have worked here a long time, have left because of uneasiness over present conditions.

Mr. Winston came, and asked that our wagon should go to Salem for articles which have been pressed for him there. When it returned in the evening the brandy which Br. Mücke had promised,—twenty-five gallons,—was put in the wagon to be taken to Bethania. The gentlemen, Williams and Winston, who returned from Salem, wanted more brandy, but no more was given than had been promised to Colonel Armstrong. The gentlemen stayed here over night.

Grass-mowing began today.

June 13. Showers interfered with the hay-making. The above mentioned gentlemen went to the mill to press corn, but found only two bushels. They insisted that when Br. Kapp ground meal he must not take toll, and they would give Tickets for it.

June 14. Hay was hauled today. Otherwise all was as usual.

June 15. Br. and Sr. Blum arrived today from Pennsylvania. This morning they left the others thirty miles from here; the wagon from Salem will bring in the rest of the party, and they expect to reach Salem this evening.

June 17. Hay-making continued, and some was hauled.

June 18. About nine o'clock our dear Brethren and Sisters, the Reichels, Jeppe Nilsons, and Br. Friedrich Peter arrived, accompanied by Br. and Sr. Marshall and the Blums and Austs. Br. Reichel held the Communion liturgy. In the afternoon at two o'clock the congregation, including the children, had a happy lovefeast. * * * It was a day full of

---

[3] The diary shows many visits exchanged between Bethabara and Salem; and Br. Ernst, of Bethania, often came to Bethabara.

blessing. Toward evening there was a hard storm with wind, thunder and rain, so there could be no evening service.

June 19. Br. Meinung came from Salem to make an inventory of things belonging to the tavern, as Br. Blum will take charge of it.

June 21. We hear that there is great unrest among people at large.

June 22. Br. and Sr. Blum went to Hope to get their child from Br. and Sr. Fritz, who have taken care of it for a quarter of a year. From Captain Schmidt, who came early this morning, we hear that he has orders to call all drafted men to Richmond today, as it is said that two thousand Tories are marching thither.[4] Toward seven o'clock there was a hard storm, with wind, thunder, lightning and rain.

June 23. Br. and Sr. Schaub and their children moved from the tavern to the former Nilson house. As no hay could be made the men began to cut barley.

June 24. The wet hay was dried and most of it was hauled in. In the eighth hour there was a hard storm, and on this account, and because everybody was tired and hot, there was no prayer meeting.

June 26. Br. Reichel held the festal services for the little boys, [whose festival had been postponed from the 24th].

Before noon rye was cut, and in the afternoon there was hay-making, but a storm toward evening spoiled the hay.

June 27. Today the town was full of militia, who demanded food for themselves and their horses, at the expense of the regiment.

June 28. The weather held up today, and some hay could be brought in. Br. Schaub, Jr. started to Pennsylvania, in company with Tobias Hirte. The wheat harvest was begun.

June 30. A company of sixty men arrived, and are to wait here for further orders.

July 1. It was possible to continue with the harvest today, and nine of the company stationed here helped with the reaping, receiving $36 apiece for the day.

July 2. All of the Brethren and Sisters who could get away went to Salem today to the funeral services of Br. Jeppe Nilson. A service was held here at nine o'clock, attended by the entire company stationed here, so there was an address on the Epistle for this Sunday,—Romans 6, beginning with verse three. Toward evening there was a hard storm with heavy rain, so that the meadow near the house was under water. In the spring-house all the milk crocks had to be raised. The horse pressed from here was returned.

---

[4] The fall of Charleston, and success of the British in South Carolina, had encouraged the Tories everywhere to rise.

July 3. Colonel Armstrong was here; he said that the company would remain until Wednesday at least.

The Committee met.[5] Of the books recently received the Brethren looked over Reichel's work on the Bible and the last volume of the Life of Zinzendorf. There was also a serious discussion about the swine that run about the town all day; it is unseemly, and besides there is danger that they will break into the gardens.

July 4. Some of the soldiers here received permission to leave, and others arrived.

July 5. Harvesting the winter grain was finished. We are thankful to our good Lord, Who has helped us in these difficult times.

July 6. Toward evening Colonel Armstrong and Captain Merrel arrived, the latter is captain of the company that is here. As the soldiers are becoming restless their meat and bread were given them to cook for themselves. About ten at night a party of cavalry arrived. Their captain led them in *brutal* behaviour, and did whatever he pleased,—they drove their horses into the oats, ordered the baker to give them bread, commanded Br. Kühnast to give them all the milk and butter they wanted, and had they been refused they would have seized what they desired.

In the children's hour there was a talk on the Text for the day. Br. Lorenz went to Bethania, and took Br. Ernst a letter from Br. Graff. Most of the soldiers attended the evening meeting, in which there was an address on the Texts of the day, and mention was made of John Hus, whose martyr death, 365 years ago today, sealed his witness to the Gospel.

July 7. The soldiers, who have been here more than eight days, went away. We were happy that we were able to get back the kettle they had borrowed to cook in, as they tried to take it away with them. The cavalry also moved on; their leader is a bad man. We had to give them a horse, and they seized four horses that came through the woods from Bethania. An Express came to Colonel Armstrong.

July 8. Today was quite peaceful in the town. Late in the evening several soldiers came in; they had been taking cattle and tools from Tories who were not at home. Hay was brought from the large meadow; it was cut fourteen days ago, and has been half ruined by the much rain. Today has been so hot that the workmen are completely worn out.

July 9. It was fairly quiet and peaceful, though several men are staying here to guard the cattle and horses of the Tories.

---

[5] It consisted of the Brn. Stach, Schaub, Sr., Schaub, Jr., Richter, Kühnast, and Lorenz Bagge, the last two ex-officio.

July 10. Another company of something over thirty men were here, and asked for and received dinner.

July 13. Oats were cut today, and wheat hauled in.

July 14. Another company of soldiers came, and remained over night. In the evening service we sang: "Oh Head so full of bruises:" and the soldiers were attentive and quiet.

July 15. The soldiers went on to Salem. Toward noon another company arrived, but did not stay long, but went on toward Salem.

In the evening the communicants had a happy lovefeast, during which hymns were sung. We thanked the dear Saviour for the end of the harvest, and for the fact that although we had had so many soldiers in the town, some of them for over eight days, yet the Eye and Guardian of Israel had protected us from harm of body or soul.

July 16. Eight or nine older girls came from Bethania to visit Sr. Engel. Toward evening they went home, with the two married Sisters who had brought them.

July 19. From Br. Michael Hauser we heard that people must take wheat to Steiner's mill for the soldiers. The proportion is to be that if I have twelve bushels I give four. Oats were brought into the shed today.

July 20. The carpenter came from Salem, with his tools, to make a new apple-press. Grass was cut, and the corn-fields were worked.

July 21. The Sisters retted late flax. Br. Richter went out yesterday to find the horse that was pressed, as we had heard that it was on the Town Fork. He finally found it and brought it home today.

July 25. Two wagons loaded with iron arrived from Philadelphia. Five hundred pounds were bought for $12 a pound.

July 26. Every one was busy gathering the fallen apples, and taking to the still-house those that were not fit for drying.

July 28. Br. Reichel and his wife came on a Visitation. They began this afternoon to speak with each Brother and Sister.

July 29. The thirty bushels of wheat, which we had to give to the army, were taken to Steiner's mill.

July 31. It rained all day. Oats were threshed in the shed. The new apple-press was used for the first time. Br. Ernst came from Bethania to confer with the Brn. Reichel and Marshall.

Aug. 2. Work was begun on cutting and drying apples.

Aug. 3. The Brethren began to sow turnip seed, and to turn under the stubble.

Aug. 4. A chaplain from General Gates' army passed on his way to Lancaster, and offered to take a letter, so Br. Lorenz wrote a few lines to Br. Ettwein.

Aug. 5. Toward evening two soldiers arrived to press wagons and horses for Captain Paschke's company. This time they took only one wagon.

Aug. 7. The soldiers who have pressed a wagon, two horses, barrels and sacks, here went further. Our neighbor, Mr. Brachten, acted as teamster for our wagon; he had to add two of his horses to the team.

Aug. 8. Today our wagon and horses left for Steiner's mill.[6] Br. Rose went along to see whether he could not have a value placed on them there, but did not succeed. Everybody here was busy with hay-making. The heat is very oppressive. In the evening there was a hard storm, and therefore no service.

Aug. 13. Sunday. There was service at nine o'clock. There was an address on the grace which the Saviour showed to our early Brethren fifty-three years ago,[7] and we wished ourselves today a fresh experience of the same.

Aug. 17. Our little girls observed their Festival today. They were fourteen in number.

Aug. 18. This morning Sr. Bagge was quickly and safely delivered of twins. The news was sent to Salem and Bethania, and Br. and Sr. Ernst came from the latter place and Br. and Sr. Marshall, Br. Prezel and Sr. Nilson from the former. At two o'clock in the afternoon was the service for the baptism of these little hearts; during the usual liturgy Br. Graff baptised Johann Lorenz and Br. Ernst baptised Maria Christina into the death of Jesus.

Aug. 19. The dry weather, which has continued for some days, has made it impossible to continue with ploughing under the stubble. Seed wheat was threshed in the shed, but the main work was with the apples, some being pressed and some dried.

Aug. 21. A package of letters was given to two travelers, John Gute and Hilmebert; they are going to Philadelphia, but will send the letters by safe hands to Lancaster. The town was full of strangers, for there is constant coming in flight from the camp.[8] In the evening meeting there was a sermon, and then several hymns were sung.

Aug. 22. The wagons began to haul manure to the fields where wheat is to be planted. Colonel Armstrong and his brother were here, coming from the camp.

---

[6] To haul flour to the army on the Peedee.   [7] In Herrnhut, Germany.
[8] After the American defeat at Camden.

Aug. 24. A beginning was made with picking peaches for brandy.

Aug. 25. Nine Tories passed under strong guard, being taken to Hillsborough. Colonel Armstrong, Shepperd and Cummings were here over night; the last two were on their way to the Assembly.

Aug. 27. This was Unity Day. Br. and Sr. Reichel, Br. Marshall and Sr. Nilson came from Salem. At two o'clock was the baptism of our negro Frank, * * * he received the name Christian.

Aug. 29. More than three hundred soldiers arrived, and camped on the meadow behind the houses, having horses and cattle with them. Colonel Armstrong and the officers who came with them made us the best of promises, and said their only object in coming was to take up the matter of the Tories. Shortly before, Aust had driven in his cattle, from which they took three oxen for slaughter. Aust was also here, but they did what they pleased. On account of the crowd the evening service was omitted.

Aug. 30. The soldiers helped themselves industriously in the orchard, and were about the town all day. Yesterday they took our meal from the mill, about twenty bushels, and Br. Ranke ground five bushels of wheat for them. Now that they had meal some one must bake for them or give them bread in exchange for meal.

There was Bible reading at the evening service.

Aug. 31. This afternoon the soldiers left. No one knew where they were going, but it was said that one company went to Salem. The meal they had was left behind, with order that it be kept for them or some other soldiers.

The wagons from our neighborhood, which took meal to the army, have come home. They went as far as the Peedee, and from there to Hillsborough. On the return trip several horses were stolen from them, so that they were obliged to take one wagon apart and load it on another. Our wagon stopped eighteen miles from here, as the horses had given out; Br. Richter and Wilhelm Volk were sent with two horses to bring it home.

Sept. 2. After a long dry spell it rained today, so that the ground was soaked.

Sept. 3. Sunday. This afternoon two hundred soldiers arrived, and as they did not want the same camping ground, but asked for the bottom meadow, it was agreed that they should take the orchard behind the still-house.

Sept. 4. Today twelve Tories were brought here, for whom we had to clear out the old Brothers House. A guard was set before the house, and this made so much confusion on the Square that we decided it would be better not to try to hold an evening service.

Sept. 5. Two wagons, loaded with lead and powder, arrived under guard of a company of cavalry. Another company brought more Tories. Some were tried, and several were whipped, one especially received more than a hundred lashes. On account of the confusion there was no evening service.

Sept. 6. Today thirteen more Tories were brought in. There was much confusion until several companies went off on expeditions, and a company from the Holston received furlough. All the meal they or we had was baked, and it looked as though there would be no bread for use the next day, but late in the evening some meal was brought in. General Stevens arrived this evening, and remained over night.

Sept. 7. In comparison with yesterday the day was quiet, though there is no end to the noise. We heard that the package of letters sent by John Gute had come back, and that one of our English neighbors had given it to the Virginia general here, who had opened it. We spoke with Colonel Armstrong about it, and he promised to see that it was returned to us.

Sept. 8. This was a very hard day, especially before noon, when a man was to be hanged, and that here in our town. We went to Colonel Armstrong, and begged that this might not happen, and the place was changed, although the soldiers and the man who was to be hanged were already on the Square. There he was tried, and acknowledged all that he had done; then the command was given to the entire company that if any knew aught against him he should speak. No one had anything particular to add, so Colonel Campbell said that no one had condemned him but he had condemned himself. Then the company was drawn up in two lines, with this man and the other prisoners between, and so they marched out to the middle bars in the field, where the man was hanged. His name was Rieth [Ried]. As he stood at the foot of the gallows he said that he deserved his sentence, and ought to die quickly.

Through the aid of Colonel Armstrong we received from the Virginia officer the package of letters that came back; Br. Rose took them to Salem to Br. Marshall.

Sept. 9. The Brn. Marshall and Herbst came from Salem to see us, whereat we rejoiced. Br. Marshall had an opportunity to speak with Colonel Armstrong and Colonel Campbell before they left. The prisoners were brought to the Square, ringed about with soldiers, and many of them were tried, and four or five were whipped. It was said that two of them ought to be hanged, but they were not executed this time, though they received more lashes instead. In the afternoon all the Virginia troops marched away; we did not know whither, but we thanked the dear Saviour from our hearts for their departure. We had feared the return of a Captain Campbell, who had been sent out with his company three days before, and he did come back with ten men; but when he found that the others had gone, and that men from our county were here to guard the prisoners, he left again, saying he would gather his company and go home, and we were thankful for this also.

Sept. 10. Sunday. At nine o'clock the church litany was prayed. At ten o'clock there was preaching on Isaiah 53, iv and v. Some of the soldiers stationed here attended both services. In the afternoon was the meeting for the children, and a reading meeting. There was a good deal of disturbance all day, and more soldiers from our county arrived. From Bethania we heard that Captain Campbell and his company arrived last evening with two or three prisoners, and after supper Geier Reit[9] was whipped. This morning there was more whipping, and toward noon he left.

Sept. 11. More Tories are being brought in, so that there are now fifty here, and in addition their women come and go, to help their husbands and friends. Yesterday two men came *express* to Colonel Armstrong, one from the Governor and the other from Salisbury. As he did not come they were sent on today.

Sr. Blum was very ill; last week she had an attack of fever, and the constant disturbance makes her worse.

Sept. 12. Colonel Armstrong arrived toward evening, and many people gathered to see him.

Sept. 13. The prisoners are still here, though we hear that one man, named Beeder, has run away.

Sept. 14. Colonel Armstrong returned from Richmond toward evening. At night he spoke with the prisoners, saying that those who would enlist in the [American] army would be set free.

Sept. 15. Hay was brought in from the big meadow and piled in stacks. We began to gather peaches.

Although only five prisoners were left here there was constant standing guard and cooking on the Square.

---

[9] Br. Lorenz' spelling of proper names is peculiar, even from a phonetic point of view. From the Salem diary it is evident that Colonel Campbell was the officer in charge in Bethabara during the early part of September, 1780. Br. Lorenz spells his name *Gamelie,* and by analogy of consonant sounds, conjoined with the usual German value of vowels, *Geier Reit* should be Kiah [Hezekiah] Wright. This substitution of consonants has persisted to the present day in the Bethania name of Grabs, which is variously pronounced (a as in father) Grabs, Graps, and Kraps.

Sept. 16. Last night the Englishman ran away. The remaining prisoners were set free on certain conditions. Other militia began to assemble here, preparing to go to the war.

Br. Lorenz was in Salem for the memorial day.

Sept. 17. Sunday. Most of the soldiers here received orders to go to the farm of James Glen, on the Atkin, and marched away. One company, that arrived late, remained over night. Some of the soldiers attended the evening service; all our meetings have been having their presence.

Sept. 18. More soldiers arrive constantly, but it was fairly quiet in the town.

Sept. 19. This morning the company of cavalry left for Richmond, so at six o'clock the French horns announced the festival of the Married People. * * * In the lovefeast Br. Peter played the organ, and sang the parts arranged for the *chorus* in the festal ode prepared for the Married People's Festival in Salem. The Married Choir here consists of fourteen couples; Br. Schaub, Jr. is absent in Bethlehem. Austs are not included in the fourteen.

Sept. 21. A company of cavalry was here for a few hours on their way to Richmond.

Sept. 28. Br. Richter is very ill, and does not think he will recover, so he made his Will and it was witnessed.

Sept. 29. Michaelmas. Br. Pfeil came from Salem to wait on Br. Richter. In the evening meeting there was an address on the service of the holy angels.

Sept. 30. The farmers began planting winter grain.

In the evening a company of sixty men arrived, half of them Virginia cavalry. They had to be cared for over night, taking supper at the tavern. There was much confusion in the town, so that we could have no prayer-meeting, but it was of the Lord's ordering, for they had expected to be in Salem for the night.

Oct. 1. Sunday. At the usual time the church litany was prayed, and many of the soldiers listened attentively. Many of our neighbors attended the preaching.

Oct. 2. This morning Br. and Sr. Reichel and Sr. Graff came from Salem. About one o'clock the congregation, including the children, had a blessed lovefeast with Br. and Sr. Reichel, who will soon set out on their journey toward Pennsylvania. * * * At the close, he and his dear wife went about the Saal, taking personal leave of the members, and many tears were shed. * * * Soon after four o'clock they returned to Salem. About five o'clock our dear Br. Richter passed into the arms of Jesus. During the morning Br. Reichel and several other Brethren had visited him, and the former held a home-going liturgy for him, in which the sick man joined; then Br. Reichel laid his hand upon his head and blessed him for his departure, and pronounced the Benediction. * * * Arrangements were made at once for sending a messenger to Salem, namely Br. Mücke, and he will order the coffin and shroud and whatever else may be needed.

Oct. 3. Many Brethren came from Salem, including Prezel and Petersen and the trombonists. At two o'clock the congregation assembled in the Saal for the funeral of Br. Johannes Richter. After this service the body was taken to God's Acre and buried during the usual liturgy. After the trombonists and bearers had eaten something they returned home.

Oct. 4. We hear that on the Atkin a party of Tories has fallen on the people, but only on those who had formerly done the same to them.

Oct. 6. Col. Armstrong was here, returning from the camp.

Oct. 9. Br. Meinung came from Salem to close the accounts for last month.

Oct. 12. On account of the rain the sowing of winter grain was interrupted. A company of Whigs[10] had to be fed here. They went on toward the Shallow Ford, and between Holder's and Volk's they met a strong company of Tories. The Whigs refused to surrender, and there was a hand-to-hand fight, in which the Tories killed one or two, and took several prisoners. Many of the Tories came here during the night to get bread to eat, but were very mannerly; they were in this neighborhood to see after the Whigs.

Oct. 13. Today was quite peaceful and quiet, and no one was here from either party. At twilight a sermon of Br. Gregor's was read. At half past eight we sang: "Oh Head so full of bruises."

Oct. 14. The orchard behind the still-house was planted in winter wheat. Toward evening Captain Lapp came with his company. They demanded food for themselves and their horses, and finally remained over night, turning their horses into the big meadow. They behaved in an orderly and modest fashion.

Oct. 15. Sunday. It began to rain last night and continued all day. We were prevented from holding our morning service by the

---

[10] Br. Lorenz calls them "eine Companie Wicks." In the *Extract der Diarii der Gemeiner in der Wachau* Bishop Graff writes: "In these days Bethabara was much disturbed, for the two parties, *Whigs* and *Tories*, moved against each other, and first one and then the other came to that town, without committing excesses, although provisions had to be furnished. Finally the Tories were defeated on the Atkin, and were scattered. On both sides some were killed or wounded, from the latter 1 and from the Whig party 4 were taken to Bethania, where Br. Bonn had to take charge of them."

arrival of several companies of soldiers, who were so cold and wet that arrangements had to be made to get them under shelter, and where they could have fire. At the same time cattle had to be killed and bread baked for them. Toward evening Colonel Paisly arrived with four hundred infantry. They were in the same condition as the others, cold, wet and hungry. Some asked to be taken into the houses, but most of them camped around the Gemein Haus, and built fires at which to dry themselves. During the night they were quiet and still.

Oct. 16. Nearly six hundred men were asking bread and meat from us, and there was also stealing or demanding a tithe of swine, chickens, sheep, ducks, and geese, and the spring-house was emptied of all the milk and the small amount of butter. The same thing happened to the apples stored in the old store building.

Oct. 17. Colonel Armstrong arrived with about 150 Virginians; but now all marched away. Four hundred men went by way of Salem, the others to the Shallow Ford or to Richmond. How glad and thankful we were to see them go, in view of the damage they had done to our garden, sheds, and indeed everywhere; and in the evening meeting we returned our thanks to our dear Lord.

Oct. 18. There was cleaning in all the houses, and wood was hauled, for they had burned more than ten cords at the Gemein Haus and at Rose's. Br. Bonn and his assistant, Joseph Dixon, came late from the Atkin, where they had attended the wounded.

Oct. 19. Br. Bonn had brought word that the wounded and the entire company would come here, so the necessary provisions were prepared; but in the afternoon we heard that they had gone to Bethania, and Br. Bonn was called thither. Late in the evening he returned and went to Salem. From Bethania came soldiers for the meat prepared for them here,—it was an ox which had been left by the others. We were very glad and thankful that they did not come here.

Oct. 20. Several soldiers were here, and also Colonel Lanier, who offered to give us money for the Tickets on public account, taking a receipt from us. The soldiers in Bethania came for bread.

Oct. 21. Corn was hauled, which during the last days had been gathered and shocked on the fields. We sent Br. Stöhr to Colonel Lanier, who had offered us money for what we had furnished on public account; he returned in the evening, having received some money.

Oct. 22. Sunday. At the usual time we began our Unity Day, with three reading meetings in the morning. In the afternoon the children had their short service, and there was a reading meeting. As we heard that more than six hundred prisoners,[11] with a strong guard, were on their way hither, the corn on the large meadow field was hauled in, so that their camp could be made there. Toward evening an officer and about thirty cavalrymen appeared and spent the night.

Oct. 23. This morning the prisoners came,[12] between five and six hundred men including their guards. They camped on the north side of the big meadow. Now there was need of bread, but little could be done in the bakery because of the press, so we asked for a guard, which was given. Our officers asked for a house for the English officers who were prisoners, and secured the old store building. As no cattle came in we had to let them have one of ours. There was much disturbance in the town, so we sent to Salem and asked for three Brethren to help us, who also came. Already on Sunday Br. Mücke had written to Br. Vogler, and he came also.

Oct. 24. Today all our meal had been used. The officers took our wagons and horses and sent them to Salem with several of the cavalry to bring meal. Arrangements were also made to shell the corn they had here and to take it to the mill. As no cattle had been brought we again had to furnish three of ours. Many of the neighbors came, bringing apples, bread, and several oxen. One of the English officers secured permission from Colonel Campbell to have a room to himself, and we had to let him have one in Kühnast's house.

Oct. 25. Our circumstances were the same as yesterday. In providing for the people who are here we had no meal left for ourselves, and could not bake. Some cattle was brought in, but three of the oxen were ours. We asked to have a guard set at our stable, so that none should be taken out, for Major Winston had threatened that if one was taken he would set the stable on fire. Many of our neighbors arrived to take the place of the militia already here, and to conduct the prisoners further.

Oct. 26. Our wagons and horses must go, as they did yesterday, to bring corn. The soldiers drove in some of our cattle, but as they did not shut them up they went off again. Br. Kapp came to ask for a guard, as the soldiers were taking meal without orders, and a guard was sent. As the families in town had no more bread the Colonels were asked that we might send some of our corn to be ground at the mill,

---

[11] Taken at King's Mountain.

[12] *Extract der Diarii, etc.* "More than 200 Tories and about 40 English officers and privates, who had been captured in an action on the Heads of the Catawba River." "The [Tory] prisoners were placed like cattle in a small, fenced-off space, where they spent nineteen days and nights, and nearly starved. The English soldiers were lodged in an empty house, and the English officers in other family houses. As no arrangements had been made for caring for so many men the burden fell on Bethabara, with only a little help from outside."

which was allowed. Toward evening Br. Herbst came to get the hides from the cattle slaughtered here.

Friday and Saturday *the 27th* and *28th,* our circumstances remained the same, except that it was a little more quiet in the town. In addition to hauling corn and going to the mill for meal, our wagons were able to bring in a few loads of our own corn. Br. Marshall came from Salem, and visited all the families in their homes, to their comfort and joy. He went back to Salem in the evening, accompanied by Br. Bonn and Oesterlein.

Oct. 29. Sunday. As there was to be preaching at the camp we had our service at half past nine. Some of the English officers and soldiers were attentive listeners. In the afternoon there was preaching in the woods between Ranke's and the big meadow. A great crowd of soldiers had gathered, and most of our Brethren; it was estimated that about two thousand were present, to whom Mr. Hill preached earnestly on the 63rd chapter of Isaiah.[13] After the service the soldiers moved their camp into the woods behind the ten-acre field. Toward evening it was more quiet, as many people went home.

Oct. 30. This morning there was much disturbance in the town, partly because many militiamen were coming in to relieve the others, and partly because a man was to be hanged. The poor sinner was led to the gallows, and drawn up, but then was pardoned. Our team, with Johann Samuel, was sent to the Town Fork to get cider. It was reported that the soldiers were planning to rob the houses, and we asked Colonel Armstrong about it, and he said we need not fear that.

Oct. 31. It was as disturbed as the other days, for there are probably more than a thousand men here and in the camp. We thank our Father in heaven that He has protected us so far from all evil, Amen.

Nov. 1. Br. Ernst, who went to Conference in Salem, stopped both going and returning. Br. Lorenz had to remain at home on account of conditions here.

As Colonel Armstrong returned, Colonel Cleveland decided to leave with his men, and certain prisoners were released. Militia from this county relieved the others, who were here in camp. The result was that the town was more quiet this evening.

Nov. 4. Br. Schaub, Jr. returned unexpectedly from his trip to Pennsylvania. Major Riht [Reed] came with orders concerning the prisoners; it is said they are to be taken to Virginia. As no cattle

---

[13] *Extract der Diarii, etc.* "In Bethabara, near the camp of the prisoners, a Baptist minister held a long thanksgiving service for the victory over the Tories, taking the 63rd chapter of Isaiah for his text. The prisoners were forced to attend this service, and many persons from the neighborhood were present."

had been brought in, the camp lacked meat and had to be content with corn.

Nov. 5. Last night hens, pumpkins and brandy were stolen. Colonel Armstrong came again, and also many people, some of whom went home while others remained in the camp.

Nov. 6. This morning we heard that last night three lower-rank English officers and a Tory captain ran away. Captain de Baas, who is here, notified Colonel Armstrong during the night, and he immediately sent cavalry after them.

Br. Meinung came to look after the accounts, but there was no time for that. In the twilight we ventured to have a service, and one of Br. Gregor's sermons was read.

Nov. 7. This morning a man was brought from the camp; he had been shot in the body through the carelessness of another man, and appeared to be in a serious condition. The man, whose name was Schmidt, was laid in the little school-house, and the English officer had to move out. Preparations were made for leaving; it was said that all the prisoners from this province who were fit for military duty had enlisted, so only the English soldiers were left, and the Militia from South Carolina, who were counted as belonging to the royal army. A company of sixty cavalry arrived this evening and remained in the tavern over night.

Nov. 8. Colonel Armstrong went to Richmond. There was much disturbance in the town because of the cavalry here. We heard that the troops would leave tomorrow, which was announced to the English officers, and it is said they will go to the lead mines. The English are much perturbed. Br. Bonn and his assistant Dixon came to see the wounded man and to bandage him, the English doctor also being present. It was suspected that the English soldiers were planning to escape, and their captain notified the officer in command, who ordered a watch set before the Brothers House.

Nov. 9. This morning about twenty English soldiers disappeared, in spite of the watch set before the Brothers House. At noon all our houses were searched, but none of them were found hidden there. The cavalry sent to look for them soon returned. In the afternoon the English officers were ordered out, and after standing in front of the tavern for two hours they were joined by the Tory officers from the camp and those who did not wish to enlist. All went as far as Ranke's, where they spent the night, though the English officers were permitted to come back and sleep in their former lodgings. The one hundred and forty Tories of the South Carolina militia who had enlisted were released, and spent the night here in the town, building many fires on the Square so that they could bake and cook. The poor men had a pitiful appearance, most of them having no clothes on their bodies. There could be no church service this evening.

Nov. 10. Br. Bonn came to change the bandages on the wounded man, but there is no hope of his recovery. It gave us much pleasure to see the soldiers march away, though we were very sorry for the poor men, who are in great need. They have been in and near Bethabara for nineteen days. They went by way of Salem toward Salisbury, first the South Carolina Tories who have enlisted, then the English soldiers, and finally the South Carolina Tories who were officers and still prisoners; they were taken to Hillsborough under guard of the local militia, both infantry and cavalry. Finally several sick men were taken in a wagon to Salisbury. We thanked the dear Saviour, Who has helped us through these trying times, and has protected us from all harm.

In the evening the Brethren belonging to the Committee met. Br. Blum had been appointed to take Br. Richter's place; he was called, informed that he was to be a member of the Committee and was greeted with kisses by the other members. While we were still in session, the man who has been waiting on Wilhelm Schmidt, the wounded soldier, came to announce that he had died, and asked for our assistance, which will be given as far as possible.

Nov. 11. Every one was busy clearing out and cleaning up inside and outside the houses. Toward evening the man who died here yesterday was buried on the Parish graveyard. A near relative had said he would be glad to see the man receive a Christian burial, so Br. Lorenz and some of the Brethren went, several English hymns were sung, and the Lord's Prayer recited.

Nov. 13. Festival of the Chief Elder. At nine in the morning the congregation, including the older children, met in the Saal for the festal morning prayers. * * * Praise, honor and might be to our Lord for this blessed and peaceful day.

Nov. 17. The farmers finished sowing winter wheat. Several of the English soldiers came from Salem to cut wood for us.

Nov. 20. The Committee met. Br. Schaub, Jr. will collect the money for the Nachrichten. He, Br. Richter and Blum will make up the Saal and book accounts for the past year. We discussed making a horn from a sea-shell, as the soldiers took ours. A company of soldiers spent the night here, on their way to the chief camp.

Nov. 21. It was rainy, so little could be done except swingle hemp. The soldiers who were here over night went toward the Shallow Ford.

Nov. 23. Br. Marshall was here all day. It was suggested that the old store building might be the best place if it was decided to establish here a Continental store of corn or meal or meat. Br. Schaub may set up his dye kettle in a room in the old Brothers House.

Nov. 24. Today and yesterday several bushels of rye were sown.

Nov. 26. Sunday. In the reading meeting the subject was the diary of the journey of Br. Grube[14] and his party from Lititz to the Indian land on the Muskingum, his stay in the three congregations, and his return with Br. Schebosch to Lititz.

Nov. 27. The Committee met. There was a discussion concerning lovefeasts, as everything is so high. It was suggested that we might use herb tea, but it was decided that if it was possible to get good tea we would continue to use that.

Nov. 30. Br. and Sr. Marshall spoke with all the Brethren and Sisters in preparation for the Holy Communion,—that is he spoke with the Brethren and she with the Sisters.

Dec. 3. Advent Sunday. At ten o'clock there was preaching, on the Incarnation of our Lord. * * * The evening meeting opened with the singing of the Hosannah chorus.

Dec. 5 and 6. Rye was threshed in the shed, and fire-wood was hauled.

Dec. 7. Colonel Armstrong came to put in order the Tickets which we received recently, but was hindered by the arrival of orders to release the militia.

Dec. 8. In addition to the usual work several large oxen were driven into the stable.

Dec. 10. Sunday. In the meeting at three o'clock, Johannes Samuel and Maria were married in the name of the Holy Trinity, and the blessing of the Lord was laid upon them.

Dec. 11. The Committee met. It was suggested that a Congregation Account should be opened for the providing of wine for Communion, paying for the Nachrichten, for books, and for the expenses of the Saal. All the Brethren were in favor of this, and it will be laid before Congregation Council. The suggestion is that each Brother shall pay 6d and each Sister 3d.

Dec. 12. Br. Schaub has made an indigo dyeing, and it seems to be good.

Dec. 13. The negro Sister, Maria, will take charge of the kitchen.

---

[14] Rev. Bernhard Adam Grube was the first minister of Bethabara, coming in November, 1753.

Dec. 14. The barley raised this year was stored in the sheds; there are seventy bushels. Now wheat threshing will begin.

Dec. 15. It rained nearly all day, so hemp was swingled for spinning. Our Saal was whitewashed and scoured.

Dec. 17. There was a lovefeast for the Saal diener and dienerinnen, those who blow the horns, and the Brethren of the Committee.

Dec. 19. Wheat was threshed; it is very full of weavils.

Dec. 20. For several days the Brethren have been in the woods looking for our cattle, but have not found them.

Dec. 21. Mr. Motsinger brought a wagon load of turnips for sale at 13d a bushel.

Dec. 23. Our wagon went to Mr. Hill, eight miles from here, for corn which Br. Schaub got for his horse.

Dec. 24. Our children had a lovefeast in the evening, in remembrance of the Holy Christ-child. Sweet and appropriate hymns were sung, then each child received a verse and a candle, and went happily homeward. For the same purpose the adult congregation gathered at eight o'clock, and sang of the birth of the Infant Jesus in old and new hymns.

Dec. 25. *Christmas Day.* The French horns played early in the morning. At ten o'clock was preaching on the gospel for the day. * * * In the evening the Hymn of Praise to the Son was sung. The weather was very stormy and cold.

Dec. 26. *Second Christmas Day.* It was Unity Day. * * * The accounts of the Saal Expenses for the year were presented to the Brethren and Sisters. The amount was £6: 6: 1, and it was decided that each Brother should pay 5sh. and each Sister 2: 6d. Our negroes went to Salem, where the negro Sambo was baptised into the death of Jesus, receiving the new name Abraham.

Dec. 27. Firewood and rails were made and brought in.

Dec. 29. The men who were driving an ox into the slaughter-house today had a narrow escape, especially one Brother who received two wounds on the head. He was glad to get off with that, for the ox was wild and nearly dragged them all away.

Dec. 30. About four o'clock one hundred and forty soldiers came from James River in Virginia, and camped between Stauber's farm and Bethabara. They made no disturbance, though some of the Brethren remained at home during the Communion.

Dec. 31. *Sunday.* The soldiers asked for preaching, which was held at half past ten. English hymns were sung, the Lord's Prayer was offered in English, the Gospel for the day was read, and comments were made upon it. In the afternoon the children had a prayer meeting for the close of the year. In the congregation meeting the Bethlehem diary for August, September and October, was read. In the evening at eight the adult congregation met, and listened to several memorabilia of German congregations for the year 1778. At ten o'clock the congregation had a lovefeast. Soon after eleven o'clock the congregation returned to the Saal, when the memorabilia of the congregations in Wachovia were read and heard with thankful hearts. As the New Year was blown in [by the French horns] we fell upon our knees, and thanked our dear Lord for all His grace and love which He has accorded to us and to all His people. We asked the continuance of His mercy, and the gift of honorable peace for this land. The soldiers made not the slightest disturbance. Amen, Hallelujah!

Memorabilia of Bethania, 1780.

[Personal items at the end are omitted.]

One of the outstanding events of this year, and one that will never be forgotten, took place on Jan. 2nd and 3rd, when our dear Br. Marshall read to us the Results of the Synod of the Unity, held in Barby in 1775. The emotion and tears of the Brethren and Sisters proved the deep impression made on every heart by the matter presented, and by the rulings of our dear Lord, which touched each one in his own circumstance. On Jan. 16th and 17th our dear Br. and Sr. Marshall spoke with each of the congregation separately, and this was a true blessing for each soul. On April 2nd, when the Older Girls here celebrated their Festival, the Brn. and Srs. Marshall and Graff were present, and Br. Marshall read the Results for the second time, the resident and the outside members being hearers. The Rules and Regulations were signed with one accord by the house-fathers of Bethania, and the local Committee was announced, which had been appointed by the Lot and was authorized to see that the Rules were observed.

We also have vivid recollections of the blessed Visitation of our dear Br. Reichel, who with his dear wife and Br. and Sr. Nilson reached Salem on June 16th, and visited here on the 25th of that month, to the joy of all, accompanied by Br. and Sr. Marshall. The unexpected home-going of our dear Br. Nilson, on the 30th of June, disturbed in no small degree the pleasure which all had felt over the coming of these Brethren; and the severe illness which overtook our dear Br. Reichel soon after increased our distress, which, thank God, was relieved by his rapid recovery. We remember thankfully the Visitation here, which took place on August 8th, 9th and 10th, when Br. and Sr. Reichel spoke with all the residents of this town, and those who are associated with us; they held many public and private meetings, with much grace and deep impression on each heart. This congregation will never forget their farewell, which took place here on Sept. 17th and 18th, when Br. and Sr. Reichel came, accompanied by Br. and Sr. Marshall.

Further we remember the great grace which we enjoyed, in that we might partake of the Sacrament fourteen times, undisturbed, to the strengthening of body and soul. Our dear Lord has accompanied each special and general Festival day with a sense of His presence, and has laid a special blessing upon it. Our hearts have found precious sustenance in the sermons from the Wochen, and in the accounts in the Nachrichten of the spread of the Gospel in Christian and in heathen lands. God the Holy Ghost has laid His blessing upon the words of the Brethren who have proclaimed the Atonement of Jesus, and many hearts have been convinced that only through the wounds of Jesus can we secure pardon for all sins and be redeemed. During this year the work of the Holy Ghost among our young people has been particularly evident, so that some have begun to be distressed about their cold, dead hearts, and to weep before the Lord; it is to be hoped that this work of grace by the Holy Ghost will continue and become general.

In these distressing and anxious times,—times such as this land had never heretofore seen,—our heavenly Father has helped us wonderfully, in spite of the fact that both the parties, which are arrayed against each other in this province, have passed through our town in large numbers, and have demanded provisions for men and horses, often paying but poorly for them. The most encouraging feature was that through the blessing of God we had a very large fruit crop, which could give some help toward the large amount of food required. Most farmers had a fairly good harvest of winter and summer grain, and we thankfully say that in the later summer there were few or no weavils to be seen, and so it was not necessary to thresh the wheat immediately, as we have done in other years, and which no one could have done this year on account of the much public hauling and other war burdens. Our great desire and prayer is that our heavenly Father will bring this ruinous war to an end early in the new year, and turn the hearts of men toward peace, and that it may not be necessary to use hunger and pestilence to accomplish this purpose. The greatest need is that the highly dangerous party spirit, which has already been injurious to some, may be put out of all hearts as inconsistent with brotherly love; especially may all double-dealing, envy, quarreling and anger be put away, of which the end is nothing but damage to a man's soul.

Bethania Diary, 1780.

[Extracts of public interest are translated, the Memorabilia having
given a sufficient outline of the Church services.]

Jan. 2. It snowed heavily, and there were no strangers in town.

Jan. 6. Br. Fischer returned with the wagon from New Bern.

Jan. 10. Andreas Volck came for me, and I rode with him to the
home of Heinrich Demuth, where I baptised Demuth's twins, George
and Andreas, and little Anna Catharina Erny.

Jan. 20. A neighbor by the name of Geiger asked baptism for his
child.

Jan. 23. The local communicant Brethren met and brought in their
votes for a new Committee.

Feb. 6. The house-fathers met. The money which has been contributed to help the poorer Brethren pay their taxes amounted to
£52 : 4:—Congress money, or £2 : 3 : 6 hard money. Three Brethren
were appointed to distribute it.

Feb. 12. The street in town is in such bad condition that the evening meetings had to be dropped this week.

March 3. Several passed on their way to Muster. We heard later
that no one volunteered.

March 9. There was General Muster in Richmond. In comparison
with other times hardly one-tenth as many passed on their way
thither.

March 16. In the house of George Hauser, Sr., Samuel Strub and
Susanna Stolz were married by George Hauser, Jr.

March 26. On Easter morning we prayed the Easter liturgy on
the Hutberg.[15] There was preaching at ten o'clock.

March 27. Peach blossoms are beginning to open.

April 2. Br. Marshall read the fair copy of the *Rules and Regulations*[16] for this congregation, which were signed by all house-fathers
resident in the town. It was announced that the Committee would
consist of the four Brn. Grabs, Ranke, Schor and Peter Hauser.

April 9. Banns were published for three couples,—Br. Holland
and Sr. M. Strub, Br. Christ and Sr. Oesterlein, of Salem, W. Grabs
of this place and Barbara Pfaff of Friedberg. The Rules and Regulations which were signed here eight days ago were read to the young
people, and they listened with interest.

---

[15] The Graveyard-hill. The name is copied from Herrnhut, Germany, where the Moravians
     laid out their graveyard on top of a hill bearing that name.

[16] Printed in full in Part I of this volume.

April 13. Br. Michael Hauser came with a report that an order had been received from Commissary Henderson that a wagon from here should bring the meat killed in Bethabara to Richmond at once. The Committee met to discuss the matter, and Br. Ranke offered to drive if a wagon and team were furnished, which was done.

April 16. Wilhelm Grabs and Barbara Pfaff were called out for the second and third times after the preaching.

April 21. Yesterday Wilhelm Grabs was married to Barbara Pfaff in her father's house in Friedberg, by Michael Hauser [J. P.]. He returned this evening, bringing her and her father.

April 22. This morning thirty horsemen came from Guilford County. Most of them came into the Gemein Haus, to see the church and the organ; the latter was played for them which pleased them, and they said that in all their lives they had heard nothing like it. In the afternoon they went on to Richmond.

May 2. This morning Adam Schumacher came for the Certificate that the Banns had been published for his marriage. At noon he was married to Anna Margaretha Hauser by George Hauser, Jr. [J. P.].

May 6. Last night the wolves killed six sheep; we heard later that it was a she-wolf with four young ones.

May 26. We hear that Mr. Cummings has returned from the Assembly and that he has brought several copies of the Militia Act. The threats therein contained, of complete ruin for those who are drafted and will not go, have brought consternation to many.

June 3. Word came from Richmond that sixteen men have been drafted from Schmidt's company, and that four horses are to be pressed. Various reports confirm the news that the advance guard of the English is not far from Salisbury.

June 12. Some of our neighbors passed this morning on their way to muster. Every third man has been called out, and has received orders to be ready to march at the first signal.

June 15. George Hauser, Sr., returned from Pennsylvania this afternoon.

June 17. Captain Schmidt came to ask for the baptism of his infant son.

June 22. A report has been received that about 2,700 men who favor the king are coming to this neighborhood from lower down on the Atkin, and the neighbors are much alarmed.

June 25. Soon after ten o'clock Br. Reichel preached. The Saal was packed with attentive hearers, in spite of the fact that many of the neighbors have been called to the Atkin to repel the expected attack.

June 26. During this week many have marched past, some mounted, some on foot. Most of them had had nothing to eat for twenty-four hours or more, and the town gathered enough together that all might be fed.

June 29. I was in Bethabara. Going and coming the road was full of soldiers, on horseback and on foot. They were well-behaved and friendly.

June 30. This morning various persons were much alarmed to find that six horses were missing, some having been in the stable and some not, and men went out at once to look for them. About the same time a report came that fifty men would arrive presently. The Committee was called together, and it was decided that for the future one man and one older boy should watch each night. It was decided further that when soldiers came and must be fed they should be divided among the houses according to their number and the means of the families, and that they should be given to eat whatever the family happened to have ready. The men and older boys were at once notified, and accepted the plans as necessary. Tonight the watch was kept for the first time, and according to agreement the bell was rung at dawn, as a sign that the watchmen were going to rest.

July 5. Br. Reitz spent the night here, on his way to look for the horses which Winston's company pressed in Salem.

July 8. The Brethren who own wagons and horses were together to agree how a wagon and four horses could be supplied if one was pressed.

July 11. The wagon mentioned on the 8th set out for Salisbury today.

July 15. A wagon came on its way to Salisbury. The officer of the guard swore vehemently that he would press a horse, as one of his could go no further, but all the horses were taken out of town during the night, so he had to drive off next day without securing one.

July 18. An Express came from Salem with word that a company of fifty men from Pennsylvania had arrived there, and were making requisition on the neighborhood for a large quantity of meal to be delivered to Baron von Kalb, who is marching across Deep River with 3000 men.

July 19. The Committee met to discuss the requisition. It was decided to notify the country members and the neighbors.

July 20. Michael Hauser, Sr., and George Hauser, Jr., asked for a list according to which the requisition could be divided proportionately according to the means of individuals.

July 21. Michael Hauser, Jr., and Sam Strub were sent among the neighbors to tell each man how much he was expected to furnish. The amount asked was 167 bushels, but pledges fell thirty-five bushels short.

July 23. The Committee met with the house-fathers, and the latter were told that the town must furnish thirty bushels of wheat, apportioned so that some should give 2½ bu., some 2 bu., some 1½ bu., and one 1 bu.

July 26. Philipp Schaus came with request that I would come to baptise his infant daughter, and also to bury his son Joseph, who passed out of time yesterday. He recently returned sick from the camp at Salisbury. I rode with him to his house, where his friends and neighbors had assembled. After an address the little daughter was baptised with the name Salome. The funeral followed immediately.

Aug. 12. Several women passed. Their husbands joined those in favor of the king, and now the women have been driven from their farms and told to go to their husbands. They were helped to food and drink, so that they could continue their journey.

Aug. 19. Br. Triebel spent the night with us. He brought word that the Americans under General Rutherford and General Gates have been completely defeated by the English.

Aug. 22. The two Armstrongs came from the south, and confirmed the report that last week the Americans were defeated by the English and scattered. This week all were busy drying and crushing peaches and apples.

Aug. 25. During these days many have passed, going to oppose the English. None of our neighbors have volunteered for this. This afternoon three soldiers, coming from the defeated army in the south, made a disturbance in the lower town because they could not get as much cider as they wanted. When Colonel Armstrong and Colonel Sheppard arrived they subsided.

Aug. 27. In the meeting of the Committee, George Hauser, Jr., was notified that he had permission to remain in the town as a resident, and he signed the Rules and Regulations.

Aug. 29. Several hundred mounted men arrived from Virginia, but soon rode on to Bethabara.

Aug. 30. The riding back and forth continues. Two large parties have passed through the town, going to seek men who are hiding in the woods.

Sept. 6. Many of the Virginians who are camping at Bethabara have been here these days, behaving passably well.

Sept. 9. Captain Campbell's company brought Geyer Wright as a prisoner, and this evening he was cruelly treated,[17] though several of the men here tried repeatedly to intercede for him.

Sept. 10. As there was much disorder in the town, and we heard that all the soldiers wanted to come into the Saal, the Communion liturgy was omitted, and instead the litany was prayed, and Br. Friedrich Peter preached on the Epistle for the day. In the evening we heard that Geyer Wright had escaped from his guards.

Sept. 11. Men passed on their way to the muster place. In the evening we heard that Jacob Stolz and Joseph Hauser were drafted.

Sept. 18. The night was disturbed by the passing of militia, for toward evening it was reported that a party of those in favor of the king were approaching this neighborhood.

Oct. 1. Yesterday and today eight wagons and many horses and much cattle have passed, fleeing from the English.

Oct. 3. It was reported from Richmond that a party had been at William Sheppard's, and though they did no more damage than to take his two stallions and the arms they could find in his house, it warned us that we might expect the same. In a meeting of the House-fathers it was therefore resolved that during these perilous times two men should be on guard each night in the upper town and two in the lower, and this was begun tonight.

Oct. 8. This evening it was reported that a party of more than a hundred of those in favor of the king had been in Richmond. They came to take back the things of which they had been robbed, and injured no one, except that John Kraus was wounded.

Oct. 9. Captain Sheppard's company came in this morning, but left again in the afternoon.

Oct. 10. Various men were here from neighboring districts, and had to be supplied with food for men and horses. At midnight another large party arrived.

Oct. 11. This morning George Aust was brought in as a prisoner, but was left here until further orders. At noon they[18] left again, in order to reach the home of Gideon Wright on the Atkin today.

---

[17] The *Extract der Diarii* says he was severely whipped.
[18] They were Tories, see following entry in the diary.

Oct. 12. Before dawn Colonel Gideon Wright and about a hundred men arrived, and inquired whether any Liberty Men were here. They were assured that at the present moment none could be found here. They remained on their horses, and were served there, and those who wished received bread, and then they set off toward Bethabara without doing anything else. It can be considered a direct act of Providence that the last of the Liberty Men set out scarcely an hour earlier, for the town has been full of them since Monday. Before midnight another company of more than a hundred passed, also for the king.

Oct. 13. At seven o'clock in the morning the latter company returned, having failed to find the former. A little later sixteen horsemen arrived; they were very wild and threatened that this town would be burned to the ground within a few days, because while the first company was passing through the lane leading toward Bethabara two guns had been fired at them. They were assured that no one from our town had done this, and that it was probably the act of spies, whom they had not seen. They took a horse and a musket away with them.

Oct. 14. The town was quiet, except that in town and in the woods several were seen who might have been spies.

Oct. 16. More than two hundred Liberty Men were in Salem, and more than six hundred in Bethabara, and they behaved badly enough. Yesterday and today a report has been current that in two places those in favor of the king have been completely defeated, and have been scattered.

Oct. 17. We visited several of our country members. Everywhere it was said that the woods were full of Liberty Men on horse-back, looking for Tories, but we saw none until we were nearly home.

Oct. 19. A Major arrived with five wounded and something over forty men, of whom half were dismissed next day. The wounded were lodged in Michael Hauser's old house, and Br. Bonn and Dixon came toward evening to bandage their wounds.

Oct. 20. The soldiers stationed here asked for a service, so a sing-stunde was held.

Oct. 21. Most of the soldiers departed, leaving eight to wait on the wounded men.

Oct. 23. It was reported that five hundred prisoners were coming, accompanied by a guard equally large.

Oct. 24. From all sides come reports of the bad behaviour of the Liberty Men, especially those from Wilkes County. Br. Bonn, who had come to dress the wounds of the men here, remained over night.

Oct. 26. Joseph Dixon came to attend the wounded men.

Oct. 27. Joseph Holder and his family passed on their way to Schemel's farm. The Liberty soldiers have taken everything from them, and beat him and his wife.

Oct. 28. Br. Bonn attended the wounded.

Oct. 29. Some went from here to Bethabara, where Mr. Hill preached in English to the prisoners.

Oct. 30. Joseph Dixon came to attend the wounded. Four of the English prisoners were here, but did not stay long.

Nov. 1. Cleveland's men were dismissed in Bethabara, and passed on their way home. They were very wild here, but the wounded Captain Parris brought them to order, and ordered them to go on, which they did.

Nov. 2. Br. Bonn and Joseph Dixon came to the wounded. Several of the English prisoners came to see the town.

Nov. 10. Joseph Dixon came to look after the wounded.

Nov. 11. During this week many of the Tories have passed, having been released.

Nov. 14. Five wagons set out for Salem and New Bern, three going for Br. Bagge and two for Mr. Cummings.

Nov. 17. Br. Bonn came to look after the wounded. The court which opened in Richmond the beginning of this week has already ended; no lawyers attended.

Nov. 23. Several discharged soldiers came, and behaved so badly that one of the soldiers stationed here quieted him with blows.

Nov. 25. The Brethren handed in their accounts of expenses for the wounded and the soldiers in attendance on them.

Nov. 26. There was a conference with the local and country housefathers about the school. Several of the latter said that if it should be a cold winter they feared they could not send their children to school for lack of clothes. They were told that as soon as possible the day school would be begun for the little boys and little girls together. The evening school for the older boys will begin tomorrow evening.

Nov. 27. Eight boys came to the evening school.

Dec. 4. Br. Joseph Dixon came to dress the wounds of the older Allen.

Dec. 5. Three of our young men rode to the fulling-mill. They had hardly arrived when one of them, Michael Hauser, Jr., was attacked by an Irishman, who shot at him and threatened to bind him. There was another Irishman with the first, who behaved better. The man of the house advised our young men to leave at once, as there were more of the same sort in the neighborhood, and they followed his advice.

Dec. 7. Mr. Allen visited us this morning for the first and last time since he has been here under treatment. In leaving he expressed regrets that he had not been to see us more often. Next day he left for home in a wagon brought by one of his sons.

Dec. 10. Daniel Wolf came with his brother-in-law Elkanah Lewis, and his mother, and brought his infant daughter, Elisabeth, for baptism.

Dec. 11. Some of our neighbors passed on their way to muster. The object was to secure volunteers from Captain Binckely's company for service against the English, but no one came forward.

Memorabilia of the Congregation and Society of Friedberg, 1780.

[Personal statistics omitted.]

We close the past year with thankful hearts for our dear Lord, Who through His great mercy has given us grace and granted us many good things for our inner and for our material life. It is to be noted, especially, that the doctrine of the Atonement of Jesus Christ has been used by the Holy Spirit to touch many hearts, and to awaken in them a longing for salvation, so that they longed even unto tears for grace and the forgiveness of their sins. Their longing to come into communion with Him and with His members has not been denied by the dear Saviour.

The Gemein Nachrichten were for us a source of blessing and upbuilding. The nearness of the Saviour was powerfully felt in the Holy Communion, which we held seven times during the year. According to His promise the Saviour has caused His presence to be felt in the Sunday and Festal Day services, especially those days on which we had visits from Br. and Sr. Marshall, Br. and Sr. Graff, and the leaders of the Brothers and Sisters Choirs. We especially remember the visit of our dear Br. and Sr. Reichel, accompanied by Br. and Sr. Marshall, in August, a visit upon which our dear Lord laid a great blessing. Doctrinal instruction of the young people was begun this fall. Recently we have reread the Results of General Synod, which made a fresh impression upon us, and by which each could test his own manner of living, and we must acknowledge with shame that some things have happened among us which were not in accord with the spirit of Christ.

With special thanks to our dear heavenly Father we record that He has cared for our temporal needs, so that all crops turned out well;

and although we were obliged to furnish much cattle, grain and the like [to the army] yet neither man nor beast was forced to suffer want. He has also graciously protected us from all harm, and has shielded those who were in danger.

[The following items are taken from the *Friedberg Diary,* 1780, with interpolations from the *Extract der Diarii der Gemeiner in der Wachau.*]

Jan. 3. In spite of the cold and snow more children came to school than we had expected; they would not permit themselves to be persuaded by their parents to remain at home.

Jan. 14. Peter Frey spoke to us about a night school to which parents might send their grown sons, so that they might learn arithmetic and writing; Pfaff had already suggested the same, and we finally agreed that they might come each afternoon from twelve to three, with which they were content.

Jan. 29. Today the collection for the heathen was gathered, and the box was opened in the presence of the two stewards, Spach and Pfaff, it amounted to 16sh. 9d.

Feb. 6. As we entered the Passion season we prayed that the Saviour, through the Holy Spirit, would give us a new and deep realization of His sufferings. In the reading meeting we listened to the beautiful Memoir of Br. Jonas Nilson, who went home in Bethabara.

[*Extract der Diarii, etc. Feb. 9.* Several Brethren from Friedberg had been summoned to Court in Salisbury, where accusation was made that they had not taken the Affirmation prescribed by the Assembly, and had not given in their taxable property, and were therefore liable for a twelve-fold tax. They were able to give both written and verbal proof to the contrary.]

Feb. 9. The Brethren returned from Court in Salisbury; they gained their point, and will have to pay the tax only three-fold instead of twelve-fold.

Feb. 14. We were notified of the departure of John Müller; during his illness he had asked that he might be buried on our God's Acre, and on *the 16th* the funeral sermon was preached to a large congregation.

Feb. 28. Br. Pfaff notified us that his daughter, Barbara, had promised to marry William Grabs.

March 5. Sunday. In a meeting of the house-fathers and mothers it was decided to buy a Bible and hymnbook for use in the Saal. Agreed also to contribute meal for the lovefeast on the congregation festival, and several offered to bake the buns.

March 9. Heinrich Hauser mentioned that a little daughter had been born, and asked for baptism for her. In talking with him I noticed that the trip to Pennsylvania with Captain Lapp had done him much harm.

March 11. A large number of adults and children gathered for our congregation festival, and toward eleven o'clock we were delighted to welcome Br. and Sr. Marshall, Br. and Sr. Graff, Br. Petersen, and the Single Sister A. Maria Krause, from Salem. Soon after there was a lovefeast for the children. After Br. Petersen had spoken with the single men, and Sr. Krause with the single women, the Society had a lovefeast, and nine persons were received as members thereof.

March 19. Sunday. After the sermon a portion of the story of this [Passion] week was read, and was listened to with attention.

March 26. Sunday. We rejoiced in the resurrection of Jesus Christ. Soon after nine o'clock we prayed the Easter litany on God's Acre, and thought of the two who have gone home,—Lorenz Vogler and John Müller. I thought the service had never been so beautiful, for few strangers were present, and in quiet the peace of God surrounded us, and a consciousness of blessing was apparent. At eleven o'clock there was the festal sermon; and soon thereafter the little son of Johannes Volz was baptised into the death of Jesus.

March 27. There was preaching, and a sermon was read. After the service the stewards presented the accounts for the half year to the house-fathers, mentioning the amount each would have to contribute.

April 2. The communicants had a conference, partly about their children, and the Brn. Martin Ebert, Sr., and Melchoir Fischer, were appointed to supervise them at the school-house. The frost today has somewhat injured the fruit blossoms; the grapes are not hurt.

April 19. Land was measured for George Hartmann and Peter Schneider, near the Middle Fork, at the beaver dam.

April 25. Today we began visiting our people, going first by way of George Hartmann's to John Müller's; she was very glad to see us, and accompanied us part way to Weesner's. Then we went to young Spach's. Finally we came to Spach, Jr.; they were in the fields planting corn, but came to the house at once to welcome us. We spent an hour with them; they lamented the loss of two horses which have been stolen from them, and we comforted them, bidding them to trust God in all things, to make it their first object to know how they stood with Him, and He would help them through with their outward affairs. On our return trip we stopped at Friedrich Boeckel's, but only the children were at home. In the evening we reached home, quite tired out. One can not blame those who live far from the School-house when they do not come to church, especially when they have no horse, though they may have a true hunger for the Word of God.

May 10. We visited the Christian Freys; they went with us part way to Tesch's where we stayed over noon. From there we went to Adam Hartmann's; they are in need of corn, and we advised them to take better care this year to clear the land and to plant at the right time. Their daughter, Ebeling's wife, took us to her farm and showed us what they had done; her husband was not at home, but was working for George Frey, and in return was to have his horse for plowing. We went on to George Frey's, and after talking there for a while we returned home.

May 18. We visited our people on the upper farms. It was a pity that Heinrich Hauser was not at home. Adam Tesches were both busy rolling logs, but came to the house as soon as they saw us. We found the Martin Eberts, Jr., busy in the field, clearing land; the loss of eleven head of cattle has distressed them. We stayed a while at the home of Johannes Höhns; then went to see Marcus Höhns, whose wife is painfully ill. Our return way was by Philipp and Peter Rothrock's. We reached home in the evening, with thanks and praise for the Saviour, and the good hope that He would do more for these souls than we could understand or ask.

May 22. We visited Peter and Johannes Volz; and then were with Valentine Rothrock.

May 27. We celebrated the Festival of the Single Sisters and Older Girls.

June 1. The beginning of this month was much disturbed, for we heard on the 1st that Charlestown had surrendered to the English. A new draft was called, and it was a signal mercy of God that our men were free. Still those who live on the road had much to bear, partly from those passing in flight, partly from the soldiers released on parole in South Carolina. They took a horse out of old Greter's stable, and he was thankful to get it back, though he had to pay $200 to ransom it.

June 8. We were happy to receive one of the printed Text Books sent to Br. Graff, for since the beginning of the war we have had no printed copies.

June 11. We visited George Ebert.

June 16. We received the good news that last evening Br. and Sr. Reichel arrived in Salem.

June 24. In the afternoon we heard a report that the Tories had risen.

June 29. About five o'clock we heard several shots in the neighborhood, which alarmed us. Soon after we learned that near George Hartmann's several soldiers belonging to Heinrich Schmidt's company had wantonly fired at Heinrich Schneider, John Hartmann and George Fischer. The two former quickly reached the woods, but they aimed twice at the latter, and had the gun not missed fire he would have been hit, for according to his story the first time the gun was aimed directly at his breast, by the second time he was into a valley where they could only see his head, and the bullet passed by his ear. The man who did it later expressed his surprise at what had happened, for his gun had never failed him before, and it is easy to see that God protected him, and shielded him from injury or death, to Him alone be the thanks and glory.

July. In the first weeks we visited our people in their fields, busy with the wheat harvest, and we were pleased to see in what an orderly manner everything was being done.

July 20. Several soldiers, Regulars, came into this neighborhood to get grain, and some had to give as much as six or eight bushels. The forethought of our loving heavenly Father, however, gave us a soaking rain, which revived the corn and the parched gardens, and gave us hope that now all would grow well, for which we give thanks.

July 30. This was a disturbed day, partly because of the pressing of horses and wagons, and partly because of a band of robbers lurking somewhere near.

Aug. 21. Br. and Sr. Reichel finished speaking with the Brethren and Sisters. Soon after there was a meeting for the communicants, during which Br. Reichel told them they should become a prayer-band, with a meeting once every four weeks. This was followed by a meeting of the Older Girls; and then the Society had a lovefeast.

August 27. Sunday. We prayed the church litany; which was followed by preaching. The other services had to be given up, for Heinrich Müller and another Captain, with sixteen horsemen, armed, came to the School-house during preaching, and ordered out our neighbor Zimmerman and his son, and that made a disturbance and distracted the minds of the hearers. One of our men wanted to go out and tell them that God had given men six days in which to work, but had sanctified the seventh day, but he was restrained.

[*Extract der Diarii, etc.* In Friedberg a party of militia made a disturbance, for they went to the School-house while Br. Beck was preaching and called out two young men who had been drafted.]

Sept. 2. All the house-fathers of this neighborhood were called to meet at Greter's, and Colonel Armstrong informed each what he was expected to furnish in grain and cattle. Adam Spach was assessed thirty bushels of grain, but was allowed to change to six bushels of grain and an ox.

Sept. 8. Friedrich Daniel Müller's wife announced the birth of a little son to her daughter, Fein's wife, and asked for its baptism, saying that she hoped it would not be refused the child because the father was not at home and could not himself ask for it. I had already heard that Fein was dead and buried, so I made no objection.

Sept. 15. I attended the [Land Arbeiter] Conferenz in Salem. Various important matters were discussed concerning the Country Congregations; for Friedberg it was decided that hereafter the Communions should be held on Saturday evenings, and also that doctrinal instruction should be commenced for the children.

Oct. 13. Although but few children have been attending school the last weeks there were a number present for the doctrinal instruction which was begun today. They are very ignorant, and with little perception, yet several showed that their hearts were touched, and tears came into their eyes, and we may hope that through the grace of the Saviour blessing will come to them through the teachings.

Oct. 19. We visited several of our people. At Friedrich Boeckel's we found no opportunity to speak with them about their souls. Lapp and his men had been there and elsewhere in the neighborhood, and had taken cattle from them, and if any man did not let it go willingly they threatened to use force; any man who had brandy had to give an unfair proportion to the men.

Oct. 21. We visited the upper farms. Heinrich Hauser and his wife were at home. Their farm work goes badly, almost backward, for he does not know whether to sow, because he does not feel safe at home. Johannes Höhns and his wife were very friendly. His experiences recently, when he took meal to the soldiers, have turned him to the Saviour, and he can not be thankful enough that He graciously helped him through, and brought him safely home.

Nov. 18. Christel Frey sent word that forty soldiers had just arrived, and asked that the service be postponed a little, as he wanted to be present. On the other hand Peter Frey and old Greter, who were already here, hurried home, as it was probable that the soldiers would pass their houses. Finally, about two o'clock, we had prayers, and then the Holy Communion.

[*Extract der Diarii, etc. Nov. 27.* Last night a band of robbers tried to break into various houses in the Friedberg settlement. They were driven away and one was captured and turned over to the authorities. In the adjoining settlement of Abbotts Creek a large quantity of stolen goods was found in a hollow tree, and those who could identify their property recovered it.]

Dec. 10. Sunday. There was preaching, and then the Results of the Synod of 1775 were read to the members of the congregation, and to the married members of the Society, for the second time. They were very attentive, and a deep impression was evident.

Dec. 22. Instead of instruction there was a song service for the children, of whom twenty-seven were present. Many recited the verses they had learned; they were attentive and quiet, and full of joy in thinking of the birth of the Christ Child.

Dec. 25. On Christmas Day we had a fair attendance at preaching. This was followed by a happy lovefeast for the children, during which they sang hymns to the dear Little Jesus; and after verses had been given to them they went home, full of childish joy.

[*Extract der Diarii, etc. Dec. 27.* The ministers of the country congregations met in Salem with the Aeltesten Conferenz. Among other things, the Rules and Regulations for the Friedberg congregation were read.]

Dec. 29. We visited Christian Frey. Johannes Schor, the boy whom he has taken, has smallpox; it has broken out well and he is not very sick.

[*Extract der Diarii, etc.* Br. George Hartmann, of Friedberg, had a narrow escape while returning from the mill. His horses shied and ran away; he and two others jumped from the wagon, and he fell against the root of a tree, and was taken up for dead and carried home, but after a while he revived. One horse was killed, having been forced against a tree by the other horse.]

Dec. 31. At noon there was the funeral of the married Sr. A. Maria Schneider. In the evening at eight o'clock there was lovefeast. In the second service the Memorabilia of Salem, Bethania and Hope were read. In the third service the Memorabilia of this congregation was read with thankful hearts, and the year was closed with prayer, all kneeling, and we commended ourselves to the gracious protection of our heavenly Father, and the care and guidance of the Holy Spirit, and so we entered with faith and peace and joy into the new year, hoping for the fulfillment of the Text for this day: "I will not always chide, neither will I keep mine anger for ever."

Memorabilia of Friedland, 1780.

[Personal statistics omitted.]

This little congregation remembers at the close of the year, with thankful hearts, all the grace which the Saviour has vouchsafed to it during the passing months. We mention first, with humble hearts, the three visits made by Br. and Sr. Reichel and Br. and Sr. Marshall, through whom the local Society was formed into a congregation, so that members might not only be Received into the Unity, but the Holy Communion might be celebrated as in other town and country congregations. We also remember thankfully the visits of Br. and Sr. Graff and other Brethren, through whom on each occasion we received a blessing. We still have a vivid recollection of the last visit of Br. and Sr. Graff, on the 18th and 19th of November, when eight persons were Received into the congregation and ten into the Society.

Our dear Br. and Sr. Toego Nissen, who had lived with us for six years, moved to Salem in the beginning of August, and were succeeded by Br. and Sr. Heinzmann.

Our dear Lord has during this year laid a special blessing on the preaching of His Word. He has filled hearts and drawn them to Himself, and has given us to know that we must put our faith in Him alone. In November we began to hold meetings during the week, that is on Wednesdays and Fridays, the service on Wednesday being for Communicants and Received, which have been well attended and conducted with blessing.

Our dear heavenly Father has provided for us, so that in spite of all the supplies demanded of us He has so blessed the remainder that we have not suffered want. Several of our Brethren who had to take to the army wagons loaded with meal He brought safe home, through many hardships and dangers.

[The following paragraphs are from the *Extract der Diarii der Gemeiner in der Wachau.*]

Aug. 6. Br. and Sr. Reichel, Br. and Sr. Marshall, and Br. and Sr. Heinzmann went to Friedland. Br. Reichel preached, and then the Society had a lovefeast during which Br. Reichel presented Br. and Sr. Heinzmann as the future leaders of the congregation, and commended them to the hearty love of the members.

Sept. 3. The Brn. and Srs. Reichel and Marshall went to Friedland and met with six persons who have been Received into the Unity, and several others who have been attending the Communion at Fried-

berg, and with them organized a country congregation. A disturbance
was made by the coming of a party of cavalry, who were calling all the
house-fathers of this section to meet at Mr. Friedrich Müller's, but
as all those present expressed their willingness to meet the demands for
supplies they rode away, so the services could be continued.

Sept. 23. The Brn. and Srs. Reichel and Marshall went to Friedland to hold the first Communion there. After a lovefeast, Br. Reichel
made an address on the Lord's Supper, * * * and then twelve persons,
not counting the Reichels and Marshalls, shared in the Sacrament. A
party of soldiers, who went through this settlement today on errands,
planned to make a disturbance, but it was warded off by the good hand
of God.

Nov. 18. As the Festival of the Chief Elder was to be celebrated
for the first time in the new country congregations, Br. and Sr. Graff
went to Friedland, spoke with the Brethren and Sisters, and held the
Holy Communion.

Hope, 1780.

[There is no regular Memorabilia of Hope congregation preserved,
but the following notes are filed with the Memorabilia of the other
congregations.]

Before Easter Br. and Sr. Fritz moved to the School-house. On
March 28th this house was dedicated by Br. Marshall, in the presence
of other Brethren and Sisters from Salem; it received the name of
Hope. At the same time the Society was organized with about twenty
members.

Br. and Sr. Reichel visited Hope on Aug. 20th, at which time a
country congregation was organized, with the Reception of four persons,
John Padget and Benjamin Chitty and their wives, to whom were added,
on Nov. 18th, Henry Slator and his wife, Margareth Booner, and
Anna, wife of Thomas Padget.

The first Communion was celebrated on Oct. 14th, with six members;
the second on Nov. 18th, with eight members.

On Sept. 13th Br. and Sr. Fritz had a special experience of protection, for during the night a wandering party fell upon them, and took
away their clothes and underclothes, though they finally gave them
back.

Br. Fritz began a school for the children.

On account of the unrest, one family, that of William Barton Peddycoard, returned to Maryland.

[To these notes are added a few paragraphs from the *Extract der
Diarii, etc.*]

Jan. 25. Br. Fritz held the first funeral in our English Settlement. A youth, Henry Crampton, while carrying in a heavy log of wood for the fire, fell on the ice and fractured his skull. This furnished the occasion for the consecration of the ground destined for the graveyard, and Br. Fritz made an address and offered prayer.

Feb. 27. Br. Fritz preached in English in our English School-house.

March 13. Br. and Sr. Fritz moved into the School-house in our English settlement, and were received with much love by their church-children.

July 8. A company of Light-horse brought through Salem, on the way to Richmond, a drove of cattle which they had taken in the Hope settlement from persons whom they suspected of being Tories. This was done without order, so they were at once returned to the owners.

July 29. A party of Light-horse created much alarm on both sides of Muddy Creek by taking weapons away from the people, and several nearly lost their lives. The present bitterness between the two parties is almost unbelievable; we thank the Saviour that He has given us grace to take no part in this unrest and molesting except to bless them that curse us, pray for them that despitefully use us, and do good to them that hate us.

Nov. 6. One of our neighbors, William Peddycoart, who has belonged to the Society of Hope, and is returning to Maryland, is taking letters and our September Diary to Br. Reichel.

Dec. 17. In Hope, Br. Fritz read an English translation of the Results of Synod to the members of the congregation and Society, in the felt presence of the Church's Head.

Dec. 24. In Hope the children had a Christmas lovefeast for the first time. Most of the members of the congregation and Society were also present, and said afterwards that they had never before had so blessed a Christmas service.

1781.

[During 1781 there were no noteworthy changes in Europe or India, but in America it was an *auserordentlicher Jahr,* as the Salem diarist declared.

On March 1st, Maryland ratified the Articles of Confederation, and the next day they were signed by all the delegates of the new United States.

In the northern states there was relatively little military activity, but in the south a most interesting situation developed. Lord Cornwallis expected an easy conquest of North Carolina, having overrun South Carolina and Georgia in the preceding year, but the tide that had turned at King's Mountain continued to run against the British fortunes. Over and over, technical victories of the British left them in untenable positions from which they were forced to retreat. After the battle of Guilford it was reported in Salem that the English had remained masters of the field, but the forces of Cornwallis were so shattered that he was forced to avoid another battle and to retreat toward the east. On the contrary, Greene's army was soon ready for another fight, and moved into South Carolina to regain that state. There the same thing occurred, and victories claimed by the British were followed by British retreats until that State and Georgia were again in American hands, except for two or three seaport towns. Cornwallis, turning into Virginia, was trapped at Yorktown, and there surrendered on October 19th.

For the Moravians this was a peculiarly difficult year, since their towns were so near the center of activities that they were constantly overrun by troops, and exorbitant demands were made upon them for supplies of various kinds. In spite of their willingness to serve the American cause in every possible way they had to endure false accusations of Toryism, and suffered much from the excesses of wandering bands of militia, out mainly for pillage under the guise of patriotism. Their honest loyalty, their compliance with all reasonable and many unreasonable demands, their kindness to the sick and wounded soldiers left in their care, gradually turned sentiment in their favor; and when the meeting of the Assembly in Salem in November gave opportunity for personal investigation by the leading men of the state, the Moravians were frankly accorded the commendation they had so richly earned.]

Memorabilia of the Congregations in Wachovia
at the close of the year, 1781.

[Written by Rev. Friedrich Peter.   A few personal statistics omitted.]

The congregations in Wachovia present themselves at the close of this year before the Lord, with truly humble hearts, but full of praise and thanksgiving that in the midst of earth's clamor and terrifying events He has led them safely.   The wonderful help of our faithful Lord and Saviour, in the unusually difficult circumstances that distinguished this year of grace, has made it noteworthy in the story of this work of God. He has furthered the growth of grace in the congregations, as a gracious High Priest has healed short-comings and sins, and through His Holy Spirit has led us on in all that pertains to the beauty and honor of His doctrine.   In the midst of war He has kept us, and He has known how to find favor for His work in spite of our weakness, so that those who lied about us could not harm us; yea, He has brought us peace even through the mistreatment which prejudice heaped upon us, and thereby we have learned wisdom and foresight, have learned to bear patiently the sorrows that came upon us, partly because we are children of God, partly by our own fault, and have learned to seek His face that He may graciously correct our errors, and that we may receive His help through all.

Who can count the wonderful and righteous things which the Lord and Saviour of His people has done for his poor children here in the Wachau?   Out of six troubles has He saved us, and in the seventh no evil has befallen us.   When in the first three months of the year the theatre of the war moved into this neighborhood, He so ordered it that no battles were fought on the soil of Wachovia.   He gave His angels charge concerning our congregation towns, and our Brethren and Sisters living without our bounds, so that no homes were burned or laid waste, as was often threatened.   Some were seized in their homes or in the fields or on the streets, some were robbed and some were wounded, but none of them lost their lives.

Certain of our families in the country congregations had much to endure, especially in Friedberg, where an epidemic of small-pox was added to the other calamities; but the Lord helped them out of it all, and gave them again days of joy, for example Friedberg on August 18th, Friedland on September 3rd, and Hope, which suffered least from the war, on August 27th, remembered before Him the founding of their congregations, and the help given through the difficult days that had passed, and brought Him their heartfelt thanks.   That meant sweet hours of grace and psalms of mercy.

Bethania and Friedland, where the English troops under Lord Cornwallis camped on the nights of February 9th and 10th, experienced great anxiety and distress and lost heavily, though at the same time they became aware of the wonderful hand of God which protected them against harm of body or soul, and cared for their supply of food, so that no one suffered need.

Before and after the passing of the English army through Salem there were incursions into Salem and Bethabara of wandering parties, especially the Wilkes militia. They caused disorder and alarm in all the streets and houses, so that we felt with gratitude that our lives and property were given to us anew by the Lord. Under these circumstances, and on the 17th of February, which was particularly noteworthy here, He comforted us with the Text for that day: *Thou art a strength to the poor, a strength to the needy in his distress, a refuge from the storm, a shadow from the heat.* Is. XXV, 4.

> So rest I now, my Saviour, in Thy arms,
> Thyself shalt be for me eternal peace.

Thus He encouraged us to be of good cheer, and so ordered things, according to His power and wisdom, that the hatred and rage of these people against us, which increased until the middle of the month of March, subsided after that time. The generality of the Continental army was convinced of our willingness to bear our share of the public burden when Colonel White's cavalry was quartered here in January, and a storehouse for ammunition was erected in Salem; they also saw that their sorely wounded, who were left here on the 5th of February when the Hospital was moved away, and who remained until April, received all possible care, and through the skill of our now departed Br. Jacob Bonn were restored to health. Several men from Virginia have written in appreciation of his ability and faithfulness; and beginning there sympathy for our circumstances has been aroused, so that even those most opposed to us have come to see that we are a quiet and peaceable people, who wish to live in peace with all men. Through the war-burdens which rested upon us the Lord has worked out one purpose for our good, for which we humbly thank Him, namely more unity of heart and more brotherly and helpful sharing in each other's circumstances. To this end He blessed a thorough discussion in the Congregation Council of January 12th, in which we resolved, by the grace of God, to lighten the war-burden for each other, and to bear it all together. For this purpose the Council elected a committee of four Brethren, Samuel Stotz, Traugott Bagge, Johann Reuz, and Peter Yarrell, who should serve as needed in conjunction with the Aufseher Collegium and the Aeltesten Conferenz. This made possible, by God's help, the erection of a magazine for the store of ammunition [for the Continental army]. During the putting up of the building a boy experienced a wonderful preservation of his life.

It is also a special cause of thankfulness to our Lord that we have retained our privilege of freedom from military service on the payment of a three-fold tax, and this in spite of objections urged by certain of our opponents.

The hand of the Lord has shielded us during the unusually severe storms of this year, so that no harm has come to us.

He also delivered Salem, which was disturbed in August by a band of highwaymen, against whom the Brethren kept constant watch; and has also helped to cast aside the injurious effect which it had on the minds of some members.

From September to November was a time of heart-searching, when the Saviour brought certain things to pass among His people. We recognized this as a preparation for the events which followed, during which the Saviour presented His people before the eyes of the world. In November, sixty-three members of the Assembly and government officials, and other gentlemen in addition, gathered in Salem to hold a meeting of the General Assembly. Lodgings were provided for all of them, for the guard of the Governor and for the militia; and after a stay of about three weeks they departed, having failed to make a House. Many, who had hitherto been opposed to us, or had had mistaken ideas concerning us, and who had now seen our organization and our services, which were held partly in English, were so well satisfied with the care taken of them in the families and other houses, that in leaving they begged that if the meeting of the Assembly for next January should be called in Salem each might be placed again in the same house in which he had been this time. We thank our dear Saviour heartily for the approval which He permitted us to win from the members of the Assembly despite our small means, and we hope for good results for our Unity congregations and settlements in Wachovia. During this time He also protected our borders from disaster, so that the alarm in the night between the 24th and 25th of November, caused by a report that the Tories were coming, proved to be needless.

Certain Brethren and Sisters, especially in Bethabara, were in danger of their lives through accident or severe illness, but the Saviour gave them back to us. Special thanks are due to Him for the passing away of the small-pox, which was epidemic in Wachovia for half the year. Friedberg suffered most, where ninety-six persons were sick with it, and five went home. In Friedland only two families were affected; and two families in Bethania also. The latter town was particularly thankful that it did not spread, for it came just at the time of harvest. In Salem, by the gracious help of the Saviour, nineteen passed through it successfully by inoculation, and twenty-four were inoculated in Bethabara.

Our reciprocal communication with our Pennsylvania congregations, whose petitions and prayers to the Lord have quickened us in these troublous times, were suspended for a while because of the war, but have not been broken, and we have kept an affectionate connection with them. The correspondence with Europe was still more interrupted, yet we thank the Saviour heartily that none of the Gemein Nachrichten, Wochen or Reden, coming by way of Pennsylvania, have been lost by sea or land, and we have received them for the nourishment of our souls, and have also received the Texts for 1782. The wonderful providence of God in regard to them is the more evident because the ship in which they came was seized, and yet they reached us, packages coming from Boston, New London and Egg Harbor from the prize vessel, and one package which had come into the hands of the Governor of the Jerseys was delivered to us safely. The loss of a few packets between here and Pennsylvania, of which one came back to us uninjured, has had no bad effect on our correspondence.

We were also rejoiced by the arrival of three Brethren from Pennsylvania during this year, Christian Ludwig Benzien and Gottfried Schulz on August 26th, and Jacob Loesch on December 18th, the angel of God having brought them safely to us.

In the interest of our trade several successful trips were made to Pennsylvania and to the lower counties of North Carolina. These, and the rich blessing of God in the grain harvest, which consoled us for the lack of fruit, helped us so greatly, that in spite of the prospect of great increase in the price, caused by wanton destruction throughout the country in addition to endless army requisitions, we were assured of enough to eat, and were able to show mercy to the needy, who passed through our towns in large numbers and in the most pitiable condition. This happened, for example, on March 4th, when the Text for the day read, *Deal thy bread to the hungry.*

In regard to the Diaconies it must be admitted that they have suffered losses, especially Bethabara, but at the same time we must acknowledge with thanks that the loss has not been nearly so great as there was every reason to think it would be. Even our Bethania Brethren have been able to recover from the hard blow dealt to them.

A house has been built for Br. Broesing on the part of the Bethabara plantation which he has taken, and he has moved thither. Br. Stöhr's new house is under roof. Br. Oesterlein has built a smithy; and Br. Schaub, Jr. has made preparations for building his house. In Salem a dwelling will be built for Br. Gottfried Schulz on the plantation of the Single Brethren, and in the town itself many improvements have been made.

The filials of Salem have been kept in affectionate connection with this congregation, partly through the Land-Arbeiter-Conferenz, partly through visits and reciprocal correspondence, for the furthering of their call of grace within and without. The Saviour has revealed Himself to them as the faithful Shepherd of their souls. The little congregation of Friedland acknowledges with thanks and humility that the inability to hold the Communion there on August 4th, because of conditions within the congregation, has had a blessed result, and has caused the Brethren and Sisters anew to determine that by the grace of the Saviour they would live to His honor and joy. A similar awakening came in Friedberg at Whitsuntide, when their Brotherly Agreement concerning congregation rules was adopted, and was signed by all communicants and those who had been Received.

In all our congregations the Gospel has been proclaimed that our Lord and Creator came from heaven out of love for us poor human creatures, and for us became a man; that through His sufferings, death and blood He gained for us freedom from sin, and righteousness before God, and through His resurrection won for us eternal life; and that since His ascension into heaven He prays for us, and has sent His Holy Spirit to be our Comforter, to lead us to Him, and to give us faith in His Atonement. This Gospel has been set before our hearts in our daily meetings, in the Bible readings, and on the festal days of special significance, as the power of God, to bless all who believe therein, and we have been kept thereby in communion with the Saviour, Who in these troubled times has given us a fairly undisturbed church and congregation life, so that we have been able in peace to celebrate the festal days of the Unity, and to partake of the most holy Sacrament of His Body and Blood in communion with our other congregations, to the comfort and strengthening of our faith.

The congregation music in Salem has been improved this year, so that the hymns and liturgies on festal days have become brighter and more pleasing, and even strangers and travelers have been touched and will remember it. We thank the Lord for this treasure, and pray that He will preserve it to us, so that our singing may become constantly more liturgical and more pleasing to Him.

The Daily Texts for this year we received from the hand of our Lord as given expressly for *us,* and in our trials we have often been encouraged by them.

The re-reading of the Results of the Synod of 1775, which has occurred this year in most of our congregations, and the communication of a Circular[1] from the Unity's Elders Conference, which was read in our Place-Congregations, reminded us of our calling to be a band of pilgrims, living only for our Lord, ready to be used by Him in His work of grace on earth, no matter what the hardship, and planning all our arrangements, our manner of life, and the education of our children according to this ideal. May He carry out His gracious wish for us, His poor children.

The *Choirs,* through the Holy Spirit, have written their Choir Principles deep within their hearts, and have been sanctified by Jesus' merits in spirit, body and soul. Each Choir, on its festal day, renewed its covenant to be a joy unto Him. The Married People and the Single Brethren and Sisters, respectively, sealed their covenant in the Holy Communion. The Choirs of single members remembered the adoption of their Choir House rules, in their important bearing on their outward life, that it might be ever more to His liking, and therefore even here they might have a contented and blessed life.

Among the *Married People,* over whom the Eye and Guardian of Israel has watched in a particular manner, the new arrangement of classes and visiting has been blessed in a more general union of hearts in love, and for the up-bringing of the children. Through the marriage of our Br. Gottfried Praetzel, on September 2nd, to the widowed Sr. Elisabeth Nielsen, the Choir has secured two dear officers, and the congregation has received a Vorsteher in place of the departed Br. Jeppe Nielsen.

> The Married Choir lifts full heart
> Of thanks, for all Thou didst impart;
> And humbly wishes that to Thee
> They and their children joy may be.

In the *Choir of Single Brethren,* during this year, our dear Lord has clearly proved to many a soul how unwearied is His patience and how great His love and Shepherd-faithfulness. On August 29th, our Br. Gottfried Praetzel closed his service as Choir Pfleger, in which he had shown much faithfulness for nearly eight years. Br. Benzien took his place, and received the blessing for his task.

---

[1] Printed in full in Part I of this volume.

> The Single Brothers Choir shall stay
> Full of His honor day by day;
> That spirit, body, soul, may be
> Their Saviour's joy eternally.

The Saviour has given to the *Choir of Single Sisters* a long wished for Curator[2] in the person of Br. Praetzel. To assist the families in their difficult circumstances was the pleasure of this Choir; and at the close of the year the Choir gave thanks to God that all its members could take part in the Communion, and that all the Older Girls had been Received.

> Thou Man, Who liv'dst so righteously,
> Regard Thy maidens graciously;
> Grant that each one, while here below,
> The selfsame quality may show.

The Friend of Children has graciously revealed Himself to our small *Choir of Children,* and has blessed them, partly in union with the congregation, partly during the children's meetings and liturgies, and especially on their festal days, June 24th and August 17th. The instruction given the little boys and the little girls made a blessed impression each time; and their instruction in school made good progress. Two children have been added to the school for little boys, and Br. Christian Stauber has become assistant in their supervision in place of Br. Martin Schneider. We pray to the Lord for our children:

> On these our children, Lord, bestow
> The merits of Thy life below;
> Thy learning and Thy industry
> Teach them to learn, to work, like Thee.
> Thine be the praise!

On Ascension Day, May 24th, in Bethabara, the married Sr. Maria Bagge, and the single Sr. A. Maria Quest were ordained Deaconesses of the Unity of Brethren by Br. Graff, and the two single Srs. Maria Elisabeth Engel and Maria Magdalena Reutz were received as Akoluthie. Sr. Reutz succeeded Sr. Engel as teacher of the little girls in Bethabara, and Sr. Engel moved to the Choir House in Salem. On December 26th, Br. Christian Ludwig Benzien was ordained a Deacon of the Unity.

---

[2] A financial adviser, and the official representative of the Single Sisters in the Aufseher Collegium.

Summary of the Brethren and Sisters in Wachovia Congregations at the close of the Year, 1781.

Salem consists of

24 married couples, or	48 persons
Widowers	1
Widows	2
Single Brethren and Boys	48
Single Sisters and Older Girls	27
Little Boys	16
Little Girls	10
	152

Associated with Salem Congregation,

3 married couples	6
Children	9
Total	167

of whom 112 are Communicants and 9 Received.

Bethabara consists of

18 married couples, or	36 persons
Widowers	2
Single Brethren and Boys	9
Single Sisters and Girls	6
Little Boys	11
Little Girls	17
Total	81

of whom 42 are Communicants and 5 Received.

Bethania consists of

19 married couples, or	38 persons
Widower	1
Young Men and Boys	16
Young Women and Girls	11
Little Boys	11
Little Girls	14
Total	91

of whom 35 are Communicants, and 8 Received.

Communicants living outside the town.................. 27
Received, outside town.. 6   33
                                                                    ——
          Total for Bethania..   124
                    to which should be added 72 children, outside the town.
Friedberg consists of
    43 Communicants
    14 Received
    60 Society Members
    95 Children
    ——
   212 Total
Friedland consists of
    19 Communicants
     7 Received
    34 Society Members
    48 Children
    ——
   108 Total
Hope consists of
    14 Communicants
     9 Received
    49 Society Members
    60 Children
    ——
   132 Total

There are therefore in the Wachovia congregations at the close of
the year 1781:
   292 Communicants
    58 Received
   183 Society Members
   363 Children
   ——
   896 Total

            The number of Thy Children grows,
            A crown for God's dear Son;
            Thousands of crowns are His reward
            For the redemption won.

Diary of the Congregation in Salem, 1781.

[Extracts translated. Items in brackets are from notes kept in English by Frederic W. Marshall in an interleaved Text Book.]

Jan. 1. We entered the new year with happy hearts, and in the felt nearness of Jesus and the believing hope that He would be with us, would let us feel His peace, would draw us closer together in brotherly union, and would graciously lead us during these hard times. Should He not be pleased to grant the prayer which we have found courage to make confidingly to Him, and should not bring these troubles to an end this year, may He continue, as hitherto, to cover us with His wings and protect us from disaster. [Friedrich Peter began to keep the diary.]

In the afternoon, the arrival of Maj. William Campbell and 105 volunteers from Bottetourt County, Va., did not interfere with the holding of the usual services. This Major Campbell kept good order, and we hear that the soldiers wish to behave better than the Virginia troops under the Colonel of the same name who were here some time ago. They had most of their provisions with them, and asked only for some corn and brandy. In the evening at half past seven they attended a happy singstunde, in the beginning of which the choir of musicians sang *Speak peace to Jerusalem;* they were attentive and respectful.

Jan. 2. The volunteers left quietly. Jacob Beroth, who lives near the mill, brought his son Johannes to the school; the boy is in his ninth year.

Jan. 3. Br. Philip Vogler brought his [step] son, Johannes Steinmann, to school; he is five or six years old. Toward evening Johann Stotz returned from Guilford, whither he had been on business for Br. Herbst. Instead of the hides, which had been promised to Br. Herbst in exchange for the leather which he delivered there, he received an Order on the Commissary in Hillsborough. This Order was given by Stotz to Br. Gottlieb Strehle, whom he met on his way to Hillsborough on the same business. Mr. Samuel Freeman, one of the Assemblymen for our County, passed on his way thither; he was friendly, and promised to speak in our behalf there if it should be necessary.

In the meeting for Bible reading we commenced the Harmony of the Gospels.

Jan. 5. Mr. Glascock came from Colonel White's Virginia cavalry, [light-horse,] to arrange for quarters, provisions and forage for three officers, twenty sick cavalrymen, and thirty or forty horses, which General [Nathaniel] Greene had ordered here to recuperate. They will probably be here two months or so. The officer spoke several times of the kind thoughts of Colonel White toward us since his last stay here; he was polite, and promised to provide everything needed for the support of the troops while they were here. Nevertheless, it required very serious consideration to decide how best to provide accommodation for man and beast.

Sarah McBain, a child of eight or nine years, of Scotch descent, came to Br. and Sr. Christ, in service, on trial. Her father is dead, and the mother, who is living in Friedland just now, wishes to have her remain here. The child has been baptised.

Jan. 7. Sunday. After prayers for the congregations among the heathen, letters and reports from various missions were read in three services. During these days Br. Samuel Stotz is collecting the offering for the heathen, and it was commended to the attention of the Brethren and Sisters.

The Boys celebrated their Choir Festival with grace and blessing.

Yesterday, Lieutenant Simons arrived on the business already referred to, and today twenty-two men came, with about forty horses and two baggage wagons. Mr. Simons was most polite, and said that he had received orders from General Greene, as well as Colonel White, that he was not to make trouble, disorder, or annoyance for the residents. He agreed that the men should be lodged in the little house of the night-watchman, and the horses placed in the sheds on the brick-yard. The first proved to be too small, so four trumpeters were placed in the house of Br. Yarrell.

This morning Mr. Cummings, our Assemblyman, passed on his way to the Assembly. He took with him our Tickets for supplies furnished, and was very friendly.

Jan. 10. This evening we had a severe storm, followed by beautiful fall weather. This winter has resembled a mild autumn.

Jan. 11. Colonel [Benjamin] Cleveland and Major Herndon, from Wilkes County, passed on their way to the Assembly, and were very polite. With them was Major Michaja Lewis, who was wounded at King's Mountain, but has recovered.

Jan. 12. Br. Gottlieb Straehle returned from Hillsborough, where he had succeeded so far with the matter entrusted to him and to Br. Stotz, that Commissioner Taylor had declared one wagon-load of leather as "pressed," and had paid for the rest in hides. The much rain had raised the streams so that he was detained two days. Some damage was done at Br. Steiner's mill. Lieutenant Hughes and another officer arrived today. The former is properly in command of the men quartered here, and he began to fit up the sheds as a stable; the store had to

12

supply nails and the mill must furnish boards. Requisitions continued on the store for grain and on the mill for meal for their use.

In the Congregation Council yesterday the dissatisfaction which was caused by the last quartering of soldiers here led to a brotherly understanding as to how the war-burdens should be regarded and handled. By unanimous vote a committee of four were selected,— Traugott Bagge, Johann Reuz and Peter Yarrell from among the married Brethren and Samuel Stotz from the Single Brethren. Working in harmony with the Aufseher Collegium and the Aeltesten Conferenz, this committee, as need arises, will consider the best interests of the congregation, and in that spirit will be our agents in the war-affairs that concern us. It was proposed to build a house near the Tavern, to be called a house for poor travelers who can not pay their way in the Tavern, but which in case of need could serve as barracks for soldiers. The Brethren of the Congregation Council considered this building further today, decided that it was practicable, appointed Br. Aust building inspector, and took up a free-will offering for it.

Jan. 13. The building subscription was explained in the meeting of all communicants today, and it will be carried out in the Choir meetings during these days. However, there arose a matter which delayed the building, for which the subscription was not sufficient. The Brn. Samuel Stotz and Johann Reuz went to see Mr. Brooks and Colonel Williams about the taxes; with the former they accomplished nothing, and the latter was not at home. They spoke with Colonel Williams here in Salem, and he told them that the assessment had not yet been made, and that the Vice-Clerk should send the list to Br. Bagge as soon as it was ready.

Jan. 14. Commissioner Brooks arrived today to arrange for the support of the troops, but he managed to fix things with the officers in such a way that they would continue to call on us for corn and meal.

Jan. 15. Although the South Fork was unusually high from the recent rains, Br. Beck crossed it safely and came to the meeting of the Land-Arbeiter-Conferenz.[1]

Jan. 16. The framework and roof timbers from the lumber shed were put up for the carpenter shop, and no one received an injury.

In the meeting of communicants Br. Marshall explained the present status of the matter mentioned under date of Jan. 12 and 13.

Today a Sergeant came from General Greene's army with twelve men and an ammunition wagon [loaded with gunpowder]. His orders were to deliver the powder to the *Conductor*[2] of Military Stores. As

---

[1] A conference of the pastors of the country congregations. Later a conference of all Moravian ministers in Wachovia took its place.   [2] The English word is used in the diary.

there is no such officer here Lieutenant Hughes was asked to let his men guard the powder, if it was stored here, so that no militia need be called in for the purpose, but he refused because his men have neither shoes nor clothes in which to serve.

Jan. 17. They sent some one to Major [Joseph] Winston to learn his opinion as to where the powder should be sent. Last evening Major [John] Armstrong arrived, who was only too glad to have the powder stay here. His brother, our Colonel, wrote to him from Salisbury on the 12th, that the British were marching toward Salisbury. The Colonel wanted to go to Charlotte, but instead went to the main army on the Peedee.

Jan. 19. This morning our next neighbor, Schumacher, Jr., overtook here in Salem a man who lodged with him last night, and stole a knife from him. On suspicion that he had stolen other things Schumacher wished to take him to a Justice, but as the man was on horseback and Schumacher on foot, when they approached the plantation the man rode ahead and called out his comrades who were hiding in the woods. A shot passed near Schumacher, but his lusty cries for help frightened the men, and they all made off hastily.

The older Christmann and Reich from Haw River came to see their sons. As Christmann was on his way home from his last visit he was attacked by three men between here and Friedland, and was forced to give them his cloak and whatever else they demanded. When he had ridden on a little further they called to him, and gave everything back. Fear of being called into the militia has driven many to hide in the woods, and as they have nothing on which to live they resort to highway robbery, which is bringing the country into a pitiable condition.

The powder wagon mentioned on the 16th quietly left.

Jan. 20. The powder wagon returned with two other ammunition wagons, a guard of thirty men, and a Conductor who will make up ammunition here. They wished to build a laboratory in which to work, and it was decided to help them, for the sake of the safety of the town. [The thirty men were sent to recover their health; they were quartered at Yarrell's.] During the following days the officers pressed wagons to haul building materials for the house, which was erected outside the town, behind the Tavern. It was 24 by 30 ft. in size, and was raised[3] by the Brethren. Meanwhile the night-watchman's house was cleared out, so that the Conductor could store the powder there. The men who had been lodged there were moved to Br. Yarrell's house.

Jan. 21. Sunday. [Two] more ammunition wagons arrived. After the litany, Br. Graff preached on the Gospel for the day. The

---

[3] *Aufgeblockt,*—used when the house raised was of logs.

officers attended the service. In the afternoon the Married People had their meeting. As the soldiers wished to attend a service a singstunde was held in the evening, instead of the liturgy, and they were attentive and quiet.

Jan. 22. Christmann and Reich returned to Haw River. The latter has declared positively that he gives his sons to the Unity.

Jan. 23. Colonel [Martin] Armstrong was here. His General has ordered him to call out half the militia, and take command of them.

Jan. 24. This week we received through Dr. Reed, in Salisbury, an order from General Greene to furnish various surgical instruments. In this we could not serve him, but were able to comply with another request and furnish leather in exchange for hides. Two of Colonel White's officers, a Captain and a Brigade Major named Boyer, arrived. We learned that their men, who are quartered here, would move in about two weeks. Meanwhile a house[4] was raised by our Brethren to serve as a magazine for the ammunition.

Jan. 25. It was unusually warm for this time of the year, and there was a storm in the evening.

Jan. 26. Today Col. Joseph Haversham, his wife and child, and seven wagons, arrived on their way to Virginia. He has lived there since his flight from Georgia, but his wife and child are now coming from Camden, with permission of the English. With them came a Captain McLane, a wounded English prisoner-of-war, going to the family of General McIntosh in Virginia. Br. Bonn helped him to a better bandaging of his wounded hand and shoulder. Colonel Haversham spoke of his pleasant visit to Bethlehem some years ago. On account of the rain only a reading meeting was held at twilight.

Jan. 27. Saturday. After a happy lovefeast, accompanied by soft music, the congregation partook of the Holy Sacrament in the midst of the quiet peace of God. We were particularly thankful that nothing from without disturbed us.

Jan. 28. The Post-Communion was attended by a number of Brethren and Sisters, who waited for it because they have the severe cough which is now epidemic. Colonel Haversham and the other officers attended the morning preaching, and the liturgy in the evening. We were comforted by the Daily Text: *When thou passest through the waters, I will be with thee; and through the rivers, they shall not overflow thee; when thou walkest through the fire, thou shalt not be burned; neither shall the flame kindle upon thee,* for all sorts of alarming rumors came in today, especially that the British prisoners, taken at

---

[4] This was also of logs.

Broad River,[5] would be brought here.   We thank God that nothing has come of it for the present.

Jan. 30.   The boy, Gottlieb Spach, was especially protected by the Saviour, as he was helping with the erection of the magazine for Continental ammunition.   The gable end of the roof was being placed, and he took hold of an imperfect timber with one hand; it broke with him and he fell from the rafters, but only dislocated one shoulder and injured one hand.   He was immediately bled, and received other needful aid.

Colonel Armstrong was here, and from him we learned that the militia as a whole is to be called out.   He and several officers from Colonel [Harry] Lee's cavalry came to see the English prisoners, but they were not here.

Colonel Haversham and his company left today for Virginia, well pleased with their visit here.   Br. Broesing went about twenty miles, to help the negroes on their way.

Jan. 31.   Two wagons, loaded with powder, lead, and balls, and two cannon, [three-pounders,] came from Salisbury to the Continental magazine here.   Colonel White and another officer arrived, to send to Virginia some of his men who have been quartered here, and to send the rest to the main body of the army.   He was very grateful for the treatment his troops had received, and inquired how they had behaved, and we could give him a good report.   An Express who came in the night to Colonel White, reported that General Greene was in camp on the Catawba, and his army in full march from the Peedee thither. [One hundred and ten acres were surveyed for Andreas Volk, near Jn. Krause.]

Feb. 1.   Colonel White sent Mr. Glascock to Hillsborough; it is said he went to secure uniforms.   During the night an Express came to him from the Catawba, and things became disturbed.   [An officer and five men were dispatched to Shallowford.]   The house for the ammunition was finished in the rain.

Feb. 2.   Last night came Mr. Hyrn, Major and Commissioner of the English prisoners.   The prisoners [about 400, taken at the Cowpen, S. C.] have been ordered to march hastily through here to Virginia. He wanted food for them and for the militia guarding them.   We furnished grain and salt, Bethabara and Bethania furnished meat.   At noon they passed without stopping, and so we escaped having them quartered on us.   Several Brethren helped in the mill as they went by.

---

[5] Jan. 17, 1781, Colonel Morgan fought Colonel Tarleton at the Cowpens, in South Carolina, on Broad River. The British loss was very heavy, the American light. General Greene ordered the prisoners sent to Virginia, planning to exchange them for Americans held in captivity since the fall of Charleston. They passed through Salem in February.

The cavalrymen who have been here began to march during the night, in detachments. The ammunition was moved from the night-watchman's house, which is in the center of the town, to the new house near the water, to the great joy and gratitude of the Brethren and Sisters. It was difficult to move, and only accomplished through the help of Colonel White.

In the afternoon a Virginia Major, Caul, arrived. We heard as a certainty that the British were on this side of the Catawba, and had had a skirmish[6] with some of the American troops, to the disadvantage of the latter, and were on their way toward Salisbury unhindered. Br. Krause took a letter from the officer to Bethania, in order to have it sent to Virginia by Express. At twilight reports from Greenland were read. Colonel White had asked for instrumental and vocal music, so a singstunde was held in the evening to please him.

Feb. 3. Colonel White and two Virginia officers took their departure. This morning was unusually quiet, but in the afternoon the noise began which continued for many days. Captain Marbury, the vice-Quartermaster, arrived. Already before that, men had been sent out to secure wagons in which to haul away the ammunition, and he pressed still more, but excused our team as we had but one for use in the town and in case of need to remove the sick. From today until the 5th many came Express to the officers who were staying here. The rest of Colonel White's company assembled here.

Feb. 4. Sunday. Colonel White's troops marched away. They thanked us for the good care taken of them, and we thanked them for their good behaviour. Four of them returned at noon from Headquarters at the Trading Ford, and were at once sent out to press wagons. A Surgeon's Mate arrived, bringing order that a house with four rooms should be made ready for the coming of the Continental Hospital. The two-story house was cleared for the purpose, the officers being moved to the Tavern. The sick and wounded were very thankful for this lodging. Br. and Sr. Meinung[7] moved to the second story of Br. Herbst's house, and the widow, Sr. Utley, was lodged in the lower story of the Gemein Haus. On account of these troubles the services closed with the reading meeting in the afternoon, and there was no meeting of the married people. Two soldiers and eight negroes came from General [Daniel] Morgan's camp, were fed, and thankfully returned thither. In the evening still another ammunition wagon came from the Pee Dee to the magazine. We hear that on the other side of the Yadkin, this

---

[6] On Feb. 1st, Cornwallis crossed the Catawba at Cowan's Ford, opposed unsuccessfully by Colonel Davidson.

[7] Mr. and Mrs. Meinung and Mrs. Utley had been living in the two-story house.

side of Salisbury, there was a bloody skirmish[8] yesterday evening. Br. Spach came from Friedberg with his wagon to haul ammunition. In Friedberg the preaching service was disturbed by soldiers from Georgia, who plundered at the homes of Christian Frey and Peter Frey. In the many threatening circumstances which have surrounded us during these days the Text for today was most comforting and strengthening:—*I, even I, am he that comforteth you: who art thou, that thou shouldst be afraid of a man that shall die, and of the son of man which shall be made as grass.*

Feb. 5. During the night a number of wagons arrived, including some from Bethania, in order to take the ammunition [to Virginia]; they were loaded, and drove off during the afternoon. Doctor Reed brought orders that the hospital also should be taken further; and it left here in the company of two wagons loaded with sick soldiers who passed through. This made it necessary to furnish additional supplies, and finally they begged the Sisters for rags for lint; all requests were made politely and the articles were received with many thanks. Scarcely had the ammunition and hospital left when other, and unwelcome, guests arrived, the same that were in Friedberg yesterday, who were out to rob and plunder. However, damage was avoided with much care and watchfulness, and they left about dusk, as did another party under Major Blair, who came at just the right time from Guilford to get lead and balls. A South Carolinian, General [Andrew] Pickens, and his men, passed during the evening, going to Virginia; during the night Captain Gamble, Adjutant-General-Quartermaster, with fifteen baggage wagons and a guard of one hundred men, passed in the same direction, after feeding their horses here. The Brn. Flex and Philip Transou went part of the way with the latter as messengers. On their return they were attacked by a drunken hussar. In reply to his question who they were they replied: *Good friends,* but thinking they might be deserters or spies he cut at them with his saber, but they ran away quickly and escaped injury. Br. Flex ran ahead, as he did not know how his companion was faring, and called the Salem Brethren to his assistance, but they met him unharmed and cheerful, to their great joy. In many alarms the Saviour was our Comfort and Protector, and, thank God, all passed off well. Today we gave heartiest congratulations to Br. Marshall for his 61st birthday. Three of Colonel White's dragoons spent the night here again, together with two sick soldiers who had just arrived, and on

Feb. 6, they went further. Today South Carolina, Georgia and North Carolina officers and men passed; some of the first named were very

---

[8] At the Trading Ford of the Yadkin, on Feb. 3rd.

boisterous, but a story invented by a friend made them hurry on. The militia company from Beloes [Belews] Creek were to muster here to-day; two came, and returned to their homes, and then two more came and remained over night. Otherwise the night was quiet. In the meeting of communicants Br. Graff spoke on the Text for today: *I, the Lord, will hear the poor and needy,* and reminded us how graciously the Lord had led us through these disturbed days, * * *.

Feb. 7.   General Morgan's Brigade-Major, named Brooks, came from the army, near Spurgeon's, and looked over the town. An officer came from General Greene asking for boots, but there were none to be had, and they both left most politely. About four o'clock in the after-noon a hundred and seventy-odd of the Wilkes Militia arrived unan-nounced. Their Captain, Herndon, first demanded brandy, which was furnished; then he wanted meat and bread or flour, and the flour was supplied; then he insisted on having meat, and some of that also was furnished. Then he and the Captains with him tried to press powder from Br. Bagge; he replied that he had none, but there was a little lead belonging to the public which was at their service if they thought wise to take it. They insisted that we had powder in the town, and that it must be given to them. Their demands were finally ended through the arrival of their senior Captain, Lenoir,[9] who brought more men. The requisitions began again about seven o'clock. In the Tavern many ate and drank as they pleased, and there they took three bundles of oats; the Single Brethren had to give them half an ox, 100 lbs. of meal, and several gallons of brandy; the store furnished corn and salt, the pottery had to supply ware, and in addition they took whatever came to hand. All these demands were made with threats, which sounded as though they sought an excuse to plunder the town. One Captain said he had inquired about the people in the town and had found that some were for and some against the common cause, and the former should now show it. Lenoir declared roundly that we were his enemies, but for the time he would not harm us except that we must give what they needed and demanded. After we had had much trouble with them, and had felt the Power of Darkness, they left about ten o'clock at night, with a show of politeness, taking the public lead, cut into small pieces. Prior to leaving, several of them went into the town, represented themselves as Tories and tried to lead the Brethren to join them, but they did not succeed, for the Saviour gave our Brethren grace to speak cautiously, and protected them from harm. After eleven o'clock three of them came back into the town, and were forbidden, by

---

[9] William Lenoir.

the nightwatch, to roam about; they claimed that they were looking for a deserter. After they left the night was quiet.

Feb. 8. Yesterday and today no meetings could be held because of the disturbances. In the morning many officers and privates were in town, they were very boisterous at the still-house, and in the Tavern things went badly, with much cursing, abuse and harsh threats so that we feared for our lives and our property. They arrested various persons who came into the town. In the afternoon a company of Georgia light-horse came through; they brought a wounded militiaman named Daniel Rash, [from Hunting Creek,] who remained here in the care of our doctor. [He had been shot through the head and knee.] Soon after all the Wilkes men left. As a last act one of the privates had seized a pair of leggins from Br. Bagge, but one of his comrades made him return them. It is to be noted that these men left just as the Brn. Bibighaus and Holder were about to set out for General Greene's head-quarters, to present a petition asking his Excellency for a Salvegarde and protection, and so they were able to start in peace. During the evening there was again some disturbance in the town, made by a Georgian who had left some work with the shoemaker, but it was soon over. The night was quiet.

Feb. 9. Fairly early the above-mentioned Georgian came to Br. Meyer and returned the two horses which Captain Herndon pressed from the Single Brethren yesterday, in place of two others which he left until he should send for them. He also took the Captain's knapsack. He asked the Holders for Colonel Cleveland's sword, and took the work ordered from the shoemaker, that is he took one finished and three unfinished shoes. He was in much haste, and was much milder than yesterday.

From Friedberg we heard a most distressing report that several of the planters in that section, and among others Martin Walk, a communicant Brother, had been arrested by men in English uniform on the charge that they were enemies of the country. In the afternoon we heard that the English army was in Bethania; we also received orders to furnish meal, which was confirmed in the evening by an English dragoon who came here. It rained all day and all night, therefore no service was held except at dusk, when reports from Greenland were read.

Feb. 10. During a little conference about the troops which are to be expected today, the Brn. Bibighaus and Holder returned from General Greene, with his answer that he could not protect us, as the English must be already in our towns. When they arrived we were worrying about them. About ten o'clock the British dragoons came, and then the entire army followed in irregular order, continuing until four o'clock in the afternoon. Among them there were many people who to save their lives had placed themselves, their wives and children under the protection of the army. Major Ross announced that Lord Cornwallis would stop for a while with Br. Bagge, which he did soon after, with him being General Lesley, General McCloud, Major England, Governor Martin,[10] and the Commissary's assistant Booth. The Brn. Marshall and Bagge received them, and were courteously treated by the Generals.[11] After a stay of about an hour and a half the Generals took a friendly leave, especially Governor Martin, the others followed them about four o'clock. The people who followed the baggage stole various things at the store and in the houses, for example the Single Brethren lost all their wash, Br. Meyer lost nine head of cattle, Br. Bonn lost £40. The Single Brethren furnished brandy and oxen, and their wagon made two trips taking meal from the mill to the camp near Friedrich Müller's. There was much work in providing the hungry soldiers with bread and meal; because of this the prayer meeting could not be held. Various Brethren were kept in the camp all night because of business; the camp extended from Friedrich Müller's to Love, about two and a half miles. In the evening some well-behaved German men were in the town; they live below Salisbury, and were going from the army to their homes, as others are doing. The night was peaceful.

Feb. 11. Sunday. Various persons arrived, returning to their homes from the army; a few who had been detained went to the army. Otherwise the day was quiet and we had a blessed Gemein Tag.

Feb. 12. The wagon of the Single Brethren returned from the English camp. During the afternoon an American lieutenant of militia and four men on horseback arrived and went on. They said that tomorrow an army of fifteen to eighteen hundred would come from the Shallowford, which led to planning for their needs in meal. We hear all sorts of alarming reports.

Feb. 13. Five militiamen came, expecting to find Major Winston and his troop here; in the afternoon they were ordered to join him in

---

[10] Josiah Martin, last royal governor of North Carolina.

[11] The Moravian custom, in early days, of using the term *Brother* for all male members without distinction, has partially obscured the fact that there were as many differences among them as in the present day in any community. The leaders in Wachovia were men of education and culture, quite capable of meeting an English Lord on terms of equality, and capable also of treating him like a gentleman although he was at the head of enemy forces. Frederic William Marshall was college bred, having studied at the University of Leipsig before taking Orders in the Unitas Fratrum, and he was a man of outstanding ability in many lines. He was a Presbyter of the Moravian Church, with the additional rank of "Senior Civilis," given only to men of such marked executive and financial ability in addition to their ministerial gifts that few men in the Church held it. Traugott Bagge, also, had been educated abroad, and had long since learned to entertain persons of distinction. It may be added that Bishop Graff was educated at the University of Jena, as was Rev. Paul Tiersch, the first pastor of Salem; and Bishop Spangenberg, in a certain sense the founder of Wachovia, took his Master of Arts degree at Jena also.

Bethabara. A sick man, named McKain, a militiaman, from Mecklenburg, arrived and asked us to take him in; he was added to the wounded men in the house of the night-watchman.

Feb. 14. Today we heard that our County-Major, Winston, and a hundred and more cavalrymen, had left Bethabara for the lower part of the county, and would come here to punish the town, since it was thought that we must be Tories because the British in their march through Bethabara and Salem had not done as much damage as in Bethania.[12] One of his parties was here, to press horses, they said, but they only took one saddle from the tanyard. Another party was out to reconnoitre, and one of their number warned us frankly about the intended punishment. Toward evening all became quiet, so that at twilight we could strengthen our souls by reading the Harmony of the four Gospels.

Feb. 15. In the morning a Land-Arbeiter-Conferenz was held in quiet, and the members were able to return safely to their homes. In the afternoon the confusion began. At noon Major Winston and Major Smith, of this county, arrived, and dined at the Tavern. They brought no men, having dismissed their companies ten miles from here, and they were very friendly. About two hundred cavalrymen from Lincoln, Mecklenburg and Rowan Counties, arrived, and were supplied with forage and provisions. Their Major Dixon, from Lincoln, and Major Davidson, from Rowan, and indeed most of the officers, were very polite, and did all they could to preserve order and not give us too much trouble; on this account, at sundown, they went near the mill to camp. Many of the officers remained here, and a Presbyterian minister, Mr. Hall, said that if any one made a disturbance during the night he and the officers would stand by us, if they knew of it. However, the night was quiet until before day of

Feb. 16, when Captain Cloud, of Surry, with thirty-five cavalrymen arrived, were supplied with provisions, and left toward evening, having been entirely polite. Major Dixon's men were much in the town, and several were very troublesome, among them three or four who forced their way into the Gemein Haus, and were driven out with the help of the officers. Then they undertook to enter the store, to see what they could steal, but this was prevented. Major Dixon came himself to get brandy for his soldiers, so that not so many would come to the town, but it did not help much. After sunset most of them were out of the town, but Captain Hammond and Mr. Peddygrew, a volunteer, and some

---

[12] Of course this was an unfair explanation. Salem suffered less because the troops passed through in the day's march, made fewer demands and had less opportunity for plunder than at Bethania and Friedland, where they camped over night.

men came from General Greene to press horses and provisions. With them came Major Michajah Lewis, his three brothers and about nine others, who hang together in a band, and they lived *at discretion* in the town. The greeting given by Hammond, Peddygrew and Lewis sounded as though the destruction of our town had been determined, since, they said, we must have shown that we held with the English, and therefore Bethabara and Salem had not suffered from them as had Bethania. They began to press horses with great sternness, but when the two first-named [the Mecklenburg officers] saw that we wished to help them to the best of our ability, and when we talked with them about things, they changed entirely. They stayed over night with Bagge's family, and they, with Major Dixon and other officers and a doctor Alexander, were very useful and ready to scatter, or to prevent the excesses of, the above-mentioned band, but enough happened which no one could help, especially in the Tavern and in the Brothers House. The greatest disturbance was in the Tavern, which ended in a fight about midnight. That the fiend had planned the overthrow of our towns may be assumed from the lies that sprang up, saying that Salem ought to be burned because it had encouraged the British army to burn Bethania. It looked as though there was no hope for Salem or Bethabara, but God's protection was sufficient for us.

Feb. 17. This was a hard day, and the powers of darkness made themselves felt. It was also a day of marvelous help from our dear Lord, Who comforted and strengthened us in our affliction through the Daily Texts: *Thou art a strength to the poor, a strength to the needy in his distress, a refuge from the storm, a shadow from the heat.* Is. XXV, 4; *Be sober, be vigilant; because your adversary the devil, as a roaring lion, walketh about, seeking whom he may devour: whom resist steadfast in the faith, knowing that the same afflictions are accomplished in your brethren that are in the world.* I Peter, V, 8, 9.

Today Hammond and Peddygrew left with Pickens' men; we furnished them with a barrel of whiskey and two steers. They took the tanner's horse with them; the store horse and the doctor's horse ran away from them during the night. The noise in town continued from morning to night; much was taken without payment or receipt. A Brother was stopped on the street, his coat was taken off his back and stolen; hardly one house remained unrobbed. The above-mentioned band was the worst. They had written down the names of Brethren whom they particularly wanted to injure. Br. Yarrell escaped their hands through the aid of the officers. Br. Bagge was twice saved from them when they had a pistol at his breast, and the other rescues of Brethren and Sisters can not be enumerated. Major Dixon's men all came in, to go from here to Pickens. He and the other gentlemen from Mecklenburg did all that they could, unostentatiously, to quiet the vicious men, who were seeking every opportunity to find evidence of treason, or of correspondence with the British, so that they might destroy us on that pretext. When he was finally obliged to march, he and the other officers, and Dr. Alexander, took a friendly leave of us, and he left a company of cavalry for two or three hours, to prevent harm to us as far as possible. But their Captain, Mr. Grimes, saw that their presence only made matters worse, so he left with courtesy, and with great pity for us. Then a party of Surry militia arrived, under the Captains Mosby and Woolridge. The former was at once willing to help us all he could, tried to straighten things out, and he and one of his under-officers spent the night at Br. Bagge's, with the intention of protecting him, and while nothing was attempted their presence doubtless had a good effect, for two or three of the band, having eaten and drunk[13] all they desired, roamed through the town all night, frightening now this and now that family, making them empty chests and show their contents, saying they were "looking for powder which the English had left here." As they also asked about hard money, fine shirts, handkerchiefs, and the like, it was sufficiently clear what they really wanted, and much was stolen, and it was a wonder of God that Salem was not totally plundered, and that no Brother suffered bodily injury.

Today the Brn. Rudolph Strehle and Lück were sent to help the Brethren in Bethabara, where General Pickens' army is stationed.

Feb. 18. Sunday. After the above-mentioned band had eaten and drunk themselves full, Major Lewis led them out of town about ten o'clock, and they took with them by force the horses belonging to the store and the doctor, which they had recaptured, refusing to give a receipt for them. The Captains Mosby and Woolridge also left, the former with very friendly adieus. Captain Murray and his party did the same. He had been here, very quietly, for two or three days, waiting, he said, to watch what the aforesaid band was going to do, so that he could report it to General Pickens. Then came six men from Montgomery County in Virginia, going to General Greene. Other parties from Wilkes returned from General Pickens' army, and some of them stole various things, among them a horse which a Captain Barton made them return. Because of the constant unrest the Sunday services had to be omitted, except that the children's meeting was held at noon, when it was most quiet.

---

[13] *Gefressen und gesoffen*, that is they had been eating and drinking like beasts. The same verbs are used in connection with them in the entry for Feb. 18th.

Feb. 19. The wounded Daniel Rash, who has been here for treatment for a week and a half, was taken home by his wife and neighbors. The afternoon was again disturbed by a party of Wilkes militia, but the Brethren and Sisters were very happy that in the twilight we could again have a gemeinstunde, after being deprived of services for four days.

Feb. 20. The party of Wilkes militia finally left politely, after having been well fed, and having had all sorts of things made by the saddler and the blacksmith. Various parties arrived on their march to the army, and remained over night, and fairly quietly. [Another sick militia man, from Mecklenburg, was also fetched away.]

Our Representative, Mr. Cummings, returned from the Assembly. He reported, among other things, that in the Assembly it had been decided that all the Brethren, Quakers, etc., must bear arms, then this decision had come to naught because one of our friends drew attention to the fact that there were not enough members present to form a House. A few days later the same proposal was made, but it was defeated by a majority vote, and some voted against it that had formerly been in favor of it. Br. Bagge received a letter from Mr. Winston, who is serving as second Colonel of the county, since Colonel Armstrong has been suspended.[14] Colonel Winston had heard of our troubles, and wrote to ask how he could protect us. Colonel Lanier,[15] who had lost most of his property when the British marched through, wrote to Br. Bagge, promising to say a good word for us whenever he had opportunity. Both received appreciative answers, and request was made for one officer and six men, who could keep order among small passing parties.

In the meeting for communicants Br. Graff spoke on the Text for the day, in reference to the Holy Communion, which we will approach with humility, believing that through it we will find strength in Him after the oppression which has come upon us.

Feb. 21. The Brn. Lorenz Bagge and Ernst were here for Aeltesten Conferenz, and returned to their stations. A poor man was brought here, whom the soldiers declared to be a Tory. They were going to let him go, when he unwisely asked for the return of some effects taken from him and the Pass given to him by a Tory colonel, whereupon they handled him very roughly before releasing him.

Requisitions for food and drink, grain and forage, smith's work, etc., continued until one troop after the other left, having spent the night

---

[14] Col. Martin Armstrong was much criticised and finally disciplined for enlisting and paroling the prisoners taken at King's Mountain, instead of holding them for exchange with Americans captured previously by the British.
[15] Col. Robert Lanier.

here. Their place was immediately taken by others, especially some under Captain Woolridge, who followed in the footsteps of those who had left, and did not take their departure until the following morning. In the twilight several men arrived from Colonel Preston's troops at Bethabara,—most of them drunk. They wanted iron for horse-shoes, and to have thirty pair made here over night. Their harsh demand for these was quickly softened by our readiness to comply. One of them, named Martin, who called himself a colonel, caused much fright in the Gemein Haus and Brothers House, and also among the families. Captain Mosby and several men returned, and spent the night; they were very orderly. Five smiths came from Colonel Preston; they were orderly men and at once began work on the horse-shoes.

Feb. 22. The first men who came yesterday from Colonel Preston's force made a disturbance all morning, and were joined by others. They had to be entertained with organ-playing and other interests. At two o'clock Colonel [John] Preston himself arrived, with Colonel Crocket, who serves under him, and his soldiers, mostly cavalry. The meeting was unusually hearty on both sides, and Colonel Preston assured us of his favor and that nothing that we had suffered from his soldiers should go unpunished. He asked for meat, meal, salt and hay, and was well content. After conditions had been set before him he ordered that none of his men should be quartered in the houses, but should be content with places assigned in the magazine, the sheds and stables, which was very good for the town in the hard rain of the next night. The man who had called himself Colonel Martin could no longer maintain his pose, and tried to ride off, but was arrested and sentenced to seventeen lashes, but he escaped during the night. Colonel Preston, his officers, and many privates, listened to the organ, and the Colonel had a most friendly conversation with Br. Marshall about our affairs, looked at the bark-mill with interest, and said once that he prized this day as one of the most pleasant in his life. In the evening he sent for Br. Bagge again, and ordered some more iron and some paper, which was furnished. In the Tavern it was as quiet as though only two men were there. The soldiers, around their camp-fires, were also orderly, and when there was a hard rain during the night they withdrew into the sheds and stables with all modesty. In the smithy work was pushed all night.

Feb. 23. About ten o'clock Colonel Preston continued his march toward Guilford. Before leaving he gave Br. Bagge a letter of thanks, written and signed by his own hand, expressing his appreciation of all the good and friendly service which had been given to him here. At leaving he spoke most affectionately to us. The other officers and privates were most polite. He left four sick men, and their horses, here to be looked after, with another man detailed to wait on them.

In the afternoon other small parties came, returning from the army or from other service. They demanded food and drink, and some of them went further. Some of those who remained over night behaved well, but some of Captain Lapp's company were antagonistic to us, though they became somewhat milder after attending the evening meeting.

Feb. 24. The men from Captain Lapp's company sneaked away, after securing brandy; the others left with courtesy. During the morning an American *flag of truce* passed, led by Surgeon Richard Pindell and Lieutenant Samuel Hanson of the Maryland troops; and a British *flag of truce,* led by Dr. Jackson and Surgeon Stewant of the 71st Regiment. They were on their way from the Cowpens, in South Carolina, to their respective armies. These gentlemen looked over the town, with approval, and went on after breakfast., At the request of the former group some money was given them on General Morgan's account. Colonel Preston sent a soldier back to the doctor, as he had carelessly shot off his thumb with his own gun. The Baptist minister, [William] Hill, and Captain Holbert, of the Dan River settlement, came on a visit. The former and Colonel Winston had planned that Mr. Hill and one or two Justices should stay here to aid us when passing soldiers made unjust demands on us, but he could not remain, for the small-pox, which was beginning to creep about on Dan River, was breaking out on him. It is quite apparent that the gentlemen do not know what we mean by a *Salvegarde,* but we see their good will toward us, so far as that goes. In the evening there arrived Col. William Sheppard, two of Colonel Cleveland's sons, and another man, who went on to the army next day. Mr. Hill went home, with many expressions of his sympathy for our circumstances.

The Saviour sent us a quiet evening, so that we might refresh our souls in His Holy Sacrament.

Feb. 25. *Sunday.* At eight o'clock there was the Post Communion. As a matter of precaution, yesterday and today a watch was set before the Gemein Haus, but there was no disturbance. Br. Graff preached on the Gospel for the day, as we entered into the holy Passion season.

Br. Rudolph Strehle took the place of Br. Zillman as night-watchman. There were no strangers in town all day, which is somewhat unusual. [Seven robbers were taken up at Tanner's, being of the Mecklenburg militia.]

Feb. 26. Things fell again into their usual channel, but not so badly. In the evening there arrived ten or twelve men from Wilkes, and two of the Lewis men. Br. Reutz' great-coat[16] and Br. Bonn's horse were returned, both the worse for use. They were tame in their manner, but next morning,

Feb. 27, they could not refrain from taking off various things on all sorts of pretexts. All day parties came and went, eating and drinking *at public expense.* Four, who said they belonged to General Pickens, pressed iron at the store and work at the smithy. These, and fourteen from Wilkes, who were returning from the army, spent the night here.

Feb. 28. The Pickens men stole three hats from Br. Reutz; the others followed their example. Both parties pressed bread from the baker, without paying for it, to take it away with them,—so it happens every day. In the afternoon Colonel Preston's Major, Joseph Cloyd, Captain Doak, Mr. Baker, and various officers and privates arrived, all on their way to the army. They were very polite and obliging, and spent the night here. In the morning the sick man left behind by Colonel Preston went away, thankful for the help given him here.

March 1. Last night a man named Robert Higgins, one of the Wilkes men who recently plundered and committed excesses here, returned, and his entrance was much as formerly. But in the morning Major Cloyd had him brought in, placed him under arrest, gave him a written statement of the accusations made against him, had his baggage searched, and made him return a handkerchief, a knife and an overcoat which had been stolen here. Then Major Cloyd and his company went on to the camp, with expressions of his appreciation. Three more men came to eat and drink at public expense. The evening and the night were quiet once again, for a wonder.

In the twilight we had a general meeting, and remembered the founding of the Ancient Unitas Fratrum, with many thanks to the dear Saviour.

At half past seven we could again have Grosse Helfer Conferenz, after an interval of six weeks. The Brethren and Sisters who have not had small-pox were asked to decide whether they would be inoculated. There have been people in our town who had it, but Br. Bonn, who has the wounded soldiers in his care, is doubtful about bringing it in by inoculation. It was decided to postpone inoculation until some one in town has small-pox.

March 2. The weather has been so mild that the cherry trees are in full bloom.

---

[16] See Salem diary entry of Feb. 17, 1781.

13

During the afternoon the rest of the Wilkes militia returned from camp, under command of Major Hernden, Captain Lenoir, etc. From some things that were said they seem to be ashamed of their former behaviour, but they were little better this time. The food which they demanded was given to them, though we afterwards learned that they had plenty with them. In spite of that the officers ordered food in the Brothers House at the point of the sword, although a meal had been prepared for them in the Tavern. The Major seemed later not to have approved of the performance, though he was present when it happened. Most of the privates left, but the majority of the officers planned to stay at the Tavern, and there was every evidence that robbery was intended for the night, but this was hindered by the coming of Col. William Campbell, of Washington County, Va., with sixty men, on their way to the army. The Wilkes men immediately left the Tavern, the officers going to the distillery, where with drawn swords they committed all sorts of excesses. Colonel Campbell and Colonel Armstrong, who had come with him, restrained them as far as they could, and it ended by our supplying them with forage for their horses, food and lodging for themselves, and bread and brandy next morning. Colonel Campbell had with him all he needed, and asked only for place for the horses, and firewood for his camp, and forty pounds of meat for the next day. At his request he and his men attended a singstunde, which they enjoyed and they were quiet and orderly. He was solicitous that no harm should befall us.

March 3. Colonel Campbell went on and thirty of his men followed later in the day. Before leaving he gave emphatic warning to Captain Lenoir of Wilkes, concerning the bad behaviour of himself and his men. Promise of *Salvegarde* for the town was secured from Colonel Armstrong. There were a good many strangers in the town, coming to make purchases. The night was quiet. [I wrote by Captain Yelpin from the State of Delaware to Pennsylvania.]

March 4. Sunday. Colonel Jacks, of Georgia, and Captain Gilpin, who had spent the night here, went on their way. The former left a negress and other things here to be taken care of; the latter took a letter addressed to Br. Neisser, in Yorktown. Today and the following day about a hundred and fifty horses passed, returning from the army for lack of forage. Various men from Virginia and sixty from Rowan, under Captains Purvians and Holmes, returned from the army; the latter took one hundred pounds of meal here.

March 5. [I returned from Bethabara to Salem, meeting many with empty horses returning from a skirmish which had been on the 2nd.

Some wounded were also brought to Salem.] The passing continued,[17] and the men must always be given food here *at public expense*. Among the large crowd in the Tavern over night was Mr. Peddygrew, who came here recently from General Pickens. All the officers spoke emphatically against the plundering and seemed to be in favor of good order. At twilight Gemein Nachrichten were read; the singstunde was omitted.

March 6. Br. Meyer's life was in danger. Several scamps aimed their weapons at him, to force him to give them brandy; but the officers interfered and they went on, though they took various things with them, on pretense of borrowing them. [There was another skirmish.] In the afternoon another severely wounded man came to join those already here, with several men to wait on them. A neighbor came for his fine young stallion, which had been recovered from the thief by Captain Purvians, and had been left here for him. James Lewis also came for the horse belonging to himself and his deceased brother Micajah, which had been left here to be fed. The night was quiet.

In the singstunde we began to use the Passion hymns and verses from the new Unity Hymn Book, singing some of them and reading others, and this will be continued during the Passion season.

March 7. Today the confusion began again. The Wilkes Captains, Joel Lewis and Franklin, in unmannerly fashion, demanded service in the Brothers House, as has been done by many others during these days. Major Shelby and four others had their horses shod here; and in the evening a number of Colonel Preston's men arrived, utterly worn out. Seven had been particularly commended to us, and they were lodged in the magazine, but they were not hungry enough to cook cornmeal for themselves; they had escaped from a skirmish that had been lost. [Some more returned from the Battle, and Captain Ewing and Lieutenant Kinder and one with fifteen wounds were brought to Salem.]

March 8. All the above-mentioned moved on. Sergeant Johann Hauser arrived with five men as a *Salvegarde* for the town. In the evening three or four of Colonel Preston's wounded arrived, among them Adjutant Ewins; Br. Bonn bandaged their wounds. With them came many of Preston's men, who spent the night here, and in one or another way were supplied with food at public expense.

March 9. Several slightly wounded men, and others who were returning from the army, went on their way. All day there were demands for

---

[17] The constant passing of militia returning from the army draws attention to the great difficulty which General Greene and all other officers experienced in holding the militia long enough to get good service from them. In all the states, north and south, this was one of the great problems of the war.

food and forage; most of the men allowed themselves to be persuaded to go further. Our *Salvegarde* was already called away. The Colonels Crocket and Preston returned, with some of their men, and a wounded Lieutenant, Sawyer, who had been shot in the side, and who increased the number of Br. Bonn's patients. In the evening the well-known Captain Campbell and three others arrived on foot; the former was somewhat subdued.

March 10. Colonel Preston looked after the wounded with all love and faithfulness. He and Colonel Crocket rode to Bethabara in the evening. There was a constant passing of militia coming from the camp. Beginning today the wounded drew their rations from the Brothers House. Several Brethren went from here to Richmond to the election of Assembly-men. In the store there was the now very rare opportunity to purchase goods from a man moving from Guilford to Virgina. The price was so high that it took three hundred Continental dollars to buy what formerly sold for one silver dollar.

March 11. Sunday. We had a blessed Unity day, with Nachrichten from the Diaspora and from the Mission fields.

This afternoon the Colonels Preston and Crocket returned, and the former found that the baggage he had thought lost had followed him here. Having spent several hours in looking after their wounded men, and having commended them to our best care, they went to their homes. As the British army is drawing nearer to us again not so many people are passing, but those that do come are troublesome. It is said that headquarters of the Continental army is at High Rock ford on Haw River, and that the British are six miles from Guilford Court-House.

March 12. In the eleventh hour of the morning, after a painful illness, our Br. Jens Schmidt went peacefully to the Saviour, and his departure was announced in the customary manner at the reading meeting.

Mr. Troy, of Salisbury, sent inquiries about two of his run-away negroes, who are supposed to be in this neighborhood. Several of our Brethren went to Richmond to the election, which was held over again today since the election of day before yesterday has been adjudged illegal. Captain Simons, of Rowan, pressed iron, black-smith's work and provisions. Captain Hammond, of General Pickens' troop, and several others were here, and behaved modestly.

March 13. More Brethren went to the election. Last evening a report spread that the British were near Richmond, which led the inhabitants there to spend the night in the woods. Colonel Sheppard was elected Senator, and John Lewis and Samuel Cummings were elected Burgesses, as they had the most votes in the boxes.

At one o'clock in the afternoon the body of our departed Br. Jens Schmidt was laid to rest, after his memoir had been read and Br. Graff had spoken on the Text of his day of home-going.

March 14. It was fairly quiet. One of the wounded placed here, Kinder by name, is dangerously ill, and it looks as though he might bleed to death. Major Balfour and lawyer McKay came to spend the night. They were followed by four men with five horses, from whose speech nothing good could be expected, but a report that the British hoped to reach Bethabara during the night caused them to break camp and depart. At twilight we continued reading the harmony of the Gospels.

March 15. Yesterday afternoon Colonel Jack came for his negress, and we took advantage of the opportunity to entrust to him the Tickets received last December from General Gates, asking him to present them and receive the payment as he is going to Maryland.

A mother whose son is a prisoner among the British, and a wife whose husband is also there, had been to visit them, and passed through on their return, very woeful. We could not help sharing in their sorrow. [There was a Battle near Newgarden.]

March 16. Colonel Alexander, Captain Brandon, &c. passed, getting out of the way of the British, thinking they would go through Rowan and Mecklenburg Counties back to South Carolina. A Hessian rifle-man arrived. He had run away at the beginning of a battle,[18] and did not know how it had ended, and he could only say that yesterday for three hours he heard heavy firing, after he left the army.

March 17. We expected to send letters and our diary to Pennsylvania today, but when the messenger reached Richmond with them Gottfried Müller had already set out, and so he brought the packet back.

This morning a stranger reported that yesterday the Continental army had been forced by the British to retreat.[19] At noon this was confirmed by an old man from the neighborhood, who had an open letter to "all friends of the country," signed by Mr. Ross, asking for a gift of old rags, meal and brandy for bandaging and feeding the wounded.[20] We collected some rags and prepared to send them. Six or seven light-

---

[18] The battle of Guilford Court-House was fought on March 15th.
[19] General Greene and his army retreated to the Iron Works on Troublesome Creek. The battle was technically a victory for the British, since they held the field, but Cornwallis had suffered such losses that he dared not risk another engagement, and on March 18th began a retreat, by way of Ramsay's Mill on Haw River, to Wilmington, N. C.
[20] Cornwallis left the American wounded at Guilford Court-House and the British wounded at New Garden Meeting House.

horse from Rowan came just in time to talk with the man, and after they had learned all about what had happened they very quietly went home. Several soldiers of the local troops came, and went on.

Today three of the wounded Virginians and their attendants left us for their homes, thankful for the care given them. During these days there have been visits from the relatives and friends of the wounded men; among others, the wife of the severely wounded Peter Kinder came to see him and stayed to wait on him; his wound continues to bleed badly.

March 18. [Spach, Sr. set off for Newgarden, and returned next day.]

March 19. Major Polk and others spent the night here; they behaved modestly.

March 21. Colonel Philips and Major Armstrong and three men came for information about the army. Yesterday the Major sent us a letter containing a friendly warning not to send help to the British hospital, but he approved when he heard that we had sent nothing except rags for the use of the wounded.

March 22. It looks as though Peter Kinder would recover, for the bleeding has ceased.

March 23. Several South Carolinians were here on their way to Virginia. They had served under Sumter, and could not say enough of the misery in South Carolina, caused by the murdering and plundering. In the evening ten or eleven Rowan militiamen arrived. They said they were on their way to join Greene's army, but they were without an officer. All but two or three were very troublesome, tried to force food in the Brothers House and so on. They were fed in the Tavern, and after giving annoyance enough they left,

March 24, at noon. Of the wounded Virginians Lieutenant Sawyers left today, fairly well restored to health.

There was a blessed celebration of the Holy Sacrament.

March 25. Sunday. The Festival of all Choirs. The Post-Communion was followed by a liturgical meeting for all, in which Br. Marshall spoke of the incarnation of Jesus for our salvation. He particularly commended the Older Girls to the thoughts and prayers of the congregation, this being their special Festal Day. In the evening the *Litany of the Life, Sufferings and Death of Jesus* was sung for the first time in the revised form appearing in the new Unity Hymn Book.

March 26. The summer arrangement of services went into effect. At twilight we read Nachrichten from the Diaspora, this service being followed by a singstunde. [Captain Sawyer, who had been shot through the breast, went home recovered.]

March 28. By a Pennsylvania wagon we received several packages of letters, the Bethlehem diary of November and December, Nachrichten and Wochen from the Unity's Elders Conference, and fourteen Text Books. Letters and our reports from December, 1780, to February, 1781, were sent north by Mr. Hill.

March 31. Br. Marshall spoke in the prayer meeting. * * * He especially recommended prayers for our dear Brethren and Sisters in the West Indies, who had been brought into great need through the terrible hurricane in October last year.

During the latter days of this month we have enjoyed an unusual peace and quiet. Today the wounded Virginian, Montgomery, and his father who has been here to wait on him, returned to their home, taking a good impression of what they have enjoyed here. It is to be hoped that the presence of the wounded here, and the visits made by their relatives and friends, may be part of a blessed plan of the Saviour on their behalf, for most of them are from New River, where many people live who have heard the preaching of the Brethren in Pennsylvania. Yesterday Peter Etter came to visit his wounded brother-in-law Peter Kinder. He is a son of Gerhard Etter of Quitopehille (now Hebron), and Br. Graff knew him as a child. He remembered Br. Graff, but was very shy. May the Saviour carry out His gracious plans for these people. Thanks be to Him for His grace and protection, and for the peace and quiet which we have enjoyed during the latter days of this month.

April. During this month a constant stream of officers and soldiers passed through Salem, and many wandering parties, which had to be provided with the necessaries of life at public charge. Among the rest there was one party with a prisoner accused of treason. The behaviour of officers and men was fairly peaceable and modest.

April 1. Sunday. Morning and afternoon we read the Bethlehem diary for the month of December, and also their Memorabilia for 1780. We thanked the Saviour with them for the quiet and peace which this beloved congregation has enjoyed during the entire year, in the midst of these hard times. A special matter for thanks and praise was the safe arrival of Br. and Sr. Reichel in Bethlehem on Dec. 28, 1780, and also the recovery of our dear Br. Nathanael [Seidel] from a severe illness.

April 2. The weather was cold and stormy. Our Burgesses,[21] Mr. Cummings and Captain Lewis, passed on their way to the Assembly. Although it was to meet at the usual time, the Governor and Council had sent a special Express to each County member, to call them together. Mr. Cummings had it much at heart that we should retain our privileges, and he made various well-meant proposals. Among other things he expressed the wish that in the laws guaranteeing our freedom we should not be confused with the Quakers, Mennonites and Dunkards, and put into the same class with them. Br. Bagge wrote a letter to a gentlemen living in the lower country, who is in the Assembly, commending the Brethren and their affairs to his usual good offices, and sent the letter by Mr. Cummings.

April 8. This was Palm Sunday, and our entrance into the Passion Week.

At five o'clock, on our God's Acre for strangers, there was the burial of a man [a continental soldier,] whose name was said to be Todewine. Two days ago Major Winston sent him to us in a litter for further care, after he had been sick for two weeks and had not improved. He was in an almost dying condition when they brought him to us, and he died last night.

April 9. The wounded Captain Ewing left us today [being almost recovered].

April 10. We continued the reading of the Passion story. This evening there was a hard storm, and during the night the cold did much damage to the fruit. [Sent a Parcell of Lettres for Pennsylvania by Hahn, Jr. of Friedland.]

April 12. The wounded Peter Kinder (or Günther) left today with his wife, who has been waiting on him here for several weeks. He showed unusual gratitude.

[The usual services for Maundy Thursday were held, closing with] an indescribably blessed Communion.

April 13. Good Friday. [The usual services.]

April 14. Great Sabbath. Mr. Guthery, a Lieutenant from Colonel Lee's dragoons, came to press a large quantity of deer-skins from the store and the leather-dresser's, for clothing for his men. Finally he let himself be persuaded to leave the skins here, and promised to spare us as much as possible. There were alarming reports that about three hundred dragoons would march through or would be quartered here, and the like. The Saviour so ordered it that they did not come, and we were able to observe the day in peace, [with the usual services].

---

[21] The 1781 diary generally uses the term Burgess instead of Representative.

April 15. Easter Sunday. The congregation assembled in the Saal at five o'clock in the morning, and after the greeting: *The Lord is risen, etc.,* they visited the graves of those Brethren and Sisters who have fallen asleep, and on God's Acre, in the presence of our risen Lord, held the Easter Liturgy. It was a mild, though cloudy morning. At the beginning of the preaching service the choir sang: *Remember Jesus Christ, Who from the dead hath risen.* In the afternoon at half past one Br. Marshall read the Easter story. In the evening at half past seven there was singstunde.

April 16. Mr. Silberberg and Mr. Nisbet, from Salisbury, have been here for the past days, spending Easter with us.

Today it snowed for the first time this winter. During the following night it froze, killing most of the fruit, and damaging the rye, which was already in ear.

April 17. Eight adults and eleven children have been inoculated for small-pox.

At twilight we remembered the laying of the corner-stone of our Gemein Saal, eleven years ago, retold the story, and gave thanks to the Saviour Who since that time has so richly blessed the services held in our Saal.

April 18. Several wagons and ten soldiers, infantry belonging to Colonel Washington, passed through the town.

April 20. During the afternoon there was a severe storm, with hail stones as large as hickory-nuts, but it did not last long and there was no wind. Our Burgesses returned from their fruitless journey. On this side of New Bern they had met a number of Burgesses, who had been waiting for the arrival of other members, but not enough had come to make a quorum, so they were scattering.

Mr. Carrington and Guthery, officers from Colonel Lee's dragoons, came for the deer-skins which were recently pressed here, taking 103 from the store and 50 from the leather-dresser. For them they gave orders on public account. They, and about thirty-five cavalrymen who were with them, attended the singstunde and listened attentively. They spent the night here, and after they had been supplied with food, hay, iron and smith-work, they left on

April 21, and were followed by their baggage. They wanted to take our team for moving the skins, but were dissuaded. In the prayer-meeting Br. Graff called attention to the inoculation for small-pox, and the arrangements for nursing made in the Choir of Married People.

April 23. Twenty-four British prisoners passed, under guard of Rowan County militia. They were being taken from Salisbury to

Henry County, Va. Mr. Beard and two women from Salisbury were shown around the town, together with Dr. Reed, who was on his way to the army with several of Washington's cavalrymen. Mr. Beard was going to Pennsylvania, and took a letter from Br. Graff to Br. Matthaeus [Heyl] in Lititz,[22] telling of our present circumstances.

April 24. Mr. Steel, of General Greene's army, passed on his way to Richmond to hasten the sending of provisions from this county and from Wilkes. Two or three familes, with about sixty head of cattle and a wagon, passed through, moving from the upper settlement on the Catawba, where the murders committed by the Cherokees made it impossible to remain. Lieutenant Simons and several of Washington's cavalry spent the night here, and

April 25, they followed the baggage wagons to the army.

Br. Broesing went to Bethabara. He has taken a small farm there, and went to make preparations for building.

April 30. The boy, Jacob Bonn, was placed with Br. Krause, on trial, to learn the cabinet-maker's trade.

Major Mazaret and several captains, with ten baggage and ammunition wagons and a guard of about twenty militia from Virginia, passed on their way to the main army. The Major, a German, was much concerned that his passing should do us no harm, and he therefore sent his wagons and men across the Wach, camping with them himself. On his way from Prince Edward Court-House hither he has taken nothing from the people without paying for it in salt. He did the same here; and asked us many questions, and was well satisfied with what he saw of the town, and in attending the singstunde, as were his officers. They left next morning.

May 3. The Single Sisters from Bethabara came to Salem, and with the local Sisters ended their Choir year.

May 4. They celebrated their Choir festival [with the usual services].

May 8. A passer-by brought Br. Marshall a letter from Br. Wollin, dated London, Oct. 29, 1780. It had come by way of Charlestown.

May 9. In the meeting for Bible reading mention was made of the home-going of the Jünger twenty-one years ago today, with thanks to the Saviour for all the blessings that the Unity of Brethren had received through this beloved servant of the Lord. The weather was cold, with a thunder-storm, hail and snow.

---

[22] Search of the Moravian Archives at Lititz shows that none of the letters from Wachovia have been preserved.

May 12. Br. Bibighaus went to Hillsborough on business for the store. In a general meeting at eight o'clock mention was made of the origin of this important anniversary in the Brethren's Church.[23]

May 13. Nine Brethren and eleven Sisters had a lovefeast in thankful recognition of the fact that within the past twelve months they have been Received into the congregation and have been permitted to partake of the Lord's Supper.

Announcement was made of the betrothal of the Single Br. Carl Opiz of Bethania to the Single Sr. Christine Jorde of Salem, and they were commended to the prayers of the congregation in view of the approaching change in their Choir standing.

May 14. The boys Michael Kirschner and Ludwig Blum went to Bethania with their masters and Br. Samuel Stotz, and there they were formally apprenticed by Justice George Hauser, Jr.

May 15. Sixty of the Virginia militia and their wagons passed through the town.

May 17. A package of letters and our diaries for March and April were sent to Pennsylvania by Mr. Peter Ikes.

May 19. Colonel Shephard and his suite passed.

May 20. For two hours there was an unusually heavy rain, which raised the streams and injured the new race at the grind-stone dam. Br. Carl Opiz came from Bethania, and was married to Sr. Christine Jorde.

May 21. Br. Bibighaus went to Mr. Eitel, but was frightened off by a French officer who asked him alarming questions, and he did not carry out his commission from Br. Bagge. (See entry on the 27th of this month.)

May 23. Day before yesterday, yesterday and today we have had severe storms, and we thank the Saviour that we have escaped injury.

May 24. Ascension Day. In the afternoon, in Bethabara, there was the reception of the three Sisters, Maria Bagge, Maria Magdalena Reutz, and Maria Elisabeth Engel as Akoluthie, followed by the ordination of the two Sisters, Maria Bagge and Anna Maria Quest as Deaconesses. Maria Magdalena Reutz will be the school-teacher for the girls of Bethabara, and will visit the girls of Bethania. Br. Andreas Broesing has been betrothed to the Single Sr. Anna Johanna Steup.

May 25. Col. Alexander Martin's brother and troops marched through Salem.

May 27. The Brn. Samuel Stotz and Bibighaus went to Salisbury on public affairs, [to get the Tickets audited]. Some goods which had

---

[23] The *Brotherly Agreement* was first signed at Herrnhut on May 12, 1727.

been bought for the store, and which were to be delivered eleven miles from here the first of last week, and which we have had much trouble in getting, (see under date of the 21st of this month,) arrived here unexpectedly in a Continental wagon on its way to Salisbury. They came in fairly good condition, and we were very glad.

May 28. Sr. Anna Maria Quest returned from Bethabara, where she has been since the 24th. With her came Sr. M. Elisabeth Engel, who will remain here.

May 30. Br. Marshall held a Choir meeting for the Single Brethren. He arranged for visiting in the Choir, taking the place of the former Choir companies.

May 31. Mr. Cummings, our Burgess, who has a very painful swelling on his hand, has come for several days of treatment by Br. Bonn. Captain Watts, of Colonel White's dragoons, came from Stanton this evening, and went on next morning. The Brn. Stotz and Bibighaus returned from Salisbury. The Auditor adjusted the Tickets given to Salem and Bethabara, and treated the Brethren with courtesy. The Tickets amounted to £145,600 : Continental currency.

During the past days new curtains have been hung in the Saal, and the tone of the organ has been improved by a box and swell.

June 1. The Georgia Colonel Pannell came on his way to the southern army, or more probably to his former home. In the afternoon General Scott arrived. He commanded the Virginia troops at the surrender of Charlestown, and has now received permission from the British to go home on parole. Both men remained over night, and the General was well pleased when we showed him our work-shops and houses.

June 2. Mr. Cummings returned to Richmond, after being in Br. Bonn's care for three days. It is reported that all American prisoners in the neighborhood of Charlestown will be sent to Virginia on the 15th of this month, for exchange.[24]

June 3. Whitsunday. [The usual services were held.]

June 4. There was a blessed Unity day, with Nachrichten from Nicobar. In the evening meeting Br. Andreas Broesing was married to Sr. Anna Johanna Steup.

Two Continental wagons, loaded with ammunition, passed under guard, going from Salisbury to Hillsborough. They took with them

---

[24] An exchange of prisoners was arranged on the Pee Dee, May 3rd, between representatives of General Greene and Lord Cornwallis. All militia held in the South were counted exchanged at once, and were set free. Officers and men of the Continental Line were sent to Virginia and were released there.

seventeen sides of leather, which were due the Continental army from our tanyard. They behaved well.

During these days the Whigs and Tories in a neighboring county have frequently attacked each other, and some have been killed or wounded. We hear most alarming reports of these attacks and of robbery and plundering.[25]

June 5. Two letters were brought by Mr. Seth [or Silas] Coffin, a Quaker; one came from Br. Sydrich at Philadelphia, and the other from Br. George Neisser at Yorktown. The latter mentioned that Friedrich Hahn, Jr., was returning, and would bring two packages from Lititz.

Col. Alexander Martin, who holds the second position in the government of this state, passed on his way to Salisbury, and was very friendly.

June 6. Repairs at the saw-mill were finished.

June 7. Since the end of May there have been frequent storms with heavy rain, so that the meadows have been flooded and the grass injured. The weather is unusually cool for the time of year.

Friedrich Hahn, Jr. arrived with letters, the Bethlehem diary for January, February and March, 1781, Gemein Nachrichten, and the Text Books for this year.

Two Captains and a Commissary passed this afternoon, with a howitzer, two cannon, and nine wagons loaded with ammunition and Continental stores. They were on their way to General Greene's army. The officers looked about the town with much pleasure. The mill gave grain.

June 8. Colonel Brisbane passed with several of his negroes, going from South Carolina to Virginia, whither he took a large number of them last year. This time he secured about thirty of them in a fort on the Congaree which the Americans have recently taken from the English.[26]

June 11. Br. and Sr. Broesing moved to Bethabara.

June 13. One hundred or more Catawba Indians arrived with wives and children, passed through quietly and camped in the neighborhood. When they were no longer with the army they remained in Virginia, but they were frightened away by the reported approach of the British,

---

[25] As the armies of Greene and Cornwallis withdrew the Tories rose, and in small bands committed many excesses, attacking the Whigs throughout the country from Guilford to the coast. The Whigs retaliated wherever they could, but suffered greatly, especially in the east, before they were able to suppress the Tories once more.

[26] After the battle of Guilford Court-House, General Greene moved into South Carolina. Camden fell on May 10th, and Augusta, Ga., surrendered on June 5th. In the interval many smaller posts were taken by the Americans.

and plan to return to their land on the Waxhaws. In the evening a company of artificers came on their way to General Greene's army, and

June 14, went on in peace. During the night several wagons returning from the army reached the mill, and passed through Salem this morning. An officer tried to press food, though he had plenty with him for all his men, but it was averted. During the night the watchman met two or three Catawba Indians near the store and sent them away. Our District-General, Francis Lock, was here, and provided himself with various necessaries in the store, paying hard money. He was friendly.

June 15. Mr. Brooks sent orders that Salem should send to Bethabara 200 lbs. meat and 20 bushels of corn for 1500 Virginia militia who were coming thither. This could not be supplied immediately, so on

June 16, Br. Samuel Stotz was sent to Bethabara, to arrange that it should be furnished there. The coming of the militia proved to be a false report, so the requisition was canceled.

June 19. The Brn. Herbst, Bagge and Samuel Stotz went to Bethabara to pay our three-fold taxes to Mr. Brooks in Tickets. He came too late to attend to the business, and was asked to get the Tickets in Salem whenever it suited him.

June 20. In the Aeltesten Conferenz Br. Praetzel was betrothed to Sr. Elizabeth Nielsen. He has been called as Congregation Vorsteher, and they will both be assistants in the care of the Married Choir.

June 21. This evening about forty recruits for Colonel White's dragoons camped beyond the bridge, and in the morning,

June 22, they went on to Virginia. Their officer, Captain Yarborough, had some clothing made here for himself, was polite, and took pains to see that no disorder occurred. Mr. George Wagner, who, with his wagon, had been pressed to take clothing to the southern army, and who was now returning to his home at Sackenaw, six miles from Bethlehem, [Pa.], took with him several letters and our diary for the month of May. A prominent family, which last year fled to Virginia from their home in South Carolina, passed through the town on their return, with a large company of negroes and all their other possessions, fleeing from Virginia because of the unrest there. All this month such families have been passing, trying to return to their homes in South Carolina or Georgia, but the circumstances which they thought favorable have changed before they finished their journey, they cannot reoccupy their former plantations, and do not know where they shall turn, and many men, formerly rich, have become very poor, so that during this month our sympathy has often been aroused.

June 24. Sunday. Fifteen little boys celebrated their Choir Festival today. In the Married Choir visiting was re-established.

June 25. Three wagons passed, having helped move Colonel Perkins' hospital from Virginia to Charlotte, North Carolina. Br. Meyer brought from Salisbury a Guinea negress, [named Betty,] twenty-five years old, who had been bought for the Tavern. As the Brethren and Sisters are busy with the harvest we are holding only one service each week-day evening,—at eight o'clock. The harvest this year is abundant.

June 29. The senior Doctor of the Southern Department of our army, Major Swann of Colonel White's dragoons, and another officer, came from Virginia on their way to the army in the south. From the south came four officers and six privates, with horses, going to Virginia. All refreshed themselves here, and the Tavern had to give forage, but no other requisitions were made. The officers attended the singstunde in the evening, to their pleasure, and both parties went on next morning.

July 1. By Mr. Temple Cole a letter was sent to Br. Neisser, at Yorktown, [Pa.]

July 2. The Sisters who are pregnant had a lovefeast and a doctrinal sermon. Tonight we had a severe thunder-storm, but the Heavenly Father protected us from harm.

July 3. Eight Continental wagons passed on their way from the southern army to Pennsylvania. At the mill they took forcible possession of fifty bushels of corn.

July 6. In the evening meeting Br. Graff reminded the congregation of the significance of this day, on which, in 1415 at Constance, John Hus, the witness to the truth, sealed his testimony for Jesus Christ with a martyr death.

July 11. Once more we have the Heavenly Father to thank for protection, when with a great crash lightning struck between the store and Br. Tycho Nissen's house.

July 14. Ninety-seven communicants partook of the Lord's Supper, including the ministers and their wives from the country congregations. [Wrote by John Leinbach to Geo. Neisser, to be left at Mr. Ogle's.]

July 17. Several members of the Assembly passed on their return to their homes. From them we learned that it had been decided to hold the next session here in Salem in November. May our dear Lord direct this according to His will, for He can turn the hearts of the mighty of this earth even as He turns the course of water-brooks.

July 21. Mr. Brooks came, and accepted Tickets for the three-fold tax.

July 22. Br. Priem is feeble and Br. Martin Schneider was transferred to the kitchen of the Brothers House for his assistance, and Br. Christian Stauber took the place of Br. Schneider in the school for little boys.

July 30. There was the first singstunde since harvest.

Aug. 4. [Received by Anton Bieler a Parcell from Pennsylvania.]

Aug. 5. After praying the Church Litany, Nachrichten from the West Indies were read. From the Bethlehem diary for April, which Br. Marshall read in the afternoon, we saw with joy what the Lord has done for that congregation, and noted their hearty sympathy for our circumstances. The heat is unusually great.

Aug. 11. The street[27] in front of Br. Triebel's house is being improved, and the gutters plastered.

Aug. 12. On account of rain the evening meeting was omitted. The night-watchman has noticed traces of thieves, so the watch was doubled. Tonight they were seen again, but when the alarm was given they ran away.

Aug. 13. This important memorial day of the Unity of Brethren was celebrated, and the Lord made it a day of blessing for us. [Court kept at Richmond, and Licenses taken out.]

Aug. 14. This afternoon two wagons set out for Pennsylvania, with Heinrich Hauser, Jacob Schor and George Hauser, Jr., in charge. They will bring goods for the store on their return trip. Br. Bibighaus, who is commissioned to make the purchases, followed them,

Aug. 15, on horseback. At twilight we began to read the *Idea Fidei Fratrum,*[28] and the Brethren and Sisters were pleased. [All this week trouble with a Gang of Thieves.] Tonight Br. Gottlob Krause shot toward the robbers to frighten them, and they sent back a ball which passed near his head.

Aug. 16. What happened yesterday has made the night-watchmen more vigorous in their action, and when a robber was discovered in the garden of the Single Sisters they shot at him and apparently wounded him severely.

Aug. 17. Fifteen girls had a blessed Choir Festival.

Aug. 21. In the singstunde hymns were used in remembrance of the first mission of the Unity to the heathen on St. Thomas, [West Indies,] forty-nine years ago, and thanks and praise were given for the spread of the Gospel since that day.

---

[27] Main Street, just north of Academy Street.

[28] *Idea Fidei Fratrum* oder kurzer Begrif der Christlichen Lehre in den evangelischen Brüdergemeinen dargelegt von August Gottlieb Spangenberg. Barby, 1779. It was reprinted at Barby in 1782 and 1789; was printed in Swedish at Gothenburg in 1782; and appeared in English in London, 1796, under the title *An Exposition of Christian Doctrine,* with a preface by Benjamin Latrobe.

BISHOP SPANGENBERG
Writing the Idea Fidei Fratum

A Quartermaster and a Treasurer arrived today, with a message from General Sumter. They wished lodgings for themselves, a house for all sorts of stores, another house for four artisans, and a smithy with five or six fire-places. They made their request courteously, accepted the apologies of the Committee, looked over the town for themselves and saw the impossibility of securing what they wished. They were told that our other two towns were still less able to accommodate them, and this was confirmed by one of their number who rode thither on

Aug. 22, and found things as we had stated. They therefore bade us a polite farewell. At our request Wendel Krause and Isaac Knoll brought militia to search the woods and if possible to rid them of robbers, which was done on

Aug. 23, with the help of several neighbors and Brethren. The remains of their camp were found, but none of them were caught. Since then we have been less annoyed by them. In the Congregation Council the war committee was asked to take charge of the preparations for the meeting here of the Assembly. Br. Herbst was added to the committee.

Aug. 25. In the prayer-meeting mention was made of the organization of the Hourly Intercession fifty-four years ago.

Aug. 26. On this Unity Day we read the memoirs of various members who have gone home, which made a deep impression. The entire Unity of Brethren, its ministers, and the Brethren and Sisters traveling on church affairs, were remembered before the Lord, and especially our Br. and Sr. Reichel who are now on their return voyage to Europe. Before the gemeinstunde we had the unexpected pleasure of welcoming our Br. Christian Ludwig Benzien, who arrived safe and well after a difficult and tiresome journey from Bethlehem. By him we received many letters and Nachrichten from Pennsylvania and Europe.

Aug. 27. Br. Gottfried Schulze arrived safely. He had accompanied Br. Benzien, but had remained with the wagon.

Aug. 28. Officers of various rank were here, among others a Commissary-General from the southern army, who told us how much pleased General Greene had been with the way we conducted ourselves during the time the soldiers were quartered here last winter, and how much he had sympathized with us during the early months of this year, adding that so far as in him lay General Greene was anxious to protect us from a recurrence of such conditions.

The Single Brethren of Bethabara, Bethania and Salem closed their Choir year, and on

Aug. 29, celebrated their Festival in a blessed manner. In the lovefeast sincere thanks were offered to the Saviour for all that He has done for this Choir since the cornerstone of their House was laid thirteen years ago. A festal ode was sung, with instrumental accompaniment. Br. Marshall made the address, * * * and then presented Br. Benzien as the Choir Pfleger, in place of Br. Praetzel, and installed him in his office. In the evening meeting of the congregation Br. Marshall read a Circular from the Unity's Elders Conference, based on the Text: *None of us liveth unto himself,* pointing out that we are called to spread the Gospel of Jesus among all nations.

Sept. 2. Sunday. In the afternoon the report of the terrible hurricane in the Barbadoes and on the west side of Jamaica was heard with general sorrow and sympathy. The Single Brethren had a lovefeast as a farewell to Br. Praetzel, and as a welcome to Br. Benzien, who succeeds him as Pfleger of the Choir of Single Brethren. In the evening meeting Br. Graff spoke on the Text for the day; then with the usual marriage doxology there was the wedding of Br. Gottfried Praezel and the widowed Sr. Elisabeth Nielsen.

Sept. 3. A package of letters which had been sent to Pennsylvania but had been lost on the borders of Virginia, was returned to us through the kindness of our friend Mr. Gallaway. [It was brought back from Dan River, where it was found in a hollow tree.]

Sept. 6. [Sent the Package of Letters again by Valentine Rothrock and others.] The married people, including the ministers and their wives from the country congregations, ended their Choir year with the Pedilavium, and on

Sept. 7, celebrated their Choir Festival in the felt presence of Jesus.

Sept. 8. In the afternoon there was a hard storm, with heavy rain, which continued during the evening, so the prayer-meeting was omitted. [There was a bloody Battle near Nelson's Ferry.]

Sept. 11. Place for a house for Br. Gottfried Schulze was staked today on the farm of the Single Brethren; Br. Schulze will take charge of the farm. Br. Benzien held his first singstunde.

Sept. 12. [Hillsborough taken by the Tories, and the Governor made Prisoner.]

Sept. 16. This remarkable memorial day for the ministers of the Unity was observed in the Grosse Helfer Conferenz.

A General-Doctor of the southern army sent an Express with a letter to Br. Bagge, saying that there had been a bloody battle[29] on the Santee,

---

[29] The battle of Eutaw Springs was fought on Sept. 8th. Both sides claimed the victory, but the ultimate advantage was with the Americans.

and asking that out of pity for the wounded we would send rags for bandages to Charlotte, whither they would be brought. This was done.

Sept. 17. The Brn. Gottfried Schulze and Johann Krause went on a visit to Pennsylvania. By them we sent many letters and our August diary.

Sept. 20. After a great heat we had a storm with heavy rain. Then the weather cooled.

Sept. 21. A Commissary from this State came to collect food and grain for the army. He had written authority to make the demand, and soldiers enough to enforce it, but he said that he did not wish to make use of it. We explained that we could not furnish what he needed from our own supplies, but only from what we had bought,[30] and he withdrew his request, and contented himself with what could be furnished by the farmers of the Friedberg and Friedland neighborhoods, and he permitted them to deliver it at their convenience.

Sept. 23. Sunday. This was a blessed Unity Day, with Nachrichten from Labrador and St. Christopher, [West Indies].

Sept. 25. This evening the Northern Lights appeared. [Our county militia came from Bethabara, &c, viz. sixty men of light-horse] under Captain Minor Smith, and some of them attended the singstunde. That they had to be supplied with food and forage, iron and smith-work, was trying, as were their repeated requests for bread at the various homes, but their behaviour was endurable. They remained until the evening of

Sept. 26, when Gov.[31] Alex. Martin arrived, and gave us a *Protection* against the demands of the militia for the food supplies which had been bought for the use of the Assembly. [Choir House Statutes introduced in Single Brothers House.]

Sept. 29. A company of the local militia passed. When the situation was explained they were ordered not to scatter here or demand anything; the latter order was not fully obeyed, but they soon moved on in peace.

Oct. 1. Winter hours began. At twilight there was a sermon from the Wochen. In the singstunde praise and thanks were rendered to the Saviour, whose glory shall forever increase among His people.

Oct. 3. Fifty Wilkes militiamen on horseback and two hundred on foot passed quietly through the town. It looked as though they wished

---

[30] Salem was gathering supplies to be used by the Assembly at its November meeting;—see under date of Sept. 26th.

[31] Governor Thomas Burke was captured by the Tories under Colonel Fanning, at Hillsborough on Sept. 12th, and was taken to Wilmington. Col. Alexander Martin, Speaker of the Senate, became acting Governor.

to improve the reputation they have hitherto had. They received from us rations of bread and brandy.

Oct. 6. We were disturbed by parties of soldiers who passed through the town and demanded bread and other articles of food.

Oct. 10. Gottfried Müller brought us a package from Pennsylvania.

Oct. 11. In the evening at half past seven Congregation Council met with all the house-fathers and house-mothers, to consider the lodging of the members of the Assembly.

Oct. 12. Br. Tycho Nissen became the night-watchman in place of Rudolph Strehle.

Oct. 18. We had the pleasure of welcoming Br. Bibighaus, who arrived with the Bethania wagon and a load of goods for the store. He brought from Pennsylvania, Nachrichten, letters, and the first part of the Text Book for 1782.

From the parts of the letters that Br. Marshall read to the communicants we learned that our Brethren and Sisters on the Muskingum had been attacked by hostile Indians and carried away captive.[32] We were much distressed for this settlement and prayed to the Saviour to rescue them from danger.

The Wilkes militia, who recently passed through, returned [without going to the army.] Here they shot an ox, which Philipp Schneider had brought for sale, and urged on by hunger they pressed upon the baker for bread and meal, but behaved fairly well, and after their commanding officer, Major Hardgrave, arrived and established order they were entirely modest.

Oct. 19. [By Valentine Rothrock received a Letter from Yorktown, Pa.]

Oct. 21. Many Continental officers and soldiers attended the services.

Oct. 30. Mr. Owen, who was captured by the English and was exchanged in Charlestown, was here on his way from Bethlehem to South Carolina. With other gentlemen he attended the singstunde. He confirmed the report, which we had already heard, that Lord Cornwallis had surrendered to the Americans.[33]

In a conference with members of the Congregation Council and all master workmen certain arrangements were made in regard to the meeting of the Assembly, and the value of certain coins was established according to the rate at which they pass elsewhere.

Oct. 31. The Brn. Lorenz Bagge and Ernst came from Bethabara and Bethania to Conferenz. While it was in session, in the tenth hour,

---

[32] Christian Indians and Moravian missionaries were made prisoners at Salem, Ohio, Sept. 4, 1781, by Indians and whites under British officers.
[33] At Yorktown, Va., Oct. 19, 1781.

our Br. Jacob Bonn had a stroke, and passed quickly and blessedly to the Saviour.[34] The entire congregation was much affected by this event, having lost their doctor and surgeon. Toward evening we had a severe thunder-storm. [Mr. Owen set out for the South.]

Nov. 1. In beginning this month, when we must expect the meeting of the Assembly of North Carolina, we take the Text for today as an encouragement from the Lord to pray to Him that He will watch over us during this critical time, establish us before the world as children of God, and make this event a benefit and a blessing to this congregation and to His entire work in North Carolina. The Text is: *Then shalt thou call, and the Lord shall answer; thou shalt cry, and he shall say, Here am I,* and we will believe that our prayer will be answered.

Nov. 2. In the afternoon at one o'clock was the funeral of our departed Br. Jacob Bonn, for which more than two hundred persons came from our other congregations and from the neighborhood. [John Hill from Maryland took possession of his land.]

Nov. 8. In Congregation Council it was announced that by direction of the Lord Br. Praetzel had become the Curator of the Choir of Single Sisters.

In the evening his excellency, Gov. Alex. Martin, arrived for the Assembly, and during these days various members came from adjoining counties. In the following week more came from the lower counties.[35] We made only one change in our church services. While they are here we will have no meetings for communicants, but public services instead; otherwise nothing will be altered. The members of the Assembly came often to our meetings, especially to the singstunden.

Nov. 13. Tuesday. We celebrated the day with three public, solemn services, remembering the consecration of our Saal ten years ago, and also joining with the entire Unity in thanking the Lord for His goodness as our Lord and Elder. At the lovefeast a psalm of thanksgiving was sung with instrumental accompaniment. In the evening service hymns were sung and instrumental selections were rendered. The gentlemen of the Assembly attended the festal services with respect and reverence, and the Governor expressed his appreciation.

---

[34] His Memoir, inserted in the "Extract der Diarii der Gemeiner in der Wachau," 1781, gives his life-story at some length. He was born April 5, 1733, in Pennsylvania, his parents having emigrated from lower Germany. He moved to Bethlehem, Pa. in May 1746; and there became a physician and surgeon. He came to Wachovia as a messenger bringing letters in 1758. In 1759 he came again, and served as Moravian doctor for nearly a year, taking the place left vacant by the death of Dr. Kalberlahn. In July, 1766, he returned to Wachovia as community doctor; and in November of that year he married Anna Maria Brendel. They had one son, Jacob, and two daughters who died in infancy. His successful practice of medicine, and his cheerful and disinterested service won the respect of every one, and in 1769 he was made a Justice of the Peace in Rowan County. When the county of Surry was erected in 1771 he qualified for the same office, and was presiding Justice of the Court for several years."

[35] From this and other entries it is quite evident that Frederic Peter, the diarist, kept notes of the daily happenings, but wrote out the fair copy at the end of each month.

Nov. 14. [The Governor went to Richmond.]

Nov. 15. Mr. Sharp, a North Carolina delegate to Congress, arrived, and spent a while here with his son. He, like the Governor, was lodged in one of the lower rooms of the Gemein Haus. Mr. John Hawersham came from Georgia, and also Mr. Harlestown, a former merchant in Charlestown; they remained several days with pleasure. In a printed sheet sent out from Philadelphia we saw the terms on which Lord Cornwallis surrendered to the Americans. [Colonel Osborne arrived, and the Governor returned.]

Nov. 17. In the singstunde, which Br. Graff held, we thanked the Saviour for the wonderful grace which He has shown to the Brethren in Wachovia since the coming of the first party twenty-eight years ago.

Nov. 18. Sunday. In the evening meeting Br. Marshall preached in English on the Text for the day to an audience so numerous that the Saal could scarcely contain them.

Nov. 19. Through the arrival of Mr. Kleinert we received a small package of letters from Pennsylvania. The most comforting news contained therein was that the reported capture of the Brethren on the Ohio was without foundation.[36] Beginning today a watch was placed before the Gemein Haus.

Nov. 21. The members of the Assembly met for the first time today, and as they were too few to form a House they adjourned to

Nov. 22. On this day they adjourned until Monday, and will then decide whether they will wait any longer for the missing members. Former Governor Caswell arrived today.

Nov. 23. Report was received that the Tories were approaching, and guards were set on all the roads so that no one could enter the town without a Pass. [I had five Officers of General Greene's Army to dinner.]

Nov. 24. Alarm was given that a party of Tories had been seen on the road to the mill and only half a mile from here, so the militia was called to arms and stationed before the Gemein Haus, where the Governor is lodged. In spite of a cold rain they remained there until

Nov. 25, about nine o'clock in the morning, when the alarm subsided. The guard, however, was posted there until the Assembly left here. Many civil and military officers, of all ranks, took this occasion to talk with Br. Marshall about our organization, and were given all the information they desired. On account of the unrest and the stormy

---

[36] The reported capture was true, but on Oct. 1st, their captors abandoned them on the Sandusky, in the midst of an utter wilderness.

weather only one service was held,—the church litany, at ten o'clock, in English.

Nov. 26. Monday. Our Saal could not hold the crowd that assembled for the singstunde, and many had to stay outside. The session of the Assembly scheduled for today was postponed until tomorrow.

Nov. 27. As they were ten members short of a quorum in the Senate, and twenty-eight short in the House of Commons, they decided to break up. In discussing where they should meet next time, which will be in January on account of the disturbed condition of the country, the majority favored meeting again in Salem. It was said that some had stayed away because they had no money to pay their expenses, and the country was not in position to furnish it to them. Colonel Taylor, Colonel Rogers, Mr. Cummings and Colonel Shepherd were appointed to confer with some of the leading men of the town, which they did, and they were told that payment for board and lodging would be accepted in food-stuffs of various kinds and at fixed prices, the charge being as now, 6sh. good money per day, or its equivalent in paper money. They were told also that we preferred not to have the Assembly meet here, on account of the interruption of work in our shops, but if they decided on this town we would show all honor to our officials, and take the best care of them that we could. Br. Bagge was asked to appear before the assembled members and further explain the matter of payment. All seemed to be satisfied with our answer. This gave us opportunity to prevent the catastrophe of having everything *on public account* if the Assembly met here again, which would have meant an official Commissary, kitchen, attendants, and the emptying of houses for the use of the members, and our offer was understood and well received. Part of them left today, [General Caswell, and also Mr. Sharp.] As a close for their sojourn among us several selections with instrumental accompaniment were sung during the singstunde for their pleasure.

Nov. 29. The Governor and the rest of the members of the Assembly left today for their homes. Sixty-three members of the Assembly and Government officials have been here, and also twenty-eight other gentlemen and officers, the Governor's guard, and two companies of militia for his protection, and all have been lodged in Salem. All were satisfied with the treatment received from the Brethren and grateful for their lodgings. [Mr. Owen and Kirshaw were here, and set off again.]

We humbly thanked our dear Lord for His gracious ordering of events, whereby we are restored to peace and the usual order of our church services, and can look forward to partaking of the Lord's Supper next Sabbath,[37] which we must otherwise have omitted. Br. Marshall spoke feelingly in the meeting of communicants, saying that the Saviour had thought graciously of His people of the Brethren's Church, whose purpose in coming to this land had been forgotten, and had openly justified them against many inimical and false ideas about them. Many a man who had forgotten God had been impressed with the question whether he should not turn and come to know Him; * * *. The spirit of the Unity was felt in our services today in a significant manner.

Nov. 30. One hundred and fifty of the Wilkes militia marched through the town today. Part of the Surry militia, who have been quartered here, left on the following day.

December. During this month our dear Saviour gave us a special blessing through His coming on our behalf, taking part in our flesh and blood. The sweet word of the incarnation and birth of Jesus refreshed our souls in peace. Besides the joys within the church He gave us other festal pleasures, which manifested to individual souls His grace and faithful care.

Dec. 1. Saturday. That we were able to celebrate the Lord's Supper in peace today was a great encouragement to us.

Dec. 4. The first snow of the season fell today.

Dec. 7. The fire-inspectors made the rounds of the town. [By a Neighbor of Bethlehem, Charles Hinkel, wrote to H. C. von Schweinitz and George Neisser. The Governor came through here on his way to Halifax. The same day some Gentlemen were publicly whipped at Salisbury by some of the Militia.]

Dec. 8. Governor Alex. Martin, who has been here since yesterday, went on to Halifax, where he and his Council will decide whether the Assembly will meet here again in January.

Dec. 10. During the morning the Brn. Gottfried Schulze and Johann Krause returned safely from Pennsylvania, accompanied by David Tanneberger. They left Br. Jacob Loesch[38] and the box of letters with the wagon.

Dec. 12. Br. Marshall made an address to the Single Brethren, and announced to them that the visiting would be replaced by companies in the Choir again.

Dec. 13. To assist the arrival of Br. Jacob Loesch, Br. Johann Krause rode to meet him on horseback.

---

[37] Saturday evening.
[38] Son of the Rev. Jacob Loesch who was in Wachovia during the colonial period.

Congregation Council was notified that Jacob Beroth, hitherto belonging to Friedberg, would now be associated with Salem as a country member, this being the beginning of an arrangement for country members[39] in connection with Salem.

Dec. 14. [By the Rothrocks received letters from Pennsylvania.]

Dec. 18. Br. Jacob Loesch arrived, having been met by Br. Krause seven miles this side of Halifax.

Dec. 19. Br. Marshall presented the Rules of the Sisters House in a meeting of the Choir of Single Sisters, and in an earnest prayer besought the Lord to give them inward grace and direct their life according to His heart.

This evening, during a heavy rain, the Brn. Michael and John Rank returned with their wagon from Pennsylvania, bringing Nachrichten and letters from Pennsylvania and Europe, and also the Old Testament Texts, and two sections of the Doctrinal Texts, for 1782.[40]

Dec. 20. The Wilkes militia, who have been scattering the Tories, returned in groups today.

Dec. 23. Sunday. In the litany service we remembered before the Lord our Indian congregations and their missionaries, who according to all reports are in grave danger.[41] In the afternoon Br. Marshall communicated a farewell letter, written by Br. Reichel from New York and addressed to all congregations of the Unity in North America. It was heard with much emotion and with tears.

Dec. 24. On Christmas Eve the children had a lovefeast at five o'clock and the adult congregation at eight. At both services a happy *Ave* and humble *Hallelujah* were rendered, that by the birth of Jesus Christ He has become our Friend, Brother, Saviour and Redeemer. Christmas verses and lighted wax tapers were given to the children.

Dec. 25. Christmas Day. At ten o'clock there was a festal sermon on the Gospel for the day.

Dec. 26. In the morning of this Unity Day there were two meetings, with the reading of memoirs and reports from European congregations. At one o'clock there was the baptism of the nine months old daughter of Reich, Sr. whom he had brought [from his home in Stinking Quarter] for that purpose. She received the name Verona. In a largely attended gathering at two o'clock Br. Graff spoke on the call-

---

[39] *Auswärtige Geschwister.*
[40] The *Losungen* or Old Testament texts, and the *Lehr Texte* from the New Testament, were printed separately for many years, though both sections were bound in one volume. Giving both Losung and Lehr Text under each date was begun in the German edition of the Text Book in 1819, but in the English edition not until forty years later.
[41] The Moravian Christian Indians on the Sandusky were having a terrible winter, facing starvation and surrounded by heathen who rejoiced in their distress and threatened the lives of the missionaries.

ing of the Unity, and especially of its ministers, first to avail themselves of the atonement of Jesus, and then to preach this grace to others and to administer the Sacraments; and then he ordained Br. Christian Ludwig Benzien as a Deacon in the Unity of Brethren, with prayer and the imposition of hands, and the choir sang the doxology.

Dec. 27. Last evening the Brethren in Friedland were disturbed by robbers,[42] overpowered them and took them to Bethania, where they were released with a warning. Today Peter Frey had the saddle and bridle stolen from his horse at our mill; he saw it at once and chased the thief, who ran through the town into the woods, but could not catch him.

Dec. 28. The Christmanns and Reichs returned to Stinking Quarter. Reich has bound his sons to Br. Samuel Stotz, through an Indenture, and has left them entirely to the care of the congregation.

Dec. 29. One hundred and eight communicants, including the ministers from the country congregations, partook of the Lord's Supper for the last time during this year.

Dec. 30. After an address by Br. Graff, and the marriage liturgy, the Single Br. George [Nathanael] Bibighaus was wedded to the Single Sr. Christina Dixon.

Dec. 31. Our New Year's Eve services, which were disturbed by the arrival of a party of soldiers, were really rendered the more solemn thereby, because at their request an additional service was held, in which the hymn was sung which Br. Ettwein has composed in view of the critical situation of our Indian congregations and their missionaries, and also the hymn of thanksgiving of our Ober-Lausitz congregations for the Peace Festival of Jan. 6, 1779. After this service the congregation had a lovefeast, during which there was sweet singing. In the following service we heard the Memorabilia, with thankful and humble hearts for all that the Lord has done for us during this extraordinary year. The closing meeting began with the anthem: *Grace be with all who love our Lord Jesus Christ in sincerity.* Br. Graff spoke on the last two Texts of the year, * * *. Then to the sound of the trombones we entered into the new year, and prayed that He would let it be for us a year of grace and peace, in which, if it be His will, peace might be once more established in this land. As an antiphone the New Year Text replied: *Before they call, I will answer; while they are yet speaking, I will hear.* In closing the benediction was laid upon the congregation.

---

[42] The diarist uses the term *Spitzbuben* for all the sneak-thieves, robbers and highwaymen who lurked in the woods at this time and preyed upon travelers and residents.

Minutes of Salem Boards, 1781.

Jan. 2. (Aufseher Collegium.) The younger Schumacher wants the bottom which is in the Salem lot and lies beside his plantation. This would cut off Schreyer's road, or make it longer. It will be best for Schumaker to make a new road at the edge of his upland, beyond the Petersbach, which will be nearly as short for Schreyer. This road must be excepted in the Lease.

Concerning the supplies which we have furnished on public account for this state we decided that the statement should be sent to the Assembly for revision. We will seek to have allowance made for the depreciation in the currency, and Colonel Armstrong is willing to help us by his endorsement.

Jacob Beroth has entered his son in the local school today. He will pay four shillings a month for him, as other parents do.

It was mentioned that the Rothrocks, Folz and others have begun to cut a road from their neighborhood toward Salem, which will shorten the road to Salisbury by two or three miles. It will be well to assist them from this end, and complete the road, and the course marked by the departed Br. Reuter shall be inspected.

Jan. 3. (Aeltesten Conferenz.) Stockburger is willing to give work to Stephen Riddle's son, and his father shall be informed when he comes for his answer.

At Hope, Br. Fritz shall speak of the anniversary of the beginning of missions, and in a meeting of the Society shall explain the collection for foreign missions and ask whether the members will contribute. If they agree the money shall be gathered next Sunday.

Small-pox has broken out at the South Fork and in other places, and if it comes nearer the Brethren and Sisters who have not had it shall be asked whether they wish to be inoculated.

Until we receive the Daily Texts in printed form the Text for each day shall be written out, and the Saal-diener[1] shall lay it on the table in the evening.

Jan. 9. (Auf. Col.) Congregation Council shall discuss how the Brethren and Sisters prefer to handle the matter of quartering troops who stay in the town, for it will fall too heavily on those to whom the demand first comes if they have to bear it alone. It should be handled to the satisfaction of all, so that the troops may be assisted, and yet not be drawn hither. The Council might appoint a Committee to attend to such matters, as has been done before, though the Committee shall main-

---

[1] Chief usher for the meeting-hall.

tain a close connection with the Collegium. If it should be found advisable to erect a house for the lodging of troops, the expense to be borne by the residents of the town, there is no objection to it.

If Matthew Brooks, County Commissioner for the *provision tax*,[2] wishes to have the grain for that tax delivered at Steiner's mill it may be done. He must keep an under-commissioner here, and pay him for his services.

Jan. 10. (Aelt. Conf.) The Brethren and Sisters in Hope are willing to contribute to foreign missions.

It was proposed that Br. Joseph Dixon should be the barber for the local Brethren and for men staying at the Tavern. No objection was raised, but as it will draw strangers to the home of Br. Bonn he shall be consulted.

Br. Spach requested that in future marriages at Friedberg should be performed by Brethren.[3] This will be discussed further with the Friedberg members when their congregation Rules are signed, probably at their Congregation Festival.

Jan. 11. (Congregation Council.) Br. Zillmann has been told to get a dog for use at night, and until the house of the night-watchman is emptied of soldiers it can be shut into the smoke-house of the Single Brethren.

Br. Steiner shall be instructed to grind the corn-meal finer for the soldiers as well as for the Brethren and Sisters. There is hope that our lack of a bolter can be relieved, for when the bolter at Bethabara wore out, a neighbor, Schoenmell by name, was found who knows how to weave bolting cloth, and enough was ordered for our mill also.

The recent quartering of the soldiers in the house of the night-watchman and at Yarrell's has made so much trouble that it will be necessary to get together and come to a general understanding of how these matters shall be managed. Of course it is a heavy load for those on whom it falls, and we must not think ill of any one who complains about it, but the following points were agreed upon:—

1) We cannot escape quartering and such war-burdens, nor can we refuse, but must realize that we must endure them as the whole country must. It follows

2) that we must provide quarters for them, and the more quickly this is done the better for us.

---

[2] The specific provision tax was laid by the Assembly which met at Hillsborough in September, 1780. It provided that "the pecuniary tax" on each £100 value of taxable property must be accompanied by one peck of corn, or by other provisions in a definitely stated ratio. Under the Act the Moravians were to pay the grain tax three-fold as they did the money tax. (See *Colonial Records*, Vol. XXIV, p. 344.)
[3] At this time most marriages were performed by a Justice of the Peace.

3) If no Commissary is with them one of the Brethren must serve in that capacity.

So far the Aufseher Collegium has looked after this matter, which properly belongs to its duty, but the Brethren who have had it actively in hand have found many difficulties and much reluctance so it seems best for Congregation Council to elect four Brethren to serve as a Committee, and take upon themselves the oversight of all war burdens which fall upon the congregation, and manage them in the best way for the congregation, keeping in touch with the Aufseher Collegium and the Aeltesten Conferenz.

The entire Council gave hearty agreement to this, and thought that the election of such a Committee would put an end to many groundless complaints, and that an active Committee of four should be elected. The following Brethren were unanimously chosen: Johann Reutz, Peter Yarrell, Traugott Bagge, and Samuel Stotz. In regard to the lodgment of soldiers the following shall be noted:—

1) They shall not be lodged in the buildings of the farm or still-house, for from the congregational standpoint it would work harm to our young men to be mixed with the soldiers, and from the economic standpoint it would be disadvantageous in that it would permit the soldiers to set the price on food which supports the entire town.

2) As long as possible the emptying of a dwelling-house shall be avoided, but if this becomes necessary

3) it will be better to double up and release a house for their use, rather than lodge them in the Choir-Houses or in homes among the families, as that would endanger the spiritual life of our people.

In case it becomes necessary to provide more accommodation for soldiers it will be wise and good to build a house somewhere, which shall not be called barracks though it would serve as such. It was proposed to build a house near the Tavern, providing it with two doors, and two fire-places in one chimney which should be in the middle of the house, making two separate rooms. Br. Meyer can use this house for travelers who can not well be accommodated in the Tavern, as has long been planned, and in case of need it will serve for soldiers.

Jan. 12. (The Committee and the Brethren of Congregation Council.) There was further discussion of the proposed building near the Tavern, which in case of need can serve as barracks for soldiers. It seems to be practicable, for Br. Herbst has on hand enough peeled logs 28 ft. and 24 ft. long which he offers to give, and which will make a house 22 ft. by 26 ft. in the clear; divided by a partition it will give two rooms each 13 ft. by 22 ft. As the site lies high there can be a dirt floor, which will be safer from fire than a floor of boards. Br. Aust was unanimously chosen building inspector.

In order to cover cost of building a free-will offering shall be gathered. As this could not be paid at once, and the Brethren ask for credit on account of the hard times, it was decided to advance the money from the Congregation Diaconie, and each who makes a subscription shall pay interest on it until paid, it being understood that no interest shall be charged for the first quarter year. Any man who gives work toward his subscription shall be credited as though it were cash, and any work exceeding a subscription shall be paid for. This proposal shall be laid before all the communicant members tomorrow.

Jan. 12. (Auf. Col.) The Brn. Stotz and Reitz will go today to Matthew Brooks or Colonel Williams and get the list of taxes laid on Salem, Bethabara and this neighborhood, so that we may provide in time the necessary money and grain, and plan how to help a neighbor pay his taxes when he has neither North Carolina currency nor public Tickets.

Jan. 15. (Land-Arbeiter-Conferenz.) Friedberg members have expressed a wish that marriages might be performed by the minister. It does not seem wise to begin this, but if the minister has been in touch with the matter from the beginning the marriage can be performed by a Justice and then there can be a lovefeast with the Choir of Married People, during which the new couple can receive the blessing of the congregation. In this case there must be no worldly dinner-parties; there is no objection to a dignified meal for the Justice and the relatives.

Jan. 16. (Auf. Col.) The married people have subscribed about £7:10:—, and the Single Brethren about £11: toward the proposed new building for the lodging of soldiers, which is not enough. Many of the Brethren are opposed to the plan, for fear that it will attract soldiers to the town, and it has been reported in the neighborhood that we will build a house for soldiers. We regret this report, but it seems that for the present the house cannot be built, and this will be announced to the communicant members this evening.

The Brn. Stotz and Reitz failed to get the tax lists from Mr. Brooks or Colonel Williams, but the latter has promised that the vice-clerk shall send it to Br. Bagge so soon as it is ready.

The Single Br. Joseph Dixon, who is studying [surgery] under Br. Bonn, will hereafter serve as barber for Brethren and for strangers, in place of Charles Holder.

The estate of the departed Br. Johann George Baumgarten has been settled. His property amounted to £200:18:8, of which the widow receives her third, that is £66:19:6. The remaining two-thirds is divided equally among the five children, each receiving £26 :15 :10, all reckoned in hard money. Br. Schreyer[4] shall give bond that he is indebted to each child in this amount.

Br. Bagge proposed that the store take over the Maryland Tickets from the various persons who hold them, paying them a stipulated sum, probably 140 for one, in hard money, and the store shall then bear all expense of redeeming them. If nothing can be obtained for them the participants shall return the money and bear the expense of trying to cash them. Br. Stotz will be asked whether the Single Brethren agree to this, and the Brn. Meyer and Steiner will probably make no objections.

Jan. 17. (Aelt. Conf.) Br. Blum[5] has promised Mr. Brooks to receive the corn brought in for the grain tax, and will take care of it partly at the Tavern and partly at the mill. He is to receive five bushels out of each hundred for his trouble.

Heinrich Wendel, who has been working as a day-laborer in Bethabara for two or three years, has told Br. Praetzel that he is concerned about his salvation and would like to become a permanent resident of the town. Close attention shall be paid to his manner of life, to see whether he would suit in the congregation.

Bethabara has found it inconvenient to maintain three cash accounts, for the Saal, the Communion, and the Nachrichten, and has proposed that they be combined into one account, toward which each Brother shall contribute six pence and each Sister three pence weekly.

Jan. 18. (Helfer Conferenz.) To protect our land from the bush fires which are all around us, leaves shall be piled and carefully burned wherever it is necessary. Br. Aust shall guard God's Acre.

Jan. 23. (Auf. Col.) It looks as though our County officers put all quartering and all requisitions on Salem and Bethabara, and demand as little as possible of Bethania, Richmond and other parts of the county, and as though General Greene has a wrong idea about Salem. Several Brethren shall speak with Colonel Armstrong and ask that no partiality be shown, and that more advance notice shall be given when requisitions are to be made. Br. Bagge shall take occasion to present to General Greene, in writing, a statement as to the manner in which Salem and Bethabara have been oppressed, partly because people have too high an idea of our ability and partly because the officers have neglected to give proper help.

Incidentally it was mentioned that the bull at the Tavern, which was to be sent away last year, is still roaming about. If Brethren

---

[4] He had married the widow Baumgarten.
[5] Living in Bethabara.

refuse to obey the orders of the Conferenz notice should be given by those who brought the complaint, or they should themselves report it, so that resolutions may not be passed in vain, or neglected at will.

Jan. 24. (Aelt. Conf.) Matthew Noeding has left us again and has gone to Friedberg. Br. Beck shall be asked to notice closely whether, as rumor says, Noeding has it in mind to marry Peter Frey's daughter.

Since the Land-Arbeiter-Conferenz spares the Aeltesten Conferenz some of its deliberations, time remaining at the morning sessions shall be used in reviewing the Results of General Synod, especially the parts pertaining especially to the Aeltesten Conferenz.

Jan. 31. (Aelt. Conf.) We hear that the elder Reich[6] is free from militia service for this time.

In Bethabara a Brother should be appointed to look after the cattle which are to be fed in town, which have been left hitherto to find forage in the forest, and should bring them into the old order so that they are not so much exposed to requisitions from the soldiers.

It would be well for a public market to be established in Salem, with some one in charge.

Feb. 6. (Auf. Col.) Oesterlein suggests that he should rent a forge from George Schmidt, and work for himself as a smith, as he has no regular employment just now. We doubt whether this will go well, as they will have to share charcoal and customers, but he shall be told that he may discuss the matter with George Schmidt, and if they can agree they shall submit the matter in writing to the Collegium.

The Brethren and Sisters shall be warned to be careful about buying from the soldiers, and especially articles of clothing, the selling of which is forbidden.

Feb. 7. (Aelt. Conf.) In a letter, Br. Fritz mentions that Mr. David Enox would like to move into one of our settlements. Br. Marshall has advised that he build near the Hope school-house, and send his children to school there.

Feb. 13. (Auf. Col.) The cornmeal which had been prepared for the militia who are expected today shall be stored in the magazine near the bridge, so that it does not have to be taken from dwelling-houses or from shops.

When Brethren go on some errand for the general good it shall be credited on their service as night-watchmen, since there is no fund from which to meet such expense.

---

[6] Then living in Stinking Quarter, on Haw River. He later moved to Friedland.

Br. Peter has presented the report of the music account. After paying the old debts and buying a rack and several strings, there is a balance on hand of one shilling and eleven pence.

Feb. 14. (Aelt. Conf.) Br. Mücke has agreed to take the eldest son of David Enox on trial, and Br. Marshall will write to the latter to that effect.

Not only the care of the two sick men in the night-watchman's house but their nursing also has been entrusted to Br. Bonn, and he asks for help. He proposes that each family in turn assist with the nursing, and it is referred to the Congregation Council Committee for consideration as to how this can be handled practically.

Feb. 21. (Aelt. Conf.) Br. Zillman is no longer able to serve as night-watchman, and he shall be told that he has been relieved and that he shall live in Br. Spieseke's room[7] and support himself by his trade.

Feb. 24. (Aelt. Conf.) On account of the uncertainty of the times the Communion shall be held in two sections, the first this evening at seven o'clock and the second tomorrow morning at eight. No public announcement shall be made [by bell or trombones]. In addition to the watch in the town a special guard shall be placed in front of the Gemein Haus to prevent unwelcome intrusions.

Two hundred and forty dollars have been put in the poor-box, largely by Colonel Preston's soldiers. We will consider how to use this for the best interest of the poor.

Feb. 26. (Auf. Col.) Colonel Preston left five sick men and an attendant here last Friday, and it seems best to issue rations to them and not let food be furnished by the families, as it is to be paid for. We will have to lend them cooking utensils.

At present many persons are lurking in the woods around us, and sometimes they are seen in town. It will be wise to advise them to report to the county officers and not to hide in this way, lest they be considered bad men and be sought out and arrested.

The Brn. Reitz and Yarrell shall be reminded to bring in the account of the magazine built for use *of the public,* without delay.

Br. Meinung may move back into the lower story of the two-story house, since there is no prospect that it will be needed further *for the public.*

There is no objection to proceeding with the inoculation for small-pox in town, and Br. Bonn hopes that he has a supply of the necessary medicine.

---

[7] The men in the Brothers House were divided into groups, each group sharing a living-room, one Brother acting as room-superintendent.

15

Those who take strangers into the Saal shall remember to remove their hats and conduct themselves with reverence, and maintain this attitude while the organ is played.

Feb. 28. (Aelt. Conf.) We have no objection to the inoculation for small-pox, but it should be suggested to the Brethren and Sisters who have not had it and who wish to be inoculated that they all do it on the same day.

Sr. Meyer's brother, who came from the army, shall be sent on as soon as possible. His presence might be dangerous for us, as he is a deserter.

March 1. (Helfer Conferenz.) When strangers ask about the *Nunnery* they shall be told that there is no nunnery here, and that there is nothing about the few single women, who do day work in the families, to arouse their curiosity.

It was mentioned that Br. Rudolph Strehle has taken the place of Br. Zillmann as night-watchman. His blowing[8] last night put him in danger of being shot, and it will be well for Br. Meyer, when there are officers in the Tavern, especially when they are on the way to the army, to explain that our night-watchman always announces the hours by blowing.

March 8. (Cong. Council.) The Srs. Reutz and Yarrell were present for the first time as members. The connection is that Single Brethren who are members of Council by reason of an office or by election and confirmation of the Lord do not lose membership by marriage, even though their places in the Brothers Choir must be filled. The wife of such a Brother does not become a member of Council automatically, but according to circumstances and the direction of the Aeltesten Conferenz.

From the 10th to the 12th of this month there will be, in Richmond, an election of a Senator and two Representatives for this county. It will be well for several of our married as well as of our single Brethren to go thither, to vote for the men who have shown themselves favorable to us during these hard times. This applies particularly to Martin Armstrong, who is being mentioned for Senator; also to Mr. Cummings, and if necessary to Mr. Freeman, all three having shown themselves to be our friends.

Yesterday the guard for which we have wished came to protect our town. It will be well for one family to take charge of them, and the burden will be made as light for them as possible. Whoever takes them in shall be paid by the other Brethren in turn.

---

[8] *Duden,* used only in connection with the blowing of the conchshell trumpet.

On account of the sick and wounded, Br. Bonn hesitates to inoculate for small-pox and so introduce it into the town. Should it enter otherwise he will at once take steps. Meanwhile the Brethren and Sisters shall gather peach blossoms[9] for it.

March 8 (Auf. Col.) If more wounded are brought to the town to stay for a while it will be better to house them in the Magazine rather than in the two-story house, or for a longer time in the night-watchman's house. We will build a chimney in the magazine, and lay boards on which they can lie.

March 16. (Auf. Col.) The Brethren who helped build the Magazine shall be allowed three shillings a day.

March 20. (Auf. Col.) The amount received for the Magazine was £6:19:6, and expenses were £15:2:8, leaving a deficit of £8:3:2. If the Brethren who subscribed toward the proposed house will pay on this the deficit will be less. The account shall be placed in the hands of the Brn. Reitz and Yarrell for further action, and the final deficit shall be paid by the Congregation Diaconie and an account[10] opened for it [on the congregation books].

March 21. (Aelt. Conf.) In Bethania rags are being gathered for the wounded, and since the hospitals have been separated they shall be sent to the Continental hospital, and Bethabara and Salem will join Bethania in what is sent. At the request of Major Armstrong a copy will be given to him of the open letter sent out from the English camp to all philanthropic men in this country.

Against the wish of the Brethren in Friedberg, Br. Beck has tried to help Martin Walk and the younger Volz. In consideration of all the circumstances it does not seem wise to meddle in the matter of the first named, but in regard to the latter the Friedberg members may ask for release if that is possible.

March 27. (Auf. Col.) Br. Zillmann shall be paid eight shillings for a cord of wood which he had on hand and the soldiers used.

March 28. (Aelt. Conf.) Br. Bonn has raised the question of sick-nurses for the married Sisters. Eight Sisters were suggested, and on some convenient day they will have a conference with Br. Bonn and arrange the matter.

The question of marriages in Bethania needs consideration. It is not proper to use the Lot in every case, but in others it should not be

---

9 Boiled into a syrup they made a mild laxative.
10 The account in Ledger A, Salem Congregation, shows that the total cost of the Magazine was £16:16: 8. Total receipts were £12: 7: 6, leaving a deficit of £4: 9: 2 which was charged to Salem Congregation Account in 1782.

omitted.   The chief thing is to consider whether the person whose marriage is suggested has yielded his or her life entirely to the Lord.

We must seize every opportunity to inculcate the idea that we are a band of pilgrims, and seek gradually to lay aside everything that does not agree with this.   Persons who wish to join the Unity must not only desire salvation, but must be willing to be guided by the Lord in all things; they must not seek ease, or expect a place of their own, but must be at home anywhere.[11]

March 29.   (Helfer Conf.)   Inoculation for small-pox will be postponed until after Easter, so the Brethren and Sisters can observe the season in peace.

Br. Strehle shall be asked to blow long notes before midnight and short notes after midnight, so that the time may be recognized more easily.

April 4.   (Aelt. Conf.)   The Banns shall not be published for Casper Stolz and Anna Hauser until he has provided a dwelling-place outside Bethania, for after his marriage they cannot live in the town.

The fence around God's Acre in Bethania has not yet been renewed. The space is too large, and the new fence shall be shorter, but the corners of the present space shall be marked with locust posts, and it shall be noted in the church book that the size has been reduced, so when needed it can be enlarged again to its former size.

April 5.   (Cong. Council.)   Br. Rudolph Strehle asks increase of pay as night-watchman.   He has been receiving 14 pence a night, and wishes 18d.   This is fair, and as it is a quarter more than he has been getting the Brethren must increase their contributions to his salary proportionately.

April 11.   (Aelt. Conf.)   Br. Ernst has written from Bethania that the house-fathers have decided to let the small-pox come into town of itself.   This is probably because they think that inoculation will cost a great deal.   Answer shall be sent that Br. Bonn does not expect to make an extra charge for inoculation, only for the medicine and the visit. Here it will amount to a little over 20 sh. per person.   In Bethabara, Samuel Johannes[12] is willing to be inoculated, and the Brethren shall be advised that those who wish the treatment shall all arrange for one day, which will be cheaper for them, as Br. Bonn must be paid for the trip.

Johann Wendel, in Bethabara, wishes to be considered as a permanent resident.   Approved.

---

[11] This point of view probably had much to do with limiting accessions during the next decades.
[12] A negro.

The position of Fremden-dienerin[13] was considered, and Sr. Betsy Nielsen was appointed.

April 18. (Aelt. Conf.) General Greene will send a delegation to the Cherokees, to discuss peace and an exchange of prisoners. We deliberated as to whether this would provide an opportunity to further our desire for the salvation of this Nation, but decided that the time was not favorable.

April 19. (Helf. Conf.) There was discussion of the reason for the first ringing of the bell. This was begun in order to notify the members living farthest away that it is time to come to the service; therefore the first time the bell is rung long, the second time only for a short while as it merely announces the beginning of the meeting. On weekdays at twilight there shall be an interval of three-quarters of an hour between the two bells, Sunday morning there shall be ten minutes, and for other services only five minutes.

We agreed to pay one shilling for one pound of butter.

The musicians wish that a better tone could be given to the organ which shrieks aloud when facing the congregation. We recently found that the tone was more pleasant when the organ was turned around, but it is not safe to have it back against the wall because of the moisture which gathers there, which would injure the organ. Br. Krause thinks that he can box up the side toward the front, and can make a top which can be opened or closed at will. This will improve the tone, and was approved by the members.

April 26. (Auf. Col.) Br. Christ requests that food-stuffs taken in barter at the pottery may be turned over to him at barter price. This brought out the thought that the taking of food for sale at a higher price is not proper, and we wish it would stop. When Brethren or Sisters order anything it should be sold to them for the purchase price.

May 1. (Auf. Col.) Br. Meyer's brother-in-law, Miller, came here as a sick soldier, but he is well now and should not remain longer.

It would be well if butter were sold in town or at the store, and tickets given to the people instead of money, the tickets to be accepted as money at the pottery.

May 3. (Helf. Conf.) There is much wild grass in the Square, and it was suggested that it might be well if the Brn. Meyer and Stockberger would put their sheep there. We think they would not injure the trees as they would have good pasturage, but the young fruit trees should be protected, and the sheep should be allowed free egress and

---

[13] A Sister appointed to look after woman visitors.

ingress during the day, though at night the gates should be closed to prevent stray cattle from coming in.

May 8. (Auf. Col.) Br. Yarrell, roadmaster, was told that if any Brethren wished to pay for work not given in road-making it should be applied to the debt incurred in recent road work. This year we will try to work over the Beloes Creek and the Shallowford roads, brace the bridge, fasten the planks, and improve the ford across the Wach and the road on both sides of it. He was reminded to include Schumacher and Schreyer among those liable for road work.

May. 9. (Aelt. Conf.) Mr. Brooks has posted Advertisements ordering that the grain tax shall be brought in, under penalty for failure. He is commissioned to collect the money tax also. He thinks that he can arrange with the Court at Richmond, which will be held next Monday, that our Tickets will be accepted for taxes, provided that several of the Brethren appear at court for that purpose. The Brn. Bagge and Samuel Stotz shall go next Tuesday.

May 15. (Auf. Col.) Yesterday the boys Michael Kürschner and Ludwig Blum were apprenticed before Justice George Hauser, Jr., the former to Br. Goetje in the shoe-shop and the latter to Br. Reutz in the hat-shop. They are to serve until they are twenty-one years of age.

Br. Schnepf is very weak from his present illness, and apparently he will soon go home. There was discussion as to how his little farm can be handled, so that there may be no interruption of the milk business through which he supplies the town.

May 22. (Auf. Col.) We hear that Stockburger has asked a man who does not belong to us to lend him money, without mentioning it to the congregation officials, and he shall be asked about it. The congregation Diaconie might make him an advance if it is necessary, but he must give a full account of his present financial condition, so that all of his debts may be known and we may be able to judge how much of an advance may be made wisely.

In regard to liquidating the public Tickets it will be best to tabulate them, giving the names of the owners, then the Brn. Stotz and Bibighaus shall take them to the Auditors,[14] who are now in or near

---

[14] A Standing Board of Auditors was created by the Assembly at the session beginning in September, 1780. It was composed of three men, elected by both Houses of the Assembly, and was authorized to adjust claims for and against the State. (*Colonial Records*, Vol. XXIV, page 325.) It was found impossible for this one Board to handle all claims, so the Assembly meeting at Halifax in January, 1781, passed an Act for Appointing District Auditors for the Settlement of Public Claims. Two Boards were appointed for Salisbury District, Matthew Lock, Benjamin Cleveland and David Wilson composing the Board serving for the part in which Wachovia lay. The Act set the price at which various commodities were to be valued; and the District Auditors were required to "transmit by their secretary to the present Board of Auditors the counter part of the Certificates by them issued, together with the vouchers." (*Colonial Records*, XXIV, page 373.)

Salisbury, and get Certificates[15] for them.

There was a conference with Br. Micksch about the lovefeasts, for which he must provide as he is the chief diener. It was agreed that all lovefeast accounts should be kept as one, except those for the separate Choirs. From this account he shall defray current expenses, and the cost of lovefeasts for the diener and musicians. Members attending the lovefeasts for those Received and Confirmed within the year shall pay as much per person as for other lovefeasts, but this shall not apply to those who attend officially. A lovefeast for communicants, with tea, for one hundred persons requires 1/4 lb. tea, which costs 6 sh., 3 lb. sugar, costing 14 sh., 100 buns, costing 16: 8d, milk and other expenses, 2 sh., in all £1 :18: 8. A congregation lovefeast for about one hundred and fifty persons requires 6 lbs. sugar, costing 28 sh., 4 lbs. coffee, costing 16 sh., 150 cakes, costing 37: 6d, milk and other expenses, 3 sh., in all £4: 4: 6. But not all pay who are counted, and there are other expenses besides the lovefeast supplies, so it is thought that for the future each member should pay 6d for a communicant lovefeast, and for a general lovefeast 8d.

May 30. (Aelt. Conf.) As summer approaches the weekday evening meetings at Friedland are less well attended on account of increased work. Br. Heinzmann shall consult with the Brethren and Sisters as to whether they wish the meetings held at some other time of day, or whether it would be better to drop them during the summer.

Hofmann's son has asked Br. Ernst to baptise him. If he has a longing for the Saviour, and believes that through baptism he will receive the forgiveness of his sins, it can be granted according to the plan agreed on in the Land-Arbeiter-Conferenz, that is through it he shall become a member of the Society. The baptism shall take place in the Saal in Bethania, in the presence of the entire congregation.

An Irishman living about sixteen miles from Bethania has asked Br. Ernst to baptise his child. As there are other children to be baptised in that neighborhood Br. Ernst shall go thither next week, and so far as possible grant their requests.

June 5. (L—A—C.) Jacob Heyne hired a servant of Friedrich Müller's, Alisbury by name, to ride a race with Mr. Powell, and promised him a hard dollar if he won the wager. This happened yesterday during preaching, and three of the Friedland men, Society members, witnessed it with pleasure. At the same time Jacob Heyne neglected to take proper care of his father's property. If persons act

---

[15] Laws regarding Auditors' Certificates varied with each Act passed. From the way in which the Certificates received at this time were handled it is evident that they were estimated in Continental currency, valued at 250 for 1 in hard money, and that they were legal tender for public taxes.

contrary to the Bible and to our rules they cannot remain members of the Society.

June 6. (Auf. Col.) Mr. Troy, of Salisbury, has a negress about twelve years old whom he offers to sell for £100 good money.

Since our public Tickets have been changed into Auditor's Certificates we will offer them in payment of our taxes[16] for last year. We can also help our country members in the payment of their taxes at the rate of 250 for 1, which is the value granted us in specie on demand.

Br. Meyer reported that the gutter between the house and kitchen at the Tavern has rotted for the second time. He must have it repaired at once, but it is hard to secure good workmen.

June 6. (Aelt. Conf.) Br. Herbst has asked George Hartmann to haul bark for him, so he will not be able to go to Salisbury until Monday to get the negro girl who is to be brought from the home of Mr. Matthew Troy and taken into the Tavern on trial.

Br. Koffler has some good wine made from wild grapes, which he is willing to sell for use in the Holy Communion. Br. Herbst shall be asked to buy as much as he can for this purpose.

June 12. (Auf. Col.) The gutters around the Gemein Haus shall be repaired until new ones can be made[17] at the proper time of the year.[18]

In a letter Br. Oesterlein asks that he may be established as a smith as he is tired of day wages. It might be possible for him to open a smithy in Bethabara, but most of the Collegium prefer to keep him in Salem, let him have a smithy at some public and convenient place, and let him continue to live in the Brothers House.

June 13. (Aelt. Conf.) The proposal to allow Br. Matthaeus Oesterlein to establish himself in an independent smithy in Salem was considered of doubtful expediency, since it would probably take the bread from Br. George Schmidt and his family and turn not only Br. Schmidt but many others against him. It was suggested that Br. Schmidt might rent his smithy to Br. Oesterlein, and support himself by the rent, his garden, and small pieces of work which he could do at the one fire in the smithy.

---

[16] These were, of course, the Certificates issued under the Act of the January session. The midsummer session of the Assembly, held in Wake County, continued the District Boards of Auditors, as "pay due for Militia duty and all other claims against the State for articles furnished or impressed, should be speedily settled and certificates granted for the same." The certificates were to be tender for public taxes at the rate of 200 for 1, [which was less than the rate granted the Moravians earlier in the year,] and all sums amounting to not less than one pound in specie were to bear interest from date if not paid before May 1, 1783. Pay to militia was "to be considered in specie." (*Colonial Records,* XXIV, page 387.)

[17] A specimen preserved in the rooms of the Wachovia Historical Society shows that roof gutters were made by splitting in half a log of the right diameter, and hollowing it out to the proper shape.

[18] That is, in winter when the sap was down, and the wood could be used without drying.

Br. Spieseke has offered to release Stauber, who has still a year to serve as apprentice, and it was decided to allow it this time. Hereafter Stauber shall receive journeyman wages. Another time this shall not be permitted so easily, but apprentices must serve until they are twenty-one, according to the law of the land.

It must not be taken for granted that persons living in the Choir Houses may go to Bethabara or Bethania for the harvest season. Martin Hauser can not secure outside help this time, because he has small-pox in his family, so we cannot refuse to allow his daughters to go and help him through the rye and wheat harvests, but with the express understanding that this does not establish a precedent.

The Congregation Festival for Bethania, coming on June 23rd, shall be postponed on account of the small-pox in Bethania.

June 18. (Auf. Col.) The light-weight gold pieces circulating in the town shall be made heavier, and this shall also be done with others which may come in. Br. Koffler can help in this matter.

June 20. (Aelt. Conf.) The Aufseher Collegium has doubts about the plan for Br. Oesterlein suggested by this Conferenz, so it was finally decided to ask the Saviour whether Br. Oesterlein shall have his smithy in Salem or in Bethabara. If the lot is drawn for Salem the suggested proposals shall be further considered; if for Bethabara a smithy shall be put up for him, and for the present he can live in the old store building. The question was then put, asking in which of the two towns he should be located, and the answer was *Bethabara.*

Br. Ernst has spoken with Martin Hauser, who says that he will try to get through the harvest without calling his daughters. He does not need them this week, but if he finds the work too heavy next week he will come for them.

On account of weakness Br. Holder must give up blowing a trombone, and Br. Oesterlein is leaving Salem, so two Brethren must be found to take their places. Br. Martin Schneider was suggested.

Br. Benzien can not make the journey hither from Pennsylvania alone. We will ask that one or two Brethren come with him who can help in the work here.

June 21. (Auf. Col.) Two other negresses have been offered to us in Salisbury, at about £100 each. One is about twelve years old, the other sixteen. Br. Meyer might, as he has suggested, go to see them and select which he prefers, and shall fix a purchase price to be paid if she proves serviceable after a trial of one or two months.

Ludwig Mellor asks that Br. Aust pay him for piece-work instead of day wages, so that he may have a larger income, as he is not receiving quite enough. We do not consider this wise, and think he can get along on what he is receiving or he would not have been able to buy a chest of drawers and other not absolutely necessary things. We know by experience that articles made on a piece-work basis are not as well made, and there is already complaint that the pottery here is not so good as that made formerly in Bethabara. It might be wise for Br. Aust to get clay from Bethabara for his pottery, but this shall be suggested to him, not ordered.

Some of the neighbors have raised spelt this year. If Bethabara makes arrangements to grind spelt at that mill, the Salem mill can make the same arrangements later.

June 26. (Auf. Col.) Br. Peter asks for an increase in his salary, as he cannot pay his way with what he has now. A half *Johannes* shall be given to him extra for the past months, and if he needs more next year it shall be given to him.

June 27. (Aelt. Conf.) In a letter, Br. Heinzmann mentioned that at the request of John Lauer he had given him a Certificate, on the strength of which Colonel Armstrong had released him from militia service. He asks what he shall do in cases like this, and Br. Marshall has written him a letter, of which a copy was read to the Conferenz. We agreed that a Certificate should not be given except to a member of a Society, who had paid the three-fold tax, and who behaved as a Brother, otherwise the giving of Certificates might endanger our privileges. John Lauer has been released by the kindness of the officer, not legitimately, and he must pay the balance due to make his taxes threefold.

Br. Meyer has bought for the Tavern a negress of twenty to thirty years of age, who has a good character.

June 28. (Cong. Council.) It is time to make the inventories of the Branches[19] and balance their accounts. This brought out the thought that not only those who conduct the Branches but also those who do business on their own account, especially those just beginning independently, ought to make an inventory and balance their accounts each year at some convenient time, that they may know whether they have lost or gained during the preceding year, what they may do without making debts, and what they may undertake without risk.

July 4. (Aelt. Conf.) Br. Oesterlein has decided to take the lot on which Br. Stoehr now lives. The money he needs to set up his business he may borrow from Br. Marshall.

---

[19] The businesses carried on for the benefit of Salem congregation, that is the tavern, store, tanyard, pottery and mill.

Br. Gottlieb Strehle was suggested as a trombone player.

July 10. (Auf. Col.) Concerning the repairs on the bridge across Muddy Creek it was decided to ask the neighbors living near to help with the work and keep up the bridge. Salem can make a contribution in money. Br. Bagge will speak with George Loesch and other neighbors about it.

When there are soldiers in the Tavern the Single Sisters shall be careful not to go pleasure-walking to the bridge nor sit down there.

It was suggested that if a hedge is to be planted around God's Acre cherry sprouts can be taken from the lower part of the Gemein Haus garden.

The Brn. Strehle and Martin Schneider ask to be allowed to clear and cultivate the lots between Mücksch and the two-story house for one year, to which there is no objection.

As there are so few good springs in the town it was decided to clear out, at public expense, a spring below the Tavern which should have good water. The Brn. Petersen and Merkly shall look after it, and shall decide upon the best way to make a road to it.

July 11. (Aelt. Conf.) Pfaff sends word that his son is planning to marry Margaretha, eldest daughter of Andreas Volk, to which we have no objection.

July 17. (Auf. Col.) Br. Meyer wishes to build a spring-house over the spring in his meadow. He must be careful to provide a good place outside where the neighbors can get water.

Br. Steiner has asked advice about the price of grain at the mill. We think that wheat can be sold for five shillings a bushel, corn for two shillings, six pence, and rye for four shillings, until the price regulates itself.

It is fair that the price of bread should be lowered when the price of grain falls, and should be raised when the price of grain rises. If that is the rule the baker can make a living, and much difference of opinion can be avoided.

July 19. (Helf. Conf.) The pedal to the swell on the organ shall be improved, so that its creaking does not disturb the devotions of the congregation.

The question whether a hedge of cherry sprouts should be planted around God's Acre, or whether the clapboard fence should be kept, was left open for further consideration.

July 25. (Aelt. Conf.) Mr. Alexander Martin will come again in a few days to hear our decision whether our Saal can be used as a meeting place for the Assembly. To do this would interfere with our church services for a month, and the Single Sisters would have to move out of the house, so we will try to keep our Saal free. It was decided to offer Mr. Martin the garret of the still-house, which is light and roomy, and the adjoining room, and if this will serve for the sessions of the Assembly we will clear it out and do our best to prepare it for the purpose.

July 26. (Cong. Council.) According to the plan of its members, the next Assembly will meet here in the beginning of November. This will make many changes in our ordinary program, but if with all modesty we hold to our chief purpose, if our conduct shows all people that we are children of God, and if we treat them in an orderly manner and with courtesy, then the Saviour will turn to good the evil that was intended against us.

It will be well if the Brethren and Sisters will plan in time for a suitable place for the sessions of the Assembly, arrange lodgings for certain persons who must have separate rooms, provide lodging and board for the members of the Assembly, etc., and care for the horses. If Brethren and Sisters think that they can do one thing or another they shall say what they are willing to undertake. It might be well for one Brother to serve as Commissary, or at least secure a *Protection* under which he can buy provisions. The advice of Mr. Alexander Martin shall be asked about these things and others which we do not sufficiently understand.

Aug. 1. (Aelt. Conf.) Yesterday Isaac Pfaff was married to Margaretha Volk by Michael Hauser, Justice, near Bethania.

Aug. 2. (Helf. Conf.) As we are to have a visit from the Assembly the necessary preparations should be made, for example the potter should make a quantity of chocolate cups, bowls, and plates, and we should provide knives and forks.

Aug. 7. (Auf. Col.) In regard to the sending of letters it will remain the rule for Br. Meinung to receive the cost of sending from the Brethren and Sisters in Salem, except that letters to Bethabara, Bethania, Friedberg, Friedland, or elsewhere near at hand shall be delivered at the store for forwarding, the postage money to be collected there and later paid over to the congregation account.

The separate Poor-fund account shall be closed at the end of this year. The money put into the collection boxes for the poor shall be placed to the credit of the congregation, which in turn shall take care of alms to poor travelers.

Aug. 8. Philipp Vogler, Sr. moved to Bethabara yesterday.

Br. Heinzmann shall consult with the Friedland house-fathers about the long-intended road through the Friedland settlement.

Early in October Br. Johann Rank will go to Pennsylvania with his brother's wagon to see about their inheritance. Friedrich Müller also plans to go to Pennsylvania this winter, and each will be told of the intention of the other, as they may wish to go together.

Cornelius Schneider has told Br. Beck that he thinks of marrying his deceased wife's sister, Christine Ebert, seventeen years of age, partly for the care of his children, and partly to avoid trouble about inheritance. As this is not forbidden by the Bible nor by the law of the land no objection was raised.

It was proposed that John Jacob Schott and his wife be received into the Friedberg Society, also the Webers, an old couple who came from Pennsylvania to join the Brethren.

Aug. 21. (Auf. Col.) For two weeks the nights have been disturbed by thieves, and it was decided to call for help from the smith, Johann Kraus, and his militiamen, who have been ordered by the Colonel to seek out such persons. Our Brethren can serve him as guides. Br. Reutz was asked to go to Kraus and make the necessary arrangements.

Aug. 22. (Aelt. Conf.) The Brethren and Sisters ask that the liturgy *O Head so full of bruises* may be sung more often. For variety it can be sung antiphonally by the Choirs, and that will be tried next time.

Aug. 23. (Cong. Council.) Br. Bagge reported what Mr. Alex. Martin said about the meeting of the Assembly. Four or five single rooms will be needed for the Governor, Speaker, etc. He will do all he can to leave our Saal free, and to prevent loss for us. On November 4th the two Speakers will come to make arrangements for the Assembly, whose members will meet a good while after that. Before they come necessary provisions must be provided, and we shall attend to that. In regard to meals, he thought it would be possible to divide the members, serving them at different places, and quite understood that lodging and meals could not always be furnished at the same place.

To work out these plans and make the necessary arrangements the Committee on war-matters was appointed, together with Br. Herbst, and other Brethren will be added if necessary.

The band of thieves has probably been scattered by the Bush-Rangers, so the strong guard which has been maintained can be dropped, and for several nights one Brother can make the rounds with Br. Strehle.

Aug. 28. (Aelt. Conf.) A circular letter[20] from the Unity's Elders Conference to all the congregations was read. It is an admonition to

---

[20] Translated in full in Part I of this volume.

all Brethren and Sisters to make our lives in all respects, through the grace of the Saviour, accord with our calling. * * * This circular letter shall be read to the entire congregation in the meeting tomorrow evening.

This gives an opportunity to speak of the costly, unnecessary and conspicious clothing, which slips in among the Brethren and Sisters now and then, and to remind them to keep to a simpler dress, and one more in accord with our calling. This supplies material for discussion in the meetings of those living in the Choir Houses.

Aug. 30. (Auf. Col.) A letter shall be written to the Governor of this state, signed by the Committee appointed to look after these matters, and it shall be sent through Colonel Armstrong. We will ask the Governor for a *Protection* for the food, drinks, sugar, coffee, etc., bought for the use of the Assembly, so that they cannot be pressed.

Sept. 5. (Aelt. Conf.) The circular from the Unity's Elders Conferenz to the congregation towns shall not be read in Bethania or the country congregations.

Colonel Armstrong is planning a trip to Charlestown, and offers to take the Tickets we received from the English[21] for supplies and try to have them cashed there, if a Brother will go with him. He will secure from General Greene a *Flag of Truce* for the purpose. If Colonel Armstrong makes this offer direct to Br. Bagge we will consider it more carefully.

Br. Rudolph Christ would like to make a visit to Pennsylvania. Conferenz cannot advise this, and Br. Marshall will speak with him about it and ask him to consider how he could pay for the trip, and how his wife and child would be supported meanwhile, as his salary could not be continued in his absence.

Br. Johann Krause also requests permission to take a trip to Pennsylvania, and expects to return before Christmas. No objection was raised to this, and as Br. Michael Rank will set out on horseback ahead of his wagon this will be a good opportunity for Br. Krause.

Br. Flex will take over the linen-weaving from Br. Praetzel, and Christoph Reich will go to him as journeyman.

Sept. 6. (Auf. Col.) It is suggested that little Jacob Meyer be given to Br. Schober to help in the making of the leather breeches and to learn the trade. Plans must also be made for taking little Samuel Meyer out of the Tavern, as it is not good for him to be there.

The Single Brethren are willing to put their plantation into the hands of Br. Schulze, who recently came from Bethlehem, he to receive one-

---

[21] Negotiations for the payment of these English tickets were attempted at intervals until 1806, but nothing was ever realized.

third of the produce for cultivating it, and they to erect the necessary buildings.

Sept. 12. (Aelt. Conf.) That the two boys, Gottlieb Fockel and Jacob Meyer, may have practice in singing they shall be used in the choir in singing the liturgy *O Head so full of bruises.* Br. Peter will instruct them in singing; and he will give Br. Oesterlein lessons in organ-playing, so that Bethabara may have an organist.

Br. Schober thinks little Jacob Meyer too young to learn breeches-making, but will see what can be done this winter. Little Samuel Meyer can sleep with Br. Priem, and eat in the Brothers House, and in the day-time he can stay with the Brethren who have charge of the school.

Cord-wood should be cut for the use of the Assembly, and for the use of the town this winter.

Sept. 13. (Helfer Conf.) Michael Hauser will come in eight days to list the property for the next tax. He asks Br. Bagge to make a list of the property of the Salem Brethren, so when he comes it will be ready and he need only list the property of persons living outside the town. Br. Stotz will do this for the Single Brethren and Br. Bonn for those who are married, and Br. Bagge will unite the two into one list. Those who are fifty years of age should be noted. It is to be hoped that the Brethren will list their property as honestly as though they were before a Justice.

Sept. 18. (Auf. Col.) There was further discussion as to the care of little Samuel Meyer and the other children during the session of the Assembly. The little boys can go to school earlier and stay later.

Peter Schneider has offered to deliver cord-wood in town, which will make this matter easier. Those who wish to order wood shall mention it to Br. Koffler.

There is a large store of wheat at the mill. The Single Brethren want fifty bushels soon. We wish it could be disposed of before the army seizes it.

Sept. 19. (Aelt. Conf.) Casper Stolz was married yesterday, and has moved to the farm near the Bethabara mill.

It was agreed that during the session of the Assembly little Samuel Meyer shall lodge and eat in the school-house, under the care of Br. Schober.

Securing freedom from militia service on the ground that a man is a member of a Society and has a Certificate from his minister to take to his officer is giving offense, and may affect our privileges. It was therefore decided that for a while there shall be no receptions into the Societies, and no one shall be given a Certificate because he is a Society member.

Lorenz, thirteen years old, son of Michael Seitz of Friedland, has received permission to come here on trial and will learn the tailor's trade from Br. Spieseke.

Advantage should be taken of the present dry weather to improve the roads. The hole near the ford across the Wach should be filled. The road to the Petersbach can be changed a little to make it shorter and better.

Sept. 21. (L—A—C.) Just now more than half the country has been called out [for military service]. To give our Certificates, and to receive many persons into our Societies, would look as though we were depriving the land of able soldiers. It was therefore proposed [and agreed] that for the present there should be no receptions into the Societies, and the former ruling shall be faithfully observed and no Certificates shall be given except in cases where the man behaves in all respects as a Brother and has paid the three-fold tax. Even then no Society member shall receive a Certificate without the approval of the Provincial Helfer [Br. Graff]. Those whose names have been placed on the muster roll without their knowledge shall take their protest directly to their Captain.

Sept. 27. (Aelt. Conf.) Authority shall be sent to our dear Br. Reichel to serve as representative of these congregations at the next Synod. It shall be signed by the members of the Aeltesten Conferenz for Salem, and by the country ministers for their congregations.

After Michaelmas schools shall be begun for the older boys and girls.

Sept. 27. (Cong. Council.) Alex. Martin, our present Governor, has given us a *Protection* for the store of provisions and liquors which we have gathered for the use of the Assembly, that they may be secured against the demands of troops marching through. This is not to be posted as a Proclamation, but is an order to be shown to the commanding officer when there is danger that force will be used.

Oct. 1. (Auf. Col.) The Committee shall meet as soon as possible to make arrangements for the Assembly. Br. Praetzel shall be a member of it.

Oct. 3. (Aelt. Conf.) Preparations for the Assembly were discussed. The members shall all be lodged in Salem. Persons who come incidentally during the time can be lodged on the neighboring farms. The horses can be sent to Bethania, Friedland, etc.

Friedrich Müller thinks that his son can become a useful man in the world, and wishes to send him here for a while so that he may attend school. It was suggested that he might come and attend the school for little boys, and when not at lessons might do all sorts of work about the Brothers House until one could see for what trade he was best fitted, but nothing can be decided until after the Assembly has left.

Oct. 8. (Aelt. Conf.) *Special meeting.* A cabbage-head was stolen from Br. Yarrell recently during the night.[22] Suspicion fell on the boy G— S—, and on the Brethren R— S— and K—, but when they were asked about it during the conversations preparatory to the Communion they denied it, and on their own responsibility partook of the Lord's Supper. Now it has become known that they did it, for the master of G— S— laid the matter once more upon his conscience, and he admitted it. Conferenz is of the unanimous opinion that the three should be severely punished.

One evening, after the boys were in bed, S— got up again and spent the night with his brother in the wagon, and C— V— did the same. The officers of the Single Brethren should be more careful and should see that everybody who belongs on the sleeping hall is there.

In regard to this matter it was decided that the three should be suspended from attendance on meetings of the communicants; S— as an apprentice, should have a whipping, administered by Br. Yarrell.

Before anything is done, however, the matter shall be taken up by the Aufseher Collegium, to whom Br. Yarrell shall give all the facts; and then S— and R— S— and K— in turn shall be called before the Collegium, and according to their consciences shall tell what they know. The Collegium shall lay before them the fact that they deserve punishment, and the two older men shall be told that they have led a younger man into sin, and deserve to be sent away from the town, and that it rests with the Lord to decide whether they can continue as Brethren or must be treated as strangers.

Oct. 9. (Auf. Col.) The necessary supply of beef cattle for the Assembly shall be furnished by the Single Brethren. To get pork, outsiders shall be told that the store will pay in salt at the rate of twenty-five to thirty shillings for a hundred pounds. The store will turn over the pork to Br. Priem, taking his Tickets in payment for the time being.

---

[22] This incident is translated in full from the Minute Books, not because it was intrinsically important but because it shows the mixture of sternness, fairness and kindness with which the Boards handled an unusual case of wrong-doing.

The road-master for Hope, Matthew Markland, shall be asked to take charge of the repairs to be made on the bridge across Muddy Creek.

It was suggested that Br. Toego Nissen be made night-watchman and in the day time serve as porter and assistant in the store, and the store can add to his salary as night-watchman what is lacking for his support.

The theft of a cabbage-head from Br. Yarrell's garden took place with the foreknowledge of R— S— and A— K—, but by the hand of the apprentice G— S—. Br. Yarrell was called, and told how he had asked many questions, and after they had denied it and lied about it he had finally brought G— S— to admit that he had done it at the instigation of S— and K—. Br. Yarrell is not in favor of giving him a whipping, and hopes that it will have sufficient effect if he is not permitted to attend services.

The boy G— S— was called, and stated that recently when he was cutting buckwheat in the lot belonging to S— the latter had encouraged him to get a cabbage-head from Yarrell's garden, which he had done by daylight, and then they and K— ate it. He said he knew nothing about the cucumbers and other garden vegetables which have been missed here and there this fall. He said also that S— had advised him not to admit the deed, but to protect himself by falsehoods. He said nothing about K— having led him astray. He was earnestly admonished, and was told that he was forbidden to attend meetings of communicants, and that he might thank the kindness of his master if when he begged his pardon the deserved punishment was remitted.

R— S— was called. He tried to twist the matter and talk himself out of it but did not succeed, and it was plain that from beginning to end he had been the instigator of the matter, including the denial of the theft and the going to Communion. He was told that for some time he had been unfaithful in his work, and the great sin of theft, lying and leading another astray was laid upon his conscience. He was told that he might not consider himself a Brother, nor go to any meeting for communicants, but he was not penitent, and so he was dismissed for the present. He would not admit that he knew anything about the cucumbers and other things taken from the gardens.

A— K— was called. He said he had known nothing about the cabbage-head until afterwards, and tried to lie about it further, though it was plain he had been a party to it. As he continued to misrepresent and try to conceal he was dismissed for the time, with instructions not to consider himself a Brother nor to attend the meetings of communicants.

Oct. 10. (Aelt. Conf.) R— S—, who was impenitent at first, has been forced to recognize his sin, and he begs that he may not be sent out of the congregation. For the present he shall not be treated as a Brother, shall be excluded from all Choir meetings, must sleep and eat alone, and must have no association with the other Brethren in the room. If he changes, and shows real repentance, his case shall be considered further. K— appears to have fallen into sin unintentionally, is very sorry, and may be treated as a Brother, but at least until the next Communion he is excluded from meetings of the communicants.

Oct. 17. (Aelt. Conf.) Br. Gottlieb Strehle has agreed to serve as clerk in the Tavern during the Assembly.

In regard to the washing for the gentlemen it will be best for each family in which there are lodgers to send the wash, with a list, to the Sisters House, and it will be returned from there to each house.

Louise Toll has asked permission to remain in Bethania, and as the Committee there has no objection Br. and Sr. Ernst shall give her permission.

It was agreed to try putting yokes on the hogs to prevent the damage they do to fields and gardens. The experiment shall be made at Bethabara and Bethania, and if it is a success in our three towns we can call it to the attention of our neighbors and our members in the country congregations, and make it the general custom in Wachovia.

Oct. 24. (Aelt. Conf.) Bethania has raised no objections to placing yokes on the hogs, so it shall be done here and at Bethabara.

Oct. 25. (Auf. Col.) The bridge on the road to the Shallow Ford is so rotten that it cannot be repaired, and instead the road-makers have improved the ford. We will let it go for this winter, but as the ford is impassable in high water we will hold the matter in mind, and find out whether the neighbors wish a new bridge, and whether to go around to another bridge when the water is high will hurt the trade of our towns.

All the chimneys in town shall be cleaned before the Assembly meets.

Br. Toego Nissen will receive his salary as night-watchman, which has been about £27:6:—a year; but as the number of residents varies the store shall supplement his salary so that he shall receive £52 a year, and his house rent. His hours in the store shall be from nine o'clock in the morning until toward evening. In view of his office as night-watchman he can take no lodgers during the Assembly, at least he shall be left until the last.

Oct. 30. (Conference of the house-fathers, masters, and heads of rooms. Minutes entered in Congregation Council Minute book.) In view of the approaching session of the Assembly the following points are to be observed:—

1) As the milk supplied within the town will hardly be enough, more shall be ordered from adjoining plantations and our other towns.

2) Particular care must be taken that no whiskey or other strong drink is sold to a negro, even when he has hard money, without a written order from his master.

3) If our guests ask that we feed their negroes also it must be understood that they will pay extra for them.

4) If a family does not want to do the washing for its guests the wife shall collect it, asking for a list, and shall say that she will "carry it to the washer-women." She shall take it to the Sisters House, and when it is clean and ready to return the charge shall be written on the above-mentioned list. It will be best if washing can be done twice a week, perhaps on Mondays and Thursdays.

5) The Brethren and Sisters, especially the latter, must be careful not to do any hand work on Sunday while the Assembly is here for that would give great offense.

6) If some of the gentlemen should come this week it will be well to lodge them in the Tavern until next Monday, on account of the celebration of the Holy Communion.

7) On account of the high price of grain the baker cannot sell bread to the visitors at the price he charges the Brethren and Sisters. They shall therefore be careful not to tell their guests the price at which they buy bread.

8) Br. Charles Holder shall assist Joseph Dixon with barbering.

9) Those who furnish meals to men who lodge in other houses shall collect for lodging also. If the gentlemen want to drink out-side of meal-times their host shall supply them and collect the extra amount.

10) In most of the other states, and in the lower parts of this state, certain gold coins are taken at a higher value than formerly. The following is therefore established as the value in our town:—English Guineas 36/8, French Guineas 36 sh., Spanish Pistoles 30 sh., French Pistoles 29 sh., English Shillings 1/8. Coppers shall be accepted without objection if not too many are offered, the larger being taken for 1d and the smaller for ½d. When we must make change for a gold coin we must be careful to give as little silver as possible, for we anticipate a scarcity of silver in the town.

Nov. 1. (Auf. Col.) Our dear Br. Jacob Bonn, a member of this Collegium, went home suddenly and unexpectedly yesterday. He has many debts, much money is owing to him, and withal he was a public man, so his estate cannot be settled without giving notice to the Court according to law. His widow has suggested the Brn. Praetzel and Reitz as Administrators, and she shall serve with them. George Hauser, Jr., Cummings and others shall be consulted as to how the property can be divided between the widow and son without a public sale.

To continue the business for the benefit of the heirs it is thought that Joseph Dixon can attend to most of the surgical calls, though he shall mention it when a case seems at all dangerous. He shall not give any medicine alone, or prescribe any without consulting with Br. Graff, without whose advice he shall not even give a purge. We think that the mercurial and other dangerous drugs should be put away in a separate place. Not so much medicine can be furnished to persons outside the town as during Br. Bonn's lifetime.

Nov. 3. (Aelt. Conf.) A— K—, of whom conditions promise better things, is re-admitted to the Communion.

Concerning G— S—, who is very sorry for his sin, the Saviour was asked; *Does the Saviour approve that G— S— shall be re-admitted to the Communion?* Answer: *Yes.*

Nov. 4. (Auf. Col.) The Justices, Colonel Armstrong and George Hauser, Jr. think that the Court will permit the settlement of Br. Bonn's estate without a public sale, and that application for such permission should be made through a lawyer. Tuesday or Wednesday of next week the two Brethren and Sr. Bonn shall go to Court and qualify as Administrators.

Nov. 7. (Aelt. Conf.) It is necessary for the congregation to have a doctor in place of our departed Br. Bonn, and Br. Marshall shall write to the Unity's Elders Conference, in the name of this Conferenz, announce his departure and ask that Br. Thürstig be sent. In a private letter to Br. Reichel he shall say that if this cannot be done some one shall be sent who is both a medical man and a surgeon.

Br. Mücke, of Bethabara, has been notified by the sheriff to appear at the next court and serve on the jury. If he is not excused willingly he cannot refuse to serve, for under the present Constitution he is allowed to take the Affirmation.

Nov. 8. (Cong. Council.) The negroes who will be lodged on the plantations shall be fed according to instructions given by their masters. Those who are fed in the houses shall have whatever is on hand there.

It looks as though we would have much trouble over paper money. It is not necessary for the Brethren and Sisters to be frightened, but they shall ask God for grace that their bearing toward the Assemblymen may be brave, polite and friendly.

We cannot refuse entirely to accept paper money, but we can explain in a friendly way that we cannot buy the necessities of life with it, and when we must we can accept it at the rate of 800 to 1. With the same politeness we will refuse to receive *Notes of Hand*. Boldness combined with foresight and courtesy will prevent many evil consequences.

If we are asked to make advances on the ground of our riches, we will explain our poverty and that we are not in position to advance anything.

If any one wishes to provide for himself it will be very good, but in that case he must furnish everything, for a divided account would lead to much annoyance.

Nov. 12. (Aelt. Conf.) In regard to the solemn services of tomorrow it was decided to hold the first at nine o'clock in the morning, the lovefeast at three, and the singstunde with instrumental music at eight in the evening. The first two shall be announced by the trombones, and all of them shall be open to the public. It shall be announced in the homes that if the gentlemen of the Assembly wish to attend they shall not be prevented from coming.

As long as there is no unusual disturbance our week-day services shall be held in their usual order. The evening meal for the gentlemen of the Assembly comes just between our two services, and they can be informed that if they wish to attend our services, which will continue as usual, they may do so. This will be a pleasant way to avoid much disorder.

R— S— is heartily sorry for his sin and his previous bad conduct, He has spoken to Br. Benzien about it, and has written a letter to the Aeltesten Conferenz in which he asks forgiveness for his sins, which have grieved the Saviour and the congregation. He asks that he may be permitted to attend the services for those who have been Received, and his request is granted gladly, and we hope that his behaviour will fulfill the words of his mouth.

The Governor has expressed a wish that the Brethren could come into closer connection with the government. We think that in many respects it would be a good thing for us to have a Justice in the town, and it was decided to ask the Brn. Bagge and Reutz whether they would be willing to accept this office, the plan being that the latter should be the active person and that the former should assist him with good advice.

Nov. 14. (Aelt. Conf.) James Wilson, who has been living at Hope, and who worked in Bethabara for a while before his trip to Pennsylvania, would like to settle among the Brethren and be freed from liability of draft. The best way would be for him to behave as a

Brother, and then have himself bound to some one. He has bound himself to Br. Stoehr for one month on trial.

When all members of the Assembly are present we will pray the church litany in English, and an English copy shall be written out, omitting the portions referring especially to the various Choirs.

Nov. 28. (Aelt. Conf.) The members of the Assembly are now leaving us, so with tomorrow our services will resume their usual order. It is plain that the members have received a good impression of our town, and especially of our services.

Dec. 1. (Aelt. Conf.) R— S— is very much ashamed of his former conduct. He does not think that we will consider readmitting him yet, but he shows such a change in behaviour that we think it wise not to make him wait longer. We therefore asked: *Does the Saviour approve that R— S— be readmitted to the Holy Communion?* Answer: *Yes.*

Dec. 5. (Aelt. Conf.) John Pratter, a Baptist, has asked permission to remain at Bethabara, and has the consent of his father. He has hired himself to Br. Mücke for one year, and this shall be considered as a time of probation.

The marriage of Br. Matthaes Oesterlein was considered and it was asked [through the Lot]: *Does the Saviour approve that Br. Oesterlein shall marry the Single Sr. C— L—?* Answer: *No.* It was asked again: *Does the Saviour approve that the Single Br. Matthaeus Oesterlein shall marry the Single Sr. C— D—?* Answer: *No.*

It was thought that Br. Oesterlein might have a suggestion to make, and that he might be consulted, so a recess was taken until afternoon at one o'clock, when Br. Oesterlein's suggestion was laid before the Lord: *Does the Saviour approve that the Single Br. Matthaeus Oesterlein marry the Single Sr. Maria Magdalena Transu?* Answer: *Yes.*

Dec. 6. (Helf. Conf.) On special occasions not only the Saal diener who are on duty that week, but all the diener shall help to preserve order. Care shall be taken that the front benches are filled first, and that visitors are shown to seats.

Dec. 6. (Auf. Col.) The town Rules were read to the Single Johann F. Schroedt, * * * and he was told that permission had been given by the Saviour for him to become a resident of Salem. He was glad to hear this, and gave his hand to the Brethren present in token of his pledge to obey the Rules.

Mr. Joseph Kershaw, of Camden, has ordered about 4500 lbs. of flour for the use of the South Carolina Assembly, and it shall be supplied from Steiner's mill.

Dec. 11. (Auf. Col.) Br. Aust and Br. Christ have agreed with the Collegium on the following scale of prices for piece-work done by the latter:—If the journeyman prepares the clay himself he shall have a half penny for each article sold for one penny. For articles sold at a higher price he shall have 10 sh. for a hundred pieces, including bowls, half pints, quarts and tea-cups (the latter counting six cups and six saucers as one dozen) of Queen's Ware. He shall have 20 sh. for a hundred pieces requiring special care in making, such as Queen's Ware tea-pots, sugar-bowls, quarts and pints with two handles, plates and spoons. To each hundred four extra shall be added for breakage, and he shall prepare the clay. Work by the day shall bring 4 shillings.

Dec. 12. (Aelt. Conf.) Br. Transu, in Bethania, gave his consent to the marriage of his daughter to Br. Oesterlein, but after careful consideration she has declined the proposal. The following questions were then asked: *Does the Saviour approve that Br. Oesterlein marry the Single Sr. J— S—?* Answer: *No. Does the Saviour approve that Br. Oesterlein marry the Single Sr. Anna Maria Hege?* Answer: *Yes.* This proposal will first be made to both of them, and then notice will be given the parents in Bethania.

Dec. 13. (Cong. Council.) The poll-tax this year is 4 shillings, of which three shillings shall be paid in North Carolina currency and one shilling in Continental currency; the three-fold tax is to be paid in the same proportion. An unmarried man is valued at £1000, and must pay tax on that and on the property he lists. A man over fifty years of age does not pay the tax three-fold.

Dec. 14. (L—A—C.) The Friedberg members who attended corn-huskings, and by their behaviour gave offense and broke their Brotherly Agreement, were not allowed to attend the last Communion. Some of them regret the offense given; others are not sorry, and accuse Br. and Sr. Beck of harsh judgment. They shall be treated with patience until the Saviour brings them to themselves.

Dec. 19. (Aelt. Conf.) Br. Oesterlein and Sr. Anna Maria Hege have accepted the proposal of marriage. The betrothal will take place tomorrow after her parents have been notified.

Dec. 27. (Aelt. Conf.) Reich, Sr., wishes to move into our neighborhood, and as Fockel in Friedland wants to rent or sell his farm Br. Heinzmann shall suggest Reich as a purchaser.

Dec. 28. (Auf. Col.) The Single Brethren report that Br. Jacob Loesch, who recently came from Pennsylvania, will work as lock-smith for their Diaconie, and the former grind-stone mill can be fitted up for his work-shop. It will be well that for the present he does as little work as possible on guns.

Bethabara Diary, 1781.

[Extracts translated.]

Jan. 2. Threshing was carried on in the sheds. A stranger brought fifty bushels of rye to the still-house. A man named John Braedt brought his two sons to work here.

Jan. 3. Mr. Henderson was here and paid several Tickets which he had given as Commissary. Many travelers passed.

Jan. 6. Colonel Armstrong arrived to check up the many Tickets which we have received for supplies furnished to the soldiers. Justice Michael Hauser was brought to witness the accuracy of our claims. The Tickets will be sent to the Assembly by Mr. Cummings who arrived toward evening on his journey thither. The receipts given by Mr. Brooks as Commissary for the supplies furnished recently to the troops and prisoners under Colonel Cleveland will be credited by Mr. Brooks on our grain tax.

Br. Lorenz went with Br. Schaub, Jr., to the home of Wilhelm Volck, who had asked for the baptism of his child. The wife of Heinrich Holder and the wife of Andreas Schwartz brought their children and asked baptism for them also. Their husbands are in the army at present. The three children received the names of George Volck, Johannes Holder and Susanna Schwartz.

Jan. 7. There were many travelers here, especially toward evening and during the night.

Jan. 8. The usual work was continued on the farm. A young man who helped with the threshing last month will make shoes with Br. Stoehr, as he is a shoe-maker. The Brethren of the Committee met for the first time this year.

Jan. 10. Last evening there was a heavy rain, and the big bottom is under water. During these days there have been many travelers here, trying to sell grain and salt. The first was priced too high, and we do not need the latter just now. About seven o'clock in the evening there was a hard storm with lightning, thunder and rain.

Jan. 11. The little flax which grew this year was brought in from the field and was threshed.

Jan. 12. Johann Samuel was quite ill yesterday with an attack of asthma, but he has begun to perspire and is somewhat better today; he was bled, and it looks as though the attack will yield.

Jan. 13. Many came offering corn, wheat, rye and barley for sale and it was taken whenever we could agree on the price.

Jan. 15. Mr. Brooks consulted with the Brn. Kuhnast and Blum about storing grain here for the use of the soldiers. Br. Blum will make a beginning with it, and will have five bushels out of each hundred for his trouble. There is little prospect that much will be delivered here, for the neighbors have already furnished a great deal when the soldiers were here the last time, and for them as for us this will be credited on the tax, if the Assembly permits.

Jan. 18. Br. Marshall was busy this morning speaking with the Brethren and Sisters living in town, and also those who have the oversight of the farms. In the afternoon he returned to Salem. Several Brethren went with him and they will look over a proposed road from Bethabara to Salem which goes over field and through the woods and may be better and shorter.

Jan. 22. Hay was brought into the stables. Colonel Lanier was here on business, partly to pay for corn, and partly to borrow several thousand dollars in gold. Many others come seeking to borrow. Several men were here from Major Schmidt's company, on their way to Salem to stand guard over the Magazine. This afternoon it was rainy, but it cleared very cold toward evening.

Jan. 23. Eight hogs were butchered today for the use of our families; they weighed 1450 lbs. Colonel Armstrong and other gentlemen were here; several of the latter attended the singstunde in the evening.

Jan. 25. Yesterday and today many have passed going from South Carolina to Virginia.

Jan. 27. Colonel Thompson left today with his negroes, after they have spent several days here. Br. George Bibighaus returned from beyond the Adkin, bringing the tax list which he had secured. In the evening at six o'clock there was a lovefeast for the communicants; we sang a prayer verse for our dear Sister Marshall, who had her birthday on the 24th, and sang verses also for the three Brethren and one Sister living here who have had birthdays this month. At eight o'clock the communicants shared in the Holy Sacrament. Sr. Lenel Schmidt has had a bad cough for several days and cannot speak, and she received the Sacrament on her sick-bed. Many travelers were here today, and many from the neighborhood also.

Jan. 28. Sunday. In the afternoon there was the short service for the children. Many living outside the town could not come because the water is up over the roads at some places.

Jan. 29. Our wagon went about five miles away for tar. Many Virginians passed, going from the army to their homes. Two officers came from Salem to get provisions, especially meat, but none has come in.

Jan. 30. Br. Meinung came from Salem to survey land for Andreas Volck in our neighborhood.

Feb. 2. An officer arrived with an order from Colonel White for meat and meal for the prisoners of war; an ox was slaughtered and corn was ground. From here the order went on to Bethania, also for provisions. Toward evening the lieutenant in charge of the prisoners arrived with a wagon to get meat, and gave order that our wagon should take the rest of the meat this evening to the prisoners at Dan River. It was a much disturbed day, for one order after the other arrived.

Feb. 3. Today the Minute Men were here from Dan River, and remained over night.

Feb. 4. The company of militia remained here, as their Captain did not arrive, and they were advised by others not to go to the Shallow Ford. Food had to be furnished them today as yesterday.

Johann Samuel returned with our team from Dan River, where he had been dismissed by Colonel Joseph Philips according to promise.

Feb. 5. Colonel Armstrong was here, as were also the militia and some of our neighbors and wagons which have been pressed. It appears that the militia do not know where to go.

Feb. 6. During last night General Pickens arrived with his men and something over twenty wagons. Corn, hay, bread and brandy were given to him at his request. He kept good order among his men. His manner was fatherly and mild, and he voiced his belief that we would take no part in anything that was partisan or low.

In the afternoon Colonel Clark arrived with more than fifty horsemen, and another company passed by the mill, all hurrying after General Pickens. So it went all day, partly with the passing of militia, partly with people fleeing from the war.

Feb. 7. The day was quiet, except for the passing of small parties of soldiers, and the coming and going of many who were moving. This continued until the evening of

Feb. 8, when a party of horsemen came from Salem for meat and bread, which was given to them, and then they returned to camp. The two express riders, who had asked for two horses here, came back during the night, returned our horses and took their own, and rode on to camp, without having much to say.

Feb. 9. We expected the return of our guests of yesterday, but instead, about eleven o'clock, a company of English dragoons arrived, bringing an order from Lord Cornwallis for brandy, meat, meal and bread, and instructions that our mill should grind all it could, and that in the afternoon our wagon should take it to Bethania, where there were more than seven thousand men. In the afternoon the Commissary came for 100 gallons of brandy, more than 300 lbs. of bread, and all the meal that was ready. The Brn. Rose and Mücke went with the load. An order was sent to Salem to Br. Bagge, and he and Br. Blum were called to Bethania, but Br. Blum could not go because of duties in the Tavern, an English scouting company having come there. They remained on their horses, and after a short time rode off again. Then came a company of German Tories, with an order for cattle for the army,—just now the question is not who are friends of the land but who are friends of the king. The last named company seized several travelers here, and took them to Bethania, to the main camp.

Feb. 10. The English army was passing through our town from eight o'clock in the morning until nearly two in the afternoon. Good order was maintained, and a guard was stationed near the tavern, where the road turns toward Salem, and another guard was placed in front of the tavern. No one was allowed in the town except those who had business there, that is the officers. Another guard was placed at the still-house. Lord Cornwallis and several gentlemen were pleased to dismount; several of us waited upon him and he was friendly and seemed satisfied. Previously two horses had been pressed here, and our wagon was not permitted to return from Bethania, but must accompany the march from there, and the Brethren who were with it were not allowed to come back until today, when they received passes. In the afternoon an officer came and took eighteen of our largest oxen and drove them to the army; Br. Stauber happened to be in town, and as the man wanted some one to go with him Br. Stauber agreed to go for us. Br. Rose had already gone to Salem to try to secure the release of our wagon and horses. We heard that our Brethren and Sisters in Bethania had suffered much from the passing of the English, and that they were in need of bread as they had not been able to have any grain ground, and we offered to help them as much as possible. Br. Schaub, Jr., went thither to see about it, but they needed nothing from us.

Feb. 11. Our Brn. Stauber, Rose and Samuel returned with our wagon and team from the army.

Feb. 12. All was quiet and still, except that some of the English left and that there were all sorts of rumors about the American army.

Feb. 13. Major Winston arrived with a company of militia. Men and officers were friendly and behaved well, though we must supply them with bread, meat, meal, brandy, and forage for their horses. Late in the evening they left the town and camped in the woods, returning

Feb. 14, early in the morning to get corn for their horses. No requisition was made for the men, but the soldiers came asking for bread. Some paid for what they took, most of them did not, and all the bread baked last night was used. In spite of protests they took five horses, and would have taken more if they could have found them. They left about noon, going toward Walker's so far as we could see. Most of the men were friends of the king, but were forced to go with the American militia or lose all their property. Last night some English Tories arrived, having run away from the army, and a spy was captured but escaped. The Tories received a Pass from Major Winston.

Feb. 15. All day it was quiet and still. Rye was threshed in the sheds, and our teamsters brought in wood. At twilight, just as we were about to hold our first meeting, Captain Cloud arrived with a company from Dan River. They stayed over night, and we had to furnish hay for their horses. They behaved well, and their Captain assured us that there would be no disturbance.

Feb. 16. The company in the tavern was called out at three o'clock this morning. The guard hailed some one, who replied: *Good Friend.* To the question: *Whose friend?* came the answer: *King George's.*

Then it was quiet until nearly four o'clock when the advance guard of General Pickens' company arrived with orders for meat, corn and meal. Preparations were at once made, and two oxen were killed, forty bushels of corn were brought into the town and as much more was ground at the mill. The General and his officers were polite and courteous, and assured us that no damage should be done; and as it would be necessary for our wagon to take the meat and meal to the camp late in the evening they promised that it should not be pressed. Our supply of bread was all taken, largely without pay. The company that was here last night returned, and it was in all respects a much disturbed time.

Feb. 17. It was again a disturbed day in the town, and several bad men rode from house to house searching for powder or arms. The bread was taken from the bake-oven, without pay. This lasted until about four o'clock when most of the men rode off to join the General. Something like seven hundred men were here, not counting those with the wagons and various stragglers. A few remained over night, but the town was quiet.

Feb. 18. From the small parties that continued to pass on their way to the General, we heard that six hundred men were coming, but they did not arrive. One of the small parties stayed over night, and all of them had to be supplied with food and drink at the expense of the country. From Salem the two Brn. Strehle and Lück came to our assistance, and from them we heard how things looked in Salem.

Feb. 19. Colonel John Armstrong arrived with 150 men, rather late at night. They asked for hay and corn for their horses, and a little bread, but no meat. They behaved well. Colonel Martin Armstrong was also here, and although he is out of commission until the next Assembly yet he does all he can for us and for the good of the county, as does his brother.

Feb. 20. About ten o'clock the above-mentioned troops went on, and soon afterwards some of Campbell's men arrived and said that he and four thousand men were coming and that we should prepare provisions for them. They took a horse to ride to Salem, and said they would leave it there. Another man came and called for our horses, which he said we had hidden in the woods. Br. Strehle took the news to Major Schmidt, and Br. Lück went to Salem to report. Major Schmidt soon came, and as our horses were still here the Major refused to allow them to be taken. Toward four o'clock Captain Campbell arrived, riding Express, and was friendly and polite. As the bad man would not give up his design, and toward evening went about the town to get a saddle and bridle, and threatened to strike Br. Kuhnast if he did not give him what he wanted, we told Schmidt and Campbell about him as they were still at the tavern. They arrested the man, and Schmidt took the saddle away from him and gave it to Br. Blum. Then the man went to bed,—his name is Wilens, and he is a Justice, though he has acted in a manner directly contrary to the last Act.

Feb. 21. Colonels Preston and Crocket arrived with 400 mounted men, coming from the mountains more than a hundred miles away. As it was rainy they took possession of all our stables, so that the cows could not be brought in and could not be milked. Most of the men were lodged in the houses, only the Gemein Haus having none. They were supplied with bread, meat and corn, and behaved very well, according to their Colonel's orders, and by nine o'clock in the evening it was so quiet that no one would have known that so many men were in the town.

Feb. 22. Soon after noon the soldiers went on to Salem, at which we were content and happy. From Richmond came Colonel Armstrong and Cummings. We asked the Colonel for a Salvegarde for our town to protect us against the wandering groups, some of whom press horses and do other things which are not right. The Colonel at once wrote an order for one, and gave it to Major Schmidt to execute. Yesterday and today some meat and corn was brought here from Richmond for the troops, which had hardly ridden off when several men came to join them, and also a small company from our county. This again disturbed the town, so that we could have no meeting, much as we wanted one.

Feb. 23. The promised guard arrived today, and also part of Major Schmidt's company.

Feb. 24. Major Schmidt's company came again today, on their way to arrest robbers who have been robbing and stealing on this side of the Adkin. Yesterday and today small companies have passed going to the camp; and some have returned from camp, especially men from Wilkes County. On account of the disturbed times it was considered best to hold the Communion by daylight.

Feb. 25. We heard from Bethania that they had not been able to have Communion because Br. Ernst was sick.

Feb. 26. Yesterday and today the town has been quiet, and some of the usual work could go on. Grass was burned along the fences.

Feb. 27. Some of Pickens' men were here; they said they were going to the army. Men from Wilkes County returned from the army, on their way home. Another party from the mountains, who said they belonged to General Pickens' corps, remained here over night. A wagon and something over twenty bushels of corn came from Richmond yesterday and today.

Feb. 28. Major Cloud and about twenty men arrived, secured what they needed for themselves and their horses, and went on to Salem. Small parties passed all day, coming from our army on all kinds of pretexts. Some of General Pickens' men passed also, going to South Carolina, where they are to rally.

March 1. Br. Lorenz went to Bethania to see Br. and Sr. Ernst, both of whom are ill, he with swollen legs and she with pains in all her limbs. Many passed coming from our army.

March 2. Colonel Campbell and his men arrived, and secured bread and meat, hay and corn. The Colonel and his men were friendly and orderly. There was an accident, however, for a Captain, who was not entirely sober, was playing with his gun with another man, thinking that the gun was not loaded. As the man pulled away the gun went off, the ball going through part of his body into his thigh. A messenger was sent for Br. Bonn, who came at once. Colonel Armstrong was here also. Colonel Campbell did not want to go to Salem, as he had provisions here for two days, but Colonel Armstrong advised him to go by way of Salem, and so they left about four o'clock. Toward evening twelve of Campbell's company arrived and spent the night. The Colonel left four men to wait on the wounded man.

March 3. Br. Bonn returned to Salem with the men who arrived last evening. The wounded man was not suffering so much, but it will be a wonder if he recovers. Br. Lorenz visited him twice today, and talked with him. The sick man asked for his prayers and thoughts and Br. Lorenz pointed him to the Saviour Who gave His life and blood for all men, for their redemption from sin.

March 4. Sunday. At nine o'clock the church litany was prayed; some of Colonel Campbell's men attended the service. At ten o'clock there was preaching on the Gospel for the day. In the afternoon there were the short services for the children. In the next service memoirs were read of several Brethren and Sisters who have been called home. Then commotion began in full force, for one party after another came from the army with riderless horses.[1] This lasted until evening and it was said that these were all Colonel Preston's horses and about fifty of his men. The men received bread, and the horses corn and hay. On account of the confusion no evening service could be held. The wounded man rested fairly easily.

March 5. The men and horses who came yesterday moved on today, except a few who want to fight first. Toward evening more of Colonel Preston's men arrived with horses; they had left some of their wounded in Salem. Colonel John Armstrong came from General Greene, with an order for meal and meat for the army; he stayed over night.

March 6. It was rainy all day, so threshing was carried on in the sheds. More men came, they said, from the camp, and more than twenty others had to be fed at the expense of the country. Many of our guests attended the evening service; there was an address on the Text for the day.

March 7. Men continued to come from the camp, and they and their horses had to be fed. Fences were mended in town and around the fields.

---

[1] The report in Salem was that they were being sent away from the army for lack of forage. (Salem Diary, same date.)

March 8. The twenty or more men who have been here two days went home this morning. In their places came others from the front, men belonging to Colonel Preston's and Campbell's troops. Colonel Armstrong and many of the officers of this county were here. Many came from the camp; they had neither shoes nor stockings, and remained here over night. Br. Meinung and Br. Stoehr went to survey land for Moses Martin. Br. Bonn was here to dress the wounds of the soldier; it looks now as though he would get better.

March 9. The soldiers left this morning, their places being taken in the afternoon by many of General Pickens' men, and in the evening he arrived with the rest of his troops. This made much disturbance in the town, for though their camp was outside they had to be supplied with corn, bread, and meat. The General and some others spent the night in the tavern. Many of Colonel Preston's men were here also. There could be no evening service.

March 10. The above-mentioned guests remained until noon. Last night they broke into the spring-house; and they took all the eggs, even from the geese that were setting. We were glad that no more damage was done by these people, who have been robbing and plundering wherever they go. Several Brethren went from here to the election of new members of the Assembly. Colonel Preston and Colonel Crocket arrived and spent the night. The fire from General Pickens' camp, between Rank's and the lower meadow, broke out, and before it could be extinguished a hundred rails were burned. The fence was probably set on fire, for it was discovered just after they left.

March 11. Sunday. Many people were here, including some of our neighbors. They made no disturbance.

March 12. Colonel Preston and his men went home today. Some of Colonel Campbell's men passed; they said all of their men had gone home and were beyond Dan River. The men who have been attending to the wounded man went home, except two. As no more Continental stores were here the guard was dismissed for the time, by order of Colonel Armstrong and Major Schmidt.

March 13. Colonel John Armstrong passed with his baggage and several men, on his way to headquarters. Others came from the chief camp, going to General Pickens. The vote for Assembly members was rejected last Saturday, and we hear that there is to be another election today, but no one was able to go from here. Br. Bonn was here to attend the wounded man; he seems to be improving and there is hope that he may recover. Before the evening service was over a shot was heard, and we later learned that our neighbors were after horse-thieves.

March 14. Plowing for oats was continued, and fire-wood and rails were cut. It was fairly quiet and still in the town. The people who were here left as quickly as possible when an English prisoner who was passing said at the tavern that the English would be here this evening. This was, however, a false alarm.

March 17. Yesterday we heard that there had been a battle[2] between the English and our army, and today we heard more about it from other men coming from the front, and a letter from Br. Marshall showed that it was true.

March 19. Yesterday and today many passed, coming from the camp with horses and wagons. Those who arrived today demanded corn-meal and brandy, and gave a Ticket instead of paying. Our wagon brought corn from Mr. Banner.

March 21. Yesterday and today it has been beautifully quiet in the town. A number of persons were here, but there was no commotion. Oats were sowed.

March 22. Twenty-three acres have been planted in oats.

March 24. A man by the name of Heinrich Clemens, who lives on the farm of the elder Schaub, asked that his still-born child might be buried on the Parish Graveyard. Br. Schaub, Jr., dug the grave, and they buried it this afternoon.

March 25. Sunday. The Festival of All Choirs was announced by the wind instruments. * * *

March 26. All went on as usual. The summer arrangement of services has begun, so after supper a reading meeting was held at seven o'clock, and the singstunde at half past eight.

March 29. It is still peaceful and quiet in the town, though more people were here than for some days. Wilhelm Volck came from Salem and brought a note from Br. Graff, and two printed copies of the Text Book, one for us and one for Bethania.

March 31. On the farm the ground was prepared for planting corn, and fences were mended. The town was quiet, though as the army has moved away from this section many more persons come in than has been the case recently.

April 2. Many of our county militia were here, though it remains to be seen where they are to go. All the officers of our county met here in conference.

April 3. The militia who gathered here yesterday went home today, as did their officers. The latter have called a General Muster for the 13th, when every fifteenth man will be called out, together with those

---

[2] The Battle of Guilford Court-House.

already drafted.[3] Br. and Sr. Holder's son David has taken small-pox.

April 5. Br. Lorenz visited Holders and Staubers. Little David Holder has broken out nicely, and is in good spirits.

Ten men and something over twenty-five horses passed. On account of the battle at Guilford they had left their wagons at Dan River, loaded with Continental stores, and were now going after them. They were from South Carolina. They asked for corn today, and will want hay when they return.

April 6. The usual farm work went on, and flax seed was sown.

April 9. Captain Schmidt's company came hither from the muster place to decide how many and who from their company should go into the Continental service.

April 10. The wounded man, John Cusick, or———, who has been at the tavern, has so far recovered that he was able to go home with his wife and her brother. He was very glad and thankful for all the love and kindness which had been shown to him here.

The Brethren of the Committee were together, to arrange for the approaching Easter services. It was also decided that, if every one was willing, it would be well to bring the small-pox into the town.[4]

April 12. Maundy Thursday. The two boys John and Nathan Bröder were taken home by their father to have small-pox. The Brethren of the Committee met, and announced to the single man Heinrich Wendel that he had received permission to become a member of the congregation. The *Brotherly Agreement* was read to him, and explained, and he gave his hand in pledge of obedience. Soon after the Pedilavium, twenty Continental wagons, loaded with salt, came from Virginia and went on to South Carolina. Br. Blum had to give them all the corn which he was holding for use of the public. At seven o'clock the congregation met again and read the story of this day. At

[3] At the session beginning in January, 1781, the Assembly of North Carolina passed an "Act to reduce the six Continental Battalions belonging to this State to four, to compleat the said four Battalions, and for other purposes therein mentioned." This Act provided that general musters were to be held on or before the 20th of March. Officers and men were to be divided into groups of fifteen, and each group was to furnish a volunteer or a drafted man to serve in the Continental Battalions of the State for twelve months. The men so raised were to meet in Salisbury on or before April 25th. The Act further provided that counties prevented by invasion from making the draft at the time specified should do it "as soon as the said hindrance is removed." (*Colonial Records*, Vol. XXIV, page 367.) The Surry County officers were evidently obeying this Act when they arranged to call out "every fifteenth man" for Continental service. The Moravian diaries do not mention a single man or group of men pressed into the Continental service because of desertion from the field during the battle of Guilford Court-House, so the forced enlistment of deserters, mentioned by some historians, did not apply to Surry troops, nor did an Act passed at the session of Assembly beginning in June, 1781. "To compel the Counties which have not furnished their quota of Continental troops as required by a late Act of the General Assembly of this State to furnish the same." (*Colonial Records*, Vol. XXIV, page 395.)

[4] By inoculation.

eight o'clock the communicants gathered, and partook of the most holy Sacrament.

April 13. Good Friday. [The usual services were held.]

April 14. Great Sabbath. This morning two dragoons came from Bethania with a press-warrant, signed by Michael and George Hauser, ordering our wagon and horses to go to Salem for deer skins. At about the same time Krüger brought deer skins which he had gotten from the tanner Doub,—they belonged to Br. Bagge. When the men returned from Salem they brought no skins, and those which were here were left here. Several drunken men were here; they had been at the muster yesterday, but had left in an hour or two.

The Brethren of the Committee conferred with Br. Kapp about his Johann George Wageman, who has finished his apprentice years and would like to remain here. Br. Kapp offered him £18 good money for a year, with food, washing and mending, with which Wageman was satisfied. The Brethren and Sisters who have children had a conference about the small-pox. They were all in favor of it if it broke out in town, but did not wish to introduce it by inoculation. At two o'clock in the afternoon the congregation, including the children, had a lovefeast, during which the story of this day was read.

April 15. Easter. The congregation was awakened early by the wind instruments. At five o'clock we met in the Saal, and greeted each other with the words: *The Lord is risen! He is risen indeed!* After singing a few verses we went to God's Acre, and there prayed the Easter Litany. At ten o'clock was preaching. In the afternoon were the short meetings for the children. In the evening there was a gemeinstunde and a singstunde. It was rainy nearly all day, but peaceful and quiet.

April 16. Easter Monday. Unity Day began with the singing of several hymns. * * * It rained and snowed, and toward evening cleared so cold that we feared frost.

April 17. This morning we saw ice, and probably all in the garden and on the fruit trees that escaped the last frost has been killed now.

April 18. About seven in the evening a company of Colonel Washington's men arrived, on their way to South Carolina. We had to supply them with meat and bread, and with forage for their horses, although there are no Continental stores here.

April 19. The wagons of the company that came yesterday did not arrive until today. They all remained for a day of rest.

April 20. The cavalry company left for the Shallow Ford. They paid in flour for the bread furnished them here. Toward evening another company of horsemen arrived, coming for the deer skins pressed recently. They went on to Salem for the same purpose.

April 25. Br. Broesing came from Salem. He plans to make a farm on some of the cleared land belonging to Bethabara, and will have timbers cut for a house.

April 26. Br. Marshall came from Salem to see about Br. Broesing's house. Search was made for a spring, and then the location of the house was determined. It will be built in the field near Stauber's.

April 27. Three Brethren and two day-laborers went into the woods to fell trees for the house. Several Virginians came from General Greene's camp, which is three miles from Pinetree.[5] They were on their way home and had to be fed; they were in needy circumstances. Yesterday and today sixteen acres of corn were planted. Br. Loretz visited at the mill and at Rank's. At Rank's and here in the town some of the children are not feeling well.

April 29. Sunday. Just as service was beginning fourteen wagons arrived from Rowan County, going to Virginia for Continental stores. They wanted corn and brandy and tar, which made a disturbance. After they left we prayed the church litany. In the evening there was a lovefeast for the one Brother and three Sisters who have been received into the congregation and have partaken of the Communion for the first time within the past twelve months.

April 30. During this month all of Br. Holder's children have recovered from small-pox.

May 2. Our negro Moses is sick, and appears to have small-pox.

May 6. Br. Bonn was here to see those who ought to have small-pox. Several were re-inoculated.

May 9. Br. Marshall came on business. In the evening he held the meeting and reminded the congregation of the home-going of the Jünger twenty-one years ago. We thought of his work and testimony with blessing, and thanked and praised the Lord, and prayed that He would hold us to the blessed principles which He gave us through His servant. Br. Marshall inspected the building in the field, then visited the residents in town, and especially those who are sick with small-pox.

May 10. The weather is raw and stormy, and sometimes hail falls instead of rain.

May 11. Br. Bonn came to see those who have small-pox, and several children were re-inoculated. This morning we saw that there had been

---

[5] Camden, S. C.

a rather hard frost, and in the gardens all the beans, cucumbers and cotton were killed again. The salad was ruined by hail on the 9th.

May 14. Several Continental wagons came from Virginia on their way to the army in the south. They got tar and brandy here, and more than forty bushels of corn at the mill. The Brethren of the Committee met. There was consideration of the wine for Communion, as the kind we prefer is very scarce, and it was decided to use some made from wild grapes. There is only enough sugar left for one lovefeast, and if no more comes in this will be saved for the lovefeast of the little boys.

May 15. Eight Continental wagons came from the south, going to Virginia for the army. Mr. Brooks sent a wagon for corn, but there was none here, and as an order was received cancelling the first the wagon left empty.

May 16. Br. Lorenz went to Salem, and Sr. Kuhnast went thither also in the small wagon to get articles from the potter-shop.

May 20. This evening thirty and more soldiers came from Richmond; they are from our district and must serve a year in the Continental army.

May 21. The soldiers, under command of Major Schmidt, left for Salisbury by way of Salem. Johann George Wageman is badly broken out with small-pox, and is very ill. The eruption burns so that he can hardly lie down, and Brethren are watching beside him; the others have it very lightly, both here and at the mill.

May 24. From Salem came Br. and Sr. Marshall, Br. and Sr. Reitz, Br. Stotz, and the Srs. Quest and Reitz. The latter will take charge of the school for little girls here, and will visit the girls in Bethania, relieving Sr. Engel who will return to Salem. Br. and Sr. Graff returned from Bethania, where they have been since Monday. Between two and three o'clock in the afternoon there was a meeting for the congregation, and Br. Graff received as Akolouthie the three Srs. Maria Bagge, Maria Elizabeth Engel and Magdalena Reitz, and ordained the two Srs. Maria Bagge and Maria Quest as Deaconesses of the Brethren's Church.

May 25. Three more of our people have broken out with small-pox. The Brn. Nathanael and John Bröder, who have had small-pox at home, have returned to work.

May 28. Our negro Christian is so ill with small-pox that we do not know how it will go with him.

May 29. The house for Br. Broesing was laid up, and finished except the roof-timbers. Br. Bonn came to see those who are sick with small-pox.

May 30. There was a distressing accident at Br. Rank's. His son John was cutting wood, and his sister was near by picking up splinters. Just as her brother chopped she reached for a splinter, and he cut the two middle fingers on her left hand nearly off. Br. Bonn was brought from Salem to bandage the hand.

May 31. Shingles were hauled for Br. Broesing's house, and as it rained hard all afternoon we were worried about our men who are just over small-pox. They returned about eight o'clock in the evening, quite wet but in good spirits. Br. Bonn, who spent last night with Br. Rank, came to see our sick, and found them all doing well.

June 1. Colonel Armstrong was here, and travelers passed north and south with their wagons and household goods.

June 2. The men have finished covering Br. Broesing's house. Br. Bonn and Joseph Dixon went to Br. Rank's to attend his little Elisabeth. The diener and dienerinnen and musicians had a lovefeast, and renewed their pledge of faithful service of the Saviour. Br. Stoehr has a sore throat. Little John Rank has broken out with small-pox.

June 5. Br. Stoehr sent for Br. Bonn, for his throat is so swollen that he can hardly swallow water. Word came that one of our mares was lying in the woods three miles from here, and could not get up. Four of our men went to see about it, and finding that her leg was broken and that nothing could be done for her they helped her out of life.

June 6. Br. Bonn went to see the little Rank girl. One of her fingers showed no sign of healing and had to be taken off.

June 7. Br. Stoehr is worse, with chills and fever, and his throat so badly swollen that he can scarcely breathe. Br. Bonn was sent for, and while he was coming Br. Stoehr tried to bring his affairs in order, and made his will.

June 8. Br. Bonn remained until noon, and finding that the swelling on Br. Stoehr's head and throat was ready to open he made an incision and there was a free discharge, which relieved him somewhat, and during the following night he slept a little. Ploughing and hoeing the corn was finished today.

June 9. Br. Stoehr was more comfortable, but he could swallow only fluids, and the free discharge from his head continues. Sr. Stoehr has fever this evening. Today the men began to cut barley. A man who has worked here for two days, and who said he had escaped from the English, was arrested by Major Schmidt as a thief and was taken to the muster place where they planned to make him enlist, but he escaped from them.

June 11. Br. Bonn and his Dixon were here to see Br. Stoehr. They amputated the little Elisabeth Rank's other finger.

June 15. Yesterday and today grass was cut and hay made. Br. Broesing and his men have planted corn.

June 16. Yesterday there was a report that 1500 soldiers were coming from Virginia, and this was confirmed today when grain was brought in from the neighborhood, and Br. Stotz came from Salem to see about the requisitions sent there. We waited for them until about three o'clock in the afternoon, when Major Schmidt arrived, and said that they had not yet crossed Dan River, and so could not get here today or tomorrow.[6]

June 17. The swelling in Br. Stoehr's throat has broken, and he is able to eat a little, and it looks as though he would recover.

June 19. Several Brethren came from Salem to see Mr. Brooks about the taxes, but he did not arrive until afternoon, and as he promised to go to Salem the Brethren went home. Men who had come from the Hope and Friedland settlements were able to talk with Mr. Brooks. Br. Stoehr is able to be up a little. Yesterday and today it was very hot.

June 20. Mr. Brooks was here, and settled the grain tax for our people and for others. Rye was cut today.

June 21. The rye was finished and wheat harvest began.

June 22. Colonel Armstrong was here; and the militia who were drafted for three months assembled, ready to march.

June 23. The militia pressed Br. Rank's wagon, and in the afternoon they pressed Br. Broesing's horse, to use with the wagon.

June 24. Br. Rank's wagon was not strong enough, so the militia pressed a wagon from Wendel Krause, and they also pressed a horse from Cornelius Sale who had a horse from Salem.

June 25. The militia left this afternoon for Guilford Court-House. Toward evening a message arrived, calling them back, and on

June 26 they returned.

June 27. Some hay was brought in, but rain interfered. The little Schaub girl began to improve. She has had small-pox and nettle-rash at the same time, but the latter has disappeared, and the postules are beginning to fill.

---

[6] This large company did not come at all; the Bethania diary says the English prevented.

June 28. As Br. Stauber stepped out of the door at night he was bitten by a snake, but he has recovered. The Brethren of the Committee were told that Br. Oesterlein wishes to build a smithy here.

July 1. This was the festival of our little boys. At two o'clock the entire congregation gathered, and had a happy love-feast with our little boys. We thanked and praised our dear Lord for all His goodness and grace, and especially for the recovery from small-pox of twenty-four persons. There are six children of members living outside our town who have not had it. We also noted with gratitude that the greater part of our harvest time has passed in peace and quiet.

July 2. Today grass was mowed and flax pulled. It was wonderfully hot. Many travelers passed, coming from South Carolina. At night there was a very severe storm, with sharp lightning and a good rain.

July 3. Today, as for several days past, the Virginia militia have come from General Greene's camp, very hungry. Some of our local militia came by on their way to Salisbury.

July 5. Hay was made, and the corn was ploughed and hoed for the second time.

July 8. George Schmidt came from South Carolina, and seized a negro who was working for Br. Broesing and took him to his brother Major Schmidt. The Major was not at home, so his brother threatened to kill the negro, but Mrs. Schmidt helped him to get away. Major Schmidt was afraid he might try to follow the negro, so on two evenings he came late and stayed at Broesing's until eleven o'clock. Four Continental wagons came in charge of an officer; they had sugar, rum and other goods.

July 9. Hay and grain was hauled, and all the wheat was brought into the sheds. Colonel Armstrong was here on business. Travelers continue to pass from the south. Br. Oesterlein came to begin building his smithy.

July 12. The Brethren of the Committee were informed that old Philip Vogler of Friedland wishes to move to Bethabara, and thinks he can support himself partly by farm work and partly by tailoring. No objection was made.

July 14. Many of our German neighbors were here. Jacob Hauser and Nicholas Doll selected men to represent them in adjusting the matter of a wagon which the former had borrowed from the latter; it was seized by the English in Bethania, and the latter has not been able to get it back.

July 15. Sunday. In the congregation meeting we began to read the book *Idea Fidei Fratrum,* and will continue on each Sunday and Wednesday.

July 17. Colonel Shepperd and Captain Lewis came from the Assembly. Among other items of interest they told us that the Assembly is to meet in Salem in November. Our hope is in the Lord, Who will help us.

July 20. In spite of rain the dry hay was brought in, grass was cut, and flax was threshed in the shed. In the fields stubble was ploughed under.

July 23. Five wagons came from Salisbury with an order for two hundred bushels of corn. They were told that there was no public corn here, so they could get only 180 bu. which Mr. Brooks had borrowed.

July 26. Some of the militia of this district mustered here, and took occasion to enroll four of our day-laborers. This evening at eight o'clock a draft was made, and these four men were included among those taken.

July 27. It was rainy all day. Toward evening a company of militia came from the Town Fork and Dan River. The men and horses made so much noise in the town that no evening service could be held.

July 28. The company that came yesterday remained today, and others joined them, including Major Winston. They caught Aust's two horses in the woods and pressed them, and also took several others which they found in the woods. When Aust heard that they had taken his horses he applied to Colonel Armstrong, who sent an order to the Captain saying that it was against the law to press horses in another district, and that these must be returned.

July 29. Sunday. We thought that we would have a quiet day, for the horsemen under Major Winston left at eight o'clock for Guilford. We began our Unity Day services with a liturgy and reading from the 13th Woche, 1779. In the second service we began to read a Memoir, and just in the middle of it the horsemen returned, and fired their guns as a sign of joy that they were allowed to go home. It disturbed us, and frightened many of us, and while they stayed we could have no service. They left about three o'clock. Colonel Armstrong came at noon, and as he had heard by Express this morning how it was with the Tories against whom the men were to march he allowed them to go home. This relieved us of these men, some of whom were so ill-mannered as to take all of the few apples we had, and go into the gardens and help themselves to whatever they pleased. Last night they did at least 40 sh. worth of damage in the tavern, where they broke panes of glass from sheer wantonness.

Aug. 3. Turnip seed was sown.

Aug. 4. The men began to haul stone for Br. Oesterlein's work-shop.

Aug. 8. It was too dry to plough, so wood was hauled for Br. Oesterlein. For a week everybody has been complaining about the great drought and the heat.

Aug. 11. The morning was cloudy, and in the afternoon there were numerous showers.

Aug. 13. Monday. Our congregation celebrated this important memorial day of the Unity of Brethren.

Aug. 14. The rain has softened the ground and three plows were put to work.

Aug. 15. Br. Blum went to court at Richmond, and secured licenses for the tavern here and in Salem. Hay was made.

Aug. 17. Our little girls had their festival today.

Aug. 18. Many travelers are passing these days.

Aug. 20. Br. Oesterlein's work-shop was raised today. Men began to make brick. Otherwise work went on as usual.

Aug. 22. An officer from Sumter's corps was here to see whether the General could establish a factory for the Southern states, but he found no suitable place.

Aug. 23. Travel continues, people going to the mountains, or coming from the mountains to Virginia.

Aug. 25. Eight Continental wagons arrived, on their way to the south. Their officer kept good order among the men. They took hay and something over twenty bushels of grain, on public account.

Aug. 27. An unusual number of travelers passed. Work continued in making hay and hauling it in.

Sept. 3. The Committee met. There was much discussion of the damage done in the fields by the swine, but no remedy was suggested except that good fences be made. Some of the Continental wagons passed on their way home.

Sept. 6. Most of the hay has been brought in. Flax was spread in the meadow.

Sept. 7. In the sixth hour the Choir of Married People solemnly closed their covenant year.

Sept. 8. Early in the morning the festival of the Married People was announced by the wind instruments. Morning prayers were at nine o'clock. At ten o'clock Br. Marshall preached on the Doctrinal Text for Sept. 7th. In the afternoon there was a hard storm. In the third hour Br. Graff presided over the festal lovefeast. The festal ode was sung by Br. Reitz. At four o'clock Br. Graff led a liturgy, and then sixteen married couples partook of the Lord's Supper. Br. Benzien played the organ for the lovefeast and Communion. In the evening Br. Praetzel led the singstunde.

Sept. 13. Many Continental wagons passed, going to Virginia.

Sept. 14. Many travelers passed, going to Virginia or to the mountains.

Sept. 19. The young people, Casper and Anna Stolz of Bethania, moved into the house near the mill, having rented the land for a year.

Sept. 20. In the afternoon there was a storm, and the rain continued until late at night. Many travelers spent the night here. Two wagons came with sugar to sell.

Sept. 21. The weather was good and rather cool. Br. Michael Hauser came to list the taxes. The General Commissary, superintendent of all the Commissaries of this part of the Province, was here. He was friendly and courteous in every way.

Sept. 22. Old Sr. Spönhauer was brought from Bethania for Sr. Blum, who was not well.

Sept. 24. This morning at six o'clock Sr. Blum was safely delivered of a little son. At noon Br. Praetzel and Br. and Sr. Meyer arrived from Salem. At two o'clock there was a meeting of adults and children for the baptism of the little son born today to our Br. and Sr. Blum. After singing several hymns there was an address on the Text for the day; then with the usual liturgy this little child was baptised into the death of Jesus in the name of the Holy Trinity. Sponsors were the Brn. and Srs. Praetzel and Meyer and Br. Mücke.

Minor Schmidt's company of horsemen gathered today. Those who came first wanted meat for their company, but we had not known of it in advance and were not prepared to give it instantly, so they shot a yoked cow on the street and cut it up. They seized two or three bushels of flour at the mill, and here had to be supplied with corn for their horses. It was an unpleasant situation for friends of the country and our neighbors from the Town Fork. The great mistake is that the Commissary does not look after the soldiers and does not provide for them. The company consisted of more than sixty men, and they pastured their horses over night in the large meadow.

Sept. 25. This morning about eleven o'clock we were rid of our guests, to our great joy.

Sept. 27. Br. Bonn came to see a sick man at the tavern, but he was so much better that he could go on north.

Sept. 28. At noon, after school, Br. Lorenz went to Bethania, and took Nachrichten to Br. Ernst. Colonel Armstrong, Mr. Brooks, and about seventy men arrived and spent the night. They brought with them what the men required, behaved well, and no one had reason to complain.

Sept. 29. The militia went to Salem and further. Colonel Armstrong and ten men returned to Richmond; he promised to come back with the next company.

Sept. 30. Sunday. At the usual time the church litany was prayed, and at the proper place the name of the infant Johann Jacob Blum was mentioned. Some of our members and their children went to Salem to visit; others from Bethania visited here.

Oct. 3. Captain Hill and his company of horsemen were here. They remained over night, and got what supplies they needed.

Oct. 4. A company of forty infantry arrived, and had to be provided with food. Colonel Armstrong and other officers were here yesterday and today. The company made no disturbance except that some who wanted to cook for themselves went about the town trying to get cooking utensils, which were not furnished because cooked food was being supplied to them from the tavern. Some of our guests attended the evening meeting.

Oct. 5. Captain Hill's company left about noon, and fired their muskets as an expression of their thanks. The infantry remained here.

Oct. 6. Meat came in for the company, and with it they repaid the meat furnished to them yesterday, and paid also for the bread they needed today and the brandy they secured from Br. Mücke. After breakfast the militia left, in spite of the rain.

Oct. 7. Several Continental wagons passed toward Virginia. The burning of the kiln of brick is finished.

Oct. 11. Br. and Sr. Broesing moved into their new house near Bethabara.

Oct. 12. Many travelers passed, many of them in very needy circumstances.

Oct. 13. The sowing of winter grain was finished.

Oct. 15. Br. John Ranke left for Pennsylvania, going first to Bethania where the wagon will be loaded.

Oct. 16. Br. Rose went to Muddy Creek, about fourteen miles away, to see after some cattle that belong here. The men began to gather corn and haul it in.

Oct. 18. They began to tear down the old tavern. The Sisters swingled flax. Many travelers were here, coming from the south. Others came from across the mountains on their way to the lower country. Many others from Virginia and Carolina went to take the place of those who came hither, so that altogether more than a hundred passed. Continental wagons came from the south to get salt for the southern army.

Oct. 21. Sunday. Congregation Council met. As there has been some complaint about the way in which provision has been made for love-feasts it was suggested that a lovefeast fund should be established, with one Brother appointed to manage it. Br. Mücke was unanimously chosen, and will have charge of it with the advice of Br. Kühnast. Members were reminded that no one must cut timber or fire-wood in the forest without permission and notice; old fallen trees may be used by any one. Br. Rose is the man to be notified when the Brethren need wood. There was a discussion of the wages to be paid day-laborers, so that all might pay the same. It was stated that sometimes a Brother might have some difficult and disagreeable work to be done, for which it would be proper to pay a few pence extra. In the gemeinstunde the congregation knelt, and thanked the Lord for all His grace and love, which He has shown to us and to all members of His Brethren's Church. We commended to His grace ourselves and all our people, Christian and heathen; and we prayed especially for this land, asking that according to His grace and wisdom He would soon give us honorable peace.

Oct. 25. On account of rain there was only one evening service; Br. Oesterlein played the organ.

Oct. 26. Repair work was begun on the old houses.

Oct. 27. Br. Aust and Möller have been working on ovens here and in Bethania.

Oct. 28. Sunday. In a short meeting of the Married People Sr. Blum and her infant son were present, and a blessing was sung for her.

Oct. 29. The Committee met. It was suggested that the swine might be yoked. No one living in the town should permit swine to run at large; if a Brother does not wish to kill all his hogs he should pen them up.

Oct. 31. At the evening meeting notice was given of the home-going of our Br. Jacob Bonn. His remains will be interred next Friday.

Nov. 1. Br. Stoehr had the logs from the old tavern laid up on his new stone foundation, and no accident occurred.

Nov. 2. Most of the Brethren and Sisters from here went to Salem to the funeral of our Br. Jacob Bonn. When we returned we found a company of militia in the town, who would have been glad for more than bread.

Nov. 3. There was threshing in the sheds, and otherwise all went as usual. The militia company left, taking the road to Deep River.

Nov. 6. Saw-logs were hauled to the mill.

Nov. 7. Br. Schaub has been having a well dug on his proposed building lot. He has found water enough at eighteen feet, so the well will be walled. Little Leonard Aust has been suffering much pain since he was kicked in the side by a young horse a few days ago, but the remedies have taken effect, and it is hoped that he will now improve.

Nov. 9. Several neighbors have asked for preaching and for the baptism of their children, so Br. Lorenz went today to the house of Johannes Krum, on Muddy Creek, where our old friends and former hearers had assembled. In the meeting a hymn was sung, followed by an address on the words of Paul: *By grace are ye saved, through faith;——not of works, lest any man might boast.* Then with the usual liturgy the following children were baptised into the death of Jesus, Heinrich Schneider, Maria Kalcklöher, Anna Elisabeth Krum.

Br. Blum went to Salem to have our remaining Tickets from 1780 signed by the gentlemen there, but found that nothing could be done until the Assembly met. Here all went as usual,—that is saw-logs were hauled and some turnips were brought in.

Nov. 10. The fire inspectors went all through the town today.

Nov. 11. It was rainy and cold. Colonel Armstrong and two officers spent the night here.

Nov. 12. The weather cleared. Br. Oesterlein began work in his smithy.

Nov. 13. The local congregation celebrated this important memorial day of the Unity of Brethren, and remembered with thanks and praise the great grace which our dear Saviour showed to His people forty years ago.

The Brn. Blum and Mücke went to court at Richmond, returning in the evening. Br. Mücke had been called as a juryman, but was allowed to come home.

Nov. 14. A house was laid up for the hens and geese.

Nov. 15. Property in this district was appraised today by the men appointed for that purpose. Br. Blum was appointed from this district.

Nov. 16. Old Br. Stach is very ill with pain in his chest.

Nov. 18. Br. Stach is very weak. Some of our neighbors assembled here, on their way to Salem to act as guard for the Assembly.

Nov. 20. Militia from various companies went toward Salem soon after noon. Most of them have orders to join General Rutherford.

Nov. 24. Wagons were here with salt, sugar, iron and rum. Some salt was bought.

Nov. 26. Yesterday and today there have been many militiamen here, going to Salem. There were also many travelers going north and going south. Some of the gentlemen of the Assembly were here. Br. Stach's fever is not so high today, and there is hope that he may improve.

Nov. 27. Our two wagons went to the Atkin for corn which Joseph Philips owes here.

Nov. 29. Poor Br. Franz Steup fell backwards as he was going up the stairs at his house, falling half the length of the stairs. He was picked up for dead, for he was quite stiff. He must be injured internally, as nothing can be seen on the outside. He was bled, and we notified Br. and Sr. Broesing, who stayed with him over night.

Nov. 30. Poor Br. Steup was able to speak this evening and recognized the Brethren. A few verses were sung for him.

Dec. 3. Br. Dixon came from Salem to Br. Steup, to see whether he could find any external injury for which something could be done, but he could discover nothing.

Dec. 4. It began to snow, and the weather was very disagreeable.

Dec. 7. The Brn. Stach and Steup were fairly well, and are steadily improving.

Dec. 8. Several soldiers with wagons returned from Williamstown, and had breakfast here. A man, who was probably a Tory, came just before day, and wanted to pour new spoons from old pewter. When the soldiers arrived he got out of sight. Shortly afterwards Major Schmidt and the younger Hoffman arrived, and hearing that he had gone toward Salem they followed him.

Dec. 9. Several travelers passed with many children.

Dec. 20. The Single Br. Oesterlein was betrothed to the Single Sr. Anna Maria Hege. Last night it rained so hard that the water has risen, and no hauling could be done.

Dec. 21. Our wagons went fifteen miles away for shingles.

Dec. 22. It snowed; then it rained, forming glaze ice; then it snowed again.

Dec. 24. This morning about four o'clock our negress, wife of the [colored] Br. Johann Samuel, gave birth to a little daughter. The child was baptised this afternoon in a meeting for adults and children, and received the name Anna Maria.

At two o'clock the diener of this congregation had a happy lovefeast. About five o'clock our children met to adore the Infant Jesus in the manger; they had a lovefeast, and at its close each child received a verse and a lighted taper. In spite of the bad weather all our children were present except the three smallest. At eight o'clock the adult congregation met to thank the Saviour for His birth, life, sufferings and death.

Dec. 25. Christmas Day. In the morning there was preaching. In the afternoon the children, the Sisters and the Brethren had their meetings. At the close of the day the *Hymn of Praise to the Son* was sung. The weather was cloudy and rainy, but the services were well attended by our members and friends.

Dec. 26. Second Christmas Day was observed as a Unity Day.

Dec. 28. Little Johannes Lorenz Bagge has not been well for several days. He has had a severe cold in the chest, and it has pleased our dear Lord and Saviour to take this child to Himself. This was announced to the congregation by the French horns, in the usual tunes.

Dec. 29. Notice of the child's death was sent to Salem and Bethania. In the evening the congregation had the last Communion of the year.

Dec. 30. Sunday. At nine o'clock was the Post-Communion. Br. and Sr. Praetzel and others came from Salem, partly on account of the funeral and partly for the wedding. In the afternoon at one o'clock Br. Praetzel held the funeral for the child Johannes Lorenz Bagge. At two o'clock there was a meeting for the adult members, during which Br. Matthaeus Oesterlein and Sr. Anna Marie Hege were united in marriage by Br. Lorenz, in the name of the Father, the Son and the Holy Ghost. Soon after the service our dear guests from Salem, and her parents from Bethania, had a happy vesper with the newly married couple. Br. Franz Steup had another attack like the one four weeks ago, becoming rigid and unable to help himself.

Dec. 31. In the afternoon our children had their last meeting of the year. In the evening at seven o'clock a messenger from Salem brought the Memorabilia of the Unity's Elders Conference, and part of it was read during the lovefeast at eight o'clock. At half past nine the congregation re-assembled, and the Memorabilia of the town and

18

country congregations were read. At eleven-thirty we met once more, * * * and when notice was given of the beginning of the new year the congregation knelt and sang: *Now thank we all our God.*

Bethania Diary, 1781.

[Extracts translated.]

Jan. 1. The reading of the Memorabilia was repeated for those who could not be present to hear it yesterday.

Jan. 9. School was begun for the little boys and girls in joint session.

Jan. 20. Two Continental officers arrived to give notice that arrangements should be made for having soldiers quartered here.

Jan. 21. Br. Yarrell came from Salem for several wagons to help haul timber for a house to be erected in Salem for the use of the soldiers, but as they were considering doing the same here no help could be given.

Feb. 1. One of the Continental wagons arrived with several soldiers from Salem, bring requisition for several loads of hay. The Brethren met, and it was resolved that George Hauser, Sr., and Schor should fill the Continental wagon, which is not large, and the others should make up two more loads. As it rained hard the next day the two loads could not be sent.

Feb. 2. Others came demanding 1000 lbs. of meat, to be ready in a few hours, so several cattle were slaughtered in haste.[1] In the evening 900 lbs. of meat were delivered at Bethabara in the belief that the English prisoners would be there. During the night the same wagons were pressed to carry provisions to the prisoners, who number six hundred.

Feb. 3. A new order came, requiring that 3000 lbs. of hay should be furnished, and that three wagons from the town and three from the country must be furnished to help move the powder magazine from Salem. After much discussion here and there two wagons and teams were made ready in the town, and left for Salem next evening.

Feb. 4. Two English deserters were brought here by several of the militia. They wanted to leave them here, but it was finally arranged that they should be taken on to Mr. Lanier by those who had arrested them. A young man was brought in about the same time, and as smallpox was breaking out on him certain Continental officers who happened

---

[1] *Extract der Diarii* says that "the Commissary, Major Heyn, was supplied with meat for the English prisoners captured at Broad River."

to be here would not allow him to be brought into the tavern. The man who was taking the deserters to Mr. Lanier therefore took the sick man on the horse behind him.

Feb. 5. Ludwig Leinbach came with the distressing news, that as a kitchen was being blocked up at Abraham Leinbach's the six and a half year old son of Abraham was killed by a falling log.

Feb. 6. Quite unexpectedly a party of Liberty Men arrived, who had been driven out of Georgia and South Carolina. They claimed that they had orders from General Greene to take away the best horses, so that the English should not get them, and they forcibly seized two of the best which they could find. So it went all day with larger and smaller parties. Some of them demanded food in rude fashion, but the dear Heavenly Father protected us from harm. Toward four o'clock Abraham Leinbach brought the above-mentioned remains, and after an address on the comforting text for the day the body was accompanied to its last resting place. Several officers belonging to passing cavalry reverently accompanied the remains. This afternoon there came a report that the English would reach Salem today, which caused much alarm among the officers here.

Feb. 7. I was in Salem at Conference. The report that the English were there was without foundation, but it was said that a party of them had been in Bryant's Settlement. All night groups of militia were passing. After midnight an Express brought word that about eight hundred of the English had reached Colonel Hound's.

Feb. 8. Yesterday and today many wagons have passed, with whites and blacks fleeing to Virginia. This evening we heard that the English army under General Cornwallis had passed the Shallow Ford about three o'clock.

Feb. 9. About noon the English really arrived here. The officers were divided among the houses. The Chief Commissary of infantry, Mr. Knecht, born in the city of Bern,[2] visited me on arrival, and I offered him my room. Several Sisters with little children, together with the older girls and the other children, retired into the school-room. The Commissary Knecht and a German Reformed preacher asked me many questions, which I answered to their satisfaction. As they arrived order was given that cattle for butchering should be furnished, and as that was neglected more than sixty were killed during the day, of which about thirty were seized here; this did not include the sheep, geese and chickens which they took. Two wagons were sent to the mill for meal, and scarcely had they left when a sharp order was

---

[2] Ernst was born in Arau, Canton Berne, and was therefore a fellow-countryman of the Commissary.

given, with threatened penalty for non-execution, for twenty good horses to be ready by six o'clock. Everything was in the greatest confusion and no one knew what to do, for all houses were filled with officers and their servants. At dusk a second written order was received, saying that the horses must be forthcoming by six o'clock, with repetition of the threats. Between eight and nine o'clock we made an attempt to explain to General Cornwallis that it was impossible to furnish twenty horses; he was not at all moved, but wrote a Pass permitting two of our young men to ride to the neighbors and bring in some horses. I had hardly reached the house when an officer arrived to seize me as hostage until the horses were furnished, but the officers lodging with me interfered, and he went away without me.

Feb. 10. At two o'clock in the morning the two boys, Jacob Hauser and Jacob Stolz, were waked and sent out to try to get several horses, but they returned much too late. About seven o'clock the army began to march. Instead of twenty horses the Colonel of artillery had to make out with seventeen, and at least six of these had been taken secretly from the English teamsters. Commissary Knecht and two assistants wrote Tickets for the residents, but as they were not particularly anxious to be exact many matters remained open. A strong guard surrounded the Gemein Haus to protect the Commissary, as the army had already moved on. The preacher and the Commissary, and the officers who had stayed with us, were most polite in taking leave, and regretted the loss that had fallen upon us. In some of the houses articles were stolen by the servants left behind.[3] We must praise our dear Saviour that He has done all things well, and none of us was injured in soul or body, though in cattle, grain, hay, brandy and fences we have lost as much as £1500, valued in good money. During the day we heard that as much as two wagon loads of meat was left lying around the countless camp fires.

Feb. 11. Sr. Feiser came in great distress, and reported that last Friday a party seized her husband and took him away by force, saying that he was a rebel and that they were for the king. In the Committee it was earnestly remarked that the controversial discussion about this or the other party must stop from now on, and that the Brethren should be asked to comply with this, so that party spirit should not again get the upper hand, for that was not proper for children of God.

---

[3] The Wachovia Historical Society Museum has a small iron pot which tradition associates with the visit of the English army to Bethania. It is said that cabbage was being cooked in the pot, and that a soldier carried it off, whereupon the irate house-wife followed the army to Salem, nine miles away, and secured an order for its return.

Feb. 12. I went to Salem to talk with the Brethren about the occurrences here. There I found out that Br. Feiser had been taken away by Liberty Men, but had been released.

Feb. 14. This afternoon Mr. Gurry[4] came bringing five bushels of corn, as he believed that the English had left us nothing. He said that the neighbors were willing to bring us a hundred bushels of corn, and also meat; but as I did not hear this from the man himself I took no further notice of it.

Feb. 15. We join with Br. Feiser in giving thanks to the Lord, Who saved him out of the hands, not of Loyalist troops but of the robbers swarming in the woods about here. Mention of the incident was made on the 11th of this month. They took him around until Saturday afternoon, and on Sunday evening he reached home.

Feb. 16. This afternoon Br. Fischer was coming from the home of Johann Kraus, and on the way was set upon by six robbers, and was very roughly handled by them because he refused to give up his horse. Several men of this type came to town this evening and remained over night.

Feb. 17. There was much passing back and forth through the town all day. Heinrich Schor, Spönhauer, Jr., and Fischer, returned in the afternoon from Bethabara without their horses, although promise of them was given yesterday.

Feb. 18. Sunday. Contrary to expectation there were many here for service. A party of Liberty Men passed through so quietly that many did not know they were here. Martin Hauser, returning from Salem, brought word that the Brethren there had been plagued on Friday and Saturday by more than twenty Liberty robbers, who had finally left the town this morning.

Feb. 19. At noon thirty mounted Liberty Men arrived, and remained for half an hour. In the afternoon two similar companies were here.

Feb. 21. I went to Salem to Conference, the Brn. Grabs and Transou going with me. Returning we met many of the Virginians, who had passed through Bethania at noon. Most of them stayed at Bethabara; those we met were going to Salem.

Feb. 22. All day there was coming and going, but they behaved fairly well. The two wagons which left here on the 4th for Virginia returned this afternoon.

Feb. 25. We heard today much about the robberies which have been committed in the neighborhood where Doll and Jacob Hauser live.

---

[4] Doubtless Malcolm Curry, of Richmond.

The robberies were the work of the men who are swarming in the woods about here.

Feb. 26. Michael Hauser left here on the 23rd, to go with the older Volz and Mrs. Walk to the camp of General Greene, to see if they could find Walk and have him released. He returned this evening, as they saw there was no chance of reaching the camp.

March 6. This morning Major Armstrong came with word that fourteen wagons of provisions must be sent from this neighborhood to the American army. In the end nothing came of this.

March 7. Casper Stolz and Samuel Strub went to Salem to keep watch there.

March 8. On this and the following days many of the Virginia militia passed, going home. As they came in small parties they behaved properly, but we had to give them food.

March 10. Some of the Salem Brethren passed on the way to Richmond to the election, some riding, some in wagons. On the return Br. Spieseke spent the night with us. From him we heard that some men had voted for George Hauser, Jr.

March 11. Toward evening the Brn. Yarrel and Bibighaus arrived, and went on to the election next day.

March 12. As the Brethren returned we heard that William Shepperd had upset the election, and that tomorrow a new vote will be taken.

March 13. We heard that William Sheppard, Commens and William Lewis were elected to the Assembly.

March 16. This afternoon it was reported that the troops under General Greene have been completely defeated by Lord Cornwallis. This brought the sigh: "Oh, if only this were the last battle!"

March 24. The three Brn. George Hauser, Sr., Heinrich Schor and Fischer left yesterday for the camp of the English army, said to be fifty miles from here on Haw River, to try to recover their horses.

March 25. Several passed from Greene's camp. They claimed to be officers, on their way to South Carolina, and said that in four weeks we would hear news from there.

March 31. It is reported that the men drafted some time ago are called to assemble at Bethabara on April 2nd, and any man who does not appear must pay a fine of £6000 or serve three years in the Continental army. The three Brethren mentioned on the 24th returned the middle of the week, safe and well but without having accomplished anything.

April 8. The house-fathers and mothers met in the Saal. Most of them were of the opinion that it would be best to wait until a case of small-pox developed in town, and then consider the question of inoculation.

April 10. Martin Walk arrived. Michael Hauser, Sr., accompanied him to Colonel Armstrong, to secure his advice about Walk's escape from prison.

April 13. Many passed on their way to General Muster at Richmond.

April 20. Br. Bagge was in Bethabara to get his deer-skins, which a Continental officer brought from Daub last week and left there, but they had been impressed again.

April 28. We visited at the home of Krieger, Sr. The two Hessian deserters who are staying there were very friendly; one is a tailor and the other a weaver. From there we went to see Daub, who has begun a new farm on Krieger's land.

May 3. Br. Spönhauer, Sr., was very ill, and asked me to rewrite his Will, made several years ago, as he wished several changes. This was done, and it was signed and witnessed today. The neighbor, Friedrich Alberty, asked me to hold the funeral service for his wife, who passed away last night about twelve o'clock.

May 4. After the morning school my wife and I went to Krieger's where many of the neighbors had already gathered. As more were present than the house could hold arrangements were made to have them gather in the shed. I spoke on yesterday's Watch Word concerning the love of Jesus for all men who are of an humble and contrite heart. All went quietly and in good order.

May 9. Heinrich Schor and George Hauser, Jr., returned from Virginia. The former brought back the stallion which the Liberty Men took by force on Feb. 6th, but was obliged to leave the horse he had ridden there for three weeks.

May 14. Peter Hauser, Abraham Transou, Michael Hauser, Jr., Samuel Strub and several country members went to Guilford County to see whether they could find the horses the English took from here on Feb. 10th.

May 16. Abraham Transou returned with Jacob Hauser, Sr., who had been taken sick.

May 17. Peter Hauser and Sam Strub returned. There is so much disturbance in the lower counties that they had turned back; old Jacob Müller, however, had decided to go to the German settlement on Reedy

Fork, and see whether his acquaintances there knew anything about the horses. Conrad and Michael Hauser, Jr., went with him.

May 19. Mr. Shepperd, his wife, some of his relatives and about thirty negroes arrived and spent the night.

May 25. In a meeting of the house-fathers it was stated that since Strub moved away there had been no grave-digger in the town, and that it was necessary to have some one who lives in town for that work. Br. Kürschner offered his services, and it was agreed that he should receive eight shillings for digging a large grave and five shillings for a small one.

May 27. At the first bell the older girls assembled, and Sr. Quest presented Sr. Reitz to them as their future Visitor.

May 31. Mr. Brooks came to collect the tax or Tickets.

June 3. Wilhelm Grabs, who played the organ for the preaching service, had to go to bed directly afterwards, as did Lazarus Hege and Jacob Stolz.

June 4. William Windfield came for me by agreement, and took me to his house, where four of the neighboring families had gathered. When I told them I would baptise their children in German they said they had never heard a German service and they would be glad to hear it. Windfield's wife was born a Messer, and some of the others understood a little German, so I spoke to them of the Covenant God had made with men, and then baptised five children:—John Windfield, John Ross, Salome Denton, Bethseba Follis and Francis Marit.

June 11. It appears that the small-pox will spread here, and there has been much friction and might be more. The house-fathers were therefore called together at noon, and they agreed that everything possible should be done to hold it in check until after harvest, and until the dog-days are over. Wilhelm Grabs, on which it is beginning to break out, was taken to Salem by his father and father-in-law, but no suitable arrangements could be made for Christian Sehnert.

June 14. It was reported that 1500 men belonging to Washington's army will pass here very soon.

June 16. Through several country members we heard that the neighbors have gathered at various places to plan for the provisions ordered for delivery at Bethabara for the expected 1500 men. They asked that a man from here would go Express to Salisbury, and George Hauser, Jr., agreed to go.

June 18. We heard that the 1500 men mentioned on the 14th will not come to Bethabara, having been hindered by the English.

June 25. Most of the men began to cut wheat. Last week they cut rye.

June 28. There have been no new cases of small-pox except at Sehnert's, where two more children have it.

June 30. Most of the town residents have finished harvesting their wheat, and each has reason to thank the Heavenly Father for the blessing He has given.

July 1. Sehnert's harvest was a problem, for he and his wife are sick and the children have small-pox. About three o'clock I took most of our young men and boys to his field and cut his wheat. We also cut part of Beroth's.

July 10. About twenty men passed, coming from Greene's army in South Carolina. They were so quiet we were hardly aware of them. Because of small-pox in town they took the road outside.

July 14. John Leinbach, who came to town with his family last evening, and who is on his way to Pennsylvania, offered to take letters.

July 17. Mr. William Sheppard returned from the Assembly. He said that twenty of the members had been captured by the English but released on parole. The others escaped by retiring into the woods, though they held the rest of their sessions. He said further that it had been resolved that the next session should be held in Salem.

July 31. We were visited by Isaac Pfaff and Margaretha Volk, who were married[5] today at the home of her father, Andreas Volk. We wished for them that they might enter their new condition of life resolved to live for the dear Saviour alone.

Aug. 3. A man named Anton Bihler came with a wagon from Pennsylvania, and brought us a small package of letters.

Aug. 14. George Hauser, Jr., and Jacob Schor left for Pennsylvania on business for Br. Bagge.

Sept. 6. The Gemein Haus was cleaned by Sisters and girls from the lower town. Eleven Continental wagons passed, but tarried scarcely half an hour.

Sept. 16. I received a letter from Br. Bagge, asking that we gather linen rags for the men who were wounded in the battle of Eutah Springs on the 8th of this month, and that we help send them to Salisbury by way of Salem. This request was laid before the house-fathers this evening.

Sept. 17. Sam Strub brought in the Hessian deserter, Fischer, who promised for a small fee to take a sack of rags to Salisbury, as he wished

---

[5] By a Justice of the Peace. *Extract der Diarii.*

to go there at any rate. George Hauser, Sr., rode with him, taking the rest of the rags, amounting to about half a sack.

Sept. 18. [*Marshall's diary.* Johann Hauser's barn and stable burned down.]

Sept. 19. Casper Stolz, who was married to A. Margaretha Hauser yesterday by Michael Hauser, [J. P.,] moved with her today to the house near the Bethabara mill.

Sept. 23. A Commissary from Salisbury was here, and ordered fifty bushels of oats, which must be delivered in Salisbury this week.

Sept. 27. Br. Peter Hauser and Michael Hauser, Jr., took to Salisbury the oats which were pressed.

Oct. 1. Ten wagons passed, going to South Carolina on service for the country. They said they were to haul rum for General Greene. The Commissary ordered corn from the fields for evening and morning, and several of the Brethren went to Plum Creek to get what he wanted.

Oct. 3. Forty men came from Belows Creek, and remained here over night. The Captain, Cummens by name, came with another man and asked modestly for something to eat; we gave it to him and he left with many thanks.

Oct. 7. There was a conference with the house-fathers concerning the meeting of the Assembly, to see what provisions they could spare for sale in Salem. Michael Hauser, Jr., told me that he had bound himself for two years and three months to the tanner and leather-dresser Daub; I wished for him that his experiences would be better than his brother Johannes had at George Frey's.

Oct. 9. The wagons that passed on the 1st returned today, but made no demands on us.

Oct. 15. Br. Johann Ranke and Gottlob Ranke set off for Pennsylvania.

Oct. 18. George Hauser, Jr., returned with his wagon from Pennsylvania.

Oct. 21. Samuel Strub received permission to become a resident of Bethania, and signed the Rules and Regulations.

Nov. 9. The road to Bear Creek was repaired, and a small bridge built across the water.

Nov. 12. Our neighbor Hofman came and asked for the baptism of his sick son, and I went with the father. When I reached home about four o'clock I found that one hundred and fifty English prisoners, under a militia guard commanded by Colonel Francis Lock, had reached Plum Creek and camped there. Toward evening some of the prisoners, with their guards, came into the town, bought brandy at the still-house, and drank themselves full. Some lay where they fell, others started a great quarreling, and this continued until ten o'clock at night when the last of them had to be driven out of town with blows.

Nov. 13. As the prisoners were not brought through the town, on their way to Virginia, until nearly noon, the first service could not be held until one o'clock. At the beginning of this meeting it was announced that in view of the disorder of last evening, which had been brought about by a shameful lust for money, and had resulted in nothing but ill-will, contention and shameful behaviour on the part of the strangers, the meetings which had been arranged for the communicant and received members would not be held.

Dec. 7. This morning a stranger arrived, saying that he had lost everything during the war and was trying to support himself and his family by pouring [pewter] spoons. It turned out later that he was a great scamp.

Dec. 8. Ten horsemen arrived, who claimed that they were searching for two murderers, one of whom was named William Ellroth. They demanded brandy and corn.

Dec. 13. Fischer's wagon returned. It had been to Edenton with others sent by James Sheppard.

Dec. 20. Michael and Johann Ranke returned from Pennsylvania. They reached Salem yesterday.

Dec. 22. The wagons of George Hauser, Sr., and Peter Hauser, returned from Edenton. They unloaded their salt in Salem.

Dec. 23. It snowed hard yesterday for the first time this winter.

Dec. 24. In spite of the bad weather and bad roads a fair number of country members and children came to the services.

Dec. 27. Early this morning the two scoundrels were brought in who attacked Heinrich Hauser on the road and frightened him badly. Next day they were released, after giving security in the amount of £500 hard money, and paying the costs which amounted to £30.

Dec. 30. George Hauser, Jr., brought me an order from Colonel Armstrong for a list of the members of this congregation, of both sexes and all ages.

Dec. 31. In the third service, at eleven o'clock, the year was closed.

Friedberg Diary, 1781.

[Extracts translated. As the order of services and the visits made by
the minister, Rev. Valentine Beck, were practically the same
as in 1780, they are omitted.]

Jan 1.   We entered the new year with a blessed sense of the presence
of God. Many friends from the neighborhood assembled for preaching
at the usual time.

Jan. 2.   The single man, Jacob Tanner, came for his certificate [of
the publication of the Banns]. I spoke with him about the guests
invited to the wedding, for it seemed to us that there were rather too
many; he promised to see that nothing was done which would be a reproach to us. As it turned out he must have found a way to avoid the
persons that we thought were too many, for they did not come.

Jan. 7.   In a meeting of communicant and received Brethren and
Sisters Br. Marshall read the draft of the *Brotherly Agreement,* and
opportunity was given for each to express his or her opinion. If any
did not wish to give an opinion in public it might be done privately.
Action was postponed, but various points were discussed, several Brethren
speaking.

Jan. 9.   The much rain has raised the South Fork, so that the whole
bottom near George Ebert's is under water, and it was impossible to cross
on the logs which had been laid there. At Nicholas Boeckel's the
little bridge was swept away, so that the children could not come to
school.

Jan. 12.   Henrich Schor has small-pox but is not badly broken out and
is doing well.

Jan. 14.   The collection for missions to the heathen was opened in
the presence of the Steward, Adam Spach, Sr.

Jan. 28.   We returned from Salem, constantly meeting soldiers, who
were all modest and polite. At Greter's we met a troop with a wagon.
Mrs. Greter told us that she had divided among them all the bread she
had in the house, and now others had come, begging her for God's sake
to give them a little, and it distressed her. I gave them what bread I
had, and they were very grateful. After we had crossed the South Fork,
which was very high, we met two more wagons, apparently loaded with
wounded.

Jan. 31.   We visited George Frey. Three of his children have small-
pox. The eldest daughter is breaking out and is not very sick; the
youngest has high fever and is very ill.

Feb. 3. Adam Spach, Sr., his son, his wagon and horses, were called out for Continental service.

Feb. 4. Sunday. The passing of soldiers made so much disturbance that those who live on the road were not able to come to service. Later Christel Frey arrived, and said that one of the passing soldiers had broken into his house and behaved badly; this frightened everybody and they hurried home. [*Extract der Diarii.* Soldiers from Georgia broke into a house and behaved badly. During these days the homes of many of our Friedberg Brethren were disturbed by soldiers, who threatened to shoot, and sometimes plundered. One Brother was beaten, dragged about by the hair, and trampled on, although he was willing to give them all they demanded. No one has lost his life, and for that we thank the Saviour.]

Feb. 5. We heard that the elder Greter had been badly treated, that he had been beaten, dragged about by the hair, and trampled upon. We were the more grieved as we heard that he had given no reason for such treatment. [*Extract der Diarii.* Wagons from Friedberg went to Salem to help in moving the ammunition.]

Feb. 6. A drunken man went to the elder Ebert's, cocked his gun repeatedly, and threatened to shoot. God protected Ebert, and helped him escape to his son, George Ebert, but before he could get into the house the man fired three times. He continued to threaten to shoot, so they had to keep a light burning all night, and they had an anxious time, not feeling sure of their lives. When the man became sober he regretted what he had done, and asked forgiveness for having behaved so badly.

Feb. 8. [*Extract der Diarii.* From Friedberg came a distressing story, for Martin Walk was seized by men in English uniform, who claimed that he was an enemy of the land, and took him away prisoner.]

Feb. 11. A child of Peter Frey has small-pox, caught from travelers who stopped there, and who had small-pox among their people.

Feb. 15. [*Extract der Diarii.* Br. Spach, who was pressed with his wagon the first of this month, returned safely today. He had to leave his wagon for a while, in order to get permission to come home.]

Feb. 17. There was quartering in this neighborhood, and many houses had from thirteen to twenty-six men with their horses, for which they had to furnish food for the men and forage for the horses. Many families were stripped almost bare of provisions, but the troops soon moved on.

Feb. 18. Toward evening we heard that while Peter and Christian Frey were here at service evil men had gone to their homes. At Peter's they threatened to shoot everybody. At Christian's only two servants were at home, and when the door was suddenly burst open they were so frightened that they did not know what to do, so the intruders did whatever they liked in the house. When Christian came home, and asked them politely not to act in that way, they attacked him with such harsh threats that he was glad to let them alone until they left of their own accord.

Feb. 25. The Brethren elected a new Steward, choosing George Frey. My wife went to Peter Frey's and found it a veritable lazaretto. The parents and eight children were all in bed. The father had only a cold, and could be up part of the time, but all the others had small-pox, and as they had no one to help them my wife stayed half a day and arranged for some one to look after the work.

Feb. 27. This morning we heard that the men who plundered in Friedland yesterday were caught last night and were under guard at George Tanner's. At noon we were frightened, for more of the neighbors were called, and it looked as though the whole settlement would be plundered; but after the men had returned the stolen articles and had promised to steal no more they were released, and passed here in good order and politely. We thanked the Saviour that we had escaped being disturbed.

March 3. Last month there was so much disturbance that the Brethren hardly dared leave their homes, but God has ordained that we have had two or three quiet days.

March 8. George Lachenauer asked that his betrothal to Christina Höhns might be announced to the congregation next Sunday.

March 13. As we were returning from Salem we met the elder Greter, who told us the tragic fate of his son George. As George was preparing to burn leaves in the woods he dropped a coal, and just then had an attack of the falling sickness, to which he was subject. As he lay on the ground unconscious the fire burned under him. When he recovered consciousness his clothing was on fire, and he jumped into a near-by spring and put it out, and with the help of a stick made his way to the house, which was only two gun-shots away. We went into the house and saw how badly the fire had injured the poor man, who was in great pain. He departed gently on *the 16th,* and on *the 17th* there was the funeral.

March. 19. We visited the families where there is small-pox, that is at the homes of Adam Hartmann, Friedrich Boeckel, John Müller's widow, and Walk.

March 21. There was the funeral of Johannes Ebeling, a child of three months, who had small-pox.

March 27. The child Sarah Walk was buried; she went home yesterday from small-pox.

April 5. We visited Cornelius Schneider. His attack of camp-fever has pulled him down, but he is beginning to improve.

April 9. We were in Salem, and I was asked by the Conferenz to advise Martin Walk to surrender himself to the authorities. This I did this evening through Peter Frey, who said that Walk was willing. He did it on the 11th, and all went well, so that he can go on with his work in peace until November Court, to which he is bound over.

April 26. At nine o'clock in the evening my wife heard a shot towards Christian Frey's. I did not notice it, and while it frightened us we heard no more so went to bed, commending ourselves to the care of God.

April 27. We heard that it was thieves who had broken in there.

April 28. We went to Christian Frey's and they told us what danger they had been in. Four rascals had broken into their house, and had behaved in a murderous fashion, and if the dear Saviour had not graciously protected them their lives would not have been safe. The men had called at the door, and when John Wolfesberger went out to them they asked if strangers were there? When he said no they seized him, but he jerked loose and went into the house. They first broke the window, then rushed into the house. When Christian spoke to them gently one of them hit him in the head, another struck Sarah across her shoulder with the flat of his sword. With a large stone they broke the paneling out of the cupboard, and with a sword cut the wood around three locks, taking all the money and whatever else they wished. After Christian had received another cut on the head he tried to get out of the house, but was given a blow on the chest with a gun by the guard at the door, so that he became faint. Finally he escaped from them and raised an alarm, when they shot after him, but God so ordered it that he was not hit. Poor Sarah, who had hidden behind the door, sank on her knees when she heard the shot; and when the rascals had left she was very happy to find her husband still living.

May 13. There was a meeting with the single men and boys, and they were asked whether they would like to be divided into two classes, from fourteen to eighteen years, and those over eighteen? There is little opportunity to get acquainted with them, and this would make it possible to see them at least once in each eight weeks. They liked the idea, and several expressed their pleasure.

May 25. We visited Peter Rothrock. All of his children are in bed with small-pox, but are not very sick.

June 3. Whitsuntide. In the second meeting Br. Marshall read again to the assembled members of the congregation the proposed *Brotherly Agreement* for Friedberg, and it was signed by all communicant and received Brethren. Time and circumstances have prevented this from taking place earlier.

July 11. Peter Schneider has been employing a man who showed him a Pass, but today the man was arrested by four men, who planned to deliver him to Captain Pierce. Schneider was taken along, but at Fischer's, where they spent the night, they accepted money from Schneider and let him go.

July 15. All the house-fathers belonging to the Society had a conference, and agreed that no one should employ a doubtful, unknown or drafted man, as it would injure the credit of our Society.

July 16. We visited John Höhns, Sr. His wife and three children are down with small-pox. The recovery of the eldest son seemed doubtful, and he went home peacefully on the following day.

July 18. We visited Heinrich Tesch. Both parents and several of the children have been sick for eight days with colds caught during harvest. He has a bad case of jaundice, but is beginning to improve.

Aug. 9. Heinrich Müller, the shoemaker, came to ask for the baptism of his little son, who is very ill.

Aug. 18. We celebrated our congregation festival. Br. Graff told the children the reason for this lovefeast, namely that on the 11th and 12th of March, twelve years ago, this combination congregation-house and school-house was consecrated. The celebration was postponed this year on account of the small-pox. Ninety-six were sick with small-pox, but only five children died.

Sept. 9. The *Brotherly Agreement* was read again to the Congregation and Society, and was heard with interest, especially by those who have recently joined the Society.

Sept. 29. The Married People celebrated their Choir festival. At the lovefeast the ode was used which was prepared for the same occasion in Salem. Forty-five persons partook of the Lord's Supper.

Oct. 3. We began to visit all of our people, going first across Muddy Creek to Philip Höhns. From there we went to Valentine Frey.

Oct. 4. We went to the upper farms.

Nov. 7. We went to our people on the South Fork and Middle Fork.

Nov. 10. At the request of the elder Br. Ebert, the widower Cornelius Schneider was betrothed to the single Christine Ebert at a little lovefeast here in the school-house.

Nov. 13. This week and last the number of school-children has increased until there are thirty-five when all are present. I take half an hour at noon to teach them verses and tunes, but singing is so hard for them that only two or three are able to remember the air. But the others listen carefully, and follow as well as they can, and it sounds as though they sang together.

Nov. 18. We had a post celebration of the Festival of the Chief Elder.

Dec. 2. We entered the Advent season and began the new Church year.

Dec. 9. On account of the persistent rain not many could come for service, so it was held in the school-room.

Dec. 24. In spite of the bad weather many children came to school. Classes lasted only until noon. Then I told them of the important event which they should remember, that is, that God our Creator and Saviour, out of great love for us, poor mortals, had become a tiny child, that we might be blest through him. They listened attentively, and after singing some Christmas verses they went happily home.

Dec. 25. So many people assembled that the Saal could not hold them all, and many had to stand outside. In the first service the sermon was on the second chapter of the Gospel of Luke. The second service was a lovefeast for the children, of whom sixty-six were present. They thanked the child Jesus in sweet songs, and at the close of the meeting each received a verse.

Dec. 31. By eight o'clock in the evening 112 persons had assembled for the watch services, which began with a lovefeast. In the second meeting the Memorabilia of Salem was read, and also the Memorabilia of Friedland. In the last service the Memorabilia of Friedberg was read, there was an address on the last Texts of this year, and the year was closed with a prayer, during which all knelt. With the coming of the new year the first Watchword and Doctrinal Text were read, and the congregation was dismissed with the New Testament benediction.

Friedland and Hope, 1781.

[There is no separate diary for Friedland or Hope for this year. The
following items are taken from the *Extract der Diarii der
Gemeiner in der Wachau.*]

Jan. 6. The three country congregations celebrated the Holy Communion after a happy lovefeast and a gracious absolution.

Feb. 4. In Friedland a beginning was made with reading the Results of General Synod.

Feb. 7. Four cavalrymen went to Friedland to press horses, and
took one by force from Br. Künzel; at the School-house, finding no
horse, they left politely.

Feb. 10. The Friedland people living near the camp lost nearly all
their forage and cattle. All sorts of excesses were committed by
wandering parties seeking food. They forced their way into the School-house also, and Br. and Sr. Heinzmann gave so long as they had anything. Toward nine o'clock there came six or eight men, to whom
they gave their last bit of bread and meat. In spite of all Br.
Heinzmann's statements they fiercely insisted upon having more, and
went through the provision closet taking anything they could find.
His wife was in bed with such a pain in her back that she could not
rest, but now she got up. When he tried to leave the house to call for
help they thrust a naked bayonet at his breast, ready to stab or shoot.
As they were about to break open the clothes chest Samuel Stotz and
three other Brethren entered the house, and then they hastily ran
away. Two Brethren remained with Br. and Sr. Heinzmann over
night.

Feb. 11. Early in the morning the English army left Friedland,
and marched away in regular order. There was no Sunday service
in Friedland, for everyone feared further disorder and dared not leave
home, but the entire day was quiet. In Hope there was preaching.
During this week the Hope neighborhood was full of evil men, bent on
robbery and plunder, yet we cannot sufficiently praise the goodness of
God for His protection of our poor Brethren, who lost nothing except
provisions. Robberies are countless in the country everywhere.

Feb. 26. Br. Fritz, [pastor of Hope,] made a visit to our friends
on Deep Creek, to their great comfort and joy. He reached home on
the *28th,* thankful for the protection of the Lord during these unsafe
times.

March 21. Late this evening Kroen and Seitz returned to Friedland, having taken bandages and rags to the army. The latter brought back four of his lost horses. Because of their long absence we had become worried about them.

April 1. Br. and Sr. Heinzmann visited at the home of Friedrich Müller, where the wife and four children are down with small-pox.

April 2. Br. Fritz and his wife went from Hope to the neighboring German settlement, where he preached, and baptised four children.

April 12. Friedland and Hope had the Pedilavium for the first time, preceding the Lord's Supper on Maundy Thursday.

April 20. This afternoon there was a hard storm. In Hope some of the hail-stones were as large as hen's eggs.

April 25. In Friedland Br. Hein has been sick with a bad leg, which has given him much pain. Today it was successfully amputated by a Hospital doctor from Guilford, to the great relief of the patient. The Brn. Bonn and Dixon from Salem assisted. Br. Heinzmann was present, and offered a prayer to the Saviour that He would make the undertaking successful, and the operation turned out to the satisfaction of every one.

April 29. Br. and Sr. Marshall, and the Brn. Praetzel and Stotz went to Friedland, where the festival of those Received during the year was held, having been postponed from Feb. 18th. At the lovefeast of the entire Society Br. Marshall reminded them that this is the twelfth year since the first six families came from Broadbay, to make the beginning of a settlement which should be served by the Brethren with the Gospel. Now, through the grace of God, it has become this little congregation.

June 4. In a neighboring county the Whigs and Tories have met often during these days, and some have been killed or wounded. The most terrible reports come in about these engagements and of robbery and theft. In Friedland it was decided to hold the week-day meetings at one o'clock on Wednesdays and Fridays, though otherwise the evenings would be the more convenient time for them.

June 10. In Hope there was a meeting of the house-fathers, in which a committee was selected to look after the support of the School-house and of the Brother and Sister stationed there.

June 29. By request, Br. Heinzmann visited a soldier who had been for some time in the Friedland settlement. He was a Catholic, born at Cologne on the Rhine, but he had been a frequent attendant on the Friedland services. Now, on his sick-bed, he could hardly speak for weakness, but when Br. Heinzmann spoke to him of the Lord Jesus on the cross, the Friend and Saviour of all men, he nodded assent.

July 15. Some of those belonging to the Friedland settlement have believed that as they belonged to the Brethren's Church they must secure Certificates from their pastor and be free from muster. Br. Heinzmann read them a letter from Br. Marshall, in which it was plainly stated that those who behaved like Brethren, and who paid the three-fold tax, might enjoy this privilege of exemption without a Certificate, and that in future Certificates would be given only to those who could qualify on these points, and then only in case of need.

Aug. 7. Br. Philip Vogler, Sr., moved from Friedland to Bethabara.

Aug. 27. Br. and Sr. Graff and other members of the Aeltesten Conferenz, went to Hope to celebrate their congregation festival, postponed from yesterday. At one o'clock there was a happy lovefeast for all adult members of the congregation and society. In the second meeting several were received into the congregation.

Sept. 3. Br. and Sr. Marshall, Br. Graff, and other members of the Aeltesten Conferenz, went to Friedland for the celebration of its congregation festival. Br. Graff preached in the first service. The lovefeast was accompanied with affectionate addresses. Br. Marshall spoke in the congregation meeting.

Sept. 27. Br. Seitz, of Friedland, took his son Lorenz to Salem, on trial in the tailor shop.

Sept. 28. In the country congregations the Married People celebrated their festival.

Nov. 24. In the country congregations the communicants celebrated the Lord's Supper. Hope also observed the day as the festival of the Chief Elder, and had a lovefeast. Br. Benzien was present, and next day held his first English meeting.

Nov. 30. One hundred and fifty of the Wilkes militia camped tonight near Friedland. They shot two head of cattle, but by the intercession of Friedrich Müller they committed no other excesses, and marched off the following day.

Dec. 27. Last week there were robbers in the Friedland settlement, and Friedrich Müller had four window-panes broken and three horses stolen. The horses were not suitable for cavalry use, and were found in the woods and returned by the Friedland men, who assembled for defense. Yesterday a neighbor, Heinrich Hauser, was stopped on his way back from Salem, was robbed of his horse and whatever he had. These highwaymen committed various acts of violence in Friedland during the evening, but were overpowered by the inhabitants and taken to Bethania. There they were released with a caution as to their future behaviour.

Dec. 30. A report that the two robbers, released on the 27th, had threatened to return to Friedland in eight or nine days led to a warning to the house-fathers to be on their guard. A false alarm made a disturbance this evening, but nothing more happened.

1782

[The surrender of Lord Cornwallis failed to bring immediate peace to America. When the news reached England it strengthened the power of the party opposing the war, but it was not until September 21, 1782, that King George III acknowledged the independence of the Colonies and instructed the British Commissioner at Paris to make peace.

In America conditions remained bad. General Washington held his army together in the north, and General Greene did the same in the south, although with numbers constantly decreasing by the expiration of terms of enlistment. In December the British troops finally evacuated Charleston, their last southern post.

North Carolina suffered greatly from wandering bands of marauders bent on murder and pillage. In the central and eastern part of the state most of this was charged to the Tories, but in the section in which Wachovia lay both parties seem to have been at fault, indeed the Moravian diaries give the impression that many of the lawless acts were committed by Whig militia, sometimes masquerading as Tories.

While various country members of the Moravian congregations were in serious danger during this year, the official standing of the church was greatly improved. The meetings of the Assembly in Salem led to better understanding on the part of the political leaders of the state, and at the April session of the Assembly an Act was passed which confirmed the title of Wachovia to Frederic William Marshall as Trustee for the Unity of Brethren, and recognized him as official representative of the Unity in the management of certain additional smaller tracts. This settled definitely the question as to whether the Moravian land in North Carolina was subject to confiscation because at the opening of the war title was held by James Hutton, an Englishman, and confirmed the claim of resident Moravians that their rights as settlers were paramount. That title continued to be held by Marshall as Trustee was owing to the fact that neither the Unity of Brethren nor the Moravian Church in North Carolina was incorporated. Neither Hutton, nor Marshall, nor their successors in the position of *Proprietor,* ever claimed or received any part of the returns from the sale of Moravian land, all going to the church for whose benefit they held title.]

Memorabilia of the Congregations in Wachovia, 1782.

[Some paragraphs omitted.]

Our Lord and Saviour has made this to be a quiet and blessed year of peace for the congregations in Wachovia, in spite of the continuing distress of the land, and He answered our prayer for more peaceful times according to the Watch-Word for the beginning of this year: *Before they call, I will answer; and while they are yet speaking, I will hear.* To Him we bring our offering of joyful thanksgiving for His unending goodness and mercy, shown to us His poor unworthy children. Therefore are we encouraged and full of hope that in the end He will fill us with joy by the re-establishment of honorable peace.

We owe Him the greatest praise, however, that He has been in our midst; that He has let us feel His peace in our festal and other meetings, and in our daily life; that He has cared for us and watched over us, has healed our infirmities, if uncleanness appeared He has taken it away; that He has made His congregations more pure and has consecrated them as His sanctuary. We prize this grace and faithfulness of our dear Saviour, and sing to Him: *Hallelujah!* But the more we recognize this, the more humbly we bring to Him an offering of tears for our many short-comings, crying *Kyrie Eleison!* Especially do we recognize that we have fallen short of the spirit of complete submission to the Saviour and to His church, and in following the customs of His house in love; and of this we have been reminded by the re-reading of the Results of the Synod of 1775, and of the Rules and Regulations of congregations and Choirs. This took place in August, when we united in prayer for the Synod of the Unity of Brethren assembled in Berthelsdorf.

Here follow certain circumstances which have been worthy of note during this year.

I. The home-going of our dear and honored Br. Johann Michael Graff, on the 29th of August in Salem, of our dear Sr. Anna Beck on the 12th of July in Friedberg, of Elisabeth Praetzel on the 29th of September in Salem, and of Maria Bagge on the 20th of October in Bethabara, have grieved us sorely. Their going home has made the work more heavy in general and in each part, yet the Lord has stood by us and has given us His help, and our mouth is full of praise and thanks that He has shown Himself to be so glorious in the midst of all our insufficiency.

II. Among the things for which we give praise are the following: 1) The two visits of Assembly members, in November of last year and January of this year, served to further establish the value of this work of God in the eyes of the people. It brought an additional blessing in April when Br. Marshall laid before the Assembly in Hillsborough the relation of the Brethren to Wachovia and to other Unity land here, and an Act was passed whereby the Brethren were confirmed in their privileges, and Br. Marshall was recognized as the authorized agent of the Unity. For this we honor and praise the providence and goodness of God.

2) The aforesaid Assembly members have brought it to pass that Br. Traugott Bagge has entered public service.

3) The long-standing matter of the Bethania land has been settled amicably, and a perpetual Lease has been given.

4) A Contract has been made between Br. Marshall and the Aeltesten Conferenz of Salem regarding the Salem land and the land of the Single Brethren.

5) The new road between Salem and Bethabara has been laid out this year and made ready for use.

6) The congregation towns have grown and new houses have been built.

The Saviour has led the country congregations, in which certain arrangements have been made which add to the attractiveness of their life. He has also laid His blessing on the visits of members of the Aeltesten Conferenz and the Land-Arbeiter-Conferenz. The Gospel has also been preached on Deep Creek, in the German settlement near Hope, and in Stinking Quarter.

The congregations of Salem and Bethabara have refreshed themselves this year with the Bible truths as presented in the *Idea Fidei Fratrum*.

The Communion seasons and festal days of the Unity have been blessed to us by the Lord, and on them we renewed our covenant to be His people, to follow His direction in love and simplicity, as in His presence. This was especially marked in Salem on Nov. 13th, when the congregation shared the Cup of Covenant, and in the other congregations on their anniversary days.

Our Father in Heaven has shielded us from harm and accident, and preserved the lives of some of the Brethren in Friedberg, who were plundered by highwaymen. He has given us our necessary food, in spite of the great drought of this year, and has blessed our trade and the work of our hands, so that the conduct of the congregation and Choir diaconies has been much easier than last year.

The journeys to Pennsylvania have been made in safety, although the roads were rendered unsafe by the coming and going of highwaymen. Correspondence with Pennsylvania has been maintained. Although the difficulties of the times have greatly interfered with our correspondence with Europe, yet with the exception of a few Beilagen we have received all of the Gemein Nachrichten, Wöchentlichen Nachrichten, and the Texts to November 10, 1783. We have greatly missed the Reden, which we have had only to the end of 1779.

We could hardly endure the pain of the news of the murder of so many of our dear Indian members on the Muskingum, but we await the time when this martyr seed shall spring up, for the glory of the kingdom of God. It was also remarkable, though painful, to note that a year ago in February, just when this, the most western part of the Unity, was filled with anxiety and fright by the war, the most eastern post, the Brüdergarten near Tranquebar, was plundered by Hyder Ali.[1] Our prayer rises to the Saviour for the missions and His whole work, that He may direct the distress of all lands so that His work may spread unhindered.

The Choirs have renewed their covenants in the presence of the Saviour on their festal days. The married people especially miss Br. Graff, whose faithful service in their behalf will never be forgotten.

[The numerous personal notices regarding all the congregations are omitted.]

Salem Diary, 1782.

[Extracts translated.]

Jan. 2. The Brn. Petersen and Samuel Stotz went to Salisbury on business. Reading of the *Idea Fidei Fratrum* was continued.

Jan. 5. The Brethren returned from Salisbury and brought word that the Assembly was called to meet here on Jan. 21st.

Jan. 6. Wilkes militia arrived, under Colonel Isaacs. Most of them camped at the Petersbach[2] over night, and had to be supplied with provisions and forage. At first they were rather wild, and the Colonel made various threats, but when they were served in friendly fashion they calmed down. Some of them attended the gemeinstunde, and were quiet and orderly.

Jan. 7. The Wilkes militia marched on.

Jan. 8. Assistant-Judge Pendleton, Colonel Senf of Saxe-Gotha, an engineer and two southern officers, were here as prisoners-of-war who

---

[1] Hyder Ali, maharaja of Mysore, had allied himself with the French against the English. The *Brüdergarten* was a Moravian mission station, in the outskirts of Tranquebar, on the Coromandel Coast, the east coast of southern India. It was begun in 1760, and was given up in 1795, partly on account of the terrible mortality among the missionaries, more than half of whom died at their post.

[2] Still called Peters Creek.

had been exchanged. They attended the singstunde, and went on to South Carolina next day.

Jan. 18. There was rain with glaze-ice, which lasted all day.

Jan. 20. Many militia returned from Greene's camp, their eighteen months of service having expired. They passed through here on their way home. Mr. Bachmann arrived with a package from Pennsylvania. It contained the remaining portion of the Texts for this year, two or three letters from Bethlehem, and especially a copy of a letter from Br. Schebosch, dated Pittsburg, Nov. 5, 1781, giving particulars concerning the capture of the three Indian congregations and their removal to Sandusky Creek.

Jan. 24. We congratulated Sr. Marshall on her 59th birthday.

Jan. 25. At twilight we read reports from Switzerland, and sang: *Oh Head so full of bruises.* Governor Alex Martin arrived, and also the Speaker and the first members of the Assembly from a distance. They were followed by others from time to time. It is worthy of note that while not so many came this time as last, yet most of them were those who were not here for the first session, so through these two opportunities Salem and the Unity of Brethren became known to most of the members of the Assembly. Beginning with today all our services were open to the public, and there was a singstunde each week-day evening at eight o'clock.

Jan. 28. Many Assembly members arrived. Some who do not like us sought quarters outside the town, without having any effect on the others.

Jan. 29. It was very cold, with a strong north-west wind.

Jan. 30. Quite unexpectedly, Governor Burke arrived this evening. He has been a British prisoner at Charlestown, but is now free.[3] The singstunde was begun with the rendering of several anthems. Among other members present was Colonel Steward, a Deputy from General Greene's army, and also Major Taylor, a Deputy from the Assembly in Virginia.

Feb. 2. The Assembly members discussed their session, and it was found that many were lacking to make a house. At first most favored waiting eight days, but at last they agreed to separate, which took place this afternoon and the following morning. In the evening there was one more service of singing with instrumental accompaniment. As they left the gentlemen of the Assembly expressed their approval of the manner in which they had been served, and under the circumstances we were glad that the session did not last longer.

---

[3] He had been paroled to James Island, S. C., where he suffered greatly and feared for his life; as his protests were disregarded he felt at liberty to escape.

Feb. 3. Sunday. In the morning the departure of the Assembly members gave every one so much to do that no service could be held.

Feb. 5. A French General, Coustaine, was here on his way from South Carolina, and with another French officer attended with pleasure a singstunde, with instrumental accompaniment, which was held at twilight in place of a meeting for communicants.

Feb. 12. By request, the number of all the members of our Societies, adults and children, of both sexes, was sent to the colonel of this county.

Feb. 14. Br. Marshall reminded the communicants that today seventeen years ago the place where Salem now stands was selected by the Saviour as the site for a congregation town. The notable Watch-Word for that day: *Let thine eyes be open toward this house night and day, even toward the place of which thou hast said, My name shall be there,* awakened the wish that the Saviour might carry out more and more His plan of peace for this town dedicated to Him, and might establish us as people after His own heart.

Feb. 17. Several wagons passed, loaded with clothing for the Continental army in the south. They were under the charge of a Captain Hamilton, who stayed some days, and showed himself most friendly.

Feb. 18. Br. Johann Friedrich Schroeth began to work in the kitchen of the Brothers House.

Feb. 25. The Brn. Samuel Stotz and Reuz went to the Furnace in Virginia, ninety miles from here. Colonel Williams, former Adjutant-General of General Greene's army, with Dr. Skinner and Dr. Pindel and a wounded Lieutenant McGuire, passed on their way to Virginia and Maryland. They were very polite.

Feb. 27. Several South Carolinians stopped here. They were prisoners-of-war, but have been exchanged. After they had refreshed themselves in every way, and had attended our services, they went on to South Carolina in a contented frame of mind.

March 1. We thanked the Saviour that we belong to the Unity of Brethren, which was begun 326 years ago, and has been so graciously renewed in this our day. The Brn. Stotz and Reuz returned from the Furnace in Virginia.

March 4. We were visited by a Captain Ziegler, who has known our Brethren in Lusatia, in Sarepta,[4] in Zeyst,[5] and recently in Bethlehem.[6] He looked about the town with pleasure.

---

[4] In Russia.
[5] In Holland.
[6] In Pennsylvania.

March 6. Today and the next day French engineers were here. They came from the army, stationed at Charlotte in Virginia. They looked around the town with interest, and busied themselves drawing its location.

March 7. Within two hours two packages reached us from Pennsylvania, one by Mr. Lawdon and one by John Volbrecht. Both contained news of the wonderful preservation of our Indian missions. Hereafter, Br. Reuz will keep the Minutes for Congregation Council and the Helfer Conferenz.

March 8. General Greene's lady was glad to be here. She continued her journey next day.

March 12. Yesterday and today the election of members of the Assembly took place in Richmond. Many of our Brethren went from our three towns to cast their vote, although it was made dangerous by the terrible commotion caused by the rough element, inflamed by strong drink. Colonel Sheppard as Senator, and Mr. Cummins and Br. Bagge as Commoners, received the most votes. Br. Bagge was harshly threatened by some, while others offered to stand by him in every possible way. However, he and our other Brethren escaped injury, though another good man was badly abused by the villains. Our Brethren were very happy when they were again in our quiet towns among God's people.

March 13. We heard with sorrow that Colonel Balfour was murdered in his own house by one of the Tories still wandering about. He was our true friend, and did us much service as a member of the Assembly. During his two or three visits here he won the affection of all by his affable manner. On the other hand we were pleased to learn that we would be spared a visit from the next Assembly, which will meet in Hillsborough.

March 16. Mr. Bachmann passed on his return to Pennsylvania, and was given a package of letters to take along.

March 21. Several Continental officers attended the singstunde. Others have been here at intervals during the month, and were pleasant and polite.

March 25. Colonel Craigh and thirteen officers, some privates and wagons, of the Pennsylvania Line spent the night here on their way north. They attended the evening services and behaved modestly.

March 30. Yesterday the advocates Mr. Penn and Mr. Kinchin passed on their way from General Court in Salisbury to that in Hillsborough. The former was very willing to be of service to us. Today the judges Spenser and Williams, and two other advocates, passed. On account of the danger of travel these gentlemen have come by Salem instead of taking the shorter way.

March 31. Easter. In the morning at a quarter past five the congregation assembled in the Saal, and after the usual Easter greeting visited the graves of those who have fallen asleep, and held the Easter litany in the felt presence of our risen Lord. The morning was clear, and unusually cold for the time of year. The cold weather during the last half of this month has frozen most of the blossoms which had been brought out by the preceding warmth.

April 2. The Brn. Gottlieb Schober and Rudolph Christ went on a visit to their friends in Pennsylvania. In place of the former, Br. Friedrich Peter took charge of most of the boys in school; Br. Benzien takes the rest, and will write the Minutes for the Aeltesten Conferenz.

April 3. Three gentlemen from South Carolina attended the evening reading meeting. They were on their way to Philadelphia, and remained until

April 4. Two of them, Governor Rutledge and Mr. Gervais, are delegates to Congress. As they were shown about the town they expressed approval of our arrangements. They also inquired concerning our circumstances, saying that it would not be just if our rights were curtailed in any way.

April 7. The Brn. Marshall and Bagge left for Hillsborough. They will present to the Assembly a Petition, asking that the Brethren may be protected against the Confiscation Act, and may be confirmed in possession of the Wachovia Tract and other pieces belonging to it.

April 13. Our neighbor, Peter Ludwig, who lives on Belows Creek, brought his infant son here, and Br. Praetzel baptised it at his home, the child receiving the name William.

April 17. A company of mounted Continental troops passed on their way to Virginia.

April 27. The road to Bethabara was cut as far as the Spangenbach.[7]

May 1. There was unusually heavy rain today and tonight.

May 4. Br. Marshall returned from Hillsborough, to our great joy.

May 5. In a separate meeting for communicants Br. Marshall reported the happy outcome of his visit to the Assembly. "We left on "April 7th for Hillsborough, going by way of Friedland, and arrived "there on the 9th. We took with us a Petition with three supplements, "these concerning Wachovia, the Metcalf land, and the land on the "Mulberry Fields, and also a draft for a Bill. This was presented

---

[7] Now called Silas Creek.

"privately to most of the members on April 12th. On the 18th it was
"introduced into the House of Commons by Mr. Sharp, former delegate
"to Congress, and was also read in the Senate for the first time on the
"same day. On the 22nd it came up for second reading in the House
"of Commons, and on the second reading in the Senate on the 23rd
"certain objections were raised, which led to an improvement in phrase-
"ology. On the 25th it came up for the third reading in the House of
"Commons, was vehemently opposed by men from Wilkes County,[8]
"the Deeds were produced as evidence, were read, and it was finally
"approved. On the 26th the Bill was read for the third time in the
"Senate, when bitter complaints were made which led to further changes
"in wording, and then the Bill was passed. The more these changes in
"wording are considered the more evident it becomes that through the
"providence of the Saviour they were much more improvements than
"limitations, and that we are the more confirmed in the quiet possession
"of our land and the right to free disposition of it. As we did not
"know how long it might be before the Act was printed, or what dif-
"ficulty might be made about it, we asked for a certified copy, signed
"by the Speakers and Clerks of both Houses, which has the force of an
"original Deed and was delivered to us on April 29th. We have had the
"gracious support of our Saviour throughout the whole proceeding, and
"He has taken the matter into His own hand." So far Br. Marshall's
report.

Col. Thomas Hutchins, Geographer-General of the United States,
was here on his way from Philadelphia to General Greene, and remained several days.

May 14. Two packages arrived from Pennsylvania. The sad news
of the cruel execution of ninety-six Christian Indians by white men,
on the Muskingum River, was communicated to the members at a noon
meeting.

May 20. Br. Bagge returned safely from Hillsborough, and brought
a letter of recommendation from the Governor to General Greene.
It asked the General to assist the Bethania Brethren to reach Charlestown and to secure payment for their English Tickets. Br. Bagge has
been appointed an Auditor for Surry County.[9]

---

[8] The constant antagonism of Wilkes militia and Wilkes politicians can only be explained
by the fact that some of their leaders had settled as squatters on the Moravian land
in the Mulberry Fields. See Wilkes County Land Suit, *Records of the Moravians in
North Carolina*, Vol. III, page 1413.

[9] The Assembly at its April session passed an Act to amend the two Acts passed at previous
sessions regarding District Auditors. It was provided that "all claims now due and
unsettled shall be liquidated in specie by the district Auditors." Traugott Bagge, James
Hunter and Charles Bruce were appointed Auditors for the Upper Board of Salisbury
District. (*Colonial Records*, XXIV, page 422. As there printed Traugott is mispelled
Fraugott.)

May 22. Captain Blake, Treasurer of South Carolina, and his family, Mr. Prioleau, Major Mitchel and several ladies arrived on their return from Pennsylvania and Virginia to South Carolina. In the evening they attended a singstunde, which was held instead of reading from the Idea Fidei Fratrum. A second sleeping-hall has been arranged over the sleeping-hall of the Single Brethren. It was occupied today by the boys and several of the Brethren, and was consecrated with hymn and prayer.

May 29. Major Will, Mr. Cochran and Captain Stone came on their return from Pennsylvania to South Carolina. The first-named said he had formerly lived in Bethlehem.

June 4. The Brn. Ernst, Schor and George Hauser, Jr., passed on their way south. They will try to reach Charlestown in order to secure payment of their English Tickets. Colonel Preston, of Montgomery County, sent back to Br. Bagge the *Greenland History* which had been lent to him, and wrote that he had read with interest and sympathy what our Brethren had endured for the good of the heathen, and that he had never before read anything like it. "Certainly," wrote he, "the hand of the Lord was with them, His wisdom guided them through "all, and His grace supported them wonderfully. Through His bless- "ing have they reaped a rich harvest, and have brought so many stupid "heathen to the Church and to Christ the great and precious Head "thereof. Such examples of disinterested fear of God are all too rare "in our times."

June 7. Friedrich Müller, who has returned from Pennsylvania, brought us a verbal report of the home-going of our dear Br. Nathanael [Seidel] at Bethlehem.

June 10. From today until the 21st the Auditors of the Upper Board of Salisbury District were in session from day to day, to liquidate the claims of the inhabitants of this county for supplies furnished on public account. Many people came in, and gave them enough to do. Mr. Hunter of Guilford assisted Br. Bagge during the first week, and Mr. Bruce, also of Guilford, helped him during the second week.[10]

Br. Rudolph Christ returned from Pennsylvania. We were glad to hear of the safe arrival of our dear Br. and Sr. Reichel; and of the Synod to be begun in Berthelsdorf on August 2nd.

June 15. Br. Ernst and his party returned. Their object had not

---

[10] Auditors Bruce and Bagge, and Bagge and Hunter, appear frequently in the Revolutionary Accounts filed with the North Carolina Historical Commission.

been accomplished, as they had been forced to turn back by reports of the great danger which would attend the effort.

June 17. Br. Tycho Nissen's house was raised and roofed.

June 20. With the usual wedding doxology, the Single Br. Gottfried Schulze was married to the Single Sr. Dorothea Schumaker, by Br. Graff. Br. Schober returned safely from Pennsylvania.

June 21. Christian Loesch came from Pennsylvania with the wagons of Heinrich Hauser and Christian Conrad. He brought a Recommendation to us, also letters and diaries.

June 24. The little boys celebrated their festival. At their lovefeast a printed Ode was used, of which Br. Schober had brought forty copies.

June 30. Br. and Sr. Gottfried Schulze moved to their newly erected house on the farm of the Single Brethren.

July 8. Governor Alexander Martin[11] spent the night here on his way to Salisbury.

July 9. General McIntosh and other officers passed on their way from Philadelphia to Georgia.

July 11. From Friedberg came the word that Sr. Anna Beck had gone to the Saviour this morning at six o'clock. Her home-going was announced here by the trombonists, and in the evening to the communicants in the usual liturgy.

July 12. A good rain refreshed the dry earth, for which we thank the Heavenly Father from our hearts.

July 15. The Memoir of Sr. Anna Beck was read.

July 21. Br. Priem went to Friedberg, to assist Br. Beck in his household affairs.

July 24. Sr. Ernst had promised that when twelve Sisters and girls from Bethania had entered the Sisters House in Salem she would give their Choir a lovefeast. Now thirteen have come from Bethania into the Sisters House here, so the Sisters had a happy lovefeast. Of these thirteen Sisters one has married here and two in Bethabara. Since the beginning of the Sisters Choir-House here in 1772 sixteen Sisters have married, one has gone home,[12] and one has left. Their living quarters have become too small, and it is necessary to think about building a new Choir-House. After this service Br. and Sr. Ernst returned to Bethania.

---

[11] Alexander Martin, as Speaker of the Senate, was acting Governor during the imprisonment of Governor Burke. After returning, Burke served until the expiration of his term, Martin being elected his successor in April, 1782.

[12] That is, she had died.

July 26. Br. Benzien, accompanied by Br. Daniel Christmann, left on a journey to Stinking Quarter. They returned on the 30th.

July 31. Br. Stockburger put up his dwelling on his new farm.

Aug. 2. Michael Seitz will learn linen-weaving; Christoph Reich will help in the bakery; Gottlieb Fockel has not done well with making keys and will go to Br. Spiesike in the tailor-shop. In a special service prayer was offered for the Synod of the Unity of Brethren, beginning today at Berthelsdorf.

Aug. 4. The singstunde was attended by several South Carolina officers recently exchanged.

Aug. 6. Our dear Br. Graff had an attack of pain in his body, but was able to attend the meeting of the Aeltesten Conferenz next day. In the following days his illness increased.

Aug. 10. The heat has been unusually great for several days.

Aug. 11. Sunday. Governor Alex Martin attended the preaching service. The masters in charge of the businesses connected with the diaconies of the congregation and Single Brethren had a lovefeast. With special thanks to the Saviour it was noted that our shops have been little disturbed this year, the most peaceful in eight years' time.

Aug. 14. Br. Bagge went to the court at Richmond, and qualified as a Justice. Br. Sam Stotz also went thither, to present the Ticket account.

Aug. 18. Br. Bagge returned from Richmond.

Aug. 19. The singstunde was attended by a Baptist preacher, who was most devout. During the service Br. Graff had a severe attack, which presaged his home-going, so Br. Marshall gave him the last blessing, in the name of the congregation and of his Choir.

Aug. 20. Johann Adam Gernand received permission to become a resident of Salem.

Aug. 29. At a quarter before two o'clock this morning it pleased our dear Lord to bring to an end the life of our beloved Br. Graff, Co-episcopus of the Unity of Brethren, and associate provincial pastor of the congregations in Wachovia, and to call him to Himself out of all care and work. At seven o'clock, after it had been announced by the trombonists with the usual home-going tunes, Br. Marshall announced the sorrowful event to the congregation, and the home-going liturgy was sung softly. Tears filled every eye, but thoughts turned to our loving communion with those whose life-work has ended. As a large number may be expected to attend his funeral, the Congregation Council planned arrangements to maintain the order and enhance the dignity of the occasion.

Aug. 30. At noon was the burial of the remains of our dear departed Br. Graff, in the presence of five or six hundred members and friends from all our congregations and from the neighborhood. First the choir sang sweetly the Text for yesterday: *No one liveth to himself, and no one dieth to himself.* Br. Lorenz Bagge spoke on this Text, and mentioned some of the most notable points in the Memoir of our Brother.[13] Then the choir sang: *Graff, our friend, sleeps, How blessedly he sleeps!* The funeral procession went to God's Acre in the usual order, and though many present were unaccustomed to the service the regularity, quiet and reverence displayed aroused respect. The number of those who bore the remains was sixteen, serving eight and eight. According to the custom of this country they wore blue coats,[14] and they had been selected from all our six congregations. After the casket had been lowered and the litany had been prayed the benediction was sung, and then this faithful servant of the Lord was left to rest in peace. The funeral procession returned in order to the Gemein Haus, and from there each went to his own home.

Aug. 31. Br. Praetzel held the prayer meeting. He spoke on the text for the day, commending to the prayers of the members the circumstances in which we now find ourselves, and also the Choir of Widows and Widowers which in other congregations celebrates its covenant day on this date.

September. In the last week of August and the first week of September the Board of Auditors was in session here.

Sept. 1. The Brn. Friedrich Peter and Benzien held the Sunday services.

Sept. 2. Br. Rudolph Strehle left for a visit in Pennsylvania, accompanied by young Weesner and a Hessian doctor from Charlestown. Br. Sam Stotz went on business to the Iron Furnace in Henry County,

---

[13] Johann Michael Graff was born in the village of Heyna, Saxony, Sept. 20, 1714, the son of Nicolaus and Margaretha Graff. The father was magistrate of the village. He was brought up a Lutheran, and while still a lad studied music, and especially the clavier. Educated by private tutors, then at the Gymnasium of Henneberg, and at the University of Jena. Became acquainted with the Brethren at Jena, and joined the congregation of Marienborn in 1739. July 3, 1740, he married Gertraut Jack. On January 21, 1741, he was ordained a presbyter of the Unitas Fratrum and served in various European congregations. In the year 1751 he and his wife were called to Pennsylvania, reaching Bethlehem in October, where they did much work among the children, until they were put in charge of the married people. In 1762 they came to North Carolina to serve the married people of Bethabara and Bethania. In 1773 he was consecrated *Coepiscopus* in Bethlehem, Pa., returning as pastor of Salem, and associate pastor of Wachovia. Of six children only two daughters outlived the father. His Memoir says that he was "patient, friendly, cheerful and loving" in character, "a true follower of Jesus."

[14] Attention is called to this interesting sidelight on the dress of 1782. When Count Zinzendorf was buried in Herrnhut, Germany, in 1760 the men all wore brown.

Virginia. Br. and Sr. Marshall went to Friedland, where the congregation festival will be celebrated tomorrow.

Sept. 7. The situation of the Choir of Married People, in view of the departure of Br. Graff and the serious illness of Sr. Praetzel, has led to the postponement of their Choir festival.

Sept. 8. *Sunday.* In the second service Br. Benzien read the Memoir of our departed Br. Graff, while the congregation shed many tears. Br. Stotz returned from the Furnace with nothing accomplished, for on account of the drought there is too little water to carry on the work.

Sept. 13. Through Mr. Kleinert we received letters, diaries and Nachrichten from Pennsylvania.

Sept. 15. Gov. Alex Martin attended the evening service, going on next day to court at Salisbury.

Sept. 17. The Married People celebrated their postponed Choir festival. Schaaf and George Müller left for Bethlehem, taking letters and diaries.

Sept. 29. At noon it pleased the Saviour to take to Himself our dear Sr. Elisabeth Praetzel, after a long and painful illness. Yesterday and today Judge Williams and the lawyers Colonel Henderson and Davie were here on their way from Salisbury to Hillsborough.

Sept. 30. Governor Alex Martin was here, taking the same route. He was most affable to the Brethren who called on him.

During this month three evil men have been arrested in this parish and taken to Salisbury. On the open highway one of them had terribly cut, stabbed and robbed five persons who were moving to Kentucky from this province with their families and four wagons. The second man had been party to the crime. The third was accused of robbing houses and stealing horses, and he had all sorts of Continental uniforms, equipment and arms, for which he could not account.

Oct. 16. We were visited by Mr. Newton, a teacher in a Latin school recently begun farther east in the state. Mr. Sharp's daughter was also here, and looked around the town with pleasure.

Oct. 25. Johann Heinrich Walther left for Pennsylvania, taking letters.

Oct. 28. Br. and Sr. Stockburger moved into their new house on the farm south of the Tavern.

Oct. 30. A Contract was prepared, and signed by Br. Marshall and the Elders of Salem Congregation, in the presence of the Aufseher

Collegium. It concerned the land belonging to Salem and to the Single Brethren.

Oct. 31. We had a hard rain which softened the dry earth.

Nov. 3. Young Weesner returned with his wagon from Pennsylvania, accompanied by Mr. Schaaf.

Nov. 9. The Brn. Rudolph Strehle and Peter Rothrock returned from Pennsylvania, bringing letters, etc.

Nov. 11. Mr. Brown brought an older package of Nachrichten than those we have received through Br. Strehle.

Nov. 14. Br. Bagge, as Justice, went to court at Richmond. Br. Marshall went with him to report the Will of Br. Nathanael Seidel and to qualify as Executor.

Nov. 15. Two-thirds of the Salem line was run and renewed, this being the best season for such work.

Nov. 17. Br. Traugott Bagge returned from court. The Single Br. Daniel Christmann was married to the Single Sr. Johanna Fischer; the lawyer Dunn attended the service.

Nov. 19. The remaining third of the Salem line was run.

Nov. 20. During these days we have been visited by several South Carolina gentlemen; also by Col. Joseph Haversham.

Nov. 26. Several officers passed, coming from General Greene's camp; their troops will follow in a few days, marching home.

Nov. 28. Br. Tycho Nissen moved into his new house aside of the Single Sisters House.[15] Friedrich Müller returned from Pennsylvania bringing a few letters.

Nov. 29. The two Boeckels brought letters and a package of Gemein Nachrichten.

Nov. 30. One hundred and fifty soldiers arrived toward evening, their commanding officers having preceded them. They spent the night here. Their quartermaster was a German, named Stozburg. They were provided with meat, meal and bread, and marched away next day. According to first reports we had expected more soldiers on their way home, but they had received orders to return to camp.

Dec. 4. Br. Christian Conrad arrived with his wagon, and goods for the store.

Dec. 7. During these days frightful threats have been made against us by certain wild men.

---

[15] It stood on the east side of Church Street, just south of the intersection with West Street. The lot adjoining on the north had been reserved for a Single Sisters House from the beginning of Salem, though the Sisters occupied part of the Gemein Haus pending the erection of their own building.

Dec. 9. Br. Joseph Dixon was installed as teacher of the little boys in place of Br. Schober.

Dec. 17. Br. Gottlieb Schober was married to Sr. Maria Magdalena Transu by Br. Friedrich Peter.

Dec. 23. William Peddycoart brought a package of letters from Pennsylvania.

Dec. 24. Some of our friends from Stinking Quarter came to spend Christmas with us.

Minutes of Salem Boards, 1782.

[The Minutes of the various Boards of Salem and Wachovia show that in 1782 the civic and church life of the Moravians was rapidly returning to normal. Long-delayed visits were made to Pennsylvania; wagoners came and went, bringing and taking letters, church diaries, and the manuscript church newspapers of the day. Businesses were inspected, some minor changes made, and new apprentices bound. Several dwellings were erected, and the first plans were made looking toward the building of a Sisters House, on the lot which had been reserved for that purpose when the town was laid out. The waterworks were repaired, some improvements were made, and the pipe line was somewhat extended. It was found that the bored logs which had been sunk in water three years before had not kept as well as had been expected, the ends having begun to rot, and it was decided that thereafter only a few should be kept on hand for quick repair work, but otherwise new logs should be bored as needed. Early in the year prices of commodities showed a downward tendency, but the summer drought affected the crop of grain which raised prices again. The Board of Elders gave the usual close attention to marriages, and to candidates for residence in the town, for reception into the congregation, and for admission to the Lord's Supper. There were few cases of serious wrong-doing; some members were suspended from the Communion for a while and were then readmitted, one apprentice received a whipping for inciting a younger boy to impudence toward his master, and one older Brother was asked to move away. Paragraphs which seem of more than passing interest are translated.]

Jan. 3. (Aufseher Collegium.) Br. Steiner has suggested that we should not be so ready to give work to soldiers, as it is being said that we favor those who have run away. It will be well not to employ such men until they have received a Pass from Major Schmidt.

Br. George Schmidt asks that two Brethren be appointed to appraise the personal property of his departed wife, so that her son in Pennsyl-

vania may receive £9 or £10. As £5 :16 :8 of her money is on hand it
would be better for Br. Schmidt to add enough to raise the amount to
£9 or £10, and then her things can be for him and his children without
further action.

Jan. 9. (Aeltesten Conferenz.) Sponhauer's wife will take a girl
from Haw River, grand-daughter of Haefner, into her house in service.
Friedrich Müller has arranged the sale of Scherzer's farm to Reich, Sr.

Br. Steup in Bethabara, in the presence of witnesses, has made Br.
and Sr. Broesing his heirs. As he has only old things and a little money
his sons in Pennsylvania shall be informed that Br. and Sr. Broesing
will received the little that was left for their care of the father during
his illness.

Jan. 10. (Congregation Council.) In view of the approaching
session of the Assembly the following points were discussed :—
1) No one shall be directed to a lodging in Salem except an actual
member of the Assembly. To other gentlemen seeking lodging it shall
be suggested that they find it on one of the near-by farms, where they
will be gladly received.
2) Each house-keeper shall be free to buy veal and pork where he
prefers.
3) Brethren and Sisters shall be careful not to accept Virginia currency, which has no value now. North Carolina currency passes at
800 to 1.
4) It shall be arranged with the officers and the Governor that the
guard shall be lodged in the Magazine building, and they may cut fire-
wood for themselves from the adjacent woods.
5) The twenty members of the Assembly who will board at the Brothers
House shall sleep at the pottery and at Br. Christ's, and help shall be
given them in regard to bedding.

Jan. 16. (Aelt. Conf.) By order of the Governor, Colonel Armstrong has written to Br. Bagge asking for a list showing the number
of members of our Denomination, married, single and children, of
both sexes, and that the list should be ready by the 19th of this month.
As the letter arrived so late Br. Bagge shall write to Colonel Armstrong
explaining why that could not be done.

Jan. 23. (Aelt. Conf.) In regard to the list asked by Colonel Armstrong it was agreed that a catalog should be made showing the names
of all who belong to our Society and of the children under sixteen years
of age; this catalog shall be kept, but another shall be made giving the
numbers according to the rubrics suggested by Colonel Armstrong, and
this shall be delivered to him.

It would be well to have certain important Nachrichten read during the meeting of the Assembly here, and selections shall be translated into English.

Jan. 24. (Helfer Conferenz.) It looks as though the value of paper money would fall below 800 for 1, and it is probable that the next Assembly will withdraw it and issue new money in place of it. It is important, therefore, that Brethren inform themselves as to its value, so that they do not lose too much.

Jan. 30. (Aelt. Conf.) The Brn. Heinzmann and Fritz have sent in the catalogs of those who belong to our Societies in their care.

It is important that the Bethabara line should be definitely determined. The exact boundary of the Bethabara Town Lot has not been established.

Feb. 6. (Aelt. Conf.) In the Bethabara catalog the two Englishmen working for Mücke and Heinrich Stöhr have been included; William Fortune has been included in the Salem catalog, with the others who belong to our Society.

Abraham Wilson would like to bring his son to learn a trade in Salem. It is evident that he would like to get him out of reach of the proposed new draft. Br. Stotz shall send him word that he can give him work cutting wood.

The Governor and other members of the Assembly have insisted urgently that the Brethren ought to appear more in public. Our need for a Justice of the Peace for Salem has been made known, and the Brn. Bagge and Reuz have been suggested. It would be well for Bethabara to have a Justice also, but for the present there seems no possibility of that. The gentlemen would also like to see one of our Brethren serve as an Assembly-man, and they have encouraged Br. Bagge to run and he has agreed. If he receives the necessary votes and becomes a member of the Assembly he can be of much service in handling our matters there. As Br. Marshall must go to the next Assembly on business for us, Br. Bagge could be of great assistance, as he is acquainted with the matter. We think this public service would be of benefit to us in many ways, and our Brethren shall be notified so far as possible, so that Br. Bagge may receive their votes.

The Bethania members wish to change the time of their congregation festival, which has been on June 23rd and is inconvenient because of harvest. Br. Ernst suggests the 19th of March, the anniversary of the laying of the cornerstone of the Gemein Haus, which was approved.

Feb. 13. (Aelt. Conf.) It is suggested that the kitchen of the Brothers House should be made more convenient, at least by making an oven for roasting meat, if not with a raised hearth with plates and hooks.

The sleeping-hall of the Brethren is too small, and it was suggested that a second sleeping-hall might be arranged over the carpenter shop.

Feb. 19. (Auf. Col.) Br. George Schmidt asks for permission to cut eight or ten cords of wood on our land to burn for charcoal, until he can get some elsewhere. There is no objection if he will cut it on the east side of town, where the avenue leading north from God's Acre has been staked out.

The lots hitherto occupied by Stockburger can now be rented for five shillings, proclamation money, a year, per lot, provided the renter will maintain the fences, keep up the alleys, and release them when needed for building purposes.

Br. Mücksch asks permission to use the house of the night-watchman for manufacturing tobacco, and other business purposes, until it is needed for something else.

The French dollars now in circulation are worth 8 sh. 10d, but may be taken for the present at nine shillings. As the coin is not yet accepted everywhere a permanent value cannot be fixed.

Feb. 20. (Aelt. Conf.) The meat-oven and raised hearth will be built in the kitchen of the Brothers House.

The additional sleeping-hall can be secured to better advantage by using the top floor of the Brothers House, now a garret. The heat from the roof can be relieved by building dormer windows. It will be for the boys and their supervisors.

Concerning the letting of blood for the Single Sisters, it was decided that Sr. Bonn should try it, and if she is not successful they may call on Br. Koffler. It must at all times be done in the Sisters House, not in the apothecary-shop.

Feb. 27. (Aelt. Conf.) A man on Dan River has offered to sell Br. and Sr. Blum a negress of sixteen years, skilled in house-hold work, for £100.

Feb. 28. (Helf. Conf.) The question has arisen whether the French leaf-dollar now in circulation shall be taken for nine shillings, as many people are passing it at less. Its actual value is less, and in Pennsylvania it is taken at 8/4, but we think it will be better to count it at nine shillings here to encourage the coming in of silver money.

March 5. (Helf. Conf.) Br. Jacob Loesch shall not do any more gun work at present, as otherwise he will be constantly called on for work for the public and it will draw too many soldiers to the town.

March 7. (Cong. Council.) During the recent meeting of the Assembly, members insisted that it was necessary for a Brother to take public office, and Br. Bagge agreed to be a candidate at the next election of Assembly-men. It will be well for two of the Brethren to take an active part in the matter, and write and distribute tickets, which are usually asked for. There should be as many Brethren as possible in Richmond on the first and on the second day of the election. It will be better for our neighbors to attend only on Tuesday. Colonel Martin Armstrong is proposed as Senator, and Br. Bagge with Mr. Cummins or Cook as Burgesses; beyond this the Brethren may vote as they please.

We cannot get a Brother from Pennsylvania to fill Br. Bonn's place as doctor, so have applied to Europe. Meanwhile Br. Joseph Dixon will do what he can as a private individual, and Br. Reutz will dispense the medicine.

March 7. (Aelt. Conf.) Br. Jacob Loesch becomes a member of Congregation Council from the Choir of Single Brethren in place of Br. Broesing, who has married.

March 14. (Auf. Col.) Br. Valentine Beck prefers that Br. Jacob Loesch should not pour pewter spoons, but leave it for him. If Br. Beck will improve the form and make a good alloy there is no objection to his proposal, but he should keep some in Salem for sale at all times. Br. Daniel Christman proposes to begin work as a cooper.

April 4. (Helf. Conf.) Mr. Brooks, who has been here to collect taxes, did not take the County tax. He has received orders to accept Certificates in place of Continental currency.

We are beginning to be short of men who can play the French horn, and will try to secure two boys who will learn.

April 10. (Aelt. Conf.) Br. Lorenz reports that he preached to a good audience last Sunday, on Deep Creek, and baptised six children. He thinks, however, that unless these people will form themselves into a Society, or will move nearer to us, the method hitherto followed will not be of much use.

April 17. (Aelt. Conf.) Several of the Brethren have adopted a new and unseemly fashion of dress, and it will be well to speak of it in Congregation Council, and draw attention to the fact that in dress also we should not follow the world.

April 18. (Auf. Col.) People are making objections to accepting the French dollar at nine shillings. Hereafter they shall be taken at 8/8, and the guinea at 37 sh.

May 1. (Cong. Council.) Changing fashions in dress shall be avoided, especially among our young people. The master-tailor can do much to assist. He who dwells in our town shall dress as a Brother. Other people may have their clothes made as they please.

May 3. (Land-Arbeiter-Conferenz.) Syberberg and Nicolaus Lund have come to Friedberg, and George Hartman has taken them in. Syberberg has made preparations to build a house.

It was recommended that members help each other block up houses, so that it may not be necessary to call in outsiders through whose presence disorder so often arises.

The so-called Dunkards, and especially the Methodists, seem to be trying hard to take over our people into their *persuasion*. The latter become constantly more busy in the neighborhood of Hope, but the last speaking with the members of that Society did not show that any harm had been done. The best thing, under the circumstances, is for our preachers to set forth the gospel, and leave the doctrines of Jesus, committed to us, to approve themselves to the hearts of men as the power of God.

May 13. (Auf. Col.) A single man, named Johann Adam Gernand, who has worked for some time in the tanyard, has asked permission to become a resident of the town. He was born in Frederic County, Md., on July 15, 1759, and was bred a farmer.

May 15. (Aelt. Conf.) The two negroes, Samuel and Christian, from Bethabara, and our Abraham, shall be called to Hope for the baptism of the negro Jupiter next Sunday. In connection with this it was agreed that when there are baptisms of adults in the country congregations the candidates shall wear not only robes but other white clothing.

Br. Meyer intends to take the old negro Caesar and his wife from Bethabara into the Salem Tavern.

May 22. (Aelt. Conf.) At the request of his father, Br. Jacob Loesch inquires whether his brother Abraham, now in Christiansbrun, can be brought here and given work? The boy is seventeen and somewhat lame in his right arm, but not enough to prevent his working. His father will pay the expenses of the journey. Br. Loesch may write to his father that if he sends the lad we will look after him.

May 30. (Cong. Council.) It was asked whether the idea was creeping in that one should marry according to preference? If this idea should become general it would be a backward step for us.[1]

---

[1] It was the belief of the Brethren at that time that marriages should be left very largely to the direction of the Lord, as part of the complete submission of their lives to Him. This is the first intimation in the Wachovia records of a changing view.

In general one can say little here about foolish clothing, though now and then certain persons show a desire to follow the fashion. The evil of individuals usually shows itself in dress, as one has seen at certain times in the leggings and ruffs. Any simple clothing can be worn without hesitation, but the heart should not be set on it. The same applies to riding and walking. Each must be guided by his circumstances. In itself it is no sin to ride, nor even questionable, we must only not allow ourselves to be turned from the calling which the Lord has given us, nor become unserviceable for the work of the Lord.[2]

May 31. (L-A-C.) Syberberg and Lund have moved into their new house.

Concerning the Methodists it was agreed, that it is not our place to criticise them, or to warn our people against them. They will alienate from us none whose hearts are fixed on the Saviour.

June 5. (Aelt. Conf.) Br. Marshall was in Friedberg last Sunday, and suggested to the Brethren there that the 300 acres, which Br. Spach entered should be surveyed and a Deed made, and that Br. Spach should then give a Deed for the School-house land, making it in the name of Br. Marshall. They were entirely willing.

June 10. (Aelt. Conf.) Some of the Brethren are disposed to give away their Auditors' Bills for half their value. We will advise them against this. Although at present they will not be accepted in the paying of taxes,[3] in time we can probably do better with them. At auctions of confiscated property they will be accepted as cash, and it may be that land in our neighborhood will be sold as confiscated and we must take an interest in it.

June 26. (Aelt. Conf.) Dr. John Rindelmann, who is living in Richmond at present, has written to Br. Marshall, expressing his love for the Brethren and his desire to be nearer their services. It may well be that he wants to build up a practice in medicine and surgery in this neighborhood. If he wishes to settle near Friedberg that will be the best place for him.

Christian Loesch has come from Pennsylvania, and wishes to remain. He learned the tanner's trade with his cousin, Friedrich Blum, at Hope in the Jerseys.

---

[2] This discussion evidently had its origin in the letter from the Unity's Elders Conference, (printed in Part I of this volume,) in which simplicity of dress was urged, and the value of walking was stressed as a means of keeping physically fit for mission service. Apparently some zealous Brethren had criticised the apparel of some of their number, and had condemned riding, and the matter reached congregation council for settlement.

[3] This applied to the Specie Certificates authorized by the Act concerning Auditors passed by the Assembly of April, 1782.

July 17. (Aelt. Conf.) The question of a boarding school for little boys will be considered if there are others of the same age as Samuel Meyer who will attend.

The Single Sisters have expressed their desire to build a new Choir House. Conferenz recognizes the need for this, for they are much crowded, and at times the increase is considerable. The trouble is that at present there is no fund out of which the cost of such a building could be met, for at least £1000 would be needed, and there must be prospect of ability to pay for it before building is undertaken. The Choir of Single Sisters has a credit of £400 with the Unity's Vorsteher Collegium, which amount was used in the building of the Gemein Haus in which they are now living, but the rest will have to be secured through collections. The first thing to do is for the Single Sisters to write to Br. Reichel, telling him of their wishes and all the circumstances, and asking whether a collection for this purpose might be taken in the European congregations, especially in the Choir of Single Sisters, with the approval of the Unity's Elders Conference. The Aeltesten Conferenz here will endorse such an appeal.

The Single Sisters should have businesses which are carried on for the benefit of their Choir Diaconie. The making of gloves, which they have begun, should be carried on in a business-like manner. The complaint that they cannot get leather from Br. Yarrell shall be taken up by Br. Praetzel, who will try to have what they need supplied by Br. Yarrell or by Doub, who lives near Bethania. Arrangements for sale shall be made, so that the profit goes to the Sisters' Diaconie.

July 18. (Helf. Conf.) The Court of Justices has appointed George Hauser, Jr., to list the taxes of residents in Captain Binkele's district. He will be here on the 20th. Houses, land, negro slaves, cattle and stock-in-trade must be given in.

Aug. 20. (Auf. Col.) Visitors to the town have complained recently that we have refused to take copper pence from them. This is injurious to our commerce. However, this does not mean that any one is obliged to accept them in large quantities, nor does it mean that farthings must be accepted as pennies.

Aug. 21. (Aelt. Conf.) When Br. Schober goes into the store he will receive from Br. Bagge £60 a year and free living quarters as his salary as salesman.

It was mentioned that Matthew Noeting plans to marry the daughter of the elder Volz, and buy a farm.

Br. Jacob Loesch is not satisfied with his circumstances, and he shall be advised to carry on the business on his own account.

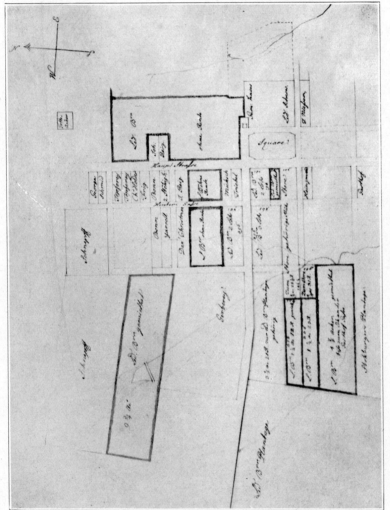

MAP OF SALEM IN 1783

Sept. 12. (Cong. Council.) This year a blessing has rested upon all our Branches, and not one has made a deficit, although the profit has varied.

It was asked whether clipped French silver coins should be taken at full value, or in the same proportion as clipped Spanish dollars? Most of the members were in favor of the latter, but we do not know what is being done in other places as they have just become evident.

Sept. 16. (L-A-C.) Friedrich Volz, in Friedberg, plans to marry Fischer's daughter, Anna Maria.

There is no objection to baptising the children of Methodists.

Sept. 25. (Aelt. Conf.) Br. Jacob Loesch will keep the evening school for the boys this winter.

Sept. 25. (Auf. Col.) Br. Marshall reported that Ellrod, who is working at the mill, would like to settle on one hundred acres on Stony Run, not far from the mill. If he should live in the neighborhood of the mill he could help there now and then, especially with the saw-mill, even though one does not wish to employ him constantly at the grist-mill.

Oct. 2. (Aelt. Conf.) Dr. Rindelmann wishes to be connected with the Brethren, and he is having a hard time in Richmond. Siverberg is moving away from Friedberg, and it can be suggested to Dr. Rindelmann that he buy Siverberg's house, move thither and practice there.

Oct. 9. (Aelt. Conf.) At the request of Br. and Sr. Reutz the little Tesch girl is attending the girls' school; now Br. and Sr. Christ request that Sally McBain may attend for two hours each morning.

Oct. 16. (Aelt. Conf.) It is deemed necessary to have something in writing concerning the Salem Land and the land of the Single Brethren. This is possible now, since the Assembly of this state has recognized Br. Marshall as the legal representative of the Unity for Wachovia. Br. Marshall presented a draft of a contract between him and the congregation, which is virtually a declaration as to the way in which Br. Marshall holds title to the Salem Land, and the conditions on which it is given over to the congregation. The draft was approved, and it shall be signed by as many of the Aeltesten Conferenz as possible, since apart from Br. Marshall, who cannot sign, we have no pastor of the congregation, no pfleger of the married people, and no preacher.[4]

Oct. 30. (Aelt. Conf.) In the afternoon at half past twelve the Contract between Br. Marshall and the Elders of the congregation concerning the Salem Land and the land of the Single Brethren was signed, the Brethren of the Aufseher Collegium being witnesses.

---

[4] All these they had lost in the death of Bishop Graff.

Nov. 5. (Auf. Col.) Mr. Walker will use the Magazine building and in it will store the Specific Tax.[5] We think he should pay £3 per year rent.

Nov. 11. (Auf. Col.) Daniel Christman has taken over the former Stockberger house for £80.

A nursery shall be laid out so that the Square can be planted in catalpa trees.

Nov. 12. (Aelt. Conf.) Several Brethren in Bethania plan to build a mill near that town, to which there is no objection. They offer to pay the congregation £10 a year, which would be considered a gratuity for the mill-site.

Several Brethren, on account of their poverty, are not in position to send their children to school in winter, or to pay the school fees. When the Brethren and Sisters in the European Diaspora heard of conditions in the congregations of Wachovia during the war they sent a free-will offering, which has now been remitted from Bethlehem and amounts to £9. We believe this can be put to the best use by helping our poor Brethren send their children to school.

Each Choir shall report to Br. Praetzel the number of Text Books which it needs. Br. Lorenz shall report for Bethabara, and Br. Ernst for Bethania.

Nov. 20. (Aelt. Conf.) The Bethania Brethren will run their line, beginning on Monday at the corner which touches the Bethabara boundary. Several Brethren from Bethabara are asked to be present.

Nov. 21. (Cong. Council.) In Br. Triebel's house more room shall be arranged for the school for little boys.

Mr. Walker intends to collect the Specific Tax this month, and George Hauser, Jr., the money tax. As there are still Tickets in town which can be used[6] it will be well to collect them, and so help each other, and if there are not enough it will be better to pay the tax in money at 2/6 per bushel than to deliver it in kind, which would cost more.

Nov. 27. (Aelt. Conf.) It will be better for the wedding of Br. Abraham Transu to take place in Bethania, for the ministers of the country congregations have so far not performed the marriage ceremony.

Careful investigation has shown that the Tickets for supplies, still on hand in Salem, are more than will be needed to pay the Specific Tax here, and the plan was approved that Bethabara should pay the tax for that town with these Tickets also.

---

[5] Otherwise known as the grain tax.
[6] Auditors' Certificates for supplies furnished, issued prior to the Act of April, 1782, were still tender for the Specific Tax.

In order to avoid loss on the Tickets which have been exchanged for Specie Certificates, which can be used only in the purchase of confiscated land and negroes, it was suggested that they be collected and sent to Salisbury, to be used in buying negroes at the vendue there on Dec. 15th. Some of these negroes can be used to advantage in our towns, the rest can be resold. The value of the Certificates and the risk shall be divided proportionately between the holders of the Certificates.

Major John Armstrong has written to Br. Bagge and to Colonel Armstrong that the English are preparing to leave Charlestown. As Flags of Truce are constantly passing between Charlestown and the camp of General Greene, Major Armstrong has hopes for the payment of our English Tickets, if we will make the journey thither, reaching the camp before Dec. 10th. We think this matter might be undertaken by Br. Stotz, who is looking after the Tickets from here and Bethabara, if Col. Martin Armstrong and George Hauser, Jr., are willing to make the journey with him. If they succeed it will be best to take a Bill of Exchange on London for the Tickets.

Dec. 4. (Aelt. Conf.) Col. Martin Armstrong will not be ready to leave for the camp for fourteen days. We do not see the end of this, but Br. Stotz shall hold himself in readiness for the trip.

It will be best that the Tickets, which we hope to use at the vendue in Salisbury, shall be collected and sent by some safe opportunity to Mr. Elliott, and we will commission him to attend to the matter.

In order to keep the Archives in proper order, and to make the entries in the Church-Book, Br. Friedrich Peter shall move them into his room.

Dec. 5. (Cong. Council.) This is not the usual time for a session of Congregation Council, but we are meeting for this reason:—Through the calling home of so many Brethren and Sisters here and in Bethabara and in Friedberg the Saviour has made great gaps in our ranks, and we keenly miss their help. Various conferences and other meetings cannot be held in their usual order because of the necessary absence of Brethren, and such meetings will have to be held as it is possible. We must therefore avail ourselves of the services of the Brethren and Sisters whom the Saviour has left to us. The married Sisters will find help in the advice of Sr. Graff. In addition to his duties as Vorsteher, Br. Praetzel will collect the contributions for the Unity from the married people. Br. Peter will take Br. Graff's place as preacher.

Dec. 5. (Auf. Col.) There was earnest discussion of the need of bringing here one or more teachers for our young people, without regard to cost, that they may be prepared for useful lives.

Dec. 10. (Auf. Col.) It is the intention that Br. Schober shall be assistant in the store here, and that as soon as possible Br. Bibighaus shall move to Bethabara and reopen the store there. The store will take over Br. Schober's leather breeches business, and continue it for the benefit of the store, allowing him £15 extra per year for it. Joseph Dixon will take from Br. Schober the business of dyeing leather for black breeches.

It will be well to collect the public Tickets for currency and specie, and be prepared to use them at public sales. We will have to be content with what we can get out of them.

Dec. 11. (Aelt. Conf.) Br. Joseph Dixon has been installed as school-teacher, and as he can not manage it alone Br. Peter will not only supervise the school but will give such instruction as is beyond Br. Dixon.

Hilsebeck's request to be received into the congregation led to the decision that it would be well to organize a Society in connection with Bethania.

Dec. 18. (Aelt. Conf.) Br. Peter reported for the school, that Br. Stauber has taken charge of the boys from the country, and those that cannot yet write. Br. Dixon takes the rest of the town boys. Arithmetic shall now begin for the little boys; they have progressed so far that they can read English with the older ones.

Dec. 28. (Aelt. Conf.) We must seek earnestly to counteract the desire of our young men to leave their professions here, thinking that outside they can get higher wages without being bound.

Dec. 30. (Auf. Col.) Br. Herbst thinks he will need £14 a year for Betsey Fockel, to cover her living expenses, clothes and school fees. The Bethabara diaconie will pay this.

Bethabara Diary, 1782.

[The Bethabara diary of this year gives the usual outline of church and congregational affairs, and of work on the farm, together with the mention of numerous visits between the various congregations. A few paragraphs are translated.]

Jan. 2. The house in which Br. and Sr. Stach live was recovered.

Jan. 3. The school for little boys commenced for the new year.

Jan. 6. At two o'clock there was the funeral of our departed Br. Johannes Franz Steup. With the usual liturgy the remains were laid in the grave on God's Acre. The bearers,[1] musicians, and those who took care of him during his last sickness, had a vesper.

Jan. 14. Br. Rose went to Wagoner's, whose wagon has arrived with a load of salt, to see whether we can get some of it, as we have needed it for a long time.

Jan. 16. The Brn. Oesterlein and Broesing returned from the Juwari,[2] bringing two boys on trial; the boy brought by the former is thirteen years old and is named Andreas Werner, and Broesing's is Jonas Werner, aged eleven years. Br. Schaub, Jr., and his day-laborers made a bridge across the Grosse Johanna, so that he can haul stone for his building.

Jan. 18. It rained all day, and was so cold that glaze-ice formed. Toward evening a company of mounted men arrived; they are searching the county for three-months men who did not go to the army.

Jan. 19. Every day soldiers are returning from General Greene's camp, their terms of enlistment having expired. Forty-nine years ago today the first Brethren were sent to Greenland as missionaries.[3]

Jan. 20. In congregation council the accounts of the congregation were read, and the members rejoiced that there was a small surplus. The majority were in favor of giving less this year, so a married couple will give 2/6 instead of 3 sh. each four weeks, if living in town; if in the country 2/3. An unmarried communicant Brother will give 1/8, and a Sister 10d.

Jan. 22. Old Br. Kühnast is sixty-eight today, and all who share in the common house-keeping[4] had a lovefeast with him.

Jan. 23. Our Brethren were out repairing bridges and roads.

Jan. 29. It was very cold today, and there was a strong north-west wind.

Jan. 31. It snowed all afternoon and into the night.

Feb. 4. Colonel Schelsie came from Salem and spent the night on his way home. A man named Themothius Ricks, from Broad River, brought a letter to Maria Handsen from her father, Benjamin Handsen.

Feb. 7. Sr. Praetzel came with Br. Vogler's wagon, returning the bedding lent to Salem from here and from Bethania.

Feb. 12. Many travelers passed.

Feb. 13. A fence was begun along one side of the town, to keep the cattle away from the houses.

Feb. 14. Br. Lorenz has a very bad cold.

---

[1] It was no sinecure to bear the remains up the long, steep path to the top of the Graveyard Hill.   [2] Uwarrie.   [3] One of them, Matthew Stach, was living in Bethabara in 1782.
[4] Those who worked the Unity farm, the minister's family and a few other officials, still had a common housekeeping, though the general Oeconomie had ceased.

21

Feb. 15. The Brn. Marshall and Meinung came from Salem. Most of the way they came through the woods, trying out the proposed new road.

Feb. 16. The proposed new road was measured; it is shorter than the present one. As planned, it will come into the old road two miles from Salem.

Feb. 18. Br. Stöhr took Sr. Rose to see Colonel Armstrong's wife, who is ill, and she advised her according to her needs.

Feb. 19. The common house-keeping killed eight hogs, weighing 1217 lbs. The weather was cloudy and rainy.

Feb. 22. Several of our Brethren began to cut out the new road toward Salem.

March 2. After the beautiful weather of yesterday it began to rain, then snowed heavily until noon.

March 7. Our Brethren opened the new road and made it passable as far as the Spangenbach. From there to the old road they cut a foot-path. The Englishman, Matthew Thompson, who has been working for Br. Schaub for four months, left of his own accord today.

March 12. Most of the Brethren from Salem and from here went to the election of new Assembly-men.

March 14. The weather was good. During these days many travelers have been coming from South Carolina.

March 22. Last night it froze, and probably all the peach blossoms have been killed. Br. Schaub, Jr., set a pump-stock in the new well on his lot.

March 26. Most of the Brethren, Sisters and children in and near the town have a cough, cold in the head, and headache.

March 31. Easter. Early in the morning we went to God's Acre and prayed the Easter Litany.

April 3. Mr. Brooks came to collect the tax, but left without having quite finished.

April 9. It rained all day and into the night. Br. Lorenz was at Deep Creek[5] last Saturday, and preached in George Lang's house to a large audience, and at request baptised six children. The greater part of these German people have ruined themselves by hiding out or by going to the English, and although they are all at home now, and have surrendered themselves, they are very poor.

April 12. Last night it rained so hard that the stream rose, but this morning it was clear, so that the usual work could be continued.

---

[5] In what is now Yadkin County. Lang was later spelled Long.

April 13. Our team went fifteen miles for a load of shingles.

April 20. During these days many travelers are passing from South Carolina to Virginia, and from Virginia to the South. John Armstrong, from Greene's camp, stopped on his way home.

April 23. The Brn. Micke and Kapp went to Virginia, the former to collect an old debt from Mr. Robersen, and the latter to buy a large kettle from the Furnace.

April 30. Fence-making continued, especially along the new lane through the orchard, going toward Salem.

May 2. A rain fructified the land, which was already rather dry.

May 14. Some of the Brethren went to court on business. Our team went to the mountains eighteen miles away for whet-stones.

May 16. Letters were received this week from Pennsylvania, and from them Br. Marshall read to us the affecting account of our Indian Brethren. Some of them came from Sandusky to the Muskingum, to get provisions from the gardens they had left there. A company of evil men fell on them, captured them, and condemned them to death. The murder of these poor sheep followed immediately. Our Brethren and Sisters sang and prayed until they were killed. According to the account there were thirty men, and sixty-six women and children. There were one hundred and sixty in the band of murderers, and they divided the booty, each receiving £20.

June 1. The two big sills for Broesing's shed were brought in with eight horses. The muster, or Court of Inquiry, for our district was held in our tavern.

June 3. George Holder's two little girls began to attend school, coming for the morning session.

June 4. Yesterday and today our teams made three trips to Salem, taking hides to the tanyard.

June 11. The Brn. Kühnast and Blum went to Salem, taking to the Auditors some Tickets which had not yet been adjusted.

June 17. Lenel Kapp entered school today.

June 27. Here and among our neighbors the cutting of wheat was begun.

June 29. Br. Schaub, Jr., prepared to make more brick on his lot, as he has not enough for his building.

This week most of the Brethren and Sisters have been suffering from vomiting, pains in the body, and diarrhoea.

July 2. All went on in the usual way.[6] It rained a little in the afternoon. The heat and drought is great.

July 7. Accounts for the half year were presented to congregation council. Expenditures were £16:3:6 and receipts were £10:15:—; unpaid and due £7:6:5. The season of fruit is beginning, and no one must go to the orchard and take fruit without permission; the house-fathers shall remind their children of this. It was also remarked that hunting and fishing on Sunday is absolutely against the law of the land, and each house-father must see that the law is obeyed. This afternoon we had a good rain, which refreshed the dry earth.

July 12. Br. and Sr. Stöhr moved into their new house.

July 13. Br. and Sr. Stöhr had a lovefeast with several friends in their new house, in token of their gratitude that they may live there.

July 17. Yesterday and today the Brethren from here went to Bethania to list their taxes with Justice George Hauser, Jr., according to the law of the land.

July 18. Two shillings per bushel was fixed as the price for apples bought at the door; when a tree is bought the value shall be appraised.

July 19. The one-third due from Br. Broesing's farm in rye, wheat and oats was brought to the sheds.

July 23. Johann Kraus was here, and asked for the burial of his youngest child on the Graveyard by the mill. The funeral took place this afternoon, an address being made at the place of burial.

Aug. 5. The master-workmen had a conference. Br. Marshall spoke of the lease that Brethren should have who occupy their own houses and lots in the town. The lane between the building lots and the meadow shall be repaired, and shall be used for the coming and going of the cattle, which shall not be allowed to stand around on the street either during the day or at night. Sr. Bonn was sent for, as Sr. Broesing was not well.

Aug. 7. Soon after noon a little daughter was born to Sr. Broesing, who had been in labor for twice twenty-four hours. Sr. Hauser was called from Bethania this morning, and her efforts were successful. As the child was weak, the heat oppressive, and most of the married Sisters there, others gathered and the child was baptised with the usual liturgy.

Aug. 26. Br. Stöhr employed a mason to coat the outside of his house with clay and lime.

---

[6] *Es war alles im gewöhnlichem gang,* is repeated over and over in this diary of Bethabara.

Aug. 29. This morning about seven o'clock a messenger brought word from Salem that our beloved Br. Graff entered into the joy of his Lord this morning about two o'clock. This was announced by the usual tunes played on the French horns. The news was sent to our country members and neighbors.

Aug. 30. Most of our Brethren and Sisters went to Salem to the funeral of our beloved Br. Graff. There was no evening service.

Sept. 1. Sunday. Wilhelm Volck came on Friday and asked for the burial of his child on the Graveyard near the mill. The service was held this afternoon at two o'clock, a rather large number being present.

Sept. 2. Yesterday the cows could not be found, but they were brought in today about noon.

Sept. 3. Yesterday and today the sills were laid for Broesing's shed, and also two or three cross pieces.

Sept. 4. About thirty men, from the town and from the country, gathered to lay up Broesing's shed, which was accomplished without accident.

Sept. 7. The Married People celebrated their festival.

Sept. 8. Sunday. In the first service the Memoir of our departed Br. Graff was read, and immediately afterward a mesenger took it to Bethania.

Sept. 12. Sr. Kapp is ill and must stay in bed. Her tongue seems lame.

Sept. 18. Many from Salem, Bethania and the neighborhood attended the funeral of Sr. Elisabeth Kapp. After the service the relatives, bearers and blowers[7] met in the Saal, and together ate white bread and coffee.

Sept. 26. It rained nearly all day. Many travelers were here, so that the tavern was filled.

Sept. 27. The guests in the tavern were still here. The Colonel from the Jerseys visited Salem. Colonel Schmidt from South Carolina called all his friends to meet here.

Sept. 28. All of the guests left except Colonel Schaa,[8] who went north next day.

Oct. 2. Br. and Sr. Schaub, Jr., moved into their new house.

Oct. 5. Colonel Schaa returned. Two horses were stolen from him and he will go to Salisbury to see about it.

---

[7] Those who played the French horns used for funerals in Bethabara. Salem had a set of trombones as well as horns.
[8] Probably meant for Shaw.

Oct. 6. Sr. Lorenz has not been well this week, and today must keep quiet with headache.

Oct. 10. Sr. Lorenz is weaker and has fever every day.

Oct. 12. Sr. Lorenz has high fever.

Oct. 17. Stone was hauled for a new kitchen and bakery for the common house-keeping.

Oct. 20. Our dear Sr. Lorenz was very weak. We noticed this morning that an eruption had broken out on her throat and head. It was evident that her end was approaching, and from three o'clock on liturgies were sung continuously around her bed. Most of the Sisters were present, and accompanied her departure with hot tears. At five o'clock this noble soul passed quietly into the arms of Jesus. The home-going was announced to the congregation by the blowers, and also by notice given in the evening meeting.

Oct. 22. Many came from Salem and Bethania for the funeral of our departed Sister. Br. Praetzel held the service making an address on the Text for the 20th. Her Memoir was read, and the choir sang: "Sleep, beloved Sister, sleep."

Today they began taking down the old bake-house, and preparing the ground for the erection of a new one.

Oct. 28. Br. Lorenz visited at the mill, where two children are sick. The opinion continues to be expressed that the illness is caused by the sick cattle. Br. Kapp has been spoken with, and has been reminded what to do when cattle die.

Nov. 17. Maria Handsen went to Bethania with the Srs. Kühnast and Reutz, where she today will be united in marriage with Gottlieb Kramer.

Nov. 21. Br. Rose and his men went to the grind-stone mountain, four miles from here, and brought back two wagon-loads of stepping stones. The little boys have no school this week.

Nov. 27. Mr. Walker was here to collect the grain tax, which was paid to him in Tickets and money. Br. Johann Ranke, and his brother's son and team, returned safely from New Bern.

Dec. 4. Br. Triebel brought two pump-stocks which he has made for use here. The re-covering of the old store building was finished.

Dec. 9. Wheat threshing continued in the shed. The wheat is badly eaten by weevils.

Dec. 12. The first cooking was done in the new kitchen.

Dec. 23. Br. Mücke secured eighty bushels of rye from Virginia.

Dec. 27. Two unmarried negresses came from Virginia to visit our Samuel; they are his sister's daughters. They went home today.

Extract from the Bethania Memorabilia, 1782.

In outward affairs we have had, in contrast with the last, a very quiet and peaceful year, and could go our way undisturbed.

The general and special festivals have been blessed to us, especially the Passion season, and the 19th of March, which at the request of the local congregation was celebrated as our congregation festival in place of the 23rd of June. His Word and Sacrament have strengthened us in body and soul. The Gospel has been preached with diligence, and many have attended the services with blessing. On the Unity days we have rejoiced to hear of the spread of the kingdom of God into all parts of the world. The re-reading of the Results of the General Synod of 1775 has encouraged our hearts to abide by the doctrine of Jesus and His apostles, to hold fast these foundation principles, and to seek to lay aside all that is contrary to them.

In the steadily continuing hard times, caused by the war on the sea and along the coast, our Heavenly Father has given us a fairly rich year of fruit and grain, in spite of the little rain and the drought of the late summer, so that we have been able to help some of the poor in these hard times.

Bethania Diary, 1782.

[Extracts translated.]

Jan. 2. Yesterday and today some of our Irish neighbors rode to Richmond to take part in the festivities there.

Jan. 7. After the afternoon school, God's Acre was laid off anew, and instead of a square of nine rods, or 148½ feet, it was made 106 ft. long and 80 ft. wide. All the graves come inside the fence.

Jan. 10. Anspach returned to Friedberg, after spending a day with Michael Hauser.

Jan 12. Some of our neighbors rode through on their way to the muster place, where the names of their families will be written down.[9]

Jan. 19. I gave George Hauser, Jr., the list which Colonel Armstrong has asked of us. It was arranged to show the number of Brethren and Sisters and children living in town, and those belonging to us living in the country, without giving their names.

Jan. 24. Agnes Standly brought her child for baptism, which her husband requested some months ago.

---

[9] A militia census was being taken in Surry County, but why women and children were included does not appear.

The house-fathers met. It was announced that Br. Peter Hauser would keep the accounts for the next half year. The names of those who had paid were read, and also the names of those who had not paid.

Jan. 25. We heard that last evening George Schmidt, brother of Heinrich Schmidt, was driven out of the town with blows, after he had behaved very badly in the tavern, had refused to listen to kind words, and was trying to do mischief.

March 2. It snowed hard this morning.

March 11. This morning the Brn. Bagge and Yarrel came on their way to Richmond, where the former will offer himself for election to the Assembly.

March 12. The Brn. Praetzel, Petersen, Samuel Stotz, Spieseke, and others from Salem, several Brethren from Bethabara, and a party from Friedland, came on their way to Richmond to cast their votes. No one came from Friedberg or Hope. Br. Bagge returned in the evening, but did not know whether he had been elected.

March 13. Early in the morning we heard that Br. Bagge was elected, although so many were against him.

March 14. Joseph Müller's brother-in-law, Spies, came for a package of letters.

March 19. In the second service Samuel Strub was baptised. The two Brn. George Hauser and Peter Hauser brought him into the Saal. Br. Graff spoke on the Text for the day, showing the difference between the Law and the Gospel. Then he questioned the candidate, who answered with a clear *Yes.* Br. Graff read the baptismal liturgy, and with the verse:

The eye alone the water sees,

the Brn. George Hauser, Jr., and H. Sponhauer, Jr., brought the water into the Saal. The congregation stood, and in an impressive prayer Br. Graff absolved the candidate from sin and the power of evil, and baptised him in the name of the Holy Trinity into the death of Jesus, with the name Johann Samuel. At the words: "Now art thou buried with Him" the Brn. Graff, Marshall and Ernst, and the two sponsors, George and Peter Hauser, laid their hands upon him. The water was removed, the candidate prostrated himself and the sponsors knelt, while Br. Graff sang:

Graciously receive his soul.

At the words: "Now live, yet not thou," he was raised by his sponsors, and the Kiss of Peace was given to him by the five Brethren above mentioned. Then Br. Graff pronounced the blessing of the Lord upon him, he was led from the Saal by his sponsors, and the congregation was dismissed after singing a hymn.

At half past one was the festal lovefeast, which Br. Graff held. He explained that twelve years ago the foundation-stone of this house was laid. Br. Marshall held the gemeinstunde, and at its close five persons were Received into the congregation,—the married Heinrich Krieger by Br. Graff, the single Jacob Stolz by Br. Ernst, the youth Joseph Hauser by Br. Benzien, the married Susanna Strub by Sr. Marshall, and the older girl Catharina Strub by Sr. Ernst. In the evening there was a singstunde of thanks and praise.

March 21. This morning there was a heavy snow storm. The following night was so cold that the early blossoms froze, and the cold continued several days.

March 30. This morning the road to God's Acre was improved. Soon after twelve o'clock was the Sabbath lovefeast; and in the afternoon the grave-mounds were renewed in the recently re-fenced God's Acre.

March 31. On Easter morning the congregation assembled at half past five, in the Saal, and greeted each other with the words: The Lord is risen! After singing several hymns we went to God's Acre, and prayed the Easter Liturgy. Soon after ten o'clock there was preaching. In the afternoon the story of the Resurrection was read. In the evening the reading of the story of Sunday was continued.

April 1. We heard that last Wednesday evening the home of Johann Hoehns was robbed by three men, and the same thing happened that night at the homes of Philip Rothrock and Peter Rothrock. Several came from Friedberg and Friedland bringing several suspected men.

April 15. Sr. Quest held morning prayers for the girls on their festal day. In the afternoon Br. Graff held lovefeast for twenty-two girls and twelve guests. Sr. Reitz played the organ.

April 17. Captain Binckele asked for the baptism of his child at his home, as his wife wished to be present.

April 21. The house-fathers met to consider a letter from Br. Bagge concerning a Pass received from the Governor for a trip to the camp of General Greene, and through his aid to Charlestown, to see whether it would be possible to secure payment of the English Tickets, given us on the 9th and 10th of February last year.

May 1. Five wagons went from here to Mr. Martin for lime for Br. Herbst.

May 5. I held the first service, after having been obliged to stay in for fourteen days.

May 12. Sr. Reutz held the services for the girls.

May 13. Court was held at Richmond this week.

May 15. I[10] was in Salem for Conference. Br. Marshall returned with me, and in the evening announced to the congregation the inhuman murder on Feb. 16th this year, when 160 militia, without orders, killed 96 of our Indian members, at Gnadenhütten.

June 3. I prepared for the trip to South Carolina. In the evening meeting I commended to the prayers of the congregation myself and the two Brn. Heinrich Schor and George Hauser, Jr.

June 4. I set off about six o'clock, accompanied by my wife and two Sisters. The Brn. Schor and Hauser followed at noon. My wife and the two Sisters returned home in the afternoon.

June 8. According to plan the youths and boys met to build a dry-house, which was finished the same day. The smaller boys cut the firewood that was left. It rained all day, which made the work hard, but they brought it to completion, and before they left they were treated to coffee and cake. Br. Friedrich Peter came this evening to hold the Sunday services in Br. Ernst's absence.

June 12. Michael Hauser's still-house was blocked up, as was Br. Transou's weave-shed on *the 13th.*

June 15. In the afternoon about 4 o'clock Br. Ernst returned from the trip toward Charlestown; the Brn. Schor and Hauser, Jr., had arrived a few hours earlier. On account of the Tories they were not able to go further than to about twelve miles this side of the Santee, some miles beyond Singelsen's mill. Soon after five o'clock lovefeast was held, and Br. Ernst took the opportunity to tell the congregation about his trip and why he had to turn back.

[The account is filed with the diary, and is as follows.]

June 4. After I, Br. Ernst, had taken leave last evening of the congregation at the time of service, and had commended myself and the two Brethren traveling with me to their thought, and had committed us all to the Saviour and to the guidance and protection of His Spirit, I set out this morning early with my wife, Lisel Hauser, and Fisher's wife. In Bethabara I took hearty leave of the Brn. and Srs. Lorenz and Kühnast, and others, and reached Salem about nine o'clock. At noon my two traveling companions, Schor and George Hauser, Jr.,

[10] Rev. Johann Jacob Ernst.

joined me. As Br. Bagge had still much to write which we were to take with us we had to wait for a while in Salem, so it was after four o'clock when I bade farewell to the dear members of the Aeltesten Conferenz, and to my wife, and other Brethren and Sisters, and commended ourselves to their thoughts, and began our journey. That evening I spent with Br. and Sr. Beck, who received me with much love; the two Brethren stopped at Christian Frey's.

June 5. In the afternoon about five o'clock we reached Salisbury, where we received a friendly welcome from Andreas Betz. From him we heard that this morning Major John Armstrong and Joel Lewis had fought with pistols and swords, and were badly wounded. After attending to several commissions, and making inquiries from Mrs. Kaehr,[11] who had recently visited her husband in Charlestown, and who told us several things, we set out again about seven o'clock, and camped for the first night in the woods, about three miles from Salisbury.

June 6. This morning at ten o'clock we reached Sassman's mill, about fifteen miles from our last night's camp, but as we could get neither oats nor corn we rode on to find Paul Beeringer. As he lives half a mile from the road, to the right, we rode on for a mile and a half to another plantation, but as we could get nothing there, and there was no hope of finding anything further on, we turned back, and Mr. Beeringer let us have two bushels of oats for six shillings. He invited us to stop on our return. From there we rode ten miles further, and stopped for the night about two miles this side of Mr. Boon. This afternoon we were for the first time wet with rain, which continued till in the night.

June 7. Soon after eight o'clock we reached Mr. Stuard's, ten miles from our last camp. As we believed that from now on we would find little forage for our horses we wanted to buy a bushel of oats from him, but when we found that he wanted six shillings a bushel we contented ourselves with a peck. About six miles from there we came to the home of Mr. Dilep, who has a spring of unparalled good water. In the afternoon we met some soldiers from the camp, who were going home. This afternoon it was again very cloudy, and toward evening it began to rain. We had to camp in the woods, six miles before the new road turns into the old road. When we had our fire burning a traveler called to us, asking that he might come to our fire, as he could go no further because of the darkness of the night, and we gladly gave permission. The rain continued until midnight.

---

[11] Kerr?

June 8. Soon after five o'clock we set out again, wet as we were, and soon after seven came into the old road, where we met many militia from the camp. The largest troop, with a wagon, had already passed. Soon after, we met three officers, and after inquiring whence we came and whither we were going they wished us much luck on the way. As we asked for the name of the man who had talked most with us he said that he was Colonel Dixon. From there on we saw nothing but burned houses and open fields; now and then houses still standing but completely ruined. At noon we came to Pfeifer's, now Ruchly's[12] mill, there we had to unsaddle and let the horses swim; our baggage was carried across by black men, swimming together. The mill and tanyard were not entirely burned, but completely ruined; everything as far as Pinetree was either destroyed or burnt. Not a sign could be seen of Mr. Sotten's plantation. At five in the evening we reached Pinetree. We did not find Colonel Kirscha,[13] but his brother received us politely, and entertained us with the story of all he had passed through during the last years. Colonel Kirscha arrived about six o'clock; he welcomed us in the most friendly way, and after I had delivered Br. Bagge's letter to him, and he had read it, he at once invited us to lodge with him. He gave us good hope that we would succeed in our undertaking; other gentlemen doubted whether we could reach there. That evening I wrote a letter to Br. Marshall.

June 9. We could not set out until ten o'clock. Colonel Kirscha advised us to go by way of Mr. Lawrence's Ferry. As we could get no corn from Colonel Kirscha except what was fed to the horses, and there was poor prospect of securing provisions further on, we could give the horses hard food but once during the day, but fortunately grass in the woods was not so scarce. Most of the plantations that we passed were either abandoned or burned, now and then one was inhabited, but they had nothing. About four o'clock we met Mr. Hampton, who gave us little hope of being able to pass the Santee Swamp, as it was full everywhere of a rabble of robbers. We spent the night in an abandoned house, two miles this side of the widow James.

June 10. About six o'clock we set out again, and toward noon reached Colonel Singelsen's mill, hoping to be able to get some food for our horses. As usual there was none to be had, and we had to go a mile off the road, where we succeeded in securing one peck. In the mill we heard that two miles further on a robber had been brought as prisoner to a Justice, and would be tried today. We therefore went there, hoping to hear something definite from the people who would

---

[12] Rugeley's.   [13] Kershaw.

be gathered.   On the way we met a lieutenant of General Greene's cavalry, who said that there was not a chance for us to get through the Swamp, as there were more than three hundred Tories in it, and while they would probably not kill us, they would rob us of everything we possessed.   He said that all the roads through the Swamp were infested in the same way; and so we decided to turn back with him.   We traveled that evening to about twelve miles from Pinetree, and camped in the woods.

June 11.   Soon after five o'clock we took up our return journey, and reached Pinetree about nine, finding Colonel Kirscha at home.   He believed that it was best that we had turned back.   We had to stop for an hour with him, while he wrote two letters, and gave me one for Br. Bagge.   He gave us a quart of rum to use on the way.   We thanked him for the love shown to us, and took a friendly leave of him.   About ten miles from there we gave our horses the last corn we had.   We could have bought a bushel yesterday, but it would have cost 20 sh. so we did not take it.   This afternoon we had a hard rain, and when we were already rather wet we found an abandoned house, into which we retired, with our horses.   We could not reach another house that evening, so wet as we were we had to camp in the woods, in a gentle rain, having come about twenty-five miles from Pinetree.   A man with whom we caught up said he had met an Express who said that peace had been made between England and America.[14]   Before we lay down we heard several cannon shots from Pinetree.

June 12.   Soon after five o'clock we left our wet camp, and came before noon out of the old into the new road.   After riding some miles along the new road we saw a plantation on our left, to which we hurried, and bought a bushel of corn for a hard dollar, feeling as though we had found it.   Toward evening we had a hard storm, with strong wind, so that we were wet through and through.   About eight o'clock we reached the home of Mr. Dilepp, who has the best spring far and wide, and spent the night there.

June 13.   At six o'clock we continued our journey, and about three o'clock reached Mr. Beeringer, who again let us have a bushel of oats. About fifteen miles from Salisbury we made our night camp in the German settlement.

June 14.   We made an early start, hoping to reach Christian Frey's this evening.   Toward the end of the German settlement we bought a peck of corn.   About ten o'clock we reached Salisbury and spent an hour with Andreas Betz, while we fed our horses.   Toward noon we

---

[14] The report was probably based on the resignation of Lord North, in March, 1782, as he was the leader of the pro-war party in England.

left there, and about two reached the Atkin, and as it was up two feet we had to let ourselves be put across on the flat. In the evening toward eight o'clock we came to Christian Frey's, and I rode on to the home of Br. Beck, reaching there about half past eight. We rejoiced to see each other again.

June 15. A little before seven o'clock my two traveling companions rejoined me, and Br. and Sr. Beck rode with us to Salem which we reached at nine. We had spent twelve days on the trip and back. I silently thanked the Lord for His leading and gracious help on this journey, so difficult in many respects. I remained in Salem over noon, and at two o'clock reached Bethabara, and at four Bethania, where I found Br. and Sr. Praetzel and my wife, well and looking for me.

[So far the travel diary.]

June 16. The house-fathers met, and decided not to purchase the Weiss land,[15] as there are too many poor people in town who cannot pay the interest on the Bethania land, and who should not undertake a larger debt by buying more.

June 24. It was decided by the house-fathers to postpone the festival of the little boys to the latter part of August, and combine that of the little girls with it, for in the midst of the harvest season few of the country members can attend. For the same reason school has been suspended.

July 11. Br. Binckele came to have his Memoir written, which was done on *the 12th* by Sr. Cramer.

July 18. With the Brn. Volck and Fischer I rode to Moser's, where, at the request of his wife and children, I held the funeral of the older Moser. Although a large number had gathered, partly English partly German, all was quiet and orderly. At the request of Catharine Spoñhauer, John Jacob's wife, I baptised their child with the name of Johannes.

July 23. The house-fathers decided to have an apple-mill made.

July 28. The Baptist preacher Christman visited me, and joined in a friendly discussion concerning the source of salvation.

July 31. The local and country house-fathers met early this morning and repaired the Gemein Haus roof, stable, etc., and cleaned out the well.

Aug. 12. We heard that Gov. Alex. Martin had passed through the lower end of town, on his way to court at Richmond.

---

[15] This was a 640 acre tract adjoining the Bethania land on the west, and just outside the Wachovia line. It appears as a Wachovia Outlot on the maps of 1766, see Vol. I this series, facing pp. 310 and 375.

Aug. 17. At ten o'clock Br. Benzien held morning prayers for the little boys and girls, and after that they were spoken with in groups. In the afternoon was their festal lovefeast, attended by thirty-three boys and thirty-two girls,—several did not come.

Sept. 7. In the lovefeast of the Married People a festal Ode was sung, and Br. Jacob Loesch, who came early from Salem, played the organ and sang the parts for the choir.

Sept. 19. The noon liturgy had to be omitted because the town was full of strangers and their wagons.

Sept. 22. In the afternoon the house-fathers met, and Br. Marshall proposed that instead of making a purchase-contract they should take the Bethania land on a long lease, bearing interest at six per cent. As some were not present the matter was held over until evening, when after a long discussion for and against it the proposal was accepted.

Sept. 26. The house-fathers met, and Br. Marshall read to them the draft of the Lease. Some remarks were made, but no changes were necessary and all were satisfied with it, so they separated. Br. Bagge and Meinung, who chanced to arrive, made fair copies of the Lease, and in the afternoon at four o'clock, after Br. Ernst had read it aloud once more, it was signed by those present and exchanged. In the evening it was read again for those who were not present in the afternoon.

Sept. 27. The negress, Rahel, passed out of Time, trusting in Jesus, and on *the 28th* she was buried on the north side of the hill behind Spönhauer's field. She was born in Virginia, and was bought by Br. Peter Hauser when she was about fifteen or sixteen years old. She had been here four years and some months, being now nineteen or twenty.

Oct. 22. Br. Sehnert is growing weaker. On the next day he made his Will, and let the events of his life be written down for his Memoir.

Oct. 25. Some cattle-drivers arrived with a herd of one hundred and fifty oxen. They meant to drive them to Pennsylvania, but turned back because of the great scarcity of food.

Nov. 4. The Brn. Marshall and Bagge spoke to us on their way to Richmond. They returned in the evening.

Nov. 15. Br. Marshall returned to Salem. Br. Bagge went to Richmond, coming back to us in the evening.

Nov. 16. Br. Bagge went to Richmond again, returning about eight o'clock in the evening.

Nov. 17. *Sunday.* After breakfast Br. Bagge returned to Salem. Soon after noon Br. Abraham Transou brought the Srs. Kühnast,

Reitz and Maria Hindsen[16] from Bethabara, and at two o'clock, in the gemeinstunde, the Single Br. Gottlieb Cramer and the Single Sr. Maria Hindsen were united in marriage. After the service the new Choir Ribbon was tied in for her[17] in the presence of her husband and Sr. Kühnast. Then a lovefeast was held in the school-room for the new couple, the above-mentioned Brethren and Sisters, and old Br. Cramer.

Nov. 23. During this week many families have passed, moving from the north to the south.

Nov. 25. Soon after eight o'clock most of the Brethren and young men from here went to the pile of stone on the Bethabara road, where they were met by four Brethren from Bethabara. From that point the line was run and renewed around the Bethania Lot.

Nov. 26. Br. Reitz came from Salem to buy cattle for the soldiers marching to Pennsylvania.

Dec. 3. I took the Memorabilia of this town to Br. Lorenz, who will take it on to Salem.

Dec. 6. Br. Reitz came to help George Hauser, Jr., collect the taxes.

Dec. 15. Sunday. At two o'clock in the afternoon was gemeinstunde, during which the Single Br. Abraham Transou and the Single Sr. Maria Pfaff were united in marriage. Soon after the service the new couple and the guests present had a little lovefeast in the home of Br. and Sr. Transou.

Dec. 17. This morning Jacob Volz and Johanna Volck were married by George Hauser, Jr.

Dec. 18. This afternoon Br. Bagge and two other Brethren from Salem brought a horse-thief, who was sent on to Richmond next day.

Dec. 24. In the afternoon at five o'clock the children had their Christmas lovefeast, at the close of which verses and candles were distributed. The adult congregation met at seven o'clock.

Dec. 25. Christmas Day. At eleven o'clock was the festal sermon. More than two hundred visitors were present, who listened attentively.

---

[16] Handson.

[17] Exchanging the pink cap-ribbon of a Single Sister for the light blue of a Married Sister.

Friedberg Diary, 1782.

[The Friedberg diary of this year contains little except records of pastoral work, schedules of church services, and outlines of sermons, the latter valuable as showing Moravian doctrine as there preached. A few paragraphs are translated.]

Jan 11. Fat hogs were impressed from several of our people, and we felt especially sorry for one family which has little and had bought a hog for its own use.

Jan. 18. The weather was bad, with glaze-ice and rain.

Jan. 19. In the lovefeast it was remarked that ten years ago the first Communion was held here, with eighteen members.

Jan. 22. During the night I was called to Simon Schneider, who is quite sick at the home of George Hartmann. I spoke to him of the Friend of poor sinners, stressing the love of Jesus.

Feb. 17. Congregation council decided to put a foundation under the passage in the lower story of the School-house.

Feb. 27. Some of the Brethren repaired the passage in the School-house. The work went well and was finished in good time.

March 9. Saturday. In the morning before eleven o'clock some of the Brethren and Sisters came from Salem to the advance celebration of our congregation festival, which properly comes on the 11th. At the lovefeast for the children at eleven o'clock Br. Marshall told the story of the beginning of this little congregation, and the consecration of the School-house and Saal thirteen years ago. He added that the Saviour should be thanked and praised for all the kindness which He has shown to this congregation, and that He receives the praises of children with special joy. In the lovefeast for adults an Ode of Thanksgiving, arranged by Br. Graff, was sung. Br. Marshall spoke on the Text for the 11th, pointing out the pitiful situation of those who cut themselves off from the world in order to live godly lives, and yet are not sure in their hearts whether they belong to the world and Satan or to the Saviour. That should not be true of us, a little congregation of Jesus, shut off from the world. We should be children of God, and that means that as we have grace and the forgiveness of sins through the blood of Jesus we should draw near to Him with faith and childlike love. Who once has tasted His friendship knows in his heart for a certainty that he not only should but will draw ever closer to the Saviour, and receive from Him grace for grace, and this is a great blessing. Then difficulties will not cause him to miss the mark, for he will have proof of the wonderful help

22

of the Saviour, and will ever more confidently and with more assurance appeal to the Saviour, as a child to his mother. This faith and child-like trust in the Saviour is the result of the covenant He has made with us, that He has become our Brother, and has poured out His blood for us, uniting poor sinners with Himself, and drawing together a company of souls who will live for Him. On His side there is assurance that He will guard the covenant forever. On our side there is poverty and weakness, but He gives us His grace and strength, and expects from us that we will patiently and quietly hold fast to Him, and be content in knowing that He will make a covenant with us. Of course it follows that we must rightly know our misery and poverty, and the worth of the death of Jesus; and it is more difficult for the Saviour to lead the children of the Unity to feel their needs, protected as they are from the things of the world, than those who plainly see their distressing condition. And without this knowledge we are not in position to enter into the covenant which the Saviour has made with us, and to abide therein. The covenant is only for poor sinners, who live by the grace of God.

In the following service of the Society was the baptism of the adult, David Zimmerman. Br. Graff spoke on the Texts of the 10th and 11th, concerning the ground of our salvation, that Jesus Christ had become a man for us, poor lost men, had taken upon Himself the hardships of human life, and had borne the sins of the whole world, had made atonement for them in Gethsemene and on Golgotha, and had poured out His blood upon the cross for the redemption of the world. * * * On this is founded the union of a congregation, consist-ing of souls who have received the forgiveness of their sins through the blood of Jesus. * * * The importance of the covenant into which he entered through baptism was then laid upon the heart of the can-didate. To the questions whether he desired to forsake the world, to be washed from sin in the blood of Jesus, through holy baptism enter into the congregation of redeemed sinners, and live for the Lord, he clearly answered Yes. The candidate knelt, and Br. Graff, in the name of Jesus Christ, pronounced him free from the power of Satan, the world and sin, and prayed that the Saviour would wash him from all sin, and through baptism accept him as His own property. Then in the name of the Holy Trinity he was baptised into the death of Jesus, receiving the name Benjamin David. Then the newly baptised man prayed, and in several stanzas the congregation promised him that the Saviour would keep his soul in the congregation of the living. As the congregation rose from prayer the new member was raised by his sponsors, and Br. Graff pronounced the blessing of the Lord upon him, and his sponsors led him out, that in quiet he might muse upon the grace received.

March 24. Palm Sunday, and the entrance into the Passion Week. Instruction was continued for the candidates for the Lord's Supper.

March 28. We heard to our sorrow that last night Johann Höhns, Philip and Peter Rothrock, were openly robbed, while they were forced to look on. Three rascals fell on Höhns in the road near his house, bound him, and would not let him or his wife stir in his house, but with pistols at their breast threatened to shoot them. The same thing happened to the two Rothrocks. This frightened us not a little.

March 31. On the holy Easter Day we rejoiced in the resurrection of our Lord Jesus Christ, and at nine o'clock prayed the Easter litany on God's Acre. In the meeting of the Society it was arranged that members of the Society should be spoken with each quarter.

April 5. I was in Salem for the meeting of the Land-Arbeiter-Conferenz. The most important decision reached was that in future, here as in Pennsylvania, candidates for the Lord's Supper in the country congregations must be approved by the Lord for Confirmation, but that meanwhile we should continue to instruct them.

April 14. Sunday. There was a lovefeast for those who within the year have been received into the congregation and admitted to the Lord's Supper,—the first such lovefeast for the congregation here.

April 18. We heard that the well-known Sieverberg and Nils Lund have moved into the neighborhood, and are staying with George Hartmann until their new house can be built.

May 11. The Single Sr. A. Maria Quest spoke with the unmarried women and girls, in view of their festival which will be held tomorrow.

May 16. Our neighbor, Thomas Lang, asked for the baptism of his infant son.

May 26. The child of Peter and Margaretha Korbman was baptised. The Brethren elected a new Committee, consisting of Peter Frey, Christel Frey, J. Adam Fischel and Martin Walk.

June 2. Br. Marshall spoke with the Committee about the School-house land. In congregation council Br. Marshall stated that it was now possible to bring the matter of the School-house land in order, and proposed that a Deed should be given; this was approved, and the Deed will stand in Br. Marshall's name.

June 16. In a Society meeting the Rules and Regulations of the congregation were read. Three weeks ago a mad dog on the main road bit several dogs of families living near. Remedies were used, and it was thought that danger had been averted, but now the dogs have gone mad. This has caused much anxiety, and parents are afraid to let their children come to school. We are thankful that no person has been injured here, though we hear that has happened in other places.

July 1. My wife was sick with high fever.

July 6. Br. Graff held the Lord's Supper for forty-six communicants. I enjoyed this high privilege with my dear wife, who was on her sick-bed and had it for her last time on earth.

July 10. Br. Reitz, Br. Yarrell and Sr. Bonn came from Salem to do what they could for my wife.

July 11. In the morning about six o'clock it pleased the dear Saviour to take my dear wife peacefully into her eternal rest. Great as was my sorrow the presence of the Saviour comforted me.

July 12. At one o'clock she was laid to rest, Br. Graff making the address. Attendance on the funeral was large, many coming from Salem and other places.

July 13. I went to Salem to rest a little, returning on the 14th.

July 21. The Single Br. Friedrich Priem came to keep me company and help me in various ways.

July 26. Neighbor Zimmerman came to see me, and expressed his wish to join our Society. I told him that if he desired this purely and simply for the salvation of his soul, and would give his whole heart to the Saviour, seek and find grace in the blood and wounds of Jesus, and so conduct himself in word and deed as to bring honor to the Saviour, we would rejoice over it. He assured me that this was his desire, and I allowed him to attend the meeting of the Society.

Aug. 29. Br. Holland brought the affecting news that it had pleased the Saviour to take His faithful servant, our dear Br. Graff, into his eternal rest. I spread the word here, and Br. Spach took it to Br. and Sr. Fritz at Hope.

Sept. 13. In the third service the Memoir of our dear Br. Graff was read.

Oct. 6. Br. Priem spoke with the single men, and I spoke with the married couples.

Oct. 26. There was a lovefeast for the postponed celebration of the Married People's covenant day. It was held by Br. Marshall.

Nov. 17. The communicant and received members had a post-celebration of the festival of the Chief Elder. There was an address on the Text for Nov. 13th, which led to the thought that though we are a poor and needy congregation yet we should have grace to share in what our Lord and Chief Elder is as the Head of His Unity, and what He will be; that we may be under His rule and special care, that He will feed us like a Shepherd, and that each member may rejoice in His individual leading.

Dec. 8.   The house-fathers and mothers were reminded that parents should be more careful about sending their children to school, and it was pointed out that it would injure them and their children if they were remiss in this respect.

Dec. 9 and 10.   Our people were busy repairing the fence around God's Acre.

Dec. 25.   Many people gathered from the neighborhood, so that the Saal could not hold them. The preaching was on Luke II, 1-14. This was followed by a lovefeast for the children, at the close of which verses were distributed to them.

Dec. 31.   In the evening the congregation and Society had a love-feast. * * * At half past eleven the congregation met for the close of the year.

Friedland and Hope, 1782.

[There is very little preserved about Friedland and Hope for the year 1782. The following extracts are taken from the *Extract der Diarii der Gemeiner in der Wachau.*]

Jan. 1.   In Friedland the Society had a happy lovefeast in thankful remembrance of the kindness of the Lord; then the communicant and received members, in their liturgical service, promised new obedience and faithfulness to the Saviour.

Jan. 15.   In the German settlement near Hope, Br. Fritz held the funeral of Philipp Wagner, and preached a sermon to a large audience.

Feb. 9.   The Land-Arbeiter-Conferenz having decided that all Society members should be spoken with each quarter-year, Br. Heinzmann made a beginning in Friedland.

Feb. 17.   The Brn. Benzien and Petersen visited Friedland. The rule was established that in the country congregations applications for membership should be laid before the communicants, that action may be taken more intelligently on information furnished by those who know them best.

March 3.   In Hope, after the Society meeting, the communicants met for the first time as a congregation council. The purpose of a congregation council was explained to them, and it will meet at eight-week intervals. The members rejoiced in the organization of a council, expecting a blessing from it.

April 1. Br. and Sr. Marshall spent the day in Friedland. After the preaching, Br. Marshall made an address to the Society, and two persons were Received into the congregation.

April 14. In Friedland, Br. Jacob Ried was elected Steward in place of Friedrich Müller.

April 28. Br. Fritz preached in the German settlement near Hope.

May 11. The communicants in the country congregations partook of the Lord's Supper. Br. and Sr. Marshall went to Hope, Br. and Sr. Graff to Friedberg, and Br. and Sr. Praetzel to Friedland. In the communion lovefeast the members were told of the results of Br. Marshall's visit to the Assembly. Celebration of the Communion followed.

May 12. At all three places the Communion liturgy was followed by public preaching. In a meeting of communicants attention was drawn to the story of this important anniversary of the Brethren's Unity. They were also informed of the resolution adopted by the Land-Arbeiter-Conferenz, that hereafter candidates for Communion, having been instructed concerning the Lord's Supper, must receive permission from the Lord to be Confirmed.

May 19. In Hope the day was made memorable by the baptism of an adult negro, the first such occasion there. The candidate was the negro Jupiter, belonging to the older Douthits.

May 26. Br. Fritz was preaching in the German settlement, so Br. Benzien held the service in Hope, and laid their Choir Principles before the unmarried men and boys. The Principles were taken from the Extract of the Results of General Synod. This was the beginning of such instruction there.

June 2. In Friedland, Br. Marshall spoke with the house-fathers about their treatment of strangers seeking work in the settlement. In Hope, their Choir Principles were read to the unmarried women from the Extract of the Results of Synod. From time to time additional information will be given them about each point. Br. and Sr. Fritz visited most of the members on their farms this week.

June 4. The Single Srs. Elisabeth Colver and Mar. Elis. Krause, returned to Salem. They have been in Hope since the 1st, taking charge of their group there.

June 30. In Hope, the Extract of the Results of Synod have been read to the congregation and Society in three meetings during this month.

Aug. 26. Br. and Sr. Marshall, Br. Benzien and other Brethren from Salem, attended the congregation festival at Hope. During the lovefeast the story was told of the organization of the little congregation two years ago, and a suitable festal Ode was sung. In the following meeting Br. Marshall spoke on the Texts of yesterday and today. This service was followed by the Holy Communion.

Oct. 26. The three country congregations had a post-celebration of the Married People's festival.

1783.

[On Jan. 20, 1783, a Preliminary Treaty of Peace[1] was signed at Paris, which virtually terminated the war. This good news was officially announced to the North Carolina Assembly by Governor Alexander Martin on April 19th,[2] and before the Assembly adjourned[3] it instructed the Governor to appoint July 4th as a day of public thanksgiving. On April 23rd, General Greene dismissed the last of his troops on furlough. On April 30th[4] a Proclamation of Congress reached North Carolina, declaring "the cessation of arms as well by sea as land," and orders were given for the release of prisoners of war.

The full Treaty of Peace was signed in Paris on Sept. 3, 1783. In October the representatives of the United States in Congress assembled issued a Proclamation[5] appointing the second Thursday in December as a Day of Thanksgiving that the Lord "has been pleased to conduct us in safety through all the perils and vicissitudes of the War," and "in the course of the present year hostilities have ceased, and we are left in the undisputed possession of our liberties and Independence." Thanks were also to be given "for plentiful harvests, the light of the blessed Gospel, and the rights of conscience in faith and worship." North Carolina was the only State that anticipated the national day of thanksgiving by celebrating the Fourth of July, and so far as is known the Moravians were the only group within the State to obey the Proclamation of Governor Martin.

General Washington took leave of his officers at New York on Dec. 4, 1783.]

Memorabilia of the Congregations in Wachovia. 1783.
[Extracts translated.]

It is impossible for man to record all the wonders of grace, faithfulness and mercy which our God and Saviour has shown to His Unity of Brethren in Wachovia during the year 1783. Yet we bring to Him the heartfelt thanks which are due, in that He has given to us and to all congregations in America, yea to the whole land, the gift of honorable peace, for which we have sighed during eight years of the stress and

---

[1] The text is given in the *Colonial Records*, Vol. XIV, pp. 748-752.
[2] *Colonial Records*, Vol. XIV, p. 773, Vol. XIX, p. 240.
[3] Friday, May 16, 1783, the House "Resolved, that the fourth Day of July be and is hereby appointed a day of General Thanksgiving and praise to Almighty God, * * * and that his Excellency the Governor notify the same by Proclamation." *Colonial Records*, Vol. XIX p. 385. Concurred with by Senate, same day. *Colonial Records*, Vol. XIX, p. 223. For text of the Proclamation see Part III, this volume.
[4] *Colonial Records*, Vol. XIV, p. 781, Vol. XIX, p. 287.
[5] *Colonial Records*, Vol. XVI, p. 906.

alarm of war. During February two parties of Light-horse marched through our settlement, and on May 22nd one hundred malcontent soldiers passed on their way home. On the day in which we remembered the rest of our Lord in the grave, that is on April 19th, just eight years after the first action of the war at Lexington, we received certain information that Preliminaries of Peace had been signed at Paris on January 20th; and on November 23rd we heard that the definite Peace Treaty between England, France, Spain and America had been signed on September 3rd. By order of the government of this State we celebrated a day of thanksgiving on July 4th, for the re-establishment of peace, and with all our hearts we rejoiced before the Lord our God with instrumental music and songs of joy. We still hold in thankful remembrance the blessed sabbatic peace of the entire day, and especially the evening procession.

The local congregations have gone their way quietly and undisturbed during this year of peace. The Gospel has also been preached to our friends on Reedy Fork, Deep Creek, in the German settlement, and at other places.

What shall the congregation of Salem say about the Saviour? Truly He has loved us as children; that is proven by His fatherly dealings with us. When the spirit of extravagance and independence turned us from His way, when we forgot His command to love Him and each other,[1] He disciplined us for the restoration of our peace. Oh, how our mouths were filled with praise and thanksgiving when as forgiven sinners we might again partake of the Supper of the Lord:

During this year earnest consideration was given to the possibility of taking the Gospel to the Cherokee Indians, so fulfilling one of the purposes for which the Saviour planted our little congregations in North Carolina. The making of a Treaty with the Indians on the Holston, after peace was established, gave opportunity for a visit to them, and the Saviour approved that Br. Martin Schneider should go thither to look into conditions and report, after which further consideration of the matter could take place. On Dec. 15th Br. Schneider went to Col. Martin Armstrong, and on the 19th set out on his journey into the Indian country. This has awakened the witness spirit in many of our Brethren. In this connection we bring our thanks to God for the news received in November that our Brethren and Sisters serving among the northern Indians are safely settled on the Huron River,[2] where they are gathering the scattered brown sheep.

---

[1] From the Diary, Minute Books and letters it appears that a controversy over the price of butter was the immediate cause of the trouble, as butter was being bought by the store for shipment out of town when the general supply in town was short.

[2] At New Gnadenhütten, now Clinton, Mich.

Our Heavenly Father has provided for our support, and has blessed our handicrafts and shops. The Diaconies of Salem congregation and of the Choirs of Salem, and the Diaconie of Bethabara, have been able to meet their obligations.

During most of the year we have been spared from sickness, but in November and December there was an outbreak of Measles, from which many of our Brethren have suffered.

Our needy Brethren and Sisters have received their share of the gift sent by the Brethren and Sisters in Europe for the relief of the Brethren and Sisters in North America who suffered during the war, and we wish God's blessing upon the kind givers.

Although peace has come, the crossing of the ocean is still dangerous, some packages have been lost, and our correspondence with Europe is not as we would wish. In June we received the encouraging news that a Visitation would be made [in America] by Br. Johannes [von Watteville] and his [wife] Benigna, and that Br. and Sr. Koehler and their party would come also. We were also glad to learn that Br. Reichel had become the correspondent for our local congregations.

During the year we have finished reading the *Idea Fidei Fratrum,* and as the Watch-Words for the year were taken from the Psalms we have read the book of Psalms in our Bible-reading meetings.

The Choirs have been blessed in their special festal days, have each had Choir Communion twice,[3] and have renewed their Choir covenants.

The congregations in Wachovia, at the close of the year 1783, consist of 340 communicants, 54 received, 203 not received, and members of the Societies, a total of 597. To these are to be added 407 children, making 1,004 persons connected with the congregations of the Brethren in Wachovia. Some of these live outside the Wachovia tract. The total population of Wachovia is about 1,100, including those who do and those who do not belong to the Moravian congregations.

Salem Diary, 1783.

[Extracts translated.]

Jan. 1. At the close of this first day of grace the Te Deum was sung, accompanied by the trombones.

Jan. 4. A bush-fire, driven against our fences by a strong north-west wind, made much trouble, but was extinguished by the rain which followed.

---

[3] Except, of course, the Choir of children.

Jan. 6.   Br. Traugott Bagge left for the Assembly at Hillsborough. Br. Benzien accompanied him, partly to meet the public men, and acquaint himself with conditions in the State, and partly to visit Stinking Quarter on his return trip, and preach there, as had been requested.

Jan. 7.   By Mr. Brown we sent a package of letters to Pennsylvania.

Jan. 9.   There was a snow-storm and glaze-ice.

Jan. 12.   The Choir of Boys celebrated their festival.

Jan. 17.   The Brn. Petersen and Stotz went to Captain Lapp, who has just returned with goods from Charlestown.

Jan. 18.   Br. Bagge returned from Hillsborough, the Assembly having dissolved.

Jan. 19. Sunday.   This is the fiftieth jubilee of the beginning of the Greenland Mission, and we took particular interest in it because one of the first missionaries going thither, Br. Matthaeus Stach, is now in our midst. The anniversary was celebrated in the following manner:—At the meeting of the congregation in the afternoon letters from Greenland were read, telling of the progress of the three congregations there, won from among the heathen. Then the congregation council and certain additional Brethren and Sisters had a happy lovefeast, which was opened by singing: *The glory of the Lord shall be revealed,* with the reply: *The glory of the Lord has been revealed.* Then Br. Stach, who came from Bethabara with his wife this morning, told the story of the beginning of the Greenland Mission, of the help of the Saviour through all difficulties, and of the blessing which attended the preaching of the Gospel to the heathen Greenlanders. Br. Benzien had composed a beautiful Ode for the day, reminding us of the most notable events connected with the Greenland mission, and this was sung at the evening service. Br. Stach was much moved to think that in his old age he might see this day, and the congregation shared in his emotion.

Feb. 5.   The Brn. Bagge and Schober set out for Charlestown, to see what the business prospect was since the English have left.

Feb. 9.   A division of General Wain's[4] troop, fifty light-horse, came from Georgia on their way to Winchester, where they will await further orders from General Washington. They camped for the night, and were provided with provisions. The officers attended the singstunde and were quiet and attentive. After singing a hymn, Br. Praetzel spoke on the Text for the day.

---

[4] General Anthony Wayne.

Feb. 13. A second division of General Wain's troops, forty in number, camped here over night, marching on to Winchester next day. Their officers attended the singstunde.

Feb. 20. The Single Brethren had a farewell lovefeast with Br. Koffler, who has faithfully served this Choir for twenty years. A fire that broke out in the Brothers House was discovered in time, and extinguished. In a public service at eight o'clock, Br. Friedrich Peter made an address on the Watch-Word for the day, and with the usual liturgy Br. Adam Koffler was married to the Single Sr. Maria Magdalena Reutz.

Feb. 21. The Friday liturgy was omitted because of a heavy rain, and during the night there was a thunderstorm.

Feb. 27. Br. Goetje took the place of Br. Koffler as Saaldiener, and Br. Tycho Nissen became forester.

March 1. The Brn. Bagge and Schober returned safely from Charlestown, though they had been much hindered on the way thither by rain and high water. A year ago the well-known Andreas Eusebius Hoecher[5] died in Charlestown. The beginning of the Unity of Brethren 327 years ago was stressed in the evening service.

March 3. Br. Priem returned from Friedberg. Br. and Sr. Adam Koffler went to Friedberg as assistants in that congregation. Br. Reutz began work on the cellar of his new house.

March 9. Br. Bagge went to Richmond to stand for re-election as Assemblyman.

March 10, and the following day many of the Brethren were at the election in Richmond. Letters were sent north with Friedrich Müller's wagon.

March 12. We learned that Martin Armstrong was elected Senator, and James Martin and Lewis[6] were elected Burgesses. Mr. Haversham's negroes passed on their way to Georgia.

March 15. Br. and Sr. George Bibighaus moved to Bethabara, where he will open a branch of the Salem store.

March 19. Since the 17th we have had heavy rain-storms, and the streams are high.

March 25. The older girls celebrated their festival. Br. Sam Stotz left for Pennsylvania and New York, where he will try to secure payment of our English Tickets. He went as far as Bethabara today, where he will be joined by the elder Br. Stauber.

---

[5] See under Eusebius, in Vols. 2 and 3, this series.
[6] William Terrill Lewis.

March 29. Br. Marshall went to Friedberg, to join the Committee in discussing the building of a new church.

April 4. With wagons going to Pennsylvania for goods for the store, we sent a package of letters.

April 5. In the prayer meeting, Br. Marshall began to read to the congregations the reports from the Synod of 1782.

April 18. Mr. James Haversham and his family, who arrived yesterday on their way to Georgia, attended all the services of Good Friday. He and his lady spoke most appreciatively of the stay of Br. Wagner in Georgia, and wished that they could again have such Brethren with them. They remained until

April 19, Great Sabbath, when they continued their journey. On the other hand his brother, Joseph Haversham, arrived yesterday, and today attended the Sabbath lovefeast, and the next day was present at the praying of the Easter litany, leaving with expressions of satisfaction with what he had heard here.

We were much impressed by the fact that on this day, which commemorated the rest of our Lord in the tomb, we received the first reliable news that rest will again be possible in this land through the peace made in Paris on January 20th of this year.

April 20. Easter Sunday. The congregation met in the Saal at five o'clock, and went from there to the graves of those who have fallen asleep, where the Easter litany was prayed in the felt presence of the risen Lord.

Br. Johann Stotz left for Bethlehem, where he will remain. He took with him letters and our diary for March.

May 4. The Single Sisters celebrated their festival. After a long drought we had a hard rain.

May 6. Through Mr. Elliott we received from Salisbury a copy of the ratification on February 3rd of the Peace Preliminaries of January 20th.

May 7. Nine packages of letters and Nachrichten arrived with Friedrich Müller's wagon, sent on by Br. George Neisser, of Yorktown.

May 18. In the children's service there was the baptism, in English, of the infant daughter of our friends James and Hannah Brown. In the evening there was the marriage of Br. Gottfried Praetzel and Sr. Maria Elisabeth Engel.

May 22. One hundred Virginia dragoons, malcontents, arrived from General Greene's camp, and camped on the brick-yard. What they asked was furnished. Some of them attended the singstunde, and

May 23, they marched on toward home, after having done much damage in Br. Meyer's field of oats by pasturing their horses there.

Today we had the pleasure of beginning a home-school[7] with three of our little boys, Samuel Meyer, Charles and Benjamin Bagge, under the supervision of the Brn. Joseph Dixon and Christian Stauber. Br. Triebel has moved into his new quarters, and his former dwelling[8] has been cleared out for the school. These three children, with the day-scholars and the members of the Aeltesten Conferenz and Grosse Helfer Conferenz, had a lovefeast, during which Br. Praetzel was installed as their house-father, and an Ode of thanksgiving was sung.

May 24. Two parties of dragoons arrived, but on being refused the pasturage they desired they went further.

June 1. Br. Feisser's wagon returned from Pennsylvania, with goods for the store.

June 6. We had a hard storm, with heavy rain, which was good for the parched earth.

June 10. During a hard storm lightning struck a fence post near the leather-dresser's shop.

June 11. There was a storm of rain and hail, and we thanked God that it did no great damage.

June 22. Br. Stauber, Sr., has returned safely from Pennsylvania.

June 26. There was a conference of the master-workmen, to consider getting rid of the many clipped, underweight pieces of money now in circulation.

June 28. Br. Sam Stotz returned safely from his journey, during which he visited in Pennsylvania and attended to business in New York. [I, by request of the claimants, went in May, 1783, to New York, which Gen. Sir Guy Carleton was then preparing to evacuate. I stated our business in a Petition to the General himself, upon which he appointed a number of Commissioners to examine all our Claims, and to register in a particular book such of them as they should find or think to merit further notice. The above-mentioned Gregory Townsend, Esq., was president of this board, and he as well as the other Commissioners expressed himself quite in favour of all the Claims * * * that they would undoubtedly be paid tho they could not say when, * * * Having settled matters so far I appointed the Rev. Ewald Gustav Shewkirk, then living in New York, by Power of Attorney.

---

[7] It is difficult to translate *Anstalt* satisfactorily. Preparation was made for the full care of these little boys, except that they ate dinner and supper with their parents. They received the scholastic instruction suited to their years, and their free time and their health habits were carefully supervised.

[8] It stood on the north-west corner of Main and Academy Streets.

* * * He gave like Power of Attorney to J. G. Wollin, of London, who died in 1792. His son and La Trobe have tried, but only received the friendly intimation that in the proper season we should not be forgotten.][9]

From letters we received the pleasant information that Br. Johannes and his Benigna will make a Visitation in North America, and will leave Barby in August, accompanied by Brethren and Sisters destined partly for the northern but chiefly for the Wachovia congregations.

June 30. Governor Martin passed on his way to Salisbury.

July 2. The pregnant Sisters of Salem and Bethabara celebrated their festal day.

July 4. According to the order of the government of this State we celebrated a day of thanksgiving for the restoration of peace. The congregation was awakened by the trombonists. At the beginning of the preaching service the Te Deum was sung, with trombone accompaniment. The Watch-Word for January 20th, the day on which the Peace Preliminaries were signed, was: *The God of Jacob is our refuge,* taken from the 46th Psalm, which gave opportunity to use this Psalm as the text for the sermon, which was preached by Br. Benzien. The service closed with the singing of: *Glory to God in the highest.* At two o'clock there was a happy lovefeast, during which a Psalm of Joy[10] [filed with the *Extract der Diarii*] was sung with thankful hearts. In the evening at eight o'clock the congregation again assembled in the Saal, and the choir sang: *Praise be to Thee, Who sittest above the cherubim.* Then the congregation formed a circle in front of the Gemein Haus, and from there passed in procession through the main street of the town, with music and the antiphonal song of two choirs. The street was illuminated. Returning to the Gemein Haus the congregation again formed a circle, and with the blessing of the Lord was dismissed to rest. Hearts were filled with the peace of God, evident during the entire day and especially during the procession, and all around there was silence, even the wind being still.

July 28. Br. Beck left for Pennsylvania in Friedrich Boeckel's wagon.

---

[9] From a report written by Samuel Stotz; undated but probably written in 1795 when another attempt was being made to collect. The report is in the Museum of the Wachovia Historical Society.

[10] The first stanza, freely translated, reads:

> Peace is with us, Peace is with us,
>   People of the Lord;
> Peace is with us, Peace is with us,
>   Hear the joyful word!
> Let it sound from shore to shore,
> Let it echo evermore,
> Peace is with us, Peace is with us,
>   Peace, the gift of God.

July 29. Br. Ludwig Moeller, and several of the younger Brethren from Friedberg, set out on horseback for Pennsylvania, intending to remain there.

Aug. 7. Br. Martin Schneider was nominated as Road-master, in place of Br. Yarrell, the nomination being confirmed by·the court some days later.

Aug. 13. The congregation celebrated this noteworthy day of the Brethren's Unity. The country ministers came to Salem for the services.

Aug. 14. The Brn. Bagge and Reutz went to court at Richmond. The former was there on the 12th also.

Aug. 17. The little girls celebrated their festal day.

Aug. 18. There was an unusually hard storm in the evening.

Aug. 24. Br. Marshall explained to the congregation the new organization of the Hourly Intercession. Some members shall serve continually on account of their offices, but others shall be drawn every eight weeks,[11] so that in turn all communicants shall belong.

Aug. 26. The congregation of Hope celebrated its congregation festival.

Aug. 27. Colonel Moore and Mr. Penn attended the rehearsal of the music for Brothers' Festival, and enjoyed it.

Aug. 29. The Single Brethren celebrated their festal day. Br. Rose, of Bethabara, brought his son, Gottfried Peter Rose, to enter the boys' boarding-school.

Aug. 31. In connection with the church litany, the blessing of the Lord was asked for the Widows and Widowers, this being their covenant day.[12] In the afternoon the Single Sisters had a lovefeast, sermon and Communion; our three Widows attended these services, which made their festal day a blessed reality.

Sept. 1. This week and the following the Auditors were in session here. Two of them had to go home on account of sickness, so they did not finish their business. The great heat has been followed suddenly by cool weather and rain.

Sept. 3. Tonight and the night following there was frost; at some places the corn was frozen.

Sept. 4. All the Taxables in our town signed a Petition against a division of our county, which some persons are trying to secure. It will be signed by all our taxable members who live in this county.

---

[11] The names of members were written on small cardboard quills, easily handled. In the Salem Archives there are several boxes of these quills, the boxes marked to indicate the Choir and whether the names had been drawn or were awaiting drawing.
[12] Celebrated elsewhere in the Unity, but not in Wachovia as their numbers were too few.

Sept. 8. Monday. The Married People celebrated their festival, postponed from yesterday.

Sept. 14. Governor Alex. Martin stopped on his way to Salisbury.

Sept. 25. Br. Peter told the children that on Michaelmas they would have their first prayer-day.

Sept. 27. Governor Martin spent the night here on his way home[13] from Salisbury.

Sept. 30. At midnight we had the pleasure of welcoming Br. and Sr. Valentine Beck, and the Single Srs. Anna Green, Elisabeth Schneider and Anna Maria Stotz.

Oct. 7. Br. and Sr. Koffler returned from Friedberg, where they have been for seven months, and Br. and Sr. Beck went thither. The evening meetings were omitted because of a severe storm, which during the night assumed almost the proportions of a hurricane, damaging buildings, fences and gardens, and blowing down many trees in the woods.

Oct. 8. About nine o'clock the wind lulled. We thank God that no serious damage was done. We hear that in Cross Creek the river has risen and has damaged goods in low-lying storehouses.

Oct. 18. On account of a rain-storm there could be no evening service, and we could only think in private of the birthday of Br. Johannes, and pray that the Saviour will give him and his company a safe crossing.

Oct. 22. Because of heavy rain there could be no evening meeting.

Oct. 26. The Srs. Graff and Quest went to Bethabara; the former will take special charge of the Sisters there, and will stay there a few days from time to time.

Oct. 31. At the close of this month it should be added that the building of a Choir House for the Single Sisters, under consideration for some time, has come so far that a committee has been appointed to advise concerning it and to make the necessary preparations this winter.

Recently there have been an unusual number of wolves in our neighborhood, and some panthers have been seen, of which one has approached our houses several nights. Mad dogs are also running about, and have done damage at various places. We thank God that we have been shielded from harm; from other places we hear alarming stories, and among us there have been things which have warned us to be on guard.

---

[13] He had a plantation known as *Danbury* on the south side of Dan River and both sides of Jacobs Creek, in what was then Guilford but is now Rockingham County.

Nov. 2. We sent letters and diaries to Pennsylvania by Mr. Fox.

Nov. 3. The Brn. Samuel Stotz and Gottlieb Schober left in a wagon for Charlestown, the latter to buy goods for the store. Today the lot for the new Sisters House was staked out, and between that and the Gemein Haus lot the digging of a well was begun.

Nov. 13. This festal day commemorated the Chief Eldership of Jesus in the Unity of Brethren, and also the organization of our congregation twelve years ago.

Nov. 21. Letters were sent north by Mr. Wagner, who came from Pennsylvania some time ago, and is now returning.

Nov. 22. This morning the affecting news came from Friedland, that our dear Br. Johann Casper Heinzman had been called home suddenly after a short attack. Br. Praetzel went thither to make arrangements for the funeral.

Nov. 23. Through Br. Sam Stotz, who wrote from Charlestown, we heard the glad tidings that a definite Peace Treaty was signed on September 3rd between England on the one side and France, Spain and America on the other. Now we can feel certain that peace has been made.

Nov. 25. The Brn. Stotz and Schober returned safely from Charlestown. The well for the Sisters House has reached water at forty-two feet, and will be walled up.

Nov. 30. Today the first snow of the season fell.

Dec. 1. With Schick's wagon we sent letters and our October diary to Pennsylvania.

Dec. 2. Br. Fritz, who came from Hope, married our negro Br. Christian, of Bethabara, to the negress Patty, who is a candidate for baptism. The marriage took place at the tavern.

Dec. 9. Br. and Sr. Reutz moved into their new house, and dedicated it to the Lord with a lovefeast, attended by the members of the Aeltesten Conferenz and the men who had helped with the building.

Dec. 11. Our Pennsylvania congregations, by the high order of Congress, are observing this as a day of thanksgiving for peace. In the prayer-meeting, which Br. Friedrich Peter held, we united with them in thanking the Lord for the re-establishment of peace, and in praying for the good of the land and those who govern it.

Dec. 13. During this week several of our Brethren and boys have developed measles and more are taking it. Through the arrival of Br. Heinrich Schneider from Pennsylvania we heard with pleasure that some of the Brethren and Sisters expected from Europe, who sailed from Hamburg and London, have reached Bethlehem safely.[14]

Dec. 14. Br. Martin Schneider will leave for Long Island of Holston River tomorrow.

Dec. 20. We received a letter from Br. Martin Schneider, written on the 19th. He reached the home of Colonel Armstrong on the 15th, and found that measles in the family would postpone the Colonel's journey to the Indian country. He therefore spent his birthday, the 18th, in Bethania, and planned that on the 19th he would set out alone, provided with a recommendation to Colonel Sevier and Colonel Martin on Long Island and a Pass from Colonel Armstrong. (He wrote later from New River that he had found a good traveling companion in Captain Nielsen.)

Dec. 24. The little children enjoyed their Christmas Eve service at five o'clock. In the evening the adults and older children had a lovefeast.

Dec. 25. Christmas. Br. Peter preached the festal sermon. In the evening the married negress Patty was baptised, receiving the name of Anna.

Dec. 26. The measles are now appearing among our little boys, who had escaped so far.

Dec. 30. Last night and today we have had a snow-storm.

Dec. 31. The adult congregation had a happy lovefeast at eight o'clock. At ten o'clock we gave thanks and praise for all the goodness of God, not alone during this year but through the eight years of the war. In the service which began at half past eleven we entered the new year to the sound of the trombones, trusting that we would receive in it new blessings from His hand.

Amen.

Salem Board Minutes, 1783.

Jan. 7. (Aufseher Collegium.) Br. Aust is willing to employ Br. Tycho Niessen in making clay pipes, which can be burned and sold in the pottery.

Jan. 8. (Aeltesten Conferenz.) Br. Oesterlein is beginning to melt copper pence, paying three shillings a pound for them. This is a good thing, and the bad silver should also be melted.

---

[14] This was not the von Watteville party, which sailed from Amsterdam on Sept. 27, 1783, and did not reach Bethlehem, Pa., until June 2, 1784.

Jan. 9. (Auf. Col.) Br. Reutz wishes to prepare to build his house. He proposes the corner lot,[1] opposite the two-story house and opposite the well, to which there is no objection.

The making of brick was discussed at length. Brick is essential for some parts of a building, but so far it has been too expensive to use for the entire building. If brick-making could be carried on properly, it would be best to use brick for the upper stories of all houses.

Jan. 10. (Land-Arbeiter-Conferenz.) Matthias Taylor, of Hope, speaks of going to the mountains to hunt beaver, thinking to improve his condition. We can not advise this, though we cannot forbid it.

Jan. 14. (Auf. Col.) As there are no roof-tiles on hand, it will be best to cover Charles Holder's house with shingles, and use the tiles from there to repair other roofs.

We believe that our tanyard will lose a good deal, and will get a bad name, if it refuses to tan hides for half as other people are doing and as people expect.

Jan. 15. (Aelt. Conf.) Joseph Dixon becomes a member of Congregation Council by virtue of his position as school-teacher. Br. Martin Schneider takes Br. Goetje's place as master-shoemaker.

Jan. 16. (Congregation Council.) If persons who visit the town do not feel that in all respects we seek their best interests we fail in the chief reason why our Saviour brought us here.[2]

Jan. 16. (Aelt. Conf.) Nathanael Pratter, who has been working on the farm in Bethabara, would like to be considered a resident.

In regard to the building of a mill near Bethania it was agreed that the mill lots and the building lot belonging to it should be valued in proportion to the lots held by the other house-holders in Bethania. Six per cent of the toll shall be paid for the use of the fall.

Jan. 23. (Auf. Col.) The contract between the Administration and Salem Congregation Diaconie provides that if the Mill and mill-land on the Wach should be sold to others the Administration should retain a sum equal to the capital on which it is receiving 5% as rent.

Jan. 23. (Aelt. Conf.) Br. Martin Schneider has received the largest vote from the Single Brethren for membership in the Helfer Conferenz, and this was approved by the Saviour, in the affirmative lot.

Jan. 28. (Auf. Col.) Br. Herbst has decided to tan for half the hides, if people ask it.

Jan. 29. (Aelt. Conf.) George and Friedrich Lang have asked Br. Lorenz Bagge to preach again on Deep Creek but this will have

[1] South-west corner of Main and Bank streets.
[2] Service of the scattered white neighbors was one of the three definite objects of the Wachovia settlement.

to wait until spring. Mr. Petri has asked him to come to the Town
Fork next Friday.

Feb. 6. (Cong. Council.) As remittances of considerable size must
be sent to Pennsylvania each year for interest and other payments,
it would be better for our commerce if money could be kept here for
circulation, and in place of that we could send products of the country,
even if there was no profit in it. The Brethren and Sisters were asked
to consider what we could buy up for the purpose, or what we could
suggest for cultivation for future use in this way. It looks as though
there might be a small trade in fur; but there is nothing except risk
in undressed deer-skins. Perhaps in time something can be done in
raising silk, though so far it has been a failure.

Feb. 7. (L-A-C.) Sarah Buttner's daughter, though she was received into the Society, does not attend the services at Hope and is
about to marry outside the Society; she shall no longer be considered
a member.

Feb. 12. (Aelt. Conf.) The need for a new building for the
Brothers House was discussed. It was agreed that it should be on
the main street, and that while it should be a separate building the
entrance to the new house should connect with the exit from the old.
A plan shall be drawn in good time, and preparations shall be made
gradually.

Feb. 18. (Auf. Col.) Several young Brethren have felled a tree
on Vogler's land and have made a canoe. As there is no use in it,
and it is to be feared that it will lead to the breaking of rules, they
cannot be allowed to keep it. If Br. Steiner wants to buy it for the
mill there is no objection.

The single man, Immanuel Dresen, who has worked for two years
in Salem, would like to become a resident. He was born Feb. 2, 1754,
on the Rhine, was brought up a Catholic, and learned from his father
the trade of a silver-smith. He also worked as a watch-maker. For a
year and a quarter he was with the Capucins on trial but did not take
the vows. He worked at his trade in Neuwied in Maestricht, then in
France. From there he went to Spain as attendant to a gentleman,
was seized as a soldier and taken to Africa, deserted with twenty-five
other men and took ship for Lisbon, where he delivered himself to a
Captain of a ship bound for Philadelphia, and served to pay his
transportation. He went to Long Island in the American service; then
served with the English, and was captured with Tarleton's Corps at
the Cowpens. Being in great need, he went into retirement, working
first at Friedland, and then here.

Feb. 19. (Aelt. Conf.) The Saviour did not approve[3] that we give Immanuel Dresen permission to become a resident of Salem. John Pratter has asked to become a resident of Bethabara.

Feb. 26. (Aelt. Conf.) The boy John Chiddy is destined for the leather goods business, and it will be well to place him for two months with Br. Christian Stauber, who will teach him to sew.

March 4. (Auf. Col.) Br. Kremser will leave the shoe-shop and work in the Single Brothers' kitchen.

Nothing could be done with the English Tickets in Charlestown. It was suggested that payment might be arranged in New York, through the American General there. Br. Stotz is planning a trip to Pennsylvania, and this may provide opportunity to see about it.

It would be well to have several hand sprinklers in the town for use in case of fire-alarms such as we have had recently. Br. Johann Krause can help in the matter.

March 5. (Aelt. Conf.) Br. Goetje shall be asked to show himself willing to mend shoes for the Sisters.

March 6. (Cong. Council.) Next week is the election, and it will be well for the Brethren to arrange that some of them go to Richmond on Monday and some on Tuesday to cast their votes. Colonel Armstrong is our choice as Senator, and Br. Bagge and Colonel Martin as Burgesses.

Many simple things happen among us which are not wrong in themselves, but as soon as they take place they change their aspect, either because of the time, the circumstances or the persons who engage in them, and then they must either have better supervision or be forbidden. Examples of this are the building of a canoe and riding around in it, skating, shooting, riding, etc.

March 7. (L-A-C.) The piece of ground in Friedland which Christoph Reich, of Haw River, has taken over, and which has been planted for him, has been stripped of fences. The seed will be ruined by cattle, and Reid, whose land adjoins, shall fence in the fields and shall be repaid by Reich.

Brethren in the country congregations shall be urged to go to the election and cast their votes for members of the Assembly who will be of real service to the public.

At the lovefeast of the Friedberg Society there can be a discussion of the plan to erect a new church building, and a committee can be elected to consider the matter and present resolutions to a meeting of the Society.

---

[3] Such decisions by lot were considered as for the moment only, and he was approved as a resident at a later time.

March 13. (Aelt. Conf.) When Casper Stolz moves to his new place near Billy Volk, he and Joseph Leinbach shall belong to the Bethania group.

It is difficult to provide the boys with bedding. Properly this should be done by the parents, but if they cannot afford it the Branches in which the boys are to work must look after it.

Demanding help in house-raising, and pressing work on the roads, is not a good thing for us, and shall be avoided.

Br. Reutz is about to dig his cellar, and the street shall be graded down before his wall is built.

March 20. (Aelt. Conf.) Ludwig Blum is under discipline for having pushed Jacob Bonn into Br. Reutz' cellar, and shall so remain until we see how it goes with Jacob Bonn, who is sick in bed.

To further observance of rules it will be well to make a plan for the taking of walks, and lay it before congregation council. The street from the bridge and leading toward Bethabara shall be the boundary between the walks. No. 1 shall comprise the road to Friedberg, to Stockburger, to Schulz, toward the Shallow Ford, to Schreyer and Schumaker. No. 2 shall have the roads toward Bethabara, Town Fork, Brushy Fork, to Vogler, and toward Friedland. On the Sunday after Communion and on Gemein Tag the Sisters shall have the use of No. 1, and the Brethren shall have No. 2; on the other Sundays it shall be reversed, the Brethren having No. 1, and the Sisters No. 2.

March 26. (Aelt. Conf.) Br. Blum, of Bethabara, has written a resentful letter to Br. Bagge, who sat as Justice in the case of Ludwig Blum. His position was probably caused by gossip from Salem, and it was decided to take up the matter with the communicant members. It will be well for Br. Traugott Bagge to have a friendly conversation with Br. Blum about the occurrence, and meanwhile Br. Lorenz Bagge can take occasion to point out that he has misunderstood.

March 28. (Auf. Col.) Br. Jacob Loesch asks whether he may now begin his gun-work. At present there seems no danger that his work would be required for regular troops, or lead to quartering in the town, and at most there would be need only for the repairing of arms for the militia if they should be called out. The Collegium therefore has no objections. The shooting range can be in the back part of the street between the store and Heinzmann's, but there must be no betting on shots.

Br. Meyer is in poor health, and wishes that a Brother could be selected to succeed him.

April 2. (Aelt. Conf.) The building committee in Friedberg consists of the Brn. Marshall, Beck and Koffler, thirteen members, and several other house-fathers. They have decided to build the new church as a separate house on the north side of the present one, but to connect the two by a diener kitchen.[4] The new house is to be thirty by thirty-five feet. Building cannot begin before fall.

Mr. Siverberg has spoken with Br. Marshall about the old Entry of 640 acres, the right to which he had bought from the Entry-taker. The Friedberg School-house stands on this land. While the claim of the Brethren to this Entry is probably safe, under a law of the recent Assembly, if the matter went into the courts, still to avoid a long-drawn-out affair it is good that in a recent conference of Br. Marshall with those who have part of the 640 acres Mr. Siverberg stated that he ceded his right in the same to Br. Marshall.

Br. Christian Loesch asks for a steady job; Br. Bagge needs help in the store, and he can go in for a while as Porter, receiving a weekly wage.

Br. Triebel has offered his garden for the use of the boys' school, and this should be accepted and the place put in order, so that the children may take their necessary exercise there.

Word has come that Br. Johann Stotz is wanted in Bethlehem, and the sooner the better. If Br. Herbst can arrange it, the journey can be made with Br. Bagge's wagon immediately after Easter.

April 8. (Auf. Col.) Br. Petersen reports that the Brethren think it will improve their lot to build a wall along the front and fill in the low place in the street.

April 29. (Auf. Col.) For lack of money the neighbors are bringing all sorts of products to town to exchange for things they wish, such as tobacco, wool, cotton, pieces of linen, tanned hides, and the like.

May 1. (Cong. Council.) There was further discussion of hand-sprinklers, and Br. Krause said he did not think they could be made out of wood to be found here.

The price of butter was discussed, but little is being brought in, so no price was set.

May 2. (L-A-C.) Philip Rothrock and his brother Peter, who attended a dance,[5] did not come to Communion, and shall be considered suspended.

---

[4] From which lovefeasts could be served.

[5] There are a number of entries in the Minute Books of 1783 which show the post-war re-action on the Moravian congregations of town and country, where the new spirit of independence led to a temporary revolt against the strict rules then obtaining. The items are translated, not so much to show problems of discipline as for the information they give regarding sports and merry-makings then in vogue outside of Moravian communities.

May 17. (Aelt. Conf.) The home-school [*Anstalt*] for boys will begin with three children, Samuel Meyer, Charles and Benjamin Bagge, under the supervision of the Brn. Joseph Dixon and Christian Stauber.

Br. Praetzel will be school-father, in which capacity he will look after the household management, the order and cleanliness of the boys. The boys will rise in summer at half past five, and in winter at six o'clock, and will go to bed at eight o'clock. They will have daily morning and evening prayers. They will take breakfast at the school, and Samuel Meyer will eat supper there. Br. Bagge's children will go home to supper at six o'clock, returning at half past six. In the middle of the day Br. Bagge's children will go to dinner at their home at half past eleven; Samuel Meyer will not go home until a quarter before twelve; they will all return to the school at half past twelve. The parents are to give each child his own comb and towel, but they will share a wash-pan, pitcher and jar. In summer the children shall each have a clean shirt twice a week; the sleeping-hall and the rooms shall be swept twice a week. The Brethren in charge must watch over the cleanliness and order, especially in regard to combing, washing, making beds and keeping them free of vermin, shining shoes, and so on.

May 22. (Auf. Col.) The committee on such matters considered what was to be done about a large party of cavalry from Washington's and White's troops, who have broken loose from their officers on the Congaree, and will pass through our town on their way to Virginia. We will have to serve them as well as we can, for example it will be better to point out a meadow for them to use than to have them seize one, better to butcher an ox for them, bake bread, and give quarters in the Tavern, at Stockburger's and in the watchman's house.

May 30. (L-A-C.) Kastner has chosen to marry the daughter of a Dunkard. It will not be wise publicly to turn him out, but the newly elected Friedland committee,—the Brn. Peter Kroen and Jacob Ried as Stewards, and the four Brn. Friedrich Müller, John Heyn, Johann Lanius and Friedrich Künzel,—can be asked whether they will recognize such a man as a Society Brother, and then they can tell the settlement of their decision.

The single women of Friedberg have asked for a post-celebration of the Single Sisters Covenant Day. Recently on Sunday, during service, there was a gathering of young people at Peter Frey's, and the same thing happened at Valentine Frey's. This must be looked into, but if the result is as we wish then the post-celebration may take place on the Monday after Whitsuntide.

June 3. (Auf. Col.) It will be sufficient for the Single Brethren to have a copy of the Minute of this Board,[6] under date of May 6th, and the plat belonging to it, and this will guarantee their rights in their lots.

An expense account shall be made out for the dragoons who were here recently. If the Auditors will allow their board some reduction shall be made.

June 5. (Cong. Council.) The cause of this meeting was a letter signed by eight members of congregation council and sent to the Aufseher Collegium. One of the signers expressed regret, and said that he was in favor of reducing the price of butter, but had no sympathy with the harsh terms of the letter. * * * After a thorough discussion it was decided that from now on only 10d should be paid for butter; and as some of the Brethren have almost no butter the store, if requested, will direct to their homes those who have butter to sell.

June 10. (Auf. Col.) It is rumored that Brethren and Sisters are availing themselves of the advice and help of conjurers and wise women. It will be necessary to discuss this in congregation council, for there are such people living not far from us.

June 11. (Aelt. Conf.) To avoid the disorder arising when everybody goes to the woods to shoot, it shall be made the duty of Br. Zillman or some other older Brother to hunt hawks and wild animals.

June 18. (Aelt. Conf.) The small group for Hourly Intercession will consist of the members of the Aeltesten Conferenz, the country ministers and their wives, and thirty-seven others.

It would be well for Br. Tycho Nissen to sing a verse occasionally during his night-watch.

June 19. (Cong. Council.) For some time it has been evident that slander and backbiting have been prevalent in this town, and that almost no rule or arrangement can be made in the congregation without arousing opposition or rebellion. If the spirit of variance cannot be broken this time it is sure to manifest itself at the next opportunity.

This condition has affected the services of the congregation, and few of the members from the upper town attend the singstunde, and but few come to the Saturday prayer meeting. There is much opposition to the musical liturgy on Friday, and it appears that it is regarded as a burden, as it interferes with the private gatherings which have been taking place during the singstunde. As innocent as

---

[6] It specified which lots were to belong to the Single Brethren, which were rented to them, and which they were to use temporarily without rent. Individuals took Leases to the property they held, but the Single Brethren were not incorporated, so this method was used.

RECORDS OF THE MORAVIANS IN NORTH CAROLINA 1853

may have been the beginning in one or another case, it is against all congregation rules, and contrary to the warnings of Synod, when such gatherings prevent members from attending the singstunden. The same applies to the custom of sitting in front of the houses in summer, talking with the neighbors, for a member who is not going to service ought to be polite enough to go home when the bell rings, so as not to prevent others from going. These illegitimate gatherings lead to a kind of *independence* of rules and regulations, the actions of the ministers of the congregation are criticised, faults in them and in other members are pointed out, amplified, and often things that have no existence are told.

It is clear that for our return there is no way except by the rule laid down by the Saviour, namely that each shall speak openly with the other.

June 30. (Aelt. Conf.) By *proclamation* of the Governor, the Fourth of July is to be celebrated as a Day of Thanksgiving for Peace. All our congregations shall be instructed to observe the day.

Br. Reichel has written that he submitted to the Unity's Elders Conference the request of our Single Sisters Choir for a kind contribution from the Single Sisters and congregations of Europe toward the proposed new building for the local Choir of Single Sisters. With the approval of the Unity's Elders Conference, the request has been sent to the Aeltesten Conferenzen in the congregations there.

It is only fair that each Sister in the Choir House here,—and the congregation,—should take part in the movement. The building proposal shall be officially announced to the congregation, which will lead to suggestions for assistance. It will be best for each room in the Sisters House to have its collection box, into which each Sister may place what she chooses each week. The head of each room shall take care of the box, and bring it to the House-conference, where the contents shall be counted and given to the Vorsteherin.

July 1. (Auf. Col.) A new fire ladder shall be made, and the old ones thoroughly repaired. A market-house would be very useful, though there is no prospect of one just now. Preparations should be made to secure the materials which must be brought from a distance for the new building for the Single Sisters.

July 2. (Aelt. Conf.) Next week is the time for Communion. Monday and Tuesday are especially set apart for conferences with the Brethren and Sisters, who are asked to open their hearts.

Kürschner, Sr., of Bethabara, has worked on Sunday, and has resented a warning. He shall be left to the civil authorities, and must pay his fine.

July 9. (Aelt. Conf.) Conferences with the members have shown that they are in a good frame of mind; they have talked over and have settled all misunderstandings among themselves. They are longing for the Lord's Supper, and we feel no hesitation in announcing it at the service tomorrow.

Concerning Br. Ludwig Moeller it was asked: *Does the Saviour approve that Br. Ludwig Moeller establish himself in Hope in the Jerseys?* The affirmative lot was drawn.

July 10. (Auf. Col.) Br. Johann Krause asks whether the price of boards will not soon be reduced at the mill? The price will regulate itself when Heinrich Schor and others in the neighborhood have begun work at their saw-mills.

July 15. (Auf. Col.) Charles Holder has undertaken to make a dozen leather fire-buckets for the Gemein Haus. Six shall hang on each side of the entry.

July 24. (Aelt. Conf.) Br. Jacob Wohlfahrt has received the largest vote from the Single Brethren for membership in the congregation council, and has been approved by the Saviour.

July 24. (Cong. Council.) In our litany there are several phrases which do not fit with the present constitution of the country. After considering two proposals it was decided to change the German, and to use the words: *Die Regierung dieser Lande und alle Obrigkeitliche Personen absonderlich in diesem Staat leiten und schützen;* the English phrase hitherto used shall be retained: *Guide and protect the dear Governors of the Lands wherein we dwell, and all that are put in authority under them.*

There was discussion of the lack of certain important buildings, for example *Anstalten,* a Widows House and a Single Sisters House. If circumstances permit the erection of one of these buildings, the room released can be used for other purposes. The building of a Sisters House will make full half of the Gemein Haus available for a girls' school or a Widows House. It is hoped that the local congregation will support this building, from which it will immediately profit. Br. Praetzel, as Curator, will have special oversight of the building, and will have a plan drawn which shall be submitted to all who understand the erection of houses, so that any errors may be corrected before anything is definitely determined.

It will soon be time to gather grapes. Special attention should be given to the prevention of disorder, and to seeing that no unripe grapes are brought in as they are unwholesome.

July 26. (Aelt. Conf.) We had intended to send an appeal to the Aeltesten Conferenz in Bethlehem, asking the Pennsylvania congregations to take up a collection for the Sisters House here, but we hesitate to do it at this time, since the Single Sisters of Nazareth are looking toward the building of a Choir House, and the Single Sisters in Lititz are planning an addition to their House.

July 31. (Helf. Conf.) The tavern must again put out a sign. Br. Holland's term as constable has expired. It would be well if a resident of the town could again be appointed.

Aug. 5. (Auf. Col.) Stockburger continues to speak of making brick on his farm. Gottlob Krause has proposed to make a burning of brick this year. The Sisters House building will require all the large and small brick that both of them can make.

The last Assembly raised the value of certain pieces of money, for example, Guineas are to be 37 sh. 4d, and Pistoreens 1 sh. 8d; the other coins remain as they have been.

Aug. 6. (Aelt. Conf.) Abraham Hauser asks permission to go to Richmond and place himself under the care of Dr. Rindelmann, and we cannot refuse him.

Aug. 12. (Auf. Col.) It will be well for Charles Holder to coat the fire-buckets with a good oil paint,—furnace paint.

The ground-plan and elevation of the proposed Sisters House was exhibited. It will be necessary to include in the Sisters House lot the back part of the lane between it and Br. Tycho Nissen, leaving the lane only fifty feet deep, but giving entrance through it into both lots. The suggestion to place the kitchen, wash-house and weave-room in an addition received the approval of most, though it will not look well from outside.

Aug. 20. (Helf. Conf.) At the last May court two roads were proposed and approved, one from here to David Murrahs', and one by way of Bernhard Fehr's to Belows Creek, which will give us a direct road to Pennsylvania. Martin Schneider has taken the position of road-master.

Sept. 16. (Aelt. Conf.) George Netter, an unmarried soldier, who has been working in Friedberg, asks for employment by the Single Brethren, and may be taken on trial.

Sept. 20. (Aelt. Conf.) We have long wished to go to the Indians of this section and teach them of their Creator and Redeemer. Col. James Martin has been appointed by the Assembly to go to the Indians twice a year, taking them messages from this State, and this appears to be an opportunity for the carrying out of our desire if a Brother could go thither with Colonel Martin. It will be well to ascertain whether Colonel Martin would be willing to take a Brother with him.

Sept. 24. (Aelt. Conf.) The children who are allowed to attend the *Anbeten*[7] shall be considered members of the Children's Congregation. If before another children's prayer-day a child misbehaves it cannot be allowed to attend.

The Brn. Marshall, Praetzel, Samuel Stotz and John Krause have been appointed a committee to superintend the building of the Sisters House.

Sept. 30. (Auf. Col.) The boards which Br. Steiner has contributed toward the building of the Sisters House can be piled on the Square. Br. Krause will have sweet-gum saw-logs cut near the mill, and boards an inch and a quarter thick shall be sawed for scaffolding.

Oct. 1. (Aelt. Conf.) Through letters from Pennsylvania we hear that Br. Lewis, of London, is coming here as doctor.

Oct. 4. (Aelt. Conf.) Br. Heinzmann writes that Br. Williard is going to marry a woman named Appel, from Stinking Quarter.

Oct. 7. (Auf. Col.) It will be well to order some iron tools from Lititz, as grubbing hoes, large cleavers, and shovels, and to order here boards, shingles and wheelbarrows. The surplus dirt from the Sisters House cellar can be used to improve the street between Heinzmann's and the tavern. A supply of water is the most serious question, but if a cistern is dug water can be turned into it during the night when summer comes.

Oct. 8. (Aelt. Conf.) The memoranda which Br. Peter has assembled concerning the protection which God vouchsafed to us during the American War shall be considered in a separate session.

Oct. 9. (Helf. Conf.) The Brethren were reminded that all who have not taken the Affirmation should do so before the limit set, that is the 17th of November. This applies particularly to the Brethren who have come from Pennsylvania recently. The Affirmation requires no more from a man than he would be obligated for as a Brother at any rate.

The paper money is beginning to depreciate in value. It will be well to wait quietly until its fate becomes clear, which will probably be soon.

Oct. 14. (Auf. Col.) The bricks which Cornelius Sale has made for Gottlob Krause are imperfect, and will not do for the outer wall.

---

[7] A service in which those present prostrated themselves in prayer. The adult Choirs used the form at certain times, and now the children were to have it as a forward step in their spiritual life.

Several of the Brethren have signed a petition for the opening of a road and ferry across the Atkin to Freeman's and Alex Long's plantations.

Oct. 17. (L-A-C.) The Brethren have been asked to furnish the number of all residents in Wachovia, large and small, which will lead to the making of a catalog of all living in Wachovia.

Oct. 28. (Auf. Col.) It was remarked that hunting could not be forbidden entirely, but the question was who should do it. If the wild animals can be driven from about our town it will keep scamps from camping near, and seizing every opportunity to steal.

Oct. 29. (Aelt. Conf.) Several Brethren in Europe, and especially one in Petersburg, have sympathized with the North American congregations in what they have suffered through the war, and have sent them a sum of money. When it has been divided, in Europe, between Pennsylvania and Wachovia, and the order for payment has been given by Br. Quandt, our share will be distributed among the most needy members in Salem, Bethabara and Bethania.

Nov. 4. (Auf. Col.) New pipes must be laid for the water-works. It was decided that the holes in the present pipes are too large, and the new ones shall be 1½ inch. A special auger shall be made, belonging to the congregation.

Nov. 6. (Cong. Council.) For some time there has been firing of guns in the woods on Sunday, which is against the law. We cannot say definitely how much of this has been done by our men. Hunting is one of the things which need to be handled with care, for several reasons. There is no objection to it when it is done openly, with the foreknowledge of the Choir Pfleger, and there is no bad company, betting, or the like. It is better for wild animals to be shot by Brethren than to have them gather around the town and attract objectionable persons. Whoever does not comply with the rules must expect to have hunting forbidden.

Bethabara has asked Br. Marshall to order a set of trombones for that town. We will order for Salem two D-sharp horns, a good bass, a set of trombones, and a supply of strings of various kinds. To cover the cost we think a general subscription can be taken when the instruments arrive.

Nov. 18. (Auf. Col.) A limit must be set for hunting and shooting, for not every one is careful for himself or for others, and there was nearly an accident recently.

Nov. 20. (Helf. Conf.) Br. Peter suggests that the liturgical service on Sunday evening shall be accompanied by trombones instead of trumpets, which is approved. We think it would be well if two of the younger Brethren would learn to play the French horn.

Nov. 26. (Aelt. Conf.) It would be difficult, under the circumstances, to arrange lodgings for Sr. Heinzmann in Salem, and it will be better for her to remain in Friedland at least for the winter, as the members there wish. She shall be consulted about this, and it shall be suggested that she send Elisabeth Hartmann to Salem as soon as possible, and take Elisabeth Schneider, of Friedland, to wait on her.

Dec. 1. (Auf. Col.) Threats have been made against Salem, the pretext being that the new paper money is refused. It will be necessary to receive it in the shops, but it will be better not to let it circulate in town but store it up for the paying of taxes. If some is left over it can be sent to a seaport, and the loss can be divided proportionately. Prices in the Branches can be raised in making sales, to reduce the loss.

Dec. 3. (Auf. Col.) Now is the time to fell trees for building material. The carpenters and masons shall have a conference to study the building plans, which have been completed. Br. Krause is opposed to making long beams of poplar.

Dec. 3. (Aelt. Conf.) Sr. Heinzmann is willing to remain in Friedland this winter and continue the school for girls.

Dec. 10. (Auf. Col.) Only oak timber shall be used for beams and rafters. Poplar also may be used for masons' laths, shores and cross beams. Moses Martin will furnish shingles 21 inches long for twenty-two shillings a thousand.

Dec. 12. (L-A-C.) Billy Peddycoart has returned from Maryland to Hope.

Dec. 23. (Auf. Col.) Br. Koffler reported that he has arranged with Br. Reitz to buy his house.[8] Br. Reitz will sell it for £210, letting him take the second lot with it.

Extract from Memorabilia of Bethabara, 1783.

Many times we have experienced the protection of our God through His angels, and especially in one instance when a child was lost from her father and from her farm and wandered more than three miles. She was found before night by her parents, who had gone out to search for her, many others from here and from Bethania having joined them in seeking her. Her finding brought much joy to young and old, and praise and thanks were brought to our dear God for

[8] Under the Lease System in Salem ownership of the improvements did not follow ownership of the land.

this as well as for other mercies which we cannot name, and for some that we did not even know.

Bethabara Diary, 1783.

[Extracts translated, especially concerning weather.]

Jan. 5. The son of Michael Gerber asked that I conduct the funeral of his father, who died yesterday.

Jan. 9. It began to snow last night and continued all day, and this evening it sleeted.

Jan. 10. The weather was very bad. Toward noon it thundered and lightened, and then rained very hard.

Jan. 23. Today it snowed.

Jan. 24. The weather was fine, and the sun melted most of the snow.

Jan. 25. It rained all day and during the following night.

Jan. 26. The poem for the Jubilee of the Greenland Mission was read, as some of the members had not heard it.

Jan. 28. The iron promised from Virginia came today. The threshing of winter grain was finished; wheat yielded 335 bushels, rye 89, and barley 88.

Jan. 30. The weather cleared with a storm.

Jan. 31. The German people on the Town Fork asked Br. Lorenz to preach for them, so he went today; he also baptised the following children: Johannes Michael Frey, Michael Frey, Johann William Petri, Anna Maria Petri and Maria Hall.

Feb. 1. A cold west wind began to blow hard, and continued all night.

Feb. 3. The cold was so intense that water froze in the rooms.

Feb. 4. The continuing cold has given many of the Brethren and Sisters bad coughs, snuffles and stiff necks. Toward evening it began to sleet and continued all night.

Feb. 5. It rained all day.

Feb. 6. Because of the continuous rain the water is high. Few children came to school. The weather cleared with a strong wind from the north-west.

Feb. 7. The weather was pleasant.

Feb. 9. It rained all morning. Many travelers were here. Three wagons came from Virginia with rye for Br. Mücke. Twelve dragoons from Greene's camp arrived and spent the night.

24

Feb. 10. The dragoons who were in Salem came here, and all went on together.

Feb. 15. James Wilson, who has worked for Br. Stöhr more than a year, has been visiting his friends for fourteen days. He returned this week, and said that at his mother's request he was going to his father's place beyond the Atkin, to stay with his mother.

Feb. 16. It rained all afternoon and during the night.

Feb. 22. From last night's rain the water is higher than it has been this month, and falls very slowly.

Feb. 25. Sr. Quest came from Salem with Sr. Elisabeth Dixon who will teach the girls' school here. Sr. Quest will install her in office, and will also introduce Sr. Catharine Leinbach into her position as head of the Single Sisters' room.

Feb. 27. The boy, George Schwarz, died on the 25th, and Wilhelm Folk asked that he be buried on the God's Acre near the mill. The boy was the son of Jacob and Barbara Schwarz, both deceased.

March 3. Supervision over our boys has been entrusted to the Brn. Renner and Wernly.

March 4. Today work was begun in burning along the fences.

March 6. Br. Meinung surveyed land for Casper Stolz about three miles below the mill.

March 13. This was a rainy day.

March 15. Br. and Sr. Bibighaus moved hither from Salem. He will re-open the store here.

March 17. Quite early in the morning there was a storm, and it rained nearly all day.

March 18. This morning there was a heavy fog which lasted until after eight o'clock. Then one storm followed another, and in the afternoon there were two hard storms with heavy rain. All low-lying land was under water, and much harm was done in the gardens.

March 19. The storm continued all night, and this morning there was much water in the bottoms. A new pump-stock was set in the cattle yard.

March 23. Sunday. The Brn. and Srs. Bibighaus and Oesterlein and the Single Sr. Elisabeth Dixon visited Bethania. Through them we heard that Br. Holder was at home with his children, and when a bush-fire approached his fence he and his children went out to fight it. When he and the children were back in the house, Elisabeth was missed. She had been sitting behind a stump, but when they looked for her she was gone. She had taken the old Shallow Ford road, had

passed Aust's plantation, and crossed the Bethania road. Seven men
went out from here on foot and on horse-back to aid in the search for
her, and brought back the glad tidings that the parents had themselves
found their child at Johannes Krause's line, more than four miles from
home, in the seventh hour. This brought general joy to children and
grown people.[1]

April 4. There was a hard storm, with hail.

April 10. The Saal diener and dienerinnen had a conference. The
wish was expressed that a set of trombones should be ordered from
Europe, which can now be done more promptly since peace has been
made between the sea-powers, which is announced in a newspaper from
Philadelphia as having taken place on January 20th of this year.[2]

Old Br. Schaub moved today into his son's house, and was given
a good room in the lower story.

April 12. When our farmers went to the fields this morning they
found that their three ploughs had been stolen, that is the share,
colter and clevis had been taken away from each. Search was made in
the woods, and notice sent throughout the neighborhood.

April 13. Palm Sunday. Reports were read from the Synod of
1782.

April 22. There was a gentle rain all day which was good for
growing things. This week and last some of the Sisters and children
have had chills and fever.

April 27. Br. Lorenz returned from Deep Creek. On Friday and
Saturday he visited most of the Germans there, and on Sunday he
preached in George Lang's house to a large gathering of German and
English listeners.

April 29. The store pays one shilling for a pound of butter, but
that prevents no one from buying it cheaper if he can. Br. Broesing
has offered to make coffins for our members; he shall be advised to
lay in a supply of lumber in case of need.

---

[1] This is the interesting foundation of a tradition which has persisted until the present day.
As told after the lapse of nearly a hundred and fifty years, the child went with companions to gather Christmas greens, was missed after they reached home, was sought
by her father and other men, and was found asleep under a cedar tree. The little girl
said that twice she had heard the call, as she thought, of another child, but she was
prevented from answering by a light touch on her lips, and with her fears strangely
soothed she had been led under the tree where she was found; her elders said that
her guardian angel had protected her from a panther. This diary entry shows a bushfire instead of Christmas greens, but supplies the child, the young companions, the
searchers, and the finding some hours later; the Bethabara Memorabilia says she was
protected by angels, and the Salem Diary notes the presence of panthers during the
year.

[2] Apparently newspaper reports were received with caution, for not until April 19th was the
news announced to the Assembly by Governor Martin, and on April 19th also the
Salem diary records it as a fact.

[At this point there is inserted in the diary the Memoir of Diserte Maria Schaub, who died on April 4th. An outline is translated, to show how wide an experience a simple Moravian woman sometimes had.]

She was born Dec. 10, 1713, at Bergen, Norway. Her parents were of good family. She lost her father early, and was brought up by her mother and friends in the Lutheran religion and the usual ways of the world. In 1742 she went to a congregation of the Unity at Herrnhaag, whereby she lost the favor of her mother, who disinherited her. On May 27, 1743, she married Johannes Schaub, at Marienborn, thirty other couples being married at the same time, all destined for Pennsylvania. With them she reached Pennsylvania at the end of the year. With her husband she served in Nazareth and in Bethlehem, in the common house-keeping, in the tavern, at the mill, and for a while she was in the Germantown *Anstalt,* and among the Indians at Gnaden-hütten. When in Bethlehem she took care of five children besides her own, until they could enter the *Anstalt.* On Nov. 4, 1755, she came to Bethabara with the first colony of married people. Here she and her husband served in the mill and in the care of the cattle, commenced the first store in Wachovia, and at various times managed the tavern. When the Oeconomie was given up in 1773 they began farming on their own account, moving to a place not far from Bethabara. During the early years, when many refugees came to Bethabara, she served them as mid-wife, and as everybody loved her she was also called into other homes in the neighborhood. She did the same service for members, when it was requested. She had six children, of whom only one survived her,—her oldest son Johannes, who is living in Bethabara, and has three children.

May 2. Through William Sheppard we heard from Hillsborough that Colonel Martin has been reëlected Governor by a majority vote; and that peace really will be established when certain particular matters between England and America are settled. Meanwhile there is a general cessation of arms.

May 6. Three gentlemen, going from Virginia to Savannah, had a statement, published on Feb. 13th, which gave the articles of peace between the warring powers, and proclaimed a cessation of arms until all points between them had been settled.

May 8. Our cart took Sr. Rose to Salem for pottery.

May 12. Mr. Micke had a bad attack of vertigo which made it necessary for him to be bled; this gave him some relief.

May 15. Br. Blum must attend court each day, as he is on the jury.

May 18. We had a good rain in the afternoon and another at night, which refreshed the dry earth. The crows have destroyed so much of the sprouting corn that it had to be replanted.

May 22. Little Elisabeth Holder was not well in school yesterday and her parents had to come for her, but we heard that she is better today. Jacob Haefner, who has worked here for more than a year and a half, chiefly as a carpenter, went to his father's home on the Catawba.

May 23. Br. Oesterlain has burned a thousand bushels of charcoal.

May 28. Br. Holder's Elisabeth continues unwell, so he went to Dr. Rindelmann, who gave him some medicine.

May 29. The corn-fields have to be watched all the time on account of the many crows.

June 3. Today was the wedding of Br. Kapp with the Single Sr. Louisa Doll, in Bethania.

June 6. Toward evening there was a hard storm.

June 10. The west side of the old Brothers House was re-roofed. In the afternoon a storm came up, and until in the night there was heavy thunder, lightning and rain.

June 11. Toward evening it rained very hard.

June 13. About eight o'clock in the evening there was a hard storm.

June 17. Before day it rained, and continued to be cloudy, so mowing of the grass was stopped, but the cutting of rye continued.

June 19. It rained early, and the weather was so uncertain that the day-laborers who had come to cut grass were sent home.

June 25. Harvest work continued. There is much complaint about the intense heat.

June 26. The cutting of wheat continued, but as it rained in the afternoon it could not be bound or stacked.

June 30. Today the winter and summer barley, and the first pulled flax, were brought in. Before noon we had a hard rain from the south. We received a letter from Br. Marshall, in which he mentioned that the government has declared Friday, July 4th, to be a Peace Festival. Preachers of all denominations are instructed to hold a solemn service on that day, and the inhabitants are bidden to do no work. This caused all the house-fathers in the town to be called, together with the Brn. Renner and Wernly. The celebration of the day was discussed, and the Brethren all favored making it as impressive as our circumstances allow. Br. Blum is to take up the offering for the heathen tomorrow, which will give him opportunity to announce the services to all members living outside the town. We will tell everybody who comes to town.

July 4. The Day of Thanksgiving for Peace was announced early in the morning by the blowing of the wind instruments. At ten o'clock there was a service, in which the Te Deum was sung, and there was a sermon on Psalm XLVI. * * * The service closed with a prayer. Some of our neighbors were present. At two in the afternoon the congregation, including the children and some of the neighbors, had a happy lovefeast, during which the Ode composed in Salem was sung. In the evening all the houses were illuminated, the bell was rung, and the congregation assembled before the Gemein Haus. Singing began with the hymn: *Oh Thou, Whose goodness no tongue can tell,* and the congregation marched in procession between the two Brothers Houses and the other houses to the tavern, along the road by Schaub's and back by Stach's to the Gemein Haus, full of praise and thanksgiving. As close the choir sang the benediction.

July 25. The heat was great. A storm passed by but we did not get the rain we so badly need.

July 26. This afternoon we had a pleasant rain, which refreshed the gardens, but the grain and our mill need more.

July 28. In our mill there are more than two hundred bushels of wheat waiting; about forty bushels a day can be ground.

July 29. This morning rain began and it still continues. This will help our mill, and everything else that needed rain.

Aug. 2. Sixty bushels of wheat were taken from the shed; it had no weevils.

Aug. 12. The Brn. Blum and Micke were at court. The former was sworn in as Justice. This afternoon we had a good rain.

Aug. 18. Toward evening we had a hard storm, with good rain, which helped our mill, where there is still much grain to be ground.

Aug. 21. The Brethren of the Committee met. It was decided to place stone steps in front of the Gemein Haus.

Aug. 24. The house-fathers were informed that Br. Stauber will move into town, and it has been suggested to him that he take charge of the school for little boys, keeping it in session all day.

Aug. 31. The Petition that our County shall not be divided was read and signed by all the residents.

Sept. 9. The weather cleared very cold.

Sept. 15. The mill for crushing corn-stalks was finished, and a trial was made with boiling the juice into molasses. It turned out well, and if we had enough of such corn-stalks it might be worth the trouble and expense.

THE PSALM OF JOY

Sept. 19. We had a fine rain, which refreshed the earth.

Sept. 30. It rained all day.

Oct. 7. Toward evening it began to rain, and during the night there was such a storm that some of the people could not sleep.

Oct. 8. Wednesday. We found that many fences around fields and gardens had been blown down, and many trees uprooted in the woods.

Oct. 18. It rained all day, with an unusually heavy downfall during the evening.

Oct. 23. In the evening we read the Memoir of the departed Br. Jacob Loesch.[3]

Nov. 4. Br. Meinung went to the Town Fork to see Mr. Winston, but he was not at home.

Nov. 10. Our wagon brought shingles from Adam Binckly.

Nov. 17. As today was the anniversary of the arrival of the first Brethren coming to settle at this place, thirty years ago, the wind-instruments announced it early in the morning; and in the evening service the story of their coming was re-told.

Nov. 18. Br. Bagge was here on business, and had a conference with most of the gentlemen of the county concerning the next election of members for the Assembly.

Nov. 19. Br. Micke found that there was a hole in his large kettle, and Br. Jacob Loesch was brought from Salem to mend it. Several Brethren from here assisted, and it was finished during the night.

Nov. 21. Br. Lorenz went to the home of John Adams and baptised several children.

Nov. 27. It began to rain last night, and continued all day, so only three children could attend school.

Nov. 30. Br. Stauber will begin the school for little boys tomorrow. During the short days the sessions will last until four o'clock in the afternoon, and in summer until five o'clock. This shall apply to the girls' school also. The parents shall supply their children with fire-wood, books, paper and ink. Br. Stauber promised to teach the children to read German and English, to write and to cipher. On Sunday he will take charge of the boys before the children's service, and attend it with them. On Saturday school shall close at noon. He shall receive £20 a year salary, and Sr. Dixon shall have £12. The children attending

---

[3] He was one of the leaders in Bethabara from 1753 to 1769, when he was recalled to service in Pennsylvania. He died November 8, 1782, eleven miles from Nazareth, Pa., while on a journey.

school, that is those four years of age and above, shall have a lovefeast tomorrow, and one parent from each family shall come with them. It rained all afternoon and snowed in the evening.

Dec. 10. We hear that little Heinrich Kapp and Johann Ranke have measles.

Dec. 18. The weather was cold and rainy.

Dec. 21. It has cleared up very cold. Two little boys in town are showing signs of measles.

Dec. 27. Since the store has goods for sale many people come here. Some of the Brethren and Sisters are suffering from vomiting and diarrhoea.

Dec. 30. Last night it began to snow and today the weather was very unfriendly. We were glad that several hogs and an ox were butchered yesterday, and that our wagon brought several bushels of salt from Friedrich Müller.

Bethania Diary, 1783.

[Extracts translated.]

Jan. 15. This morning I rode with Br. Heinrich Schor to Mr. Windfield, and in the afternoon I baptised eight children there.

Jan. 25. This week we began to read the *Idea Fidei Fratrum.*

Jan. 29. The old woman, Susanna Beeringer, born in Regensburg, came from Friedland, bringing me a letter from Br. Heinzmann.

Feb. 10. Some of the young men began to dig a hole in the cellar of the Gemein Haus, to free it of water.

Feb. 13. Today the above-mentioned hole was finished. It had to be dug fourteen feet deep to find sand. Before evening the cellar was paved with broad stones.

March 16. Sunday. This afternoon there was the baptism of the infant son of Dr. Rindelmann, who received the name August Wilhelm.

March 19. The water was so high that the country members did not reach here until toward ten o'clock. The Brn. Friedrich Peter and Reitz came from Salem to furnish the music for the festal services.

March 22. Br. Transou's leg has become worse instead of better, although it was lanced seven weeks ago, so he sent for Peter Schneider, who ordered an herb poultice which seemed to have a good effect.

April 4. This morning Br. Feiser and Friedrich Fischer left for Pennsylvania.

April 6. Br. Transou had himself taken to Salem, in order to be under the care of Br. Peter Schneider, since his leg does not improve here. His wife went along to wait on him.

April 19. At one o'clock was the lovefeast for Great Sabbath. As there were many outsiders in town who wanted to come into the Saal the members were told to assemble without having the bell rung.

April 20. On Easter morning at five o'clock we met in the Saal, gave each other the usual Easter greeting, then went to the Hutberg where we prayed the Easter litany. Preaching was at ten o'clock. As the weather was fine a great crowd was present.

April 21. Br. Transou and his wife returned from Salem. His leg is a little better.

April 24. Br. Marshall came from Salem and inspected the mill site, where half of the race has been finished, and wood has been cut for the dam and mill-house.

May 3. Br. Philip Schaus came with three horses, and we rode with him to his plantation, stopping at the younger Hilsebecks, where only the wife and her mother, old Mrs. Fiscuss, were at home. At their parents' (Br. and Sr. Hilsebeck) we were received with much joy. Br. and Sr. Philip Schaus were very glad to have us in their house again.

May 4. In the second service, Richard, the little son of Benjamin Bennett, was baptised; they have recently come from Virginia. Through a letter from Colonel Armstrong we heard that the Brethren, and all others who did not bear arms, were relieved by the Assembly of the three-fold tax.

May 18. This morning the elder Krieger came to me with Peter Ludwig, and asked that I publish the Banns for Johann George, son of the former, and Catharine, daughter of the latter.

May 23. Digging for the mill-race is finished. Br. Bulitschek and his son John are preparing to build the mill.

May 25. The new Committee consists of George Hauser, Sr., and George Hauser, Jr., from the upper town, and Cramer and Beroth from the lower town. Concerning the contract between the Brn. Heinrich Spoenhauer and Philip Transou, representing the house-fathers, and the Brn. Michael Ranke, George Hauser, Sr., Heinrich Schor and Peter Hauser, who are building the mill, several points remain to be adjusted.

June 3. At noon there was the wedding of the widowed Br. Jacob Kapp and the Single Sr. Louise Doll. Immediately after the ceremony

Sr. Kapp's new Choir ribbon was tied in, and then we had dinner together in the home of Br. and Sr. Schor.

June 6. This morning I had a return of my old leg malady, and could not hold the school.

June 10. This evening I began the antimony cure, and during the following days the Saviour blessed it to my improvement.

June 15. The house-fathers met. All accounts were presented for their inspection, notes were signed by those who were back in their rent, and the mill contract was read and signed.

June 18. Christian Conrad's brother Johannes came from Pennsylvania with Kettner's wagon.

June 22. Various residents in the upper and in the lower town were sick, but when they began vomiting and purging they became better.

June 23. An Irish woman purloined various articles in a house, and hastened away on her horse. The theft was soon discovered, she was pursued and captured, and the stolen articles were found between the saddle-pad and saddle-tree. She was brought back, the Justice ordered twelve lashes to be administered outside the town, and then she was sent away.

June 26. Jacob Hauser was worse. Medicine given to cause vomiting and purging had a good effect. Dr. Rentelman was brought to him. Wilhelm Grabs and Elisabeth Ranke are also worse.

June 29. Colonel Armstrong brought me an order from the Governor that the 4th of July shall be observed in this Province as a Day of Thanksgiving.

Two outsiders, Muzzel and Christian Schaus, had a fight, and as several Justices were present they were arrested and tried. Colonel Armstrong was indignant that they had created such a disturbance on a public street in town on Sunday, and immediately after a funeral [Jacob Hauser's], and that they had no more fear of God. They were fined ten shillings apiece.

June 30. Some of the sick are improving, another is not, and others are sickening. Gov. Alex. Martin was here for an hour on his way to Bethabara and Salem.

July 1. The rest of the wheat and spelt was cut.

July 4. This being the appointed day for the Peace and Thanksgiving Festival the first service was held at ten o'clock. First the Proclamation was read, then the portion of the litany referring to the government of the land was prayed standing, then on our knees we thanked the Lord of Lords for His gift of peace. The 46th Psalm was read, as the 12th verse was the Watch-Word for Jan. 20th when Peace was agreed upon in Paris, and this was followed by an address based on this Psalm. An unexpected number of outsiders were present.

July 17.   Br. Bagge came to list the property of the residents.

July 20.   Johannes Conrad will leave for Pennsylvania in the morning.

July 29.   A drove of cattle was driven through on their way north.

Aug. 3.   Just at preaching time a great drove of cattle was driven through, so that the service had to be postponed a while.

Aug. 7.   Another great herd of cattle was driven through the town, on the way to Pennsylvania.

Aug. 14.   Br. [Philip Christoph] Vogler came from Salem, and was married to the widowed Sr. Sehnert.

Sept. 10.   Several Brethren and outsiders are building the foundation for the mill-house.

Sept. 18.   We visited Bulitscheks, where we met Nilson, who expressed regret over his separation from the Brethren.

Sept. 29.   On this Feast of Angels [Michaelmas] the children were told of the service of the holy angels, who gladly do the will of their Lord and our Saviour, especially when children love the Saviour.

Sept. 30.   About the middle of this month sickness broke out among the cattle in town. Measures were taken with some of the cows, to prevent spread of the disease, and at the close of the month we see no further signs of it.

Oct. 7.   There was a severe storm during the afternoon and especially during the night. Fences and trees were blown down, roofs damaged, and some thought they felt the earth quake.

Oct. 12.   Joseph Knause arrived this afternoon, coming from Pennsylvania.

Nov. 3.   Br. Hege tore down the old school-house, which he bought some years ago, as Abraham Transou wishes to use the lot.

Nov. 7.   The house which Abraham Transou built last year was rolled over to his new lot.

Nov. 9.   From letters recently received we learn that the Brethren and Sisters destined for America are to come on three different ships.

Nov. 29.   During the week several persons have gone to bed with measles.

Dec. 3.   Three wagons, loaded with tobacco, left for Charlestown.

Dec. 20. Forty-five persons have had measles, and most of them, thank God, have already recovered.

Friedberg Diary, 1783.

[A few extracts translated.]

Jan. 19. In the third meeting we read the poem[1] composed for the Jubilee, which is being celebrated today in Salem.

Feb. 23. The house-fathers met, and for the first time discussed the building of a new Saal, as the present one has become too small.

March 2. Br. Priem took leave of the Brethren and Sisters, who expressed their thanks for the service he has rendered here.

March 3. Br. Priem returned to Salem, and Br. and Sr. Koffler came hither as assistants in the work of the congregation.

March 12. Our congregation festival was celebrated. Fourteen years ago eighteen persons were present, and the Society was begun with thirteen married couples; now the number has increased to thirty-seven couples. Br. Marshall suggested that the house-fathers elect a building committee.

April 20. We rejoiced in the resurrection of our Lord Jesus Christ, and at ten o'clock prayed the Easter litany on God's Acre.

April 27. Those who during the year have been received and admitted to Communion had a lovefeast, attended also by the Saal-diener and musicians. Peter Schneider becomes a diener, and George Fischer joins the musicians.

May 25. There was preaching, but no other service could be held because we heard that soldiers were marching past, and the Brethren wanted to be at home.

June 1. The unmarried women and girls have asked for a post celebration of the Sisters Festival. They were called together by Sr. Koffler, who inquired about the recent unseemly conduct of two of them, and affectionately urged them to give themselves entirely to the Saviour. This had a good effect, especially on those who had erred, and who begged with tears for forgiveness. In the Society meeting the Brotherly Agreement was re-read, and two or three points were emphasized.

---

[1] This Ode, composed by Br. Benzien for the celebration of the Jubilee of the Greenland Mission, is copied into the Extract der Diarii der Gemeiner in der Wachau for 1783. It covers four closely written pages, and is arranged for solo, duet, chorus and congregation. It outlines the history of the mission, referring particularly to Matthew Stach, one of the first missionaries to Greenland, who was present in Salem when the Ode was sung.

June 9. The unmarried women and girls had a blessed festal service. Sr. Quest held morning prayers, Br. Praetzel preached, and then they had a lovefeast.

July 4. In the day appointed by government for the observance of a Day of Thanksgiving we gladly took our part. The congregation assembled in the Saal at ten o'clock. The Proclamation of His Excellency Governor Alexander Martin was read, and we sang: *Now thank we all our God.* The 46th Psalm served as topic for the sermon.   * * * Then followed a prayer, and the *Te Deum* was sung. The congregation and Society and the children had a lovefeast, during which many hymns of thanksgiving were sung.

July 6. Peter Sehnert, who lives in the neighborhood, asked for the baptism of his infant son.

July 16. We had an unexpected visit from the Brn. Praetzel and Benzien. They proposed that I make a journey to Pennsylvania, and I agreed to go.

July 27. Br. Beck took a hearty leave of the Brethren and Sisters, and asked for their constant prayers to the Saviour in his behalf while he was away. [Beginning with the account of Br. Beck's departure the diary was kept by Br. Koffler, until Oct. 1st.]

Sept. 30. We closed the month with thankful hearts. The Watch-Word for the day was: *Thou, Lord, givest a gracious rain,* and this was literally fulfilled, for after a long drought the Lord did give us a gracious rain, for which we were heartily thankful.

Oct. 1. Yesterday at midnight we reached Salem, coming from Bethlehem, where on Aug. 26th I married the Single Sr. Maria Beck. During our stay of a few days in Salem we visited Bethabara, and in Salem partook of the Holy Communion. On

Oct. 5th we came to Friedberg, where I preached on the Epistle for the day.

Oct. 7. Br. and Sr. Koffler moved back to Salem, and we returned to Friedberg with the same wagon.

Oct. 12. Sunday. The congregation, Society and children had a lovefeast as a farewell to Br. and Sr. Koffler and a welcome to Sr. Maria Beck. Br. and Sr. Koffler served this congregation for seven months and Br. Priem for thirty-two weeks. Sr. Maria Beck was born in Heidelberg, [Pa.] where her parents are still serving the congregation from which several of our members came.

Dec. 8. A neighbor named Jacobi asked that one of his children might attend our school, and I could not refuse for I saw that he was thinking of his and his children's salvation and wished to become better acquainted with us.

Dec. 24. Although it looked like rain so many people assembled that the Saal could not hold them. Before the sermon we thanked God the Father that He had sent His well-beloved Son, our Lord Jesus Christ, to become our Saviour, taking upon Him our flesh and blood. Then the children had a happy lovefeast, and again Christmas verses were distributed to them.

Dec. 31. In the evening the congregation and Society met for the close of the year, and to thank the Lord for the countless mercies which He has shown to us.

Friedland Diary, 1783.

[The Friedland diary as filed begins with April, 1783. It contains little except church services, of which enough notices are translated to show what was customary.]

April 2. In the evening a printed sermon was read and a singstunde was held.

April 4. The service could not be held because of rain.

April 6. After the church litany there was preaching, and then a well-attended service for children.

April 11. My wife and I went to Land-Arbeiter-Conferenz in Salem. In the evening there was a liturgy, with a sermon read from the Wochen.

April 13. Palm Sunday. I began to read the story of the Passion Week, and preached on the wonderful manner in which He, the true God, gave Himself to death in order to save us, lost men. In the second service there was the baptism of an infant. The communicant and received members had a meeting in which the approaching celebration of the Lord's Supper was announced.

April 14. There was the funeral of Carl Christoph Künzel, who passed away on the 12th. He was born in Broadbay, New England, Jan. 24, 1765, and was baptised there. He came to Wachovia with his parents and seven other families, led by Br. Soelle, and was lodged in Salem until February, 1775, when a Society was formed in Friedland, with fourteen married couples, and the new school-house was dedicated; then he and his parents moved hither.

April 16, 17 and 18. The reading of the account of the sufferings of our Lord was continued. The services were well attended and were blessed. On Maundy Thursday, after being spoken with individually, twenty-five Brethren and Sisters had a gracious Absolution and Pedilavium, a happy lovefeast, and a blessed Communion. On the afternoon of the 18th, Good Friday, the communicants and received had a liturgy.

April 20. On Easter morning, before sunrise, I greeted the assembled congregation with the words: *The Lord is risen,* and they answered in tones full of emotion: *He is risen indeed.* After singing a suitable hymn we went to God's Acre, singing most of the way, and there we prayed the Easter litany. At ten o'clock many were present to hear the reading and preaching concerning our risen Lord. Then there was a well-attended children's meeting for young and old.

April 21. On second Easter Day the story of the Resurrection was read, and there was a sermon on that theme. In the second service I read the interesting Memoirs of several Brethren who have gone home.

April 27. Sunday. The church litany was prayed, and was followed by a sermon. In the second service I made an address and baptised an infant. In a meeting of the house-fathers Br. Peter Kroen was elected by a majority vote to succeed Br. Künzel as Steward.

May 4. Because of necessary field work the week-day meetings have been dropped for the summer.

May 11. There was a reception of ten persons, followed by a lovefeast for the entire Society. Toward the close of the day the house-fathers met, the Rules and Regulations of this Society were read, and were signed by the three house-fathers Christoph Reich, Jeremias Elroth and Jann Schneider.

May 25. The house-fathers decided that in addition to the two Stewards, Peter Kroen and Jacob Ried, they would elect four men as a committee, and there being no objection the four following were selected: Friedrich Müller, Jann Hein, Johannes Lanius and Friedrich Künzel. Class was begun again for the single men today; the Class for the single women was begun eight days ago. Each group will meet every fourteen days.

June 8. Many people came for the Whitsuntide preaching.

June 29. The introduction to the *Idea Fidei Fratrum* was read, and was heard with much attention.

July 4. We celebrated the Peace Festival with happy hearts and voices. The preaching was on Psalm 46, then we commended to Him the entire land, and especially His children whom He has planted therein. In the second meeting I read from the history of the Unity the account of the Peace Festival in Herrnhut on March 21st, 1763.

July 27. We prayed the church litany, with the change in wording made since the establishment of peace, a prayer for those who govern this land and especially this State being inserted.

Aug. 18. We were very thankful that no harm was done by the lightning which struck twice between the School-house and Seiz's during the unusually severe storm.

Aug. 31. Br. Schober was here to secure signatures to the petition to the Assembly asking that our county may not be divided.

Sept. 3. Our congregation festival was celebrated. In the first service for adults and children the story was told of the beginning of this Society and consecration of the Saal in 1775, and the organization of the congregation in 1780.

Sept. 27. The Saviour laid His blessing upon our post celebration of the Married People's Covenant Day. Thirteen more attended the lovefeast than last year. Twenty-five communicants partook of the Lord's Supper.

Oct. 6. I began school with seven children.

Oct. 8. The first evening meeting was held according to the winter schedule.

Oct. 10. In the evening the liturgy: *O Head so full of bruises,* was sung, and a sermon from the Wochen was read.

[Beginning with the 1st of November the diary was written by Sr. Heinzmann, who continued to keep it for more than a year. The first seven entries are evidently copied from Br. Heinzmann's notes, but on the 20th the words become her own.]

Nov. 13. We celebrated the festival of the Chief Elder with the congregation in Salem.

Nov. 16. The festival of the Chief Elder was celebrated here.

Nov. 20 and 21. There was speaking with our received and communicant Brethren and Sisters. At its close my husband remarked that he was well pleased with the conversations.

Nov. 22. My husband rose as usual, but felt faint and had to lie down again. I sent for a neighbor and the wife came. My husband did not speak again except a few minutes before his end when he said: "Oh Jesus, oh God, oh Thou dear Saviour." So he quietly and blessedly fell asleep about seven o'clock in the morning. Word was at once sent to Salem, and about noon our dear Br. Praetzel arrived.

Nov. 23. Br. Friedrich Peter came to hold the Sunday services. In the third meeting was the baptism of Br. Michael and Sr. Anna Maria Vogler's infant son, Johannes, born on the 21st of this month.

Nov. 24. The funeral of my dear husband was held, to which many came from Salem. Br. Benzien made the address. All of the congregation here assembled looked upon him with sorrow, and bewailed their loss.

Nov. 29. Br. and Sr. Praetzel came to celebrate the Holy Communion with the congregation.

Dec. 7. Br. Benzien came to preach, and in the second service there was reading from the *Idea Fidei Fratrum*.

Dec. 25. Br. Toego Nissen held the festal services. There was a lovefeast for the children.

Dec. 28. Br. Benzien held the Sunday services. There was a conference of the house-fathers about the observance of New Year's day.

*Offering of Praise and Thanksgiving of the Congregations in Wachovia
for the Protection of God during the North American
Disturbances, from the Year 1774 to the Year 1783.*

> Honor and praise the Highest Good,
>   The Father of all mercy,
> The God of wonders manifold;
>   The God Who mind and spirit
> With His abundant comfort filled,
> The God Who lamentations stilled,
>   Be to our God the glory!

1774. This was still a year of peace, although the fire which was to devastate the land glimmered under the ashes.

1775. The reciprocal correspondence between here and Europe was somewhat interrupted by the increasing war-unrest, and the reduced number of ships sailing the ocean. In spite of that Br. and Sr. Marshall made a safe voyage to Europe where he attended the Synod at Barby as our delegate.

In spring the North Carolina Assembly fell out with Governor Martin, refused him obedience, and formed itself into a Congress, which disbanded after a few sessions and after calling another Congress to meet in Hillsborough in August. On March 9th an Advertisement was posted, calling all house-fathers to meet in Richmond on the 24th of the month to elect Delegates to Congress. From New Bern and other places printed and written papers were sent to us, giving encouragement and urging participation in the procedure. Among these was one from our Delegates in the General Congress, addressed to Br. Bagge, which had been sent from Philadelphia by an Express rider on July

7, 1775. Extraordinary militia drills were begun, Minute Men were organized, regular troops were enlisted, and all these preparations were pushed.

In August the Brn. Bonn, George Hauser, Sr., and Bagge were elected by the Delegates as members of the Committee for this county, and when they refused to serve they were summoned to appear before several members of the aforesaid Committee, who pressed them hard. In Friedberg a loyalist Justice posted an Advertisement on the School-House, calling all Taxables to appear before him and take the oath of loyalty to the King. On the other hand orders were given for taking the Oath of Fidelity to the Country. We held aloof from all these things. But already in the latter part of September we were called upon for supplies for the outfitting of newly enlisted soldiers; and in December we had to give up several hundred pounds of lead, which was in the stores of Salem and Bethabara, it being claimed that those who received it would pay for it in cash.

Means of support were impaired during this year by the circulation of the new Congress Money, in which bills were paid for goods for the soldiers, especially clothing. In spite of this, God so blessed the work of our hands that our members were able and willing to show their active interest in the fate which befell the congregation of Sarepta.

1776. The year 1776, during which American Independence was declared and the fire of war broke into full flame, was a year full of distress and unrest, but a year in which God spread His wings over His congregations and protected them from harm.

When two wagons from Salem and seven from Bethania brought salt and other goods from Cross Creek to our settlement and store, we were accused of having sent the wagons to assist Gov. Josiah Martin in bringing an army into the land, and further that when it was found that no such army existed the wagons had brought ammunition which we were hiding to use against the country. This led to a war-commission, which made a rigid examination in our three towns on Feb. 14th and 15th. Under these circumstances we found great comfort in the Watch-Word for the 14th: *Say to them that are of a fearful heart, Be strong and fear not,* and that for the 15th: *So saith the Lord—Fear not thou, oh my servant Jacob,* and God turned the hearts of the Commissioners, so that they were convinced of our innocence in the matter to their entire satisfaction. They also accepted from us a written Declaration that we would not meddle in political matters, that we would seek the good of the country, would help to bear its burdens and would obey all commands, though we asked freedom from the bearing of arms, which was against our conscience. They also gave us a written Protection, which stood us in good stead when we were called to muster.

In February, March and April our towns had some experience with troops, marching against the malcontents near Cross Creek, and returning. All the lead in Salem was taken for the army. The officers and soldiers took whatever they wished from the store and shops, and much provision had to be furnished. Some of the militia had planned to live at discretion in Bethabara, and were much disappointed when the Colonel's order interfered.

There was much alarm in the land, caused by fear that Governor Martin would land with troops, and the enlisting of soldiers, foraging, pressing of wagons, seizing arms from the Tories, and gathering supplies, went steadily forward, and our Brethren, especially in Friedberg, suffered thereby.

In March the Brn. Graff and Bagge were called to Salisbury to receive a package which had come from Europe and had been held by the Committee of Safety. It was opened in their presence, and when the Brethren had assured them that it contained nothing relating to the war the Committee dismissed the Brethren in peace and with courtesy.

July 11th an order arrived from Brigadier Rutherford, in Salisbury, calling upon the Brethren to join the expedition against the Cherokees on Broad River, who had been murdering, and any man who would not go must furnish a substitute or pay a fine of £10. The Brn. Bonn and Bagge were sent to Salisbury to take up the matter with the General, but he had already left, and we heard no more about it.

On June 22nd, Communion day, Salem had a great fright, for murderous men behaved badly in the town and especially in the Brothers House. Although several of the Brethren were severely wounded with tomahawks God preserved their lives. The murderers were arrested by the authorities, and all necessary protection and assistance was promised.

In this year we had also a visit from the Council of Safety, which spent two days in Salem, attended the church services, and looked about the town. This led to a change in the opinions which some had about us and which had led them to insist that we must take the Oath, must bear arms, etc., from which we had excused ourselves.

1777. As we did not receive the Texts for this year we used those of 1771. The Watch-Word for the 17th of May: *Like as a father pitieth his children, so the Lord pitieth them that fear him,* which encouraged us in the midst of the Regulator disturbance of 1771, suited admirably this time because of the report that a storm was threatening Salem.

In respect to the new Constitution of the land we made the rule, by the grace of God, that we would be obedient to those who had the rule over us, according to Romans XIII. Although we established our reputation as true citizens among those of the government who noted that we gave honest lists of our property in the two tax assessments of the year, still it must be admitted that some difficulties would have been avoided if all parts of our settlement had acted in one spirit and with due foresight. But God's hand brought to naught all evil designs against us, and gave us patience under mistreatment.

The Act concerning the State Oath and the Militia Act made us much trouble. We declared in writing and by word of mouth that the Oath and the bearing of arms was against our conscience, but that we were willing to pay our share in money in lieu of the latter.

During this year there were visits in Salem from all sorts of people, and from honorable gentlemen who noted that it was the residence of a people of God. Among those who came was the Vice President from Charlestown, Mr. Henry Laurence, who spent some days there and showed his old love for the Brethren.

During these warlike times several successful trips were made for the store, to Petersburg, Cross Creek and Charlestown, although the paper money began perceptibly to fall in value, which greatly disturbed trade and commerce and caused much loss in our work-shops. It should also be noted that during this year and later we furnished coast towns with articles which formerly were brought into the ports and sold from there into the up-country. This did not apply to North Carolina only, but also to South Carolina, Virginia, Maryland and Pennsylvania.

1778. In August, 1778, we sent a Petition to the General Assembly, which met in called session at Hillsborough, protesting against the Oath of Abjuration which was being demanded of us. We gained nothing except that we might have until the next session, in January, to think about it, and meanwhile might continue to exercise our rights as citizens. Br. Heckewälder went to Pennsylvania to obtain for us the advice of our Brethren there, who were in the same case, and returned in safety.

During this time we suffered all sorts of annoyances, for without a shadow of right persons who thought that the Brethren would not be protected by the authorities entered land belonging to the Unity of Brethren, both within and outside of Wachovia, although this was contrary to a recent law. Wonderful was the Watch-Word for Oct. 8th, when this report spread: *The meek shall inherit the earth, and shall delight themselves in the abundance of peace.*

Threats also were generally made, and we were not always careful enough, so that the world had some reason to work us harm. But God helped us in every time of need, and often moved the hearts of honest and understanding men, yea, even of our enemies, to come to our rescue, and show themselves favorable to us.

During this year all Parishes were abolished, for no denomination was to rank above another, and so our Dobbs Parish came to an end.

Means of support during this year were uncommonly difficult to secure, partly because of the paper money being put into circulation on every hand, which was brought to our town in large quantities by outsiders, though they would hardly receive it at all in exchange for the wares which they offered at greatly increased prices; partly because of the supplies that had to be furnished, the high taxes, and the fines for refusing militia service, which amounted to £25 a man. This brought loss to the Diaconies, for in this year we began to buy what we could get for paper money, though we could not sell it again for nearly as much as it cost.

1779. The year opened with a somewhat dismal outlook, for it was credibly reported that most of the Wachovia land,—including Salem and Bethabara,—had been entered by others, and that surveying would begin directly after New Year. The more were our hearts filled with praise and rejoicing when our Lord gave grace to our Brn. Praetzel and Heckewälder, who left for the General Assembly in Hallifax on Jan. 8th, taking another Petition, so that they secured a hearing and were able to bring back a favorable Resolution, stating that if we would take the Affirmation of Allegiance in the form prepared for us we should not only be left in the peaceful possession of our land but would be excused from military service on the payment of a three-fold tax. This Affirmation of Allegiance was taken by most of the Brethren without hesitation before Justice Dobson, and in this respect we have since been left in peace.

On Nov. 5th, Br. and Sr. Marshall returned in safety from Europe, to our great joy, having been absent five years.

The rapidly falling value of the currency, and the enormously high prices of the necessaries of life created a huge loss in the Diaconies. Moreover commerce and trade were greatly interrupted by small-pox, brought into Salem by Pulaski's Corps during their four days' stay in the town. In addition unpaid fines and the three-fold tax had to be met. In spite of the fact that there was a poor crop also, through God's providence we did not suffer want.

1780. In March, Br. Marshall waited upon the Judges of the Superior Court at Salisbury, and presented to them the new Deed to Wachovia and other tracts, asking to have it registered; this they refused to permit, and it looked as though there was a disposition to confiscate our land. Soon after, he and Br. Bagge were cited to appear before the Commissioners of Confiscated Estates, and list the English property in their hands; however they were treated indulgently.

In June we had the pleasure of welcoming Br. and Sr. Reichel, who arrived with other Brethren and Sisters in the midst of the tumult, he being an official Visitor. Many people in the country were in flight, fearing that since the fall of Charlestown the English would over-run the land.

The English came as far as Camden and the Cheraws. In our neighborhood more than a thousand Tories gathered, who did many deeds of violence. To put a stop to this the militia was called out, and scoured the land pressing horses, arms and provisions, and living at discretion in many places. Our towns were constantly visited, but no payments were made. In addition all sorts of demands were made for provisions. This happened just at the time of harvest, which was greatly hindered by the lack of available men.

Meanwhile three thousand regulars came from the north to Cross Creek, where they were joined by seven thousand militia, and marched against the English. For their support, requisitions were made on the wheat that had just been harvested, and a Captain and sixty men came to Salem to secure the grain from that town and vicinity. Wagons and horses were pressed, mostly from our members, to take flour to the army. Battle was joined, and General Gates was defeated. Two wagons belonging to our members were in and near the battle; one wagon and its horses were lost, though the teamsters escaped. Others came back to Hillsborough, worn out and losing many horses, —the Bethania wagons lost six. But, thank God, not one of the men was injured.

Bethabara suffered a special loss in August, when several hundred of the Virginia militia were called hither to hunt for Tories, stayed in that town for three weeks, brought in a number of prisoners, and ate up all the provisions on hand. On Sept. 13th Br. and Sr. Fritz were protected from bodily injury when sixteen Light-Horse broke into the School-house at Hope.

Bethabara had a hard time again in October, when the secret Tories were being sought and therefore openly joined others under Gideon Wright. The militia were called out against them, and defeated them on Oct. 13th. Five hundred of the militia went to Bethabara, and as it was raining they forced their way into the houses, lived entirely at discretion, committed excesses, and nearly ruined the entire establishment. After receiving certain information that the Tories had been scattered, they finally left; and General Smallwood also marched away from Salem, where he had been posted with some two hundred regulars and about fifty of the Guilford militia, among whom he held strict discipline.

After the militia from this state and from Virginia had defeated at King's Mountain another party of Tories and English who had marched to the Catawba from South Carolina, they brought the prisoners, without warning, to Bethabara. There were three hundred prisoners, fifty being English, and a militia guard of five hundred men, and they stayed at Bethabara nineteen days, using up everything that remained after the last quartering. The farm, also, was greatly injured by the pressing of horses and men, for it was just at the time when seed should have been sown. Later the prisoners were divided, and Salem, on whom heavy requisitions had already been made, had to take in the English prisoners for ten days. Bethania had four wounded soldiers, but they were more a protection to the town than a burden.

During this year the currency fell three separate times, and on one occasion the loss was £500, estimated in hard money. Great losses also came through the constant requisitions, the high tax, which was three times that of the preceding year, the grain demanded as an advance on the next year, and especially by the lack of food-stuffs caused by the poor harvest of the preceding summer.

1781. In the year 1781 the theatre of the war approached our towns and neighborhood. This caused many alarming scenes, but God held His hand over us, and protected our towns from destruction and our members from death. It was a special providence of God that neither battle nor skirmish took place on Wachovia ground.

On Jan. 7th twenty-two men, forty horses and two baggage-wagons belonging to General Greene's army were quartered in Salem, where they remained until Feb. 4th.

On Jan. 12th a Committee of four Brethren was organized, who should look after all matters connected with the war, serving in collaboration with the Aeltesten Conferenz and the Aufseher Collegium. They caused barracks to be erected outside the town, which spared the town much trouble. On Jan. 20th three, and later more, ammunition wagons arrived, under guard of a Conductor and thirty men. The powder was placed in the house of the night-watchman until a magazine could be built, and on Feb. 2nd the ammunition was moved thither.

On Feb. 2nd the English taken on Broad River marched through Salem under guard, and our three towns were called on to furnish provisions.

On Sunday, Feb. 4th, a hospital came to us, and was lodged in the Two-story house. The preaching service in Friedland was disturbed by Georgia soldiers belonging to General Pickens' troops, which plundered several plantations, and treated some of our members badly, giving them blows.

On Feb. 5th the hospital and store of ammunition were moved away, wagons being pressed from our Brethren in Bethania and Friedberg. In the evening General Pickens' troops marched through Salem, and also Captain Gamble's Adjutant and General Quartermaster, with fifteen baggage-wagons and a guard of a hundred men. They all camped at Bethabara over night. It was a day of terror, with some distress and danger, but our towns were still protected from disaster. In the doubtful outlook we were encouraged by the call of the Saviour in the Watch-Word for this day: *Israel, forget me not,* and the promise given on the 6th: *I, the Lord, will hear the poor and needy, I, the God of Israel, will not forsake them,* and we were reminded to look ever to Him, and believe that His help was sure.

On Feb. 7th and 8th, Salem was alarmed by one hundred and seventy of the Wilkes militia, who were joined by a party of Georgia militia. They tried by deception to draw out an admission that we were Tories, and when that did not succeed they committed all sorts of excesses on the pretense that we must be enemies of the country, lived at discretion, and with oaths and harsh threats swore they would plunder us.

Not knowing that the English army was near, on the 8th we sent the Brn. Biwighaus and Charles Holder to General Greene with a petition for protection, which looked to many people as though we had been spying in order to tell the English. It was a wonder of God that these Brethren returned safely on the 10th, shortly before the English army reached Salem.

Feb. 9th several persons in Friedberg were arrested as enemies of the country, among them Martin Walk, who escaped after suffering much misery and returned to his home. Bethania was much distressed by the army under Lord Cornwallis, which made camp there on the 9th at noon. A sharp order was given that twenty horses must be furnished, but in the end they lost twenty-three, besides thirty head of cattle and all their fowls, while their fences were completely ruined. But for the praise of God it should be noted that young and old were preserved from injury to body or soul.

On Feb. 10th the English army marched through Bethabara and Salem, when large requisitions were made for cattle, meal, bread and brandy, wagons were pressed, and much was stolen by the camp followers.

The English army camped for the night near Friedland, and the neighboring farms lost nearly all their forage and cattle, and all sorts of excesses were committed. Br. Heinzmann experienced special protection, being rescued just in time by the visit of several Brethren from Salem, who came as eight soldiers, with bayonets at his breast, were trying to force him to give them food, of which he had none.

Feb. 15th, 16th, 17th and 18th were days of darkness and terror for our towns. Salem was afflicted by Major Dixon's troops from Mecklenburg, to whom were added two parties of General Pickens' men and several wandering parties. They made large demands for supplies, and impressed large quantities, committing many excesses, though the officers tried quietly to avert them. When two parties of the Wilkes militia arrived there was no escape. On the pretext that we were traitors to the country, and that we were carrying on a clandestine intercourse with the English, they committed the most terrible excesses, and lived entirely at discretion. The same thing happened at Bethabara, where a free party of seven hundred under General Pickens were camped. It looked as though the ruin of our towns had been agreed upon; but we were spared a complete plundering of the towns, and the Brethren and Sisters escaped with their lives although loaded guns were held at their breasts. The wonderful hand of God was particularly with the Brethren who had to mingle with the soldiers, who might carelessly have killed them with their loaded guns, and yet no accident occurred. On Feb. 17th, the darkest and the worst day, we were comforted by the Watch-Word: *Thou art a strength to the poor, a strength to the needy in his distress; a refuge from the storm, a shadow from the heat.*

> So rest I now, my Saviour, in Thy arms,
> Thyself shalt be for me eternal peace.

The passing of all sorts of free parties and regular troops, especially General Pickens' and Colonel Preston's, going to and returning from Guilford, lasted until nearly the end of the month, and was accompanied by many demands for provisions, by excesses and alarm. Some Brethren were protected by God when their lives were really in danger. Salem notes another special providence of God in that on March 2nd, when the Wilkes militia had planned another plundering, and were already committing excesses and robbing on the main street of the town, Colonel Campbell arrived from Virginia with sixty men and put a stop to it, Colonel Armstrong assisting him.

Bethabara also was protected, for as General Pickens' troops left on March 10th, after making a great disturbance, they left a fire burning, which before the Brethren were aware had burned a hundred fence-rails, but was then extinguished.

Some Virginia soldiers, wounded in a skirmish in Guilford, remained in Salem until some time in April, being lodged partly in the house of the night-watchman and partly in the tavern. The good care taken of them and the sympathy shown, and the successful, even remarkable service given to them by Br. Bonn, together with the good treatment given to the troops quartered in Salem in January, finally, through God's leading, gave us a good reputation with the commanding officers of the Continental army, which counteracted the prejudice against us, and brought to naught the evil intentions of evil men.

The misery of this period cannot be described, and to all else small-pox was added in Friedberg. In Bethania and in Friedberg, and also in Friedland, highwaymen attacked Brethren in their houses, or on the public roads, on the pretext that they belonged to one or the other party, and robbed and injured them. The more should we praise the wonderful hand of God, Who preserved the lives of our Brethren, and finally put an end to the distress.

During this year several journeys were made on account of our commerce, for example to Pennsylvania and to other places, and they were successful.

It is not surprising that the Diaconies had heavy losses, especially in Bethabara, but we have found means to live and to help many others. This happened especially on the 4th of March, when the Watch-Word was: *Break bread to the hungry.*

A wonderful Providence protected our Nachrichten from Europe this year. Among others we have received packages of Nachrichten from Boston, New London, and Egg Harbor, taken from prize ships, and a package which was delivered into the hands of the Governor of the Jerseys. In November, Salem had a visit from sixty-three members of the Assembly and the government of North Carolina, which together with the Governor's guard and the militia were lodged to their satisfaction.

1782. In January another, though smaller, group of Assembly members met in Salem, for the most part those who had not been here in November. They remained scarcely two weeks. In this way Salem became known to most of the leading men of the State, and the Brethren were recognized as a people of God. The Saviour brought it about that the approval thus won had a blessed result, for when the Assembly met in Hillsborough in April, and Br. Marshall laid before it the uncertainty regarding Wachovia and other tracts belonging to the Unity of Brethren, an Act was passed confirming the Brethren in their privileges, and recognizing Br. Marshall as the person holding title for the Unity.

Br. Bagge took public office as a member of the Assembly, Auditor and Justice of the Peace.

1783. Several parties of soldiers marched through our towns, returning from the army to their homes, among them a party of malcontents, who made a disturbance when taking leave of Salem.

The Assembly reduced our three-fold tax to a simple tax.

Finally, in this year we had the great joy of knowing that Peace Preliminaries had been signed at Paris on Jan. 20th, and ratified on Feb. 4th. On the 4th of July, by order of the government of the State of North Carolina, we solemnly and happily celebrated the Day of Thanksgiving for Peace. On Nov. 23rd we received certain information that on Sept. 3rd peace had been established between America and Great Britain, by the signing of the Peace Treaty.

To our God and Lord alone be the glory!
Amen!

PART III
ARCHIVE PAPERS

Bethania Diary, 1779.

[Since Vol. III of the *Records of the Moravians in North Carolina* was published the diary of Bethania for the year 1779 has been found. The items of general interest follow, to give information which would otherwise be lacking in the history of the Bethania congregation.]

Jan. 1. The three wagons which went from the upper town to Charlestown on Nov. 26th returned this evening.

Jan. 7. Evening school began for nine boys.

Feb. 3. We heard that Captain Dobson would be in Bethabara tomorrow, to take the Affirmation from those who had not already taken the State Oath, and to give them Certificates.

Feb. 4. Toward noon nine Brethren went to Bethabara, namely Ernst, Grabs, Hege, Sehnert, Beroth, Cramer, Ranke, Fischer and Bulitschek, the latter a country member; also the five boys Wilhelm Grabs, Abraham and Philip Transou, Gottlieb Cramer and Gottlob Ranke. In the Gemein Saal they all took the Affirmation before the above mentioned Justice [Captain Dobson], who signed a Certificate for each of them.

Feb. 9. Yesterday and today many passed on their way to court. Br. Bulitscheck came to tune the organ.

Feb. 13. We hear that Adam Binckely and George Aust with their teams have returned from the army in Georgia.

Feb. 16. We heard that last evening a draft was made at Peter Hauser's, and John Clean was chosen in place of Rudolph Nieds who belongs to Ekel's company.

March 17. Word came from Richmond that Johannes Strub, who volunteered as ensign to accompany Captain Schmid to Georgia, was wounded, and on the 11th of February died in a hospital there.

March 19. The two Leinbachs, Benjamin and Joseph, came for Certificates [of Moravian membership].

March 20. Abraham Leinbach did the same and the three took them to the home of Colonel Williams, where General Muster was held today.

March 21. It rained hard all day. In the afternoon there was a meeting of those house-fathers who have hitherto paid fines caused by the draft. They were asked if they desired to continue this, and whether they would share the fines imposed by the last draft made in 1778?

They were unanimous in their wish to continue as heretofore. We hear that the three Leinbach Certificates were accepted, but the men must take an Affirmation that they have conscientious objections to bearing arms.

March 24. We hear that Spönhauer, Sr., wishes to take the younger George Hausers into his house, when his son Heinrich Spönhauer moves to his farm.

March 29. We hear from Richmond that Mr. Sheppard and George Hauser, Jr. were severely injured by the stallion belonging to the former.

April 4. The Easter liturgy had to be sung in the Saal as it rained heavily. In spite of the bad weather more people were in town than we expected, among them Captain Eckel and his wife.

April 10. Spönhauer, Jr., a road-master, will visit Bethabara.

April 20. Spönhauer, Jr., his wife and two children moved to his father's farm, and the George Hausers, Jr., came from there into the house of Spönhauer, Sr.

April 23. We hear that Captain Schmid returned yesterday from Georgia, and that his company, although scattered, will follow soon.

April 25. We heard that a band of horse-thieves and robbers had been seen up on the Yadkin, prepared to rob and plunder everything that came their way. Therefore some of the men from here went out to look after their horses.

April 26. We heard this morning that last night the elder Sheppard and his son John were robbed.

April 27. Br. Heckewälder came with a cavalry officer who arrived in Salem with fifty men yesterday, and came here to seek provisions for them.

April 28. A wagon-load of corn was sent to Salem, most of it furnished by the neighbors.

May 25. Br. Strub has been ill for several days, the result of a spider's bite.

June 26. Most of the men finished the wheat harvest today. The rye was cut last week.

July 21. Various men passed on their way to muster.

July 22. Colonel Sheppard and his lady arrived, coming from Hillsborough where they have just been married. They visited the Gemein Haus, and the organ was played for them.

July 24. This week many people have passed, some coming from the new land, others going to the Hollow seeking the men who, it is said, are taking horses and cattle from the settlers.

July 28. I took to Br. Schaub, Jr., at Bethabara, a list of all Brethren living in Bethania or in the adjacent country.

July 30. We heard that at the General Muster yesterday ten men were drafted from this district, among them Abraham Hauser, Kastner and Lanius. Martin Hauser secured the release of his son, Abraham.

Aug. 1. Gottfried Müller's servant came with a letter, in which Müller announced the birth of a son, and asked that I would come to Richmond to baptise the child as it was very weak. I went at once, but the child went home shortly before I arrived.

Aug. 4. Ludwig Blum came with the news that the negro Jacob had run away from Salem. He brought an Advertisement, which was at once posted on the tavern, and a copy was sent to Richmond by a traveler who was going thither.

Aug. 6. We hear that Colonel Armstrong has returned from the south.

Aug. 11. Most of the men from the upper town have been in Richmond at court today and yesterday.

Aug. 14. A man named Schnabely came from Virginia. His wife ran away with a man named Kohlhup, and stopped in this neighborhood at the farm of the departed Johannes Schor. The man said that the two had made off with almost his entire property while he was in Pennsylvania.

Aug. 25. One hundred and sixty head of cattle were driven through the town on their way to Virginia. It is said they are for the prisoners from Burgoyne's army.

Sept. 4. Today men passed, going to muster, and most of the young men from the upper town went also. In the evening we heard that Christian Conrad volunteered to accompany the soldiers who have been ordered to protect the surveyors who are to run the line between Virginia and North Carolina toward the west.

Sept. 7. Christoph Ellroth's son-in-law, John Winscot, with his wife and children, stopped on their way to Holston, and asked for the baptism of the infant, Robert, born on July 25th of this year.

Sept. 9. The Brn. Kühnast and Blum came early this morning to confer with several of the Brethren about the wagons which have been pressed. It was agreed that two horses, Transou's and Ranke's, and a teamster, Samuel Strub, shall go from Bethania, and that Bethabara shall furnish a wagon and two horses.

Sept. 13. Samuel Strub set out for Richmond with the wagon that was pressed.

Sept. 20. Br. Carl Holder brought two horses, which will take to Richmond the wagon from Salem left here on the 17th. Casper Stolz volunteered as teamster.

Sept. 21. The Salem wagon drove off today. Samuel Strub, who has been feeding his horses here, rode with it.

Oct. 9. In the evening at six o'clock was the Communion lovefeast. Shortly before it began Colonel Armstrong and Colonel Scheppert arrived, and wished an opportunity to hear the organ, so following the lovefeast arrangements were made to gratify them.

Oct. 21. Casper Stolz and Samuel Strub returned. Last month they left with the wagons pressed in Salem and Bethabara, and accompanied the men who were running the line [between Virginia and North Carolina] as far as Long Island [of Holston River].

Oct. 29. Five wagons set out for Charlestown. Michael and Peter Hauser went on their own account, Ranke, Schor and George Hauser, Sr., went for Br. Bagge.

Nov. 6. Two officers passed, coming from the Continental Corps in Georgia. They confirmed the report that more than a thousand Americans and Frenchmen were defeated near Savannah.

Nov. 26. The five wagons returned from Charlestown. They were away four weeks and a day.

Dec. 1. Toward noon I rode with George Hauser, Sr., and Heinrich Schor to Ludwig Wolf's, where a fair number of people had gathered for the funeral of Catharine Wolf, maiden name Dietz.

Dec. 2. We heard that this evening there was a draft made at the tavern. Br. Steiner's man, Ellroth[1] by name, and Friedrich Müller's servant were drawn, together with an Irishman from the neighborhood.

Dec. 14. Tobias Hirte came to see whether he could get reeds for pipe-stems. He returned on the 16th to gather the reeds.

Dec. 23. In the presence of the Brn. Grabs and Michael Hauser, George Hauser, Jr., signed the agreement by which he becomes a resident of Bethania for a year.

---

[1] Usually called Adam of the mill to distinguish him from Adam, son of Christopher Ellroth or Elrod.

*Travel Diary of Bishop Johann Friedrich Reichel, Lititz, Pa., to
Salem, N. C., and return.   1780.*

[These travel diaries were translated in full for *Travels in the American
Colonies* edited by Newton D. Mereness; published by the Macmillan Co., New York, 1916.   Only a bare outline is therefore given
here, to show the route traveled, and any special item that should be
recorded.   In addition to the four teamsters there were ten persons in
the party,—Bishop and Mrs. Reichel, Rev. and Mrs. Jeppe Nilsen,
Mr. and Mrs. Gottfried Aust, Mr. and Mrs. Jacob Blum, Miss Maria
Magdalena Reutz and Johann Friedrich Peter.]

The party left Lititz, Pa., on May 22, 1780.   In the sixth hour
they reached Anderson's Ferry across the Susquehannah.   It required
two hours to get the two wagons and three riding horses across, by
means of two flats.   The charge was $56.00 for each six-horse wagon,
and $8.00 for a horse and rider.

On the 23rd and 24th they passed through Yorktown [York], and
Peter-Town [Petersburg,] and camped on the Maryland line on the
second night.   On the 25th at Danitown [Taneytown] Md. the people
were celebrating the festival of Corpus Christi, in the Catholic church.
On the way thither the party passed the home of Adam Loesch, and
spoke with him; he was planning to sell his house and move to Holston
River, in Virginia, four hundred miles away.   Reached Frederictown
[Frederick] Md. on the 26th, where they stopped at the inn of Mr.
Grosh.   There they found that Congress money was worth forty to one,
some said thirty to one, and they exchanged silver for Congress money,
as they were going into Virginia "where there is little money and silver
is little used."

In Virginia they saw one-roomed cabins in the woods, built of unhewn logs, without windows; the chimneys were built at the gable end,
of logs.   Everywhere there were negroes moving about.   On the morning of the 27th they found that Br. Reichel's chest had been stolen,
also Hauser's sickles and clothing.   "This neighborhood is far-famed
for robbery and theft."   Crossed the Potomac into Virginia, and
camped for the night at Louisburg [Leesburg,] Va.   On the morning
of the 27th and of the 29th much time was lost looking for the Carolina
riding horses, which each time had set off toward home, but were caught
when they stopped to feed.   On the night of the 29th they camped eight
miles beyond Redhouse; "Redhouse is 25 miles from Louisburg, 130
miles from Lititz, and 195 miles from Bethlehem."

On the 30th the party passed Nevill's Tavern and Germantown,—
"When one is in the town one asks where the town is."   The road

was rough, hilly and marshy, and Conrad's wagon stuck in a hole, and it took ten horses to pull it out. Hauser's wagon broke several times, and had to be repaired. On the 31st they forded the Rappahannock, and spent the night at the home of Mr. Shelton, where they had "a room with four beautiful double beds."

June 1st they reached the Rapidan, but the water was so high from the rain of the preceding day that they could not cross until the 2nd. On the 3rd they made twenty-three miles, their longest distance for one day; camped at night at Bird's Ordinary. The night of the 4th was spent half a mile from Peyne's Tavern. On the 5th they crossed James River; also heard that Charlestown had been forced to surrender to the British. "This made a great stir in Virginia." On the 6th the party passed Cumberland Court-House; and on the next day crossed the Appomattox on a bridge. On the 8th crossed a bridge over the little Roanoke, and passed Charlotte Court-House. "In the afternoon it was clear, and we crossed marshy ground on a corduroy road half a mile long, to drive over which would certainly be good medicine for a hypocondriac. We spent the night in a pretty, open spot, where we ate the first *Journey-cakes*[1] with a good appetite." On the 8th forded Stanton River, where the banks were so steep that it took eight horses to pull Conrad's wagon out. On the 10th the roads were so bad that everything fell out of the wagons. "Here we made a new arrangement. Br. and Sr. Nilsen and Br. and Sr. Aust rode double on two of the horses, and Sr. Reichel rode for the first time alone, the rest went afoot." Noon was spent at the high Bannister Bridge. The night camp was half a mile from Old Halifax, 100 miles from Salem.

On the 11th Sr. Reichel had a headache. "At noon as she lay on a bed in the shade a hog jumped over her because the dog was after it, and this cured her." Camped for the night at Lynch's Tavern. On the 12th Br. Jeppe Nilsen was so weak that he could not ride, but had to stay in the wagon most of the time. Hauser was made happy by the arrival of his men, Jacob Stotz and Samuel Strub of Bethania, who came to help him. Stopped at noon at the Sandy River. On the 13th the party had "a miserable road, ruts filled with sand by the rain, stony, hilly, and full of holes." "This morning we crossed the Carolina line." "In spite of the recent rains we passed safely over Smith's River and Matrimony Creek." On the 14th the party crossed the Mayo River soon after noon, and shortly thereafter were met by the Brn. Marshall and

[1] The words Journey Cakes are written in English in the diary. Philologists have differed as to the relative age of this form and the generally accepted form Johnny-cake, the latter being usually given as "of negro origin." The early date of this use of Journey Cake, and the ease with which this type of corn-bread could be made at a camp fire while on a journey, point to it as the original form, and Johnny-cake as a later corruption.

Herbst, the wagon of the Salem Single Brethren, and the teamsters Broesing and Heinrich Stöhr, who had come to assist them in. On the 15th they crossed Dan River, reaching Salem about six in the afternoon, "thankful to the Saviour, Who had guided and led us like children, and had given us to feel His peace and presence throughout the entire way."

June 16th the wagons, left behind the preceding day, arrived in Salem. "And so here we are in Salem, in this town of the Lord's peace!"

[The return trip, from Salem, N. C., to Lititz, Pa., was made over the same road, except that the party turned aside to visit Caroll's Manor and Manakasy. This time there was but one wagon, lightly loaded, and besides the teamsters the party consisted only of Bishop and Mrs. Reichel and Christian Heckawälder. A few War references only are translated here, together with the paragraphs on the two Maryland congregations.]

The party left Salem on Oct. 5, 1780. On the 8th "we met two wagons from Jersey on their way to Rowan County, and the teamsters told us that the road from Redhouse to Halifax (a distance of 200 miles) swarmed with soldiers, going to Carolina." The 9th they "met wagons coming from Petersburg, whose owners told us that a French fleet with 7000 men and a number of cannon on board had run in to Southkey. Toward evening we reached Stanton River, where we met soldiers going to Carolina." On the 13th "we saw the first traces of the army, said to be going from Virginia to North Carolina, for we met perhaps a hundred militia-men, traveling, however, without any organization." On the 15th, at the home of Captain Bradley, they "heard that General Arnold, who had planned to betray General Washington into the hands of the English, had deserted to them."

On the 18th they went to Caroll's Manor, stopping at the home of Mr. Johnson. "This man and Schau's family are the only Brethren still living at Caroll's Manor, the rest have moved away, some to Wachovia, the others elsewhere. Br. Reichel spoke much with Mr. Johnson about the school-house here and the land belonging to it, both of which lie practically abandoned, for Heil, who lived there for a while, has let it go to ruin, instead of taking care of it, since the Brethren have moved away. They would like to have a Brother here again as teacher, but they are too few, and not able to support him, much as they would like to do so." From the 19th to the 24th they were in Manakasy, Md. where Bishop Reichel held several services for the Brethren living there. On the 25th the party reached Yorktown, and next day Br. Heckewälder set out for Lititz, where, Oct. 30th, Bishop and Mrs. Reichel also arrived, "to the great joy of the entire congregation."

Extract from letter, Bishop Graff to Nathaniel Seidel.

[From Archives in Bethlehem, Pa.]

Salem, June 28, 1780.

This will be brought to you by our Br. Johannes Schaub, Jr. of Bethabara, formerly tavern-keeper there. Br. Matthew Weis, the dyer, his god-father and an old friend of his father's, has several times offered that if Schaub would come to Bethlehem, and pay his own expenses while there, he would teach him how to dye. Schaub now desires to settle in Bethabara, and there establish a dye-house,—the lack of which our Brethren and Sisters have keenly felt hitherto, as they had to send all yarn to Pennsylvania to be colored, which cost a good deal and some was lost. With this in view Br. Schaub now goes to you, with full approbation of our Conference. * * *

Letter, Marshall to Andresen.

[Translated in full from a copy of a letter written by Rev. Frederic William Marshall to Rev. Joachim Heinrich Andresen, a member of the Unity's Elders Conference.]

Month of September, 1780.

My dearly beloved Br. Andresen,

Without doubt you will have wondered why you have heard nothing from me since my arrival here, but when everything is so uncertain one does not know what to write, and there was no possibility of sending a letter with assurance that it would go through. Everything had to go by way of Pennsylvania, and I wrote to Brethren there at every opportunity, so I feel sure that you have not been without a general idea of our circumstances. Our life has been fairly quiet, and without marked disturbance, but we have been constantly uncertain in regard to our possessions, and have been therefore the more aware of the nearness and blessing of our dear Lord, which we must not fail to mention.

On our arrival in Salem I found rich fulfillment of my hope that since the Lord had called away so many of the active members here He intended to take matters into His own hands. I have thanked Him many times for this, and can never be grateful enough for the help He gave to our dear Br. Graff, on whom everything rested, including many matters which it had not been the intention that he should handle. He so directed this His servant (especially in the office left vacant by the death of Br. Wallis) that taking it all together I believe Wachovia has passed through these difficult times as well, I might almost say better, than other congregations led by much more experienced men, and this although the complications here were as great as anywhere.

When we arrived in America, by express permission of the Governor of the Jerseys and the President of Pennsylvania, we were received by General Manwell at Elisabethtown, and were sent on with a Pass to Bethlehem. I soon after called on the President of Pennsylvania, Mr. Reed, and the former President of Congress, Mr. Henry Laurence, in Philadelphia, and I was welcomed without any hesitation, and remained in Pennsylvania for half a year, so had no fear that I would not be allowed to stay here. In spite of this the lawyers, and others who were familiar with conditions, thought that I must appear before the Governor and the Assembly before I could be considered, unquestionably, a resident; but this might mean risk and waste of time, and would have required a journey of some weeks, so I decided not to go. Now so long a time has passed that there appears to be no question that I am a quiet and peaceful citizen of the land.

My first duty was the publication of the Results of General Synod, which were heard with the more interest because the members had been waiting for them. In Salem the reorganization of the Conferences followed. In Bethabara, in place of an Aufseher Collegium and a Grosse Helfer Conferenz, a Committee was appointed.

In regard to Bethania, we resolved not to withhold from them such parts of the Synodal Results as they could understand, or such as might apply to them; resolved also, when opportunity offered, to have a heart-to-heart talk with them. He, Who had manifested Himself to the Synod, made Himself felt here also, pointed out where they had hitherto erred and the cause thereof, and awakened a desire that the Rules and Regulations, which had been under consideration for eight years, might now be finished and signed. This was done, and a Committee was proposed by them and approved by the Lord.

When I compare their circumstances with what I saw in Pennsylvania at various places, it appears to me that the life on a farm lends itself to a patriarchical mode and to daily worship of God in the home, better than to residence in a congregation town, with numerous and daily meetings, and with strict Choir organization. Even when persons trained in the Choir Houses marry and take charge of a farm, the care of cattle and other farm work does not always permit rigid adherance to rules, and by oft repeated exceptions the opposite of what they have done becomes their custom, and the rules become burdensome.

In Friedberg and Friedland the Abstract prepared for the Diaspora was communicated with blessing.

In the English Settlement there was at first complaint that though they had built a school-house there was little prospect of securing a teacher for their numerous young people. We took the matter under advisement, and the Lord gave us Br. and Sr. Fritz for this position, and when they moved thither a close Society was organized and the settlement received the name of *Hope.*

During our absence in Europe our little Choir of Married People in Salem and Bethabara was much reduced by the home-going of members, although the congregation in general had remained about the same in size because of the birth of children. Certain marriages could not be longer postponed. Br. Lorenz Bagge, the only minister in Bethabara, needed a helpmate, and the widowed Sr. Fockel was provided for us by the Lord. The elderly Br. George Schmid could no longer get along in his household affairs, and as the widowed Sr. Bachhof was not unwilling, and the Saviour approved, she was united with him in marriage for his assistance. Our Tavern needed an assistant, and Br. Holland, the only man we had for the place, was married to the Single Sr. Maria Strub; and the Single Br. Rudolf Christ was married to Elisabeth Oesterlein for assistance in the pottery. The two widowers, Aust, the master-potter in Salem, and Bluhm, who had been managing the farm in Bethabara, could no longer remain unmarried, and as they could not find suitable Sisters for wives here we had to send them to Pennsylvania for that purpose. As Br. Schaub, Jr., hitherto tavern-keeper in Bethabara, wished to establish a dye-house it was decided that on his return Br. Bluhm should take charge of the tavern there, and Br. Peter Rose, who was giving up the plantation near Salem, took Br. Bluhm's place on the Bethabara farm. We thanked the Lord for directing the working out of these difficult questions. As the Single Br. Philip Vogler took over the Salem plantation, he was married to the widowed Sr. Steinmann. It would seem as though these marriages would have put an end to the already small Choir of Single Sisters, but it is really larger than formerly, partly through women from New England, and from the country near us, who have been living in Salem for some time in service, partly through daughters of Bethania parents who have received permission to move into the Choir House here or in Bethabara. In the same way the Choir of Single Brethren shows an increase.

Although the children in the town are not numerous, still we felt the need of an organized school for little boys, where they might spend the greater part of the day under supervision, and learn what is necessary; this was at last arranged, with Br. Christian Heckewaelder for the older and Gottlieb Schober for the younger boys, to their evident advantage. Since that time Br. Graff has held doctrinal instruction for them. Catharine Sehner has taken charge of the girls' school, in place of Sr. Oesterlein, who has married. Sr. M. Elis. Engel holds a school for girls in Bethabara, where hitherto there has been only a school for boys.

Before our departure from Europe Br. Hutton made a deed to me for Wachovia, and Charles and Mary Metcalf drew up a Power of Attorney to certain Brethren here, under which they were to transfer to me the Metcalf lands, of which the title deeds are in our hands here. Both documents were attested under the Lord Mayor's seal. Br. Hutton's deed to me was signed and sealed before our company left Portsmouth, and we took the precaution to have it witnessed by several Brethren of our party, so that in case of need they could testify here. When I was in Philadelphia I inquired expressly whether the seal of the Lord Mayor would be accepted as valid, and no doubt was expressed, so I did not think it necessary to go to the expense of having the Brethren travel to Philadelphia as witnesses. When I took the papers to General Court at Salisbury, to secure from the Chief Judges an order to have them recorded, men objected to honoring the Lord Mayor's seal on the Power of Attorney, believing that the Metcalf lands came under the Confiscation Act. I therefore did not produce Br. Hutton's deed, but sent it to Pennsylvania where the aforesaid Brethren could witness it before the President of Pennsylvania.

In each County, Commissioners were appointed, with wide powers, to seek out property subject to confiscation and sell it at public auction, and to call such persons as they saw fit and demand that they take the Oath, and in case of refusal to put them in jail. For this purpose I and Br. Traugott Bagge were summoned, and gave in a description of all the land belonging to Br. Metcalf. They thought it came under the Confiscation Act, and ordered us to appear at the next County Court, but because of much disturbance then it was postponed to another time, and has not yet come up,—perhaps before it does peace and amnesty will have arrived.

The two pieces of Cossart land, lying in Wilkes County, sixty miles from here, were sold to a gentleman in Salisbury, Mr. Montgomery, for £2500 hard money, on which £1000 was paid. During these disturbed times certain squatters have settled there, and when the present owners tried to eject them the question was raised whether Cossart had a right to sell the land or whether it came under the Confiscation Act. It looks as though the matter would have to be settled in the

Courts,[1] and should the case be lost not only would we lose the land and the unpaid balance of £1500 and interest, but the £1000 already received would have to be given back.

Under these circumstances we have not thought it wise to make any use of Hutton's deed to me, for fear of raising a question concerning that part of our land in which we are as yet undisturbed.

When I returned from Europe I had many applications for the purchase of land, and I could have sold much had it not been for the difficulty about the paper money, which must be accepted under the law though it had less than the one-hundredth part of its value commercially. After selling a few small pieces I decided it was better to make no sales for the present. Even the rents are being poorly paid, and when we try to force settlement currency must be taken at the above-mentioned value.

Heavy as the taxes are for those of us who bear no arms and must pay a three-fold tax, still the burden is not nearly so great as the loss occasioned by the falling value of the paper money. In the three-quarters of a year that I have been here the value has fallen from 20 to 100 per cent, and many will not accept it at all.

The past winter was unusually severe, and no one remembers such continuous cold and so much snow. In addition the last harvest had been rather poor, and finally there was a great rise in prices. This made travel impracticable, and with the exception of a few packages which had been sent before we left Pennsylvania we received nothing from you or from anywhere in Europe for six months. As soon as travel became possible the march of troops destined for this province made provisions still scarcer, and no one dared travel for fear that wagon and horses would be seized for the army. There were also heavy rain-storms, which brought greater floods than those of nine years ago, and did much damage to bridges and to the Salem mill. We therefore remained in complete ignorance when and how Br. and Sr. Reichel would come hither, and whether the Brethren and Sisters (Huebners, Nielsons, and others) expected from Europe had arrived in Bethlehem. Finally a wagon was sent from here, accompanied by another, and was so fortunate as to reach there in safety, and just as Br. Reichel had sent forward some necessary things and could travel back with them. Three Single Brethren, who had set out in another wagon shortly before them, arrived here on the 31st of May, as advance messengers for those

---

[1] A summary of the Wilkes County land suit was given in Vol. III, *Records of the Moravians in North Carolina*.

we were expecting, and bringing letters from Europe and Pennsylvania. How good it was to have news after being cut off for so long can hardly be understood by those who are accustomed to regular post service. On June 17th they were followed by Br. and Sr. Reichel, and the Single Br. Johann Friedrich Peter, together with Br. and Sr. Aust and Bluhm and the Single Sr. Reitz. They came in the two wagons above mentioned, and their arrival filled us with joy and fulfilled our wish. That the Saviour had provided for this trip of His servants was evident, for the party aroused the wonder of all the persons they met, who could not understand why they were coming hither just when others were fleeing from this province, and in the three and a half months since their arrival there has been no other opportunity for Bethlehem to send us letters, although as a usual thing there is no lack of opportunity in summer.

Br. and Sr. Nielsen as assistant leaders of the Married People's Choir, Br. Nielsen as Vorsteher, and Br. Friedrich Peter as Reader, were at once presented to the congregation in their several capacities, and were heartily welcomed. Our dear Jeppe entered into his office with such good spirits, and made himself so much at home, that everybody had the best of hopes for his success. But scarcely had the Saviour showed him to us when, on June 30th, He took him away through a stroke, and so unexpectedly that he was probably not aware of what was happening. In the evening he laid himself down to sleep, weary, but not knowing that anything was the matter with him, and soon after midnight he awakened in the presence of the Saviour.

With the coming of Br. and Sr. Reichel a new spirit developed within the congregation and without its bounds, running parallel and without interference the one with the other, and having a remarkable effect in each. The English took Charlestown and came half the distance from there here, to Camden and the Cheraws, indeed it was reliably reported that they were only one day's march from this place. This induced the so-called Tories to rise, and more than a thousand gathered, did all kinds of deeds of violence to those by whom they had formerly suffered and finally joined the English. To scatter these, and to prevent further risings, the militia were called out, who scoured all the country, pressing horses, arms and provisions, and living *at discretion* in various places. We had frequent visits from them, but no pay. In addition to this there were official demands for brandy, steel, iron and leather. The grain, forage and provisions on the farms of the Tories who had risen were assigned to the wandering bands of militia for their free use. As these were scattered in rather large parties, and the leader of each was the judge, acts of violence occurred in many places. One of the worst things about this was that it came just at harvest time, and the already few available men were hindered in their work. During this time the need was so great that various travelers, and the wounded who came from the south, said that in three days they had been able to get no food, only water, and their first request was for a piece of bread. Meanwhile three thousand of the regular Continental troops were assembled at Cross Creek, where they were joined by about seven thousand militia, and preparations were made to march against the English. For their use requisitions were made on the new crop of wheat. A Captain, with sixty men, made headquarters in Salem, and brought in grain from the neighborhood. The Salem mill was required to grind this grain without taking toll; and many soldiers were here from time to time, who had to be provided with bread, meat and brandy daily. Then wagons and horses were pressed, mostly from the surrounding country, to take the flour to the army. The English appeared to weaken, but in the middle of August there was a battle and General Gates was defeated. Several wagons belonging to our members were in or near the battle; one wagon and team were lost, though the teamsters escaped; others retired to Hillsboro, both men and horses suffering from bad treatment and great hunger, and finally many horses were lost, (Bethania men alone lost six,) though, thank God, none of the men suffered actual bodily injury.

It was feared that the Tories would seize this opportunity to rise, and several hundred of the Virginia militia were called on for help. Part of them came through Salem, keeping good order, and new requisitions for meal and meat were made in the surrounding country. They took prisoner numerous suspected persons, and finally gathered in Bethabara, where they spent twelve days. There things went badly because of the numbers present, and Bethabara suffered in many ways,—in her corn-fields, meadows, and orchards, at the mill, in the brewery and distillery, where all the reserve stores were taken. Finally another Continental army gathered at Hillsboro, and General Gates ordered all the leather which could be made ready in the Salem tannery, though he promised to pay for it. The German officer sent here for the leather was a reasonable and modest man.

In spite of all these circumstances Br. and Sr. Reichel were not disturbed in their business, so long as they were here. They saw and spoke with all the Brethren and Sisters, first in Salem, Bethabara and Bethania, and then in Friedberg, Friedland and Hope. Services were held for each village and for each Choir, and necessary changes in organization were made. Our congregations are small, but because of the distances between the places it takes some time to make the rounds. I will mention only the most important things, for all will appear in the diaries and through the report of Br. Reichel. Tycho Niessen, in Friedland, had asked to be relieved, and Br. Heinzmann, who had asked to be released from his office as Vorsteher of the Single Brethren, was proposed for the place, and was united in marriage with the widowed Sr. Reuter. Tycho Niessen and his family moved to Salem. This led to a complete change in the Single Brothers Choir, where the Brn. Petersen and Samuel Stotz took joint charge of the Vorsteher's office, and Br. Praezel became Choir Pfleger. At the same time the House Conferences, Groups, and the general arrangements of the House, were reorganized, and we promise ourselves much blessing in them.

Friedland is an old Society, most of whose members came hither from Broadbay in New England in order to be near the Unity, and they were joined by a few from Pennsylvania. Among them were several who had been Received into the congregation, and some communicants who belonged to the country congregation of Friedberg. Because of their distance from Friedberg they could not receive the proper care, so in future they will have their own Receptions and Communions. In Hope the same thing was true, and in addition the services in Friedberg were held in German, so that the English members enjoyed neither pastoral care nor doctrinal instruction. It was therefore essential that Hope should be organized as a separate congregation. Since Br. and Sr. Fritz have lived among them the improvement is evident, and there is more brotherly union.

In order to serve these congregations it was necessary to ordain pastors, so on Sept. 16th, at the close of the conference with all the country ministers over the plan for this entire work, the Brn. Heinzmann, Fritz and Friedrich Peter were ordained Deacons by Br. Reichel. At the same time four Brethren and Sisters were Received as Akoluthie.

Salem especially enjoyed the visit of Br. and Sr. Reichel partly because he re-read the Synodal Results, omitting the doctrinal sections, held conferences with the parents regarding the education of their children, and completed various details of organization; partly because they could share in the congregation and Choir festivals and Communions occurring during the time of their sojourn here. We cannot be sufficiently thankful for the quiet which we enjoyed on those special days.

Bethabara had to endure a severe test before the Married People there could celebrate their festival. Their circumstances have already been mentioned, and when the militia marched away a number of prisoners were left behind, in the former Brothers House, under a strong guard.

In Bethania the Holy Spirit continued to point out the matters in which they had been remiss, of which good work there were many evidences during this Visitation. Special joy and hope for the future was caused by the Reception of one Older Boy and four Older Girls, by which parents as well as children were greatly stirred, and the young people particularly felt a new impulse to follow the call.

In Friedberg no changes were made, but the visit was pleasant and blessed on both sides, as for some years this country congregation has had a fair increase in numbers and a favorable life.

Attached to this are the remaining abstracts of our accounts for the year. I will not guarantee that there are no errors in the first part of the accounts, because of the great irregularity in currency matters; since we have adopted an entirely new method, and enter everything as in hard money, there is little chance for mistake. It is easy to understand that under such conditions as now exist there must be many losses in our financial affairs. In these times the man who makes a bare living can not lose anything, but the better established a business is the more it must lose on account of the constant requisitions, sometimes without pay, sometimes for paper money which no one receives willingly and only at a small value, and sometimes for a receipt only which one does not know where to present for payment. Not only does borrowed capital lie buried in work-shop and houses, though it continues to draw interest, but the above-mentioned requisitions have forced the opening of House accounts, and in consequence a man who has money does not know where to put it to keep it safe.

F. W. M.

Order and Instructions to Major Hartmann. [Copy.]

Sir

You will please to proceed forthwith to Salem in the County of Surry in this State and apply to the Society of Moravians for 1000 prs. of Shoes, for the Use of the Maryland Troops serving in this Department. You may assure the Society, that upon the Delivery of your Certificate signifying your having received the Shoes, that I will pay them the price thereof with the Depreciation allowed. The Society is likewise requested to supply you with a Waggon and Team, to bring the Shoes to the Troops wheresoever they may be in this State, which shall be faithfully sent back upon the Delivery of the Shoes. You will acquaint the Society that the United States in Congress assembled will have a due Sense of this supply being chearfully furnished to their Army, and that every Indulgence and Protection will be granted to them in Consequence thereof. All just Demands which the Society may now have upon the Army in this Department shall be paid with the Depreciation allowed, so soon as the Accounts or Certificates are produced to the proper Officer in this Army. Given at my Headquarters in Hillsboro this 3ᵈ Day of Sept. 1780.

Horatio Gates Genˡ
& Commander in Chief.

To Mr. Traugott Bagge.
Surry County

Bethany Sep. 17th 1780

Sir

I received yours dated Salem Sep. 16th and have Noticed the Contents. I have in a hurry directed a few lines to Mr. Jacob Meyers, also to Mr. Charles Holder, which I desire them to execute, as Subjects of this State & to call any asistance present to put the same in execution if there is Need. I have no person here to send to your Town at this Juncture But shall not neglect such your request, which is & may be of escential Service to myself, and the peacable Inhabitants of your Salem, pray Sir encourage your people to asist in commanding & keeping the peace under the direction of Mr. Holder, & to take in custody all Roi[s]ters, suposed deserters and other evil disposed persons which may either disturb the Good pople of Salem or any other peacable Subjects of this or any of the United States, that has Occasion to travel through your Town, this I think is highly Necessary for the good of every well disposed person as well Inhabitants as those traveling about ther lawfull affiairs—in so doing you will much Oblige

Sir your Very Hble Servant

Martin Armstrong J. P. & Colº Surry Regᵗ Militia.

Part of Letter, Marshall to Nathanael Seidel.

[From Bethlehem Archives.]

* * *In Bethabara everything is much disturbed by the continuing presence of many soldiers; and as no proper advance orders had been given for provisions for the troops the supply of meal is exhausted, all their hogs, their winter butter, much of the cattle and corn, all the oats, all the dried fruit, brandy, fire-wood and rails have been used. * * * Far and wide the land is much reduced, partly laid waste, so that we

can look for high prices if not actual hunger, if God does not give Peace. * * *

Receipt, or Ticket.

[There are twelve similar receipts in the Museum of the Wachovia Historical Society. Why they were not paid is not known. Michael was not a Moravian.]

11 November, 1780.

Received of Barnet Michael Ten Dozen Sheaves of Oats and One Bushel of Corn for the Use of the Riding Horses and Waggon Horses belonging to Gen¹ Gates's Family.

Chrisⁿ Richmond, Secy to Gen¹ Gates.

Extract from a letter, Marshall to Henry XXVIII, Count Reuss,
Jan. 2, 1781.   Copy in Salem Archives.

Difficulties in the entire land have greatly increased, and the farm and household affairs in Bethabara have been almost ruined. The occasion was as follows: For a considerable time all those who were more or less suspected as Tories had been sought out, whipped and beaten, houses had been burned, cattle driven away, and farms ruined. This induced those who feared like treatment to decide to declare themselves openly and enroll under Gideon Wright. On the other hand those who had been active against the Tories were afraid that they would be attacked. A man from Maryland, William Peddycoart, who had lived for five years in Wachovia, for sheer fear of the Tories left his farm and went back to Maryland. Finally all the militia were called out, and on Oct. 13th Gideon Wright's crowd were defeated and scattered. Nevertheless, with the same object in view, General Smallwood came to Salem with one hundred regulars and about fifty of the Guilford militia; strict order was kept, and the General expressed his great disapprobation of the excesses committed here by the militia. Five hundred militiamen went to Bethabara, and as it was rainy they forced their way into the houses, and as no arrangements had been made for their food they seized all stores in the town and neighborhood, killed cattle, and in all ways lived "at discretion." Finally they had definite news of the scattering of the Tories, and then they marched away, and General Smallwood also left Salem.

Some time thereafter several hundred South Carolina militia and Tories and some Englishmen, who had been surrounded on the Catawba in North Carolina at King's Mountain by militia from this state and

Virginia, and had been defeated after a hard fight, were brought to Bethabara. The English officers and soldiers were quartered in the town, but the rest had to camp under the open sky, although it was already very cold. It grieved every humane man to see them thus, and besides in the beginning they suffered hunger and later they ate raw meat and raw corn from the cob. Fortunately for Bethabara it did not rain the whole time they were there, for had it been necessary to bring these men also into the town the misery would have been indiscribable. The reason for this long quartering was that no one knew where to place such a large number of prisoners; and the officers who were in charge of them did not venture to dispose of them without instructions from higher authority, although they were finally obliged to do it. Bethania had four wounded officers quartered there, but it was more of a protection for them than a burden.

Order.

Salem, Feb. 3, 1781.

Mr. Bagge,—Please to deliver to Mr. John Hughes forty seven lb Iron, for the Use of Col^o Whites Regiment.

Wm. Reynolds C.M.

Residents of Salem to General Greene.

Salem Febr. the 8th 1781.

Sir The Underwriters would not presume at present to take up any of Y^r Exc^{ys} precious Time, if it was not the highest Necessity that obligeth them to it.

Conscious of the Integrity of our Hearts, wherewith we allways willingly bear our Share of the Difficulties of these Times, we boldly apply to the Testimony of the Generals Smallwood, Stephens, Colonells White, Washington, Majors Call & Hartmann, Captains Marbury, Gamble & other Officers of the Regulars, who have lately either been quartered here, or came thro' this Place, whether we did not readily supply them with every Thing they wanted & our small Settlement could afford. Tho' this Town was but inhabited in the Years 1772 & 1773, which was 2 & 3 Years before the breaking out of this War, & consequently is but in its Infancy, not containing quite 20 Dwelling houses, & scarce one hundred grown persons, Men & Women included, besides the Difficulty of all Beginners that we owe great Part of our Stock in Trade & our Houses to others, we have never been behindhand with any Part of the County but rather unsupported by the County Commissioner the whole Weight of providing for the Troops is always fallen upon us.

The Commissioners of Military Stores however will attest, that we expressly built a large Loghouse, for the Reception of their Stores, & Col° White that we made sheds for his Horses, that large and small Houses were emptied for the Hospital & the Soldiers here quartered.

But these are not properly the Difficulties we labour under, for we are willing to the utmost to bear our Share in the Calamities of the Times and all the Officers & Men will bear us Testimony that what we did & were able to do for them, we allways did with Chearfullness. But the great Excesses at all Times committed by the Militia, both here & at the old Town called Bethabara; and within a few Days past, since the regular Troops, the Hospital & Magazine of Ammunition were gone from hence, the renewed Excesses of some Georgia & South Carolina people traveling thro' here, the Robberies committed in our Neighbourhood, the unreasonable Treatment we just now received of a couple of hundred Militia from another County, come here under pretence of going to join Y^r Exc^{ys} Army, but far from that seeming to have much Time on their Hands, and continually exacting new Quantities of Brandy, Meat, Bread, Flower, Corn, Salt, pressing of Horses & shoeing their own, with horrid Imprecations, striking the People, coining of Stories, & threatening not to leave this Place, before they have killed a Number of us, besides many pretences to pick a Quarrel or invade People's Properties. These Sir, are the Grievances, which in the Distress of our Hearts we cannot help laying before Y^r Exc^y

The exemplary good Order always observed by the regulars which were here quartered, together with the express Declaration of Genl Smallwood, Col° White & others, make us bold to hope, that Y^r Exc^y will condescend to send a few of Y^r Regulars here to protect the Place, with such further Instructions, as Y^r Excellency in Y^r Wisdom will think proper, and if it could be at the same Time, to grant us a Protection in Writing. * * *

To Mr. Bagge, Salem. (Both letters on one small sheet.)

Sir, I am truly sorry for the Distress of your People & will do everything I can to prevent the like usage for the future, furnish me with a little Paper & Inform me what you think necessary & it shall be done if in my Power. Your friend &c

Jo Winston
20th Feby 1781.

Excuse the want of paper.

Sir, If in my Power to be of Service you may make free Perhaps it may have some weight with a person or those who tell me they intend Greater Dammage than you have as yet suffered. for my part I am ruined

R. Lanier.

To Mr. Traggat Bagge.

Richmond   March 19th 1781.

Sir, I understand that your People is sending down to Newgarding Meeting-house som things for the seport of the wounded in the hospitle there   I know of non there but the Enemy, without a Requist from General Green or the Surgen General I would advise you not to send one sixpence worth to that place   I hope you are sensable that our wound and theres was never put in one hospitle, and that any thing sent for the Seport of our wounded or prisnors mus be sent by a Flagg from General Green   I wish you would send me a coppy of the orders you recev^d. I am Your Humb^l Servt

Jn° Armstrong.

Translated from a letter to Mr. Bagge in Salem.

Honored friend,   I must tell you to my sorrow but still more to yours that we had a General Muster last Friday and when I reached home late I found that two of Colonel Lee's dragoons had pressed a hundred and two of your deer-skins which they had already taken out of my house * * *

Your friend Johannes Daub

April 4th 1781

George Davidson to Mr. Bagey.

Dr Sir   I take thy opurtunity of writing to you as a frend as I am in great want of Lether for the publick * * * Sir I hope you will do every thing that is in your power to git as large a quantity as you can and as soon as posabill. * * *

May ye 12 1781

Extract from a letter, Marshall to a member of the Unity's Elders Conference.

Perhaps you will wonder that I have said no more about the terrible time of plundering, and I cannot deny that it has been a remarkable period, in which each morning we were glad to see each other again, and to know that no one had suffered injury to his person, and that neither the town nor a part of it had been burned. But most of the details have been entered in the diaries, and they did not take place by order of those in authority nor of the army officers, but by mob violence of a released hungry militia. We must say for the regular troops, those belonging to the army of this country, and those belonging to the English, that their officers kept good order among them, and the excesses were committed only by camp followers, single soldiers, and especially by the militia. * * *

Salem June 21st 1781

Receipt.

July 9th 1781   North Carolina   Roan County

this may certify that Barneat Michel heath holed fourrigh with his wagon and two horses one Day for tha Publick Store Raceved by me

Charles Hinkel Captin and
A S Qor master

William Preston to Doct^r Bonn.

Sir   Several of the Militia from Montgomery County on their march to Hillsborough have taken sick and are unable to travel further than this Place untill the Recover. I beg the Favour of you to Visit them & to administer such Medicines as you Judge necessary to relieve them as also to have them put into some comfortable Place untill they are able to follow & you shall be paid for the same.

Salem July 23^d 1781

Note of thanks.

The Officers commanding and belonging to the Regiment of Militia from Montgomery County in Virginia, beg leave to return Thanks in behalf of themselves and the soldiers under their Command, to Mr. Bagge and the other Gentlemen and Inhabitants of the Town of Salem, for their polite behaviour, the hospitable manner in which they received and treated the Troops; and the Inconvenience to which they put themselves to entertain them, and to make their stay, one Night, Comfortable.

Signed by Order

Wm Preston.

Participants in Maryland Ticket.

Salem Store, George Smith, Jacob Bonn, Jacob Meyer, Samuel Stotz, Jacob Steiner, Christoph Kuhnast, 49 men living in the neighborhood, Total amount 38084¾ dollars.

William Read to Traugott Baggie, Esq.

Charlotte September 14th 1781

Dear Sir   Enclosed you will find an address to the People of your part of the Country—I know that a hint of our wants is sufficient for you to influence every person immediately under your direction in our favour, you will please forward said request, & facilitate the business all in your power—Such has been the loss of the Enemy that good authority says they cannot take the field again this Campaign unless they are considerably reinforced—a Brick House which the flying British took shelter in was our bane & caused most of our loss but never was there a severer conflict or a battle more obstinately fought on both sides.

Address to the good People of the Moravian Settlement.

As an action has lately happened between the contending Armies wherein though our army have come off victorious we have suffered much having two hundred wounded,—And as there is a great scarcity of bandages & lint in the Department; I do hereby call upon the humanity of the Inhabitants to make every possible exertion in furnishing old Linnen for dressings—a People remarkable for christianity cannot fail in making use of this opportunity to exercise the most blessed of Christian virtues; for the present situation of our suffering Brother Soldiers really call for charity in a most striking manner.

Charlotte, Septr 14th 1781

Thomas Sumter to Mr. Traugott Baggar.

29th Sepr 1781

Sir

I send Mr Shealds with ten Guineas and one half Joehanus to pay for the Shoes, the overplus of the Money to be laid out in Saddle tacks.

I also send by him Twenty Guineas and four half Johannes to be laid out in Leather, one third Saddle Leather the other two thirds Shoe Leather in an equal proportion of Sole and Uper Leather * * *

Extract from a letter F. W. Marshall to Bishop Reichel.

Oct. 1781.

You can hardly imagine how discouraging it is to prepare a letter to Europe when we do not know who will take the letter from here, when we have not heard from Bethlehem for a long time whether the road thither is practicable, and nothing can be written to us from there before the letter starts on a dangerous voyage. * * *

Extract of a letter Marshall to Wobeser, for the Unity's Elders Conference.

Salem 1 Oct. 1781.

Our dear Lord has wonderfully ordered our income and support for the past year. In the beginning of last winter there was a great increase in prices. The supply of food in the country was small, and ours was used and supplied to the soldiers, and beef cattle were nearly all killed. With concern we saw the last animal driven past, and wondered how it could last. Grain rose in price, and the few cattle left in the county were hidden in the woods. Under these circumstances we had to buy a good part of our grain, and for four or six weeks at a time a supply of fresh meat was rare. Then several circumstances combined to bring prices down. The army moved away, many people fled to Virginia, the Indian murders of settlers in Kentucky prevented the moving thither usual at this season, for example last year the numbers passing through our towns reached into thousands. The mild winter made it possible for the cattle to find most of their food out of doors instead of being fed in the barns, and as their numbers were greatly reduced at any rate not so much was needed for them. Finally, when some of the people realized that their supplies would be more than they needed, fear that they would have to give up their store for Tickets induced them to bring various things for sale, and so the price of grain fell and beef cattle could be secured at a season when ordinarily not one could be had. Under the circumstances the cattle had to be butchered as it was brought in, and so from time to time we were fed, like Elijah by the ravens, and no one suffered want.

As Quit Rents are hated in America, and in Pennsylvania have been annulled by law, and here it is forbidden to pay them to an English proprietor, it is uncertain how we will be able in the future to collect ours.

As the yearly tax on land must be paid partly in grain and partly in money, and I did not know whether the three-fold tax would be collected from me, or only the tax for old men, and in either case it would require a large quantity of corn, so I let it be known that I would accept grain in payment of rent, at the price set by the Act of Assembly. This brought in a fair quantity, which would not have been nearly enough for the three-fold tax, but as only a little more than the simple tax fell on me there was some left over, which served Bethabara well in the requisitions made soon after, as I let them have it for the lower price to which it had meanwhile fallen.

Extract of a letter, Benzien to Reichel.

Salem the 5 Oct. 1781.

Were it not for the distance, I would have sent you our travel diary, especially as we took a road not well known to us, which I would not recommend to any one. In Friedrichstown we saw that if we took the road by Nolan's ferry we would be in constant danger of being pressed, so we took the way over the Blue Mountains by Winchester, Staufers Town, Millerstown, Stanton, and Stone-House, the road which properly leads to Holston and Kentucky. Then we turned back across the Blue Ridge and had unexpectedly bad and fatiguing days of travel. We also had much to suffer from the great heat and severe storms. Most of the horses were sick, the wagons broke down and had to be mended in a neighborhood where no one lived and there was neither smith nor wagon-maker to be found, and our rest was constantly disturbed by sea-ticks of which we found plenty. But we stayed well, were hindered by no one, and were not once asked for our Pass.

Extract from letter, Marshall to Henry XXVIII, Count Reuss.

Nov. 1781.

The Assembly, which should have met on the 5th of this month, assembled very slowly. The Governor at that time [Alex Martin], and the gentleman who had been Governor [Thomas Burke], a Delegate from the General Congress, and two gentlemen of the Council, lodged with us [in the Gemein Haus] and appeared to be entirely satisfied with such accommodations as we were able to give them.

A Proclamation.

By the Honourable Alexander Martin, Esquire, Speaker of the Senate, Captain-General and Commander in Chief, for the Time being, in and over the said state. Dec. 25th, 1781.

[This is a printed sheet, tendering pardon to all loyalists who have enlisted or will enlist in the Continental service. The text is given in full in the *Colonial Records,* Vol. XVII, page 1049.]

Extracts from a letter, Marshall to Count Henry XXVIII.

Salem, March 7, 1782.

In the hope that my letter of Nov. 1781, has reached you I will continue the story and tell you of the results of the Assembly which met here in that month. * * *

On Saturday night the alarm was given that the Tories were coming to seize the Assembly, as had been threatened, (though it was only a party of horse-thieves who fired at a sentinel who spoke to them). All were called to arms and preparations for defense were made. When the first alarm had subsided I invited the members of the Assembly and the officers into my room, where in turn all were served with a hot drink and cold cake. This led to many modest questions about our organization, which I explained to them until day broke and they separated.

All possible preparations were made for the accommodation of so many guests, and beds, etc, were borrowed from several hours' ride all around us. As during these times the Assembly had often had worse accommodations our arrangements made a good impression on them.

At first men of unkind intention toward us made trouble about paying, wishing to give Tickets or paper money, by which the town would have lost two-thirds of the value, but this disposition gradually changed and part was paid in hard money and part in receipts for meat and the like, which brought some loss but not as much. After careful consideration I decided to accept no pay from my own guests.

Our music and singing had a great effect on them, and they listened with wonder and respect. An old, gray-haired gentleman came to me expressly before leaving and said that he had always heard that we were a religious people, which was largely the reason that he had made the long trip to come here, but it had far surpassed his expectations. He was convinced that God was in our midst, and if he could do anything for us in the Assembly, personally or by his influence, he would do it gladly.

On account of an approaching large draft for the army, lists were made of the residents of the entire county. We were called upon to give the Colonel the number in all our Societies, adults and children, of both sexes. In Surry County this amounted to 693; no such order was given in Rowan County. Whether this was the only county in which such a count was made we do not as yet know.

Certificate, (In Wachovia Historical Society Museum.)

Salisbury 4 April 1782. I certify that Peter Michel substituted Philip Long as a Soldier in one of the Continental Battalions of the State of North Carolina for one year to commence this day.

Edm Gamble D.D.

Letter, Marshall to Unity's Elders Conference.

June 20, 1782.

[The letter gives a full explanation of the English law which led to the making of a Deed to James Hutton as Proprietor of Wachovia, the insertion of the Trust clause, the transfer of the title to Marshall, the danger of confiscation under the North Carolina confiscation Acts, and the action of the Assembly in confirming the title to Marshall. Much of the information has already appeared in this and preceding volumes of this series.]

Translation of letter, Adam Spach to Traugott Bagge.

I can now give you better information about the matter. When I reached home the Under Commissary was in my house, and notified me to furnish cattle. He said they had orders from Governor Martin that by the 1st of August provisions and forage for three months for 2000 men and horses must be delivered at Salisbury. If the people did not furnish it willingly he would have to press it. In that case he would bring a Justice and a lawful officer and take what he wanted, and the man must pay the cost which would run to £40. So much in the way of information from your well-known Br.

Adam Spach.

Dated 25th July, 1782.

Extracts from the Report of the Visit in Stinking Quarter, between Reedy Fork, Trevisons Creek and Christoph Reich's on Haw River, from 26th to 30th July, 1782. Written by C. L. Benzien.

Since the last visit in Stinking Quarter, more than two years ago, our friends there have fallen into distress and need, especially during the time when both armies were near them, and through their own fault since most of them behaved as Tories. Three lost their lives, among them the well-known Schumacher. Heinrich Streder and Joh. Sommer have not dared to appear to this hour, since they went with the English army, and their families doubt whether they are still living. Others have gone to the mountains, among them Kummerling and Philipp Ludwig, whom I find on a list made by Br. Ernst. Through these circumstances the others have become subdued, are behaving with caution, and are obeying the orders of the authorities.

I traveled thither with Br. Daniel Christmann, and in the evening arrived at the home of his brother Jacob Christmann. Two years ago this man built a large school-room over his spring-house where he has taught his own children and others who were entrusted to him, instructing them in reading and writing, which he had learned from the Brethren in Pennsylvania. Last winter he had more than thirty children, and on Sundays he gave them religious instruction also. * * *

The corn-fields look astonishingly bad, and people doubt whether they will have any harvest, even if it rains soon. * * *

Jacob Hold and Reich told so many stories of deeds of violence which are still taking place in the neighborhood, that one could not listen without sorrow. Last week a man was made a cripple for a minor matter, and another was murdered. * * * I was told that Jacob Hold is known to be an ardent Tory. Perhaps it was as well, all things considered, that I did not go to his house this time. * * *

Heinrich Herd returned this afternoon from Wachovia. He is building a large stone house, and says that services can be held there. * * *

The following heads of families I have seen on my trip to Reedy Fork, some in their homes, others met elsewhere. Jacob Christmann, Sr.; Jacob Christmann, Jr., at present school-teacher; Christian Fahl, church superintendent; Heinrich Herd; Joh. Drollinger; Andreas Schmidt. These seven seem most interested in a closer connection with the Brethren, though the desire seems to be increasing among those whose names follow. They were all very friendly. Ludwig Eisely has much influence. George Zimmermann is reader in this church and at

Bohn's school-house. Bastian Geringer is a dear man. Jacob Sommer, Sr.,—his wife runs the still-house. Peter Sommer is his son. Jacob Trog. Father Reizmann. Captain Henrich Weizel, miller on the Reedy Fork, was in church for the first time after a long interval, and visited us in our lodging and was very friendly. Daniel Hofheins and his father. Henrich Kopp's place we missed, to his true sorrow; he is a good friend of the Brethren. Jacob Wenig is a simple heart. Martin Weirich and Jacob Weirich, two new attendants on the services, are fine men. Adam Schillig is the well-known Dunkard. George Streder. I also learned to know Jacob Bohn, Adam Weitzel and Esslinger from Bohn's school-house, six miles from here; Bohn and Weitzel appeal to me especially.

Extracts from Report, Marshall to the Unity's Vorsteher Collegium.

Salem, the 1 Oct. 1782.

The Wachovia Administration has lost much through the sale of indigo, and has a supply lying in Philadelphia which will cause additional loss. On the other hand the taxes, set high in paper money, were not collected for so long a time that they were smaller when called for. Little has been done with land this year, partly because there is no money in the hands of people, and partly because I have learned by experience that it is not wise to make a land contract with men unless they pay cash down. * * * The Deed to Wachovia is properly registered, but nothing more has been done about the Cossart and Metcalf land. * * * With the residents of Bethania it has been agreed that they are to pay 6% yearly on the agreed value of £800, together with the Quitrents, and are to receive from me a Lease for fifty years, renewable for ever. This rent begins at Michaelmas.

Extracts from letter, Marshall to Count Henry XXVIII.

Salem, the 10th Dec. 1782.

In Bethabara the former store building, which was ruined during the war, was re-covered and arranged as a dwelling. The business formerly carried on there will be continued as a branch of the Salem store, and a new store building will be erected. * * *

In Virginia, North and South Carolina, there are places where the ground contains mineral (presumably copper ore), and in the bottoms, especially in a dry season, many-colored water stands in the puddles and swamps. The cattle drink this and then in fall their intestines apparently dry up, and the fattest cattle seem to die first. Persons drinking milk from these infected cows become painfully ill, the sickness hangs on for years and often results in death. This disease is commonly known as *distemper*. It has been observed that where the bottoms are cleared, so that the stagnant water is dried up by the sun, the sickness ceases.

Extracts from letter, Marshall to Unity's Aufseher Department.

Salem, on the 17 Apr. 1783.

Concerning the Pennsylvania estates which have come to me through the Will of Br. Nathanael Seidel, the Executors there and other Brethren in authority will have informed you from time to time. So far as I know all is going quietly there, and nothing has arisen which makes my presence necessary. The field here is so insufficiently manned that no one in Wachovia would agree to my moving to Pennsylvania.

Should peace come now I think it would be necessary to have certified copies of Br. Nathanael's Will made, and send them to all the places in the West Indies where we have property which stood in his name, and have them registered there so that I am put in possession. It has occurred to me that my Brethren might find it advisable to appoint some one, born in England or a naturalized British subject, to whom I might convey all my rights in the West Indian estates, who could administer them without question.

After I had written the above, Mr. James Haversham stopped on his return to Georgia, after having refugeed in Virginia for three years. * * * He told me that the papers relating to our two lots in Savannah and the out-lots belonging to them had been burned along with his departed father's papers. From my papers I gave him a copy of Br. David Nitschmann's town and out-lot, in the Second Tything, Anson Ward, No. 3, and the two lots standing in Br. Spangenberg's name, No. 4, with information as to where they had been recorded, and he promised to try to save them for us. Br. David Nitschmann has gone home, and Br. Joseph is old, and something should be done about them, or some one appointed in America to look after them. The Deeds are in Bethlehem.

English permit.

Office of Police, 28th April, 1783.

This certifies that Samuel Staats and Sigmund Leishinksky from Pennsylvania and North Carolina, having complied with the Commander in Chief's order of the 27th March last, is permitted to reside in this City seven days.

Wm. Walton, Magis. of Police.

Extracts from letter, Marshall to Reichel.

Begun June 12th,
finished July 22nd, 1783.

I wonder that during these four years of war our letters have come so safely, and so far as I know nothing of importance has been lost, even though they have arrived irregularly, and were a long time on the way.

In Friedland Br. Heinzmann has been ill with attacks resembling apoplexy, and has fallen three times. The drawing of a small amount of blood has given relief for the time being. The whey-cure and other remedies have been tried, but without results.

Nothing particular has happened in land matters. Sale has been offered to several people who have settled upon the Metcalf tracts, but acting upon the advise of busy-bodies they have neither moved away, nor paid rent, nor signed a contract for purchase, and it has not seemed wise to move them by force.

Br. Michael Hauser, of Bethania, has resigned his office as Justice of the Peace, and Br. Blum, of Bethabara, has been appointed though the Dedimus has not yet arrived.

[Of the following Proclamation there is a manuscript copy in the Salem Archives. It does not appear in the *Colonial Records,* though the order of Assembly for it is recorded there.]

State of North Carolina

> By his Excellency Alexander Martin Esquire Captain General and Commander in chief of the State aforesaid.

A PROCLAMATION

Whereas the honorable the General Assembly have by a Resolution of both Houses recommended to me to appoint Friday the Fourth of July next being the anniversary of the declaration of the American Independence, as a Day of Solemn Thanksgiving to Almighty God, for the many most gracious interpositions of his providence manifested in a great & signal manner in behalf of these United States, during their conflict with one of the first powers of Europe:—For rescuing them in the Day of Distress from Tyranny & oppression, and supporting them with the aid of great & powerful allies:—For conducting them gloriously and triumphantly through a just and necessary War, and putting an end to the calamities thereof by the restoration of Peace, after humbling the pride of our enemies & compelling them to acknowledge the Sovereignty and Independence of the American Empire, and relinquish all right & claim to the same:—For raising up a distressed and Injured People to rank among independent Nations and the sovereign powers of the world. And for all other Divine favors bestowed on the Inhabitants of the United States & this in particular.

In conformity to the pious intentions of the Legislature I have thought proper to issue this my Proclamation directing that the said 4th Day of July next be observed as above, hereby strictly commanding and enjoining all Good Citizens of this State to set apart the said Day from bodily labour, and employ the same in devout and religious exercises. And I do require all Ministers of the Gospel of every Denomination to convene their congregations at the same time, and deliver to them Discourses suitable to the important Occasion, recommending in general the Practice of Virtue & true Religion, as the great foundation of private Blessings as well as National happiness & prosperity.

Given under my Hand & the great Seal of the State at Danbury the 18th Day of June in the Year 1783 & seventh Year of the Independence of the said State

Alex: Martin

By his Excellencys
Commande   God save the State.
P. Henderson Pro Sec.

A Proclamation.

[This printed Proclamation of Pardon and Oblivion for the Loyalists, dated Halifax, July 28, 1783, and signed by Governor Alexander Martin, is given in full in the *Colonial Records,* Vol. XVI, page 850.]

Extract from letter, Benzien to.........

........................1783.

I do not like it that the work of the Saviour in Carolina is entirely restricted to Wachovia, and everywhere else there is, as it were, a thick darkness. This was manifest on our visits to Stinking Quarter and Deep Creek where very few permanent results can be seen and the preaching moves the people for only a short time. But I believe that the Saviour does not have us here in vain, especially if He can make His purpose increasingly clear to us, of which there seems to be a comforting prospect.

Extracts from letter, Marshall to Unity's Vorsteher Collegium.

Oct. 28, 1783.

It cannot be denied that this country is in the condition of a patient convalescing from fever, who begins to be conscious of his weakness and still needs medicine and care. The land itself, the people of property, commerce, public and private credit, the currency in circulation, all are laid waste and ruined.

Although during the past year seven hundred and fifty acres of land have been surveyed for purchasers, it has not been entered in the capital account because only a very small amount has been paid, and therefore the property still belongs to the Unity. The 497 acres given up by Samuel Perry have been re-entered at the price at which they were sold.

Amidst the calamities of this year the most fortunate thing for Salem was that throughout the country all business was on the basis of hard money. Some time ago it was noticed that the French, stationed in Virginia, and also the English, had brought in much hard money. Sales increased, partly because more things could be secured, partly because prices went down. In other places no stores had been reopened, so there was good trade in our store, in the pottery, which had again secured glazing, and in the tannery, where there was a stock of leather. The heavy loss made two years ago was entirely covered and a clear profit remained, and this seemed a good time to reopen a store at Bethabara.

The more I am conscious of failing strength the more I am anxious to bring everything into good order. I find, however, that the Administration work constantly increases, and would advise that an assistant be given to me, who could continue to carry on the work in case of my home-going or incapacity, though so long as the Saviour gives me strength I am most willing to serve where and as I am needed.

Men resident in Wachovia, 1775 to 1783.

[The following lists have been compiled from various church registers and congregation catalogs in the Salem Archives; the list of men living on separate plantations is taken from a tax list of 1780. Names of women and children are omitted. The date following the name is the year of birth.]

Salem.

Aust, Gottfried, 1722
Bagge, Traugott, 1720
Baumgarten, Johann George, 1722
Beck, Johann Friedrich, 1751
Benzien, Christian Ludwig, 1753
Beroth, Jacob, 1740
Bibighaus, George, 1754
Blum, Heinrich, 1752
Bonn, Dr. Jacob, 1733
Broessing, Andrew, 1742
Christ, Rudolph, 1750
Christmann, Balthaser, 1760
Christmann, Daniel, 1756
Dixon, John, 1762
Dixon, Joseph, 1761
Flex, Johannes,
Goepfert, George, 1729
Goetje, Peter, 1747
Graff, Bishop Johann Michael, 1714
Heckewälder, Christian, 1750
Heinzmann, Johann Casper, 1723
Herbst, Johann Heinrich, 1727
Hill, Philipp,
Holder, Charles, 1744
Holland, John, 1743
Hurst, James, 1720
Koffler, Adam, 1727
Krause, Gottlob, 1760
Krause, Johann, 1742
Kremser, Andreas, 1753
Lick (Lück), Martin, 1759
Marshall, Rev. Frederic William, 1721
Meinung, Ludwig, 1743
Merkly, Christopher, 1713
Meyer, Jacob, 1725
Miksch, Matthew, 1731
Möller, Ludwig,
Nissen, Toego (Tycho), 1732

Oesterlein, Matthew, 1752
Peter, Rev. J. Frederic, 1746
Petersen, Nils, 1717
Pfeil, Johann Fr., 1711
Praetzel, Gottfried, 1739
Priem, Johann Fr., 1718
Reitz (Reuz), Johannes, 1752
Renner, Johann George, 1714
Reuter, Christian Gottlieb, 1717
Rose, Peter, 1733
Schaaf, Jeremias, 1718
Schmid, Jens, 1732
Schmidt, George, 1719
Schmidt, Johann Christian, 1760
Schneider, Martin, 1756
Schnepf, Daniel, 1718
Schober, Gottlieb, 1756
Schreyer, Johann Peter, 1735
Schroeter, Johann, 1758
Schumaker, Adam, Jr., 1755
Schulz, Gottfried, 1750
Sehner, Peter, Jr., 1749
Spach, Johann Gottlieb, 1764
Spieseke, Thomas, 1730
Stauber, Christian, 1761
Steiner, Jacob, 1734
Stockburger, Johann George, 1731
Stotz, John, 1751
Stotz, Samuel, 1752
Strehle, Ch. Rudolph, 1751
Strehle, Gottlieb, 1756
Strub, Johann Jacob,
Transu, Philip, Jr., 1761
Triebel, Christian, 1714
Wallis, Johann George,
Walther, Johann Heinrich, 1728
Wohlfahrt (Welfare), Jacob, 1755
Wageman, Andreas, 1758
Yarrel, Peter, 1749
Zillmann, Heinrich, 1713.

Salem (continued)

Gernand, Joh. Adam, 1759
Rasp, Melchior, 1715
Reich, Christoph, Jr., 1763
Reich, Matthaeus, 1764
Spach, Gottlieb, 1764
Stauber, Franz, 1765

Bethabara.

Aust, Johann George,
Bagge, Rev. Nic. Lorenz,
Blum, Jacob, 1739
Fockel, Gottlieb, 1724
Holder, George, 1729
Kapp, Jacob, 1729
Kapp, Joseph Friedrich, 1761
Kühnast, Christoph, 1715
Leinbach, Ludwig, 1743
Lung, Jacob, 1713
Mücke (Micke), Johannes, 1749
Nilson, Johannes,
Nilson, Jonas, 1712
Rank, John, 1737
Richter, Johannes, 1716
Schaub, Johannes, Jr., 1744
Schaub, Johannes, Sr., 1717
Schemel, Johannes, 1746
Schmidt, Christoph, 1715
Stach, Rev. Matthew, 1711
Stauber, Paul Chr., 1726
Steup, Joh. Franz, 1716
Stöhr, Joh. Heinrich, 1746
Vogler, Philip Martin, 1754
Wageman, Joh. George, 1760
Wernly, Heinrich, 1746

Bethania.

Beroth, Johannes, 1725
Binkele (Pinkley), Peter, Sr., 1704
Binkele, Peter, Jr.,
Boeckel, Joh. Nicholas, 1741
Bulitschek (Bolejack), Jos. Ferdinand, 1729
Conrad, Christian, 1744
Conrad, Johannes, 1747

Ernst, Rev. Joh. Jacob, 1730
Feiser, Peter, 1743
Fischer, Casper, 1720
Grabs, Gottfried, 1716
Grabs, William, 1755
Hauser, Abraham, 1761
Hauser, George, Jr., 1755
Hauser, George, Sr., 1730
Hauser, Jacob, Jr., 1764
Hauser, Jacob, Sr., 1733
Hauser, Johannes, 1754
Hauser, Martin, 1733
Hauser, Michael, Jr., 1758
Hauser, Michael, Sr., 1731
Hauser, Peter, 1740
Hege, Balthaser, 1714
Kirschner, Joh. Christian, 1717
Kramer, Adam, 1719
Kramer, Gottlieb, 1762
Krieger (Krüger), Heinrich, 1753
Krieger (Krüger), Jacob, 1755
Künzel, Friedrich, 1737
Loesch, Jacob, 1760
Loesch, Joh. Christian, 1758
Leinbach, Abraham, 1744
Leinbach, Benjamin, 1746
Leinbach, Joseph, 1752
Müller (Miller), Jacob, 1721
Müller, Joseph, 1741
Opiz, Carl Gottlob, 1754
Ranke, Gottlob, 1761
Ranke, Michael, 1729
Schauss, Philip, 1728
Schor (Shore), Heinrich, 1735
Schor, Johannes, 1760
Schulz, George, 1730
Schulz, Johannes, 1703
Sehnert, Peter, Sr., 1713
Seiler, Johannes, 1751
Spönhauer, Heinrich, 1716
Spönhauer, Joh. Heinrich, 1750
Strub, Johannes, Jr.,
Strub, Johannes, Sr., 1719
Strub, Samuel, 1757
Transou, Abraham, 1756
Transou, Philip, Jr.
Transou, Philip, Sr., 1724
Volk, Andreas, 1722.

Friedberg.

Beck, Rev. Valentine, 1731
Boeckel, Friedrich, 1743
Ebeling, Ludwig, 1758
Ebert, Johann George, 1752
Ebert, Martin, Jr., 1750
Ebert, Martin, Sr., 1724
Fischel, Johann, 1762
Fischel, Johann Adam, 1730
Fischer, George, 1757
Fischer, Melchior, 1726
Frey, Christian, 1731
Frey, George, 1741
Frey, Heinrich, 1752
Frey, Johannes, 1753
Frey, Joh. Peter, 1746
Frey, Johann Valentine, 1748
Frey, Michael, 1747
Frey, Peter, 1749
Frey, Valentine, 1721
Greter, George, 1749
Greter, Jacob, Jr., 1764
Greter, Jacob, Sr., 1708
Hartmann, Adam, 1729
Hartmann, George, 1724
Hartmann, James, 1760
Hartmann, Johannes, 1757
Hauser, Heinrich, 1754
Hoehns (Hanes), Johannes, 1750
Hoehns, Marcus, 1719
Hoehns, Philip, 1752
Ingram, David, 1764
Jans, Johannes, 1760
Knauss, Joseph, 1750
Lund, Nils, 1728
Miller (Müller), Johannes, 1763
Miller, John, Sr., 1726
Miller, Heinrich, 1751
Miller, Michael, 1753
Moll, Johann, 1749
Nöting (Nading), Matthes, 1756
Pfaff, Isaac, 1755
Pfaff, Peter, 1727
Rippel, Henrich, 1757
Rothrock, Peter, 1746
Rothrock, Philip, 1746
Rothrock, Valentine, 1752
Schmidt, Jos. Christian, 1761

Schneider, Cornelius, 1751
Schneider, Heinrich, 1754
Schneider, Peter, 1744
Schott, J. Jacob, 1748
Spach, Adam, Jr., 1753
Spach (Spaugh), Adam, Sr., 1720
Spach, Johannes, 1762
Tanner, Jacob, 1756
Tesch, Adam, 1757
Tesch, George Heinrich, 1761
Tesch (Desch), Heinrich, 1733
Volz (Folz), Andreas, 1751
Volz, Friedrich, 1759
Volz, Johannes, 1755
Volz, Joh. Jacob, 1753
Volz, Peter, Jr., 1749
Volz, Peter, Sr., 1726
Walk, Martin, 1737
Weber, Leonard, 1722
Wesner, Jacob, 1762
Wesner, Johannes, 1764
Wesner, Matthias, 1730
Zimmerman, Benjamin David, 1763
Zimmerman, Christian, Jr., 1762
Zimmerman, Christian, Sr., 1726
Zimmerman, Johannes, 1760

Friedland.

Clayton, William, 1765
Elrod, Jermias, 1755
Fiedler, Joh. Peter, 1752
Fockel, Samuel, 1719
Hahn, George Friedrich, 1744
Hein (Hine), Jacob, 1713
Hein, Jacob William, 1761
Hein, John, 1749
Kastner, Anton, 1743
Kröhn (Green), Conrad, 1763
Kröhn, Peter, 1722
Kröhn, Philip, 1753
Lagenauer, George Fr., 1755
Lagenauer, Jacob Fr., 1751
Lanius, John, 1751
Miller, Frederic, 1745
Reid, Jacob, 1735
Reid, Johannes, 1763

Friedland (continued)

Rominger, Christian, 1762
Rominger, Jacob, 1743
Rominger, Michael, Jr., 1759
Rominger, Michael, Sr., 1709
Schelhorn, Joh. Jacob, 1740
Schneider, David, 1762
Schneider, Johann, 1756
Schneider, Philip, 1760
Seiz, Joh. Michael, 1765
Seiz (Sides), Michael, 1737
Vogler, George Michael, 1759
Vogler, Lorenz, 1752
Vogler, Philip Christoph, 1725

Hope.

Blake, John, 1750
Bohner (Booner, Boner), William, 1747
Boyer (Bucher), Henry, 1729
Butner, Thomas, 1741
Chitty (Chiddy), Benjamin, 1743
Douthid, Abraham, 1762
Douthid, Isaac, 1756
Douthid, James, 1749
Douthid, John, 1709
Douthid, Thomas, 1753
Douthid, William, 1746
Elrod, Adam, 1744
Elrod, Adam (miller), 1753
Elrod, Christopher, Jr., 1757
Elrod, Christopher, Sr., 1721
Elrod, John, 1762
Elrod, Robert, 1759
Fritz, Rev. Christian,
Goslin, John, 1756
Hamilton, Horatio, 1756
Jones, Michel, 1761
Maas, Henry, 1756
Markland, Jonathan, 1757
Markland, Matthew, Jr., 1761
Markland, Matthew, Sr., 1727
McKnight, George, 1765

McKnight, Roger, 1763
Peddycoart, Basil, 1740
Peddycoart, John Jac., 1750
Peddycoart, William Barton, 1739
Padget (Badget), John Jr., 1763
Padget, John, Sr., 1723
Padget, Thomas, 1752
Riddle, Stephen, 1730
Smith, Daniel, 1736
Slator, Henry, 1747
Spoon, Adam, 1736
Taylor, Matthias, 1752
Wainscot, John, 1749

Scattered on farms. Tax list 1780.

Adamson, Sim
Binkele, Adam
Boger, Jacob
Cooper, John
Endsly, James
Fiedler, Gottfried
Fiedler, Peter
Folk, William
Garland, Samuel
Hampton, Ez.
Hill, Henry,
Hill, William,
Krause, John
Krause, Wendel
Lauer, John
McPherson, Joseph
Noll, Jacob
Padget, John
Perry, Samuel
Pfau (Faw), Jacob
Pool, William
Rosenbaum, Alex
Rothrock, Jacob
Scherzer, Philip
Schmidt, Capt. Heinrich
Schneider, Peter
Schumaker, Adam, Sr.
Stolz, Philip
Wolf, John Adam

For additional names see Index.

For variant spellings see text.

INDEX

A

Abbotts Creek, 1543, 1544, 1549, 1556, 1571, 1578, 1652.

Abraham (a negro), 1515, 1579, 1804.

Accidents, 1517, 1523, 1576, 1577, 1619, 1633, 1636, 1652, 1655, 1659, 1671, 1682, 1746, 1753, 1761, 1765, 1776.

Acts of Assembly of N. C., 1515, 1516, 1539, 1540, 1544, 1607, 1640, 1690, 1784, 1786, 1792, 1805, 1850, 1855, 1867, 1878, 1885, 1913.

Adams, 1564.

Adams, John, 1865.

Adamson, Sim, 1925.

Administrator of Unity in N. C., 1512, 1582, 1784, 1846, 1904, 1921.

Administrators of estates, 1735.

Advent Sundays, 1578, 1579, 1635, 1779.

Advertisements, 1720, 1891.

Atkin, see Yadkin River.

Aeltesten Conferenz, 1500, 1501, 1514, 1521, 1525, 1526, 1528, 1546, 1547, 1552, 1558, 1560, 1565, 1568, 1570, 1571, 1581-1612, 1617, 1652, 1659, 1668, 1680, 1696, 1702, 1709-1738, 1782, 1786, 1791, 1797, 1799-1810, 1840, 1844, 1845-1858, 1897.

Affirmation of Fidelity and Allegiance, 1513, 1534, 1538, 1551, 1599, 1607, 1647, 1735, 1856, 1879, 1889.

Akoluthie, 1512, 1515, 1566, 1663, 1693, 1752, 1903.

Alberty, Friedrich, 1769.

Alexander, Colonel, 1687.

Alexander, Dr., 1678, 1679.

Alisbury, 1721.

Allen, Sr., 1573, 1645, 1646.

America, 1835, 1836, 1844, 1862.

American Colonies, 1511, 1784.

Ammunition, 1542, 1570, 1668, 1672, 1673, 1692, 1694, 1695, 1764.

Ammunition, Store-house for, 1658, 1659, 1669, 1670, 1671, 1672, 1681, 1685, 1714, 1715, 1717, 1740, 1800, 1808, 1881, 1908.

Amusements, 1847, 1848, 1850, 1851, 1852, 1853.

Anderson's Ferry, 1893.

Andresen, Rev. Joachim Heinrich, 1896.

Angels, 1517, 1523, 1538, 1568, 1577, 1613, 1628, 1657, 1660, 1858, 1869.

Anna (a negress), 1845.

Antigua, 1528.

Anspach, 1817.

Apprentices, 1557, 1582, 1586, 1596, 1609, 1692, 1693, 1708, 1720, 1723, 1731, 1732, 1750, 1799.

Arbitration, 1505, 1506. 1809

Archive Papers, 1887-1921.

Arms, 1500, 1548, 1549, 1643, 1671, 1849, 1880.

Armstrong, Col. John, 1746, 1747, 1813.

Armstrong, Maj. John, 1548, 1560, 1618, 1624, 1642, 1669, 1688, 1693, 1717, 1744, 1768, 1809, 1821, 1909.

Armstrong, Col. Martin, 1530, 1543, 1545, 1548, 1551, 1553, 1560, 1561, 1562, 1563, 1566, 1567, 1568, 1569, 1570, 1575, 1591, 1603, 1605, 1616, 1617, 1618, 1619, 1620, 1622, 1624, 1625, 1626, 1627, 1629, 1630, 1632, 1633, 1635, 1642, 1651, 1669, 1670, 1671, 1680, 1684, 1693, 1709, 1713, 1716, 1724, 1728, 1735, 1739, 1740, 1741, 1744, 1745, 1746, 1747, 1753, 1754, 1755, 1756, 1759, 1761, 1769, 1773, 1789, 1800, 1803, 1809, 1811, 1817, 1835, 1838, 1845, 1848, 1867, 1868, 1884, 1891, 1892, 1905.

Arnold Benedict, 1895.

Arrests, 1539, 1578, 1604, 1652, 1674, 1675, 1683, 1708, 1819.

Articles of Confederation, 1656.

Ascension Day, 1618, 1663, 1693.

Assembly meetings in Salem, 1697, 1699, 1701, 1702, 1703, 1704, 1705, 1725, 1726, 1727, 1729, 1730, 1731, 1733, 1734, 1735, 1736, 1737, 1756,

1762, 1771, 1772, 1784, 1785, 1787, 1788, 1800, 1801, 1884, 1913, 1914.

Assembly of North Carolina, 1513, 1515, 1527, 1534, 1535, 1540, 1559, 1581, 1619, 1625, 1640, 1656, 1659, 1667, 1680, 1690, 1691, 1697, 1701, 1709, 1739, 1756, 1771, 1786, 1787, 1790, 1791, 1801, 1807, 1834, 1837, 1875, 1878, 1879, 1885, 1913, 1919.

Auditors 1607, 1649, 1720, 1792, 1793, 1796, 1813, 1842, 1852, 1885.

Auditors Bills, 1805.

Aufseher Collegium, 1514, 1515, 1520, 1523, 1525, 1528, 1529, 1533, 1534, 1537, 1538, 1539, 1545, 1547, 1559, 1560, 1561, 1563, 1571, 1572, 1574, 1576, 1578, 1581-1611, 1658, 1663, 1668, 1709-1738, 1797, 1799-1810, 1845-1858, 1897.

Augsburg Confession, 1515, 1548.

Augusta, Ga., 1695.

August Thirteenth, 1515, 1557, 1624, 1698, 1757, 1842.

Aurora Borealis, 1528, 1701.

Aust, Gottfried, 1517, 1530, 1533, 1541, 1546, 1583, 1584, 1585, 1595, 1603, 1606, 1608, 1610, 1617, 1620, 1668, 1712, 1713, 1723, 1737, 1760, 1845, 1893, 1898, 1922.

Aust, Johann George, 1625, 1628, 1643, 1756, 1861, 1889, 1923.

Aust, Johann Gottfried, 1521.

Aust, John Leonard, 1761.

Aust, Maria, 1551, 1893.

Austria, 1511.

B

Baas, Captain de, 1633.

Bach, 1574.

Bachhof, Rosina, 1521, 1522, 1523.

Bachman, 1541, 1547, 1788, 1790.

Bader, 1567.

Bagge, Benjamin, 1840, 1851.

Bagge, Charles, 1840, 1851.

Bagge, Johann Lorenz, 1518, 1624, 1763.

Bagge, Maria Christina, 1518, 1624.

Bagge, Maria, m.n. Leibert, widow Fockel, 1624, 1663, 1693, 1752, 1785, 1816, 1898.

Bagge, Rev. Nic. Lorenz, 1512, 1517, 1525, 1539, 1542, 1548, 1566, 1614, 1615, 1619, 1622, 1632, 1680, 1702, 1739, 1746, 1751, 1759, 1761, 1763, 1796, 1803, 1808, 1811, 1816, 1826, 1846, 1849, 1859, 1861, 1865, 1898, 1923.

Bagge, Susanna Elizabeth, 1617.

Bagge, Traugott, 1498, 1512, 1523, 1527, 1537, 1539, 1540, 1542, 1543, 1550, 1553, 1556, 1558, 1561, 1566, 1569, 1572, 1581, 1583, 1592, 1594, 1597, 1599, 1601, 1604, 1605, 1608, 1609, 1610, 1611, 1645, 1658, 1668, 1674, 1675, 1676, 1678, 1679, 1680, 1681, 1690, 1693, 1696, 1700, 1705, 1711, 1712, 1713, 1720, 1725, 1727, 1728, 1729, 1736, 1742, 1750, 1769, 1771, 1786, 1790, 1791, 1792, 1795, 1798, 1800, 1801, 1803, 1806, 1818, 1819, 1821, 1822, 1825, 1826, 1837, 1838, 1842, 1848, 1849, 1850, 1865, 1869, 1875, 1876, 1877, 1885, 1892, 1899, 1905, 1907, 1908, 1909, 1910, 1911, 1915, 1922.

Balfour, Colonel, 1790.

Balfour, Major, 1687.

Baker, 1683.

Bakery in Salem, 1549, 1572.

Banner, 1748.

Banns, 1539, 1567, 1584, 1610, 1611, 1617, 1639, 1640, 1693, 1718, 1774, 1867.

Baptisms, 1494, 1515, 1517, 1518, 1542, 1553, 1557, 1561, 1562, 1579, 1584, 1614, 1615, 1619, 1624, 1625, 1636, 1639, 1640, 1642, 1646, 1648, 1651, 1707, 1721, 1739, 1758, 1761, 1763, 1770, 1772, 1778, 1781, 1791, 1803, 1804, 1807, 1812, 1814, 1817, 1818, 1819, 1824, 1828, 1829, 1832, 1839, 1845, 1859, 1865, 1866, 1867, 1871, 1874, 1891.

Baptists, 1632, 1682, 1737, 1795, 1824.

Barbadoes, 1497.

Barby, 1566, 1582, 1637.

Barter, 1576, 1580, 1597, 1598, 1600, 1670, 1705, 1719, 1731, 1850.

Barton, Captain, 1679.

Battles, 1543, 1544, 1548, 1555, 1558, 1559, 1560, 1567, 1571, 1572, 1629, 1642, 1656, 1671, 1672, 1673, 1684, 1685, 1687, 1700, 1702, 1748.

Baumgarten, Johann George, 1582, 1712, 1922.

Baumgarten, Maria, 1517, 1521, 1554, 1556, 1557, 1558, 1583, 1713.

Beard, 1580, 1692.

Beard, Jr., 1553.

Bechler, George, 1536.

Beck, Anna, m.n. Leinbach, 1785, 1794, 1830.

Beck, Johann Friedrich, 1922.

Beck, Maria, m.n. Beck, 1871.

Beck, Rev. Valentine, 1512, 1556, 1572, 1612, 1650, 1668, 1714, 1717, 1727, 1738, 1774, 1794, 1803, 1821, 1824, 1841, 1843, 1849, 1871, 1923.

Beeder, 1627.

Beeringer, Paul, 1821, 1823.

Beeringer, Susan, 1866.

Beilagen, 1787.

Belews Creek, 1549, 1564, 1674, 1772, 1791, 1855.

Bell in Salem, 1517, 1523, 1536, 1539, 1719, 1853.

Bell tower, Salem, 1534, 1535, 1536, 1538, 1540, 1586, 1587, 1588, 1599, 1601.

Bennett, Benjamin, 1867.

Bennett, Richard, 1867.

Benzien, Christian Ludwig, 1660, 1662, 1663, 1699, 1700, 1708, 1723, 1736, 1758, 1782, 1791, 1795, 1796, 1797, 1819, 1831, 1832, 1837, 1841, 1870, 1871, 1875, 1913, 1916, 1920, 1922.

Berger, 1552.

Beroth, Jacob, 1666, 1707, 1709, 1922.

Beroth, Johannes, 1508, 1666, 1867, 1889, 1923.

Berthelsdorf, 1557, 1795.

Bethabara, 1512, 1513, 1514, 1515, 1517, 1518, 1519, 1545, 1547, 1550, 1551, 1557, 1559, 1563, 1564, 1565, 1569, 1571, 1572, 1573, 1576, 1580, 1584, 1585, 1594, 1595, 1596, 1599, 1610, 1611, 1612-1637, 1644, 1658, 1659, 1660, 1664, 1671, 1677, 1679, 1681,

1687, 1692, 1694, 1696, 1713, 1714, 1717, 1718, 1722, 1723, 1739-1764, 1801, 1810-1816, 1818, 1838, 1843, 1857, 1858-1866, 1877, 1879, 1880, 1881, 1882, 1883, 1884, 1902, 1903, 1904, 1905, 1906, 1907.

Bethabara Committee, 1612, 1614, 1615, 1634, 1636, 1739, 1749, 1750, 1757, 1897.

Bethabara land, 1801, 1808, 1824, 1825, 1826.

Bethabara Town Lot, 1801, 1814.

Bethania, 1493, 1498, 1508, 1512, 1514, 1518, 1519, 1521, 1523, 1526, 1532, 1540, 1557, 1559, 1562, 1566, 1572, 1573, 1574, 1579, 1584, 1585, 1598, 1599, 1629, 1630, 1637-1646, 1658, 1659, 1660, 1664, 1671, 1675, 1677, 1708, 1713, 1717, 1718, 1723, 1733, 1741, 1742, 1752, 1764-1773, 1792, 1794, 1817-1826, 1866-1870, 1876, 1881, 1882, 1886, 1889-1892, 1897, 1902, 1904, 1907.

Bethania Committee, 1500, 1501, 1504, 1507, 1514, 1582, 1586, 1637, 1639, 1641, 1733, 1897.

Bethania Congregation Festival, 1801, 1817, 1818, 1819, 1866.

Bethania land, 1505, 1507, 1526, 1605, 1611, 1786, 1808, 1917.

Bethania Society, 1810.

Bethany, see Bethania.

Bethlehem, Pa., 1516, 1530, 1532, 1533, 1536, 1547, 1570, 1589, 1619, 1637, 1689, 1695, 1698, 1702, 1850.

Betty (a negress), 1697.

Betrothals, 1521, 1527, 1534, 1539, 1552, 1558, 1567, 1578, 1619, 1693, 1696, 1738, 1762, 1776, 1779.

Betz, Andreas, 1821, 1823.

Bibighaus, Christina, m.n. Dixon, 1708, 1838, 1860.

Bibighaus, George, 1527, 1528, 1536, 1538, 1553, 1554, 1568, 1569, 1573, 1575, 1577, 1578, 1675, 1693, 1694, 1698, 1702, 1708, 1720, 1740, 1768, 1810, 1838, 1860, 1922.

Bible, 1497, 1499, 1503, 1504, 1524, 1540, 1541, 1574, 1584, 1609, 1612, 1622, 1625, 1647, 1836.

Biehler, George, 1618.

Bieler, Anton, 1698, **1771**.

Binckele, Joseph, 1586.

Binkele, Adam, 1865, 1889, 1925.

Binkele, Peter, Jr., 1923.

Binkele (Pinkley), Peter, Sr., 1824, 1923.

Binckely, Captain, 1646, 1806, 1819.

Birthdays, 1553, 1568, 1673, 1740, 1788, 1811, 1843, 1845.

Blair, Major, 1673.

Blake, Captain, 1793.

Blake, John, 1925.

Blue Ford, 1528.

Blum, Anna, 1518, 1530, 1621.

Blum, Elisabeth, m.n. Koch, 1518, 1546, 1547, 1613, 1620, 1627, 1758, 1760, 1893.

Blum, Frederic, 1805.

Blum, Heinrich, 1922.

Blum, Jacob, 1517, 1533, 1537, 1541, 1546, 1547, 1584, 1610, 1613, 1614, 1615, 1617, 1620, 1621, 1634, 1713, 1740, 1742, 1744, 1749, 1757, 1761, 1762, 1802, 1813, 1849, 1862, 1863, 1864, 1891, 1893, 1898, 1919, 1923.

Blum, John Jacob, 1758, 1759, 1760.

Blum, Ludwig, 1557, 1593, 1693, 1720, 1849, 1891.

Boeckel, Friedrich, 1648, 1651, 1776, 1798, 1841, 1923.

Boeckel Joh. Nicholas, 1508, 1774, 1798, 1923.

Boger, Jacob, 1925.

Bohemia, 1527, 1551.

Bohn, Jacob, 1917.

Bohn's School House, 1917.

Bohner (Booner, Boner), William, 1925.

Bonn, Anna Maria, m.n. Brendel, 1539, 1703, 1735, 1802, 1814, 1830.

Bonn, Dr. Jacob, 1512, 1523, 1525, 1527, 1534, 1544, 1545, 1548, 1550, 1558, 1559, 1562, 1563, 1568, 1571, 1572, 1523, 1574, 1583, 1584, 1608, 1611, 1614, 1615, 1629, 1630, 1632, 1633, 1634, 1644, 1645, 1658, 1670, 1676, 1678, 1679, 1683, 1685, 1686, 1694, 1703, 1710, 1712, 1715, 1717, 1718, 1729, 1734, 1735, 1746, 1747,

1751, 1752, 1753, 1754, 1759, 1760, 1761, 1781, 1803, 1876, 1884, 1911, 1922.

Bonn, Jacob, Jr., 1521, 1593, 1692, 1849.

Books, 1524, 1541, 1554, 1582, 1584, 1589, 1622, 1635, 1647, 1698, 1793.

Boon, 1821.

Booner, Joseph, 1553.

Booner, Margaret, 1654.

Boote, 1527, 1528, 1529.

Booth, Commissary, 1676.

Borrowing money, 1504, 1720, 1724, 1740.

Boyer, Major, 1670.

Boyer (Bucher), Henry, 1925.

Brachten, 1614, 1624.

Braedt, John, 1739.

Brandon, Captain, 1687.

Brandy, 1545, 1576, 1588, 1598, 1611, 1620, 1623, 1625, 1633, 1651, 1666, 1674, 1676, 1677, 1682, 1684, 1685, 1701, 1702, 1734, 1741, 1748, 1751, 1752, 1759, 1773, 1902.

Bread, 1535, 1544, 1554, 1559, 1562, 1572, 1584, 1590, 1622, 1625, 1626, 1629, 1630, 1631, 1674, 1676, 1683, 1684, 1701, 1702, 1725, 1734, 1741, 1742, 1743, 1750, 1759, 1761, 1774, 1798, 1815, 1851, 1902.

Brewery, Bethabara, 1564.

Brick and Tile, 1539, 1588, 1611, 1757, 1759, 1813, 1846, 1855, 1856.

Brisbane, Colonel, 1695.

Broadbay, Maine, 1526, 1781, 1872, 1903.

Broad River, 1671, 1811.

Broeder, John, 1749, 1752.

Broeder, Nathanael, 1749, 1752.

Broessing, Andreas, 1541, 1546, 1589, 1660, 1671, 1692, 1693, 1694, 1695, 1751, 1752, 1753, 1754, 1759, 1762, 1800, 1803, 1811, 1861, 1895, 1922.

Broessing, Anna Johanna, m.n. Steup, 1693, 1694, 1759, 1762, 1800, 1814.

Brooks, Major, 1674.

Brooks, Matthew, 1539, 1575, 1576, 1668, 1696, 1697, 1710, 1712, 1713, 1720, 1739, 1740, 1752, 1754, 1756, 1759, 1770, 1803, 1812.

Brotherly Agreement, 1493, 1498, 1507, 1661, 1693, 1738, 1749, 1774, 1778, 1870.

Brotherly love, 1501, 1532, 1557, 1609, 1638, 1658.

Brothers' Garden, 1497, 1787.

Brothers House, Salem, 1517, 1520, 1526, 1527, 1529, 1535, 1537, 1545, 1550, 1567, 1569, 1577, 1578, 1581, 1584, 1587, 1588, 1590, 1594, 1597, 1603, 1605, 1678, 1681, 1684, 1685, 1686, 1688, 1698, 1700, 1701, 1710, 1715, 1723, 1729, 1731, 1789, 1793, 1800, 1801, 1802, 1838, 1847, 1848, 1849, 1877, 1903.

Brothers House, new, 1847, 1850.

Brown, 1798, 1837.

Brown, Hannah, 1839.

Brown, James, 1839.

Brown, John, 1539, 1588.

Brown, William, 1558, 1559.

Bruce, Charles, 1792, 1793.

Bryant, 1556.

Bryant, Col. Samuel, 1549, 1551.

Bryant's Settlement, 1765.

Budget of Congregation Expenses, 1504, 1516, 1601.

Buford, Colonel, 1543, 1544.

Bulitschek, John, 1867.

Bulitschek, Joseph Ferdinand, 1556, 1867, 1869, 1889, 1923.

Burgoyne prisoners, 1541, 1891.

Burke, Gov. Thomas, 1700, 1701, 1788, 1794, 1913.

Butter, 1554, 1622, 1630, 1719, 1835, 1850, 1852.

Butner, Thomas, 1925.

Buttner, Adam, 1508.

Buttner, Sarah, 1847.

C

Caesar (a negro), 1804.

Cairo, 1497.

Caldwell, Captain, 1561, 1565.

Call, Major, 1672, 1907.

Camden, 1511, 1512, 1555, 1559, 1567, 1624, 1670, 1695, 1737, 1751, 1880, 1901.

Campbell, Captain, 1572, 1627, 1643, 1686, 1744.

Campbell, Col. William, 1562, 1563, 1564, 1565, 1574, 1626, 1631, 1684, 1744, 1745, 1746, 1747, 1884.

Campbell, Maj. William, 1666.

Candles, 1503, 1579, 1707, 1763, 1826.

Carleton, Sir Guy, 1840.

Caroll's Manor, 1895.

Carrington, 1691.

Carteret, 1579.

Caswell, Gov. Richard, 1512, 1537, 1704, 1705.

Catalogs of Wachovia, 1773, 1789, 1800, 1801, 1817, 1857, 1891, 1915, 1922.

Catawba Indians, 1695, 1696.

Catawba River, 1512, 1548, 1555, 1573, 1631, 1671, 1672, 1692.

Catholics, 1598, 1781.

Cattle, 1505, 1516, 1529, 1535, 1542, 1551, 1553, 1562, 1574, 1580, 1584, 1585, 1594, 1595, 1615, 1617, 1622, 1625, 1630, 1631, 1632, 1635, 1636, 1647, 1649, 1651, 1655, 1674, 1676, 1702, 1713, 1714, 1719, 1731, 1742, 1743, 1744, 1760, 1811, 1815, 1816, 1825, 1826, 1866, 1869, 1891, 1912, 1915, 1917.

Cavalry, 1559, 1562, 1565, 1569, 1574, 1619, 1622, 1628, 1631, 1633, 1634, 1641, 1654, 1658, 1672, 1677, 1679, 1681, 1691, 1741, 1744, 1750, 1756, 1758, 1759, 1765, 1780, 1782, 1791, 1851, 1859, 1860.

Census, 1773, 1789, 1800, 1801, 1817.

Certificates, Auditor's, 1720, 1722, 1803, 1805, 1808, 1810, 1905.

Certificates given to Brethren, 1889.

Certificates, Moravian, 1538, 1541, 1544, 1545, 1548, 1591, 1605, 1724, 1729, 1730, 1782, 1889, 1890.

Charity, 1496, 1504, 1516, 1559, 1590, 1642, 1660, 1687, 1688, 1715, 1717, 1726, 1751, 1771, 1774, 1808, 1817, 1836, 1911.

Charlestown, 1511, 1512, 1523, 1527, 1528, 1529, 1530, 1540, 1541, 1567, 1621, 1649, 1692, 1694, 1702, 1704, 1728, 1784, 1792, 1793, 1809, 1819, 1837, 1838, 1844, 1869, 1880, 1889, 1892, 1894.

Charlotte, N. C., 1543, 1697, 1701, 1911.

Cheraws, 1901.

Cherokees, 1692, 1719, 1835, 1877.

Chiddy (Chitty), John, 1848.

Chiddy (Chitty), Mary, 1598.

Chitty (Chiddy), Benjamin, 1561, 1598, 1654, 1925.

Chief Elder, 1494, 1515, 1566, 1577, 1634, 1654, 1703, 1779, 1782, 1830, 1844, 1874.

Children, 1502, 1514, 1516, 1519, 1523, 1524, 1547, 1558, 1562, 1568, 1581, 1582, 1620, 1628, 1648, 1651, 1663, 1664, 1665, 1697, 1765, 1845, 1866, 1898.

Children's meetings, 1524, 1528, 1529, 1548, 1552, 1558, 1562, 1569, 1579, 1581, 1603, 1616, 1617, 1618, 1621, 1622, 1624, 1627, 1630, 1637, 1652, 1663, 1679, 1697, 1698, 1740, 1750, 1757, 1763, 1794, 1824, 1825, 1826, 1831, 1842, 1843, 1845, 1856, 1872.

Choir System, 1502, 1514, 1516, 1619, 1527, 1528, 1532, 1563, 1569, 1582, 1589, 1602, 1612, 1662, 1688, 1693, 1728, 1737, 1748, 1787, 1796, 1808, 1832, 1836.

Christ, Elisabeth, m.n. Oesterlein, 1898.

Christ, Rudolph, 1530, 1531, 1533, 1534, 1535, 1537, 1583, 1586, 1587, 1589, 1610, 1617, 1639, 1719, 1728, 1737, 1791, 1793, 1800, 1807, 1922.

Christian (a negro), 1515, 1561, 1625, 1636, 1752, 1804, 1844.

Christiansbrun, 1804.

Christman, Rev., 1824.

Christman, Balthazer, 1518, 1568, 1609, 1922.

Christman, Barbara, 1518, 1520.

Christman, Daniel, 1540, 1541, 1589, 1600, 1795, 1798, 1803, 1808, 1916, 1922.

Christman, Jacob, Jr., 1578, 1916.

Christmann, Jacob, Sr., 1532, 1568, 1578, 1610, 1669, 1670, 1708, 1916.

Christmann, Johanna, m.n., Fischer, 1798.

Christmas Day, 1515, 1579, 1636, 1652,

1707, 1763, 1779, 1799, 1826, 1831, 1845, 1875.

Christmas Eve, 1579, 1636, 1655, 1707, 1763, 1773, 1779, 1826, 1845, 1872,.

Church history, 1582, 1584.

Churton, William, 1558.

Citizenship, 1500, 1547, 1551, 1584, 1591, 1598, 1607, 1609, 1814, 1856, 1874, 1878.

Clark, Colonel, 1741.

Clayton, William, 1924.

Clean, John, 1889.

Clemens, Heinrich, 1748.

Cleveland, Col. Benjamin, 1574, 1575, 1632, 1645, 1667, 1675, 1682, 1720, 1739.

Clinton, Sir Henry, 1511.

Clothing, 1728, 1796, 1803, 1804, 1805.

Cloud, Captain, 1677, 1743.

Cloyd, Maj. Joseph, 1683, 1745.

Cochran, 1793.

Cochran, Robert, 1610.

Coffee, 1597, 1721, 1728, 1815, 1820.

Coffin, Seth or Silas, 1695.

Coffins, 1606, 1629, 1861.

Cole, Temple, 1697.

Colver, Elisabeth, 1515, 1526, 1566, 1832.

Coly, 1545, 1553.

Commerce, 1847.

Committee, Special, of Salem, 1658, 1668, 1699, 1709, 1711, 1715, 1727, 1728, 1730, 1851, 1881.

Communion, Holy, 1513, 1514, 1515, 1518, 1520, 1531, 1536, 1540, 1547, 1553, 1557, 1563, 1564, 1567, 1571, 1580, 1591, 1598, 1603, 1612, 1614, 1615, 1618, 1639, 1646, 1651, 1654, 1662, 1670, 1680, 1682, 1688, 1690, 1697, 1706, 1708, 1715, 1722, 1734, 1740, 1745, 1758, 1763, 1778, 1782, 1786, 1827, 1829, 1830, 1832, 1833, 1842, 1854, 1872, 1873.

Conch-shell horn, 1634, 1716.

Confirmation, 1518, 1531, 1564, 1607, 1799, 1829, 1832.

Confiscation Acts, 1516, 1526, 1539, 1540, 1784, 1791, 1805, 1809, 1880, 1899, 1915.

Congaree River, 1695, 1851.

Congregation Account, Bethabara, 1613. 1634, 1635, 1811, 1814.

Congregation Account, Salem, 1500, 1504. 1516, 1591, 1596, 1600, 1601, 1635, 1717.

Congregation Council, Bethabara, 1613, 1614, 1635, 1760, 1811, 1814.

Congregation Council, Bethania, 1501.

Congregation Council, Hope, 1831.

Congregation Council, Salem, 1515, 1522, 1541, 1551, 1560, 1582, 1586, 1589, 1590, 1592, 1593, 1599, 1600, 1601, 1602, 1603, 1607, 1609, 1658, 1668, 1699, 1702, 1703, 1707, 1709, 1710, 1715, 1716, 1718, 1724, 1726, 1727, 1730, 1733, 1735, 1738, 1790, 1795, 1800, 1803, 1804, 1807, 1808, 1809, 1837, 1846, 1847, 1848, 1850, 1852, 1854, 1857.

Congress, Continental, 1511, 1570, 1704, 1791, 1792, 1834, 1875, 1904.

Congress money, 1532, 1560, 1569, 1590, 1639, 1876, 1893.

Conjurers, 1852.

Conrad, Christian, 1546, 1562, 1770, 1794, 1798, 1891, 1923.

Conrad, Johannes, 1508, 1869, 1923.

Consilium abeundi, 1604, 1605, 1799.

Constable, 1855.

Continental Currency, 1596, 1599, 1738, 1803.

Continental troops, 1512, 1530, 1544, 1559, 1560, 1562, 1563, 1564, 1567, 1568, 1576, 1580, 1595, 1597, 1599, 1608, 1624, 1641, 1642, 1650, 1656, 1658, 1668, 1671, 1673, 1682, 1686, 1687, 1692, 1694, 1697, 1702, 1704, 1744, 1748, 1749, 1752, 1754, 1757, 1764, 1768, 1770, 1771, 1784, 1788, 1789, 1790, 1791, 1798, 1809, 1811, 1821, 1826, 1834, 1837, 1838, 1839, 1840, 1851, 1859, 1860, 1876, 1880, 1881, 1884, 1892, 1895, 1902, 1906, 1907, 1910, 1915.

Contracts, 1560, 1582, 1588, 1596, 1604, 1608, 1614, 1786, 1797, 1807, 1846, 1867, 1868.

Contributions, weekly, 1601, 1602, 1713, 1811.

Cook, 1803.

Cooper, John, 1925.

Copts, 1497.

Corn Tax, see Tax, Specific.

Cornwallis, Lord Charles, 1511, 1512, 1559, 1656, 1658, 1672, 1676, 1687, 1694, 1695, 1702, 1704, 1741, 1742, 1765, 1766, 1768, 1784, 1882.

Cossart land, 1899, 1917.

Cotton, 1752, 1850.

Counterfeit money, 1555, 1609.

Country congregations, 1514, 1515, 1519, 1561, 1563, 1565, 1566, 1598, 1602, 1603, 1651, 1652, 1654, 1668, 1697, 1707, 1780, 1782, 1786, 1804, 1808, 1829, 1831, 1832.

Court Martial, 1549.

Court of Inquiry, 1813.

Court of Surry County, 1516, 1523, 1525, 1558, 1577, 1581, 1583, 1614, 1618, 1645, 1698, 1703, 1720, 1757, 1761, 1798, 1813, 1820, 1824, 1842, 1855, 1862, 1864, 1889, 1891.

Coustaine, General, 1789.

Covenant Day, see Festal Day.

Cowan's Ford, 1672.

Cowpens, 1671, 1682, 1847.

Craigh, Colonel, 1790.

Crampton, Henry, 1523, 1655.

Crocket, Colonel, 1681, 1686, 1744, 1747.

Cross Creek, 1533, 1535, 1537, 1538, 1542, 1545, 1558, 1559, 1569, 1573, 1575, 1577, 1578, 1596, 1597, 1599, 1610, 1843, 1876, 1877, 1880, 1902.

Cummens, Captain, 1772.

Cummings, Samuel, 1529, 1534, 1535, 1561, 1568, 1569, 1570, 1577, 1579, 1617, 1619, 1625, 1640, 1645, 1667, 1680, 1687, 1690, 1694, 1705, 1716, 1735, 1739, 1745, 1768, 1790, 1803.

Cummings, Thomas, 1617.

Cup of Covenant, 1570, 1619, 1786.

Curator of Single Sisters, 1663, 1703, 1854.

Curry, Malcolm, 1767.

Currency Certificates, 1810.

Currency depreciation, 1527, 1528, 1532, 1535, 1544, 1585, 1590, 1591, 1596, 1601, 1709, 1735, 1736, 1800, 1801, 1856, 1878, 1879, 1881, 1900.

Currency of North Carolina, 1560, 1596, 1712, 1738, 1800, 1801, 1856, 1858.

Currency rates in Salem, 1514, 1528, 1534, 1560, 1582, 1590, 1593, 1596, 1702, 1736, 1800.

Cusick, John, 1746, 1749.

Customs, general, 1503, 1602, 1606, 1712, 1721, 1738, 1796.

Customs, Moravian, 1502, 1676, 1826.

D

Daily Word, see Texts.

Danbury, 1843.

Dancey, Abraham, 1539.

Dan River, 1539, 1542, 1546, 1551, 1570, 1572, 1614, 1682, 1700, 1741, 1743, 1747, 1749, 1754, 1756, 1802, 1843, 1895.

Daub, Johannes, 1615, 1750, 1769, 1772, 1806.

Davidson, General, 1567.

Davidson, Major, 1677.

Davidson, George, 1909.

Davie, Lawyer, 1797.

Davie, Maj. W. R., 1555, 1558.

Deacons, 1515, 1566, 1663, 1708, 1903.

Deaconess, 1663, 1693, 1752.

Deaths, 1514, 1518, 1520, 1525, 1532, 1538, 1550, 1552, 1558, 1569, 1575, 1576, 1613, 1616, 1629, 1634, 1637, 1642, 1647, 1652, 1655, 1686, 1691, 1703, 1734, 1763, 1765, 1769, 1776, 1777, 1778, 1785, 1793, 1794, 1795, 1797, 1809, 1814, 1815, 1816, 1825, 1830, 1831, 1844, 1859, 1872, 1874, 1892.

Debts, 1501, 1504, 1614.

Dedications, 1526, 1533, 1654, 1793.

Deeds, Moravian, 1545, 1553, 1554, 1880, 1899, 1900, 1915, 1917, 1918.

Deep Creek, 1542, 1619, 1780, 1786, 1803, 1812, 1835, 1846, 1861, 1920.

Deep River, 1641, 1761.

Deer-skins, 1600, 1690, 1691, 1750, 1751, 1769, 1847, 1909.

Delaware, 1684.

Demuth, Andreas, 1639.

Demuth, George, 1639.

Demuth, Heinrich, 1639.

Denton, Salome, 1770.

Deserters, 1542, 1548, 1555, 1590, 1598, 1675, 1716, 1764, 1769, 1771.

Diaconie of Bethabara, 1660, 1810, 1836.

Diaconie of Salem Congregation, 1516, 1574, 1576, 1590, 1591, 1593, 1596, 1601, 1604, 1608, 1660, 1712, 1717, 1720, 1724, 1786, 1795, 1836, 1846.

Diaconie of Single Brethren, 1516, 1569, 1590, 1604, 1608, 1660, 1738, 1786, 1795, 1836, 1852.

Diaconie of Single Sisters, 1590, 1660, 1786, 1806, 1836.

Diaconie of Unity Administration, 1523, 1601.

Diaspora, 1526, 1686, 1689, 1808.

Diener (in Saal), 1507, 1536, 1568, 1636, 1709, 1721, 1737, 1753, 1763, 1838, 1861.

Dienerin, 1536, 1568, 1581, 1636, 1753, 1861.

Dilep, 1821, 1823.

Discipline, church, 1499, 1501, 1503, 1504, 1506, 1591, 1592, 1593, 1594, 1604, 1605, 1661, 1722, 1731, 1732, 1733, 1735, 1736, 1737, 1738, 1773, 1799, 1835, 1847, 1850, 1852, 1870.

Distemper, 1918.

Distillery, Bethabara, 1589, 1614, 1623, 1739, 1742, 1859.

Distillery, Bethania, 1772, 1820.

Distillery, Salem, 1611, 1675, 1684, 1726.

Dixon, Colonel, 1822.

Dixon, Major, 1677, 1678, 1679, 1883.

Dixon, Christina, 1708.

Dixon, Elisabeth, 1860, 1865.

Dixon, John, 1922.

Dixon, Joseph, 1571, 1572, 1630, 1633, 1644, 1645, 1710, 1712, 1734, 1735, 1753, 1754, 1762, 1781, 1799, 1803, 1810, 1840, 1846, 1851, 1922.

Doak, Captain, 1683.

Dobbs Parish, 1879.

Dober, Leonard, 1560.

Dobson, Capt. William, 1879, 1889.

Doctrinal Texts, see Texts.

Doctrine, 1494, 1499, 1501, 1514, 1524,

1526, 1552, 1569, 1582, 1584, 1598, 1646, 1651, 1661, 1718, 1746, 1804, 1827, 1828, 1830, 1872, 1899.

Dog-days, 1770.

Dogs, 1710, 1829, 1843.

Doll, Louisa, 1863, 1867.

Doll (Dull), Nicholas, 1615, 1755, 1767.

Douthid, Abraham, 1538, 1925.

Douthid, Isaac, 1538, 1925.

Douthid, James, 1925.

Douthid, John, 1527, 1538, 1610, 1832, 1925.

Douthid, Thomas, 1538, 1925.

Douthid, William, 1610, 1925.

Douthit, Sarah, 1610.

Doxology, 1566, 1700, 1794.

Drafts, 1537, 1542, 1544, 1605, 1621, 1640, 1643, 1649, 1650, 1736, 1748, 1749, 1754, 1756, 1768, 1801, 1889, 1891, 1892, 1915.

Drollinger, Johann, 1916.

Drought, 1786, 1797, 1799, 1817, 1839, 1871, 1916.

Dresen, Immanuel, 1847, 1848.

Drunkeness, 1565, 1566, 1604, 1611, 1673, 1681, 1750, 1773, 1775, 1790.

Dunkards, 1690, 1804, 1851, 1917.

Dunn, Lawyer, 1525, 1798.

E

Early Easter Service, 1532, 1616, 1639, 1691, 1750, 1791, 1812, 1819, 1839, 1867, 1873, 1890.

Easter, 1532, 1616, 1648, 1691, 1718, 1749, 1750, 1791, 1819, 1829, 1867, 1870, 1873.

Easter Monday, 1532, 1585, 1616, 1750, 1873.

Ebeling, Johannes, 1777.

Ebeling, Ludwig, 1649, 1923.

Ebert, Christine, 1727, 1779.

Ebert, Johann George, 1649, 1774, 1775, 1923.

Ebert, Martin, Jr., 1923.

Ebert, Martin, Sr., 1648, 1775, 1779, 1923.

Eclipse, 1574.

Edenton, 1773.

Education, 1502, 1516, 1593, 1594, 1595, 1676, 1809, 1831.

Eisly, Ludwig, 1916.

Eitel, 1693.

Ekels, Captain, 1889, 1890.

Elections, 1529, 1530, 1584, 1615, 1686, 1687, 1716, 1747, 1768, 1790, 1803, 1812, 1818, 1838, 1848, 1865, 1875.

Elliot, 1809.

Ellroth, William, 1773.

Elrod, Adam, 1925.

Elrod, Adam (miller), 1807, 1892, 1925.

Elrod, Christopher, Jr., 1610, 1923.

Elrod, Christopher, Sr., 1598, 1610, 1891, 1925.

Elrod, Jeremias, 1873, 1924.

Elrod, John, 1925.

Elrod, Robert, 1925.

Embroidery, 1592.

Endsley, James, 1925.

Enerson, Maria, 1567.

Engel, Maria Elisabeth, 1612, 1617, 1623, 1663, 1693, 1694, 1752, 1839, 1899.

England, Major, 1676.

England, 1511, 1523, 1524, 1582, 1835, 1844, 1862.

English fleet, 1529.

English officers, 1573, 1575, 1576, 1577, 1631, 1632, 1633.

English Settlement and School-house, 1513, 1514, 1523, 1527, 1530, 1532, 1533.

English troops, 1511, 1527, 1528, 1541, 1542, 1543, 1545, 1546, 1548, 1551, 1553, 1555, 1558, 1559, 1561, 1567, 1568, 1572, 1573, 1574, 1576, 1577, 1628, 1631, 1633, 1634, 1640, 1642, 1656, 1658, 1672, 1675, 1676, 1682, 1686, 1687, 1717, 1741, 1742, 1765, 1766, 1767, 1768, 1769, 1780, 1784, 1881, 1882, 1883, 1901, 1906, 1910.

Ernst, Rev. Joh. Jacob, 1508, 1512, 1548, 1565, 1572, 1582, 1584, 1585, 1586, 1591, 1616, 1620, 1623, 1624, 1632, 1680, 1702, 1718, 1721, 1723, 1733, 1745, 1759, 1765, 1766, 1793, 1794, 1801, 1808, 1818, 1819, 1820, 1825, 1889, 1923.

Ernst, Juliana, m.n. Carmel, 1794, 1819, 1820.

Erny, Anna Catharina, 1639.

Enox, David, 1714, 1715.

Esslinger, 1917.

Estates, 1582, 1603, 1712, 1734, 1735, 1799, 1800.

Etter, Gerhard, 1689.

Etter, Peter, 1689.

Ettwein, Bishop John, 1623, 1708.

Europe, 1516, 1584, 1660, 1707.

Europe, Moravians in, 1514, 1537, 1601, 1707, 1708, 1836, 1853, 1857.

Eutaw Springs, 1700, 1771.

Ewins, Adjutant, 1685.

Ewing, Captain, 1685, 1690.

Executions, 1564, 1565, 1626, 1632.

Expresses, 1551, 1553, 1562, 1563, 1622, 1627, 1641, 1671, 1672, 1690, 1700, 1741, 1744, 1756, 1765, 1770, 1823.

F

Fahl, Christian, 1916.

Faith, 1501, 1592, 1599.

Fanning, Col. Edmund, 1701.

Farms, 1505, 1506, 1517, 1524, 1526, 1533, 1536, 1537, 1541, 1545, 1560, 1587, 1588, 1600, 1606, 1660, 1661, 1692, 1700, 1720, 1728, 1729, 1730, 1739-1764, 1769, 1794, 1797, 1814, 1897. See also Bethabara diaries.

Fehr, Bernhard, 1855.

Fein, 1651.

Feiser, Anna Margaretha, m.n. Moser, widow Demuth, 1766.

Feiser, Peter, 1766, 1767, 1840, 1866, 1923.

Fences, 1587, 1593, 1636, 1725, 1745, 1746, 1747, 1748, 1757, 1811, 1813, 1836, 1865.

Ferguson, Patrick, 1512.

Festal Days, 1532, 1548, 1558, 1562, 1564, 1565, 1588, 1612, 1621, 1624, 1628, 1637, 1639, 1646, 1648, 1649, 1662, 1663, 1667, 1688, 1692, 1697, 1698, 1700, 1748, 1755, 1757, 1778, 1781, 1782, 1786, 1787, 1794, 1815, 1817, 1819, 1825, 1829, 1837, 1838,
1839, 1841, 1842, 1843, 1851, 1870, 1871, 1874.

Fever, 1563, 1627, 1753, 1830, 1861.

Fiedler, Gottfried, 1925.

Fiedler, Joh. Peter, 1924, 1925.

Fire-fighting equipment, 1528, 1581, 1606, 1616, 1848, 1850, 1853, 1854, 1855, 1860.

Fire Regulations, 1503, 1507, 1581, 1597, 1609, 1610, 1614, 1706, 1713, 1733.

Fires, 1527, 1576, 1613, 1616, 1713, 1747, 1772, 1776, 1836, 1838, 1848, 1860, 1884.

Fischel, Johann, 1923.

Fischel, Johann Adam, 1612, 1829, 1923.

Fischer, 1771.

Fischer, Anna Maria, 1807.

Fischer, Casper, 1508, 1639, 1767, 1768, 1773, 1824, 1889, 1923.

Fischer, Catharine, 1518.

Fischer, Christina, 1820.

Fischer, Friedrich, 1866.

Fischer, George, 1650, 1870, 1923.

Fischer, Johanna, 1564, 1798.

Fischer, Melchoir, 1648, 1778, 1807, 1923.

Fiscuss, Maria Eva (wife of Friedrich, 1867.

Flag of Truce, 1682, 1728, 1809.

Flax, 1505, 1623, 1739, 1749, 1755, 1756, 1757, 1760, 1863.

Flex, Johannes, 1578, 1673, 1728, 1922.

Floods, 1517, 1538, 1551, 1618, 1693, 1740, 1774, 1860, 1900.

Flour, 1556, 1557, 1737, 1750, 1758.

Flux, 1552.

Fockel, Anna Johanna, 1518.

Fockel, Elisabeth, 1617, 1810.

Fockel, Gottlieb, 1729, 1795, 1923.

Fockel, Samuel, 1738, 1924.

Fogler, see Vogler.

Follis, Bethseba, 1770.

Folk, see Volk.

Folz, see Volz.

Food scarcity of, 1535, 1542, 1554, 1559, 1562, 1572, 1573, 1590, 1626, 1631, 1641, 1702, 1755, 1774, 1825, 1881, 1900, 1902, 1912.

Forestry, 1505, 1506, 1595, 1603, 1760, 1800, 1802, 1838, 1858.

Fortune, William, 1801.

Foundation principles, 1591, 1592, 1593, 1609, 1662, 1817, 1832.

Fourth of July, 1834, 1835, 1853, 1863, 1868, 1885, 1919.

Fowls, 1505, 1630, 1633, 1747, 1761.

Fox, 1844.

France, 1511, 1523, 1524, 1835, 1844.

Frank, see Christian.

Franklin, Captain, 1685.

Free-holder, 1530.

Freeman, Samuel, 1529, 1530, 1535, 1617, 1666, 1716.

Fremden Dienerin, 1719.

French Fleet, 1895.

French horns, 1628, 1636, 1637, 1748, 1757, 1763, 1803, 1815, 1858.

French officers, 1789, 1790, 1892.

Frey, Christian, 1570, 1649, 1651, 1652, 1673, 1775, 1776, 1777, 1821, 1823, 1824, 1829, 1923.

Frey, George, 1649, 1772, 1774, 1776, 1924.

Frey, Heinrich, 1924.

Frey, Johannes, 1924.

Frey, Joh. Peter, 1578, 1647, 1651, 1673, 1714, 1775, 1776, 1777, 1829, 1924.

Frey, Johannes Michael, 1859.

Frey, Johann Valentine, 1924.

Frey, Michael, 1859, 1924.

Frey, Peter, 1708, 1851, 1924.

Frey, Sarah, m.n. Schneider, 1777.

Frey, Valentine, 1778, 1851, 1924.

Friedland, 1512, 1514, 1515, 1519, 1526, 1532, 1542, 1544, 1545, 1549, 1552, 1553, 1557, 1560, 1563, 1567, 1571, 1577, 1585, 1591, 1598, 1599, 1653, 1654, 1658, 1659, 1661, 1665, 1677, 1701, 1708, 1721, 1726, 1738, 1754, 1776, 1780-1783, 1818, 1831-1833, 1844, 1858, 1872-1875, 1882, 1883, 1897, 1903.

Friedland Anniversary, 1526, 1657, 1797, 1874.

Friedland Committee, 1851, 1873.

Friedland Society, 1560, 1563, 1653, 1665, 1831, 1832, 1851, 1873.

Friedberg, 1512, 1514, 1515, 1518, 1519, 1525, 1539, 1556, 1560, 1579, 1591, 1599, 1646-1652, 1657, 1659, 1661, 1665, 1673, 1675, 1701, 1710, 1712, 1717, 1738, 1775-1779, 1818, 1827-1831, 1839, 1842, 1843, 1851, 1870-1872, 1876, 1877, 1882, 1897, 1904.

Friedberg Anniversary, 1529, 1647, 1648, 1657, 1710, 1778, 1827, 1870.

Friedberg Church, 1839, 1848, 1849, 1850, 1870.

Friedberg Committees, 1829, 1848, 1849.

Friedberg land, 1805, 1929, 1850.

Friedberg School-House, 1647, 1650, 1779, 1827, 1850, 1870.

Friedberg Society, 1648, 1650, 1652, 1665, 1778, 1781, 1828, 1829, 1830, 1848, 1870, 1872.

Fries, Rev. Peter Conrad, 1528.

Fritz, Rev. Christian, 1512, 1513, 1515, 1521, 1522, 1523, 1524, 1527, 1530, 1531, 1532, 1533, 1538, 1560, 1565, 1566, 1576, 1621, 1654, 1655, 1709, 1714, 1780, 1781, 1801, 1830, 1831, 1832, 1844, 1880, 1903, 1925.

Fritz, Christina, m.n. Loesch, widow van der Merk, 1515, 1531, 1566.

Fruit trees, 1505, 1514, 1533, 1613, 1638, 1639, 1648, 1683, 1691, 1719.

Fugitives, 1530, 1541, 1542, 1543, 1545, 1546, 1547, 1555, 1559, 1560, 1562, 1567, 1568, 1569, 1571, 1575, 1624, 1642, 1643, 1649, 1687, 1696, 1715, 1741, 1753, 1765, 1912.

Fulling-mill, 1645.

Fulneck, 1521.

Funeral Chorales, 1550, 1763, 1794, 1795, 1815.

Fur, 1847.

G

Galloway, 1700.

Gamble, Captain, 1572, 1673, 1882, 1907.

Gamble, Edmund, 1915.

Garland, Samuel, 1925.

Gates, Gen. Horatio, 1511, 1512, 1559, 1560, 1562, 1563, 1569, 1574, 1577,

1578, 1599, 1611, 1624, 1642, 1687, 1880, 1902, 1905, 1906.

Geiger, 1639.

Gemein Haus, Bethabara, 1630, 1744, 1864.

Gemein Haus, Bethania, 1640, 1766, 1771, 1801, 1819, 1824, 1866, 1890.

Gemein Haus, Salem, 1523, 1535, 1536, 1555, 1576, 1601, 1672, 1677, 1681, 1682, 1704, 1715, 1722, 1725, 1796, 1798, 1806, 1841, 1854, 1913.

Gemein Nachrichten, 1516, 1520, 1521, 1526, 1541, 1567, 1568, 1575, 1579, 1589, 1612, 1616, 1634, 1635, 1638, 1646, 1660, 1685, 1686, 1689, 1695, 1698, 1701, 1702, 1707, 1759, 1787, 1798, 1801, 1884.

Gemein Ort, 1499, 1501, 1503, 1657.

Gemein Saal, Bethabara, 1615, 1635, 1636, 1750, 1861.

Gemein Saal, Bethania, 1504, 1640, 1643, 1818, 1819.

Gemein Saal, Salem, 1527, 1528, 1532, 1544, 1546, 1547, 1553, 1562, 1569, 1577, 1579, 1581, 1595, 1691, 1694, 1703, 1704, 1705, 1709, 1716, 1725, 1727, 1737, 1841.

Gemeinstunde, 1528, 1547, 1586, 1614, 1680, 1750, 1760, 1787, 1819, 1826.

Gemein Tag, see Unity Days.

Gemein Vorsteher, 1514, 1547, 1548, 1604.

General Court, 1527, 1647, 1790.

Georgia, 1511, 1542, 1543, 1546, 1555, 1575, 1656, 1670, 1673, 1675, 1684, 1696, 1765, 1775, 1837, 1838, 1839, 1882, 1890.

George III, 1511, 1536, 1784.

Gerber, Michael, 1859.

German Reformed, 1765.

German settlements, 1517, 1786, 1823, 1831, 1832, 1835, 1859, 1861.

Gernand, Johann Adam, 1795, 1804.

Gervais, 1791.

Glascock, 1666, 1671.

Glen, James, 1628.

Gnadenhütten, 1820.

God's Acre, Bethabara, 1582, 1613, 1614, 1615, 1616, 1629, 1750, 1811, 1812.

God's Acre, Bethania, 1504, 1639, 1718, 1770, 1817, 1819, 1867.

God's Acre for Strangers, see Parish Graveyard.

God's Acre, Friedberg, 1647, 1648, 1829, 1831, 1870.

God's Acre, Friedland, 1873.

God's Acre, Hope, 1524, 1655.

God's Acre, Salem, 1527, 1532, 1550, 1552, 1603, 1606, 1691, 1713, 1725, 1791, 1796, 1802.

God, the Father, 1507, 1513, 1517, 1538, 1543, 1546, 1550, 1563, 1580, 1592, 1612, 1632, 1638, 1646, 1650, 1652, 1678, 1697, 1786, 1817, 1885, 1919.

Goepfert, George, 1620, 1922.

Goetje, Peter, 1517, 1541, 1542, 1592, 1598, 1720, 1838, 1846, 1848, 1922.

Gold, coins, 1723, 1734.

Goode, Major, 1549.

Good Friday, 1531, 1616, 1690, 1750, 1839, 1873.

Goslin, John, 1925.

Gospel, 1517, 1661, 1786, 1804, 1817, 1834, 1835.

Grabs, Gottfried, 1508, 1527, 1582, 1639, 1767, 1889, 1892, 1923.

Grabs, William, 1508, 1518, 1524, 1527, 1535, 1639, 1640, 1647, 1770, 1868, 1889, 1923.

Graef, 1539.

Graff, Gertraut, m.n. Jack, 1521, 1522, 1529, 1535, 1546, 1547, 1553, 1558, 1560, 1561, 1563, 1567, 1569, 1573, 1586, 1628, 1646, 1648, 1653, 1654, 1752, 1782, 1809, 1832, 1843.

Graff, Bishop Johann Michael, 1512, 1520, 1521, 1522, 1524, 1525, 1526, 1527, 1529, 1532, 1535, 1540, 1541, 1544, 1546, 1547, 1553, 1558, 1560, 1561, 1562, 1564, 1567, 1568, 1569, 1572, 1573, 1574, 1578, 1579, 1586, 1591, 1607, 1608, 1612, 1624, 1637, 1646, 1648, 1653, 1654, 1663, 1669, 1676, 1680, 1682, 1687, 1689, 1697, 1700, 1704, 1707, 1708, 1730, 1735, 1752, 1758, 1778, 1782, 1785, 1787, 1794, 1795, 1796, 1797, 1807, 1815,

1818, 1819, 1827, 1828, 1830, 1832, 1877, 1896, 1922.

Grain, 1514, 1516, 1526, 1539, 1551, 1554, 1555, 1556, 1562, 1563, 1576, 1583, 1584, 1598, 1605, 1607, 1610, 1611, 1614, 1615, 1617, 1623, 1632, 1635, 1636, 1638, 1642, 1647, 1649, 1650, 1651, 1660, 1666, 1668, 1671, 1674, 1691, 1695, 1696, 1697, 1710, 1713, 1725, 1729, 1734, 1739, 1740, 1741, 1743, 1745, 1751, 1756, 1758, 1772, 1773, 1799, 1816, 1859, 1863, 1868, 1880, 1881, 1890, 1912.

Granville, John, Earl, 1558.

Grapes, 1595, 1601, 1648, 1752, 1854.

Gravestones, 1608, 1613.

Great Sabbath, 1532, 1616, 1690, 1750, 1835, 1839, 1866.

Green, Anna, 1843.

Green (Kröhn), Philip, Jr., 1585.

Greene, Gen. Nathanael, 1512, 1578, 1656, 1666, 1667, 1668, 1670, 1671, 1674, 1675, 1678, 1679, 1687, 1694, 1695, 1696, 1699, 1704, 1713, 1719, 1728, 1746, 1751, 1765, 1768, 1772, 1784, 1788, 1790, 1792, 1809, 1819, 1834, 1881, 1907.

Greenland, 1672, 1675, 1793, 1811, 1837, 1859, 1870.

Grego, Christian, 1571, 1629.

Greter, George, 1776, 1924.

Greter, Jacob, Jr., 1924.

Greter, Jacob, Sr., 1539, 1544, 1549, 1578, 1649, 1651, 1774, 1775, 1776, 1924.

Greter, Maria, m.n. Frey, 1774.

Grimes, Captain, 1679.

Grind-stone mountain, 1816.

Grube, Rev. Bernhard Adam, 1567, 1635.

Guilford County, 1536, 1571, 1619, 1640, 1666, 1673, 1681, 1686, 1756, 1769, 1781, 1793, 1881, 1883, 1884, 1906.

Guilford Court-House, 1553, 1563, 1564, 1580, 1656, 1686, 1687, 1695, 1748, 1749, 1754, 1768.

Günther, see Kinder.

Gute, John, 1624, 1626.

Guthery, Lieutenant, 1690, 1691.

H

Haefner, 1800.

Haefner, Jacob, 1863.

Hahn, Friedrich, Jr., 1690, 1695.

Hahn, George Friedrich, 1924.

Halifax, 1706, 1707.

Hall, Maria, 1859.

Hall, Rev., 1677.

Hamilton, Captain, 1789.

Hamilton, Horatio, 1541, 1925.

Hammond, Captain, 1677, 1678, 1686.

Hampton, 1822.

Hampton, Ez., 1925.

Handicrafts, Trades and Professions, 1503, 1504, 1514, 1517, 1522, 1523, 1533, 1535, 1536, 1557, 1567, 1582, 1583, 1586, 1591, 1592, 1594, 1595, 1596, 1597, 1598, 1600, 1609, 1618, 1620, 1623, 1660, 1680, 1690, 1692, 1694, 1696, 1705, 1710, 1714, 1720, 1723, 1728, 1729, 1730, 1738, 1782, 1786, 1795, 1802, 1803, 1804, 1805, 1806, 1810, 1816, 1836, 1840, 1846, 1847, 1848, 1849, 1858, 1860, 1892.

Handson, Maria, 1525, 1811, 1816, 1826.

Handson, Benjamin, 1811.

Hanson, Lieut. Samuel, 1682.

Hanging Rock, 1544, 1545, 1546, 1551, 1555, 1558.

Hardgrave, Major, 1702.

Hard money, 1534, 1544, 1555, 1560, 1576, 1581, 1582, 1583, 1590, 1591, 1593, 1596, 1598, 1604, 1608, 1639, 1696, 1702, 1713, 1722, 1723, 1724, 1734, 1773, 1802, 1803, 1806, 1807, 1823, 1840, 1845, 1855, 1893, 1911, 1912, 1921.

Hard times, 1601, 1602, 1666, 1689, 1712, 1817, 1879.

Harleson, 1704.

Harmony of the Gospels, 1666, 1677, 1687.

Hartmann, Adam, 1649, 1776, 1924.

Hartmann, Elisabeth, 1525, 1555, 1858.

Hartmann, George, 1525, 1537, 1579, 1648, 1650, 1652, 1722, 1804, 1827, 1829, 1924.

Hartmann, James, 1924.

29

Hartmann, Johannes, 1535, 1536, 1567, 1650, 1924.

Hartmann, Major, 1563, 1599, 1904, 1907.

Harvests, 1514, 1516, 1546, 1548, 1550, 1561, 1606, 1613, 1621, 1622, 1623, 1638, 1646, 1650, 1659, 1660, 1697, 1723, 1753, 1754, 1755, 1770, 1771, 1817, 1824, 1834, 1859, 1890, 1902.

Hauser, Abraham, 1855, 1891.

Hauser, Anna, 1718, 1729.

Hauser, Anna Margarethe, 1518, 1640, 1772.

Hauser, George, Jr., 1508, 1518, 1554, 1586, 1587, 1598, 1605, 1611, 1639, 1640, 1642, 1693, 1698, 1720, 1735, 1750, 1768, 1769, 1770, 1771, 1772, 1793, 1806, 1808, 1809, 1814, 1818, 1820, 1826, 1890, 1892, 1923.

Hauser, George, Sr., 1508, 1533, 1534, 1546, 1549, 1584, 1615, 1617, 1639, 1640, 1764, 1768, 1772, 1773, 1818, 1867, 1876, 1892, 1923.

Hauser, Gertraut, 1518.

Hauser, Heinrich, 1648, 1649, 1651, 1698, 1773, 1782, 1794, 1924.

Hauser, Jacob, Jr., 1766, 1923.

Hauser, Jacob, Sr., 1755, 1767, 1769, 1868, 1923.

Hauser, Johannes, 1685, 1772, 1923.

Hauser, Joseph, 1643, 1819.

Hauser, Maria Christina, 1518.

Hauser, Maria Elisabeth, m.n. Spönhauer, 1820.

Hauser, Martin, 1723, 1767, 1891, 1923.

Hauser, Michael, Jr., 1508, 1531, 1570, 1604, 1642, 1645, 1769, 1770, 1772, 1923.

Hauser, Michael, Sr., 1508, 1526, 1554, 1581, 1582, 1583, 1604, 1623, 1640, 1642, 1644, 1726, 1729, 1739, 1750, 1768, 1769, 1772, 1817, 1820, 1892, 1919, 1923.

Hauser, Peter, 1508, 1582, 1639, 1769, 1773, 1818, 1825, 1867, 1889, 1892, 1923.

Hauser, Petrus, 1508.

Haversham, James, 1839, 1918.

Haversham, John, 1704.

Haversham, Col. Joseph, 1542, 1543, 1670, 1671, 1798, 1839.

Haw River, 1517, 1518, 1588, 1669, 1670, 1686, 1687, 1714, 1768, 1800, 1916.

Hebron, 1689.

Heckwälder, Christian, 1516, 1518, 1520, 1521, 1558, 1568, 1569, 1570, 1581, 1589, 1604, 1890, 1898, 1922.

Hege, Anna Maria, 1531, 1738, 1762, 1763.

Hege, Balthaser, 1508, 1869, 1889, 1923.

Hege, Juliana, 1518, 1520, 1521, 1525, 1564.

Hege, Lazarus, 1770.

Hessians, 1543, 1567, 1597, 1602, 1687, 1769, 1771, 1796.

Heyl, 1553, 1554.

Heyl, Rev. Matthaeus, 1692.

Heyn, Major, 1764.

Hides, 1568, 1569, 1574, 1599, 1632, 1666, 1667, 1670, 1813, 1850.

Higgins, Robert, 1683.

High Rock Ford, 1686.

Highwaymen, 1659, 1669, 1708, 1767, 1782, 1786, 1797, 1884.

Hill, 1689.

Hill, Captain, 1759.

Hill, Henry, 1925.

Hill, John, 1703.

Hill, Philip, 1922.

Hill, Rev. William, 1574, 1632, 1636, 1645, 1682, 1925.

Hillsborough, 1523, 1561, 1562, 1563, 1565, 1567, 1569, 1573, 1575, 1577, 1578, 1607, 1618, 1625, 1634, 1666, 1693, 1694, 1700, 1701, 1790, 1791, 1837, 1862, 1875, 1890.

Hilmebert, 1624.

Hilsebeck, Catharine (wife of Friedrich), 1867.

Hilsebeck, Friedrich, 1810.

Hilsebeck, Jacob, 1867.

Hein, Eva, 1531, 1588.

Hein (Hine), Jacob, Sr., 1781, 1924.

Hein, Jacob William, 1721, 1924.

Hein, John, 1851, 1873, 1924.

Heintz, Hoft, 1614.

Heintzmann, Anna Catharine, m.n. Antes, widow Kalberlahn, widow

Reuter, 1515, 1557, 1653, 1780, 1781, 1858, 1874, 1903.

Heinzmann, Rev. Johann Casper, 1512, 1515, 1517, 1523, 1524, 1525, 1526, 1527, 1532, 1537, 1540, 1541, 1552, 1553, 1555, 1557, 1560, 1566, 1588, 1589, 1595, 1619, 1653, 1721, 1724, 1726, 1738, 1780, 1781, 1782, 1801, 1831, 1844, 1856, 1874, 1875, 1883, 1903, 1919, 1922.

Helfer Conferenz, Grosse, 1514, 1515, 1521, 1544, 1547, 1551, 1554, 1556, 1581-1608, 1683, 1700, 1713, 1718, 1719, 1725, 1729, 1737, 1790, 1801, 1802, 1803, 1806, 1840, 1846, 1855, 1856, 1857, 1897.

Hemp, 1634, 1636.

Henderson, Colonel, 1797.

Henderson, Michael, 1529, 1530, 1615, 1617, 1640, 1739.

Henry XVIII, Count, 1568, 1906, 1913, 1914, 1917.

Herbst, Johann Heinrich, 1523, 1524, 1525, 1535, 1545, 1546, 1547, 1556, 1564, 1574, 1580, 1581, 1582, 1586, 1587, 1590, 1599, 1603, 1604, 1608, 1610, 1626, 1632, 1666, 1672, 1696, 1699, 1711, 1722, 1727, 1819, 1846, 1850, 1895, 1922.

Herd, Heinrich, 1916.

Herndon, Captain, 1674, 1675.

Herndon, Major, 1667, 1684.

Herrnhut, 1547, 1557, 1558, 1624, 1639, 1873.

Hilsebeck, Maria Eva, m.n. Fiscuss, 1867.

Hinkel, Capt. Charles, 1706, 1910.

Hirte, Tobias, 1549, 1617, 1621, 1892.

Historical Outlines of Years, 1510-1513, 1656, 1784, 1799, 1834.

Hoecher, Andreas Eusebius, 1838.

Hoehns, Christina, 1776.

Hoehns (Hanes), Johannes, 1649, 1651, 1778, 1819, 1829, 1924.

Hoehns, Marcus, 1556, 1649, 1924.

Hoehns, Philip, 1778, 1924.

Hofheins, Daniel, 1917.

Hofmann, 1721, 1772.

Hofmann, Jr., 1762.

Holbert, Captain, 1682.

Hold, Jacob, 1916.

Holder, Charles, 1558, 1566, 1585, 1586, 1604, 1610, 1675, 1712, 1723, 1734, 1846, 1854, 1855, 1892, 1905, 1922.

Holder, David, 1749.

Holder, Elisabeth, 1858, 1860, 1863.

Holder, George, 1618, 1629, 1749, 1751, 1813, 1860, 1923.

Holder, Heinrich, 1739.

Holder, Johannes, 1739.

Holder, Joseph, 1645.

Holland, 1511, 1520.

Holland, John, 1517, 1520, 1521, 1534, 1535, 1586, 1587, 1617, 1639, 1830, 1855, 1898, 1922.

Holland, Maria, m.n. Strub, 1898.

Hollow, The, 1536, 1891.

Holmes, Captain, 1684.

Holston, Captain, 1565.

Holston River, 1522, 1540, 1626, 1835, 1845, 1891, 1892, 1893, 1913.

Holy Ghost, 1497, 1501, 1546, 1612, 1638, 1646, 1647, 1652, 1820.

Hope, Congregation Festival, 1832, 1842.

Hope, N. C., 1512, 1514, 1515, 1519, 1523, 1527, 1530, 1532, 1533, 1535, 1538, 1542, 1549, 1560, 1561, 1565, 1571, 1585, 1591, 1598, 1610, 1654, 1655, 1657, 1665, 1709, 1710, 1714, 1732, 1754, 1780-1783, 1804, 1818, 1831-1833, 1880, 1898, 1903.

Hope, N. J., 1805, 1854.

Hops, 1614.

Horns, 1634, 1636.

Horses, 1538, 1542, 1543, 1544, 1549, 1550, 1551, 1560, 1562, 1563, 1567, 1570, 1571, 1573, 1574, 1575, 1579, 1590, 1595, 1604, 1608, 1619, 1621, 1622, 1623, 1624, 1625, 1629, 1631, 1636, 1638, 1640, 1641, 1643, 1649, 1650, 1652, 1667, 1678, 1679, 1682, 1683, 1684, 1685, 1721, 1730, 1741, 1742, 1743, 1744, 1745, 1746, 1748, 1753, 1754, 1756, 1765, 1766, 1768, 1769, 1775, 1780, 1781, 1782, 1822, 1823, 1840, 1880, 1890, 1891, 1892, 1893, 1902, 1908.

Horse-thieves, 1536, 1555, 1625, 1641, 1643, 1648, 1747, 1767, 1782, 1815, 1826, 1890, 1891, 1914.

Hosannah Chorus, 1635.

Hospital, Continental, 1658, 1672, 1673, 1697, 1717, 1882, 1908.

Hound, Colonel, 1765.

Hourly Intercession, see Stundenbeter.

Householders, 1521, 1597, 1602, 1606, 1609.

Houses in Bethabara, 1614, 1619, 1621, 1625, 1630, 1631, 1635, 1660, 1661, 1744, 1751, 1752, 1753, 1759, 1760, 1761, 1810, 1813, 1815, 1816, 1820, 1863, 1917.

Houses in Salem, 1516, 1541, 1547, 1557, 1566, 1570, 1586, 1587, 1588, 1591, 1594, 1595, 1596, 1606, 1608, 1610, 1661, 1667, 1668, 1669, 1671, 1672, 1694, 1711, 1712, 1714, 1715, 1717, 1722, 1726, 1764, 1794, 1798, 1799, 1802, 1804, 1806, 1808, 1838, 1840, 1843, 1844, 1846, 1849, 1854, 1858, 1881, 1908.

Hübner, John Andrew, 1532, 1537, 1542.

Hudspeth, Sheriff, 1582, 1583.

Hughes, John, 1907.

Hughes, Lieutenant, 1667, 1669.

Hunt, 1555.

Hunter, James, 1792, 1793.

Hunting, 1500, 1848, 1852, 1857.

Hunting Creek, 1675.

Hurst, James, 1922.

Hus, John, 1551, 1622, 1697.

Hutchins, Col. Thomas, 1791.

Hutton, James, 1527, 1784, 1899, 1900, 1915.

Hyder Ali, 1511, 1787.

Hymns, 1494, 1524, 1526, 1529, 1531, 1536, 1539, 1547, 1568, 1580, 1581, 1591, 1617, 1619, 1623, 1629, 1634, 1636, 1661, 1685, 1703, 1708, 1763, 1788, 1819, 1864.

Hymn Books, 1524, 1582, 1584, 1685, 1688.

Hyrn, Major, 1671.

I

Ide (negress), 1557, 1606.

Idea Fidei Fratrum, 1582, 1584, 1698, 1756, 1786, 1787, 1793, 1836, 1866, 1873, 1875.

Ikes, Peter, 1693.

Impressment, see under Supplies Furnished, Bread, Meat, Horses, etc.

Independence, 1609, 1784, 1834, 1850, 1853, 1876, 1919.

India, 1511, 1787.

Indians, 1535, 1542, 1556, 1635, 1692, 1695, 1702, 1704, 1707, 1787, 1835, 1855, 1912.

Indian War, 1498.

Indigo, 1917.

Indigo dyeing, 1517, 1613, 1635, 1896, 1898.

Industry, 1504.

Ingram, David, 1924.

Infantry, 1549, 1550, 1551, 1565, 1571, 1572, 1630, 1634, 1641, 1759.

Inoculation, 1683, 1691, 1709, 1715, 1716, 1717, 1718, 1749, 1750, 1751, 1769.

Inventories, 1724.

Ireland, 1511.

Irishmen, 1553, 1556, 1645, 1721, 1817, 1868.

Iron, 1545, 1564, 1577, 1604, 1623, 1681, 1683, 1686, 1691, 1701, 1762, 1859, 1907.

Iron Works, 1687, 1789, 1796, 1797, 1813.

Isaacs, Colonel, 1787.

J

Jacks, Captain, 1684, 1687.

Jackson, Dr., 1682.

Jacob (negro), 1522, 1580, 1891.

Jacobi, Johann Nicholas, 1871.

Jamaica, 1497.

James (widow), 1822.

James River, 1545, 1636.

Jans, Johannes, 1924.

Jesus Christ, 1496, 1499, 1502, 1503, 1513, 1526, 1531, 1535, 1550, 1558, 1569, 1580, 1598, 1636, 1638, 1666, 1688, 1697, 1706, 1781, 1791, 1827, 1870.

Johannes, Tag, 1548.
Jolibet, 1540.
Jones, Michel, 1925.
Jorde, Christine, 1693.
Joseph, Br., see Bishop Spangenburg.
Journey-cakes, 1894.
Jünger, see Zinzendorf.
Jupiter (a negro), 1804, 1832.
Jury service, 1530, 1558, 1577, 1735, 1761, 1862.
Justices of the Peace, 1530, 1538, 1603, 1640, 1682, 1703, 1710, 1712, 1726, 1729, 1735, 1736, 1739, 1744, 1772, 1795, 1798, 1801, 1806, 1849, 1864, 1868, 1879, 1885, 1915, 1919.

K

Kalb, Baron von, 1641.
Kalberlahn, Dr. Hans Martin, 1703.
Kalcklöher, Maria, 1761.
Kalmucks, 1497.
Kapp, Anna Maria, 1617.
Kapp, Elisabeth, m.n. Everitt, 1815.
Kapp, Heinrich, 1866.
Kapp, Jacob, 1537, 1619, 1620, 1631, 1750, 1813, 1816, 1863, 1867, 1923.
Kapp, Joseph Friedrich, 1923.
Kapp, Louisa, m.n. Doll, 1863.
Kapp, Magdalena, 1518, 1539, 1586, 1813.
Kastner, Anton, 1851, 1891, 1924.
Kentucky, 1522, 1533, 1534, 1556, 1617, 1797, 1912, 1913.
Kershaw, 1705.
Kershaw, Colonel, 1822, 1823.
Kershaw, Joseph, 1737.
Kinchin, Lawyer, 1790.
Kinder, Lieut. Peter, 1685, 1687, 1688, 1689, 1690.
Kings Mountain, 1512, 1573, 1607, 1631, 1656, 1667, 1680, 1881, 1906, 1907.
Kirschner, Joh. Christian, 1508, 1517, 1770, 1923.
Kiss of Peace, 1525, 1555, 1818.
Kleinert, 1560, 1704, 1797.
Knauss, Joseph, 1869, 1924.
Knecht, Commissary, 1765, 1766.
Knoll, Isaac, 1699.
Koehler, Anna Johanna, m.n. Kohler, 1836.

Koehler, Rev. Johann Daniel, 1836.
Koffler, Adam, 1603, 1605, 1722, 1723, 1729, 1838, 1843, 1849, 1858, 1870, 1871, 1922.
Koffler, Maria Magdalena, m.n. Reuz, 1838, 1843, 1870.
Kohlhup, 1891.
Kopp, Heinrich, 1917.
Korbmann, Anna Catharina, 1829.
Korbmann, Margaretha, 1829.
Korbmann, Peter, 1829.
Kramer, Adam, 1508, 1826, 1889, 1923.
Kramer, Gottlieb, 1508, 1816, 1826, 1867, 1889, 1923.
Kramer, Maria, m.n. Handson, 1816, 1826.
Kramer, Maria Barbara, m.n. Eyerich, 1824.
Krause, Andreas, 1614.
Krause, Anna Maria, 1529, 1648.
Krause, Gottlob, 1698, 1855, 1856, 1922.
Krause, Maria Elisabeth, 1515, 1522, 1566, 1832.
Krause, Johann (of Salem), 1521, 1538, 1539, 1540, 1570, 1586, 1609, 1672, 1692, 1701, 1706, 1707, 1719, 1728, 1848, 1850, 1854, 1856, 1858, 1922.
Krause, John, 1571, 1614, 1643, 1671, 1727, 1767, 1814, 1861, 1925.
Krause, Wendel, 1699, 1754, 1925.
Kreiter, Leonard, 1537.
Kremser, Andreas, 1559, 1597, 1609, 1848, 1922.
Krieger (Krüger), Heinrich, 1750, 1769, 1819, 1923.
Krieger (Krüger), Jacob, 1923.
Krieger, Johann George, 1867.
Krieger, Nicholas, 1867.
Kröhn (Green), Conrad, 1924.
Kröhn, Peter, 1780, 1851, 1873, 1924.
Kröhn (Green), Philip, Jr., 1585.
Kröhn, Philip, Sr., 1542, 1544, 1924.
Krum, Anna Elisabeth, 1761.
Krum, Johannes, 1761.
Kühnast, Christoph, 1573, 1603, 1613, 1614, 1615, 1622, 1631, 1634, 1740, 1744, 1760, 1811, 1813, 1891, 1911, 1923.

Kühnast, Rosina, m.n. Arndt, 1752, 1816, 1825, 1826.
Kummerling, 1916.
Künzel, Carl Christoph, 1872.
Künzel, Johann, Friedrich, 1780, 1851, 1873, 1923.
Kürschner, Johann Michael, 1518, 1693, 1720, 1853.

L

Laborers, 1503, 1548, 1549, 1561, 1565, 1566, 1590, 1597, 1614, 1615, 1620, 1713, 1739, 1756, 1760, 1778, 1799, 1801, 1811, 1812, 1846, 1847, 1863.
Labrador, 1701.
Lagenauer, George, Fr., 1545, 1548, 1562, 1776, 1924.
Lagenauer, Jacob, Fr., 1745, 1924.
Lamps, 1537.
Lancaster, 1624.
Land Arbeiter Conferenz, 1602, 1606, 1609, 1651, 1661, 1668, 1677, 1712, 1713, 1721, 1730, 1738, 1786, 1804, 1805, 1807, 1829, 1831, 1832, 1846, 1847, 1850, 1857, 1858, 1872.
Lang, Elisabeth, 1619.
Lang, Friedrich, 1524, 1526, 1619, 1846.
Lang, George, 1524, 1812, 1846, 1861.
Lang, Thomas, 1829.
Lanier, Col. Robert, 1522, 1555, 1573, 1580, 1610, 1618, 1630, 1680, 1740, 1764, 1908.
Lanius, John, 1851, 1873, 1891, 1924.
Lapp, Captain, 1571, 1629, 1648, 1651, 1682, 1837.
Lauer, John, 1724, 1925.
Laurence, Henry, 1878, 1897.
Law, 1500, 1853, 1857, 1868.
Lawlessness, 1517, 1527, 1545, 1552, 1554, 1555, 1556, 1562, 1563, 1565, 1570, 1572, 1575, 1577, 1578, 1580, 1601, 1604, 1605, 1622, 1625, 1632, 1642, 1643, 1644, 1645, 1650, 1652, 1654, 1655, 1656, 1657, 1658, 1669, 1673, 1674, 1675, 1676, 1677, 1678, 1679, 1681, 1683, 1684, 1685, 1688, 1695, 1698, 1706, 1708, 1727, 1743, 1744, 1745, 1747, 1756, 1757, 1766, 1767, 1768, 1773, 1775, 1776, 1777,

1780, 1781, 1782, 1784, 1790, 1791, 1797, 1798, 1813, 1823, 1829, 1882, 1883, 1890, 1901, 1906, 1908, 1910, 1916.
Lawrence's Ferry, 1822.
Lead, 1567, 1570, 1579, 1626, 1673, 1674.
Leap Year, 1520.
Leases, 1608, 1709, 1786, 1814, 1825, 1858, 1917.
Leather, 1545, 1563, 1567, 1568, 1569, 1570, 1573, 1578, 1580, 1599, 1610, 1666, 1670, 1694, 1806, 1902, 1909, 1912.
Leather-dressing, 1595, 1596, 1597.
Lee, "Light-Horse Harry," 1512, 1671, 1690, 1909.
Lee, Thomas Sim, 1611.
Leinbach, Abraham, 1765, 1889, 1890, 1923.
Leinbach, Benjamin, 1889, 1890, 1928.
Leinbach, Catharine, 1587, 1588, 1860.
Leinbach, John, 1697, 1771.
Leinbach, Joseph, 1849, 1889, 1890, 1923.
Leinbach, Ludwig, 1765, 1923.
Lenoir, Captain William, 1674, 1684.
Lesley, General, 1676.
Letters of Protection, 1563, 1566, 1599, 1701, 1728, 1730, 1908.
Letters, see Postal Facilities.
Lewis, Elkanah, 1646.
Lewis, James, 1685.
Lewis, Joel, 1685, 1821.
Lewis, Capt. John, 1687, 1690, 1756.
Lewis, Dr. John, 1856.
Lewis, Maj. Micajah, 1667, 1678, 1679, 1685.
Lewis, William, 1768, 1838.
Liberty-Men, 1542, 1567, 1644, 1645, 1765, 1767, 1769.
Liberty of Conscience, 1501, 1513.
Lick, Magdalena, 1567.
Lick (Lück), Martin, 1609, 1679, 1744, 1922.
Light-Horse, 1513, 1536, 1548, 1549, 1550, 1551, 1556, 1561, 1562, 1568, 1571, 1576, 1579, 1618, 1640, 1650, 1655, 1666, 1675, 1687, 1701, 1835, 1837, 1838.

Lime, 1819.

Lincoln County, 1677.

Linen, 1500, 1565, 1850, 1911.

Litanies, 1528, 1552, 1571, 1614, 1615, 1627, 1628, 1643, 1648, 1650, 1688, 1698, 1705, 1707, 1737, 1746, 1759, 1791, 1796, 1812, 1829, 1839, 1842, 1854, 1872, 1874.

Lititz, 1518, 1533, 1536, 1541, 1547, 1635, 1692, 1695, 1855, 1856, 1893, 1895.

Little Boys, see Children.

Little Girls, see Children.

Liturgies, 1521, 1522, 1525, 1527, 1528, 1529, 1531, 1532, 1547, 1550, 1555, 1561, 1564, 1569, 1576, 1603, 1616, 1619, 1620, 1624, 1629, 1643, 1661, 1663, 1670, 1688, 1691, 1708, 1727, 1729, 1756, 1758, 1761, 1794, 1795, 1810, 1816, 1818, 1819, 1825, 1831, 1832, 1838, 1852, 1857, 1872, 1873, 1874.

Locke, Col. Francis, 1548, 1696, 1772.

Lock, Matthew, 1720.

Loesch, Abraham, 1804.

Loesch, Adam, 1893.

Loesch, Christian, 1794, 1805, 1850.

Loesch, George, 1725.

Loesch, Rev. Jacob, 1865.

Loesch, Jacob, Jr., 1660, 1706, 1707, 1738, 1802, 1803, 1804, 1806, 1807, 1825, 1849, 1865.

London, 1575, 1692.

Long, see Lang.

Long, Alex, 1857.

Long Island of Holston, 1845, 1892.

Long, Philip, 1915.

Lord's Prayer, 1634, 1636.

Lord's Supper, see Communion.

Lot, The, 1500, 1514, 1536, 1583, 1587, 1588, 1589, 1596, 1598, 1637, 1703, 1717, 1723, 1735, 1737, 1738, 1789, 1829, 1832, 1846, 1848, 1854.

Lovefeasts, 1521, 1526, 1532, 1533, 1535, 1537, 1547, 1553, 1555, 1557, 1563, 1568, 1569, 1577, 1579, 1580, 1586, 1591, 1601, 1614, 1615, 1616, 1620, 1623, 1628, 1635, 1636, 1637, 1647, 1648, 1650, 1652, 1653, 1654, 1655, 1693, 1697, 1700, 1703, 1707,

1708, 1712, 1721, 1740, 1750, 1751, 1753, 1755, 1758, 1760, 1763, 1778, 1779, 1782, 1794, 1795, 1811, 1813, 1819, 1820, 1825, 1826, 1827, 1829, 1830, 1833, 1837, 1838, 1839, 1840, 1841, 1842, 1844, 1845, 1848, 1864, 1866, 1867, 1870, 1872, 1873, 1875.

Lawdon, 1790.

Lower Counties, 1539, 1660, 1703, 1769.

Loyalty, 1551, 1592, 1599, 1607, 1656.

Ludwig, Catharine, 1867.

Ludwig, Peter, 1791, 1867.

Ludwig, Philip, 1916.

Ludwig, William, 1791.

Lund, Nils, 1804, 1805, 1829, 1924.

Lung, Jacob, 1613, 1923.

Lusatia, 1526.

M

Maas, Henry, 1925.

Magazine, see Ammunition, Store-house for.

Manakasy, Md., 1575, 1895.

Marbury, Captain, 1672, 1907.

Marit, Francis, 1770.

Market in Salem, 1714, 1853.

Markland, Jonathan, 1925.

Markland, Matthew, Jr., 1565, 1925.

Markland, Matthew, Sr., 1523, 1585, 1600, 1732, 1925.

Marriage, 1495, 1501, 1502, 1503, 1516, 1517, 1518, 1522, 1523, 1524, 1533, 1534, 1535, 1539, 1540, 1552, 1553, 1555, 1557, 1558, 1561, 1569, 1578, 1583, 1586, 1587, 1588, 1590, 1602, 1605, 1606, 1611, 1612, 1617, 1635, 1639, 1640, 1662, 1693, 1694, 1700, 1708, 1710, 1712, 1717, 1726, 1727, 1729, 1737, 1738, 1763, 1771, 1772, 1774, 1794, 1798, 1799, 1804, 1807, 1808, 1826, 1838, 1839, 1844, 1847, 1851, 1867, 1869, 1871, 1890, 1897.

Marriage License, 1584.

Married People, 1502, 1514, 1519, 1528, 1546, 1547, 1552, 1562, 1564, 1565, 1569, 1590, 1602, 1617, 1628, 1662, 1664, 1670, 1691, 1696, 1697, 1700, 1712, 1757, 1760, 1778, 1782, 1787, 1797, 1815, 1825, 1826, 1830, 1833, 1843, 1868, 1874, 1898, 1901.

Marshall, Elisabeth, 1515, 1521, 1523, 1526, 1528, 1529, 1535, 1558, 1560, 1561, 1563, 1567, 1570, 1571, 1580, 1610, 1618, 1620, 1624, 1635, 1646, 1648, 1653, 1740, 1752, 1781, 1788, 1797, 1819, 1832.

Marshall, Rev. Friedrich Wilhelm, 1498, 1512, 1515, 1516, 1521, 1523, 1525, 1526, 1527, 1529, 1530, 1534, 1535, 1539, 1540, 1541, 1542, 1545, 1548, 1552, 1554, 1558, 1560, 1561, 1563, 1564, 1565, 1567, 1569, 1570, 1571, 1574, 1577, 1580, 1589, 1591, 1604, 1605, 1610, 1611, 1618, 1620, 1624, 1625, 1626, 1632, 1635, 1637, 1646, 1648, 1653, 1666, 1668, 1673, 1676, 1681, 1688, 1689, 1694, 1698, 1700, 1704, 1706, 1707, 1714, 1724, 1728, 1735, 1740, 1751, 1752, 1774, 1781, 1782, 1784, 1786, 1789, 1791, 1795, 1797, 1798, 1801, 1805, 1807, 1812, 1813, 1818, 1819, 1820, 1822, 1825, 1827, 1829, 1830, 1832, 1839, 1849, 1850, 1856, 1863, 1670, 1875, 1879, 1885, 1894, 1896, 1905, 1906, 1910, 1912, 1913, 1914, 1915, 1917, 1918, 1919, 1921, 1922.

Martin, 1681.

Martin, Gov. Alexander, 1525, 1542, 1558, 1619, 1695, 1701, 1703, 1704, 1705, 1725, 1726, 1727, 1730, 1736, 1788, 1794, 1795, 1797, 1801, 1819, 1824, 1834, 1841, 1843, 1862, 1868, 1871, 1913, 1914, 1915, 1920.

Martin, Col. James, 1838, 1845, 1848, 1855, 1856.

Martin, Gov. Josiah, 1676, 1875, 1876, 1877.

Martin, Moses, 1579, 1747, 1858.

Mary (a negress), 1515, 1518, 1578, 1605, 1606, 1611, 1635, 1763.

Maryland, 1656, 1682, 1687, 1703, 1804, 1893.

Masinger, 1543.

Maundy Thursday, 1531, 1690, 1749, 1781, 1872.

May Twelfth, 1693.

Mazaret, Major, 1692.

McArthur, Major, 1551.

McBain, Sarah, 1667, 1807.

McCloud, General, 1676.

McGuire, Lieutenant, 1789.

McIntosh, General, 1670, 1794.

McKain, 1677.

McKay, 1687.

McKnight, George, 1925.

McKnight, Roger, 1925.

McLane, Captain, 1670.

McPherson, Joseph, 1925.

Meal, 1556, 1559, 1562, 1565, 1573, 1580, 1584, 1620, 1631, 1635, 1641, 1651, 1668, 1674, 1676, 1681, 1684, 1702, 1710, 1714, 1741, 1748, 1798.

Measles, 1836, 1844, 1845, 1866, 1869, 1870.

Meat, 1580, 1615, 1622, 1630, 1633, 1635, 1640, 1671, 1674, 1676, 1681, 1684, 1696, 1731, 1741, 1759, 1764, 1798, 1851, 1902, 1912.

Mecklenburg County, 1541, 1547, 1548, 1562, 1567, 1568, 1677, 1679, 1680, 1682, 1687, 1883.

Medicine and Surgery, 1512, 1544, 1545, 1550, 1552, 1557, 1559, 1562, 1563, 1571, 1572, 1577, 1610, 1611, 1615, 1624, 1637, 1670, 1671, 1688, 1691, 1694, 1703, 1712, 1717, 1718, 1735, 1739, 1745, 1753, 1754, 1761, 1762, 1763, 1770, 1776, 1777, 1778, 1781, 1795, 1802, 1803, 1805, 1811, 1812, 1813, 1816, 1829, 1859, 1862, 1866, 1867, 1868, 1890, 1894, 1917, 1919.

Meinung, Ludwig, 1534, 1535, 1560, 1578, 1579, 1581, 1585, 1586, 1588, 1618, 1621, 1672, 1629, 1715, 1726, 1741, 1747, 1812, 1825, 1860, 1865, 1922.

Memoirs, 1603, 1647, 1687, 1699, 1703, 1746, 1756, 1794, 1796, 1797, 1815, 1816, 1824, 1825, 1830, 1862, 1865, 1873.

Memorabilia, 1513, 1516, 1520, 1580, 1612, 1637, 1646, 1652, 1653, 1657, 1708, 1763, 1764, 1779, 1785, 1826, 1834, 1856, 1858, 1875.

Memorabilia of the Revolutionary War, 1875-1885.

Memorial Days, 1515, 1557, 1558, 1566, 1577, 1624, 1628, 1693, 1698, 1700, 1757, 1832, 1838, 1865.

Mennonites, 1690.

Merkly, Christopher, 1594, 1605, 1725, 1922.

Meredith, Captain, 1551.

Merrel, Captain, 1622.

Metcalf, Charles, 1558, 1899.

Metcalf lands, 1527, 1540, 1558, 1791, 1898, 1917, 1919.

Metcalf, Mary, 1558, 1899.

Methodists, 1804, 1805, 1807.

Meyer, Jacob, Jr., 1517, 1523, 1587, 1728, 1729.

Meyer, Jacob, Sr., 1517, 1523, 1525, 1548, 1553, 1576, 1578, 1583, 1587, 1589, 1592, 1593, 1605, 1606, 1608, 1610, 1611, 1675, 1676, 1685, 1711, 1713, 1716, 1719, 1722, 1723, 1725, 1758, 1804, 1849, 1905, 1911, 1922.

Meyer, Maria Dorothea, m.n. Miller, 1758.

Meyer, Maria Magdalena, 1517, 1523, 1532, 1587.

Meyer, Samuel, 1728, 1729, 1805, 1840, 1851.

Michael, Barnet, 1906, 1910.

Michaelmas, 1568, 1608, 1628, 1730, 1843, 1869.

Michel, Peter, 1915.

Middle Fork (Wach), 1648, 1778.

Midwifery, 1758, 1814, 1862.

Miksch, Maria Christina Henrietta, m.n. Peterman, 1581.

Miksch, Matthew, 1533, 1534, 1535, 1547, 1566, 1576, 1578, 1579, 1586, 1587, 1721, 1725, 1802, 1922.

Militia, 1512, 1536, 1537, 1539, 1541, 1542, 1543, 1544, 1545, 1548, 1551, 1553, 1554, 1559, 1560, 1564, 1565, 1567, 1571, 1573, 1574, 1576, 1577, 1596, 1605, 1615, 1618, 1621, 1622, 1623, 1625, 1626, 1627, 1628, 1629, 1630, 1631, 1632, 1635, 1638, 1640, 1643, 1650, 1659, 1670, 1671, 1674, 1676, 1682, 1685, 1694, 1699, 1701, 1702, 1704, 1705, 1709, 1710, 1714, 1730, 1741, 1743, 1744, 1745, 1747, 1748, 1754, 1756, 1758, 1759, 1761, 1762, 1765, 1772, 1788, 1800, 1811, 1849, 1876, 1877, 1880, 1881, 1895, 1901, 1902, 1906, 1908, 1910.

Militia Service of Moravians, 1512, 1513, 1515, 1542, 1544, 1545, 1575, 1599, 1659, 1680, 1729, 1730, 1736, 1782, 1876, 1877, 1878, 1879, 1890.

Milk, 1720, 1721, 1734.

Mill near Bethabara, 1537, 1539, 1571, 1614, 1620, 1625, 1631, 1632, 1710, 1713, 1724, 1729, 1741, 1742, 1743, 1752, 1758, 1772, 1860, 1864.

Mill near Bethania, 1808, 1846, 1867, 1868, 1869.

Mill below Salem, 1517, 1520, 1521, 1537, 1538, 1539, 1542, 1546, 1548, 1549, 1552, 1554, 1555, 1556, 1557, 1565, 1566, 1576, 1578, 1593, 1594, 1601, 1609, 1611, 1623, 1624, 1667, 1668, 1671, 1676, 1695, 1697, 1710, 1724, 1725, 1729, 1737, 1807, 1846, 1847, 1900, 1902.

Miller, 1716, 1719.

Miller, Frederic Daniel, 1527, 1533, 1548, 1549, 1556, 1559, 1571, 1593, 1651, 1654, 1676, 1721, 1727, 1731, 1781, 1782, 1793, 1798, 1800, 1832, 1838, 1851, 1866, 1873, 1924.

Miller, Capt. Heinrich, 1650, 1778, 1924.

Miller (Müller), Johannes, 1924.

Miller, John, Sr., 1525, 1647, 1648, 1776, 1924.

Miller, Michael, 1924.

Ministers, 1499, 1500, 1501, 1504, 1507, 1512, 1566, 1592, 1601, 1635, 1697, 1699, 1700, 1712.

Ministers' Conference, 1514, 1668.

Minute Men, 1741, 1876.

Missions, Foreign, 1495, 1496, 1499, 1516, 1522, 1524, 1550, 1560, 1582, 1584, 1593, 1638, 1647, 1667, 1686, 1709, 1774, 1787, 1793, 1811, 1837.

Missions, Home, 1496, 1498.

Missions to Indians, 1707, 1708, 1719, 1787, 1788, 1790, 1792, 1813, 1820, 1835, 1855.

Mitchel, Major, 1793.

Molasses, 1860.

Moll, Johann, 1924.

Möller, Ludwig, 1723, 1760, 1842, 1854, 1922.

Moore, Colonel, 1842.

Montgomery, 1689.

Montgomery County, 1910.

Montgomery, Hugh, 1527, 1528, 1529, 1530, 1899.

Moravia, 1527, 1551.

Moravian position toward Revolutionary War, 1513, 1515, 1542, 1544, 1545, 1547, 1548, 1550, 1551, 1557, 1562, 1565, 1566, 1568, 1570, 1580, 1582, 1584, 1590, 1591, 1592, 1594, 1599, 1607, 1609, 1610, 1612, 1620, 1638, 1641, 1647, 1649, 1655, 1656, 1657, 1658, 1659, 1666, 1668, 1670, 1671, 1672, 1678, 1680, 1681, 1689, 1699, 1706, 1709, 1710, 1711, 1712, 1713, 1715, 1724, 1726, 1729, 1730, 1735, 1736, 1749, 1758, 1766, 1775, 1778, 1782, 1784, 1876, 1878, 1907, 1908, 1910.

Morgan, Col. Daniel, 1512, 1671, 1672, 1674, 1682.

Mortgage, 1528.

Moseley, Captain, 1553, 1679, 1681.

Moser, 1559, 1824.

Moses (negro), 1751.

Motsinger, 1636.

Muddy Creek, 1534, 1600, 1655, 1725, 1732, 1760, 1761, 1778.

Mücke (Micke), Johannes, 1589, 1614, 1620, 1629, 1715, 1735, 1737, 1742, 1758, 1759, 1760, 1761, 1801, 1813, 1859, 1862, 1864, 1865, 1923.

Mücke, Magdalena, m.n. Hirt, 1758.

Mulberry Fields, 1528, 1529, 1791.

Müller, George, 1797.

Müller, Gottfried, 1687, 1702, 1891.

Müller, Jacob, 1769, 1923.

Müller, Joseph, 1818, 1923.

Murder, 1535, 1575, 1578, 1692, 1784, 1787, 1790, 1813, 1820.

Murrah, David, 1855.

Murray, Captain, 1679.

Music, Instrumental, 1514, 1547, 1565, 1568, 1572, 1578, 1579, 1580, 1615, 1636, 1640, 1672, 1700, 1705, 1715, 1729, 1736, 1753, 1757, 1788, 1803, 1825, 1841, 1857, 1864, 1865, 1914.

Music, Vocal, 1514, 1535, 1555, 1568, 1572, 1579, 1580, 1581, 1603, 1635, 1661, 1666, 1672, 1691, 1700, 1705, 1708, 1727, 1729, 1753, 1788, 1796, 1816, 1825, 1837, 1841, 1914.

Muskingum River, 1542, 1567, 1635, 1702, 1787, 1792, 1813.

Muster, 1541, 1542, 1544, 1591, 1615, 1639, 1640, 1643, 1646, 1674, 1748, 1749, 1750, 1754, 1756, 1769, 1813, 1817, 1889, 1891, 1909.

Muzzel, 1868.

N

Nachrichten, see Gemein Nachrichten and Wochen.

Nash, Abner, 1537.

Nazareth, Pa., 1855.

Negroes, 1497, 1515, 1518, 1533, 1542, 1545, 1546, 1555, 1556, 1560, 1605, 1606, 1611, 1613, 1619, 1636, 1671, 1672, 1684, 1686, 1687, 1695, 1696, 1697, 1722, 1723, 1724, 1734, 1735, 1740, 1751, 1755, 1763, 1770, 1802, 1804, 1809, 1816, 1825, 1832, 1838, 1844, 1893.

Neighbors, 1514, 1609, 1846.

Neisser, Rev. George, 1537, 1684, 1695, 1697, 1706, 1839.

Netter, George, 1855.

New Bern, 1527, 1534, 1537, 1546, 1577, 1579, 1639, 1645, 1816, 1875.

New Garden, 1687, 1688, 1909.

New Gnadenhütten, 1835.

New River, 1530, 1533, 1538, 1579, 1689, 1845.

Newspapers, 1524, 1861.

Newton, 1797.

New Year, 1520, 1666, 1774, 1836.

New Year's Eve, 1513, 1520, 1580, 1637, 1708, 1763, 1773, 1779, 1831, 1845, 1872.

New York, 1838, 1840, 1848.

Nicobar, 1497, 1694.

Nieds, Rudolph, 1889.

Nielson, Captain, 1845.

Night-watchmen, Bethania, 1641, 1643.

Night-watchmen, Salem, 1541, 1543, 1546, 1547, 1556, 1566, 1595, 1675,

1682, 1696, 1698, 1702, 1704, 1710, 1714, 1715, 1718, 1727, 1732, 1733, 1851, 1852.

Nilson, Elisabeth, 1514, 1541, 1546, 1547, 1592, 1605, 1620, 1624, 1625, 1637, 1662, 1696, 1700, 1719, 1893.

Nilson, Jeppe, 1514, 1541, 1546, 1547, 1548, 1550, 1552, 1620, 1621, 1637, 1893, 1894.

Nilson, Johannes, 1518, 1533, 1869, 1923.

Nilson, Jonas, 1614, 1621, 1647, 1923.

Nisbet, 1691.

Nissen, Christian, 1518, 1553.

Nissen, Toego (Tycho), 1512, 1515, 1531, 1532, 1552, 1553, 1557, 1595, 1608, 1653, 1697, 1702, 1732, 1733, 1794, 1798, 1838, 1845, 1852, 1855, 1875, 1903, 1922.

Nitschmann, David, 1560.

Noll, Jacob, 1925.

Noly, 1553.

North Carolina, 1512, 1558, 1673, 1784, 1834.

Nöting (Nading), Matthes, 1567, 1601, 1602, 1714, 1806, 1924.

Notions Store, 1590.

November Thirteenth, 1515, 1577, 1634, 1703, 1736, 1761, 1786, 1844.

Nursing Service, 1717.

O

Oath of Abjuration, 1878, 1889.

Oath of Allegiance to English, 1575, 1876.

Oath of Fidelity, 1876, 1878.

Odes, 1700, 1703, 1758, 1778, 1794, 1825, 1827, 1833, 1837, 1840, 1864, 1870.

Oeconomie, 1517, 1583, 1614, 1811, 1812, 1816.

Oesterlein, Anna Maria, m.n. Hege, 1738, 1763, 1860.

Oesterlein, Elisabeth, 1516, 1534, 1535, 1537, 1586, 1589, 1617, 1639, 1899.

Oesterlein, Matthew, 1543, 1569, 1574, 1632, 1660, 1714, 1722, 1723, 1724, 1729, 1737, 1738, 1754, 1757, 1760,

1761, 1762, 1763, 1811, 1845, 1860, 1863, 1922.

Ohio, 1497, 1542, 1702, 1704.

Older Boys, 1503, 1519, 1562, 1569, 1571, 1594, 1603, 1664, 1667, 1793, 1837, 1849.

Older Girls, 1503, 1518, 1519, 1532, 1623, 1637, 1649, 1650, 1663, 1664, 1688, 1770, 1819, 1820, 1838.

Opiz, Carl Gottlob, 1508, 1517, 1518, 1541, 1542, 1620, 1693, 1923.

Orange County, 1558.

Ordinations, 1515, 1566, 1663, 1693, 1708, 1903.

Organs, 1565, 1590, 1640, 1681, 1694, 1716, 1719, 1725, 1729, 1758, 1760, 1770, 1825, 1889, 1890, 1892.

Orphans, 1504.

Osborn, Colonel, 1707.

Owen, 1702, 1703, 1705.

P

Padget, Anna, 1654.

Padget (Badget), John, Jr., 1925.

Padget, John, Sr., 1527, 1561, 1598, 1654, 1925.

Padget, Mary, 1598.

Padget, Thomas, 1654, 1925.

Paisly, Colonel, 1630.

Palatinate, 1526.

Palm Sunday, 1690, 1829, 1861, 1872.

Pannell, Colonel, 1694.

Panthers, 1843.

Pardon, 1574.

Parris, Captain, 1645.

Parish Graveyard near Bethabara Mill, 1634, 1748, 1814, 1815, 1860.

Parish Graveyard in Salem, 1552, 1558, 1587, 1608, 1690.

Paschke, Captain, 1553, 1554, 1555, 1556, 1557, 1563, 1624.

Passes, 1531, 1560, 1568, 1569, 1599, 1603, 1742, 1743, 1766, 1778, 1799, 1819, 1845.

Passion Week, 1616, 1647, 1682, 1685, 1690, 1817, 1829, 1872.

Passion Week Manual, 1690, 1819, 1872.

Patty (a negress), 1844, 1845.

Peace, 1501, 1523, 1524, 1536, 1543, 1612, 1637, 1638, 1760, 1784, 1785, 1823, 1834, 1836, 1839, 1841, 1844, 1853, 1861, 1862, 1863, 1869, 1873, 1885.

Peddycoart, Basil, 1925.

Peddycoart, John Jac., 1578, 1925.

Peddycoart, William Barton, 1575, 1654, 1655, 1799, 1858, 1906, 1925.

Peddygrew, 1677, 1678, 1685.

Pedilavium, 1531, 1749, 1781, 1873.

Peedee River, 1542, 1556, 1557, 1559, 1562, 1624, 1625, 1669, 1671, 1672, 1694.

Pendleton, Judge, 1787.

Penn, Lawyer, 1790, 1842.

Penn, Major, 1570.

Pennsylvania, 1514, 1556, 1660, 1698, 1704, 1707, 1803, 1813, 1826, 1829, 1838, 1844, 1855, 1893, 1897, 1918.

Perkins, Colonel, 1697.

Perry, Samuel, 1921, 1925.

Peter, Rev. J. Friedrich, 1514, 1515, 1541, 1546, 1547, 1552, 1565, 1566, 1575, 1580, 1591, 1612, 1620, 1628, 1643, 1657, 1666, 1703, 1715, 1724, 1729, 1791, 1796, 1799, 1809, 1810, 1820, 1838, 1843, 1844, 1857, 1866, 1874, 1893, 1901, 1903, 1922.

Peter, Simon, 1508.

Petersbach, 1517, 1709, 1730, 1787.

Petersen, Nils, 1515, 1529, 1552, 1553, 1555, 1571, 1573, 1595, 1629, 1648, 1725, 1787, 1818, 1831, 1837, 1850, 1903, 1922.

Petitions, 1581, 1675, 1791, 1792, 1842, 1864, 1874, 1878, 1879, 1907.

Petri, 1847.

Petri, Anna Maria, 1859.

Petri, Johann William, 1859.

Pfaff, Anna Barbara, 1518, 1639, 1640, 1647.

Pfaff, Isaac, 1726, 1771, 1924.

Pfaff, Maria, 1826.

Pfaff, Peter, 1527, 1535, 1585, 1647, 1725, 1924.

Pfau (Faw), Jacob, 1925.

Pfeifer's Mill, 1822.

Pfeil, Jacob Friedrich, 1554, 1568, 1628, 1922.

Pfleger, 1515, 1552, 1662, 1700, 1857.

Phelps, Captain, 1538.

Phelps, Major, 1539, 1576.

Philadelphia, 1704.

Philips, Col. Joseph, 1688, 1741, 1762.

Pickens, Gen. Andrew, 1673, 1679, 1683, 1685, 1686, 1741, 1743, 1745, 1747, 1882, 1883, 1884.

Pierce, Captain, 1778.

Pinetree, 1559, 1751, 1822, 1823.

Pipes, Tobacco, 1845.

Pindell, Dr. Richard, 1682, 1789.

Politics, 1501, 1534, 1548.

Polk, Colonel, 1547.

Polk, Major, 1688.

Pool, William, 1925.

Postal Facilities, 1516, 1529, 1532, 1534, 1536, 1537, 1559, 1564, 1567, 1574, 1575, 1577, 1580, 1581, 1622, 1624, 1626, 1660, 1687, 1689, 1690, 1692, 1693, 1695, 1696, 1697, 1698, 1699, 1700, 1702, 1704, 1706, 1707, 1726, 1771, 1787, 1790, 1797, 1798, 1836, 1837, 1839, 1844, 1900, 1901, 1912, 1919.

Pottery, Salem, 1528, 1534, 1537, 1583, 1585, 1587, 1593, 1601, 1604, 1608, 1610, 1611, 1674, 1719, 1723, 1724, 1726, 1738, 1752, 1800, 1807, 1845, 1862, 1921.

Potomac River, 1545, 1549, 1553, 1554, 1567.

Powder, 1626, 1668, 1669, 1674, 1764.

Praetzel, Elisabeth, m.n. Engel, widow Nilson, 1696, 1700, 1758, 1763, 1785, 1797, 1811, 1832, 1839.

Praetzel, Gottfried, 1515, 1528, 1552, 1591, 1601, 1624, 1629, 1662, 1663, 1696, 1700, 1703, 1713, 1728, 1735, 1758, 1759, 1763, 1781, 1791, 1796, 1806, 1808, 1809, 1816, 1818, 1832, 1837, 1839, 1840, 1844, 1851, 1854, 1856, 1871, 1874, 1875, 1903, 1922.

Pratter, John, 1737, 1848.

Pratter, Nathanael, 1846.

Prayer, 1497, 1501, 1525, 1548, 1550, 1551, 1573, 1580, 1592, 1609, 1650, 1651, 1666, 1689, 1702, 1703, 1708, 1760, 1781, 1785, 1795, 1820, 1874.

Prayer Meeting, 1514, 1525, 1558, 1571, 1795, 1796, 1839, 1844, 1852, 1856.

Presbyterians, 1677.

Press-warrant, 1750.

Preston, Col. John, 1681, 1682, 1683, 1685, 1686, 1715, 1744, 1746, 1747, 1793, 1883.

Preston, William, 1910, 1911.

Prices, 1506, 1530, 1538, 1581, 1583, 1586, 1587, 1588, 1589, 1590, 1594, 1595, 1596, 1598, 1599, 1600, 1604, 1606, 1607, 1608, 1610, 1611, 1613, 1614, 1615, 1617, 1621, 1623, 1636, 1660, 1686, 1705, 1709, 1711, 1717, 1719, 1720, 1725, 1731, 1734, 1799, 1802, 1808, 1810, 1814, 1821, 1823, 1852, 1854, 1858, 1861, 1879, 1893, 1912, 1921.

Priem, Johann Friedrich, 1698, 1729, 1731, 1794, 1830, 1838, 1870, 1871, 1922.

Prioleau, 1793.

Prisoners, 1563, 1564, 1565, 1573, 1575, 1576, 1577, 1597, 1602, 1625, 1626, 1627, 1628, 1629, 1631, 1632, 1633, 1634, 1643, 1644, 1645, 1670, 1671, 1680, 1687, 1691, 1694, 1702, 1719, 1739, 1764, 1772, 1773, 1787, 1789, 1834, 1881, 1882, 1902, 1904, 1907.

Proclamation Money, 1585.

Proclamations, 1572, 1834, 1853, 1868, 1871, 1914, 1919, 1920.

Proprietor of Wachovia, 1512, 1527, 1554, 1558, 1784, 1786, 1915.

Provision Tax, see Tax, Specific.

Psalm of Joy, 1493, 1864.

Public Accounts of North Carolina, 1557, 1630.

Pulaski's Corps, 1553, 1554, 1597, 1879.

Purvains, Captain, 1684, 1685.

Q

Quakers, 1554, 1680, 1690, 1695.

Quartering of troops, 1709, 1710, 1711, 1713, 1716, 1764, 1775, 1880, 1881, 1884, 1902, 1907, 1908.

Quest, Anna Maria, 1526, 1663, 1693, 1694, 1752, 1770, 1819, 1829, 1843, 1860, 1871.

Quitopehille, 1689.

Quit-Rents, 1912, 1917.

R

Rahel (a negress), 1825.

Rainord, 1555.

Ramsay's Mill, 1687.

Ramsour's Mill, 1512, 1548, 1551.

Rank, Catharine, 1518.

Rank, Elisabeth, 1753, 1754, 1868.

Rank, John, 1604, 1632, 1633, 1707, 1727, 1747, 1751, 1753, 1754, 1759, 1772, 1773, 1816, 1923.

Rank, John, Jr., 1753, 1866.

Ranke, Gottlob, 1508, 1772, 1816, 1889, 1923.

Ranke, Michael, 1508, 1582, 1595, 1639, 1640, 1707, 1728, 1773, 1867, 1889, 1891, 1892, 1923.

Rash, Daniel, 1675, 1680.

Rasp, Malchoir, 1582, 1588.

Rawdon, Lord, 1555.

Read, Dr. William, 1670, 1673, 1692, 1911.

Reading Meeting, 1514, 1516, 1520, 1521, 1526, 1627, 1630, 1635, 1647, 1672, 1686, 1791.

Reception of members, 1514, 1515, 1518, 1525, 1533, 1538, 1561, 1563, 1598, 1603, 1610, 1611, 1648, 1653, 1654, 1664, 1665, 1693, 1781, 1799, 1819, 1832, 1873.

Reden, 1660, 1787.

Redhouse, Va., 1893.

Reed, Major, 1575, 1632.

Reedy Fork, 1578, 1769, 1835, 1916, 1917.

Regulators, 1877.

Reich, Christoph, 1517, 1708, 1728, 1795.

Reich, Christoph, Sr., 1669, 1670, 1707, 1708, 1714, 1738, 1800, 1848, 1873, 1916.

Reich, Matthews, 1517, 1708.

Reich, Verona, 1707.

Reichel, Bishop Johann Friedrich, 1514, 1515, 1516, 1521, 1541, 1543, 1545, 1546, 1547, 1548, 1549, 1550, 1551, 1552, 1553, 1554, 1555, 1556,

1557, 1560, 1561, 1562, 1563, 1565, 1566, 1567, 1568, 1569, 1570, 1574, 1575, 1576, 1577, 1591, 1596, 1597, 1598, 1599, 1603, 1604, 1605, 1612, 1620, 1623, 1625, 1628, 1629, 1637, 1638, 1640, 1646, 1649, 1653, 1654, 1689, 1699, 1707, 1730, 1735, 1793, 1806, 1836, 1853, 1880, 1893-1895, 1900, 1901, 1902, 1919.

Reichel, Mrs., 1514, 1545, 1546, 1547, 1553, 1569, 1570, 1591, 1620, 1623, 1625, 1628, 1653, 1689, 1699, 1893.

Reid, Jacob, 1563, 1832, 1848, 1851, 1873, 1924.

Reid, Johannes, 1924.

Reizmann, 1917.

Renner, Johann George, 1860, 1922.

Rent, 1537, 1802, 1808, 1814, 1846, 1867, 1900, 1913, 1917.

Reports to U. E. C., 1896-1904, 1906, 1910, 1912, 1913, 1914, 1917, 1918, 1921.

Respect for officials, 1507.

Reuter, Anna Catharina, 1515, 1552, 1553, 1555, 1557, 1583, 1586.

Reuter, Christian Gottlieb, 1709, 1922.

Reuz (Reitz) Johannes, 1517, 1541, 1542, 1551, 1557, 1567, 1569, 1570, 1591, 1601, 1603, 1606, 1608, 1641, 1658, 1668, 1683, 1711, 1712, 1715, 1720, 1727, 1735, 1736, 1752, 1758, 1789, 1790, 1801, 1803, 1807, 1826, 1830, 1838, 1842, 1844, 1846, 1849, 1858, 1866, 1922.

Reuz, Maria Magdalena, 1518, 1546, 1663, 1693, 1752, 1770, 1816, 1819, 1820, 1826, 1838, 1893.

Reuz, Magdalena, m.n. Lick, 1567, 1716, 1752, 1844.

Reynolds, William, 1907.

Rice, 1537.

Richmond, Christian, 1906.

Richmond, N. C., Court-House and Town, 1525, 1529, 1536, 1541, 1542, 1548, 1551, 1558, 1570, 1571, 1577, 1579, 1584, 1615, 1618, 1621, 1627, 1628, 1630, 1633, 1639, 1640, 1643, 1645, 1655, 1686, 1692, 1694, 1698, 1704, 1713, 1716, 1720, 1745, 1752, 1759, 1761, 1768, 1769, 1790, 1795,

1798, 1803, 1805, 1807, 1817, 1820, 1824, 1825, 1838, 1842, 1855, 1875, 1889, 1890, 1891, 1892, 1909.

Richter, Johannes, 1518, 1568, 1569, 1622, 1625, 1628, 1634, 1923.

Ricks, Timotheus, 1811.

Riddle, Stephen, 1610, 1709, 1925.

Ried, 1564, 1565, 1626.

Ries, Valentine, 1619.

Rindelmann, August Wilhelm, 1866.

Rindlemann, Dr. John Herman Friedrich, 1805, 1807, 1855, 1866, 1868.

Rippel, Henrich, 1924.

Roads, 1533, 1571, 1577, 1585, 1593, 1600, 1709, 1720, 1725, 1726, 1730, 1733, 1740, 1772, 1786, 1791, 1811, 1812, 1813, 1821, 1822, 1823, 1849, 1855, 1857, 1860, 1861, 1894, 1913.

Road-Masters, 1532, 1571, 1585, 1600, 1720, 1732, 1842, 1855, 1890.

Robbery, see Lawlessness and Thieves.

Rocky Mount, 1559.

Roberson, 1813.

Rogers, Colonel, 1705.

Rominger, Christian, 1924.

Rominger, Jacob, 1924.

Rominger, Michael, Jr., 1924.

Rominger, Michael, Sr., 1563, 1924.

Rose, A. Rosina, m.n. Böckel, 1811, 1862.

Rose, Gottfried Peter, 1842.

Rose, Peter, 1517, 1524, 1533, 1564, 1575, 1624, 1626, 1630, 1742, 1760, 1811, 1816, 1898, 1922.

Rosenbaum, Alex, 1522, 1925.

Ross, John, 1770.

Ross, Major, 1676, 1687.

Rothrock, Jacob, 1925.

Rothrock, Peter, 1649, 1707, 1709, 1778, 1798, 1819, 1829, 1850, 1924.

Rothrock, Philip, 1649, 1707, 1709, 1819, 1829, 1850, 1924.

Rothrock, Valentine, 1649, 1700, 1702, 1924.

Rowan County, 1554, 1558, 1609, 1687, 1703, 1751, 1915.

Rowan County Militia, 1548, 1677, 1684, 1686, 1688, 1691.

Rugeley's Mill, 1822.

Rules and Regulations, 1498, 1499, 1504, 1514, 1520, 1523, 1526, 1585, 1592, 1597, 1598, 1601, 1609, 1637, 1639, 1642, 1652, 1707, 1722, 1737, 1772, 1785, 1829, 1847, 1849, 1850, 1853, 1873, 1897.

Rumors about the War, 1537, 1539, 1540, 1543, 1546, 1553, 1555, 1558, 1559, 1568, 1574, 1580, 1620, 1640, 1644, 1656, 1659, 1670, 1676, 1686, 1687, 1690, 1702, 1742, 1748, 1754.

Rutherford, Gen. Griffith, 1525, 1529, 1548, 1553, 1555, 1560, 1642, 1762, 1877.

Rutledge, Governor, 1791.

S

Saal, see Gemein Saal.

Saal Diener, see Diener.

Sackenaw, 1696.

Salaries, 1504, 1586, 1587, 1591, 1593, 1594, 1595, 1601, 1602, 1604, 1608, 1728, 1729, 1732, 1733, 1750, 1806, 1809, 1865.

Sale, Cornelius, 1588, 1754, 1856.

Salem Archive Papers, 1513.

Salem Archives, 1498, 1809, 1842.

Salem Board Minutes, 1581-1612, 1709-1738, 1799-1810, 1845-1858.

Salem Congregation Register, 1809.

Salem Diary, 1520-1580, 1666-1708, 1787-1799, 1836-1845.

Salem Land, 1709, 1725, 1786, 1798, 1802, 1807.

Salem Memorabilia, 1513-1519, 1657-1665, 1785-1787, 1834-1836.

Salem, N. C., 1512, 1514, 1519, 1523, 1529, 1558, 1584, 1593, 1594, 1596, 1598, 1641, 1644, 1658, 1659, 1660, 1664, 1677, 1694, 1696, 1713, 1717, 1746, 1764, 1767, 1789, 1801, 1876, 1877, 1879, 1881, 1882, 1883, 1884, 1885, 1890, 1892, 1893, 1895, 1902, 1903, 1907, 1910, 1921.

Salisbury, 1525, 1527, 1530, 1542, 1543, 1551, 1553, 1554, 1565, 1568, 1569, 1576, 1577, 1578, 1580, 1581, 1634, 1640, 1642, 1647, 1669, 1670, 1672, 1687, 1691, 1692, 1694, 1706, 1709, 1720, 1752.

Salisbury, 1755, 1771, 1790, 1797, 1809, 1839, 1841, 1843, 1877, 1915.

Salt, 1535, 1537, 1542, 1560, 1569, 1573, 1575, 1576, 1578, 1579, 1671, 1674, 1681, 1692, 1731, 1739, 1749, 1762, 1773, 1811, 1866, 1875.

Salveguarde, 1675, 1682, 1684, 1685, 1686, 1716, 1745, 1908.

Sandusky Creek, 1704, 1707, 1788, 1813.

Santee River, 1700, 1820.

Santee Swamp, 1822, 1823.

Sambo, see Abraham.

Samuel, Anna Maria (a negress), 1763.

Samuel, Johannes (negro), 1578, 1595, 1605, 1611, 1632, 1635, 1718, 1739, 1741, 1742, 1763, 1804, 1816.

Sarepta, 1497.

Sassman's Mill, 1821.

Satan, 1517, 1540, 1678, 1828.

Savannah lots, 1918.

Savier, Colonel, 1845.

Saviour, 1494, 1495, 1496, 1497, 1499, 1514, 1521, 1533, 1540, 1546, 1547, 1549, 1554, 1558, 1564, 1567, 1570, 1573, 1592, 1598, 1599, 1605, 1623, 1634, 1646, 1647, 1657, 1673, 1682, 1689, 1701, 1704, 1706, 1746, 1763, 1777, 1785, 1789, 1820, 1827, 1828, 1834, 1835, 1868, 1895.

Saw-mills, 1618, 1695, 1761, 1807, 1854, 1856.

Sawyer, Lieutenant, 1686, 1688, 1689.

Schaaf, 1797, 1798.

Schaaf, Jeremias, 1537, 1554, 1922.

Schaub, Diserte Maria, m.n. Schumacher, 1862.

Schaub, Johannes, Jr., 1517, 1549, 1575, 1585, 1613, 1615, 1621, 1622, 1628, 1632, 1634, 1635, 1636, 1661, 1739, 1742, 1748, 1811, 1812, 1813, 1815, 1861, 1891, 1896, 1898, 1923.

Schaub, Johannes, Sr., 1614, 1622, 1748, 1761, 1861, 1862, 1923.

Schauss, Christian, 1868.

Schauss, Joseph, 1642.

Schauss, Philip, 1642, 1867, 1923.

Schauss, Salome, 1642.

Schebosch, 1635, 1788.

Shelhorn, Joh. Jacob, 1924.

Schelsie, Colonel, 1811.

Schemel, 1645.

Schemel, Johannes, 1923.

Scherzer, Philip, 1800, 1925.

Schick, 1844.

Schillig, Adam, 1917.

Schmid, Jens, 1521, 1577, 1610, 1686, 1687, 1922.

Schmidt, Colonel, 1815.

Schmidt, Major, 1745, 1747, 1752, 1753, 1754, 1755, 1762, 1799.

Schmidt, Andreas, 1916.

Schmidt, Christoph, 1618, 1923.

Schmidt, George, 1521, 1522, 1523, 1528, 1566, 1605, 1611, 1714, 1722, 1799, 1802, 1898, 1911, 1922.

Schmidt, Helena, m.n. Gründling, 1615, 1740.

Schmidt, Johann Christian, 1922.

Schmidt, Jos. Christian, 1924.

Schmidt, Rosina, m.n. Kaske, widow Biefel, widow Bachhof, 1898.

Schmidt, Wilhelm, 1633, 1634.

Schnebely, 1891.

Schneider, Anna Maria, 1652.

Schneider, Cornelius, 1727, 1777, 1779, 1924.

Schneider, David, 1924.

Schneider, Elisabeth, 1843, 1858.

Schneider, Heinrich, 1567, 1650, 1761, 1844, 1924.

Schneider, Johann, 1873, 1924.

Schneider, Martin, 1516, 1533, 1535, 1554, 1558, 1559, 1568, 1608, 1663, 1698, 1723, 1725, 1835, 1842, 1845, 1846, 1855, 1922.

Schneider, Peter, 1535, 1562, 1570, 1604, 1648, 1729, 1778, 1866, 1867, 1870, 1924.

Schneider, Philip, 1702, 1924.

Schneider, Simon, 1827.

Schnepf, Daniel, 1582, 1603, 1720, 1922.

Schober, Gottlieb, 1516, 1520, 1521, 1568, 1605, 1608, 1728, 1729, 1791, 1794, 1799, 1810, 1837, 1838, 1844, 1874, 1898, 1922.

Schober, Maria Magdalena, m.n. Transou, 1799.

Schoenmell, 1710.

Schools for boys in Salem, 1516, 1520, 1521, 1562, 1568, 1581, 1593, 1594, 1596, 1601, 1602, 1608, 1663, 1666, 1698, 1709, 1729, 1730, 1731, 1791, 1799, 1805, 1807, 1808, 1809, 1810, 1840, 1842, 1850, 1851, 1898.

School for girls in Salem, 1516, 1535, 1586, 1589, 1593, 1594, 1595, 1601, 1602, 1730, 1807, 1809, 1854, 1898.

Schools in Bethabara, 1612, 1617, 1618, 1663, 1693, 1752, 1759, 1810, 1813, 1816, 1859, 1860, 1864, 1865, 1866.

Schools in Bethania, 1500, 1602, 1645, 1764, 1765, 1769, 1817, 1824, 1889.

Schools in Friedberg, 1602, 1647, 1651, 1774, 1779, 1871.

School in Friedland, 1602, 1858, 1874.

School in Hope, 1602, 1654, 1714.

Schools, non-Moravian, 1578, 1614, 1797, 1916.

Schor (Shore), Heinrich, 1508, 1582, 1639, 1764, 1767, 1768, 1769, 1793, 1820, 1854, 1866, 1867, 1868, 1892.

Schor, Jacob, 1698, 1771.

Schor, Johannes, 1518, 1616, 1652, 1891, 1923.

Schor, Margaretha, 1613.

Schott, J. Jacob, 1585, 1727, 1924.

Schreyer, Johann Peter, 1517, 1557, 1558, 1561, 1709, 1713, 1720, 1922.

Schreyer, Maria, m.n. Fiscus, widow Baumgarten, 1517, 1557, 1558.

Schroeth, Johann, Ferdinand, 1561, 1597, 1598, 1737, 1789, 1922.

Schulz, George, 1614, 1923.

Schulz, Gottfried, 1660, 1661, 1699, 1700, 1701, 1706, 1728, 1794, 1922.

Schulz, Johannes, 1619, 1923.

Schulz, Maria, 1614.

Schumacher, 1916.

Schumacher, Adam, Jr., 1561, 1570, 1571, 1577, 1603, 1640, 1669, 1709, 1720, 1922.

Schumacher, Dorothea, 1518, 1561, 1794.

Schumaker, Adam, Sr., 1561, 1925.

Schwarz, Andrea, 1739.

Schwarz, Barbara, 1860.
Schwarz, George, 1860.
Schwarz, Jacob, 1860.
Schwarz, Susanna, 1739.
Schweinitz, Rev. Hans Christian Alexander von, 1706.
Scott, General, 1694.
Sehnert, Catharine, 1516, 1535, 1541, 1586, 1589, 1595, 1899.
Sehnert, Christina Margaretha, m.n. Born, 1869.
Sehnert, Christian, 1770.
Sehnert (Sehner), Peter, Jr., 1871, 1922.
Sehnert, Peter, Sr., 1508, 1771, 1825, 1923.
Seidel, Rev. Nathanael, 1689, 1793, 1798, 1896, 1905, 1918.
Seiler, Johannes, 1923.
Seiz, Lorenz, 1730, 1782.
Seiz, Michael, Jr., 1795.
Seiz (Sides), Michael, 1508, 1537, 1730, 1780, 1782, 1924.
Senf, Colonel, 1787.
Senior Civilis, 1676.
September Sixteenth, 1515, 1566, 1628, 1700.
Service, Christian, 1494, 1496, 1497.
Services, Church, 1520, 1522, 1524, 1526, 1531, 1539, 1540, 1547, 1549, 1557, 1562, 1564, 1569, 1574, 1577, 1579, 1586, 1612, 1617, 1618, 1646, 1653, 1666, 1689, 1697, 1698, 1701, 1703, 1704, 1705, 1715, 1725, 1736, 1746, 1748, 1825, 1852, 1872.
Services, Moravian Church, for Assemblymen, 1703, 1704, 1736, 1737, 1788.
Services, Moravian Church, for soldiers, 1549, 1562, 1572, 1579, 1622, 1623, 1628, 1632, 1634, 1644, 1666, 1670, 1672, 1682, 1684, 1691, 1692, 1697, 1701, 1708, 1746, 1759, 1787, 1789, 1790, 1837, 1838.
Shallow Ford, 1550, 1556, 1572, 1600, 1629, 1630, 1634, 1671, 1741, 1750, 1765.
Sharp, 1704, 1705, 1792, 1797.
Shaw, Colonel, 1815.
Shealds, 1911.

Sheep, 1603, 1630, 1640, 1719.
Shelby, Major, 1574, 1685.
Sheppard, Capt. James, 1551, 1570, 1643.
Sheppard, John, 1890.
Sheppard, Col. William, 1529, 1561, 1571, 1615, 1625, 1642, 1643, 1682, 1686, 1693, 1705, 1755, 1768, 1771, 1790, 1862, 1890, 1892.
Shewkirk, Rev. Ewald Gustav, 1840.
Shoes, 1563, 1597, 1598, 1599, 1674, 1675, 1747, 1848, 1904, 1911.
Sickness, see Medicine and Surgery.
Sick soldiers, 1557, 1558, 1559, 1576, 1634, 1656, 1666, 1669, 1672, 1673, 1677, 1680, 1682, 1683, 1690, 1715, 1717, 1719, 1910.
Silas Creek, 1791.
Silk, 1847.
Silver coins, see Hard Money.
Simons, Captain, 1686.
Simons, Lieutenant, 1667, 1692.
Singelsen's Mill, 1820, 1822.
Singing, 1603.
Single Brethren, 1514, 1515, 1519, 1535, 1541, 1547, 1552, 1555, 1562, 1569, 1589, 1590, 1595, 1596, 1599, 1602, 1606, 1608, 1611, 1646, 1661, 1662, 1664, 1674, 1675, 1676, 1694, 1699, 1700, 1706, 1713, 1716, 1728, 1729, 1731, 1786, 1794, 1798, 1803, 1807, 1838, 1842, 1846, 1852, 1855, 1898.
Single Sisters, 1514, 1517, 1518, 1519, 1527, 1528, 1563, 1574, 1586, 1587, 1595, 1602, 1607, 1646, 1649, 1662, 1663, 1664, 1692, 1703, 1707, 1716, 1725, 1726, 1794, 1802, 1806, 1826, 1829, 1832, 1839, 1842, 1853, 1860, 1898.
Singstunde, 1521, 1522, 1535, 1538, 1543, 1548, 1552, 1567, 1572, 1614, 1616, 1644, 1666, 1670, 1672, 1691, 1698, 1700, 1701, 1702, 1703, 1704, 1705, 1736, 1750, 1758, 1788, 1793, 1795, 1819, 1837, 1839, 1852, 1872.
Sisters House, New, 1798, 1799, 1806, 1843, 1844, 1853, 1854, 1855, 1856, 1858.

Sisters House, Salem, 1520, 1522, 1525, 1543, 1546, 1555, 1564, 1587, 1663, 1698, 1707, 1716, 1723, 1733, 1734, 1794, 1798, 1802, 1806.

Siverberg, 1691, 1804, 1805, 1807, 1829, 1850.

Skinner, Dr., 1789.

Slator, Henry, 1654, 1925.

Slaves, 1515, 1518, 1522, 1557, 1561, 1578, 1579, 1594, 1605, 1606, 1607, 1613, 1697, 1722, 1723, 1724, 1751, 1663, 1698, 1707, 1716, 1723, 1733, 1845.

Small Pox, 1652, 1657, 1659, 1682, 1683, 1691, 1709, 1715, 1716, 1717, 1718, 1723, 1749, 1750, 1751, 1752, 1754, 1755, 1764, 1765, 1769, 1770, 1771, 1774, 1775, 1776, 1778, 1781, 1879, 1884.

Smallwood, General, 1563, 1571, 1572, 1577, 1881, 1906, 1907.

Smith, Daniel, 1598, 1925.

Smith, George, 1755, 1818.

Smith, Capt. Henry, 1544, 1548, 1549, 1555, 1570, 1571, 1578, 1591, 1621, 1640, 1650, 1677, 1740, 1744, 1749, 1818, 1889, 1890, 1925.

Smith, Capt. Minor, 1701, 1758.

Smith River, 1539.

Smithy, Bethabara, 1722, 1723, 1724, 1755, 1757, 1761.

Smithy, Salem, 1567, 1681, 1683, 1685, 1686, 1701, 1714, 1722, 1802.

Snakes, 1755.

Snow, 1520, 1523, 1538, 1639, 1691, 1692, 1706, 1750, 1763, 1773, 1811, 1817, 1819, 1837, 1844, 1845, 1859, 1866.

Societies, Moravian, 1514, 1519, 1526, 1533, 1721, 1724, 1729, 1730, 1789, 1810, 1851.

Sommer, Jacob, Sr., 1917.

Sommer, Johann, 1916.

Sommer, Peter, 1917.

Sotten, 1822.

South Carolina, 1511, 1512, 1526, 1542, 1545, 1549, 1555, 1557, 1558, 1617, 1618, 1621, 1633, 1634, 1649, 1656, 1673, 1687, 1688, 1695, 1696, 1702, 1740, 1745, 1749, 1750, 1755, 1765,

1768, 1772, 1789, 1791, 1793, 1795, 1812, 1820, 1906.

South Fork of Muddy Creek, 1549, 1668, 1709, 1774, 1778.

Spach, Adam, Jr., 1567, 1648, 1924.

Spach (Spaugh), Adam, Sr., 1567, 1579, 1647, 1651, 1673, 1688, 1710, 1774, 1775, 1805, 1830, 1915, 1924.

Spach, Johannes, 1648, 1924.

Spach, Johann Gottlieb, 1671, 1922.

Spain, 1511, 1835, 1844.

Spangenbach, 1791, 1812.

Spangenberg, Bishop August Gottlieb, 1522, 1531, 1553, 1582, 1676, 1918.

Speaking, 1546, 1618, 1623, 1635, 1637, 1648, 1650, 1731, 1740, 1804, 1825, 1829, 1830, 1831, 1853, 1854, 1872, 1874.

Specie Certificates, 1805, 1809, 1810.

Spek, 1532.

Spelt, 1724.

Spenser, Judge, 1790.

Spiders, 1890.

Spies, 1818.

Spieseke, Thomas, 1569, 1715, 1723, 1730, 1795, 1818, 1922.

Spönhauer, Catharine, m.n. Volk, 1824.

Spönhauer, Elisabeth, m.n. Lum, 1758, 1800.

Spönhauer, Heinrich, 1508, 1769, 1890, 1923.

Spönhauer, Joh. Heinrich, 1767, 1818, 1867, 1890, 1923.

Spönhauer, Johannes, 1824.

Spönhauer, John Jacob, 1824.

Spoon, Adam, 1925.

Springs in Salem, 1725.

Square in Salem, 1586, 1719, 1808, 1856.

Stach, Rev. Matthew, 1540, 1622, 1762, 1810, 1811, 1837, 1923.

Stach, Rosina, m.n. Stach, 1837.

Standly, Agnes, 1817.

Standly, Anna Elisabeth, 1817.

Standly, Isai, 1817.

Statistics of Wachovia Congregations, 1518, 1519, 1613, 1664, 1665, 1836.

Stauber, Christian, 1663, 1698, 1723, 1810, 1840, 1848, 1851, 1922.

Standly, Anna Elisabeth, 1817.

Stauber, Johanna, 1618.

Stauber, Paul Chr., 1619, 1636, 1742, 1751, 1755, 1838, 1840, 1864, 1865, 1923.

Statistics of Moravian Congregations, 1519.

Steel, 1692.

Steiner, Abraham, 1498, 1518, 1520.

Steiner, Anna, 1555.

Steiner, Jacob, 1530, 1537, 1546, 1561, 1710, 1713, 1725, 1847, 1856, 1911, 1922.

Steiner's Mill, see Mill below Salem.

Steinmann, Johanna Elisabeth, m.n. Moll, 1517, 1539, 1540, 1588, 1619.

Steinman, Johannes, 1540, 1541, 1666.

Stephens, General, 1564, 1626, 1907.

Steup, Anna Johanna, 1693, 1694.

Steup, Joh. Franz, 1762, 1763, 1800, 1810, 1923.

Steward, Colonel, 1788.

Stewart, Surgeon, 1682.

Stinking Quarter, 1532, 1540, 1541, 1568, 1589, 1610, 1707, 1714, 1786, 1795, 1798, 1837, 1856, 1916, 1920.

Stockburger, Johann George, 1520, 1585, 1587, 1594, 1605, 1606, 1709, 1719, 1720, 1795, 1797, 1851, 1855, 1922.

Stöhr, Dorothea, m.n. Schütz, 1753.

Stöhr, Johanna Elisabeth, 1617.

Stöhr, Joh. Heinrich, 1536, 1545, 1546, 1585, 1610, 1614, 1618, 1620, 1630, 1660, 1724, 1737, 1739, 1747, 1753, 1754, 1761, 1801, 1812, 1814, 1860, 1895, 1923.

Stolz, Anna, m.n. Hauser, 1718, 1729, 1758, 1772.

Stolz, Casper, 1718, 1729, 1758, 1768, 1772, 1849, 1860, 1892.

Stolz, Jacob, 1605, 1643, 1766, 1770, 1819.

Stolz, Philip, 1925.

Stolz, Susanna, 1639.

Stone, Captain, 1793.

Store in Bethabara, 1596, 1809, 1838, 1860, 1861, 1862, 1866, 1917, 1921.

Store in Salem, 1512, 1536, 1550, 1565, 1566, 1573, 1575, 1577, 1579, 1585, 1593, 1596, 1597, 1599, 1600, 1601, 1608, 1611, 1667, 1668, 1674, 1677, 1678, 1679, 1683, 1686, 1690, 1691, 1693, 1694, 1696, 1698, 1702, 1713, 1719, 1724, 1726, 1731, 1732, 1733, 1798, 1806, 1807, 1809, 1838, 1839, 1844, 1850, 1852, 1878, 1911, 1921.

Storms, 1536, 1659, 1691, 1693, 1695, 1697, 1700, 1755, 1781, 1840, 1842, 1843, 1865, 1869, 1874.

Stotz, Anna Maria, 1843.

Stotz, Jacob, 1894.

Stotz, John, 1569, 1666, 1667, 1839, 1850, 1922.

Stotz, Samuel, 1515, 1552, 1555, 1558, 1559, 1566, 1573, 1578, 1596, 1598, 1603, 1605, 1658, 1667, 1668, 1693, 1694, 1696, 1708, 1711, 1712, 1713, 1720, 1729, 1752, 1754, 1780, 1781, 1787, 1789, 1795, 1796, 1797, 1801, 1809, 1818, 1837, 1838, 1840, 1844, 1848, 1856, 1903, 1911, 1918, 1922.

Stozburg, Quartermaster, 1798.

Streder, George, 1917.

Streder, Heinrich, 1916.

Streets in Salem, 1587, 1593, 1698, 1802, 1849, 1856.

Strehle, Christian Rudolph, 1679, 1682, 1702, 1716, 1718, 1725, 1727, 1796, 1798.

Strehle, Gottlieb, 1568, 1666, 1667, 1725, 1733, 1744, 1922.

Strub, Catharine, 1819.

Strub, Johann Jacob, 1922.

Strub, Johannes, Jr., 1889, 1923.

Strub, Johannes, Sr., 1534, 1770, 1890, 1923.

Strub, Johann Samuel, 1508, 1584, 1639, 1642, 1768, 1769, 1771, 1772, 1818, 1891, 1892, 1894, 1923.

Strub, Maria Margaretha, 1534, 1535, 1586, 1617, 1639.

Strub, Susanna, m.n. Stolz, 1819.

Stuard, 1821.

Stundenbeters, 1555, 1561, 1617, 1699, 1842, 1852.

Sugar, 1597, 1721, 1728, 1752, 1762.

Sumner, General, 1562.

Sumter, General, 1511, 1555, 1558, 1559, 1561, 1688, 1699, 1757.

Sumter, Thomas, 1911.

Supplies, Depots for, 1554, 1609, 1610, 1635, 1713, 1740, 1747, 1749.

Supplies for Assembly meeting, 1701, 1727, 1734, 1735, 1736, 1772, 1914.

Supplies furnished American troops, 1513, 1516, 1526, 1529, 1530, 1545, 1549, 1550, 1557, 1559, 1562, 1563, 1565, 1567, 1569, 1570, 1571, 1573, 1574, 1575, 1576, 1580, 1584, 1589, 1592, 1594, 1595, 1599, 1611, 1612, 1615, 1617, 1618, 1620, 1621, 1622, 1623, 1625, 1626, 1628, 1629, 1631, 1638, 1640, 1641, 1642, 1643, 1645, 1647, 1651, 1653, 1654, 1656, 1660, 1666, 1667, 1668, 1671, 1672, 1673, 1674, 1677, 1678, 1680, 1681, 1682, 1683, 1684, 1685, 1686, 1688, 1691, 1695, 1696, 1697, 1701, 1702, 1709, 1713, 1714, 1715, 1717, 1739, 1740, 1741, 1743, 1744, 1745, 1746, 1747, 1748, 1749, 1750, 1752, 1754, 1756, 1757, 1758, 1759, 1760, 1761, 1764, 1765, 1766, 1768, 1772, 1775, 1780, 1782, 1787, 1793, 1798, 1808, 1826, 1837, 1839, 1851, 1876, 1877, 1880, 1883, 1890, 1901, 1907, 1908, 1912, 1915.

Supplies furnished English troops, 1658, 1675, 1676, 1728, 1741, 1742, 1765, 1766.

Surinam, 1497.

Surry County, 1529, 1530, 1581, 1692, 1792, 1789, 1842, 1864, 1874, 1915.

Surry County troops, 1529, 1541, 1543, 1544, 1567, 1631, 1632, 1634, 1674, 1677, 1679, 1688, 1701, 1706, 1747, 1748, 1752, 1755, 1756, 1762, 1890, 1905.

Surveying, 1507, 1534, 1558, 1578, 1579, 1648, 1671, 1741, 1747.

Susy (negress), 1594.

Swann, Major, 1697.

Swine, 1622, 1630, 1733, 1740, 1757, 1760, 1812, 1827, 1866, 1894.

Switzerland, 1788.

Sydrich, 1695.

Synods, General, 1513, 1514, 1515, 1516, 1520, 1523, 1526, 1541, 1562, 1566, 1592, 1593, 1601, 1612, 1637, 1646, 1652, 1655, 1662, 1714, 1730, 1780, 1785, 1793, 1795, 1817, 1832, 1839, 1853, 1861, 1875, 1897.

T

Tanner, George, 1776.

Tanner, Jacob, 1612, 1682, 1774, 1924.

Tanneberger, David, 1706.

Tannery, Salem, 1545, 1563, 1568, 1590, 1593, 1599, 1601, 1608, 1610, 1677, 1678, 1681, 1695, 1724, 1804, 1807, 1813, 1846, 1921.

Tar, 1740, 1751, 1752.

Tarleton, Col. Banistre, 1512, 1543, 1544, 1559, 1671.

Tavern in Bethabara, 1517, 1620, 1621, 1628, 1633, 1713, 1742, 1743, 1757, 1760, 1761, 1813, 1815.

Tavern in Bethania, 1818, 1892.

Tavern in Salem, 1517, 1520, 1523, 1527, 1534, 1536, 1543, 1545, 1546, 1548, 1549, 1554, 1555, 1557, 1558, 1562, 1563, 1566, 1571, 1574, 1575, 1576, 1578, 1579, 1585, 1586, 1587, 1590, 1592, 1593, 1594, 1604, 1605, 1608, 1611, 1672, 1674, 1675, 1677, 1678, 1681, 1684, 1688, 1697, 1710, 1711, 1713, 1722, 1724, 1725, 1728, 1733, 1734, 1757, 1797, 1804, 1805, 1806, 1807, 1840, 1844, 1851, 1855.

Taxes, 1500, 1523, 1525, 1555, 1556, 1581, 1593, 1594, 1613, 1647, 1668, 1712, 1720, 1722, 1729, 1738, 1740, 1754, 1762, 1770, 1805, 1806, 1808, 1858, 1868, 1879, 1881, 1917.

Taxes, Special, on Moravians, 1513, 1516, 1523, 1525, 1527, 1544, 1551, 1581, 1583, 1593, 1594, 1605, 1607, 1614, 1639, 1647, 1659, 1696, 1697, 1710, 1712, 1722, 1724, 1730, 1738, 1739, 1754, 1770, 1782, 1803, 1808, 1812, 1814, 1867, 1879, 1881, 1885, 1900, 1913, 1917.

Tax, Specific, 1607, 1710, 1712, 1713, 1720, 1739, 1740, 1754, 1808, 1816, 1913.

Taylor, Colonel, 1705.

Taylor, Commissioner, 1667.

Taylor, Major, 1788.
Taylor, Matthias, 1846, 1925.
Tea, 1635, 1721.
Te Deum, 1836, 1841, 1864, 1871.
Tennessee, 1512.
Terror, 1560, 1565, 1641.
Tesch, Adam, 1649, 1924.
Tesch, George Heinrich, 1924.
Tesch (Desch), Heinrich, 1649, 1778, 1924.
Text Books, 1532, 1541, 1579, 1589, 1612, 1620, 1649, 1660, 1662, 1666, 1689, 1695, 1702, 1707, 1709, 1748, 1787, 1788, 1808, 1836, 1877.
Texts, 1513, 1520, 1525, 1528, 1532, 1533, 1540, 1544, 1547, 1549, 1551, 1552, 1555, 1559, 1560, 1570, 1573, 1575, 1578, 1619, 1622, 1627, 1652, 1658, 1660, 1662, 1670, 1673, 1678, 1680, 1687, 1700, 1703, 1704, 1708, 1709, 1746, 1758, 1779, 1785, 1789, 1796, 1828, 1841, 1871, 1876, 1877, 1879, 1882, 1883.
Thanksgiving Day, 1844, 1853, 1885, 1919.
Thanksgiving services, 1574, 1834, 1835, 1841, 1844, 1853, 1863, 1864, 1868, 1869, 1871, 1873, 1885, 1919.
Thieves, 1554, 1555, 1556, 1562, 1565, 1567, 1570, 1572, 1577, 1578, 1625, 1630, 1634, 1650, 1652, 1657, 1669, 1673, 1675, 1676, 1678, 1679, 1682, 1683, 1685, 1698, 1699, 1708, 1727, 1745, 1747, 1753, 1766, 1767, 1776, 1777, 1780, 1782, 1784, 1797, 1819, 1822, 1829, 1857, 1861, 1868, 1890, 1893, 1910.
Thompson, Colonel, 1740.
Thompson, Matthew, 1812.
Threats against Brethren, 1526, 1543, 1546, 1561, 1565, 1572, 1573, 1592, 1599, 1644, 1645, 1657, 1674, 1675, 1677, 1678, 1798, 1858, 1879, 1882.
Thürstig, Dr., 1735.
Tiersch, Rev. Paul, 1676.
Tickets, 1530, 1557, 1559, 1569, 1573, 1578, 1597, 1607, 1611, 1620, 1630, 1635, 1666, 1667, 1687, 1691, 1693, 1694, 1696, 1697, 1709, 1712, 1713, 1719, 1720, 1722, 1731, 1739, 1748, 1761, 1770, 1795, 1808, 1809, 1810, 1813, 1816, 1905, 1906, 1910, 1911, 1912, 1914.
Tickets, English, 1728, 1766, 1792, 1793, 1809, 1819, 1838, 1840, 1848.
Tobacco, 1802, 1850, 1869.
Todewine, 1690.
Toll, Louise, 1733.
Tories, 1515, 1536, 1542, 1543, 1548, 1549, 1551, 1553, 1558, 1561, 1562, 1564, 1565, 1567, 1570, 1571, 1572, 1573, 1574, 1575, 1576, 1577, 1590, 1592, 1607, 1610, 1618, 1621, 1622, 1625, 1626, 1627, 1629, 1631, 1633, 1634, 1638, 1640, 1642, 1643, 1644, 1645, 1650, 1655, 1659, 1674, 1680, 1695, 1700, 1701, 1704, 1707, 1742, 1743, 1756, 1762, 1767, 1781, 1784, 1790, 1812, 1820, 1823, 1877, 1880, 1881, 1901, 1902, 1906, 1914, 1918.
Town Congregations, 1606, 1657, 1662, 1728, 1786.
Town Fork, 1623, 1632, 1756, 1758, 1847, 1859, 1865.
Townsend, Gregory, 1840.
Traders, 1532, 1597, 1611.
Trading Ford, 1672, 1673.
Tranquebar, 1787.
Transou, Abraham, 1508, 1518, 1589, 1769, 1808, 1825, 1826, 1869, 1889, 1923.
Transou, Johannes, 1508.
Transou, Maria, m.n. Pfaff, 1826.
Transou, Maria Magdalena, 1518, 1525, 1737, 1738, 1799.
Transou, Philip, Jr., 1673, 1922, 1889.
Transou, Philip, Sr., 1508, 1738, 1767, 1820, 1826, 1866, 1867, 1891, 1923.
Travel Diary, Reichel's, 1893-1895.
Travelers, 1516, 1523, 1532, 1533, 1534, 1535, 1540, 1571, 1574, 1587, 1617, 1692, 1699, 1711, 1739, 1740, 1742, 1753, 1755, 1757, 1758, 1759, 1760, 1762, 1811, 1812, 1813, 1815, 1825, 1826, 1859, 1891, 1902.
Trevison's Creek, 1916.
Triebel, Christian, 1516, 1554, 1568, 1582, 1594, 1595, 1596, 1620, 1642, 1808, 1816, 1840, 1850, 1922.
Trinity, The, 1555, 1635, 1758, 1818, 1828.

Trog, Jacob, 1917.
Trombones, 1629, 1703, 1723, 1725, 1794, 1795, 1815, 1836, 1841, 1845, 1857, 1861.
Troublesome Creek, 1687.
Troy, Matthew, 1687, 1722.
Trumpets, 1858.
Turnips, 1636, 1761.
Two-story House, 1587, 1588, 1672, 1715, 1725.

U

Unitas Fratrum, 1512, 1527, 1558, 1601, 1683, 1718.
United Colonies, 1511, 1656, 1784.
Unity of Brethren, 1497, 1499, 1503, 1513, 1523, 1526, 1546, 1551, 1557, 1692, 1699, 1708, 1789, 1795, 1834, 1838.
Unity Days, 1496, 1532, 1542, 1614, 1616, 1619, 1625, 1630, 1636, 1676, 1686, 1694, 1699, 1701, 1707, 1750, 1756, 1763, 1817.
Unity land in North Carolina, 1558, 1582, 1583, 1605, 1671, 1784, 1786, 1878, 1900, 1917, 1921.
Unity Sustation, 1504, 1516.
Unity's Aufseher Collegium, 1918.
Unity's Elders' Conference, -493, 1494, 1516, 1568, 1591, 1662, 1689, 1700, 1727, 1728, 1735, 1763, 1805, 1806, 1853, 1896, 1910, 1912, 1915.
Unity's Vorsteher Collegium, 1806, 1917, 1921.
Utley, Sarah, 1540, 1672.
Uwarrie, 1811.

V

Vegetables, 1505, 1752, 1761.
Vesper, 1810, 1815, 1820.
Virginia, 1512, 1543, 1544, 1553, 1555, 1564, 1567, 1568, 1569, 1577, 1579, 1611, 1632, 1656, 1670, 1671, 1673, 1686, 1688, 1692, 1695, 1696, 1697, 1740, 1749, 1751, 1754, 1757, 1773, 1788, 1837, 1851, 1859, 1893.
Virginia troops, 1512, 1544, 1561, 1562, 1563, 1569, 1572, 1578, 1579, 1580, 1589, 1626, 1627, 1628, 1630, 1636, 1642, 1643, 1658, 1666, 1671, 1672,

1679, 1684, 1688, 1689, 1692, 1693, 1694, 1696, 1740, 1751, 1755, 1767, 1768, 1839, 1880, 1884, 1902, 1910.
Visitations, 1514, 1546, 1547-1570, 1601, 1612, 1623, 1637, 1836, 1841.
Vogler, Anna Maria, m.n. Künzel, 1874.
Vogler, Christina Margaretha, m.n. Born, widow Schnert, 1869.
Vogler, Elisabeth, 1617.
Vogler, George Michael, 1537, 1545, 1548, 1874, 1924.
Vogler, Johanna Elisabeth, m.n. Moll, widow Steinmann, 1898.
Vogler, Johannes, 1874.
Vogler, Lorenz, 1648, 1924.
Vogler, Philip Christoph, 1508, 1537, 1726, 1755, 1782, 1869, 1924.
Vogler, Philip Martin, 1517, 1536, 1537, 1539, 1541, 1560, 1587, 1588, 1589, 1619, 1666, 1811, 1847, 1898, 1923.
Volbrecht, John, 1790.
Volk, Andreas, 1571, 1614, 1629, 1639, 1641, 1671, 1725, 1771, 1824, 1923.
Volk, George, 1739.
Volk, Johanna, 1826.
Volk, Margaretha, 1725, 1726, 1771.
Volk, Wilhelm, 1625, 1739, 1748, 1815, 1849, 1860, 1925.
Volunteers, 1567, 1639, 1642, 1646, 1666, 1889, 1891.
Volz (Folz), Andreas, 1924.
Volz, Friedrich, 1807, 1924.
Volz, Joh. Jacob, 1826, 1924.
Volz, Johanna, m.n. Volk, 1826.
Volz, Johannes, 1648, 1649, 1924.
Volz, Peter, Jr., 1649, 1717, 1924.
Volz, Peter, Sr., 1543, 1601, 1709, 1768, 1806, 1924.
Vorsteher, 1514, 1547, 1552, 1555, 1597, 1604, 1661, 1696, 1809, 1901.
Voyages, 1537, 1542.

W

Wach, 1535, 1538, 1560, 1578, 1606, 1692, 1720, 1730.
Wachovia, 1512, 1513, 1526, 1591, 1657, 1659, 1665, 1676, 1704, 1784, 1795, 1917, 1918, 1920.

Wachovia Historical Society, 1722, 1766, 1841.

Wachovia Land, 1516, 1527, 1534, 1555, 1648, 1713, 1741, 1747, 1791, 1879.

Wachovia, Title to, 1516, 1527, 1540, 1545, 1549, 1553, 1554, 1784, 1786, 1791, 1792, 1807, 1880, 1885, 1899, 1915, 1917.

Wageman, Andreas, 1922.

Wageman, Joh. George, 1613, 1750, 1752, 1923.

Wager, 1721.

Wages, 1590, 1604, 1713, 1714, 1717, 1718, 1738, 1740, 1760, 1770, 1810.

Wagoner, George, 1696.

Wagoning, 1533, 1534, 1537, 1539, 1541, 1542, 1559, 1562, 1567, 1577, 1584, 1595, 1616, 1617, 1623, 1638, 1645, 1651, 1653, 1687, 1689, 1696, 1698, 1702, 1706, 1707, 1750, 1751, 1755, 1757, 1758, 1759, 1760, 1762, 1767, 1771, 1772, 1788, 1789, 1790, 1797, 1798, 1799, 1811, 1837, 1838, 1839, 1840, 1844, 1869, 1889, 1892, 1902.

Wagons, 1556, 1557, 1559, 1562, 1567, 1575, 1577, 1595, 1599, 1603, 1604, 1615, 1624, 1625, 1631, 1632, 1640, 1643, 1696, 1706, 1741, 1742, 1750, 1755, 1756, 1759, 1762, 1764, 1774, 1775, 1794, 1811, 1813, 1819, 1859, 1865, 1866, 1880, 1882, 1891, 1892, 1900.

Wagner, 1844.

Wagner, John George, 1839.

Wagner, Philip, 1831.

Wainscott, John, 1891, 1925.

Wainscott, Robert, 1891.

Walk, Martin, 1539, 1675, 1717, 1768, 1769, 1775, 1776, 1777, 1825, 1882, 1924.

Walk, Sarah, 1777.

Walker, 1808, 1816.

Walker, Robert, Sr., 1559.

Walks, 1593.

Wallis, Johann George, 1922.

Walther, Johann Heinrich, 1517, 1521, 1571, 1577, 1589, 1797, 1922.

War expenses, 1592, 1594, 1595, 1658, 1668, 1711, 1852.

War Committee, see Committee, Special, Salem.

Washington, Captain, 1543.

Washington, Col. William, 1512, 1543, 1691, 1750, 1851, 1907.

Washington, Gen. George, 1511, 1512, 1770, 1784, 1834, 1837, 1895.

Waterworks, Salem, 1528, 1533, 1582, 1586, 1594, 1595, 1799, 1857.

Watteville, Benigna, m.n. von Zinzendorf, 1836, 1841.

Watteville, Bishop Johannes von, 1836, 1841, 1843, 1845.

Watts, Captain, 1694.

Waxhaws, 1544, 1555, 1696.

Wayne, Gen. Anthony, 1837, 1838.

Weather, see Bethabara diaries, also Salem diary of 1780.

Weber, Leonard, 1727, 1924.

Weevils, 1636, 1638, 1816, 1864.

Weirich, Jacob, 1917.

Weirich, Martin, 1917.

Weis, Matthew, 1896.

Weiss land, 1824.

Weizel, Adam, 1917.

Weizel, Capt. Heinrich, 1917.

Wells, 1761.

Wendel, Heinrich, 1713, 1749.

Wendel, Johann, 1718.

Weinig, Jacob, 1917.

Werner, Andreas, 1811.

Werner, Jonas, 1811.

Wernly, Heinrich, 1860, 1863.

Wesner, Jacob, 1924.

Wesner, Matthias, 1556, 1648, 1924.

Wesner, Johannes, 1796, 1798, 1924.

West Indies, 1520, 1524, 1528, 1560, 1689, 1698, 1700, 1918.

Wetteravia, 1526.

Whet-stones, 1813.

Whigs, 1573, 1629, 1638, 1695, 1781, 1784.

Whippings, 1626, 1627.

White, Colonel, 1658, 1666, 1667, 1670, 1671, 1672, 1694, 1696, 1697, 1741, 1851, 1907.

Whitsunday, 1539, 1588, 1618, 1661, 1694, 1778, 1851, 1873.

Widowers, 1519, 1522, 1664, 1796, 1842.

Widows, 1504, 1515, 1519, 1521, 1662, 1664, 1796, 1842.

Widows' House, 1854.

Widows' Society, 1605.

Wild animals, 1843, 1852, 1857.

Wilens, 1744.

Wilkes County, 1528, 1567, 1644, 1667, 1692, 1792, 1899.

Wilke's Militia, 1644, 1658, 1674, 1675, 1678, 1679, 1680, 1682, 1683, 1684, 1685, 1701, 1702, 1706, 1707, 1745, 1782, 1787, 1792, 1882, 1883.

Will, Major, 1793.

Williams, Col. Joseph, 1529, 1545, 1620, 1668, 1712, 1789, 1889.

Williams, Judge, 1790, 1797.

Williamstown, 1762.

Williard, George, 1856.

Williard, Susanna Catharine, m.n. Appel, 1856.

Wills, 1504, 1527, 1605, 1613, 1614, 1628, 1753, 1769, 1798, 1825, 1918.

Wilmington, N. C., 1536, 1538, 1579, 1687, 1701.

Wilson, Abraham, 1801.

Wilson, David, 1720.

Wilson, James, 1736, 1860.

Windfield, —— m.n. Messer, 1770.

Windfield, John, 1770.

Windfield, William, 1770, 1866.

Wine, 1554, 1604, 1722, 1752.

Winston, Maj. Joseph, 1549, 1550, 1551, 1553, 1575, 1620, 1631, 1641, 1669, 1676, 1677, 1680, 1682, 1690, 1743, 1756, 1865, 1908.

Witness-congregation, 1551, 1700, 1708.

Wochen, Wöchentlichen Nachrichten, 1516, 1612, 1619, 1638, 1660, 1689, 1701, 1756, 1787, 1872.

Wohlfahrt (Welfare), Jacob, 1854, 1922.

Wolf, Catharine, m.n. Dietz, 1892.

Wolf, Daniel, 1646.

Wolf, Elisabeth, 1646.

Wolf, John Adam, 1925.

Wolf, Ludwig, 1892.

Wolfesberger, John, 1777.

Wollin, J. G., 1692, 1841.

Wolves, 1640, 1843.

Wool, 1850.

Woolridge, Captain, 1679, 1681.

Worldliness, 1495, 1498, 1591, 1602, 1606, 1712, 1728, 1803, 1805.

Wounded soldiers, 1544, 1545, 1572, 1573, 1574, 1629, 1630, 1633, 1634, 1643, 1644, 1645, 1656, 1658, 1667, 1670, 1672, 1675, 1680, 1682, 1683, 1685, 1686, 1687, 1688, 1689, 1690, 1701, 1717, 1746, 1747, 1749, 1774, 1781, 1789, 1881, 1884, 1902, 1907, 1909, 1911.

Wright, Gideon, 1571, 1572, 1616, 1643, 1644, 1880, 1906.

Wright, Giery, 1575.

Wright, Hezekiah, 1627, 1643.

Wutrobe, Johann, 1603.

Y

Yadkin River, 1538, 1543, 1548, 1549, 1551, 1554, 1559, 1565, 1568, 1569, 1570, 1572, 1574, 1580, 1615, 1628, 1629, 1630, 1640, 1641, 1643, 1762, 1824, 1857, 1890.

Yarborough, Captain, 1696.

Yarrell, Maria, m.n. Everson, 1567, 1716.

Yarrell, Peter, 1567, 1569, 1570, 1596, 1597, 1658, 1667, 1668, 1669, 1678, 1710, 1711, 1715, 1720, 1731, 1732, 1764, 1768, 1806, 1818, 1830, 1842, 1922.

Yelpin, Captain, 1684.

Yorktown, Pa., 1532, 1537, 1577, 1684, 1702, 1893, 1895.

Yorktown, Va., 1656, 1702, 1704.

Young people, 1502, 1503, 1553, 1579, 1585, 1609, 1638, 1639, 1646, 1804, 1809.

Z

Zeisberger, David, Jr., 1537.

Ziegler, Captain, 1789.

Zillman, Heinrich, 1566, 1682, 1710, 1715, 1716, 1717, 1852, 1922.

Zimmerman, Benjamin David, 1828, 1924.

Zimmerman, Christian, Jr., 1650, 1924.

Zimmerman, Christian, Sr., 1650, 1830, 1924.

Zimmerman, Johannes, 1924.

Zimmermann, George, 1916.

Zinzendorf, Count Nicholas Lewis, 1538, 1692, 1751.

Zinzendorf, Life of, 1541, 1584, 1622.

DATE DUE

PRINTED IN U.S.A.

Rev. Frederic William Marshall